A History of the Muslim World Since 1260

A History of the Muslim World Since 1260

The Making of a Global Community

Vernon O. Egger
Georgia Southern University

Upper Saddle River, NJ 07458

Library of Congress Cataloging in Publication Data

Egger, Vernon, (date)
A history of the Muslim World since 1260 : the making of a global community / Vernon O. Egger.
p. cm.
Includes bibliographical references and index.
ISBN-13: 978-0-13-226969-8
ISBN-10: 0-13-226969-4
1. Islamic countries—History. I. Title.

DS35.63E34 2008
909'.09767—dc22

2007024458

Executive Editor: Charles Cavaliere
Senior Editorial Assistant: Maureen Diana
Senior Marketing Manager: Kate Mitchell
Managing Editor: Mary Carnis
Production Liaison: Marianne Peters-Riordan
Operations Specialist: Maura Zaldivar
Cover Design: Bruce Kenselaar
Director, Image Resource Center: Melinda Patelli
Manager, Rights and Permissions: Zina Arabia
Manager, Visual Research: Beth Brenzel
Image Permission Coordinator: Ang'John Ferreri
Photo Researcher: Melinda Alexander
AV Project Manager: Mirella Signoretto
Cartographer: Pristine Graphics
Full-Service Project Management: Pine Tree Composition, Inc.
Composition: Laserwords
Cover Art: Courtesy Library of Congress: A chart of the points of the compass from Katip Celebi's Tuheftul - Kibar fi Esfaril-Bihar (The Naval Wars of the Turks), Istanbul, 1729.
Printer/Binder and Cover Printer: R.R. Donnelley & Sons

Credits and acknowledgments borrowed from other sources and reproduced, with permission, in this textbook appear on pages 519–520.

Pearson Education LTD.
Pearson Education Singapore, Pte. Ltd
Pearson Education, Canada, Ltd
Pearson Education-Japan
Pearson Education Australia PTY, Limited
Pearson Education North Asia Ltd
Pearson Educación de Mexico, S.A. de C.V.
Pearson Education Malaysia, Pte. Ltd

4 5 6 7 8 9 10 0BRV 15 14

ISBN-13: 978-0-13-226969-8
ISBN-10: 0-13-226969-4

Contents

Preface

This book continues the narrative begun by *A History of the Muslim World to 1405: The Making of a Civilization*. That volume traced the emergence of Islam as a religion and its spread from the Arabian Peninsula eastward to the Indus River valley and westward to the Atlantic Ocean. It focused on the development of a civilization that rivaled Chinese culture as the most sophisticated in the world. The book concluded with an examination of the impact on Islamic civilization of a series of catastrophes that occurred in the thirteenth and fourteenth centuries. The catastrophes—the Reconquista in the Iberian Peninsula, the Mongol invasions, and the conquests of Timur Lang—administered such a psychological and material shock to the majority of the world's Muslims that they seemed a fitting conclusion to the first volume. Conveniently, they also fell at the midpoint in Muslim history from the rise of Islam to our own generation.

The present volume, *A History of the Muslim World since 1260: The Making of a Global Community*, begins by revisiting the catastrophes of the thirteenth and fourteenth centuries, for they were not merely the end of a story, but the beginning of one, as well. That point has been appreciated only in recent years. The fact that we can share it today is due to a transformation in the historiography of the Muslim world. Before 1970, many of the preeminent scholars in the fields of Islamic studies and the history of the Muslim world assumed that the thirteenth- and fourteenth-century catastrophes rendered the history of the Muslim world between the mid-thirteenth century and the early nineteenth century unworthy of serious study. So little historical research had been done on that long period that the assumption could be neither verified nor confirmed. Over the past thirty years, scholars have started to fill out the picture of Muslim history during those centuries. Much remains to be done, even at the basic level, but we can now at least trace the outlines of the period's history. As a result, we are beginning to see how the profound dislocations of the thirteenth and fourteenth centuries reshaped the histories of North Africa and of the eastern Muslim world. New states were created and new religious themes emerged. Some of the new states even rose to become among the most powerful in the world.

The subtitle of this volume derives from another important development of the post-fourteenth-century period: This is when Islam became a world religion. Prior to the fourteenth century, the overwhelming majority of Muslims lived in southwestern Asia, North Africa, and the Iberian Peninsula. After the fourteenth century, Islam spread widely. Today, half of the world's Muslims are found in the four countries of Indonesia, Pakistan, India, and Bangladesh, and Islam has become the majority religion in Africa between the Sahara and the equator. More than fifteen million Muslims now live in Western Europe and North America. Muslims across the world inhabit a great diversity of cultures, and they are engaged in a quest to integrate the elements of the Islamic tradition that they consider essential with the features of their respective societies that they value most.

This book is divided into three parts. Part One, entitled "Mongol Hegemony, 1260–1405," is the transition from the first volume and is identical to the concluding section of the earlier book. Its two chapters examine the decisive period of the thirteenth and fourteenth centuries. It argues that the extreme violence of the campaigns by the Mongols and Timur left a mixed legacy. On the one hand, it obliterated governments and material culture in a region extending from the Mediterranean Sea to northern India; on the other hand, it created the conditions for an even more luxuriant growth of Islamic culture over a far wider area than before.

Part Two is called "Muslim Ascendancy, 1405–1750." It comprises Chapters 3 through 7. It surveys the development of economies, states, societies, and religious traditions from West Africa to Southeast Asia. This period is the least studied in all of Muslim history, and yet knowledge of it is essential for understanding developments in the twenty-first-century Muslim world. In addition to the dramatic geographical expansion of the religion that took place during these centuries, critical changes took place in Islamic doctrine, ritual, and institutions. The earlier assumption that little of consequence happened during this period could not have been more misplaced.

Part Three is called "The World Turned Upside Down, 1750–Present." It includes Chapters 8 through 12. The theme of this section is the unprecedented weakness that afflicted Muslim countries after the mid-eighteenth century. For a millennium following the early seventh century, Muslims had been accustomed to success. Their religion was the final and complete revelation of the three great monotheistic traditions. Even when their normally victorious armies lost, they took solace in the fact that their culture was superior to that of the barbarian victor. The great majority of the time, the barbarian eventually converted to Islam, and the Muslims won after all. Islamic civilization had been so advanced that medieval Europeans eagerly translated thousands of texts from Arabic to Latin. As late as the early eighteenth century, Europeans were awed by the might and splendor of the Ottoman, Safavid, and Mughal empires.

After 1750, by contrast, foreigners found little of interest in predominantly Muslim countries other than raw materials that could be consumed in their industrializing economies. During the course of the eighteenth century, Muslim societies perceptibly fell behind those of Europe in the fields of science and technology. During the nineteenth and early twentieth centuries, almost all of them came under European control. Today, after half a century of independence, most Muslim countries are suffering profound economic, political, and cultural weaknesses. Some Muslims have felt humiliated by these circumstances, and they have constructed a new, politicized version of Islam that enables them to lash out violently against targets that they regard as the cause of Muslim weakness. We should not be *reductionist* and claim that religions are simply products of their social and economic environments, but we should also not be *essentialist* and speak of them as though they are unaffected by the vicissitudes of history. The interaction between the expression of faith and contemporary social conditions should be clear throughout the book, and it is clearly visible in the various forms that Islam takes today.

Most readers would benefit from prefatory remarks regarding the organization and the thematic emphasis of the two-volume work as a whole. First, a word about organization. In the first volume, each of the chapters that treated the period up to the invasion by Chinggis Khan in the early thirteenth century explored developments in the Muslim world as a whole. Since for most of that period the Muslim world extended from the Iberian Peninsula to the Indus River, such an approach was feasible. For the last section of that book (Part One of this volume), the time period and the geographic scope are greatly reduced, because I consider the Mongol period and the conquests of Timur to have constituted a decisive watershed in Muslim history. The period covers the thirteenth and fourteenth centuries, and the territory involved is restricted to the region from the Balkan Peninsula and the Nile River in the west to northern India in the east. During the period covered in Part Two of this volume, the Muslim world expanded enormously. In addition to the sheer geographical scope involved, a number of important developments were taking place in Islam that, to my knowledge, no other single book treats. Since I am convinced that knowledge of those developments is essential for understanding modern Islam, I devoted each chapter of that section to one of five geographical regions. Part Three, by contrast, reverts to the first model of treating the entire Muslim world as a unit. Each of the four final chapters covers a chronological period, rather than a geographical region.

The reason for the shift in organization for Part Three is directly tied to a change in thematic emphasis at that point in the book. The two-volume project began as an analysis of the history of the Muslim world, treated as a unit of world history. Religion was to be one of several elements that would receive equal attention. When I was about one-third of the way through the project, the terrorist attacks of September 11, 2001, occurred. Those events and the subsequent American invasions of Afghanistan and Iraq naturally generated a flood of commentary about Islam in the news media and trade books. The bulk of the analysis has been so execrable that I felt compelled to adjust this project to serve as a counterpoint to it. Whereas the constant evolution of Islam is one of several themes for most of the project, it becomes dominant in Part Three of this volume so that the reader can place global jihad within its proper context. Social, economic, and political trends continue to be treated in Part Three, but religious developments take center stage. All historical writing reflects the issues and concerns of the generation within which it is written. That basic truth applies to this project *a fortiori*.

Acknowledgments

I wrote this book during a fortuitous time. It would not have been possible without the work of scholars who have published the results of their research in recent years. Because this work was intended to be a textbook rather than a work of original scholarship, I assumed that it would not require the use of footnotes. In retrospect, I wish that I had begun citing sources, because some of the more recent works in particular fields have come to conclusions that challenge many general assumptions held by scholars in other fields of Muslim history. In a few cases, I have cited sources when it was clear to me that an assertion required documentation; in other cases, the note is a response to readers of the manuscript who asked for a citation. I have listed the sources that I have found most valuable for my own purposes—and that I recommend to other readers—at the end of the relevant chapters.

I wish to express my appreciation to the members of the staff of the Interlibrary Loan office of the Henderson Library at Georgia Southern University for their consistently excellent help and to staff members of the various libraries within the University System of Georgia who responded quickly to requests to borrow their books through the marvelous GIL Express system.

The quality of this book was enhanced immeasurably by the comments, insights, and corrections that I received on the manuscript from Kimberly Katz, Towson University; Roger Adelson, Arizona State University; Gene R. Garthwaite, Dartmouth College; David Commins, Dickinson College; and Byron Cannon, University of Utah. They invested a great deal of time in the analysis of most or all of the manuscript, thereby improving my writing, providing me with new information, and saving me from several egregious errors. Thanks go to Chuck Thomas for his review of my translation of a primary source document that was in a German version. That the book still has shortcomings despite the herculean efforts of these scholars is due solely to my own limitations.

I am grateful to Charles Cavaliere at Prentice Hall for his patience, courtesy, and encouragement throughout this project. My wife, Mary, has shared my attention with this project for several years. Her patience and generosity have been priceless, providing yet more evidence for why I love her. And to Krista and Rachel, who often must have wondered if I were writing my own version of *The Neverending Story*, go my thanks for giving me the benefit of the doubt.

Note on Transliteration, Dating, and "the Muslim World"

Any work that treats of the Muslim world faces the challenge of the transliteration of words from one alphabet to another. Scholars need a comprehensive system that represents in the Latin alphabet all the vowels and consonants of other alphabets, but nonspecialists can find such a system more confusing and alien than useful. The problem is a serious one when transliterating only one language; in this book we have to deal with several. I have tried to compromise between accuracy and ease of use.

For the most part, this book spells geographic place names as they appear on modern English-language atlas maps (Khorasan, Baghdad, Cairo). In some cases, no consensus exists among cartographers on the spelling of place names, and so this book occasionally provides alternate spellings (Zaragoza/Saragossa, Qayrawan/Kairouan). In a few cases, this book uses names that are more easily understood by English speakers than some that are more culturally authentic. An example is the Greek-based "Transoxiana" for the Arabic phrase *ma wara' al-nahr.* In two cases, I simply could not follow the standard spelling, because they are patently incorrect: I use Riyad for Riyadh, and Hadramawt for Hadhramawt.

In the interest of trying to make transliterated words less of an obstacle to the task of understanding the material, I have also used the more popular spellings for some words, even when doing so seems inconsistent with the practice of the book as a whole. Thus, I discuss "Sunnis and Shi'ites" rather than "Sunnis and Shi'is" or "Sunnites and Shi'ites." I have also transliterated "Saudi Arabia" conventionally, although I use "Sa'ud" when referring to the family prior to the creation of the Kingdom in 1932.

For personal names and technical words in the Arabic, Persian, and Turkish languages, this book uses a simplified version of the Library of Congress system. The book does not distinguish between long and short vowels nor does it provide diacritical marks for the vowels of words from any language. For the Arabic language, no attempt is made to indicate the so-called velarized consonants, and no distinction is made between the two forms of the letter "h." The Arabic letter *dhal* appears underlined as *dh,* and represents the sound of the *th* in the English word *then; kh* is similar to the *ch* in the Scottish *loch; gh* is best described as the sound made when gargling. The *q* is pronounced farther back in the throat than the *k.* The symbol ' represents a glottal stop, the sound that begins each syllable of the English expression "uh-oh." The symbol ' represents an Arabic consonant with no English equivalent, but it is important in words such as 'Ali or Shi'ite. Phonetically, it is a "voiced guttural stop" produced in the very back of the throat, by constricting the larynx to stop the flow of air. An approximation may be achieved by making a glottal stop as far back in the throat as possible. The Turkish ğ is unvoiced; it lengthens the vowel preceding it.

The prefix *al-* is the definite article in Arabic, meaning "the." Before most letters in the alphabet, the prefix sounds the way it is spelled, but it assumes the sound of certain letters when it precedes them (t, th, d, dh, r, z, s, sh, n). Thus, al-Rahman is pronounced ar-Rahman.

Notes regarding the significance of names containing 'Abd, Abu, and Ibn may be found in the glossary. Understanding the terms makes the learning of Arabic-based names easier and more meaningful.

In a book on Muslim history, the most logical (and considerate) way of dating would be to use the A.H. ("Anno Hejirae") system, which is based on the Islamic calendar, the first year of which began in July 622 on the Gregorian calendar. Most readers of this book, however, are English-speaking non-Muslims, who, in my experience, are usually confused by, rather than helped by, the use of the A.H. dating system. It is explained in the glossary.

The title of this book is *A History of the Muslim World.* The phrases *the Muslim world* and *Muslim history* appear frequently throughout both volumes. The terms are admittedly problematic: Substituting the words *Christian* or *Buddhist* for *Muslim* in either phrase makes the awkwardness of the connotations more clear. The terms would have no currency today but for the concepts of the *dar al-islam* and the *umma,* which are the bases for my use of them.

The *dar al-islam* is a term from Islamic law, which drew a distinction between the Dar al-Islam ("the abode of Islam"), where Muslims and non-Muslims lived under a Muslim ruler, and the *dar al-kufr* ("the abode of unbelief"), where non-Muslims ruled. The religious scholars who devised Islamic law assumed that Muslim rulers would enforce Islamic law and that non-Muslim rulers would not. They also decreed that if an army from the Dar al-Kufr should capture part of the Dar al-Islam, Muslims in the affected area had the obligation to move to the remaining areas of the Dar al-Islam. The Dar al-Islam was a useful concept until imperialists began seizing large chunks of Muslim-ruled territory in the second half of the eighteenth century. By 1920, almost all Muslims were subject to non-Muslim rulers. Even after they gained their independence, most Muslims continued to live in secular states. With the advent of imperialism, the Dar al-Islam ceased to have meaning, at least temporarily.

The *umma* is the "community of believers," a group of people who share the conviction that, as Muslims, they are living in accordance with the final revelation from God. The ideal of community is often more theoretical than real. Throughout their history, Muslims have found numerous ways to erect differences between themselves and to engage in ferocious fighting with each other over national or sectarian differences. If this were not enough to vitiate the concept of the Umma, Muslims have also frequently allied with non-Muslims against fellow Muslims. The concept of the Umma has historically been weak when Muslim states are strong; when Muslims feel weak, the Umma is important as a reassurance that they belong to a large community that may be a source of assistance. In those circumstances, the sense of belonging to the Umma transcends cultural frontiers and national boundaries and is sometimes strong enough to obliterate sectarian differences, such as those between Sunnis and Shi'ites. The importance of the Umma grew during the age of imperialism, and it stimulated a high level of communication among various Muslim nationalities as they sought solutions to their subjugation. It is also strong today, when it is common for Muslims to feel threatened when Muslims on the other side of the globe are attacked, regardless of how small or remote the region.

Thus, although the terms *Muslim world* and *Muslim history* lack the precision of *Greenland* or *Australian history,* respectively, they are not meaningless. In this book, the term *Muslim history* refers to the events that took place in *the Muslim world,* by which is meant the Dar al-Islam, those parts of the Dar al-Islam that were captured by non-Muslims, and those communities of Muslims where the conviction of belonging to the Umma stimulated the forging of bonds with other Muslim societies. In this book, the phrase *Islamic history* refers to specifically religious developments rather than to elements of the larger culture.

Introduction: The Making of a Civilization 610–1260

The Formative Period, 610–950

The Prophet Muhammad began his mission in the city of Mecca, on the western edge of the Arabian Peninsula. In the year 610, he began to receive a series of revelations that would later be collected into the book of scripture known as the Qur'an. His teachings provoked hostility from some of the Meccan elites, and tensions rose until the lives of his followers were in danger. In 622, he accepted an invitation extended to him by a delegation from the oasis community of Medina, which asked him to mediate a civil conflict that was tearing the community apart. His 220-mile trek to Medina is known as the Hijra. Because of the significance of the event for later Islamic history, Muslims mark the year in which it occurred as the first year on the Islamic calendar.

At Medina, Muhammad began implementing his vision of a community of believers who attempt to live in submission to the will of God. Islam's first mosque was constructed adjacent to his home, and the site became the center of political and religious affairs in the city. During the Prophet's decade in Medina, the Qur'an's twin themes of monotheism and social justice became more fully developed, and Muslims came to understand that Islam was the fulfillment and completion of Judaism and Christianity: The Hebrew prophets and Jesus had previously brought God's message, but their followers had corrupted and misunderstood their teachings. Muhammad was bringing the message yet again, this time to the Arabs. Jews and Christians were "People of the Book" due to their possession of the scriptures, but their understanding of God and His purposes was deficient.

Muhammad's vision of a community of believers in which merit was based on one's relationship with God was incompatible with the interests of the Meccan elites, whose status was based on tribal hierarchy and wealth. Friction between Mecca and Medina led to a series of three sharp battles, and Medina won two of the three. Muhammad's military achievement and his skillful diplomacy attracted support from around the peninsula. He rapidly built up his military and political power as well as his religious following. Mecca finally capitulated without a struggle in 630. Many more tribal leaders from across the Arabian peninsula then sought out Muhammad and made alliances with him. When he died two years later, he was the recognized leader of some two-thirds of the peninsula.

The Muslim community was unprepared for the Prophet's death. His stunned companions were initially immobilized, but they soon met together and selected a successor, or caliph, to Muhammad. The caliph was to be responsible for religious and political guidance, but was not expected to continue Muhammad's prophetic role. The choice of Abu Bakr as the first caliph was not to everyone's liking, for a group of Muslims thought that Muhammad had already designated his cousin and son-in-law, 'Ali, to be his successor. A further complication for the new caliph was that several of the Arabian tribes refused to recognize him, and refused to send tribute. Abu Bakr began a military campaign to force them back into the new Muslim state. As the campaign pushed farther north into the peninsula, it made a seamless transition into a war of conquest of regions outside the peninsula.

Two great empires lay on the northern frontiers of Arabia. Bordering the Mediterranean Sea was the Byzantine Empire, which was the successor to the Roman Empire. Its language of administration was Greek, and its official religion was a version of Christianity that has come to be called Orthodoxy. To the east lay the Sasanian Empire, which occupied the region from Iraq to western Afghanistan. Its administrative language was a form of Persian, and the religion of the court was Zoroastrianism, although the region of Iraq contained large numbers of Jews and Nestorian Christians. By 640, the Muslim Arabs had conquered Syria and Egypt from the Byzantines and had taken Iraq from the Sasanians. Within a decade, the Sasanian Empire had been destroyed.

There is evidence that the Arab Muslims expected all polytheists to convert to Islam. They did not, however, expect Christians and Jews to convert to Islam. The Prophet's designation of the Jews and Christians as People of the Book meshed with the needs of the new elite. Under the new administration, all non-Muslims would pay a head tax and a tax on property, whereas Muslims paid a tax only on property. Because of a need for revenue, for several decades the Arabs actually discouraged many non-Muslims from converting. Talented Christians and Jews served in important government posts for the next several centuries.

In 656, 'Ali finally became the fourth caliph, but his entire caliphate was consumed by a civil war. It was during this war that his followers came to be called *Shi'ites* (from a word that means "partisan"). For five years, Mu'awiya, a rival from the Meccan clan of Umayya, challenged 'Ali's right to be caliph, and the two men amassed huge armies in defense of their respective claims. In 661, 'Ali agreed to a request to mediate the conflict so that Muslims would not shed each other's blood. Some members of his army were outraged at his agreement to negotiate, saying that the chosen one of God would never be willing to give up his rightful position. They left his army, gaining the label of *Kharijites* (from an Arabic word meaning "to leave"). Shortly thereafter, one of the Kharijites assassinated 'Ali. Kharijites subsequently gained a reputation for regarding anyone who disagreed with them to be heretics who deserved to be killed.

The death of 'Ali opened the way for Mu'awiya to become the fifth caliph. Two decades later, on his deathbed, rather than leaving the choice of the new caliph to a council, he designated his own son. This was the beginning of the Umayyad dynasty, which made Damascus its capital. The Umayyads ruled the Muslim world until 750. They instituted several important administrative reforms and annexed North Africa from Tunisia to Morocco, most of the Iberian Peninsula, the Indus River valley, and lands within Transoxiana, the area that lay to the north of the Amu Darya River (which roughly defines the border of modern Uzbekistan and Turkmenistan). Despite their accomplishments, they were unpopular. Their practice of dynastic succession reeked of monarchy rather than of qualification by integrity and spirituality. They favored certain Arab tribes to the exclusion of others, and they were accused of violating the modest and sober values of Islam by indulging in wine, women, and song.

The inhabitants of the Iraqi city of Kufa had been among the staunchest supporters of 'Ali during the civil war. In 680, they invited his sole surviving son, Husayn, to the city to lead a revolt against the Umayyads. Husayn's entourage was intercepted near the village of Karbala, where Husayn and nearly all of his family were massacred. The bloody deaths triggered among many of the Kufans a sense of remorse, grief, and guilt for not having come to the aid of the helpless band. The event at Karbala appears to have transformed Shi'ism from a sentiment that 'Ali's descendants possessed a right and a natural ability to be caliph, to a conviction that only they possessed the blessing of God to rule due to a unique, God-given spiritual ability. From this time on, numerous politico–religious movements arose that were carried out in the cause of installing an Alid (one of 'Ali's descendants) as caliph. Different groups of Shi'ites existed, each one recognizing a different Alid as its leader. In his spiritual capacity, the Alid leader was referred to as Imam.

In 750, the Umayyads were overthrown by another clan, the Abbasids. The Abbasids tried to exterminate the Umayyads, but one member of the former ruling family escaped to North Africa, and then to the Iberian Peninsula, where he gained the allegiance of most of the local Arab army garrisons. The Abbasids established their capital at Baghdad and began consolidating their authority. They managed to secure control over all the areas that the Umayyads had ruled except for the regions west of Tunisia.

For over a century, the Abbasid caliphal court was rivaled only by the Chinese imperial court for grandeur and spectacle. The caliphs were powerful and sophisticated, and their realm stood in sharp contrast to contemporary Western Europe, where Charlemagne was struggling to find people who could read. The Abbasids began a systematic program of translating scientific, mathematical, medical, and philosophical texts from other languages into Arabic. This intellectual enterprise resulted in a dazzling intellectual renaissance in which the contributions of India, Iran, Greece, and Rome were not only preserved, but synthesized and reworked into novel patterns. It laid the foundation for the intellectual advances of the next several centuries, including the development of modern mathematics and remarkable advances in medicine, optics, pharmacology, astronomy, agricultural sciences, and numerous other fields.

In addition to the emergence of philosophy and science, the early Abbasid period was the setting for four important religious developments. One was the formation of the three most politically influential branches of Shi'ism in subsequent Islamic history: the Zaydis, the Isma'ilis, and the Imamiya. Among the numerous Shi'ite groups that followed various Imams within 'Ali's family was one that focused on a specific chain of Imams that began with 'Ali and continued through his elder son Hasan, but then ignored Hasan's sons and recognized Husayn as the third Imam. The next Imam for this group was Husayn's surviving son, 'Ali Zayn al-'Abidin, and then one of 'Ali Zayn's sons, Zayd. Zayd won a devoted following because of his teaching of the centrality of the duty of ensuring justice. He burned with hatred for the Umayyads, and he believed that inaction in the face of oppression was a sin. He raised a revolt against the Umayyads in 740, in the course of which he was killed. His followers, the Zaydis, continued to follow Imams who were Alids, but they were not convinced that an Imam had to have been the son of another Imam. They also did not regard their Imams as infallible. The important criterion for an Imam was that he was an Alid who took an activist stance against injustice. Because duty was more important than doctrine to the Zaydis, they did not develop a sense of identity that contrasted as sharply with the majority of Muslims as the other Shi'ites did. They went on to found small states in remote areas such as the mountains of Iran and Yemen.

The most influential line within Shi'ism respected Zayd but did not regard him as an Imam. Instead, these Shi'ites believed that the Imamate passed from 'Ali Zayn to Zayd's half-brother, Muhammad al-Baqir. Muhammad al-Baqir was a quiet scholar, not an active soldier. Toward the end of his life, he designated his son, Ja'far al-Sadiq, to be the sixth Imam. Sometime around the year 760, Ja'far named one of his sons, Isma'il, to be his successor. Isma'il, however, died soon thereafter, plunging the community into confusion, for the Imam's designation of his successor was regarded as an infallible choice. Ja'far, however, was still alive, whereas Isma'il was dead. The evidence suggests that Ja'far never designated another successor. Upon his death in 765, his followers splintered into numerous factions. In this book we will be following the history of two of them. One regarded Ja'far's choice of Isma'il as determinative and followed Isma'il's son, Muhammad ibn ("son of") Isma'il. The other group followed one of Isma'il's brothers, Musa al-Kazim.

The group that followed Muhammad ibn Isma'il came to be known as the Isma'ilis. After Muhammad died several years later, their activities became lost to history for a century. They disappeared into secret cells, and they apparently taught their followers that Muhammad ibn Isma'il would soon return, bringing justice to a world that had failed to follow God's teachings. During the last quarter of the ninth century, leaders claiming to be from this group appeared in Iraq and Syria, engaging in active missionary work and teaching the need for social revolution. One of their leaders made his way to North Africa at the beginning of the tenth century. Soon his followers overthrew the governor of what is now Tunisia and the Isma'ilis took his place. The new government, led by the Isma'ili Imam, denied the legitimacy of the Abbasid caliphate. The new state became known as the Fatimid Empire.

The Shi'ites who followed Musa al-Kazim remained a public group. They were known as the Imamiya, and they avoided political confrontation with the Abbasids. The Imamate passed down from father to son until 874, when the eleventh Imam died. Most of his followers thought that they had become leaderless, and they fragmented into two dozen factions. One group among the Imamiya, however, proclaimed that the eleventh Imam had been survived by an infant son, who became known as Muhammad al-Muntazar. They asserted that God was protecting him from his enemies, and that he would return to lead his people in the fullness of time. Because God is hiding him, he has become known as the Hidden Imam. From 874 to 941, he was in the Lesser Concealment (sometimes rendered *Lesser Occultation*), during which he communicated with spokesmen within the Imamiya. After 941, however, he has been in the Greater Concealment. In the Greater Concealment, the Imam is still the spiritual guide and light of the world, but there is no longer any direct communication between the Imam and his followers. The most learned and spiritual among the Imamiya can obtain guidance from the Imam through dreams and visions. Because the Imamiya believe that there have been only twelve Imams, they are widely known as the Twelver Shi'ites.

A second major development during this period was the rise of a Sunni self-consciousness. Non-Shi'ites did not have an Imam to consult, and so many of them began seeking religious guidance from collections of anecdotes (*hadith*) that conveyed the Prophet's extra-Qur'anic sayings and narratives of his behavior in certain situations. These Hadith were believed to portray accurately the Prophet's *sunna,* a word that suggests "practice," "way," or "custom." The Muslims who used them as models for their own practice began calling themselves *ahl al-sunna wa al-jama'a,* or the People of the (Prophet's) Sunna and of the Community. The term *Sunni* refers to these people, who accepted the idea that the caliphate was a legitimate institution, even when they realized that it needed to be more responsive to the people's needs and to the requirements of God's will.

A third development during the eighth and ninth centuries that merits notice here was jurisprudence. As Muslims moved out of Medina into regions as far west as the Pyrenees Mountains and as far east as the Indus River, they encountered new customs and laws. Many of the existing laws worked well enough, but pious Muslims wanted their lives to conform to the rules and principles laid out in the Qur'an. During the late Umayyad era, religious scholars (*'ulama';* hereafter *ulama*), began discussing with each other how to formulate a comprehensive system of guidelines for living in accordance with God's will. They studied the Qur'an even more assiduously, and they began examining the Hadith for guidelines. By synthesizing the Qur'an and the Hadith, these individuals began codifying rules that embraced all aspects of life, including marriage, divorce, inheritance, theft and murder, and religious ritual.

It is important to note that the development of these regulations was the result of initiatives made by private individuals and was not a governmental activity. The Abbasid government encouraged this juristic activity and appointed many of the ulama to be judges (*qadis*), but Islamic law, or the Shari'a, was recognized by Muslims everywhere as the result of a sincere effort by pious scholars to discern God's will. Inevitably, scholars from different regions used a variety of techniques to determine guidelines, and local customs helped to shape their conclusions. In the ninth century, there were literally hundreds of juristic traditions, or "schools," of Islamic law. By the early tenth century, however, most scholars had agreed with a reform movement that proposed a common set of four techniques: The Qur'an and Hadith were the basic sources of principles, but a scholar could make analogies with other cases and could also employ *ijtihad*, or independent judgment. As a result of this synthesis, the number of legal traditions gradually dwindled until there were only four major Sunni ones: the Maliki, Shafi'i, Hanbali, and Hanafi. In general, Shi'ites were not active in developing legal texts during this period because they could consult their Imams for guidance. The eminent scholar and Imam, Ja'far al-Sadiq, however, had laid the foundation for a Shi'ite school of law, and his teachings were revived and expanded during the Greater Occulation. His school is called the Ja'fari school.

A fourth major development of this era was Sufism. Sufism was the result of a yearning to attain purity of heart and to experience a deeply spiritual relationship with God. It is the primary expression of mysticism in Islam. It is similar, although not identical, to the mystical expressions within Christianity exemplified by Meister Eckhart, St. John of the Cross, St. Teresa of Avila, and Thomas Merton. Sufis sought to spend as much time as possible in prayer and the contemplation of the attributes of God. They often fasted and deprived their body of comforts in order to focus their spiritual life.

Tension developed between Sufis and non-Sufis. Some Sufis were openly contemptuous of the religious habits of most Muslims, which often went little beyond performing the five daily prayers, attending the Friday sermon, giving alms, and abstaining from the consumption of pork and alcohol. Some Sufis neglected to participate in such rituals, claiming that they were prescribed only for the masses, who could not respond to the deeper, more spiritual, aspects of the faith. A few Sufis even claimed that their religious experiences had enabled them to realize that they were God Himself, a patently blasphemous claim within the context of the uncompromisingly monotheistic Islamic tradition. By the mid-tenth century, however, Sufi leaders had developed a theoretical framework for helping initiates understand that the mystical experience required being grounded in the Shari'a, including the rituals of worship. Although some ulama never overcame their suspicions of the heretical possibilities latent within the mystical path, Sufism rapidly became popular both among the masses and among the learned elite.

By the mid-tenth century, the small movement that the Prophet had founded in Mecca was transformed into a civilization that stretched across 5000 miles from Iberia to western India. Intellectually, religiously, and economically, it was dynamic and creative. Politically, however, the dream of a united Muslim community had collapsed. Shi'ites had never accepted the caliphate of non-Alids, and the Abbasids had not been able to restore caliphal control over areas west of Tunis. During the late ninth century, some of the caliph's Iranian governors began withholding taxes, and in 910, the Fatimids created a rival caliphate in North Africa. Shortly thereafter, in 929, the Umayyad rulers of Iberia declared their own caliphate. The Abbasid caliph may well have asked himself whether things could get worse. He was soon to discover that things could, indeed, get worse: In 945, a group of military adventurers from a mountainous area on the southwestern shore of the Caspian Sea seized Baghdad, the rest of Iraq, and western Iran. The new rulers, the Buyids, allowed the caliph to remain in his palace as a figurehead, but they exercised all real military and political power. For most of the next three centuries, the Abbasid caliph was merely a reminder of what had been.

A Civilization Under Siege, 950–1260

Historians of Western Europe like to point out that the violence experienced by the peoples of that region from at least the ninth century through the eleventh century (and both ends of that spectrum could be extended) contributed to the poverty, illiteracy, and overall misery of life characteristic of the era. Some of the violence was self-inflicted, in the form of feudal competition, and some of it was inflicted from outside, in the form of invasions from Muslims, Norsemen, and Magyars. It was only when the violence began to wane toward the end of the eleventh century that urban life could resume and the amenities of civilization could appear. It was only then, too, that people had the confidence to explore new avenues of thought, even when they conflicted with traditional dogmas.

For much of the Muslim world, the wavelengths of violence and stability did not correspond chronologically with those of Europe. The ninth and tenth centuries were eras of relative stability and of excited intellectual inquiry for the Muslim world, but the tenth century inaugurated a long era of astonishing levels of violence. To read a short summary of it can be mind-numbing, but it is worth taking the risk of numbing our minds here. Once we have recovered our equilibrium, we should have a better understanding of why subsequent Muslim history took the course that it did.

Not long after the Buyids became the masters of Baghdad, the Isma'ili Fatimids began to act upon their ambition of ruling the Muslim world. In 969, they conquered Egypt and went on to take over the Holy Cities of Mecca and Medina and to conquer much of Syria. They founded Cairo as their new capital city. By virtue of their control of trade routes to West Africa and the major route between the Mediterranean Sea and the Indian Ocean, they made enormous profits from trade. From the latter part of the tenth century to the late eleventh century, they seemed poised to dominate the Muslim world.

During the second half of the eleventh century, however, plague, famine, and turmoil within the Fatimid military ranks weakened the regime. Then, in 1094, a schism developed when the caliph–Imam died. Two of his sons claimed the Imamate, but supporters of one, al-Musta'li, killed the other claimant, Nizar. The followers of Nizar fled to mountain strongholds in Syria and Iran, creating the Nizari branch of Isma'ilism. The Musta'lis controlled Egypt and were the group who were still identified as the Fatimids.

Meanwhile, the Buyids were surprised by an invasion from the east. In 1055, the Buyid holdings in Iran and Iraq were captured by the Saljuq Turks. The Saljuqs were part of a large Turkish migration from Central Asia that had begun in the mid-tenth century. At the turn of the eleventh century, the Saljuqs adopted a Sunni Muslim identity. In the 1030s, they moved into Khorasan (roughly, the region of modern northeastern Iran, Turkmenistan, and western Afghanistan), and in 1055 they seized Baghdad. They claimed to be "saving" the Abbasid caliph from the Twelver Shi'ite Buyids. In fact, however, the caliph remained a figurehead while the Saljuq leader, or *sultan,* exercised real power.

In the 1060s, a Saljuq chieftain rebelled against the sultan and withdrew with his followers into eastern Asia Minor. Leaders of the remaining, and larger, group of Saljuqs, called the Great Saljuqs, consolidated their control over Iran and Iraq. They also began plans to conquer Syria and Egypt from the Isma'ili Fatimids. They justified the attack on fellow Muslims in the same way that they had justified attacking the Buyids: Shi'ites, they argued, were heretics, and should be fought. As the Saljuq campaign against the Fatimids began in 1071, the Byzantines decided to attack the Great Saljuqs in retaliation for raids that isolated bands of Saljuq herders had been conducting in northwestern Iran and eastern Anatolia. At the Battle of Manzikert near Lake Van, the army of the Great Saljuqs obliterated the Byzantine army. The entire Anatolian plateau now lay open to the Turkish herdsmen, whose widespread presence there would soon prompt some observers to coin the name of "Turkey" for the region.

Traditionally, the Turkish herdsmen had engaged in raiding their neighbors in their spare time. Now, they had the opportunity to raid Christian settlements and receive religious credit for it. This was the inauguration of what came to be known as the *gazi* tradition in Anatolia. *Gazi* means "raider," and it derives from the Arabic word that was applied to the nomadic raiders of the Arabian Peninsula. Henceforth, however, *gazi* gained the additional connotation of *mujahid,* or "one who engages in *jihad.*" In the manuals of the Shari'a, the two terms were not at all similar, because jihad was theoretically governed by specific rules. An offensive jihad was conducted against areas not ruled by a Muslim caliph (the *Dar al-Kufr,* or "Abode of Unbelief"). Only a Muslim caliph was to declare and lead such a war, and he was to do so only after demanding that the non-Muslims convert to Islam or submit to the caliph and pay the protection money required of non-Muslims. If war ensued, it was to follow explicit rules of a "just war." A defensive jihad was obligatory on all Muslims when non-Muslim armies invaded the *Dar al-Islam* ("Abode of Islam"). Its purpose was to repel the invader. Gazis, by contrast, were raiding Christian settlements because they sought plunder; the main reason they did not raid Muslim settlements was because Muslim rulers punished them when they did so. Gazis did not hold grudges against the Christians; they frequently welcomed their victims into their bands after a raid to enable them to recoup some of their losses. Life on the frontier was much less rule-bound than life in the capital cities.

In the aftermath of Manzikert, Byzantine factions began quarreling with each other over rights to the throne in Constantinople, and one faction requested aid from the Saljuq group that had split from the Great Saljuqs in the 1060s. Byzantines even gave the Turkish band the city of Nicaea, east of Constantinople, for use as its headquarters. This group of Saljuqs soon became known as the Saljuqs of Rum, because the Arabs had called Byzantine territory (the area covered by the eastern half of the Roman Empire) *Rum,* or "Rome." The Saljuqs of Rum, like the Great Saljuqs, began to acquire the trappings of urban life and to patronize art and architecture. They became rivals of the Byzantines, but not their mortal enemies. Over the next century, the Byzantines found themselves far more threatened by fellow

Christians to the west than by the Saljuqs, with whom they cooperated as often as they fought.

The Great Saljuqs continued with their campaign against the Fatimids and conquered Syria from them. By 1090, however, Fatimid "special forces" groups had established themselves in remote and seemingly impregnable fortresses in Syria and Iran. The most famous of the strongholds was Alamut, in the Elburz Mountains of northern Iran. From these outposts, Fatimid agents conducted assassinations of Saljuq officials. They were the first of the legendary "Assassins." In 1092 they murdered the powerful Saljuq prime minister, Nizam al-Mulk. A few months later, the Saljuq sultan died. At that point, the Saljuq *amirs* (princes) began quarreling with each other over who had the right to the throne. The result was a devastating civil war. Although a new Saljuq sultan established power over Iran and Iraq, the region of Syria was subsequently ruled by a myriad of petty Saljuq princes. They jealously defended their small principalities not only against each other, but also against the Fatimids, the Saljuq sultan, and the Assassins (who, after 1094, welcomed the Nizari refugees from Egypt and embraced their cause).

The Battle of Manzikert, the Saljuq civil war of 1092, and the Fatimid schism of 1094 set the stage for a famous episode in the history of southwestern Asia: the crusades. In 1094, the Byzantine emperor had secured himself against fellow Byzantine rivals and wanted to begin rebuilding his army, which had still not recovered from the devastation of Manzikert. He sent a delegation to ask the pope to help him recruit Frankish cavalrymen for his army, because he was facing actual threats from Normans, Serbs, and Bulgarians to the west and a potential threat from his sometimes-friendly rivals, the Saljuqs of Rum. In 1095, the pope translated this call for army recruits as a call for volunteers who would go to the aid of the Christians of the East. In 1096, a massive army of Frankish knights began its slow march across Europe. The crusaders had no intention of joining the Byzantine army, and when they arrived at Constantinople, their arrogance and independence alienated the emperor.

The crusaders continued their march to Jerusalem, and what had begun as a campaign to aid the Christians of the East quickly turned into a cold and often hostile relationship between the Catholic Franks and the Orthodox Byzantines. The crusaders endured some difficult sieges of Muslim cities, but in general they found that the fragmentation of Saljuq power in Syria and the Fatimid schism had left the region vulnerable to outside invaders. The crusaders captured Jerusalem in 1099 and set up a string of feudal principalities from Jerusalem northward to the Taurus Mountains. Had the First Crusade been attempted a decade earlier, it would have confronted the united power of the Great Saljuqs, and the results would have been quite different.

In the western Muslim world, the Umayyad dynasty continued to consolidate its power in the Iberian Peninsula. Prior to 929, it had claimed only the status of an amirate, or rule by a prince. The area ruled by the Umayyad prince and other Muslim chiefs covered roughly the southern two-thirds of the peninsula and was referred to as Andalus. To the north lay an arc of territory occupied by feuding Christian kingdoms. The Umayyad rulers were based in the city of Cordoba from the time of their arrival there in 756. By 929, the Umayyad ruler had forced all rival Muslim chiefs to submit to him. Even then he might not have claimed to lead a caliphate had it not been for the growing power of the Fatimid caliphate, which was still based in Tunisia. Because both rivals were trying to bring the Maghrib (North Africa west of Libya) into their sphere of influence, however, he felt compelled to claim the same level of political authority as the Fatimid Imam.

Andalus had always been difficult to rule due to tensions among the various Arab tribes that had migrated there and to Arab tensions with Berbers, who had formed a large component of the conquering Muslim armies of the period 711–720. Many Berbers, who were indigenous to North Africa, had become Muslim, but Arabs often regarded them as second-class Muslims. The tensions among the Arab tribes and between Arab Muslims and Berber Muslims were a much greater threat to Umayyad control than any challenge from the Umayyads' Christian and Jewish subjects.

In 1003, aggressive governors in Andalus challenged the Umayyad caliph in Cordoba, and a civil war broke out. It raged until 1031, when the caliphate collapsed. Andalus became divided into numerous city–states, each as jealous of its independence as the Saljuq city–states in Syria proved to be in the 1090s. Christian kingdoms in the north began to take advantage of the Muslims' political divisions in the process known as the Reconquista, or "reconquest." Several Muslim cities fell to Christian sieges. The most shocking loss was when the large city of Toledo fell, in 1085. At that point, several leaders of Muslim city–states launched a joint appeal for help from a new Berber empire in the Maghrib.

Although Berbers had represented the single largest ethnic group in North Africa for many centuries, they had characteristically been subjects rather than masters. The Romans and Byzantines had ruled over them, and then the Arabs had taken over North Africa. Individual Berbers, such as St. Augustine, attained high levels of achievement, but rarely as political leaders. That all changed in the eleventh century. In the 1030s, a religious reform movement arose among a group of Berbers in the region between modern Senegal and Morocco. Its leaders were called the Almoravids, and they soon turned their movement into a powerful political and military force. By 1069, they had control of Morocco, and by 1082 they ruled the area from the Atlantic to Algiers. It was to the Almoravid Empire that the frightened Muslim leaders of Andalus appealed for help in 1085. The Almoravids responded by defeating the Christian armies that threatened the remaining Muslim city–states. Much to the dismay of most Andalusis, the Almoravids did not go home but rather incorporated Andalus into their empire.

The Almoravid victory did not last long. The Berbers of the Maghrib were divided into several groups, whose dialects were sometimes mutually unintelligible. Linguistic and other differences caused friction among them. During the early twelfth century, yet another religious reform movement arose among a group of Berbers just a few miles south of the Almoravid capital of Marrakech. These Berbers were rivals of the group that constituted the core base of the Almoravids, and their religious emphases exacerbated the existing differences they had with the Almoravids. Known as the Almohads, they destroyed the Almoravids by 1147, and they soon had an even larger empire than that of their predecessors. The Almohad Empire patronized the arts and intellectual life more lavishly than the Almoravids had done, and numerous spectacular architectural works in Morocco and in Andalus remind us of its vibrant cultural life.

By the early thirteenth century, however, the Almohads had weakened. In 1212, a coalition of Iberian Christian kingdoms defeated the Almohad army not far from Cordoba. The Christians then resumed quarreling among themselves rather than continuing their campaign, but in 1236 they allied once again to fight the Muslims. Between 1236 and 1248, they captured all of Andalus except for the southern province of Granada. Simultaneously, the Almohad Empire collapsed in North Africa and was replaced by yet another Berber dynasty, the Marinids (1269–1465). The Reconquista was a series of crusades in the same sense that the more famous ones in the eastern Mediterranean were. They were conducted in the name of Christ, the pope continually urged reluctant kings to launch them, and soldiers fought in the expectation of material reward as well as spiritual glory. The major difference between the two sets of crusades was that the Reconquista achieved long-term success: None of the captured territorities reverted to Muslim rule.

By contrast, the crusades in the eastern Mediterranean were only temporarily successful. As early as 1147, the largest of the crusader states fell to Muslims, and Jerusalem fell in 1187 to Saladin, the ruler of Egypt. His conquest of Jerusalem sparked the Third Crusade, but even the legendary Richard Lionheart of England could not regain the holy places of Christianity from Muslim rule. The Fourth Crusade of 1204 was intended to be a direct attack on Egypt, in order to deliver a blow at the heart of the Muslim power that ruled Jerusalem. Instead, Venetian merchants and Frankish knights set out for Constantinople. The crusaders captured the city, looted its art and treasure, and murdered and raped many of its inhabitants. Merchant–princes from Venice began ruling the city, and the Byzantine royal family had to flee to cities in Anatolia. The crusades, which were intended to help the Christians of the East, had now devastated Eastern Christianity's greatest city. The remaining crusades were failures, and only a few isolated crusader castles remained.

While the smoke was rising over Constantinople, a Mongol chieftain was gathering a confederation in a region northwest of China. The chieftain, who became known as Chinggis Khan, was sufficiently powerful by 1206 to launch an attack on China. He won large swaths of territory there, and he might have continued to focus on Chinese territory had not a Muslim ruler in Transoxiana insulted him. Chinggis felt compelled to set an example of the ruler in order to deter any such insolence in the future. Between 1219 and 1222 he conducted a campaign of destruction and terror in Transoxiana and eastern Iran on a scale not seen since Alexander the Great had engaged in an orgy of blood-letting 1500 years earlier.

In 1256, Chinggis Khan's grandson, Hulagu, led a second Mongol military campaign into Iran. His first major goal was the destruction of the Nizari castles, which had proved impregnable until that time. Hulagu captured them all and killed all the Nizaris he found, forcing the survivors to flee. He then destroyed Baghdad in 1258. His next target was Egypt. There, in 1250, a group of Turkish cavalrymen within the royal army had overthrown Saladin's Ayyubid dynasty and had taken power themselves. The cavalrymen were called *mamluks* (Arabic for "owned"), because as boys they had been sold into slavery from their homes north of the Black Sea and Caspian Sea. In Egypt, they were trained in military skills until they proved their worth and reliability as top-flight cavalrymen. Then they were manumitted and enrolled in the elite unit of the Egyptian army. The mamluks who seized power in 1250 had not intended to rule, but after a few years, they became convinced that no one was more worthy than the cavalrymen themselves to do so. The Ayyubid Empire thus became the Mamluke Empire (this book uses *Mamluke* to designate the mamluks in their capacity as state actors). This was the state that Hulagu set out to destroy in 1260.

As Hulagu was poised to attack, he received word of the death of the Great Khan in China, and he thought it was prudent to return to China to safeguard his interests in the coming succession crisis. He left only a fraction of his army in Syria. The Mamlukes attacked and destroyed this garrison at the Battle of `Ayn Jalut, near the Sea of Tiberias. This was the first time that a Mongol army had been defeated. Hulagu found out—too late to save his army in Syria—that he did not need to return to China after all. He established his headquarters at Tabriz, in northwestern Iran, and he did not attack the Mamlukes during the remaining five years of his life. The Mamlukes, meanwhile, earned widespread admiration for defending the realm of Islam.

Despite the rising level of violence during the period 950–1260, Muslims made extraordinary advances in the arts and sciences. In mathematics, science, medicine, and philosophy, their legacy became clear when Western Europeans began translating their work into Latin. Particularly after 1085, when Castile captured the city of Toledo, monks and Christian kings began systematic projects to translate Arabic texts into Latin, much as the Muslims had done in the ninth century to obtain texts from other languages. The Muslim scholars whom the Latins respected the most included Ibn Sina (known in Europe as Avicenna, famous for his philosophical texts and his medical encyclopedia, which was used in European universities into the seventeenth century), al-Razi (Rhazes, medicine), Ibn Rushd (Averroes, philosophy), al-Ghazali (Algazel, philosophy), al-Khwarizmi (Algorismi—the origin of *algorithm*—who devised algebra), and Ibn al-Haytham (Alhazen, optics). The work of these and numerous other scholars contributed to the stimulation of an intellectual awakening in thirteenth-century Western Europe.

Muslims were also advancing what most people consider to be religious knowledge as such (although many Muslims consider true knowledge to be religious knowledge, properly understood). Al-Ghazali's fame in Europe was actually misplaced: His summary of philosophical thought that the Europeans admired was actually written to help his students criticize certain tendencies among philosophers. Al-Ghazali himself was more concerned to advance the realms of theology and Sufism. There is no more space here to enumerate the details of religious scholarship than there is for the secular sciences, but three other scholars must be mentioned, since they played a major role in subsequent Islamic thought. One was Ibn al-`Arabi, who was born in Andalus but migrated to Syria. He devised a complex, multilayered philosophical exposition of the Sufi experience that became the basic philosophical underpinning for most literate Sufis over the next several centuries. Another writer was al-Rumi, whose Sufi poetry in the Persian language became the best loved of all Sufi writings from Anatolia to India. The other intellectual was al-Suhrawardi, an Iranian whose philosophical exposition of Sufism employed the metaphor of God as Light and the metaphor of the soul's knowledge of God as Illumination.

Finally, mention must be made of two institutions that emerged toward the end of this period. Both played major roles in enabling Islam to survive the formidable challenges that were rising to confront it. One was the *madrasa,* which supplemented mosques as centers of education. Madrasas might be privately endowed or supported by the state, but they provided teachers, lodging, and, often, stipends for the poor. They provided advanced education and were the primary institution that produced ulama.

Another institution that emerged during this period was the Sufi lodge, which might be called a *ribat, tekke, zawiya,* or *khanaqa.* The emergence of the lodge enabled Sufis to live in proximity to a spiritual teacher, rather than occasionally visiting the home of such a teacher. This development led to a greater emphasis on the teacher–disciple relationship, and to the emergence of *tariqa*s, or "paths" (usually rendered "orders" or "brotherhoods"). Each spiritual master (usually called *shaykh* or *murshid* by Arabic speakers and *pir* by Persian speakers) developed his own progressive series of stages to reach spiritual enlightenment, and each order was distinguished from the others by its particular pattern. Each order also had its own distinctive *dhikr* (chant or invocation) that enabled its members to achieve the state of mind that enhanced the meditative experience.

By the middle of the thirteenth century, Muslims had created a flourishing civilization that was the envy of most of the rest of the world. Europeans, in particular, were voraciously devouring whatever they could glean from the texts found in libraries in Andalus and Sicily. The development of Islamic law, educational institutions, economic networks, and artistic traditions represented a high degree of intellectual, social, and economic attainment. Muslims were justifiably proud of those achievements. They were very concerned, on the other hand, about two other developments. One was that Muslims had not found an answer to the problems of political organization. The original vision of a community of believers united within a single, moral, and just state had long since dissipated into the mundane reality of ambitious and power-hungry individuals and cliques seizing and holding power for their own ends. Despite its cultural cohesion, the Muslim world was hopelessly fragmented politically; worse, there was no linkage between the religious vision and the political reality.

The other worrisome development was the success of the Reconquista and the Mongol invasions. Very few Muslims have ever possessed the world-denying, vale-of-tears perspective that has been a powerful current within Christianity. (Note the absence of the monastic tradition within Islam.) Muslims have regarded Muhammad's creation of a God-centered society to be paradigmatic for their times: God will bless and extend the arena within which Islam is practiced by a righteous people. Why, then, was God allowing these terrible things to happen to His community? Many Muslims began to question what had gone wrong. Had they strayed from the path that God had expected them to follow? At the very time that Western Europe was becoming more secure, more prosperous, and more confident, much of the Muslim world had become less secure, less prosperous, and less confident.

PART ONE

Mongol Hegemony, 1260–1405

The Mongol conquests dwarfed those of the Arabs, which had occurred some six centuries earlier. Between 1206 and 1260, the Mongols subjugated northern China, Central Asia, Iran and Iraq, eastern Anatolia, the Caucasus, and the vast steppe region from Mongolia to the area now occupied by eastern Poland. By 1279, they completed the conquest of southern China, as well. On the one hand, then, the achievement is greater than the Arabs on sheer scale. On the other hand, the Mongols did not create a civilization, and most of their conquests were lost within three generations.

The Mongols are not easy to dismiss as a destructive, one-time wonder, however. Despite the fact that they soon lost control of their possessions, their legacy was remembered, revered, and emulated for centuries thereafter throughout much of the vast region they had conquered. In western and central Europe, too, the legacy lingered, but in a peculiar fashion: Rumors that a great force to the east had brutalized part of the Muslim world during 1219–1222 sparked hope in Europe that a potential ally, perhaps even a Christian king, existed in the east that would help to destroy Islam. This was the origin of the legend of Prester John, a great Christian king in the East with whom the Europeans should join forces against Islam. The hope was so strong that when, in 1238, the Nizari Imam at Alamut and the Abbasid caliph in Baghdad jointly dispatched an embassy to Europe, appealing for help against the Mongols, they were rebuffed. Europe, particularly in the person of the Pope, was pursuing a diametrically opposed policy of attempting to form a great Christian alliance with the Mongol Great Khan—whom some thought to be Prester John—against the world of Islam. Even the crushing Mongol defeat of European knights three years later at Liegnitz did not dissipate the fantasy of Prester John, who continued to fascinate and lure Europeans for hundreds of years to come.

But the Mongols were not only the stuff of memory and legend. They transformed the world. These horsemen from the steppes who destroyed so many cities quickly began to rebuild urban economies once they assumed power. Few of their leaders appear to have appreciated the importance of agriculture, and that sector usually languished as a result. Long-distance trade, on the other hand, flourished as never before. From the Pacific to the Black Sea, bandits were held in check, caravanserais were constructed, and diplomatic contacts were established. The famous career of the Venetian Marco Polo in the last third of the thirteenth century would be unthinkable without the Mongols. He and his father and uncle traveled from Constantinople to Beijing and back with less fear for their lives or property than they would have felt had they journeyed anywhere in the Mediterranean basin. Taking advantage of the *pax Mongolica*, Venice quickly established a vast trade network that extended from the Pacific to Scandinavia.

The Mongol Empire affected the histories of all its neighbors as well as of peoples beyond their immediate reach. The history of a large part of the Muslim world was irrevocably altered. The Mongols and their desperately ambitious scion Timur Lang dominated western Asia for only a century and a half, but Mongol hegemony had such a profound influence on the course of Muslim history that it merits a separate section in this book. Chapter 1 establishes the historical framework for the period. It examines the history of the three Mongol states whose rulers eventually converted to Islam, traces the rise of three other powerful Muslim states during this period, and explores the destructive effects of the plague and Timur Lang on western Asia. Chapter 2 examines the cumulative effects of these and other events on Muslim intellectual and religious life. The evidence undermines the widely held view that the Mongol era caused Islamic civilization to decline. Despite frequent outbreaks of political chaos and the long-lasting economic depression of some regions, Islamic culture continued to thrive and break new ground in a wide variety of fields. More striking still, the period marks a transition from an era of several centuries during which the frontiers of the Muslim world had remained largely static to an age of remarkable expansion. In many respects, the period of Mongol hegemony marks the beginning of a golden age of Muslim history.

CHRONOLOGY

1210–1236	Reign of Iltutmish, founder of Delhi sultanate
1219–1222	Campaigns of Chinggis into Muslim world
1240s	Batu founds Saray, begins to administer his Qipchaq khanate
1250	Mamlukes seize power in Egypt and Syria
1253–1260	Hulagu's campaign
c.1250–c.1290	Career of Hajji Bektash
1260	Mamlukes defeat Hulagu's army at 'Ayn Jalut
1260–1265	Hulagu is first ruler of Il-khanate, establishes Maragha observatory
1261	Byzantines regain Constantinople from Latin Kingdom
1269	Marinids replace Almohads in Morocco
1271–1295	Marco Polo's adventures in the Mongol Empire
c.1280–1326	Career of Osman, founder of Ottoman dynasty
c.1280–1334	Career of Shaykh Safi al-Din
1291	Mamlukes capture the last Crusader castle in Syria
c.1290–1327	Career of Ibn Taymiya in Mamluke Empire
1310–1341	Third, and most successful, reign of Mamluke ruler, al-Nasir Muhammad
1313–1341	Reign of Uzbeg, and the Islamization of Qipchaq khanate
1325–1351	Reign of Muhammad ibn Tughluq of Delhi
1325–1349	Ibn Battuta's journey east; serves Ibn Tughluq seven years
1326–1362	Reign of Orhan of Ottoman sultanate
1334	Schism in Chaghatay khanate, Transoxiana is lost
1335	Collapse of Il-khanate
c.1335–1375	Career of Ibn al-Shatir
1347	First wave of plague
c.1350–1390	Career of Hafez
c.1350–1398	Career of Baha' al-Din Naqshband
c.1350	Consensus has been achieved in most *madhhabs* that, theoretically, *ijtihad* is no longer permitted
1359–1377	Civil war in Qipchaq khanate; Toqtamish secures control by 1383
c.1360–1406	Career of Ibn Khaldun
1368	Ming dynasty overthrows Yuan dynasty of the Mongols in China
1370	Timur's career begins in Transoxiana
1381–1402	Timur's campaigns from Ankara to New Saray to Delhi
1405	Death of Timur

CHAPTER 1

The Great Transformation

By 1248, the Christian kingdoms of the Iberian Peninsula had seized all Muslim territory north of the Strait of Gibraltar except for the small principality of Granada. Over the next century and a half, they secured their control over this area, confirming that the Reconquista had succeeded in destroying one of the most populous and culturally creative zones of the Muslim world. Simultaneously, a similar process of conquest and consolidation of power was taking place in the eastern Muslim world. During the 1250s, the second major Mongol invasion of southwestern Asia took place. Millions of Muslims were now under the rule either of Christian Europeans or of pagan Mongols. For the first time since the Islamic calendar began, half or more of the world's Muslims were subject to governments dominated by non-Muslims.

In spite of the similarities, the situation in the eastern Muslim world differed from that of the Iberian Peninsula. The challenges facing Muslims in Iberia were insidious and chronic, but those in the east were violent and episodic and transformed the eastern Muslim world in profound ways. Whereas the Iberian Muslim community slowly suffocated under increasing restrictions, Muslims in three of the four Mongol empires rejoiced at the conversion of their rulers to Islam by the early fourteenth century. Their joy was short lived, for all three dynasties suddenly lost their grip on power in the middle third of the fourteenth century. Anarchy and widespread destruction became the order of the day. As the dynasties were collapsing, the worldwide epidemic of plague began its deadly work, leaving large areas of the Muslim world underpopulated. The first wave of the plague had hardly subsided when a half-Turk, half-Mongol warlord named Timur Lang began his career. His inexplicably vicious campaigns ranged from Delhi to Damascus and caused the horrors of Chinggis and Hulagu to pale by comparison. From 1380 to 1405, the very mention of his name sent panic into the hearts of multitudes, and his conquests laid waste to vast regions. The region from the Aegean Sea to the Ganges River had been violently shaken, with consequences that would reverberate for centuries.

The Mongol Khanates

Shortly before his death in 1227, Chinggis Khan gave each of his four sons a portion of his great empire. He did so in accordance with the ancient Mongol custom of establishing a home for the eldest son at the furthest distance and assigning the youngest to tend the family hearth. Accordingly, Jochi, the eldest, received the steppe land that lay north of the Aral sea and extended westward "as far as the hooves of Mongol horses have reached," whereas Tolui, the youngest, received the ancient Mongol homeland that is now eastern Mongolia. The second son, Chaghatay, and the third son, Ogedai, divided the lands that lay between those extremes. Ogedai succeeded his father as Great Khan, and his son Guyuk replaced him in the 1240s. In 1251, Tolui's eldest son Mongke became the Great Khan.

From his capital at Qaraqorum in modern Mongolia, Mongke (1251–1259) planned a new campaign of expansion. Leaders of Christian Europe hoped that he was Prester John, and they appealed to him to join them in a crusade against Islam, but he was unwilling to do so unless the Christian rulers and the Pope submitted themselves to him. Confident that the Lord of the Sky had entrusted the world to the Mongols, he embarked upon an ambitious campaign of conquest on his own terms. He sent one brother, Qubilai, to conquer the Sung dynasty in southern China and another brother, Hulagu, to subjugate southwestern Asia. When Mongke died, he was succeeded by Qubilai (1260–1294), who completed the conquest of China and is regarded as the first ruler of the Yuan dynasty (1279–1368) in China. He symbolized his new status by moving his capital from Qaraqorum to Beijing.

During the rule of Mongke and Qubilai, the Mongol domains became more or less institutionalized: The Great Khan ruled over Mongolia and China; Jochi's son Batu and his successors ruled over the Golden Horde in the vast steppe that extended from north of the Aral Sea almost to the Baltic Sea; the Chaghatay khanate ruled over the area that now comprises the Chinese province of Xinjiang and eastern Afghanistan, as well as the territory north of the Amu Darya River; and Hulagu's Il-khanid regime comprised Iraq, eastern Anatolia, the southern Caucasus, and Iran to just east of Herat (see Map 1.1).

The Qipchaq Khanate

Europeans from the sixteenth century on referred to the domain of Batu's successors as the Golden Horde. The origin of the name is lost in obscurity. The English word *Horde* derives from the Mongol word *ordu,* meaning "camp" or "domain," but the meaning of the term *Golden* has spawned considerable debate, with no consensus having emerged. The name Golden Horde is commonly used in English to refer to the entire period of the dominance of the Mongols on the Eurasian steppes. Europeans have also frequently referred to the people of the Golden Horde as *Tatars,* a word that has been very loosely used throughout history. Understood in its linguistic sense, however, it has some value, because the various Tatar dialects belong to the Qipchaq division of the Turkic languages. In fact, the Golden Horde's neighbors in the east knew it as the Qipchaq khanate, which is a more appropriate name for it. For ease of reference, this discussion will refer to the khanate as the Horde.

At its height, the Horde dominated the area from eastern Poland to the Siberian forests. The core was the vast, grassy plain known as the Qipchaq steppe that extended from northwest of the Black Sea to northeast of the Caspian Sea. This sea of grass was broken by three of the great rivers of Russia: the Dnieper, the Don, and the Volga. Batu had no doubt immediately recognized that the level, endless plains were ideal for his horse culture. The rivers complicated travel on an east–west axis, but facilitated travel and trade on a north–south axis.

This core region of the khanate was populated by numerous ethnic groups, but was dominated by the Qipchaq Turks. Batu's followers quickly became assimilated into the majority Turkish culture when their Mongol leaders intermarried with local Qipchaq elites and adopted the local language. The "Mongol" elite of the khanate always boasted of their lineal ties with Chinggis Khan and retained certain aspects of their Mongol culture, but they were soon indistinguishable from their Qipchaq subjects.

Our knowledge of the first century and a half of the history of the khanate is frustratingly scanty, due to Timur Lang's destruction of its cities in the 1390s. What we know about it is derived largely from the observations of outsiders and from archaeological evidence. It began with Batu, whose invasion in the late 1230s was as catastrophic for Russia as Chinggis Khan's invasion was for Khorasan. Catapults and battering rams pummeled cities into ruins, and thousands of people were slaughtered. The scale of the destruction is detected by art historians, who note that Russian artisanal skills declined permanently in the area.

The Horde exercised direct control over the Qipchaq steppe, but exacted tribute in a system of indirect control over the forested north and west. The latter region covered a vast area that included Russian, Ukrainian, Polish, Lithuanian,

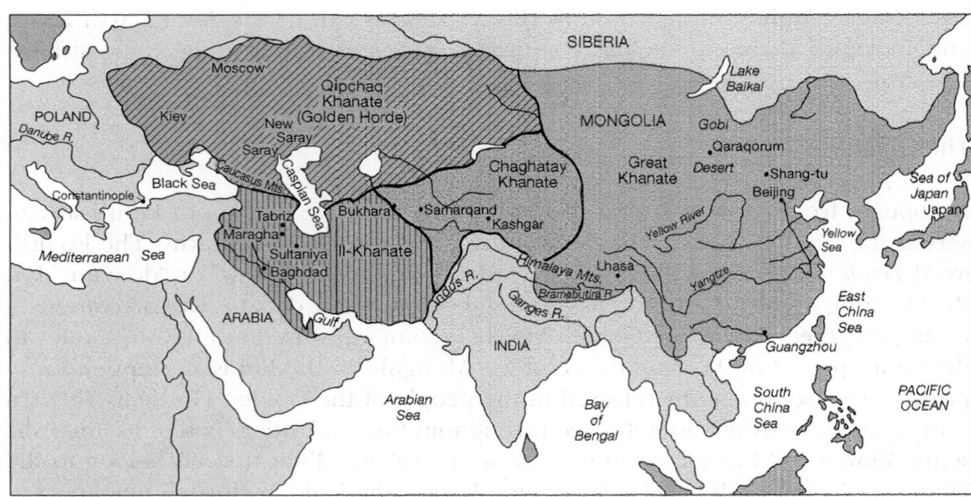

MAP 1.1 The Mongol Empire, c. 1300.

and Latvian cities. The most important among these were Kiev, Novgorod, and Moscow. The ruling elite preferred to remain nomadic, whereas a majority of the population was settled. Unlike the Mongols in China and Iran, who assimilated to the local culture, the Qipchaqs did not live among the Russians or in any way become integrated into Russian society. On the whole, the rulers resisted the urge to raid and loot their territory, but retribution for failing to pay the quite heavy tribute was typically severe, and the armies would often engage in slave raiding even in areas that had not been targets of punishment.

The economy of this new empire was quintessentially Mongol, based on pastoralism and long-distance trade; the leaders of the Horde were interested in agriculture only insofar as it generated the revenue among the Russians that enabled them to pay tribute. Pastoralism was the means of subsistence that most Mongols wanted to retain, but they recognized the benefits that long-distance trade could bring. The security that the various Mongol regimes quite successfully enforced across the huge region from the Pacific Ocean to the Black Sea enabled merchants of all nationalities to benefit from the new commercial possibilities. Batu, like other Mongol rulers, was interested in trade, which would augment the revenues derived from taxes on peasants and townsmen. In pursuit of this objective, he established his capital of Saray near the Volga delta, situated at the crossroads of trade routes that connected China with eastern Europe in one direction and Scandinavia with Iraq and Iran, in the other. It rapidly became a commercial center with a distinctly international air. From the forested zones to the north came amber, furs, timber, Russian slaves, and honey, to be exchanged for textiles, tools, and scientific instruments from the Muslim heartland and for spices from the east.

Merchants from all nations were encouraged to live in the capital, and a wide variety of religious missionaries—Muslim, Russian Orthodox, Greek Orthodox, and Nestorian—were tolerated. The Russian Orthodox Church supported Mongol rule precisely because of the Horde's religious tolerance, and especially because of the tax exemption the regime allowed the Church. The Horde established correct relations with the Byzantines once the latter had recaptured Constantinople from the Italians in 1261, but they also welcomed Italian traders to Saray. Trade was encouraged with both the Latin Catholics and the Greek Orthodox, despite their hostility toward each other. The Mamluke regime took particular pains to foster good relations with the government at Saray because of the abundance of Qipchaq boys available to be shipped to Egypt as mamluks. Many Egyptian and Syrian craftsmen made their way to Saray to create objects of art in the Mamluke style. By contrast, the Horde's relations with its fellow Mongol regime, the Il-khanids, were hostile throughout the thirteenth century due to competing claims over the Caucasus. Several expensive wars drained the resources of both Mongol powers.

Too much can be made of the fact that Batu's brother Berke (1257–1267) was the first Mongol khan to convert to Islam. He did not pressure the remainder of the Mongol elite to convert, and he tolerated the Jesuit and Orthodox Christian missionaries who proselytized in his realm. Until the early fourteenth century, only one other khan converted to Islam, and shamanism remained the focus of the religious life of the masses. Nevertheless, Islam slowly became the dominant religion in the khanate. It had been the religion of the leaders of the Bulghar Turks along the middle Volga from the tenth century, but the religion had not expanded westward. During the era of the Horde, however, the caravans that plied the long-established routes between Syria and the lower Volga provided a means for Muslim merchants, scholars, and craftsmen, as well as wandering preachers, to make their presence felt in the realm. Mosques, the call to prayer, Ramadan observance, and numerous other signs of a growing Muslim presence provided strong witness to a vibrant Islam.

The definitive turning point in the religious history of the Horde was the conversion in 1313 of the khan Uzbeg (1313–1341). Like Berke, he did not force other members of the elite to convert, and Christianity maintained a strong and tolerated presence, but Uzbeg did expel shamanistic priests. During his reign Islam became well established as the dominant religion, at least in the urban centers. Muslims coming in from Syria or Egypt would have felt comfortable in the larger cities, particularly the capital, which Uzbeg moved upriver to New Saray on a site near the present city of Volgograd. By the end of Uzbeg's reign, the new city had large mosques and madrasas, and qadis were dispensing justice in Shari'a courts.

Uzbeg's rule represented the height of the Horde's wealth and prestige. Under him the Horde had become an international power feared and respected by other nations. Even during Uzbeg's lifetime, however, his eastern European vassals were beginning to become restless. During the reign of his two sons, Lithuania gained its independence and other regions began challenging Mongol power. With the death of Uzbeg's son Berdi-beg in 1359, the last of Batu's descendants was gone. The rival leaders within the Horde began fighting each other, and in the midst of the chaos, Moscow refused to pay tribute. A distant cousin of Berdi-beg, Toqtamish of the White Horde, seized New Saray in 1377. He crushed Novgorod and Moscow, and by 1383 he had restored Mongol control over Russia. The Horde seemed as strong as it had ever been, but Toqtamish's ambitions exceeded his good judgment. He unwisely challenged Timur Lang, who was building his power in Transoxiana. As we shall see, Timur would administer a defeat to the Horde that would shatter its mystique in the eyes of its subjects, and it would never again be so formidable.

The Il-khanate

In the aftermath of Chinggis Khan's conquest of eastern Iran during 1219–1222, a formal Mongol authority was set up only in the area of the former Khwarazmian Empire. In Khorasan and Transoxiana, anarchy reigned, interspersed with occasional Mongol raids. Hulagu's campaign through northern Iran, Iraq, and Syria in 1253–1260 inflicted further destruction in the predominantly Muslim world. Hulagu, however, proved to be a gifted administrator in the areas he had just devastated. He established his headquarters in northwestern Iran immediately after the destruction of Baghdad, and his state came to be known as the Il-khanid Empire. The name comes from *il-khan,* meaning "subject khan," in the sense of being subject to the Great Khan in China.

Like Qubilai and the leaders of the Horde, Hulagu valued the wealth that trade generated. He realized that he needed thriving cities in order to benefit from trade and that he would need a strong agricultural sector to feed the population of those cities. The southern half of Iran had not been harmed by the Mongol invasions of 1219–1222 and 1253–1260, but the northern half was in ruins. The irrigation system of qanats in Khorasan had not been rebuilt since the destruction of Chinggis Khan, and the riverine system of irrigation in Iraq had been destroyed during Hulagu's own campaign. He ordered the rebuilding of cities and the restoration of the irrigation works, but he was able to accomplish little in the five years remaining in his life. In his short reign, he did lavish patronage on art and architecture, inaugurating a policy that would eventually make his royal city of Tabriz widely admired for its beauty. He also built an astronomical observatory at Maragha, some sixty miles south of Tabriz, which became the most highly regarded scientific institute in the Muslim world.

Hulagu's efforts to rebuild Iran were handicapped by the fact that he was surrounded by enemies. The Mamlukes, the Horde, and the Chaghatay khanate were all hostile to him, forcing him to disperse his troops to confront them. The greatest threat was the Mamluke Empire, and Hulagu initiated contacts for an alliance with Louis IX of France against it, beginning a diplomatic correspondence between France and the Il-khans that lasted well into the next century. Hulagu's death in 1265 interrupted his plans to revive the economy that he and his predecessors had shattered so thoroughly in their conquests.

The next several rulers of the Il-khanid realm were remarkable for their lack of ability. For thirty years, the khanate was subject to constant infighting among the ruling elite and was the victim of neglect of the economic infrastructure. The population had suffered a catastrophic decline due to a combination of mass murder, famine, and flight, and it remained low. The peasants suffered particular hardship, for the Il-khanid rulers actually increased the taxes on villages compared to preconquest levels, even though both population and production had fallen precipitously. Mongol nomads stole peasants' livestock and grazed their horses on what had been prime cultivated fields. Most towns on both sides of the Euphrates were deserted, and Marco Polo described Baghdad as having been a "trading town" when he passed through it in 1272. Other major cities such as Nishapur lay in ruins until the early fourteenth century.

The early Il-khans were hostile to Islam. They had come out of a shamanistic background, but several of the leaders found Buddhism attractive. Many Buddhist monks came with Hulagu's expedition, and others arrived soon after he set up his capital. Buddhism remained strong among the male Mongol ruling elite, but many of the rulers, from Hulagu on, had Nestorian wives or concubines. For the first several decades of Il-khanid rule, the rulers clearly were more sympathetic to Buddhism and Christianity than to Islam. During this period, the Nestorian and Jacobite churches thrived across Iran as never before.

From the accession of Ghazan in 1295, those policies were reversed, and Christianity and Buddhism went into irreversible decline in the Il-khanid realm. Ghazan (1295–1304) was the greatest of the Il-khans after Hulagu. A Buddhist, he proclaimed his conversion to Islam in the first year of his rule and ordered the destruction of churches, synagogues, and Buddhist temples throughout the realm. He initiated many reforms in order to build up his regime's wealth and prestige. He began the restoration of irrigation systems, reduced taxes and exchange rates, and reformed the system of weights and measures. The agricultural economy began a slow recovery, and for over two decades, tax revenues showed a steady increase.

In contrast to the agricultural decline throughout the thirteenth century, the Il-khanid regime boasted a sparkling urban life in certain areas. Hostile relations with the Mamlukes had interrupted the historic long-distance trade with Syria and Egypt, but trade with China intensified. The Il-khans were also as eager to please Italian and other European merchants as were their cousins in the Horde. Tabriz thrived on the new commercial life. Its location placed it on excellent trade routes. Iranian and Iraqi scholars and artists who had not fled to other lands in the face of the Mongol conquests made their way to Tabriz to enhance their careers. Hulagu's astronomical observatory at Maragha became famous for thousands of miles. Nasir al-Din al-Tusi, who had joined Hulagu's retinue at the siege of Alamut, was its first director, and it attracted astronomers and mathematicians from as far away as Andalus and China. It surpassed anything that Europe would offer until the career of Tycho Brahe in the late sixteenth century.

Under Uljaytu (1304–1316), Il-khanid literature, history, architecture, and painting blossomed. He constructed a new capital at Sultaniya, for which he commissioned magnificent tombs, mosques, bazaars, and schools. Because of close

An illuminated manuscript from the Il-khanid period, revealing Chinese influences.

trading relations with the Great Khan in China, Chinese styles and techniques began to influence the plastic arts of the Il-khanate. The Chinese influence is particularly striking in the manufacture of porcelains and in the emergence of Persian miniature painting.

Just as it appeared that the Il-khans had established a regime that would enable them to create a stable administration and a thriving economy, family feuds broke out into the open. Uljaytu's son Abu Sa'id (1316–1335) was a devout Muslim, fluent in Arabic and Persian, musically talented, and determined to continue the rehabilitation of his empire's economy. In 1335, however, he was poisoned, and anarchy broke out as ambitious chieftains struggled for supremacy. By midcentury, Iran and Iraq had been carved up by numerous successor states headed by Mongol, Turkic, Iranian, or Arab families. The populace once again sank into poverty and despair, and then, as we shall see, the northern arc of Iran was devastated by Timur Lang. Not for two centuries did the area begin to recover economically.

The Chaghatay Khanate

The Chaghatay khanate was separated from the Il-khanid realm by the Amu Darya River and by a line of fortresses east of Herat. In the west, only the grazing areas of some Mongol and Turkic pastoralists separated it from the territory of the Horde. In the east, its territory extended into modern Xinjiang province in China, which encompasses the remarkable Tarim Basin.

The Tarim Basin consists largely of an absolutely barren desert the size of the state of Texas. The desert is surrounded by a series of oases that served not only as fertile crop-producing areas, but also as rest areas for the southern Silk Road. The oases exploit the fertile alluvial soil that has been washed down over the ages from the mountains ringing the basin on three sides. These are some of the most formidable mountain ranges in the world. To the west are the Pamir Mountains; to the north are the Tien Shan Mountains; and to the south are the Kunlun Mountains. All three ranges are covered perpetually in snow and are laced with numerous glaciers. Their average altitude is over 20,000 feet, and all have peaks that exceed 24,000 feet. The Pamirs have subranges that run east and west and others that run north and south; merchants on the southern Silk Road often experienced dizziness and nausea while crossing it. The Tien Shan are formidable barriers to transit between the Tarim and Mongolia, but predatory bands found ways to get through. The Kunlun, on the other hand, constitute an impenetrable barrier to Tibet in the south.

The Chaghatay khanate thus extended over vast steppe land, some of the world's most inaccessible mountains, and the sophisticated urban oases of Transoxiana. The khans themselves retained the original features of the Mongol traditions more than did their cousins in the Horde, Il-khanate, or Yuan dynasty. Whereas the Yuan and Il-khan dynasties became urbanized quickly and the Horde fostered the development of mercantile interests in their capital of New Saray, the Chaghatays remained nomadic in lifestyle and outlook. The ruling family did not settle down into one of the great cities. The closest to a capital that it had was an encampment between Lake Balkhash and the Tien Shan. The ruling family never lost its contempt for urban life, and it treated cities as fields to be harvested. The khans plundered and looted their own cities more than once. The fate of Bukhara is representative. Within twenty years of its destruction in 1220 by Chinggis Khan, it had largely recovered its prosperity. By the early 1270s, Marco Polo, passing through Khorasan, heard that it and Samarqand were the most splendid cities in Iran. However, in 1273, and again in 1316, the Chaghatay rulers sacked, burned, and depopulated Bukhara.

Kebek (1318–1326) was the first Chaghatay to prefer urban life to a nomadic existence, and under him Samarqand and Bukhara enjoyed a revival. Despite his efforts at rebuilding those cities, however, as early as 1334 the great Moroccan traveler Ibn Battuta found many of the mosques, colleges, and bazaars of Bukhara in ruins again. Because of the antipathy of most of the Chaghatays to urban life, we have little evidence to indicate that any of the rulers other than Kebek patronized literature and the arts. On the other hand, it is clear that long-distance trade continued to be conducted through Transoxiana throughout the thirteenth and fourteenth centuries. The repeated rebuilding of the cities of Transoxiana, and the pronounced Chinese influence on Il-khanid arts, speak eloquently of a well-established commercial life linking China and southwestern Asia that refused to die even in a hostile cultural environment.

The ruling elite of the Chaghatay khanate was a loose coalition of Mongols, Turks, and Uighurs (a Turkic-speaking people who inhabited the oases of the Tarim), in addition to a few Muslim Iranians who were appointed governors of Transoxiana. As in the Horde, Turkish culture soon became predominant. Shamanist religious practices remained strong among the nomadic population, although Buddhism made inroads, particularly among the nomads of the Tarim. The Uighurs, on the other hand, gradually Islamized, as did the Turkic nomads who settled down in Transoxiana.

In 1326, a new khan, Tarmashirin (1326–1334), came to the throne. He had been a Buddhist ("Tarma" in his name derives from "dharma"), but he became the first Chaghatay ruler to convert to Islam. When he converted, he required all the important leaders in the khanate to follow suit. The order antagonized his chieftains in the east, and they became restive. When Tarmashirin was unsuccessful in his attack on Delhi in 1327, these chieftains seized the opportunity to revolt. After seven years of civil war, the khanate split in 1334. The Tarim basin and the area north of the Tien Shan Mountains were paired in an unlikely entity that became known as Moghulistan. It remained a regional political actor for two more centuries, and members of the House of Chagatay exercised at least nominal authority in the area into the twentieth century. Ironically, the more wealthy Transoxiana was bereft of a central government. A handful of tribes dominated the area, and the towns and cities became prey to the raids of nomads and seminomads. The merchants and ulama of Samarqand and Bukhara could only hope for a leader to arise who would restore to their cities the vitality and glory of their fabled past. By the last quarter of the century, they would find him in Timur Lang.

Thus, all four of the Mongol empires collapsed quite suddenly within a period of just over thirty years. The Chaghatay khanate splintered in 1334, leaving only a minor principality behind; the Il-khans disappeared in 1335; the Horde collapsed in 1359; and in Beijing the Chinese overthrew the Yuan dynasty of the Great Khan in 1368. The only descendant of Chinggis Khan who still exercised authority was in isolated Moghulistan, and the only other Mongol with a powerful state was Toqtamish, who seized power in Saray in 1377. Despite the short period of formal Mongol rule, the Mongol legacy would continue to exercise a powerful effect on the imagination of the peoples of Central Asia.

New Centers of Islamic Culture

For six hundred years, the most influential forces shaping the legacy of the Qur'an and the Hadith into an Islamic civilization had been the creative communities of Iraq and Iran. Their decline had begun even before the Mongol threat, but the invasions of Chinggis Khan and Hulagu, followed by decades of Mongol misrule, were devastating in their effect. Now, as Iran and Iraq suffered, Muslim military power and cultural vibrancy shifted to the geographical fringes of the historic heartland. The Mamluke Empire, the Delhi Sultanate, and the Ottoman Sultanate assumed the dominant roles for the Islamic world in the thirteenth and fourteenth centuries. All three of them left permanent legacies for Islamic history.

The Mamluke Empire

The irruption of the Mongols into western Asia profoundly altered the geopolitics of the eastern Mediterranean. Egypt under the Mamlukes now rose to a position of influence that it had not enjoyed since Hellenistic times. By virtue of their triumph over Hulagu's army at 'Ayn Jalut in 1260, the Mamlukes of Egypt gained the respect and gratitude of Muslims everywhere. The regime continued to enhance its reputation for military prowess by repelling an Il-khan invasion of Syria in 1281, eradicating the last of the Crusader strongholds from the Syrian mainland by 1291, and preventing further Il-khan attempts to annex Syria during the period 1299–1303. As a result, the Mamlukes expanded the control over Syria that rulers in Cairo had aimed for since early Fatimid times, and they occupied the Holy Cities of the Hijaz.

The Mamlukes constituted one of the most formidable military forces in the world from the thirteenth through the fifteenth centuries. Although that fact alone would merit their place in history, they attract attention primarily because of their unusual recruitment policy. Muslim governments had relied upon slave soldiers since the early ninth century, but the Mamluke regime is distinguished by the fact that the rulers themselves were of slave origin. The staffing of the highest positions in the state relied upon a well-organized system of slave importation and training. Slave merchants combed foreign markets—primarily in the Qipchaq steppe—for young boys ten to twelve years of age. They sold the boys to the sultan and to the several dozen amirs who were the most powerful men in the empire other than the sultan himself. These included the vizier, other chief court officials, provincial governors, and military officers. Each official then provided several years of training for the boys.

The "curriculum" included instruction in the basic rituals of Islam and rigorous drilling in the cavalry arts of the bow and the lance. The sultan, of course, was able to provide the most elaborate program. His slaves lived together in barracks, were drilled in the arts of cavalry warfare, and were taught basic literacy. They learned that their survival depended on loyalty to their master and to their fellow recruits. Upon completion of the training, their master granted them their freedom and gave them their military equipment and an estate to supply the revenue to maintain the expenses of their horses, arms, and armor.

The graduates of the sultan's school became members of the "royal mamluks," who numbered 5000–6000 during the late thirteenth and early fourteenth centuries. Enjoying the highest status of all the troops, they demanded to be stationed in or around Cairo rather than at posts remote from the center of power. The mamluks of the amirs were stationed in the provinces and at the homes of their masters. The Mamluke army, then, was characterized by an organization not unlike a feudal army of contemporary western Europe. At its core were the sultan's troops, who were loyal to him; supplementing them were the dozens of regiments that were loyal to their respective amirs, who in turn were loyal to the sultan. When the corps of the mamluks were supplemented by cavalry of the auxiliary units (freeborn troops who included local Egyptians, Syrians, and foreign soldiers of fortune), the regime could mobilize 40,000–50,000 cavalrymen, in addition to infantry.

Regardless of who their master was, the mamluks were intensely loyal to him and to their brothers in arms. This loyalty, by virtue of which the master was viewed as the mamluks' father and they called each other brothers, also meant that it was almost impossible for a mamluk who was transferred from one amir to another to be accepted by the new group. The sense of exclusivity also meant that the mamluks always felt a social distance between them and the society they ruled. They passed laws prohibiting civilians (Muslim as well as non-Muslim) from riding horses. They also adhered to a policy of marrying slave women (usually from the areas where they themselves were born), and even their concubines were not of local origin. Some exceptions occurred, but local marriages were rare. Because the mamluks' sons by such wives and concubines were not slaves, they did not receive the training of the slave boys and found themselves overlooked in the competition for the best positions. They could serve in the lower status auxiliary units, but with the exception of several of the sultans' sons and brothers, they did not advance to the highest ranks. Thus, the perpetuation of the regime required the continual purchase of new slaves.

The Mamluke system was remarkable for its combination of power and latent anarchy. On the one hand, it fostered an esprit de corps among its soldiers that, combined with the high level of training, resulted in a formidable military force. On the other hand, the system of purchasing and manumitting slave troops created a system of cliques and factions that was a constant threat to peace and security. The system was most vulnerable during the process of succession to the leadership of the state. Each sultan wished to pass his office to his son, but the amirs demanded the right to ratify the choice of the next sultan. The amirs were not being presumptuous: They were adhering to the traditions of their common Turkish background, and they were well aware that the new sultan's "family" of troops would expect to displace the existing bureaucratic and military officials. Those who were threatened with the loss of their positions sought out allies among the other amirs, and those already in office did the same. Such a transition of power almost always led to fighting and scores of deaths.

The dynamics of this process were in evidence from the early years of the empire. Baybars, a talented and ruthless sultan, ruled for seventeen years (1260–1277). He named his son to succeed him, but his son was overthrown by Baybars' own troops. In 1293, another sultan was overthrown by a conspiracy of amirs, and his ten-year-old brother, al-Nasir Muhammad, was installed on the throne by yet another faction. He was deposed a year later, then reinstalled in 1299, only to be deposed again in 1309. By this time in his mid-twenties, the young ex-sultan seized the throne himself in 1310 and enjoyed the longest and most successful rule in Mamluke history (1310–1341). The nature of the Mamluke system guaranteed political instability, and its entire history was punctuated by frequent violence among the mamluks themselves. Fortunately, although the Egyptian and Syrian citizens whom the mamluks ruled were occasionally harassed and often exploited by them, they were not frequent victims of the political violence, which was largely restricted to the ruling elite themselves.

The mamluks who seized control of Egypt and Syria in 1250 from their "masters" in the Ayyubid dynasty were Qipchaq Turks. Their homeland was the Qipchaq steppe, which, as we have seen, had become the domain of the Horde a few years before the coup d'état in Cairo. The Mamluke regime needed a constant supply of slave soldiers, but the traditional supply route for them by 1260 lay through hostile Il-khanid territory. Baybars began a two-pronged diplomatic effort to develop a new supply route. In a fortuitous development for him, the Byzantines now reappeared in diplomatic affairs for the first time in several decades. The Byzantine royal family had been living in exile in Nicaea ever since the Venetians conquered Constantinople in the so-called Fourth Crusade of 1204. After decades of Byzantine frustration, the emperor Michael VIII Palaeologus (1259–1282) recaptured Constantinople from the Venetians in 1261. Threatened by the Venetians to the west and Turkish raiders to the east, the emperor needed to be on good terms with both Berke of the Horde and Baybars of the Mamlukes. He agreed to facilitate the mamluk trade between the Horde and Egypt, and he refurbished an Umayyad-era mosque in Constantinople as a gesture of good will to Baybars. He even made a promise to give Egypt military aid if needed.

Baybars also cultivated diplomatic relations with the Horde. The alliance became progressively easier to maintain because both regimes were Muslim, the Horde was continually assimilating to the Qipchaq culture into which the mamluks were born, and the two empires had no reason to quarrel over territory. On the other hand, both empires had hostile relations with the Il-khans, with the result that the natural trade routes through Iran and Iraq were never accessible. The two Muslim allies therefore maintained good relations with the Christian Byzantines in order to keep the shipping route open between Egypt and the Black Sea. The trade route opened up opportunities for merchants to purchase boys who were of Greek, Georgian, and Slavic origin as well, some of whom became mamluks. Beginning in the late thirteenth century, however, the largest number of non-Turkish mamluks were Circassians, members of an ethnic group whose origin was the area of the Caucasus on the northeastern shore of the Black Sea.

Baybars was as careful to develop economic ties as he was to cultivate diplomatic contacts. Mediterranean trade in the thirteenth century was dominated by Europeans. The fleets of Italian city–states by that time had obtained a near monopoly of naval power. By virtue of Baybars' campaigns against the Crusader ports of Syria and Palestine (he captured all the remaining Crusader forts except Acre), the once-flourishing Italian trade with Syria was destroyed. Baybars realized that he could redirect that trade to Egypt, and he negotiated treaties with several Italian maritime powers in an effort to secure a share in the profits of the Mediterranean trade. Egypt's maritime commerce grew steadily in volume over the next century, and Alexandria experienced an economic boom as a result. The Mamlukes regained the dominant position in the trade between the Mediterranean and the Indian Ocean that Egypt had lost during the era of the Crusades. They maintained good relations with Venice and Genoa, whose ships transported most of the slaves from the Black Sea and whose merchants purchased the spices that came to Egypt from India and the East Indies.

Realizing the need for a vibrant economy to support their military machine and their high standard of living, the Mamlukes supported the crafts and manufacturing as well as trade. During the early fourteenth century, they invested in huge paper-making factories and sugar refineries. They encouraged the export of sugar to Italy, southern France, Catalonia, Flanders, England, and the Baltic Sea. The most important Egyptian industry continued to be the manufacture of cotton and linen textiles, both of which were in great demand during this period in both the Muslim world and in Europe.

With their wealth, the Mamlukes patronized learning and the arts. During the Mongol devastation of Iran and Iraq in the first half of the thirteenth century, both Damascus and Cairo had welcomed scholars and merchants fleeing the destruction of their homelands. Due to the influx of Iranian and Iraqi scholars, and the destruction of Baghdad in 1258, the two cities became the greatest centers of Islamic learning during the late Ayyubid period. As the capital city of the Mamluke empire, Cairo surpassed Damascus in importance and imperial stature, and it remained the cultural capital of the Muslim world at least until the late fifteenth century. Through patronage of culture, Mamluke sultans attempted to legitimize their rule by winning favor with the ulama and the masses alike. One time-honored way for rulers to impress upon the public the grandeur of their reign is through the construction of impressive buildings, and the Mamlukes were no exception in this regard. They vied with their predecessors in endowing magnificent madrasas, mosques, Sufi lodges, and hospitals, in addition to constructing enormous tombs for themselves. Some of the most impressive buildings to be found in Syria and Egypt to this day are the result of Mamluke patronage of monumental architecture.

Baybars installed a member of the Abbasid family as caliph in Cairo after he consolidated his power. It is impossible to assess the actual impact of this symbolic act. The caliph was not recognized outside the empire, and he wielded no influence in the government. On the other hand, his presence was politically useful for the government and psychologically important for many Egyptians and Syrians. More tangible were changes that the regime made in the patronage of the religious institutions. Previous Muslim regimes had favored one or another school of law, but the Mamlukes were the first to endow all four schools and to appoint qadis for each one.

The period 1260–1341 was the high point of Mamluke history, and the third reign of al-Nasir Muhammad (1310–1341) was its apogee. During al-Nasir's reign, there were neither famines nor plagues in the empire, a stark contrast with the late Fatimid and early Ayyubid periods. The population grew, and prosperity soared. The death of al-Nasir Muhammad in 1341 marked the end of the golden age for the Mamlukes, even though they would continue to rule for almost two hundred more years, until 1517. Beginning in the last decade of the thirteenth century, ethnic rivalry between the Qipchaqs and the Circassians escalated, and fierce clashes broke out when al-Nasir Muhammad died. Struggles between the two groups caused chronic violence for the next forty years. Members of al-Nasir's family held the office of the sultanate during that time, but they were puppets of the factions who placed them on the throne. Thus, political instability in the Mamluke Empire occurred simultaneously with the collapse of the Mongol khanates.

To complicate matters, the plague, or Black Death, struck the Mamluke realm with at least the level of ferocity in 1348 that it did Europe, killing one-fourth to one-third of the population. For the next century and a half, the epidemics recurred at a rate of more than once per decade, causing the population to continue to decline. As agriculture and commerce plummeted, a Circassian group of Mamlukes seized power in 1382, and the Qipchaq era was over. The Circassians dominated the empire until their defeat at the hands of the Ottomans in 1517.

The Delhi Sultanate

The Arab invasions of 711–713 established an Islamic presence in the middle and lower Indus valley, but in terms of both geography and influence, the settlements there remained on the periphery of the Islamic world for several centuries. The Abbasids lost control of the area in the ninth century, and several of the towns in the valley soon came under the control of Isma'ilis who looked to Fatimid Cairo for guidance. In the eleventh century, however, Mahmud of Ghazna expanded his aggressive and predatory Muslim state into the Indus basin. The Ghaznavids inaugurated an era of seven centuries that would witness a series of powerful, autonomous Muslim states in South Asia (the area south of the Hindu Kush and Himalaya mountain ranges). Usually ruled by Turks or Afghans, each dynasty attempted to maintain an identifiably Muslim court in an overwhelmingly Hindu society. The model they found most congenial was the Islamic–Persian style that developed in northeastern Iran with the Samanid court of the tenth century. Until the advent of the Mughals, the greatest of these Muslim states was the Delhi Sultanate.

Mahmud of Ghazna laid the foundations for a powerful Muslim presence in South Asia. He raided the Punjab area as early as 1002 and captured Lahore in 1030. When the Saljuqs chased Mahmud's successor out of Khorasan ten years later, Lahore increasingly became the most important city in the remaining areas of the Ghaznavid Empire, and it developed into a thriving center of Islamic culture.

In 1173, an Afghan family from the region of Ghur seized power in Ghazna and began a systematic conquest of Ghaznavid holdings in the Punjab, which they accomplished by 1192. Not content with the Punjab, these Ghurids conquered Delhi in 1193 and occupied areas as far east as Bihar on the lower Ganges. Their military power can be gauged by the fact that, while they were conquering the Punjab and the Ganges, they were also winning Khorasan from the shahs of

Khwarazm, often regarded as the greatest Muslim military power of the day until their defeat by Chinggis Khan. The Ghurid realm grew until it extended from Bihar through Khorasan. But just as the Ghurids were poised to create a major state in South Asia, their ruler was assassinated in 1206, leaving no son to inherit the throne. The general who conquered Delhi for the Ghurids took over the reins of power in both Delhi and Lahore. But he in turn died in a polo accident in 1210. His former military slave, Iltutmish, then seized power. Iltutmish (1210–1236) is regarded to be the founder of the Delhi Sultanate, although it was over a decade before he made Delhi preeminent over Lahore.

Although the Delhi Sultanate was composed of several different dynasties, it is regarded as a single period in Muslim–Indian history because of the continuity of the ruling elite. Historians disagree on the issue of its duration. Some point out that it was the dominant state in South Asia from 1210 to 1398 and limit their treatment of the sultanate to the three dynasties of that period. Other historians include two later dynasties, in which case the sultanate's history is considered to last until the arrival of the Mughals in 1526. Regardless of how one defines the duration of the sultanate, each dynasty began of either Turkish or Afghan lineage. Like almost all other Muslim regimes (the major exception was that of the Mamlukes), the rulers might choose wives or concubines of strikingly different ethnic origin, but the patrilineal system of tracing one's ancestors made it natural for each generation to see itself as the heir to the founder of the dynasty and to identify with his ethnic origin.

The early Delhi Sultanate experienced the same degree of political turbulence that the Mamluke regime did. The entire period from 1210 to 1320 was one of political tumult among the ruling elite itself. Powerful amirs attempted to check the power of others, and violence often resulted. Between 1236 and 1296, ten sultans reigned, eight of whom averaged a reign of less than three years. Only one of the ten is known to have died a natural death. Despite having to confront almost constant challenges within the elite and violent changes of dynasties in 1290 and 1320, the sultanate successfully withstood threats from the Mongols. A Mongol expedition actually sacked Lahore in 1241, but between 1290 and 1327, the Chaghatay khanate's attacks were repulsed at least nine times.

In the periods between internal clashes and Mongol attacks, the sultanate expanded its area of control. By 1230, Iltutmish dominated a wide arc based on the Indus and Ganges river valleys. In that year, he sought and won recognition from the Abbasid caliph in Baghdad as the legitimate Muslim ruler of the area. By the early fourteenth century, the sultanate had extended its authority to Gujarat and the Deccan plateau, in addition to controlling most of the Ganges valley and the Punjab. Until the 1320s, the regime exercised authority in the conquered areas by a variety of means. The sultanate ruled directly in some areas, and in other areas it exacted tribute from Hindu or Muslim princes who were allowed to rule with little oversight.

The most influential of the Delhi dynasties was that of the Tughluq family, whose effective rule was from 1320 to 1388, although members of the family remained on the throne until 1413. Muhammad ibn Tughluq (1325–1351) was the most famous of the family. He was a fascinating figure of undoubted intellectual and creative talents, but his administration was a disappointment. On the one hand, he continued his father's military campaigns and managed to extend the authority of the sultanate over almost all of South Asia. His domain extended from the Himalayas almost to the southern tip of the peninsula, and from the Punjab to Bengal. He also defeated the Chaghatay ruler Tarmashirin at the very gate of Delhi in 1327, the event that indirectly resulted in the division of the Chaghatay khanate into Transoxiana and Moghulistan. He was an accomplished scholar, proficient in both Arabic and Persian, and he recruited numerous new qadis from abroad in a major effort to facilitate the implementation of Islamic law. Toward his Hindu and Jain subjects, he practiced a conciliatory policy of offering them high positions in the government, allowing them to build new temples, and inviting them to court to debate philosophical and theological issues.

Although these policies seem like the strategies of an accomplished politician, Muhammad actually found it difficult to devise realistic policies for some important issues. His fastidious need for symmetry made it impossible for him to tolerate the variety of relations that existed between the central government and the multitude of provinces that were at least nominally subject to it. He instituted a uniform policy of direct rule for all regions, provoking widespread resentment in the areas that had been allowed a degree of autonomy by previous Delhi sultans. The biggest problem was in the Deccan plateau. The area was hundreds of miles south of Delhi, and the Hindu rulers there had no intention of yielding on the issue of indirect rule. Muhammad thought that he could resolve the problem of distance by moving the capital from Delhi to the more centrally located site of Dawlatabad in the Deccan, but the change was implemented in a heavy-handed fashion that provoked resentment among his own followers.

These and other unpopular measures were followed by a catastrophic drought and famine in the Punjab and the Ganges valley during the years 1335–1342. The suffering brought on by the drought became the pretext for widespread rebellions throughout the northern tier of the sultanate, forcing Muhammad to lead his army on repeated campaigns to the northern as well as southern provinces of his realm. He responded to the uprisings, and even to the whisperings of criticism of his policies, with brutal punishment that caused him to develop a reputation for cruelty. By the end of his rule, he had lost control of his southern possessions, including Bengal, and the support of most of his remaining subjects.

The reign of Muhammad's cousin Firuz (1351–1388) stood in sharp contrast to that of his own. Firuz practiced clemency where Muhammad had been brutal, although he responded to Muslim criticisms of his cousin's religious toleration by destroying newly built Hindu temples and promoting proselytizing efforts among the Hindu majority. He made a concerted effort to assist the agricultural sector of the economy by constructing irrigation projects, and he promoted employment by building a new capital city near Delhi. In the end, however, he had not made a convincing case for the continuing authority of Delhi. When Firuz died in 1388, a power struggle broke out among his sons and grandsons. Many of the Hindu and Muslim rulers of the provinces took advantage of the confusion to renounce their allegiance to the dynasty, plunging the sultanate into a civil war that lasted a decade.

Delhi was not on a major trade route and probably would never have become the center of the sultanate had it not been for the Mongol threat. Chinggis Khan's return route to Mongolia in 1222 passed through the Punjab, persuading Iltutmish to establish his headquarters at Delhi rather than at the Ghurid capital of Lahore. On the other hand, the valley of the Indus, the Punjab, and the Gangetic plain were all rich agricultural regions that supplied Delhi with wealth, and the acquisition of

Gujarat granted the city access to the wider world of commerce. Gujarat was famous for its fine cotton cloths as well as for its role as an entrepôt. Commodities shipped there from Southeast Asia or East Africa would be transshipped to yet another port, such as Hormuz in the Persian Gulf.

As the capital of a rich and powerful regime, Delhi attracted soldiers, merchants, craftsmen, scribes, and scholars. Like Cairo and Damascus, it was a haven for refugees fleeing the depredations of Chinggis Khan and Hulagu. The Delhi sultans welcomed and offered patronage to foreign scholars and artisans, whose work enhanced the glory of the regime. Outstanding ulama were appointed to serve as qadis and administrators in the government, particularly during the reign of Muhammad ibn Tughluq, who seems to have been willing to trust foreign officeholders more than local ones. Most of the intellectuals who emigrated to Delhi came from Khorasan and Transoxiana, reinforcing the Persianate cast of the elite culture that had been bequeathed by the Ghaznavids to the Punjab. Poetry, music, and historical works composed in Persian flourished under the regime. Architecture, likewise, reflected the styles that had been developing in Iran and Central Asia. Magnificent mosques, Sufi lodges, madrasas, tombs, and palaces incorporated the vaulted halls, pointed domes, blue faience tiles, and gold plating of the Persian-speaking region. No contemporary Muslim city exceeded the architectural splendor of Delhi.

The sultanate shared many common characteristics with those of Muslim regimes to the west, but it was distinctive in one major feature: Not in several centuries had the Muslim rulers of any other major state represented such a small minority of the population. The population of the sultanate at its height (ca. 1310–1340) was remarkably complex linguistically. Over one thousand languages and dialects were spoken in South Asia. From the perspective of a Muslim government, however, the issue of religion was more vexing than that of language. During the thirteenth and fourteenth centuries, the Muslims of the sultanate were a tiny minority of the total population. For many Muslims the ultimate responsibility for any Muslim ruler was the protection and advancement of the faith. Although opinions varied regarding what this duty actually entailed, for most it seems to have included the enforcement of the Shari‘a, the toleration of Jews and Christians within certain prescribed guidelines, and the eradication of polytheism.

In the Delhi Sultanate, the tension between the religious duty of the ruler on the one hand and the social reality on the other reached a level inconceivable in the rest of the Islamic world. The sultans depended on millions of Hindu laborers, troops, bureaucrats, carpenters, masons, metallurgists, bankers, and merchants. The Ghaznavids, the Ghurids, and the early sultans at Delhi exploited the religious issue when they raided Hindu towns and temples, but as the later sultans began to consolidate their holdings, they followed a more pragmatic policy. The fourteenth-century rulers Muhammad ibn Tughluq and his successor Firuz exemplify the range of possibilities available to the Muslim rulers of South Asia in their treatment of non-Muslims. The former's generosity to Hindus and Jains was criticized by devout Muslims, and the latter's punitive measures against non-Muslims contributed to the outbreak of the civil war that followed his death in 1388. As we shall see, the disorder of that period exposed northern India to perhaps the greatest catastrophe that it has ever experienced: the invasion of Timur Lang.

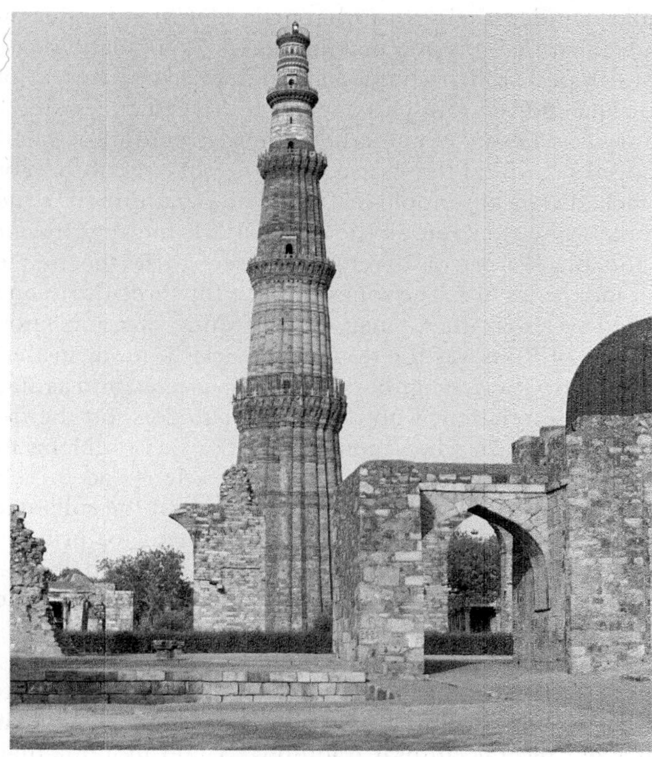

The thirteenth-century Qutb mosque in Delhi.

The Ottoman Sultanate

The third of the great Muslim states to emerge on the periphery of the Islamic heartland in the thirteenth century was that of the Ottomans. During the second half of the fifteenth century it achieved the status of an empire, and it went on to become one of the greatest and most durable states in world history. It collapsed only after World War I. During the period prior to the fifteenth century, when its territory was relatively compact and its reputation was only regional, its status may best be described as that of a "sultanate."

Until the Saljuq defeat of the Byzantines at Manzikert in 1071, Anatolia was hostile territory to the Muslims and represented a seemingly impenetrable barrier to Muslim expansion. After the battle, the entire peninsula lay open to unlimited Turkish migration for a quarter of a century. In 1098, the knights of the First Crusade discovered that Nicaea (Iznik), just a few miles east of Constantinople, was the capital of the Saljuq Sultanate of Rum. They forced the sultanate back onto the Anatolian plateau, where the Saljuqs established their capital at Konya.

For the next two centuries, the pattern of settlement in Anatolia did not change much. The Turks controlled the central plateau and the east. The majority of the population under their control remained Christian peasants, although conversions and emigration ensured that the Christian population was slowly declining throughout this period. Three independent Christian states lay on the periphery of the peninsula. On the southern shore was the Armenian kingdom of Cilicia (sometimes known as Lesser Armenia). In the extreme west was the Byzantine state, which moved its capital to Nicaea when the soldiers of the Fourth Crusade captured and sacked Constantinople in 1204. The Byzantines returned the capital to Constantinople when they retook the city in 1261, but their former subjects in Trebizon, on the Black Sea coast, refused to recognize the new emperor and insisted on their independence. The zones between the three Christian states and the Turkish-controlled area were the domain of the frontier warriors known as *gazis*.

The Sultanate of Rum was the dominant Turkish power in the peninsula. It frequently cooperated with its neighboring Christian states, and as an urban society, it sometimes had tense relations with the gazis, or raiders, on the frontiers. Occasionally it restrained the gazis when their activities caused problems for their diplomatic relations with the Christian states. Despite the often peaceful relations with its neighboring Christian kingdoms, however, the history of the sultanate was punctuated by violence. For several decades, it had to contend for primacy with several other Turkish dynasties in the area, and after having established its supremacy, it had to subdue challengers. In addition, the dynasty followed the Saljuq tradition according to which the sons of the ruler fought each other for control of the sultanate upon their father's death.

Despite the frequent violence, however, the sultanate managed to establish an urban culture that was more vibrant than had been seen in Anatolia in several centuries. It synthesized several cultural traditions. Saljuq monumental architecture incorporated Byzantine styles, an emerging Turkish Sufi musical repertoire adapted Orthodox Christian musical themes for its own purposes, and Turkish immigrants were influenced by local customs and mores in countless ways.

Persian models of government, art, and literature also influenced the culture of the Rum sultanate. The early sultans admired the Persian cultural tradition, but the Persian influence became even stronger when Konya became a haven for Iranian refugees fleeing the destruction caused by Chinggis Khan in the 1220s. The products of the newly arrived scholars, architects, and craftsmen transformed Konya into a lively cultural center. It became famous for its beautiful mosques, madrasas, caravanserais, and other monuments, as well as for the mesmerizing lyrics of the great Sufi poet Rumi, whose career unfolded there. Although non-Muslims probably constituted ninety percent of the population in the early thirteenth century, Konya's prestige aided in the Islamization of the sultanate. The visibility of mosques, the ubiquity of the call to prayer, and the fact that Islam was the religion of the ruling elite played important roles in the growing Islamic identity of the Anatolian plateau.

Mongol armies shattered the sultanate as decisively as they had destroyed other regimes and societies from China to central Europe. Batu of the Golden Horde challenged the sultanate at Kose Dagh in 1243 and won a decisive victory. The Saljuq army disintegrated, and Konya never again wielded effective influence outside its own environs. The sultanate withered away during several decades of tortured civil war, until it disappeared in the early fourteenth century. In 1260 Hulagu asserted his authority in the eastern half of the peninsula, and that region became part of the Il-khanate.

Although the Il-khanid regime continued to nourish the Persian strain in the high culture of eastern Anatolia, it also sparked a new wave of Turkish immigration into the peninsula. The second half of the thirteenth century witnessed the migration of tens of thousands of Turks into the area. Hulagu's conquests had left many of them displaced and in desperate straits; others had served as troops and were now in quest of further military adventures; and still others were simply taking advantage of new opportunities that had arisen in the wake of Hulagu's victories. As they entered Anatolia, the process of the Turkification of the peninsula accelerated. In the central region of the peninsula, neither the Il-khans nor the sultanate of Rum wielded effective authority, and it became a no-man's-land of anarchy. Many of the new immigrants resorted to sheer banditry to survive. Others continued to the fringes of the peninsula, where they augmented the existing groups of gazi fighters.

The Turkish migration began just as the Byzantines gained their revenge on their Latin enemies. When Michael Palaeologus unexpectedly recaptured Constantinople from the Venetians in 1261, the Byzantines eagerly anticipated a revival of imperial power. Unfortunately for them, they now faced a conjunction of challenges. To the west, rival Christian states—both Orthodox and Catholic—were planning to seize the wealthy Byzantine capital; and to the east, the new Turkish migrants were swelling the ranks of the gazis. The gazis were discovering that, when the Byzantines had relocated their capital to Constantinople, they had neglected their defense structure in Anatolia. After midcentury, the ambitious gazi chieftains who until then had been held in check by both Nicaea and Konya now began to carve out independent principalities in the western third of the peninsula. Many of the Turkish newcomers joined the ranks of the successful raiders, enabling some of the chieftains to establish thriving bases of power even along the Aegean coast. By the end of the century, some were hiring renegade Byzantine sailors to help them raid Aegean islands. Although the Byzantine emperor's diplomacy had protected his realm from the Sultanate of Rum, the Horde, the Mamlukes, and the Il-khans, it was futile against the gazi tradition, which had gained a new life with the arrival of large numbers of Turkish immigrants.

One of the gazi regimes was led by a chieftain named Osman, who was born about 1260. He developed a power base at Soghut, only a few miles east of Bursa. From there, Osman had opportunities to tax merchants who were using the trade route that connected the Aegean with Central Asia, and he could raid Byzantine territory. By virtue of his successful raids, he attracted a growing number of gazis and adventurers. Many of the latter included Christians. Thus, the early Ottomans reflected the typical gazi band, which was not a group related by kinship ties, but rather a mixture of many different peoples, Turkic and Turkicized, who chose to participate in a dynamic organization.

At some point (possibly long after Osman's death), Osman's group became known as Ottomans, or "followers of Osman." Taking advantage of the Byzantines' deadly rivalries with the Bulgars, Serbs, Venetians, Genoans, and other Christian powers, they laid an extended siege to Bursa and took it in 1326, just after Osman died. His son Orhan (1326–1362) made Bursa his capital city, and from there he captured Nicaea (1329; later renamed Iznik) and Nicomedia (1337; later renamed Izmit), the last major Byzantine cities in Anatolia.

Osman and Orhan, like all contemporary successful leaders of volunteer military forces, had to provide outlets for the energies, appetites, and religious fervor of their followers. Success necessiated further success, for victories generated new recruits who expected glory and treasure, and the veterans of previous campaigns soon felt the need for new exploits. There is little doubt that Orhan would have eventually crossed the Dardanelles on his own, due to the fact that beyond it lay a vast territory that was Christian, wealthy, and increasingly riven by conflicts among weak states. As it turned out, however, in 1345, he was invited to cross by a Byzantine faction vying for power in the capital city, just as earlier Byzantines had invited the Saljuqs into western Anatolia at the end of the eleventh century. After enabling his Byzantine ally to gain the throne, Orhan remained interested in the Balkans. By 1361, he had captured territory from the Dardanelles to the old Roman capital of Adrianople (modern Edirne), which he made into his own capital.

The Ottomans arrived in the Balkans at an opportune time for their ambitions. The Byzantine Empire had shrunk to a mere shadow of its former self and comprised little more than the suburbs of Constantinople; the Serbian Empire of the great Stephen Dushan had lost most of its vitality at his death in 1355; and the peoples of the Balkans were suffering from the constant warfare of numerous petty states. Few of the inhabitants of the area, powerful or weak, felt a loyalty to a Balkan state at the time. Many of them sensed that the prospect of Ottoman overlordship could be no worse than what they were already experiencing. Due to the chaotic conditions, the Ottomans were able to recruit Christian knights to serve in their army, and in some battles, other Christians defected to the Ottoman side. Many Orthodox noblemen and soldiers of fortune made successful careers out of service to the Ottoman state. Many Christian peasants and townsmen benefitted from the stability offered by the Ottomans of this era, in contrast to the anarchy and exploitation characteristic of the Balkan Christian states of the fourteenth century.

Orhan's son Murat I (1362–1389) took advantage of the vacuum of power in the region. He consolidated his hold on Thrace, conquered Macedonia and southern Bulgaria, and forced the Byzantines to pay tribute to, and provide troops for, Ottoman campaigns. In 1389, his army, composed of Turks and Christian vassals, defeated a far larger force of Serbs and their allies at Kosovo. Murat was killed in the battle, and his son Bayezit (1389–1402) became sultan.

Murat and Bayezit laid the foundations for a future Ottoman Empire. Murat began the process of building a more reliable army than that of either the gazis or Turkish tribesmen in general, both of whom he regarded as unpredictable and independent minded. He created a unit of soldiers who were prisoners of war, and he instituted a centralized bureaucracy in order to collect the taxes required to support his growing empire. Bayezit expanded upon these initiatives. He implemented a levy of male children on Christian villages in the Balkans, who were then educated as Muslims and trained for either the military or the civilian administration. This recruitment mechanism was known as the *devshirme* system. The slaves in the military served in what came to be known as the Janissary corps (from "Yeni Çeri," or "New Force"). The Janissaries rapidly became the Ottoman army's primary infantry unit and were stationed around the sultan on the battlefield. Originally armed with pikes and bows and arrows, they later became famous for their effective use of gunpowder weapons.

As a result of his policies and leadership ability, Bayezit became a remarkably successful conqueror. Relying on the loyalty of his Christian vassals and Janissaries, he quickly conquered the western half of Anatolia from Turkish rivals, acquired large areas north of the Danube, and, in 1395, laid siege to Constantinople itself (see Map 1.2). By this time, all of the major European leaders had become aware of the potential threat of the Ottomans to their security, and they responded to the appeal of the Byzantine emperor for aid. The king of Hungary organized a huge army that attracted knights from France, Burgundy, England, Germany, and the Netherlands. This military force moved down the Danube in 1396, destroying Ottoman forts along the way. At the fortress of Nicopolis, however, Bayezit confronted the coalition's army and utterly destroyed it, sending a wave of terror throughout Europe.

While the siege of Constantinople continued, Bayezit turned to Anatolia again in 1397, and began conquering its eastern regions. By this time, the defunct Il-khanate's domain in eastern Anatolia had been replaced by several Muslim Turkish overlords. Bayezit won battle after battle, until he had conquered the bulk of the peninsula. His territory, extending from the Caucasus to the Danube, was poised to become an empire. His brutal Anatolian conquests, however—accomplished with the aid of large numbers of Balkan Christians—had alienated many Turkish families in Anatolia, whose own hopes for leadership had been destroyed. They looked to Timur Lang to get their revenge.

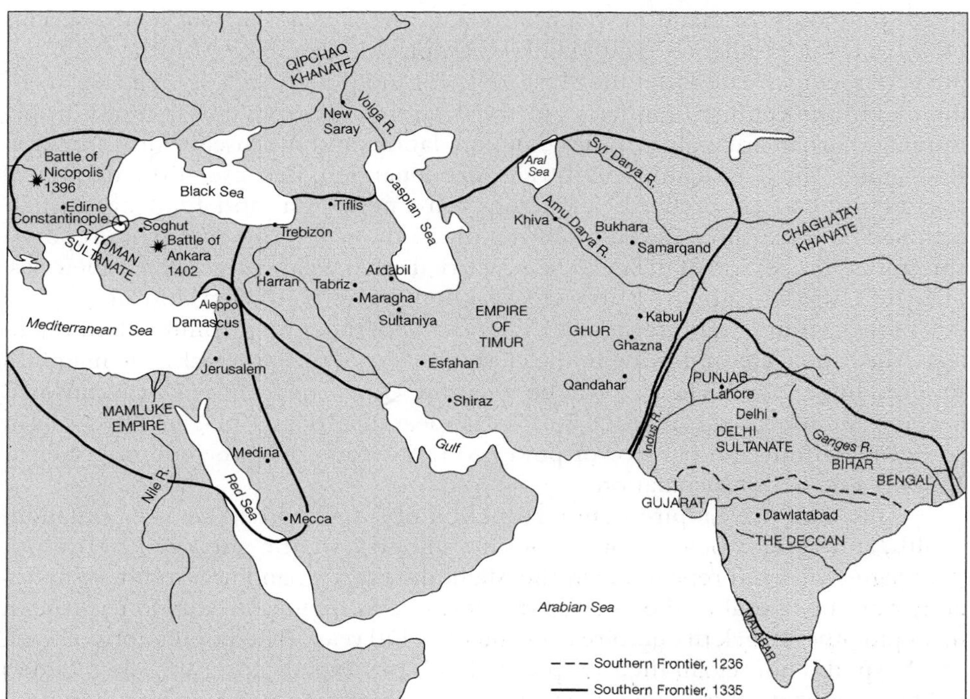

MAP 1.2 The Eastern Muslim World, Late Fourteenth Century.

Scourges

The fourteenth century was a difficult one for much of the world's population. The travails of the inhabitants of Europe are justly famous: famine, wars, the schism within the papacy, and the plague, which reduced the population by thirty to fifty percent. China also suffered from epidemics during this century, as well. For much of the predominantly Muslim world, however, the second half of the century was probably more wretched than for any comparably sized area on the planet.

Plague

The plague had already felled millions of people in China and India when it swept into southwestern Asia and Europe in 1347. Its sudden appearance and high mortality rate were shocking enough, but the symptoms of the disease made it even more terrible. Victims developed fever and shivering, and blackened swellings appeared in the neck, armpits, and groin, filled with dark and foul-smelling pus. Sometimes the swellings burst, causing the victim intense agony, and the stench of the escaping pus was so strong that many family members could not approach the victim. (The discolored swellings gave the disease its popular name, Black Death.) Many also experienced purple or red skin discolorations, internal bleeding, bloody urine, diarrhea, or vomiting. Many died from what appeared to be pneumonia, for their lungs filled with fluid, and they died of asphyxiation.

From Transoxiana to Egypt and Andalus, the Dar al-Islam suffered a serious blow from the pestilence. The Mamluke Empire's experience with the plague is the best-documented case in the Muslim world, and it suggests a population loss by the end of the century of at least one-third, a rate comparable to that of Europe. Rural and urban areas alike suffered depopulation, and the disease killed the livestock upon which agriculture and transport depended. Because of the depopulation of rural areas, orchards and crops were neglected, and food production dropped. Disease spread even more rapidly in the cities; the chronicles report a continuous procession of the dead being carried out the city gates to the cemeteries. Many of Cairo's neighborhoods were abandoned and had fallen into ruin by the end of the century. Hardest hit of all, it seems, were the royal mamluks. Refusing to leave the capital city and living in the close quarters of their barracks, the mamluks suffered huge losses. The struggle between the Qipchaqs and the Circassians had become intense by the time of the first appearance of the plague; what role it played in shifting the balance of power to the Circassians (who seized power in 1382) is a matter of speculation.

The Mamluke Empire entered a period of sustained decline in population, wealth, and military power. For reasons not understood, the pneumonic variety of the plague recurred repeatedly in the Mamluke Empire, and as a result, the mortality rates of several of the later epidemics were as high as the first one. At least fifty epidemics struck the empire over the next 170 years. The populations of Syria and Egypt did not regain their preplague levels for several centuries. The regime's military power itself declined markedly due to the high rate of death among the royal mamluks.

Mamluke agriculture entered in a centuries-long state of depression, and the thriving industries of the fourteenth century went into steep decline. The one bright spot amid the gloom of the plague was that the Mamluke Empire did witness a boom in construction. New buildings, particularly madrasas, mosques, fountains, and tombs, went up in large numbers. Many of these may have been endowed by individuals hoping to escape the plague by their good works and by others grateful for having been spared from the plague. At any rate, as a result of the increased opportunities for constructing and decorating such buildings, urban artisans who survived the epidemics were well paid. In addition, Egypt continued to benefit from its role as an entrepôt in the international spice trade. Its spice merchants joined the artisans as the only groups who prospered during the period from the mid-fourteenth to late fifteenth century.

Apart from the urban areas of the Mamluke Empire, our knowledge of the impact of the plague on the Muslim world is surprisingly limited. It is clear that the plague caused numerous villages in Palestine (within the Mamluke Empire) to be abandoned, and much agricultural land there reverted to the control of nomads. The ports of North Africa and of Granada were also hit hard by the epidemic. The disease struck the Iberian Peninsula during a war between Granada and Castile. It hit Granada's army before that of Castile, causing some Muslims to consider converting to Christianity as a prophylactic. Fortunately for their faith, the disease was soon raging among troops of Castile, as well. Alfonso XI, the king of Castile, was the only ruling monarch of Europe to die of the Black Death. The Ottomans were involved in the Byzantine struggle for the throne in the same year that the plague struck Constantinople (1347), but we do not know how the disease affected their campaigns.

Timur Lang

Shortly after the first incidence of the plague, another destructive scourge struck southwestern Asia. This was the army of the warrior Timur Lang, known to Europe as Tamerlane ("Temur Leng" is more accurate as a Turkic rendering of his name, but less widely used). The ferocity and wanton destructiveness of his campaigns still provoke amazement and horror, and the victories of his undefeated army changed the course of history for numerous regimes. He came of age as the Mongol states were collapsing, and he found the heirs to those states to be easy prey. More impressive was the ease with which he defeated the Mamlukes, the Delhi Sultanate, and the Ottomans.

Timur (1336–1405) was born in the immediate aftermath of the schism within the Chaghatay khanate that erupted during the reign of Tarmasharin. He grew up near Samarqand, where the settled population was dominated by nomadic and seminomadic Turko–Mongol tribes. Timur himself could claim descent from the Mongols through his mother and from Turks through his father. During the 1360s, he developed a series of alliances with local chieftains and became a powerful actor in the affairs of Transoxiana.

In about 1370, Timur seized control of Samarqand and declared his intention of restoring the glory of the Mongol empire. He spent the next decade securing control of the frontiers of Transoxiana. True to the classic model, victories begat victories, for the vanquished armies became the reservoir for new recruits into his own army, and his forces grew exponentially. Unlike the armies of light cavalry characteristic of the Chinggisid conquests, however, Timur's armies gradually became a composite force. One element that made him such a formidable opponent was that he realized the advantages of combining the mobility of light cavalry with the shock force of heavy calvary. He also utilized infantry when it served his purposes, and he gradually adopted the new technologies of rockets and siege artillery.

In 1381, Timur began the conquests that made his place in history. His own explanations for the campaigns are not recorded, and historians have had to speculate on his motivations. To some observers, the needless bloodshed and physical destruction of the campaigns suggest that they were simple plundering operations, carried out to keep his volatile troops satisfied with booty. Other historians have speculated that the campaigns were begun in order to create a great commercial network that would allow Samarqand to recapture its glory, and that the accompanying violence was a technique to intimidate the local populations to submit to his authority.

Whatever Timur's motives may have been, by 1385 he had captured Herat, Khorasan, and all of eastern Iran, and during the course of the next year he conquered Esfahan and Hamadan, thus destroying the petty dynasties that had emerged in the aftermath of the collapse of the Il-khanid regime. Over the next nine years, he conquered Iraq and the Caucasus. During the 1390s, he led two punitive expeditions against Toqtamish of the Horde. Toqtamish, self-confident after having seized power over the Horde in 1377, dared to encroach upon Timur's territory in Transoxiana. Timur retaliated and punished him in battle, but Toqtamish foolishly challenged Timur again Azerbaijan. This time, Timur systematically destroyed all the commercial cities in the Horde from the Black Sea to the Aral Sea. Although Timur was not able to capture Toqtamish, the latter's reputation was destroyed, and the destruction of the cities of the steppes caused irreparable harm to the economy of the Tatars.

During Timur's campaign against Toqtamish, revolts broke out all over Iran against his occupation. He brutally suppressed the revolts. Whole cities were destroyed, their inhabitants massacred, and towers were built of their skulls. After reestablishing control of Iran, Timur invaded the Delhi Sultanate in 1398. The Indian army, exhausted by the decade of civil war that followed the death of Firuz, was crushed. The killing and wanton destruction that characterized the Delhi campaign may be unsurpassed in history. The chroniclers report that Timur ordered the execution of tens of thousands of Hindu captives before and after the battle for Delhi. Thousands of them are said to have been skinned alive. The sack of Delhi went on for several days before the city was set afire and left in smoldering ruins. Members of the Tughluq dynasty continued to claim sovereignty in Delhi until 1413, but the city remained devastated. Over the course of the next century, Delhi slowly established itself as a regional power, but it would take over a century for it to eclipse its rival Hindu and Muslim states again.

Timur returned to Samarqand in 1399 with a vast amount of wealth with which to enhance the only city that he appears ever to have appreciated. He also brought back a herd of Indian war elephants, a novel weapon that he wanted to add to his arsenal. As usual, he spent only a few days inside the walls before retiring to his rural pavilion. Before the end of the year, he set out on a campaign to the west, and he again secured control over Azerbaijan. While there, he received emissaries from Turkish chieftains in Anatolia who were under his protection and learned that Bayezit had invaded their territories. Bayezit's action was an affront to Timur's honor and resulted in a tense confrontation between two of the most powerful men in the world. Neither one had a clear picture of the other's power, and both were reluctant to force the issue without more intelligence. Timur sent a diplomatically worded dispatch to Bayezit, warning him to keep his distance from areas under Timur's authority. Bayezit replied not only arrogantly, but insultingly. Timur then attacked and destroyed the Ottoman outpost of Sivas, which had been under the command of one of Bayezit's sons.

Assuming that he had taught Bayezit his lesson, Timur then turned to the Mamlukes and attacked the city of Aleppo in 1400. The Circassian Mamlukes, reeling from the effects of recurring bouts with the plague, of famines caused by inadequate floods of the Nile, and of a worsening balance of trade with Europe, were in no position to contest the mighty Timur. Aleppo was sacked, and in 1401, Timur moved on to Damascus. There, the young Mamluke sultan had assembled his army, but when he heard of a rebellion in Cairo, he returned to his capital in haste. The abandoned army, confused and leaderless, straggled back to Cairo in disarray. The inhabitants of Damascus, now defenseless, agreed to pay Timur a heavy ransom not to be attacked. Once inside the walls, however, Timur increased the ransom demand tenfold. When the citizens protested, he ordered the city to be sacked, and the inhabitants were massacred. He spared the city's artisans, whom he sent to Samarqand.

By the fall of 1401, Timur was no longer concerned by a potential threat from the Mamlukes, and he headed toward the Caucasus for the winter. Learning of a rebellion in Baghdad, he ordered the city destroyed. Leveled for the second time in little more than a century, it would require more than four centuries for the city to become even a regional town again. Once in the Caucasus, Timur received news of Bayezit's continuing challenge to his claims in eastern Anatolia, and he resolved to decide the issue the following season. In July 1402, the two armies met at modern Ankara. Timur used his Indian war elephants to launch the attack. Once the battle had been joined, Bayezit's Turkish allies abandoned him, leaving him to fight Timur with his Balkan Christian vassals. He was defeated and captured, and died in captivity eight months later. Timur's army pursued the remnants of the Ottoman army all the way to the Dardanelles, where the Ottoman survivors were ferried across (for a price) by Genoese and Venetians.

Bayezit's sons began fighting each other for control of the Ottoman holdings, and they almost caused the destruction of everything that their ancestors had achieved. For the next nine years, their civil war allowed most of the local leaders in Anatolia and in the Balkans to regain their political independence, and both areas lapsed into near anarchy. To contemporaries, it appeared that the Ottomans were finished.

Timur now began to prepare for the climax of his career: a campaign against the Ming dynasty in China. He set out from Samarqand in December 1404, but fell seriously ill as he approached the Syr Darya River. He died in February 1405. Contrary to

In the Presence of Timur

Anyone trapped within a city besieged by Timur would be consumed by anxiety of the worst kind. Such a fate befell one of the era's greatest scholars, Ibn Khaldun, when Timur besieged Damascus. The scholar's experience with Timur soon became "up close and personal" when the conqueror announced that he desired to see him. Timur received Ibn Khaldun graciously, and then informed him that he wanted him to write a detailed description of the Maghrib. Ibn Khaldun spent the next five weeks in Timur's camp writing his report, and he left a record of his experiences during that time. Foregoing an opportunity to portray Timur as a monster, he reveals a human side to Timur as well as his own obsequiousness in the presence of absolute power.

[After asking for the report on the Maghrib] he gave a signal to his servants to bring from his tent some of the kind of food which they call "rishta" and which they were most expert in preparing. Some dishes of it were brought in, and he made a sign that they should be set before me. I arose, took them, and drank, and liked it, and this impressed him favorably. [Then] I composed in my mind some words to say to him which, by exalting him and his government, would flatter him. . . .

The news was brought to him that the gate of the city had been opened and that the judges had gone out to fulfill their [promise of] surrender, for which, so they thought, he had generously granted them amnesty. Then he was carried away from before us, because of the trouble with his knee, and was placed upon his horse; grasping the reins, he sat upright in his saddle while the bands played around him until the air shook with them; he rode toward Damascus. . . .

When the time for Timur's journey approached and he decided to leave Damascus, I entered to him one day. After we had completed the customary greetings, he turned to me and said, "You have a mule here?"

I answered, "Yes."

He said, "Is it a good one?"

I answered, "Yes."

He said, "Will you sell it? I would buy it from you."

I replied, "May Allah aid you—one like me does not sell to one like you; but I would offer it to you in homage, and also others like it if I had them."

He said, "I meant only that I would requite you for it with generosity."

I replied, "Is there any generosity left beyond that which you have already shown me? You have heaped favors upon me, accorded me a place in your council among your intimate followers, and shown me kindness and generosity—which I hope Allah will repay to you in like measure."

He was silent; so was I. The mule was brought to him while I was with him at his council, and I did not see it again. . . .

Then on another day I entered to him and he asked me: "Are you going to travel to Cairo?"

(Continued)

I answered, "May Allah aid you—indeed, my desire is only [to serve] you, for you have granted me refuge and protection. If the journey to Cairo would be in your service, surely; otherwise I have no desire for it."

He said, "No, but you will return to your family and to your people."

SOURCE: *Anthology of Islamic Literature From the Rise of Islam to Modern Times,* with an introduction and commentaries by James Kritzeck. New York: Holt, Rinehart and Winston Inc., 1964, pp. 281–284.

Muslim practice, his body was embalmed and sent to Samarqand, where it was buried in the impressive tomb that he had constructed for that purpose, the Gur-e Amir. At his death, his sons and grandsons fought over the succession and lost all the territories that Timur had conquered, except for Transoxiana and western Afghanistan.

Timur's legacy would boast of impressive cultural achievements in Samarqand and Herat over the next century. Timur himself adorned Samarqand with beautiful architecture, gardens, and the equivalent of a national library, where books were copied, illustrated, bound, and stored. Elsewhere, however, the result of Timur's career was sheer destruction. The area from Delhi to Damascus had been laid waste, and combined with the effects of the plague in Syria and Iraq, the populations of a huge area experienced suffering and despair beyond comprehension.

Some historians have pointed out that Chinggis Khan and his Mongol successors usually employed cruelty as a means to gain submission. Timur, like Alexander the Great, seems to have simply enjoyed watching rivers of blood flow. What makes Timur's cruelty more difficult to explain is that all of his opponents were Muslim regimes. If he had been a pagan like his Mongol ancestors, his barbarity might be dismissed as a symptom of his hostility to an alien culture. Timur, however, like many of his fellow Turks and Mongols in Central Asia, easily combined residual shamanism with a commitment to Islam. In the name of Islam, he systematically destroyed the Jacobite church in northern Syria and western Anatolia, as well as the Nestorian church in Central Asia. He also claimed to be serving the cause of Islam in invading the Delhi Sultanate, which of course was ruled by Muslims. But his motives for the utter destruction of large numbers of Muslims across a wide swath of territory remain obscure.

Conclusion

The fifteenth century dawned on an eastern Muslim landscape utterly transformed from its contours of the early thirteenth century. From Syria and the Russian steppes in the west to India in the east, the whole order had been reworked several times in a century and a half. Muslim regimes, Mongol regimes, civil war, the plague, and Timur Lang had transformed the political and social order the way a tornado scrambles anything in its path. The Mongol conquests of the thirteenth century inflicted catastrophic damage upon Iraq and Khorasan. They had also inadvertently boosted the fortunes of the nascent Mamluke, Ottoman, and Delhi regimes by causing tens of thousands of intellectuals, craftsmen, and artists to flee to those havens. In the fourteenth century, the plague and Timur's campaigns laid waste once again to Iran and Iraq, but also threatened the very existence of the Mamluke, Ottoman, and Delhi states and societies. By the time of Timur's death in 1405, Delhi had been reduced to the status of a local pretender, and Ottoman power appeared to be destroyed. The Circassian Mamlukes had been humiliated by their failure to defend Damascus, and recurring waves of the plague kept them weaker than their Qipchaq predecessors.

The Mongol conquests, it should be remembered, were only the latest wave of violence and suffering to afflict the Muslim world. On the other hand, they were so destructive that they caused mass migrations of peasants, nomads, craftsmen, intellectuals, and merchants to areas not under the immediate threat of Mongol attack. One important consequence was that the ethnic composition of many parts of the Muslim world would be changed for centuries to come. Moreover, regions which up to that time had been peripheral to mainstream developments in the Dar al-Islam now became thriving centers of commerce and culture due to the influx of refugees from the Mongol advance.

The period 1260–1405 represents a major watershed in Muslim history. It witnessed a degree of destruction and suffering that can hardly be imagined, and yet the thoroughness of the changes that took place created the conditions for new societies to assert themselves. A comparable period in western European history would be that of the Frankish conquests and the Norsemen's raids, or from the sixth through the late tenth centuries. The cumulative effect of this period was that, by the beginning of the fifteenth century, the political structures of the central and eastern sections of the Dar al-Islam had been so shaken that a contemporary outside observer could be forgiven for wondering if Islamic civilization had a future. As it turned out, that civilization was about to rise, phoenixlike, and become the most dominant force in the world for several centuries.

FURTHER READING

The Mongol Khanates

Adshead, S. A. M. *Central Asia in World History.* New York: St. Martin's Press, 1993.

Kwanten, Luc. *Imperial Nomads: A History of Central Asia, 500–1500.* Philadelphia: University of Pennsylvania Press, 1979.

Morgan, David. *The Mongols.* Oxford: Basil Blackwell, 1986.

Vernadsky, George. *The Mongols and Russia.* New Haven, Connecticut: Yale University Press, 1953.

New Centers of Islamic Culture

Ahmed, Aziz. *Studies in Islamic Culture in the Indian Environment.* Oxford: Oxford University Press, 1962.

Ayalon, David. *Islam and the Abode of War.* London: Variorum, 1994.

———. *Outsiders in the Lands of Islam: Mamluks, Mongols and Eunuchs.* London: Variorum Reprints, 1988.

Cahen, Claude. *The Formation of Turkey*. Translated and edited by P. M. Holt. Harlow, U.K.: Longman, 2001.

Canfield, Robert L., ed. *Turko–Persia in Historical Perspective.* Cambridge, U.K: Cambridge University Press, 1991.

Ikram, S. M. *Muslim Civilization in India.* Edited by Ainslie T. Embree. New York and London: Columbia University Press, 1964.

Inalcik, Halil. *The Ottoman Empire: The Classical Age, 1300–1600.* Translated by Norman Itzkowitz and Colin Imber. New York and Washington: Praeger Publishers, 1973.

Kafadar, Cemal. *Between Two Worlds: The Construction of the Ottoman State.* Berkeley, California: University of California Press, 1995.

Irwin, R. *The Middle East in the Middle Ages: The Early Mamluk Sultanate (1250–1382).* Carbondale, Illinois: Southern Illinois University Press, 1986.

Jackson, Peter. *The Delhi Sultanate.* Cambridge and New York: Cambridge University Press, 1999.

McCarthy, Justin. *The Ottoman Turks: An Introductory History to 1923.* London and New York: Longman, 1997.

Scourges

Adshead, S. A. M. *Central Asia in World History.* New York: St. Martin's Press, 1993.

Dols, Michael. *The Black Death in the Middle East.* Princeton, New Jersey: Princeton University Press, 1977.

Manz, Beatrice Forbes. *The Rise and Rule of Tamerlane.* Cambridge, U.K.: Cambridge University Press, 1989.

CHAPTER 2

Unity and Diversity in Islamic Traditions

In 1325, a young Moroccan named Ibn Battuta embarked upon the hajj. Others from his hometown who had traveled to Mecca before him had usually been away for two to three years. Thus, he knew that he would be gone for an extended period, but it is doubtful that he had any idea at the time just how long it would be before he saw home again. In fact, after he had completed the rituals of the pilgrimage, he decided to travel the extent of the Muslim world. He sailed along the coast of East Africa, ventured into the realm of the Horde in southern Russia, lived for seven years in India, and may even have sailed through the straits of Southeast Asia on his way to China. He did not return home until 1349. His return trip was fraught with numerous perils, for he had to make his way through the collapsing states of the mid-fourteenth century as well as avoid becoming a victim of the plague, which was ravaging much of the world at the time.

Ibn Battuta's career opens a window upon Muslim cultures of the fourteenth century. Muslim states, as a rule, proved ephemeral in the face of the cataclysms of the thirteenth and fourteenth centuries. More impressive was the strength of the ideas and institutions that had evolved within the Muslim world over the previous several centuries. Scholars in many disciplines had not ceased producing original work, and Ibn Battuta visited many whose fame was spread all across the Dar al-Islam. The *Shari'a,* or Islamic law, provided cultural continuity when states failed, and Ibn Battuta financed his travels by serving as an itinerant *qadi:* Everywhere he went, his credentials qualified him to adjudicate disputes according to Islamic law, and local Muslims paid handsomely for his services. By the mid-fourteenth century,

Sufi lodges and orders were widespread throughout the Muslim world. Ibn Battuta visited many different Sufi masters, enjoyed the hospitality of numerous Sufi lodges, and marveled at the variety of Sufi expression wherever he went.

Intellectual Life in the Fourteenth Century

The widespread elimination of Muslim states by the Mongols, the collapse of the newly Islamized Mongol regimes themselves, the catastrophe of the plague, and the utter ruthlessness of Timur were spectacularly destructive and severely demoralizing events. Many European historians of the nineteenth and twentieth centuries, viewing the Muslim experience of the thirteenth and fourteenth centuries through the prism of the subsequent rise of Europe to world dominance, found it easy to assume that Islamic civilization had been shattered and left moribund. That view can no longer be defended.

The End of the "Golden Age"?

Unlike early medieval western Europe after the collapse of Roman administration, the Muslim world never suffered from a cessation of its cultural life. As had happened earlier during times of great turmoil, Islamic law continued to function, precisely because it was not dependent upon the stability of any particular regime. Also as before, the new states, even the transitory ones, attempted to gain legitimacy for themselves by patronizing scholars and artists who exemplified the best of Islamic civilization.

Even though Islamic civilization did not collapse in the fourteenth century, a shift in the locus of cultural creativity did slowly occur. Until the thirteenth century, the level of intellectual production in the Muslim world had been vastly superior to that of Europe. With the work of scholars such as Albertus Magnus, Robert Grosseteste, and Roger Bacon (all of whom were inspired by translations of Arabic manuscripts), however, European thought began to value mathematical and experimental methods in the practice of natural science. The twelfth- and thirteenth-century translation of Arabic versions of Greek texts prompted a desire to read the Greek originals, and in the process of searching for them, scholars discovered previously unknown texts by Plato, Aristotle, and other intellectuals. Although philosophy remained largely within the framework set by the Church for two more centuries, numerous new currents in philosophy emerged, laying the foundation for humanism and other secular developments of the fifteenth and sixteenth centuries.

These changes did not take place overnight. Cultural production in the Muslim world continued to flourish in many quarters, and the visual arts were about to enter their most creative phase. In the fields of pure mathematics and astronomy, as well, the Muslim world continued to eclipse Europe until the mid-sixteenth century, when Copernicus made his breakthrough. Even in the field of astronomy we must remember that the Copernican thesis was not readily accepted in Europe. The rejection of the geocentric theory flew in the face of the everyday experience of everyone, but also seemed heretical to both Protestants and Catholics. Since the Bible contains several passages that refer to the sun's movement around the earth and never mentions a possible revolution of the earth around the sun, most Christians were reluctant even to consider the new theory. Not until the late seventeenth century was the geocentric view decisively discredited in scientific circles, and the Catholic Church had so much institutional prestige invested in it that it continued to adhere officially to the notion until 1860. In science and mathematics, therefore, we can say that Protestant Europe began to move beyond Muslim achievements by the late seventeenth century. It was also during this period that European universities finally began to discard Ibn Sina's seven-hundred-year-old book of medicine in favor of the new European discoveries in physiology, based upon the work of Vesalius and Harvey.

The reversal of fortunes in the scientific and philosophical productivity of Europe and the Muslim world has given rise to much speculation about "what went wrong" for the Dar al-Islam. Often forgotten in the discussion is the fact that Europe's subsequent development was unique and unpredictable. Its science and technology eventually dwarfed that of all other regions of the globe, not just the predominantly Muslim regions. The cultural systems of China, India, Southeast Asia, and the Americas all contained elements that had been more sophisticated than their European counterparts, but by the late eighteenth century, their technological prowess was eclipsed. The European aberration is actually the topic that needs explanation, and we still cannot provide an adequate one. Much of the speculation has been based on misplaced assumptions about historical inevitability and progress, rather than on a careful analysis of how history actually takes place.

The contrasting trajectories of the intellectual history of Europe and the Muslim world are of particular interest due to their common heritage. They shared many features: Their monotheistic traditions were remarkably parallel, and they enjoyed the same access to the Greco–Roman traditions of architecture, philosophy, engineering, medicine, and political thought. The advantages the Muslim world enjoyed were a more direct access to the creative traditions of China and India and not having to overcome the disastrous collapse of Roman administration that western Europe suffered after the fourth century. A major advantage for western Europe was that it no longer suffered from outside invasions after the mid-tenth century, and subsequently enjoyed a period of economic growth that resulted in political centralization and cultural sophistication. The Muslim world, by contrast, began suffering from sustained violence from the same, mid-tenth century, period.

Muslim religious scholars became increasingly intolerant of speculative thought. Innovation (*bid'a*) in religious affairs had always been frowned upon due to the perceived obligation to act strictly in accord with the Qur'an and the Prophet's own behavior, but the charge of "bid'a" was increasingly effective in limiting the scope of intellectual inquiry. By the thirteenth century, when Muslims felt hemmed in by aggressive Christian enemies to the west and ruthless pagan Mongol enemies to the east, philosophical speculation had practically ceased.

At this time, it is as impossible to explain the growing conservatism of Muslim intellectuals as it is to explain the increasing creativity of European intellectuals. A multitude of factors played a part, and it is possible that we will never be able to discover many of the most important ones. It does, however, seem useful to keep in mind two elements of the Muslim experience. One is the conjunction between the sense of collective insecurity, on the one hand, and the growing reluctance to allow challenges to established religious doctrine, on the other. A confident society is likely to allow more scope to intellectual inquiry than one that fears for its future. The other element is the fact that Muslim philosopher–scientists required the patronage of ruling families for their economic support, whereas, by the twelfth century, European scholars were beginning to organize autonomous universities. European scientists and philosophers enjoyed legal protection as communities of scholars. They benefitted from the exchange of ideas and the criticism that came from belonging to a faculty, and they could respond to threats to their livelihood by going to court. Muslim scholars, however were attached individually to the palaces of ruling dynasties. They shared ideas with fellow scholars, but at a distance. If their ideas were criticized by local religious leaders or by public opinion, the patron usually found it expedient to dismiss them. Under those conditions, it was next to impossible for a school of thought to develop based on an original idea.

Thus, it is possible to say that the period of Mongol hegemony represents a period during which Muslim philosophical thought practically disappeared except as an adjunct to theology and law. The fields of prose, poetry, the sciences, and mathematics, however, continued to boast the work of outstanding talents, and the visual arts were entering their most spectacular period. Scientists and mathematicians continued to make important revisions to existing knowledge, but their isolation from each other and their dependence on the good will of a ruler limited the scope of their work. Their plight was similar to that of the vast majority of intellectuals in the world at the time.

Against All Odds

A remarkable feature of the period of the Mongols and of Timur is the vibrancy of the religious, artistic, and intellectual life of the Muslim world. The cultural and intellectual life of the Dar al-Islam showed that it had securely established itself across a wide area, and even the hammer blows of the fourteenth century could not destroy it. As we have seen, even the Mamluke Empire, which may have experienced the worst effects of the plague of any region in the world, made contributions to art and architecture which are still regarded with awe. The intellectual life of Muslims, too, continued to flourish. Philosophy continued to be suspect because of its association with challenges to the authority of revelation, but the use of disciplined reason was highly valued in most theological and legal circles. Historical and scientific studies also continued to flourish wherever manuscripts survived or were copied and where patronage made scholarship possible. Sometimes these conditions made vibrant scholarship possible in the most unlikely of settings.

Ibn Taymiya

One of the greatest Muslim religious scholars of the fourteenth century was Ibn Taymiya (1262–1327). He was born in 1262 in the city of Harran, located near today's border between Syria and Turkey. Fearing the effects of the onset of Hulagu's rule, his family moved to Damascus while Ibn Taymiya was a small child.

For the rest of his life, he lived under Mamluke rule. Through a combination of formal education and independent study, he mastered the disciplines that focused on the study of the Qur'an, Hadith, jurisprudence, rational theology, philosophy, and Sufi metaphysics. His keen intellect, his deep knowledge of the religious sciences, and his forceful personality combined to create one of the most influential thinkers in Islamic history.

Ibn Taymiya's career was committed to the cause of Islamic reform. He was convinced that certain doctrines and practices had arisen that were not sanctioned by the legitimate sources of the faith, and he became a tireless advocate of the need to return to what he regarded as the purity of early Islamic history. He argued that the two sources of all religious truth are the Qur'an and the Hadith as interpreted by the first generation of Muslim scholars. As a member of the Hanbali school of law, he believed that whatever is commanded in those sources must be obeyed, and whatever is not mentioned in them must not be required. Although he was proficient in the methods of philosophy and rational theology, he was bitterly critical of the conclusions that philosophers and theologians drew from them.

He was particularly critical of philosophers who asserted that scripture had been deliberately couched in metaphors and pictorial images so that common people could understand it. He also found fault with certain features of Sufism, although he was not opposed to Sufism as such. He did, however, object to common Sufi practices such as the pilgrimages that were made to the tombs of saints, and he rejected the monism of Ibn al-'Arabi. One of his greatest contributions to subsequent Islamic history was his criticism of fellow jurists for accepting without question the decisions of jurists of previous generations. He was convinced that scholars of the Shari'a had an obligation to continue interpreting the will of God as it applied to contemporary society, provided that all such decisions were firmly grounded in the two major sources of law, extended where necessary by analogical reasoning.

Ibn Taymiya was what today we would call a "public intellectual." He brought his passionate concerns to the attention of both the public and the authorities, not just to the small group of his fellow intellectuals. Because some of his criticism threatened other intellectuals, popular religious leaders, and the interests of government officials, he became the center of controversy and conflict. From at least 1298 until his death in 1327, he was repeatedly brought before the courts on various charges—"anthropomorphism," his attacks on rituals at saints' shrines, and his support of a revision to the Shari'a that would make it more difficult for a man to divorce his wife, among others—and was jailed several times for a total of at least five years for his "offenses." His funeral attracted thousands of admirers, many of whom he had criticized for un-Islamic practices, but who respected him for his courage, brilliance, and integrity.

Ibn Taymiya's moral courage and his uncompromising dedication to truth as he understood it has made him a role model for many Islamic reformers to the present day. He is particularly remembered today for his evaluation of Ghazan, the Il-khan ruler whose army occupied Damascus for a year after defeating the Mamlukes in 1300. Ghazan, as we have seen, was a professed Muslim, but Ibn Taymiya never forgot that the Mongols had destroyed much of the civilization of the Islamic world and had frightened his family out of their home in Harran. He led an opposition group to the Mongol occupation of his adopted city, and afterward he wrote extensively on the duty of believers to oppose rulers who professed to be Muslim and performed the basic rites, but who in fact failed to apply the Shari'a. As a result, he is revered today by Muslim activists who challenge the oppressive and corrupt governments of their countries and advocate the creation of an Islamic state.

Ibn al-Shatir

Until the late twentieth century, the focus of historians of astronomy on the Copernican tradition caused them to ignore the original work of Muslim astronomers. In fact, from the tenth century on, a large number of Muslim astronomers recorded important observations and made significant contributions to astronomical theory. Some of the most important Muslim astronomers lived during the period from the thirteenth to the sixteenth centuries, an era when many western historians assumed that Islamic scholarship had died. One of the most important astronomers in history was Ibn al-Shatir of Damascus (1306–1375), whose career spanned the last, turbulent decades of the Qipchaq period of Mamluke rule. He was a young man in Damascus when Ibn Taymiya died there. Ibn al-Shatir was the *muwaqqit*, or timekeeper, for the congregational mosque of Damascus, and he was chief of the mosque's muezzins. He designed and constructed his own versions of several observational and computing instruments, including the quadrant and sundial. His large sundial for the congregational mosque of Damascus still stands, and a portable one is preserved in the Aleppo Museum.

Even more impressive is Ibn al-Shatir's work in astronomy. He stands in the tradition of what has come to be known as the "Maragha school" of astronomy. As we have seen, Hulagu's observatory at Maragha attracted scientists from China to Andalus. The astronomers at Maragha engaged in much observational work, but are best known for their revision of existing astronomical theory. Ibn al-Shatir, although not at Maragha itself, continued in this tradition. At the center of the debate was the work of Ptolemy, the great second-century geographer and astronomer. In addition to having established the basis for determining latitudes on earth, he proposed a geocentric (earth-centered) model of the universe that incorporated the important observations and theories up to his time in a brilliant synthesis. It rapidly became the paradigm that explained the structure of the universe as seen from earth. Its basic features remained unchallenged until the sixteenth century, when Copernicus proposed his heliocentric (sun-centered) theory.

The Muslim astronomers did not offer a heliocentric theory, for, at the time, such a theory was contrary to the evidence of the senses as well as unnecessary, since the Ptolemaic theory was highly accurate in predicting eclipses and other celestial events. What concerned them was the inconsistency between Ptolemy's model and the mechanics that he proposed to explain how it worked. A major problem was that Ptolemy assumed for philosophical purposes that celestial orbits were perfectly circular, but actual observations demonstrated that they acted in an elliptical fashion. He had attempted to explain the discrepancy by proposing that the spherical orbits moved uniformly around an axis that did not pass through the center of the sphere (an "eccentric" circle, rather than a "concentric" one).

Another problem was that, over the centuries, astronomers found that the assumption of the perfect uniformity of the velocity of planets ran counter to their observations. Planets appeared to wander in random patterns and to speed up or slow down. Rather than abandoning the Ptolemaic model, however, astronomers proposed that a given planet actually moves in a small circular orbit (an "epicycle"), which is itself centered on the rim of an orbit around the earth. This corollary seemed adequate until so many epicycles had to be proposed that the entire model became unwieldy. When the dozens of epicycles were combined with the eccentric orbits, the Ptolemaic model was beginning to look like a Rube Goldberg machine. The Copernican "revolution" was provoked in part because Copernicus could not believe that God had designed such an awkward instrument.

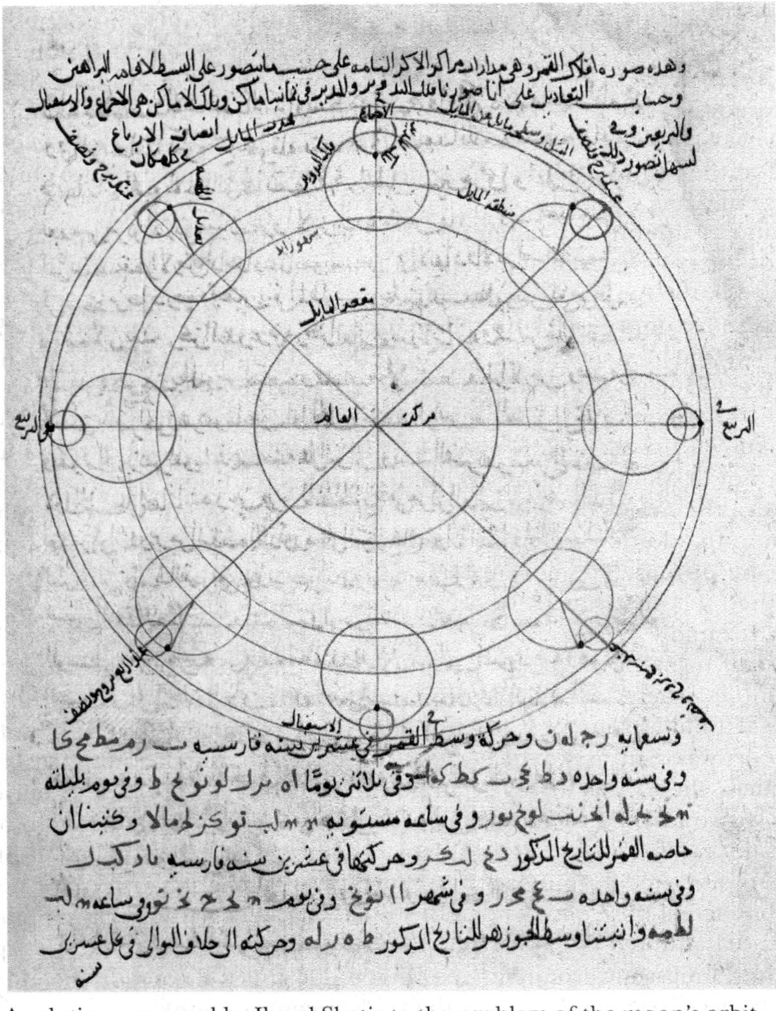

A solution proposed by Ibn al-Shatir to the problem of the moon's orbit around the earth.

Ibn al-Shatir, too, was concerned with the problems of the eccentrics and the epicycles. Like all other astronomers of the fourteenth century, he saw no need to challenge Ptolemy's basic model, but rather to make it internally consistent. Starting with the assumption that celestial orbits are the result of a succession of uniform circular motions, he developed models of orbits of the moon and the planets that did not require eccentrics. His highly sophisticated geometry allowed him to accomplish what the master Ptolemy could not. His geometric models, which assume a geocentric universe, show up in a revised form two hundred years later in the heliocentric model of Copernicus. Since the late 1950s, when Ibn al-Shatir's manuscripts were first discovered by European scholars, historians of science have been wrestling with the remarkable similarity of the models of Ibn al-Shatir and of Copernicus. They are aware that just because Ibn al-Shatir came up with such models prior to Copernicus does not mean that someone else could not devise them, but two considerations cause them to think that they must have been transmitted in some form to central Europe, where Copernicus could have had access to them. One reason is that no such models existed in the European tradition from which Copernicus could borrow. The other is that it is inconceivable that Copernicus would come up with the models himself, since they cause, rather than solve, problems for his theory. The lack of a theory of gravity in the Copernican model renders Ibn al-Shatir's models problematic in a heliocentric context: Without gravity, Copernicus has no explanation for why celestial bodies orbit the sun, whereas the Ptolemaic model utilized the Aristotelian theory that planets and moon "desire" the earth. The discovery of a "missing link" between Ibn al-Shatir and Copernicus would provide a fascinating glimpse of late medieval intellectual history.

Ibn Khaldun

Ibn Khaldun (1332–1406) was descended from one of the great families of Seville. His great-grandparents fled the city just before its fall to Castile in 1248 and settled in Tunis, where Ibn Khaldun was born. As the scion of a wealthy and powerful family, he received the best education possible, but was forced to migrate west in 1352 after the plague epidemic took the lives of his parents and teachers. For most of the rest of his life he served as a government minister. He found advisory positions in the Marinid capital of Fez, and then at Granada and several small principalities in modern Morocco and Algeria. Life as a government minister in that era was notoriously unpredictable and dangerous, but Ibn Khaldun seems to have had a knack for making enemies that made his own career even more unpredictable and dangerous than most: In every position that he held, he was either jailed or forced to leave town. Perhaps seeking a more stable career line, he sailed for Egypt in 1382, the same year that Sultan Barquq seized power and inaugurated the Circassian period in Mamluke history. Barquq recognized Ibn Khaldun's achievement as a scholar and a jurist, so he appointed him professor of Maliki law and then to be the senior Maliki qadi of Egypt. Even in Egypt, Ibn Khaldun encountered political problems and temporarily lost his posts. Because he was so adept at establishing contacts with important patrons, however, he always regained his positions.

Soon after Barquq's death in 1400, Timur began his invasion of Syria. The new Mamluke sultan insisted that Ibn Khaldun join his entourage as he went to Damascus to repel the attack. When the sultan returned in haste to Cairo, however, and his army straggled after him, he left Ibn Khaldun behind in the defenseless city. Timur asked to see him. Ibn Khaldun was thereupon lowered over the city's walls by ropes in a scene strikingly evocative of an episode in the life of the Christian theologian and missionary Paul fourteen centuries earlier. He spent five weeks in Timur's camp, serving as "scholar in residence." Ibn Khaldun recorded his experiences in the camp in a remarkably informal style. (See the extract in Chapter 1.) Timur wanted detailed knowledge of the Maghrib, and Ibn Khaldun presented enormous quantities of oral and written information, but in a way that portrayed the area as strong and united, rather than as the weak and divided region that it actually was. Whether the information he provided had anything to do with the fact that Timur did not venture south of Damascus is a matter of conjecture. Ibn Khaldun managed to obtain a safe conduct for himself and several of his friends, but witnessed the murderous sack of the city and the burning of the great congregational mosque for which Ibn al-Shatir had served as timekeeper. Ibn Khaldun died in Egypt in 1406, a year after Timur.

Ibn Khaldun is best known for the *Muqaddima*, or "Introduction," to his history of the Arabs and Berbers. In 1374, after a particularly exhausting period of government service in North Africa, Ibn Khaldun had sought refuge with a Berber tribe in what is now Algeria. He stayed with them for four years, and it was during this time that he wrote the *Muqaddima*, a massive introduction (the English translation is in three large volumes) to an even larger work of history. Its originality and profundity have had a major influence on Egyptian historians of the fifteenth century, Ottoman historians, and social scientists and philosophers of our own time. Many consider it to be the first work of genuine social science. While it is too complex to be summarized in a few dozen words, mention can be made of its most famous features. It includes a survey of the full range of Islamic learning, but concentrates on the dynamics of historical change. Ibn Khaldun's positivism is revealed in his blistering critique of the metaphysics of philosophy and is expressed again in his theory of history, which he believes to be governed by rational or natural laws. He stresses the role of climate, geography, economics, and ecology in creating the distinctive characteristics of given societies.

Most famously, Ibn Khaldun proposes a theory of historical change based on his understanding of North African history: An aggressive and simple nomadic community conquers an existing state and then develops a dynamic community characterized by ethnic, religious, or lineal solidarity. As the nomads become assimilated to the urban society they have conquered, however, the second generation becomes corrupted by the vices of urban civilization, and in particular tends to reject the loyalty-based political authority that had made the state possible in the first place. The third and final generation loses both its solidarity and its martial spirit, and becomes the easy prey of yet another vigorous nomadic community. Ibn Khaldun offered numerous examples from the time of the Arab conquests through the Berber dynasties of the Almoravids, Almohads, and Marinids to support his theory. The destructive campaigns of Timur, coming after he had written his book, could only reinforce his conclusions.

Hafez

The rebirth of Persian literature that began in the ninth century produced numerous talented poets. The epic poet Ferdowsi (ca. 940–1020) and the mystical poets Farid al-Din 'Attar (ca. 1120–ca. 1220), Sa'di (ca. 1193–1292), and Jamal al-Din al-Rumi (1207–1273) are still revered in Iran. Speakers of Persian, literate and illiterate alike, can recite from memory numerous verses of their poetry, and can harmonize Ferdowsi's celebration of pre-Islamic Iran with the religious themes of the others. As beloved as these poets are, however, the favorite poet of many Iranians is Hafez (ca. 1325–ca. 1390). Widely regarded as the greatest lyric poet in Persian, Hafez honed his craft in the midst of the chaos of the immediate post-Il-khanid era.

Hafez lived almost his entire life in Shiraz. When he was about ten years old, the Il-khanid ruler Abu Sa'id was poisoned, and the Il-khanid regime disintegrated. Various chieftains throughout the former empire seized power in the provinces. In Shiraz and western Iran, the Muzaffarid dynasty proved to be dominant until Timur conquered the area in 1387. Local revolts continued throughout Hafez's life, however, and Shiraz changed hands several times. Hafez's family was not prominent in the community, but he managed to acquire a deep knowledge of the Islamic sciences, Arabic, and Persian literature. He is said to have written several commentaries on religious texts and to have taught the Qur'an. (His name is actually an honorific, deriving from the Arabic word *hafiz*, which literally means "memorizer," specifically one who has memorized the entire Qur'an.)

Hafez was a deeply spiritual Sufi, but he did not possess an ascetic nature. He saw no contradiction between a love for God and a robust delight in the pleasures of the senses, and he composed poetry celebrating both. He became so renowned in Shiraz for his verses that he became a court poet for the Muzaffarids, although he fell out of favor with them in 1368. His sensual lifestyle and love of wine provoked the ulama to criticize him, and at his death, some of them did not even want him buried in a regular cemetery.

Hafez specialized in the type of poetry known as the *ghazal*, a lyric poem of six to fifteen couplets. By the fourteenth century, Arabic and Persian poetry had developed certain conventions that were beginning to make poetry stilted and formal. Hafez deliberately chose to write about everyday experience in simple and colloquial language, avoiding artificial display. The listener detects a remarkably humane and honest spirit in the poet. Unlike most court poets, he wrote few panegyrics, and even when he satirized hypocrites, he did not use the insults commonly hurled by other poets.

Hafez continued the Persian Sufi tradition of allusive images. His poetry contains many references to lovers (both male and female), wine, idols, mosques, birds, flowers, and other potent symbols. On the other hand, even at its most materialistic, it is often couched in Islamic terminology. Western students of his poetry have often wondered whether his language is allegorical and needs to be "decoded" for its spiritual message, or whether it is simply the sly musings of a profligate. Neither approach is adequate for the great Persian poets. Ambiguity of meaning is intrinsic and essential to their poetry. The cultivation of ambiguity was born in the midst of political and religious tension. Iranians chafed under the political dominance first of Arabs, and then of Turks and Mongols. Iran was a religious cauldron, as well. Both Zoroastrianism and Manichaeism (a religion that arose in third-century Iran and was severely persecuted by both Christians and Muslims over the next millennium) contained elements that still appealed to some Iranians. As a result, literally minded interpreters of the Qur'an bitterly criticized Muslims who were philosophically or mystically inclined, out of suspicion that they were being seduced by the older religions. In this political and religious hothouse, poets with serious themes learned to express themselves through double entendre, symbol, and metaphor. Everyday experience became inextricably entwined with the mystic's hunger for union with God.

Ibn Battuta

Ibn Taymiya, Ibn al-Shatir, Ibn Khaldun, and Hafez were intellectuals of the first order whose work is still the object of scholarly inquiry. Other intellectuals of similar stature could be treated here who worked in the natural sciences, historical studies, and religious studies. It seems appropriate to close this section, however, with Ibn Battuta (1304–1368), who was a minor intellectual but whose career, as suggested at the beginning of this chapter, demonstrates the scope and depth achieved by Islamic civilization by the fourteenth century. Ibn Battuta may have qualified as the most widely traveled individual prior to modern times. Born in 1304 in Tangier, he had the typical education of a young man who was preparing for a career as a qadi. Like many other young scholars, after his preparatory training he was ready to seek certificates from the more celebrated ulama in the great centers of Islamic studies. Thus, he embarked upon the hajj in 1325, planning to combine the fulfillment of that religious duty with the experience of studying with some of the more famous scholars of the two Holy Cities and of the Mamluke Empire. By the time he had completed the hajj, however, he had developed a passion for seeing the world. Over the next two decades, he became a citizen of the world, and before returning to Morocco in 1349, he had traveled at least 60,000—and perhaps as many as 75,000—miles.

Ibn Battuta could not have timed his travels better if he had had the hindsight of history and returned in a time machine. He passed through Cairo during the third reign of the Mamluke al-Nasir Muhammad, and thus saw Egypt and Syria at their most prosperous and stable period for centuries before or after that time. He sailed south along the African coast as far as modern Tanzania. Later, he was introduced to Orhan, the Ottoman leader; to Abu Sa'id, the last of the Il-khan rulers; and to Uzbeg, the great khan of the Golden Horde. (He even accompanied one of Uzbeg's wives—a Byzantine princess—to Constantinople so that she could give birth to her child in her father's palace.) He took advantage of Muhammad ibn Tughluq's generosity to foreign scholars and served the Delhi Sultanate as a qadi and administrator of a huge mausoleum complex. After serving the sultan for seven years, he spent several months as a qadi in the Maldive Islands and may have traveled as far east as China, although features of the account of his trip to Sumatra and Beijing cause some scholars to think that this section was composed by the editor of his book.

The People's Poet

The poetry of Hafez, like that of many of the great Persian poets, can be read on at least two levels. Its literal meaning expresses the values of the secular sophisticate, but its words can be interpreted as metaphors for Sufi mystical theology. After Hafez's death, his poetry became popular even in the Ottoman Empire and in Muslim India, where Persian literature benefitted from court patronage. On the level of popular culture, many people used his poems for divination: They would open a copy of his collection of poetry, the Diwan, at random and place their finger on a poem, expecting it to give them guidance for the day.

THE BODY'S CUP

Last night I saw angels knocking at the tavern door;
they shaped and cast a winecup from Adam's clay,

and I was drunk with potent wine poured
by ascetic angels who dwell behind the sacred veil.

The sky couldn't bear that burden of love along,
so they cast the dice and my poor name came up.

Seventy-two sects bicker over fairy tales;
forgive them, they don't know the truth.

Thank you God for making peace with me;
the Sufis dance and raise their cups to you.

The candle laughs flame, but the true fire
harvests bodies of countless ecstatic moths.

The brides of poetry have combed my hair.
Only Hafiz has ripped the veil from wisdom's face.

On his way back to Morocco from the Indian Ocean basin, Ibn Battuta began to see evidence of the problems that would have made his trip impossible had he begun it later. As he came through Iran and Iraq, he had to dodge the chaos and anarchy that followed the death of Abu Sa'id, and in Syria he witnessed the devastation of the plague. By the time he reached Cairo, it, too, was reeling from the epidemic, as well as from the violence that had begun to diminish the quality of life there since the death of al-Nasir Muhammad seven years earlier. He returned home to Morocco in 1349, but his travels were not over. During the remaining twenty years of his life, he visited both Granada and Mali.

The significance of Ibn Battuta's career goes well beyond the actual number of miles that he traveled. A contrast with the extensive travels of Marco Polo, which had taken place some fifty years earlier, is instructive: Whereas Polo's travels took place almost entirely in strange and alien cultures, Ibn Battuta always found a Muslim community in which his skills were valued. Polo could not possibly have traveled as extensively as he did had he remained within a Christian, Latin, or Greek culture. By contrast, Ibn Battuta found mosques, schools, Sufi communities, and the recognition of the Shari'a as the legal norm in an uninterrupted zone from Morocco to the steppes of Russia and Central Asia, and all around the rim of the Indian Ocean basin. Everywhere he went, he found that his mastery of the Arabic language was useful to him, either as a lingua franca or as a skill that qualified him for remunerative positions as a religious specialist. He found the areas on the periphery of the Islamic heartland to be the most rewarding, for there he was invariably given a lavish welcome, including money, robes, horses, and wives. In those areas, the members of the Muslim community were eager to have a religious authority who could advise them on how to follow the Shari'a, and the local rulers were eager to have their own authority legitimized by their patronage of specialists in the Islamic sciences. Ibn Battuta's career reveals in strikingly personal and concrete detail that, despite the catastrophes of the thirteenth and fourteenth centuries, the Islamic world had become the largest cultural continuum in the world.

The most honored intellectual activity in the Muslim world was jurisprudence, or *fiqh*. This valuation was justified: Not only did Muslims consider Islamic law to reflect God's will, but, as we have seen repeatedly, the independence of Islamic law from any given regime enabled societies to continue even when their governments were destroyed. Thus, the Shari'a was one of the most important elements in the "glue" that held Islamic civilization together. As the law books proliferated, however, many jurists began to question what their role was. If they did not make the law, but only inferred from the sources what God's will was, would there come a time when they had no more original work to do?

The Queen of the Sciences

The delineation of Islamic law had begun at the initiative of private scholars, and it continued to be elaborated in the same, unofficial manner. Qadis, it is true, were appointed by specific regimes, and their jobs depended upon the good will of those regimes. But the existence and perpetuation of the law itself was totally independent of the patronage of governments. A myriad of "schools," or traditions of interpretation, arose in the eighth century, but most of them failed to attract a sizable following and disappeared. The number of viable schools continued to decline, and by the end of the tenth century a consensus had been established that no new schools could emerge. The appearance of a new school, after all, would imply a rejection of the methods of fiqh that had been used up to that time.

By the fourteenth century, the Sunni community had consolidated into four main traditions. Until the thirteenth century, it was not uncommon to hear of riots between the followers of two competing law schools, but thereafter such clashes were less likely to happen. Despite the differences among them, their adherents came to recognize the legitimacy of the others. Ibn Battuta's experience was typical in this regard. He was trained in the Maliki school of North Africa, and yet his services were welcomed in communities in which the Hanafi, Hanbali, or Shafi'i traditions predominated.

Members of the public accorded high respect to a scholar who engaged in fiqh (a *faqih*). Since scholarship of any kind was regarded to be a form of worship of God, the study of jurisprudence was considered one of the highest acts of piety. The faqih was also respected for his intelligence and perseverance: One was accepted as a faqih only after a long and rigorous course of study. He had to demonstrate that he could derive a legal ruling from the Qur'an or Hadith, know when to stress the literal rather than the metaphorical meaning of a text, realize whether a general rule fit a specific case, and refer to the entire corpus of his school's literature in order to cite a precedent.

Despite the insistence of all the schools that their work was not original, but rather was the methodical deduction of the will of God from the Qur'an and Hadith, all the schools tacitly admitted that the process of fiqh involved at least some degree of *ijtihad,* the "effort" or "exercise" of one's judgment or reasoning. Everyone acknowledged that such judgment had to be employed when interpreting texts or assessing the authenticity of Hadith, and the jurists who defended its use in fiqh argued that it had to be exercised when extending the principles established by the Qur'an and Sunna to problems not directly addressed by those texts. These faqihs had been careful to point out that they advocated the use of reasoning only when it was subordinate to the dictates of divine revelation. Some early faqihs, notably in the Hanbali school, campaigned vigorously against analogical reasoning. By the twelfth century, however, even the members of the Hanbali school (as we have seen in the case of thirteenth-century Ibn Taymiya) had come to realize that the practice of finding analogies between cases was unavoidable and that the logic and good sense of the faqih had to come into play.

The period of the most original work in fiqh was the eighth through the twelfth centuries. Most of the problems of ritual, family law, and criminal law had been identified during the first three centuries, but the eleventh and twelfth centuries witnessed an increased sophistication of legal concepts, as well as a growing precision in the use of language. As the issues to be addressed declined in number, and the actual work of the faqih became that of framing the legal issues with more clarity and subtlety, it was becoming clear that some faqihs were more original than others. Some were able to recast an issue in a new light, while others were more comfortable simply applying the results of a precedent to a current case.

The "Closing of the Gate of Ijtihad"?

During the twelfth century, the fact that fewer faqihs were doing original work led some Sunni scholars to voice the opinion that the era of engaging in ijtihad was now past. In the rhythmic and rhyming style so popular in Arabic prose, this sentiment was often expressed in the phrase "*insidad bab al-ijtihad,*" or the "closing (blocking) of the gate (door) of ijtihad." Those who expressed this opinion regarded the earlier members of their legal schools to have been intellectual and spiritual giants and felt that it was disrespectful and even impious to think that further ijtihad could be exercised. This sentiment was expressed most frequently by members of the Hanafi and Maliki schools and by some members of the Shafi'i school.

Other legal scholars insisted that the exercise of juristic judgment was a continuing need. They argued that there was no reason to think that intellectual abilities and spiritual qualities had declined over the generations. Moreover, since there was now more legal knowledge available to scholars precisely because of the work of those past generations of jurists, there was more opportunity to make wise judgments than ever before, assuming that jurists made the effort to apply sound reasoning to their decisions. Most members of the Shafi'i school took this position. More surprising, in light of the antirationalist origins of the Hanbali school, the Hanbalis after the twelfth century were the most adamant in their insistence on the necessity of practicing ijtihad.

The issue of the closing of the gate of ijtihad slowly grew more controversial within the Sunni community. In the thirteenth century, some scholars began ranking each other in terms of their proficiency in exercising original judgment. Some rankings included up to seven grades of proficiency, ranging from very original to extremely imitative. The rankings provided ammunition to some scholars to argue that the number of genuine *mujtahids* (practitioners of ijtihad) was decreasing, that the day would soon come when no qualified scholars would be alive, and that ijtihad could no longer be practiced. The Hanbalis were contemptuous of this position and argued that ijtihad was an obligation imposed on the totality of Muslim scholars and that to stop exercising it would be a sin. This was the position of Ibn Taymiya, and his differences with other faqihs over this issue was a major irritant for many of his critics.

By the second half of the fourteenth century, the majority of Sunni scholars had come to agree that ijtihad was no longer an option for faqihs. They argued that *taqlid* ("imitation" of previous scholars) was the only option for "modern" jurists. Taqlid came to be understood as the unquestioning acceptance of a previous decision or doctrine without inquiring into the reasons and evidence that were the basis for them. Most Hanbalis and a few Shafi'is continued to claim the right to practice ijtihad, but they were in a conspicuous minority. Many Hanafis considered them heretical for doing so.

The sentiment that led to the near consensus to terminate ijtihad can be appreciated in light of a conservative understanding of Islamic law. Most jurists would have agreed that the Shari'a, as God's law, is ultimately unknowable. Fiqh, they would argue, represents the efforts of the jurists to discover God's law, and thus the jurists' writings are works of jurisprudence rather than statements of God's law. In daily life, however, with concrete decisions having to be made, it was easy to slip into the habit of referring to the statements of the jurists as the Shari'a: The jurists needed to feel that what they were doing was worthwhile, and the community needed to have confidence in the rules they were accepting. A Hadith that quoted the Prophet as saying that his community would never agree upon error reassured them that they in fact had approximated God's will. Since God's will does not change, one did not have to worry about revising laws; besides, revisions would smack of human agency rather than divine decree.

In practice, ijtihad could not stop. Legal experts, even Hanafis, continued to employ it, but few faqihs admitted that they were doing so, and those who witnessed it pretended not to see it. New problems continued to arise that needed ijtihad in order to be solved. Jurists who were active in solving those problems understood their work in a different light from that of the outspoken advocates of taqlid. They believed that the work of all jurists throughout Islamic history had been approximate and had been achieved within a specific time and region. Circumstances, they knew, change from time to time and from society to society, and therefore ijtihad was necessary. Their work can be seen most vividly in the careers of the most preeminent jurists in Muslim societies, who were called upon to give rulings (*fatwas*) on vexing questions that other jurists could not provide. Such a legal authority, usually known as a *shaykh al-islam* or *mufti,* could issue thousands of fatwas on a wide variety of issues during his career.

The very fact that fatwas from muftis were necessary because other jurists could not agree on an issue seems to the eyes of the twenty-first century to be evidence that ijtihad continued. Nevertheless, taqlid became the official practice of the period after the fourteenth century. As a result, the fundamentals of the law did not change for centuries. The legal concepts that had developed during the creative eleventh and twelfth centuries remained unchanged until the nineteenth century. Discussions among jurists tended to be over hypothetical cases or even over issues that had once been important, but were no longer relevant. The occasional mujtahid did make revisions in practice when necessary, and sometimes a mufti's defense of his novel decision entered into the corpus of juristic tradition. On the whole, however, jurists understood that their primary mission was not to codify the law and to make the process of adjudication more streamlined and efficient. They continued to learn the body of decisions that had been recorded in the legal books and tired to apply them to their own circumstances with as little innovation as possible.

Twelver Shi'ite law faced similar issues, but underwent a different evolution. The Shi'ite jurists who advocated ijtihad won a tenth-century victory over those who opposed the exercise of reason. The opponents of ijtihad would have to wait until the late seventeenth century to (temporarily) close the "gate." The advocates of the use of reason continued to develop more sophisticated arguments for its employment. During the fourteenth century, when the Sunnis were achieving a near consensus on agreeing that ijtihad was no longer possible, the great Shi'ite jurist 'Allama al-Hilli was reorganizing jurisprudence so as to make reasoning its central feature.

The practical results of the apparent contrast between Sunni and Shi'ite jurisprudence were not as great as one might think, however. The actual Shi'ite experience after the fourteenth century was the mirror image of that of the Sunnis: Whereas the Sunnis claimed that ijtihad was no longer acceptable, but found to their embarrassment that they continued to practice it, the Shi'ites claimed to practice it, but found that the scope within which reason could be exercised was quite limited. Shi'ite jurists understood that they must exercise what they called "prudence and caution" in their decisions, so as not to stray from the path of the Imams. This self-censorship limited the number of original initiatives that a jurist might make.

The Varieties of Religious Expression

The members of any major religion exhibit a wide variety in their patterns of ritual behaviors and beliefs. Protestants, Catholics, and Orthodox Christians all belong to the same religion, and yet differ considerably from each other. Even within Protestantism or Catholicism, the range of expression is great: If a Catholic bishop from Paris were to spend a month in the home of fellow Catholics in a village in Haiti, he might well experience moments when he would wonder what religion his hosts practiced, after all. Muslims are equally diverse in their beliefs and practices. Muslims from North Africa, Central Asia, and the littoral of the Indian Ocean inevitably received the Islamic tradition through the filter of their respective cultural heritages. The remarkable fact about Islam is that it has a common identity at all. Unlike most monotheistic traditions, it has no institution with the authority to enforce orthodoxy. During the period of Mongol hegemony, many of the myriad expressions of Islam were becoming organized into institutional form and would be prepared to affect history in profound ways over the following centuries.

"Orthodoxy" and "Heterodoxy"

Throughout history, the various Christian denominations have enforced orthodox doctrines and practices within their respective churches. Persons who claim to be within a particular tradition, but who preach or teach contrary to orthodoxy ("correct doctrine") and engage in other than orthopraxy ("correct practice"), are labeled "heretics." In earlier centuries, heretics were severely disciplined, often by execution. Since the Enlightenment, the typical response of the officials of the Church in question has been to exclude the person from membership. Islam does not have the equivalent of a pope or patriarch who can enforce conformity. Several individuals have claimed such a role, to be sure: During the first two centuries of Islamic history, some of the Umayyad and Abbasid caliphs attempted to enforce correct religious practices; the *Imams* of the various Shi'ite groups served such a function; and subsequent caliphs of many splinter groups all over the globe claimed such authority. In every case, however, the actual authority of a given leader extended over a limited territory or period of time. The majority of Muslims were unaffected.

Islamic history has witnessed many instances in which the charge of *kufr* ("unbelief," the equivalent of "heresy") has been leveled at various individuals and groups who claimed to be Muslim. The seventh-century Kharijites stimulated one of the most intense of these crises, for they regarded all Muslims who disagreed with them to be outside the pale, while other Muslims considered that attitude itself to be un-Islamic. This conflict gradually resolved itself over the next couple of centuries as the extreme Kharijites died out in the battles they provoked, and the surviving Ibadi Kharijites of North Africa and Oman were known primarily for their puritanism and reluctance to interact with outsiders, rather than for their aggression.

Early Shi'ites who elevated 'Ali (or other personages) to the status of a divinity were regarded as having compromised the monotheistic status of Islam. The extremist Shi'ites were gradually marginalized when the major Shi'ite groups officially denied deifying 'Ali or anyone else. Two important groups that were excluded from the Muslim Umma in this fashion still play important roles in the countries of the eastern Mediterranean. The Druze, who deified al-Hakim, the eleventh-century Fatimid caliph, were forced by popular pressure to seek refuge in the mountains of Lebanon and southern Syria. Farther north, the Nusayris sought refuge in the mountains of the Lataqiya province of western Syria. The Nusayris were the followers of the ninth-century figure Ibn Nusayr, who had preached the divinity of the eleventh Imam, and thus split from the group that subsequently became the Twelver Shi'ites. His group came to be associated with a divine trinity of 'Ali, Muhammad, and Salman the Iranian, in which 'Ali takes precedence as the God of the Qur'an. Because of this worship of 'Ali, the Nusayris are often called Alawis. The Nusayris worship in homes instead of mosques, do not observe Ramadan or the hajj, drink wine at religious services, and hold to the doctrine of transmigration of souls. For these reasons, Muslims have frequently persecuted Nusayris as heretics, although in the 1970s, the Nusayri ruler of Syria, Hafez al-Asad, obtained a ruling from Syrian Sunni ulama that declared him to be a Muslim.

Early Sufis who claimed to have experienced union with God during their mystical experiences were also ostracized. Once again, the central issue at stake was the compromising of the doctrine of the unity of God, which to most scholars also entailed a radical distinction between the Creator and his creatures. Al-Hallaj, the most famous of the extreme Sufis, was even executed by the state in 922 as a threat to public peace. Sufi leaders then began working toward a consensus on the doctrine that union with God was not a legitimate claim for the mystical experience.

With the exception of the execution of al-Hallaj, these examples of spiritual disciplining were largely collective affairs in which private religious scholars managed to win a consensus among other scholars and influential men of affairs to exclude (and even persecute) groups that had violated basic Islamic tenets. The key to understanding the continuity of Sunni Islam is an appreciation of the insistence upon fidelity to the text of the Qur'an and to the Sunna ("practice") of the Prophet as revealed in the Hadith. The various schools of Islamic law insisted upon the centrality of those two sources; theologians condemned the practice of philosophical speculation not limited by the truths of revelation; and Sufi orders developed traditions that reputedly linked their practice to the practice of the Prophet. The Sunni tradition was one of self-censorship. It was inevitably conservative and traditional in spirit, leading to the withering of an independent philosophical tradition and the closing of the gate of ijtihad.

In order to maintain a consensus across the vast Muslim world, scholars corresponded frequently with each other about their own work. They went on journeys to study with scholars greater than themselves. Most importantly, the practice of the hajj ensured that scholars would travel from every part of the Muslim world to Mecca, where they would be kept up to date on current thinking on theology and practice. Meccan scholars served as the touchstone for piety. They had absolutely no authority to enforce any doctrine or practice on anyone in any region, but pilgrims who came to Mecca seeking to study under such scholars for a period of time could learn whether their home community practiced a version of Islam that reflected the Meccan standard. Many pilgrims throughout history returned to their homes to begin reform movements, jolted by their experience on the hajj. Their reform movements could be campaigns of persuasion or of force.

This Sunni tradition of self-censorship was somewhat different from the attainment of a consensus within the various Kharijite and Shi'ite traditions. The Kharijites (Ibadis) comprised a relatively small number of Muslims, but they were scattered from Iran to North Africa. They maintained a high level of scholarly activity, and they maintained communications over vast distances in order to stay current with each other. Their political leaders were religious authorities, as well, and they maintained an effective discipline within their oases.

The Shi'ite communities that had the good fortune of being led by a "visible" Imam had direct access to the keeper of the consensus, for the Imam by definition possessed the authority to define truth. He could enforce any doctrine and maintain tight discipline. The communities that had a "hidden" Imam were a step removed from that sense of certainty, but still had confidence that the Hidden Imam maintained at least indirect communication with their religious scholars. As we have seen, the dominant school of religious scholars within the Twelver Shi'ite community did not share the opinion of most Sunnis that the gate of ijtihad ever closed. When they were left without a visible Imam, they were confident that pious, consecrated reason was capable of determining the will of the Hidden Imam. They developed the doctrine that the Hidden Imam would never allow his community to be misled by an erroneous ruling. If it should ever happen that (1) two jurists' rulings be in opposition, (2) one be totally wrong, and (3) the methods of jurisprudence not be able to detect the error, the Hidden Imam would intervene in person. Since he has never intervened, the members of the Twelver community can be confident that no rulings have ever been in error.

Thus, Islam had no Vatican, synod, or rabbinate to determine orthodoxy or orthopraxy. The scholarly consensus served as a remarkably effective method for obtaining cohesion among large groups of Muslims across a vast swath of the planet. The achievement is all the more impressive when one remembers that the vast majority of Muslims were illiterate. Just as it is impossible to appreciate Luther's accomplishments in the years after 1517 without realizing that most contemporary Europeans were illiterate and lightly Christianized, one cannot appreciate the fact that "Islam" exists today without understanding the far-flung, multiethnic, decentralized, and largely illiterate society in which the small group of private scholars labored to conserve the heritage of the Prophet.

Cohesion and a common sense of identity did not mean homogeneity, of course: Muslims developed distinctive differences in the expression of their faith. Sunnis, Shi'ites, and Kharijites formed three quite distinct groupings. Subsects formed within each of these traditions, and yet were regarded to be within the bounds of acceptable doctrine and practice. Some Muslims were persuaded that a scrupulous performance of ritual was the height of piety; others felt that ritual had to be balanced by a spiritual communion with God; and yet others regarded ritual as the mere outward expression of piety, placing emphasis on a mystical experience. The Qur'an and the Hadith (Sunni or Shi'ite) remained central, however.

The Proliferation of Sufi Groups

Historians assume a linkage between the upheavals of the twelfth and early thirteenth centuries, on the one hand, and the rise of Sufi lodges and orders during those centuries, on the other. In the face of the sufferings and uncertainties of the period, the small communities established by Sufis provided spiritual and material support, as well as the possibility of common defense. The subsequent disasters of the Mongol era from the mid-thirteenth century to the end of the fourteenth century were accompanied by a rapid increase in the number of Sufi organizations and an even larger increase in the percentage of Muslims who identified with Sufism. Once again, it appears that Sufism responded to a deep need. In damaged and leaderless societies, the new Sufi orders (*tariqas*) satisfied social and religious needs that were not being met in any other way. The lodges (variously known as *ribats*, *zawiyas*, *khanaqas*, and *tekkes*), became centers of local worship, teaching and healing, and politics.

Sufism Triumphant

Sufism first appeared in the Muslim East (Iraq and Iran) in the eighth century. By the beginning of the tenth century, it was established in Andalus, and a century later it had secured a foothold in Morocco. By the fourteenth century, Sufism had become integrated into the everyday religious life of many—if not most—Muslims. Believers performed the ritual and moral duties of the Shari'a obediently and willingly and understood these to be the public expression of their faith and commitment. The Sufi dimension was the inner, emotional, personal relationship that they sought with their Creator God. Sufism could assume a wide range of expressions: Some adherents lived permanently in a lodge following the teachings of the founder of the order, and others were wandering mendicants, but most lived ordinary lives at home with their families and occasionally attended meetings of the local chapter of an order in order to recite mystical litanies.

Along with the work of intellectuals and artists and the consensus of the Shari'a, Sufism was one of the critical universal features that held the Umma together in the absence of a central authority. Each order had its own distinct devotional practices and ethical system that were used in lodges and mosques wherever the order was found. A given order's common tradition, authoritative texts, network of lodges, and distinctive lifestyle became elements that the culturally and ethnically diverse societies of Islam shared in common.

Sufism was also important because it provided women an acceptable avenue of both religious expression and religious leadership. Over the centuries, mosques had practically become preserves of males. The increasing exclusion of women from urban public spaces, coupled with the requirements of modesty during the ritual of the prescribed prayers, resulted in a consensus in most parts of the Muslim world that the community was better served if women performed their prayers at home. The expression of women's religious needs therefore frequently took the form of maintaining folk cults and performing pilgrimages to local shrines. Certain pious women themselves became the objects of intense veneration: In Cairo, both al-Sayyida Nafisa (great-granddaughter of Hasan, celebrated for her learning and piety) and al-Sayyida Zaynab (daughter of ʿAli) are revered in magnificent tomb–mosques. (*Sayyida* is an Arabic word normally meaning "lady" or "Mrs"; here, it implies both lineal descent from the Prophet and the status of sainthood.)

Sufism did not shatter any gender barriers, but in most locales it did encourage women's participation in Islamic rituals. Some Sufi preachers ministered primarily to women; a few lodges that served a largely male clientele were staffed primarily by women; women held their own Sufi meetings; some women became preachers; and other women were accorded the status of saint. It is clear that a number of women were initiated into Sufi orders. One young fourteenth-century male even received from his grandmother a *khirqa,* the robe that a Sufi novice received from his mentor.

Sufi masters—the heads of lodges and the teachers of the mystical path—rarely limited their services to their formal disciples. Usually known as *shaykh* in the Arabic-speaking communities and *pir* in Persian-speaking regions, they served the entire community, whether it be urban or rural. They provided spiritual guidance, mediation, and medical cures. Their primary function was to serve as a religious specialist, teaching their students how to achieve the mystical experience. For local residents, however, they also served as spiritual counselors, led prayers in mosques, and helped as needed at times of special rites, such as circumcision, marriage, and funerals. Some of the shaykhs, particularly in Morocco, were well versed in the Shariʿa, and were able to give definitive rulings on legal matters and thought.

Sufi shaykhs also mediated disputes. They provided arbitration in disputes among local residents and between local residents and the conquerors who came and went with dizzying frequency. Their zawiyas would become busy centers where disciples would live and learn; local inhabitants would come for religious services, spiritual counsel, and food; and local tribesmen would come to settle conflicts. The lodge would typically be located at an intersection of trade routes or near water sources, making the site easily accessible to as many people in the area as possible. In rural areas it was usually fortified, in order to provide a refuge for local residents from raiders.

Religious specialists throughout history have often been called upon to provide aid to those in need of medical attention, since they are believed to be able to intercede with God. That was particularly true in the premodern period, when modern medicines were not available. Sufi shaykhs were believed to have the power to heal persons and animals and to bestow blessings that enabled petitioners to become prosperous, bear children, and restore affection in a marriage relationship.

A Sufi shaykh with outstanding spiritual gifts might become revered as a "saint." The status of saint, or "friend of God," was accorded to notable martyrs, Shiʿite Imams, companions of the Prophet, and noteworthy ascetics. Sufi shaykhs achieved the distinction by their combination of exceptional piety, ecstatic states, the power of intercession, and extraordinary miracles. Most saints were credited with the gifts of clairvoyance and telepathy. Some were said to be able to fly, to be in two places at once, to ride rainbows, and to end droughts.

People far and near sought out saints in order to share in the power of their spiritual gifts. Their authority was enhanced even further when they combined evidence of spiritual power with an esteemed genealogical descent, either from a notable local family or, especially, from the Prophet's family. Saints were thus in a good position to provide an alternative source of authority in the absence of a strong central government. By virtue of their personal qualities and, perhaps, their family lineage, they possessed an authority that enabled them to keep the peace within an impressive radius of their zawiya, intercede for the poor with the wealthy landowner, and assure that travelers could enjoy both hospitality and safety.

A saint's service to his community did not end with his death. He was usually buried at the site of his zawiya, and his tomb would typically become the object of pilgrimages, as individuals continued to look to him as a source of aid. The shrine was regarded to be the repository of the spiritual power (*baraka*) that inhered in the saint in death as in life. Pilgrims came to shrines to ask for healing and the other blessings that the saint had provided during his lifetime. There they touched or kissed the tomb, made small gifts or sacrifices, attached written requests to the shrine, celebrated the major religious festivals of the year, and observed the death day of the saint.

After the saint's death, the zawiya complex might actually increase in importance, for it boasted the attraction of the shrine in addition to the services of the saint's successor and his disciples. Its influence would typically spread into an even wider radius, providing the services of a market, religious education, the settling of tribal disputes, and the distribution of food to the poor. Over time, the shrine

A Sufi saint's tomb in Morocco.

would typically become the recipient of gifts from grateful local residents and develop a wealthy endowment, able to exercise power at the spiritual, political, and economic levels.

Sufism as Social Critique

The practice of pilgrimage to shrines did not attract much controversy before the eighteenth century. The veneration of holy men and women—or of sacred places and objects—is a phenomenon common to all the major religious traditions and should be seen as a normal aspect of premodern Islam. It was the Muslim parallel to the contemporary Western Christian traffic in relics and visits to shrines such as Canterbury, Santiago de Compostela, and Jerusalem. The practice was validated by mainstream Sufism and sanctioned by most jurists, who cited passages from the Qur'an and the Hadith supporting the doctrine that some individuals have superior spiritual power. A handful of religious scholars opposed the veneration of saints, however: Ibn Taymiya vehemently attacked the practice as a flagrant violation of the Shari'a. The great Hanbali scholar practiced Sufi meditation techniques himself and did not oppose Sufi spirituality. On the other hand, he regarded shrine visits to be a remnant of pre-Islamic idolatry, and he accused supplicants at shrines of being "grave worshipers." His diatribes had no impact on the practice, and only landed him in jail. The masses, the majority of religious scholars, and government officials (throughout the Muslim world, not just the Mamlukes) agreed that the veneration of living and dead saints was a valid Islamic practice.

The veneration of saints drew the ire of Ibn Taymiya because he thought it compromised features of Islamic monotheism. Other critics of Sufism focused on the fact that some of the movement's features had taken on the trappings of a fully mature social institution. Indeed, the more elaborate shrines were eloquent testimony to the power, wealth, and systematization that had come to characterize much of the Sufi experience by the thirteenth and fourteenth centuries. This development was criticized by some individuals who were aware that Sufism had begun as a critique of the material and institutional elements of society, and that ascetic tendencies were always latent within the movement. In the thirteenth century, a rejection of mainstream Sufism appeared in the form of "Sufi deviancy." It was characterized by mendicancy, celibacy, asceticism, and the deliberate tweaking of what today would be called middle-class sensibilities.

Forms of deviancy had manifested themselves throughout most of Sufi history. From at least as early as the tenth century, individuals known as the *malamatiya* ("those who draw blame upon themselves") were Sufis who were so concerned not to parade their virtue that they deliberately invited the contempt of their neighbors by committing unseemly, and even unlawful, acts. Most other Sufis, however, recognized that, while the malamatiya might be overzealous and overly conscientious in obeying the precept to avoid trying to impress the world of one's purity, they were sincere and pure of heart.

During the thirteenth century, Sufi deviancy became a much larger movement and was viewed with hostility by much of society. Several groups emerged, including the Qalandars, Haydaris, Abdals, Bektashis, and Madaris. Their individual members were usually called dervishes. "Dervish" is the Turkish pronunciation of the Persian word *darvish,* which suggests "wandering mendicant." Dervishes first appeared in Syria and Egypt in the thirteenth century, but soon became more characteristic of the region that includes Anatolia, Iran, and India.

In some ways, the life styles of dervishes suggest parallels with the Cynics, who became notorious in the Hellenistic world of the eastern Mediterranean beginning in the fourth century B.C.E. Typically, dervishes showed their contempt for social conventions by rejecting family life and choosing celibacy; rarely bathing; wearing unusual clothing (such as turbans with horns) or abandoning clothing altogether and going nude; shaving all bodily and facial hair (a practice that went contrary to the Shari'a); and using forbidden hallucinogens and intoxicants.

Beyond the obvious characteristics shared by many of the dervishes lay differences in their attitudes toward communal life. Some were solitary mendicants, who tended to exhibit the more extreme of the unconventional traits we have described. It is these individuals that European travelers and novelists of the nineteenth century made famous as "wild-eyed dervishes." Others also wandered across the countryside, but did so as a group of disciples who followed their shaykh. Still others maintained a permanent community, but their lodge was distinctively decorated and they themselves were clearly marked off from their fellow townsmen by their clothing and behavior.

The cultural elite of Muslim societies consistently identified the dervishes as the riffraff of society, and frequently accused them of being impostors and frauds. In fact, a considerable number of the dervishes were the sons of the elite. They rejected the comfortable and staid world of their fathers, and engaged in behavior that scandalized and disappointed their families. Like the Cynics (and hippies), they were engaged in a countercultural critique of dominant social norms. Unlike those two groups, most of the dervishes were also sincerely seeking a close spiritual relationship with God. They thought that establishing a relationship with God required severing their ties with the world of conventional morality.

Sufism, Syncretism, and Shi'ism

During the Mongol period, Sufi deviancy was most likely to be found in Anatolia, northern Iran, and northern India. The arc that stretched from Anatolia across northern Iran was also the primary setting for the rise of some Sufi groups that would exercise much more influence on subsequent Muslim history than did the Sufi deviants. Their story is the result of the Turkish migrations into the era.

During the century of Mongol rule of Iran, the composition of the population underwent a significant change. Under the Il-khanate, Iran was opened to the migration of large numbers of Turkish and Mongol peoples. Many of them made the long journey all the way into western Anatolia, where they played important roles in the early history of the Ottoman Sultanate. Most of those who entered the Iranian cultural area, however, settled in Transoxiana and in the region that comprises both Azerbaijan and eastern Anatolia. In both Transoxiana and Azerbaijan/eastern Anatolia, the Turkish-speaking peoples gradually came to outnumber the speakers of Persian. One result of this change in the ethnic composition of the area was a significant modification of the economy. Because many of the Turkish immigrants continued their nomadic existence, large areas of Iran, Azerbaijan, and eastern

Anatolia were converted from agriculture into grazing areas for the service of a pastoral economy. In order to adjust, many erstwhile villagers began to practice semipastoralism: They cultivated the valleys that remained under cultivation and took herds of sheep into the mountain highlands during the summer for grazing. Other than the short-lived reforms of Ghazan (1295–1304), the agricultural economy of the region from the Amu Darya River to the headwaters of the Euphrates River suffered alternate bouts of destruction and neglect for several centuries.

The decline of urban life and the long-term absence of state security institutions also encouraged the development of new forms of social and religious organization in the region. With the decline of central governments, the traditional social organization that the Turks brought with them from Central Asia remained important for purposes of security. This structure was based on what has been called a household state: A chief ruled over a large group of people related by kinship ties or alliances. He was aided by his family and by lesser chiefs and their followers, whose support was won by leadership ability and martial skills. The system was financed by raiding and by extorting revenues from nomads, peasants, and towns under its control. It was very unstable, however, for the authority of the chief was constantly challenged by ambitious subordinates. Rebellions were common, and the ensuing violence wreaked havoc among defenseless subject populations.

It was within this unstable and violent environment that Sufism began making inroads. As early as the twelfth century, Sufis had been working among the Turks of Transoxiana. The most revered of these was Ahmad Yasavi (d. 1166). Yasavi met with considerable success due to his technique of setting religious and moral education to music, using the lute as an accompaniment. From the mid-thirteenth to mid-fourteenth centuries, several other Sufi-led movements appeared among both peasant and nomadic communities from Transoxiana into rural Anatolia. There, shaykhs served the functions mentioned earlier: They were healers, mediators, and religious guides, and they resisted the oppression and exploitation of the poor by the household states.

Given the insecurity and oppression that characterized the era, it is understandable that the doctrines that flourished in the Sufi communities stressed deliverance and rewards. Popular religious figures included those of the Mahdi, who would come at the end of time to create a just order; the Qutb, the figure in Sufi circles who served as the axis for the world and a haven for oppressed peoples; and ‘Ali, Muhammad's closest companion, cousin, and son-in-law, whose combination of religious piety and martial valor provided a role model for serious young men. ‘Ali was particularly popular among Sufis of this era, and many of the newly emerging Sufi orders constructed *silsilas,* or spiritual genealogies, that traced their teachings back to him. For some groups, ‘Ali became as prominent as Muhammad, although the groups seem not to have viewed themselves as Shi‘ite. Unlike the urban Sunni and Shi‘ite scholars, distinctions such as "Sunni" and "Shi‘ite" do not seem to have been important to them.

Of the many Sufi groups that emerged at this time among the primarily Turkish-speaking peoples, four are particularly worthy of notice because of their subsequent historical importance. The Naqshbandi order, attributed to Baha' al-Din Naqshband (1318–1398) of Bukhara, later became highly influential in Central Asia and India. One of its distinguishing characteristics was the teaching of a "silent dhikr":

Whereas most orders practiced a communal, vocal dhikr, the silent dhikr enabled an individual to engage in it mentally and thus under practically any circumstance and at any time. The order arose in the highly sophisticated atmosphere of Bukhara, and despite its subsequent dissemination among the rural population of the Ottoman realm, Central Asia, and India, it was always characterized by a careful attention to normative ritual and doctrine.

By contrast, several groups that emerged at this time exhibited syncretistic qualities that reflected their origins in the multireligious and multiethnic rural area between central Anatolia and Azerbaijan. After the battle of Kose Dagh in 1243, when Batu defeated the Sultanate of Rum, the region's cities went into decline. With Hulagu's creation of the Il-khanate in 1259, the region was inundated by Turkish and Mongol immigrants. The influence of the Shari'a-minded ulama was no longer as strong as it had been. In contrast to the strict adherence to the Shari'a practiced by the Naqshbandi order and the rural shaykhs of Morocco, Sufi leaders of eastern Anatolia and Azerbaijan tended to stress the universal aspects of Islam in their preaching. They relaxed their ritual requirements, making it easier for shamanistic Turks and local Christian peasants alike to make the transition into their communities.

One example of this trend was the career of Hajji Bektash. Scholars have traditionally thought that Bektash lived until 1337, but recent research suggests that he died in the last quarter of the thirteenth century. He was a learned Sufi shaykh who emphasized the importance of the mystical way and taught his followers that the details of the Shari'a, including the daily prayers, were not important. As a result, his original movement is regarded as an example of Sufi deviancy. Over the next two centuries, as the Bektashi movement developed in the melting pot of Anatolia and Azerbaijan, it acquired many doctrines and practices that, had it not been so secretive, would almost certainly have caused it to be ostracized or even persecuted. Nevertheless, it became highly popular all across Anatolia and eventually in the Balkans.

Similarities between the mature Bektashi order and the Nusayri sect are striking. Its members considered many elements of Islamic ritual and worship, such as performance of the *salat* (five daily prayers) and observing the fast during the month of Ramadan, to be unimportant. Bektashis did not attend mosques, but rather held a communal weekly prayer in a private home. Ostensibly Sunni, the Bektashis revered the Twelve Shi'ite Imams, but scandalized the Twelver Shi'ites by their extremist practice of worshiping 'Ali as the center of a trinity of 'Ali, Muhammad, and "God." They denied the doctrine of the resurrection of the body and taught instead that souls are reincarnated into other bodies. They initiated new members with a reception of wine, bread, and cheese, a practice that seems to have been borrowed from a heretical Christian group of Anatolia called the Paulicians.

The Bektashis were usually found in towns and cities, and they were tightly organized under their leader. The Alevi (the Turkish spelling of "Alawi") movement was closely related to it and seems to have been the result of a schism in the historical development of Hajji Bektash's group. The Alevis tended to be rural, located in central and eastern Anatolia, and less educated than their urban counterparts. Their practices and doctrines were almost identical to those of the Bektashis, however. Because they were scattered among farming villages and nomadic

PART TWO

Muslim Ascendancy, 1405–1750

It is no exaggeration to describe as catastrophic the blows suffered by the Muslim world in the thirteenth and fourteenth centuries. Soon after Timur's death, however, the course of Muslim history was reversed. For the next three centuries, the twin themes of Muslim history were expansion and dynamism. The frontiers of the Muslim world expanded dramatically as Islam became deeply rooted in regions as diverse as West Africa, East Africa, Central Asia, South Asia, and Southeast Asia. The stage was set for South Asia and Southeast Asia to become the world regions that now contain more than half the world's Muslims. In addition, new Muslim states arose that wielded enormous political and military power. By the early sixteenth century, the Ottoman, Safavid, and Mughal empires extended in an unbroken arc from the Danube River to the foothills of Nepal.

The period treated in Part Two provides the foundation for understanding the formation of the modern Muslim world. Many of the ideas, institutions, and practices that we now associate with both Sunni and Shi'ite Islam date from this period. It was also a period of major innovations in the fields of military technology, art, economic organization, and political systems. Given the importance of this period, it is all the more remarkable how little the general outline of its history is known in Western Europe and the Americas. It has the disadvantage of competing for attention with topics in contemporary European history such as the Renaissance, the Age of Discovery, the Protestant Reformation, the Scientific Revolution, the Enlightenment, and the emergence of modern states, economies, and ideologies. These topics claim our attention in part because they so clearly shaped the world on both sides of the Atlantic and in part because we seek in them an explanation for the global dominance of Europe in the nineteenth and twentieth centuries.

What is lost in this approach to the study of history is the realization that, throughout the era under review, no European could have been confident that Europe would eventually dominate the globe. To the contrary, at least until the end of the seventeenth century, Europeans feared being overwhelmed by Muslim power. Not until well into the eighteenth century were some individuals within both

Europe and the Muslim world becoming aware of how the balance of power had shifted in dramatic fashion. In fact, what is emerging in recent research is that many important changes that took place in the Muslim empires between the fifteenth and seventeenth centuries echo developments in contemporary central and western Europe. Among the most notable were the triumph of regional political claims over universal ones, challenges by new religious groups to the dominant religious traditions, new relationships between the religious establishment and governments, and the increasing use of vernacular languages in religious literature.

The Muslim world doubled in geographical extent during the period from the fifteenth to the eighteenth centuries. The inclusion of numerous new cultures into the realm of Islam renders the concept of "Islamic civilization" problematic as a unit of historical analysis. The first volume of this work was an attempt to show how an Islamic civilization arose over a period of several centuries. As long as the literature of that civilization remained almost exclusively in the Arabic and Persian languages, a case can be made for the notion of an Islamic civilization that was a stage in the ongoing development of Middle Eastern civilization. However, as indigenous Muslim communities arose in Java, Bengal, Xinjiang, the Horn of Africa, and Hausaland, religious literature began appearing in local languages. Mosques and their decorative motifs assumed the forms of local architectural traditions, and many Islamic concepts and doctrines were interpreted in light of local religious and moral traditions.

By the seventeenth century, the Muslim world extended across several civilizations. From that time on, we can continue to speak of the Muslim world, but probably not of Islamic civilization. Islam had become multicivilizational. That is not to say that the Muslim world no longer had a sense of identity or that its members could not communicate well with each other. On the contrary, scholars of all lands continued to communicate in Arabic or Persian much as medieval European scholars communicated in Latin. They traveled extensively and studied with each other, exchanging ideas and views. Muslims continued to view themselves as members of the Umma—the community of believers—and they recognized their common allegiance to a core of values and beliefs and their common grounding in a particular historical tradition.

In Part Two, then, we will see that most of the Muslim world experienced a remarkable dynamism and expansion during the fifteenth, sixteenth, and seventeenth centuries. Some societies, naturally, were not so fortunate. Muslim community life was almost annihilated in the Qipchaq steppe, where a weak tradition of urban life rendered Islamic institutions vulnerable to civil disorder, and in Kerala and the Philippines, where Iberian Christian crusaders made a determined effort to destroy Islam. The most significant setback, however, was in the Iberian Peninsula, where Muslim society had flourished for centuries. Granada, the only Iberian Muslim principality to survive the thirteenth century intact, fell to Spain in 1492, the same year that witnessed the expulsion of Iberian Jews. For the first time in almost eight hundred years, no independent Muslim state existed in the peninsula. Shortly afterward, Spain began persecuting its large Muslim minority. By 1614, the country's rulers had expelled the entire Muslim population.

It is understandable that not all regions of the Muslim world experienced growth during the period from the fifteenth through the seventeenth centuries.

What is harder to understand is why, after three centuries of robust expansion, the bulk of the Muslim world rapidly declined in economic and political power during the few decades prior to the mid-eighteenth century. During this period, the Ottoman Empire lost its dominant position in Eastern Europe and both the Safavid and Mughal empires suddenly collapsed. Simultaneously, the economies of Southeast Asia and Central Asia withered. The political and economic declines did not march in tandem—several areas remained generally prosperous while they fragmented politically—but the pattern of a rapid loss of political power throughout the Muslim world is unquestionable. Each region had its own unique factors that created political or economic crises, but the overall trend suggests a general crisis that has not yet been adequately described or explained.

The Ottoman Empire

The Ottoman sultanate appeared to be dead after Timur Lang smashed its army in 1402. It quickly recovered, however, and by the sixteenth century it had become transformed into the most powerful empire in the world other than China. Its social and religious institutions influenced large areas of the Muslim world for centuries, and its struggles with Spain, the Habsburg Empire, Russia, and the Safavid Empire of Iran gave rise to a large number of today's cultural and political boundaries.

The Creation of an Empire

After Timur's defeat of Bayezit, the Ottoman sultanate nearly disintegrated. As Bayezit was dragged off to die in captivity, his four sons began to contest for leadership of the realm. In a scenario strikingly reminiscent of the fratricidal conflicts that crippled the Saljuqs from the eleventh to the thirteenth centuries, the brothers fought each other in a brutal civil war for more than a decade. It was the perfect opportunity for a European attack to have delivered a fatal blow against the Ottomans, but the European nations were too preoccupied with fighting each other to focus on their common enemy. Some of the Ottomans' vassals in both Rumelia (the Ottoman holdings in Europe) and Anatolia did assert their autonomy, but they proved to be unpopular rulers with their subjects. They fought numerous wars with each other, and they also imposed higher taxes than the Ottomans had levied. Merchants and peasants alike wistfully recalled the "good old days" under the Ottomans.

By 1413, Bayezit's son Mehmet I defeated all his brothers and became the new sultan. He managed to retain the key cities of Rumelia, and under his aggressive leadership the Ottoman army now recaptured western Anatolia and much of the territory in Rumelia that had been lost in the chaos of the civil war. His son Murat II succeeded him in 1421. He was an able ruler, but his energies were devoted more to the defense of the sultanate than to its expansion. By this time, Hungary and Venice were the primary European states that threatened the Ottomans, and they began a series of attacks on the Ottoman western front during the 1430s and 1440s. By 1444, the Hungarians and their allies had driven the Ottomans out of several areas of the Balkans. Under pressure, Murat signed a treaty that renounced several Ottoman claims there. At that point, when the morale of the Europeans was at its highest, Murat abdicated the throne in favor of his twelve-year-old son, Mehmet II.

The reason for Murat's abdication is still a puzzle, although there is evidence that it may have been the result of a state of psychological depression. At any rate, it left the realm vulnerable to an opportunistic attack. Indeed, the Pope promptly called for a crusade, and in the summer of 1444 knights and foot soldiers by the tens of thousands gathered in Hungary for war. The Ottoman response to the crusade demonstrated how the administrative structure of the government at Edirne had evolved since Osman's day. The Ottoman elite comprised several competing ethnic and social groups: Turkish chieftains, devshirme recruits, and Balkan Christian nobility. Previous Muslim regimes had deliberately kept such ethnic military groupings separate in order to play one off against the other. In the event of a crisis, the groups would often fall upon each other in a desperate struggle for survival, and the regime would collapse. By contrast, when the Europeans threatened a state headed by a twelve-year-old boy, the powerful groups at the top of the Ottoman hierarchy did not fragment. They had become tied into a centralized bureaucratic structure that was in their interests to keep alive. Imperceptibly, they had accepted an Ottoman identity and helped to create a state that would continue to exist even in the face of unexpected changes in leadership. Now, confronted with a potentially fatal threat, all sides within the ruling elite agreed to ask Murat to come out of retirement, if only to lead the army against the Europeans. He did so, and in November 1444, the Ottomans shattered the invading force at Varna. Murat once again retired, but a unit of the Janissaries refused to serve under the boy-emperor, Mehmet II. Murat was persuaded to resume his sultanate in 1446.

Despite having been deposed, the teen-aged Mehmet benefited from his father's resumption of the sultanate. During the next five years he gained administrative experience as well as intensive academic training. In 1451, his father died and Mehmet II inherited the throne as a remarkably talented and well-trained nineteen-year-old. Two years later, he achieved what Muslim leaders had failed to do for seven centuries: He captured the legendary city of Constantinople and turned it into his capital. The conquest was the result of meticulous planning. Mehmet built a fort on the European side of the Bosporus that matched the one that the Ottomans already held on the Asiatic side; he constructed a fleet to blockade the city from reinforcements; he contracted with a Hungarian gunsmith to provide huge cannons to bombard the walls of the city; and he assembled an army that is soberly estimated to have included 100,000 troops. After a furious bombardment that lasted two months, the huge walls caved in. The defenders, who were outnumbered more than ten to one, had no chance once the walls were breached.

Some historians curiously downplay the significance of the conquest, noting that the Byzantine Empire had long ceased to exert meaningful political influence beyond the immediate environs of the city itself, and that the city's population had shriveled to a tenth of its former size. It is true that the conquest would have been much more difficult had Mehmet faced the metropolis that Constantinople had been in its glory days, but the achievement was nevertheless monumental in both symbolic and practical terms. For centuries, Constantinople had been the epitome of Christian urban life. Despite its shrunken population, no city in western Europe could compete with its physical dimensions or with its cultural heritage. It was also a shield for Christian Europe against Muslim armies. Its fall in 1453 was both a severe psychological blow and a genuine military liability for Christendom. For Muslims, on the other hand, the capture of the city resulted in profound euphoria. The Byzantine city had always been a major obstacle to the expansion of Muslim power. Its fall appeared to be a harbinger of a glorious era for Islam. The Ottoman Empire thereafter enjoyed immense prestige for having been the power that captured Constantinople and transformed it into its capital, Istanbul.[1] For Ottoman administrative purposes, the capture of the city removed a serious obstacle to Ottoman communications between Rumelia and Anatolia, and it secured imperial control over the overland trade routes from east to west as well as the water route from the Black Sea to the Mediterranean.

The capture of Constantinople was Mehmet II's most prestigious military victory, but just as important strategically were the defeat of the Serbs in 1459—which led to the definitive annexation of Serbia—and the defeat in the east of Uzun Hasan's White Sheep confederation in 1473. Uzun Hasan was a powerful Turkic chieftain who ruled eastern Anatolia and most of Iraq and Iran. Ambitious and sophisticated, he purchased muskets from the Venetians and other western powers for use against the Ottomans. By 1472 he felt strong enough to march against Bursa. This was a miscalculation, for Mehmet launched a major attack on him and drove him back into central Anatolia before utterly defeating him on the upper Euphrates River in 1473. Mehmet's victories between 1453 and 1473 secured a vast territorial base for the Ottoman Empire. Mehmet was also responsible for outfitting the Ottoman army with gunpowder weaponry. Although the Ottomans may have used muskets and cannon as early as the Anatolian campaigns of Murat I in the 1380s, it was Mehmet II who made muskets and artillery the standard equipment of the Janissary corps.

By the early sixteenth century, this new composite army of cavalry, infantry, and artillery had developed into one of the most formidable in the world. Its effectiveness was first demonstrated in a war against Iran that was precipitated by Ottoman anxiety over the ambitions of the Safavid Sufi order. The Safavids had actively recruited among the population of central and eastern Anatolia since the mid-fifteenth century. Their message had received an enthusiastic response from many Anatolian Turks who feared Ottoman expansion. In addition, many pastoralists felt a genuine attraction to Safavid religious teachings and practices, which bore striking similarities to the Bektashi and Alevi movements, with which they were already familiar.

In 1501, Isma'il, the charismatic young leader of the Safavids, won a string of impressive military victories in Azerbaijan. He then assumed the title of shah, declaring his intention of implementing a temporal empire. Soon, he controlled eastern Anatolia and eastern Syria. Almost immediately, pro-Safavid revolts began occurring within the Ottomans' Anatolian realm. For several years, numerous pro-Safavid rebellions flared up as far west as the Aegean coast. Ottoman sultans became increasingly concerned about Isma'il's influence among their subjects. Bayezit II (1481–1512) killed thousands of Shi'ites and deported large numbers of others to the Peloponnesus in 1502, but the revolts continued. In 1511, a huge, pro-Safavid revolt erupted near Antalya. Bayezit sent an army to suppress it, but thousands of the Ottoman soldiers defected from the army and joined the rebels. When the revolt's leaders gained control of central Anatolia, they began leading an army toward Bursa with the intention of besieging the city. An Ottoman army intercepted the expedition and defeated the rebels only after a major battle.

The growing disorder prompted several of Bayezit's sons to begin maneuvering to replace their father. Isma'il contributed to the confusion by aiding two of the brothers, thus incurring the wrath of a third brother, the ruthless and taciturn Selim. In 1512, Selim deposed his father, becoming Sultan Selim I (1512–1520). Then, in accord with Turkish tradition, he killed his brothers in order to preclude the risk of sibling rivalry. After securing his position, he began making plans to strike a decisive blow against the Safavids themselves. In the spring of 1514, he led his army through Anatolia, punishing pro-Safavid Turkmen. Selim even had to purge his army of Safavid sympathizers during the campaign itself.

The Ottomans and Safavids finally met each other at Chaldiran. Some 70,000 Ottoman soldiers—including 12,000 Janissaries wielding muskets and cannon—faced some 40,000 Safavid cavalrymen. The Safavids chose not to rely upon gunpowder weapons. They were familiar with them: The Safavids and Uzun Hasan had employed muskets on a limited basis, but the mountainous terrain of Azerbaijan rendered the transport of cannon a practical impossibility. Besides, in the hands of the skilled Safavid cavalryman, the arrow and saber were devastatingly effective.

The Battle of Chaldiran raged for hours, and many on the Ottoman side began to fear that their army would be annihilated. The Ottoman left wing was routed, but the Janissaries managed to set up their formation behind a barrier of gun carriages and wagons linked together by chains, which kept the Safavid horsemen at bay. The 200 cannon, 100 mortars, and thousands of muskets fired volley after volley, killing many of the Safavids, including high-ranking leaders. Finally, the smoke, noise, and blood-letting caused the Safavid army to collapse in confusion. It retreated from the field. Both sides had suffered horrible losses, but the Ottomans had clearly won. They continued unopposed to the Safavid capital of Tabriz, which they occupied. Shortly thereafter, they pulled back to the region of Lake Van. Although the Safavids remained dangerous enemies of the Ottomans, they were never again able to challenge them for supremacy in Anatolia.

Selim made military history again two years later. In August 1516, he led a campaign into Syria, which the Mamlukes had retaken shortly after Timur's death in 1405. The Mamluke Empire, which had begun in 1250, was still intact. Despite relying on a vicious power struggle rather than on dynastic succession to determine each generation's ruler, the state had lasted two and one-half centuries. It also still managed to rule Syria and the Holy Cities as well as Egypt. By the time of Selim's invasion, however, the empire was much weaker than it had been at its peak in the early fourteenth century. Egypt and Syria were still reeling from continued epidemics of the plague. The population in both provinces had continued to decline, and their economies were weak. The fine products that had made the Mamlukes famous—textiles, glassware, and inlaid work—deteriorated in quality during this period to the extent that the local inhabitants began to import such items from Europe. This economic weakness accelerated during the first decade of the sixteenth century after Portugal became established in India in 1502. The Portuguese tried to divert all trade between India and Europe around the tip of southern Africa, and began a blockade of the Red Sea and Persian Gulf. The result was a temporary but precipitous drop in tariff revenues in Egypt from long-distance trade.

Ominously, too, the Mamluke ethos did not easily accommodate gunpowder weapons into its system. Like the Safavids, the Mamlukes had experimented with artillery and muskets as early as the 1480s, but they did not revise their military organization in order to incorporate the weapons into their system. Unlike the Safavids, the Mamlukes did not have the argument of mountainous terrain to justify not using muskets and artillery: Egypt and the most valuable regions of Syria were situated on plains that would have accommodated wheeled artillery. The Mamluke army resisted gunpowder weapons because its decision makers were cavalrymen, and gunpowder transferred the striking power and the weight of the economic resources of any army to the infantry.

As a consequence, Selim's army faced Mamlukes who insisted as a point of honor on making cavalry charges directly into the teeth of musket and artillery fire. Courageous as the Mamlukes were, they were literally blown away during battles in Syria and Egypt, and by January 1517 the Mamluke Empire was gone, its territory now securely within the Ottoman fold. As spectacular as the conquest of Constantinople had been in raising the prestige of the Ottomans, their conquest of the Mamlukes enhanced their prestige even more. Because Mecca and Medina were part of the Mamluke domain, Selim now became the ruler of the Holy Cities and the guardian of the pilgrimage routes.

The conquest of Constantinople, the defeat of the Safavids, and the annexation of the Mamluke Empire transformed the Ottoman state into an empire. Its expansion did not stop there, however. Selim's son, Suleyman I (1520–1566), captured Iraq from the Safavids, annexed Hungary, captured the island of Rhodes from the Knights of St. John, and occupied much of the North African coast. He laid siege to Vienna in 1529 and might well have captured the city had winter weather not forced him back to his own capital. By the end of his reign, the empire comprised the Balkans south of the Danube River; autonomous provinces in modern Hungary, Romania, and southern Russia; all of Anatolia; and almost the entire Arab world to the frontier with Morocco. In the eastern Mediterranean it included all the Aegean islands (Cyprus was taken in 1571 and Crete was conquered between 1645 and 1669).

Society

For roughly two centuries, the Ottoman Empire was one of the world's greatest powers. At the beginning of the seventeenth century, it occupied an area of 800,000 square miles and contained twenty-five to thirty million people (see Map 3.1). (By comparison, the British Isles had approximately seven million people in 1600; France had almost nineteen million; and Spain had about ten million.) The population of the Ottoman Empire was diverse, containing large numbers of Turks, Armenians, Magyars, Arabs, Greeks, Slavs, and Berbers, as well as many smaller groups.

The empire also comprised many religious groups, including Sunni and Shi'ite Muslims, several Christian denominations, and Jews. The Muslim and Christian communities, in particular, were further distinguished by their various social classes and their urban or rural identities: The differences between the urban and rural expressions of these religions could be quite striking. As in every major society of the era, the majority of the population were peasants. Only a small minority were nomads, but in eastern Anatolia, Iraq, the Arabian Peninsula, and North Africa, their influence was considerable. Compared to Europe, the empire had a much higher percentage of population living in huge cities (such as Istanbul and Cairo) and large cities (such as Edirne, Izmir, Aleppo, and Damascus).

The status of free women in the Ottoman Empire changed over time, particularly among the upper social strata. Among the early Ottomans, the mores of their Central Asian heritage prevailed: Women moved about freely, left their faces uncovered, and played an active role in the economic production of the household. As the Ottomans became urbanized, wealthy, and influenced by urban Islamic values, however, women's public roles changed just as they had throughout Muslim history. On the one hand, women's public roles became more circumscribed; on the other hand, women's legal rights were formalized due to the impact of the Shari'a.

These two developments became evident during the reign of Suleyman I (1520–1566). By that time, the wealthy Muslim women of Istanbul did not have the freedom of movement of local Christians. Some men even stipulated in the marriage contract that their wives would never be allowed to step outside their homes. Even when they were allowed to leave the home, their faces were covered by a veil that made it impossible for anyone to see their features. Such women, however, might be quite powerful individuals. In the palace, the mothers of the sultan's sons exerted tremendous influence, whether they were wives or concubines. They lobbied to obtain for their sons the most powerful positions possible, they advised the sultan (whether consort or son) on policy decisions, and they granted huge sums of money for the construction of mosques, hospitals, and schools.

Even women outside the palace could wield considerable power. Unlike their contemporaries in Europe, they were able to buy, own, use, and sell property without any restrictions by their male relatives. They could lend or borrow money, enforce their rights in court when necessary, and serve as executors of wills. Legally, they could not be forced into marriage, although family pressures are known to have infringed upon this right. As in many other societies (such as that of the Byzantines), their sequestration was a sign of their families' wealth—it showed, like the binding of the feet of wealthy Chinese women, that their labor was not necessary for

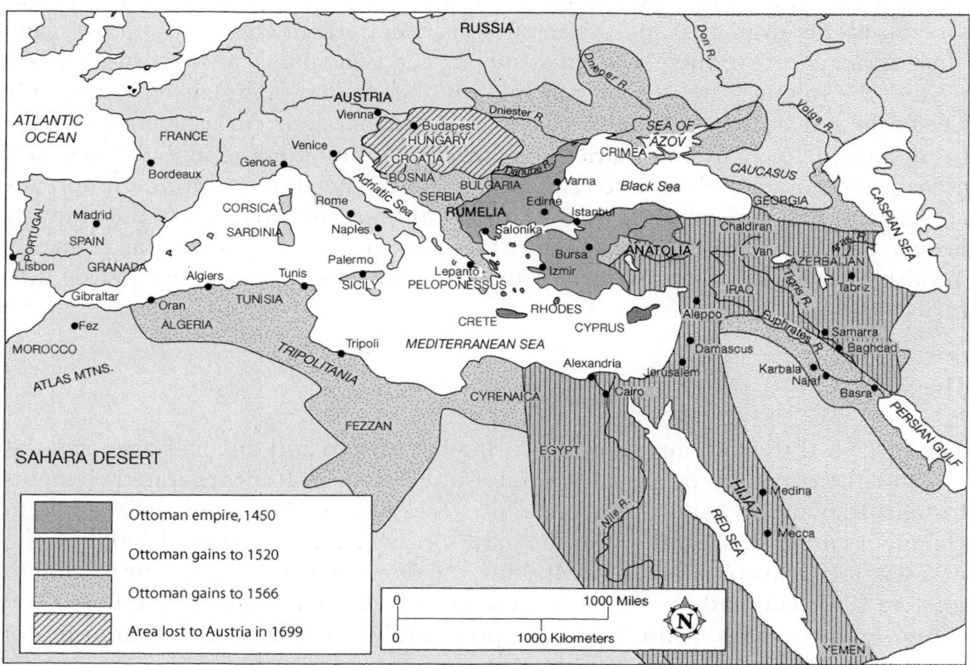

MAP 3.1 The Ottoman Empire to 1699.

the maintenance of the family. Sequestration and veiling were also regarded as demonstrations of piety, but they were characteristics primarily of prosperous families. Poor women, on the other hand, whether in the city or in the village, often appeared in public without their faces covered, for they were actively involved in labor.

Ottoman society, like many other premodern societies, exploited a large slave population. The trade in slaves was a major element in the Ottoman economy. Istanbul's slave markets were enormous, siphoning human chattel from a huge Afro-Eurasian hinterland. Some of the slaves were captured in war by the regular army, others were captured by pirates in the Mediterranean or Black Sea, and still others were transported into the empire as "commodities" of long-distance trade. We are accustomed to thinking of slaves as being forced into the most menial and oppressive types of work, but it should be obvious by now that this was not always the case in the Ottoman Empire. Slaves played an even more visible role in the Ottoman Empire than they did in the Mamluke Empire, where they were technically manumitted at the end of their training. The recruits of the Ottoman devshirme remained slaves all their lives, and yet they joined the highest ranks of administrators in the land. The Shari'a forbade the offices of the sultan and the highest religious dignitaries from being held by slaves, but the vizier, other top government officials, military officers, and many provincial governors were life-long slaves who wielded enormous power. Viziers and other powerful slaves in the civilian and military administration possessed their own slaves.

Most slaves, of course, were not obtained to staff powerful offices. On the other hand, they were rarely sought to provide cheap labor for agriculture or industry (although they were used extensively in the navy's galleys). Most were personal servants and bodyguards, and there was a thriving trade in concubines. Like many Muslim rulers before them, Ottoman sultans had concubines as well as wives, and most of the sultans were themselves children of concubines. A glance at the family tree of the sixteenth-century sultans demonstrates that their Turkish gene pool had been overwhelmed by the Slavic element of their mothers, grandmothers, and great-grandmothers. When one remembers that the heads of government bureaus and the military were also largely of Slavic origin, that the language of the elite was heavily Persianized and Arabized, and that the large cavalry force was primarily Turkish, the cosmopolitan nature of the Ottoman enterprise comes quickly into focus.

The State

The success of the Ottoman Empire during its first two and one-half centuries was due in large part to its remarkable administrative system. It incorporated elements from its Iranian, Byzantine, and Saljuq predecessors, and it continually adapted to changing circumstances. Because the early Ottomans were constantly conquering new territory that contained non-Muslims, the Ottomans thought it only natural to tolerate Christians and Jews, who formed the majority of the population for several centuries. The state's institutions were profoundly affected by the relationship of the ruling class with the non-Muslim subjects.

The Sultan

The first ten Ottoman sultans were men of unusual ability. They were highly charismatic and they all personally led their armies and civil administrations. Before they ascended the throne, they were trained by long service in various administrative and military positions. Until 1611, the sons of sultans succeeded to the throne in the traditional Turkish manner of a struggle among the brothers. Each gathered an army and fought the others until one emerged triumphant. Any surviving losers were garroted. This ruthless process of natural selection seems to have resulted in the survival of the fittest.

In 1421, Mehmet I added the title of *caliph* to his long string of honorifics, but he was not claiming a unique status in the Muslim world. Numerous petty chieftains had appropriated the title ever since it was cheapened in the tenth century, when three caliphs contested for power. Since 1260, the Mamlukes had retained the services of a descendant of the Abbasid family upon whom they conferred the title of caliph, as well. He had no power and was simply a puppet of the state. Mehmet laid claim to the title only because he knew that fellow Muslims would not take him seriously as a chief of state without it.

When Selim went to war against the Safavids and the Mamlukes, he was in the awkward position of making war on fellow Muslims rather than engaging in jihad against infidels. Like many rulers before and after him, he justified his wars against Muslim states by claiming that they were heretics, but he knew that such a claim rang empty in many quarters. His defeat of both powers, however, provided him with the opportunity to secure his preeminent status. Upon defeating the Mamlukes, he dismissed the puppet caliph in Cairo and began to emphasize his own responsibility for the sacred precincts of Mecca and Medina.

Despite the rapid ascent of Ottoman power between the capture of Constantinople in 1453 and the annexation of the Holy Cities in 1517, sultans knew that they could not aspire to be the spokesman for the entire Muslim world. Like sixteenth-century Safavid and Mughal rulers, Ottoman sultans faced a vastly expanded Muslim world that made a mockery of universal claims. Despite occasional wars among these rulers, they recognized that the others had their respective spheres of influence. They often engaged in formal diplomatic relations with each other as equal powers. No single individual claimed that, by virtue of his office, he held hegemony over other rulers. The Muslim world, which had always been multipolar in fact, had finally become institutionalized as such, although political and religious theory still did not recognize it.

The long, quiet death of the caliphate was not a controversial issue as long as the empires were vibrant, for religious scholars and the masses alike could assume that their respective leaders were fulfilling the caliphal function by virtue of their success. Awkward moments did occasionally arise in the matters of war and peace, however. Rulers confronted two major complications. One was that wars with other Muslim empires were problematic from the perspective of Islamic law, because fighting fellow Muslims was hard to justify except on the basis of stamping out heresy.

The other problem was that the doctrine of jihad became less and less consistent with political reality. The Shari'a prohibited the making of peace with non-Muslim states except under extraordinary circumstances. Theoretically, the normative relationship between the Muslim world (the *Dar al-Islam,* or the Abode of Islam) and non-Muslim areas (the *Dar al-Harb,* or the Abode of War) was supposed to be continual jihad. The collective duty of jihad was to respond to the caliph's call to go to war against non-Muslim neighbors. The individual duty of jihad was to defend the Dar al-Islam if it were attacked, regardless of whether a caliph was present to lead. Muslim monarchs, however, discovered that they occasionally had to go to war with fellow Muslims to accomplish their goals and that they occasionally needed alliances with non-Muslim states for the same reason. When a Muslim ruler concluded a treaty of alliance with a non-Muslim ruler, his partner in peace expected him to restrain zealous subjects from engaging in jihad. Thus, like earlier Muslim dynasties, the Ottomans, Safavids, and Mughals had amicable relations with both Muslims and non-Muslims and fought both Muslims and non-Muslims. The practice of international relations in Muslim countries was hardly distinguishable from that of European nations. The concept of jihad lost its clarity, and individuals in later generations would reinterpret it to serve their own purposes.

Whatever Muslims thought about jihad and the caliphate, the Ottomans ruled over a large population of non-Muslims who had little interest in those issues. As a result, Ottoman sultans worked hard to establish justice as the principle that legitimized their rule. In addition to their lavish support of the court system that enforced the Shari'a, they paid careful attention to issues that fell outside the purview of Islamic law. All Muslim regimes employed non-Shari'a laws to fill gaps that the Shari'a did not cover. These laws included new regulations that the state needed to carry on its business as well as traditional laws that the empires' subjects—both Muslim and non-Muslim—were accustomed to following. Ottoman administrators were more diligent than previous ones had been in compiling provincial law books that reflected customary usage in a given area. This body of non-Shari'a law, or *kanun,* gradually became very large, and it occasionally contradicted the Shari'a. When Ottoman administrators codified kanun regulations into books, the differences between them and the Shari'a became more obvious. The muftis during the reign of Suleyman resolved many of the inconsistencies between the two systems of law, and Suleyman received the credit: Although Europeans know him as Suleyman the Magnificent, Muslims refer to him as Suleyman the Law-Giver.

The *Devshirme*

As impressive as the sultans were as individual leaders, even they realized that without a stable and efficient bureaucratic apparatus, the Ottoman regime was unlikely to be any more durable than that of the Saljuqs had been. A sophisticated administrative system distinguished the Ottomans from the many short-lived dynasties that preceded them. At the dawn of their own history they had been a loosely organized band of independent-minded gazis, but over the decades their leaders gradually created a remarkably complex administration. It proved to be a hybrid bureaucracy, having emerged under the guiding hands of religious specialists and administrators from the cities of the old Sultanate of Rum, the Byzantine Empire, and the Mamluke Empire, as well as from the Ottomans' own innovation of the devshirme.

A sophisticated bureaucracy began to emerge as early as the reign of Murat I (1362–1389). Prior to the capture of Constantinople, Turks played the most important role in the army and the administration, but Mehmet II attempted to balance the power of the Turks in both institutions by expanding the levy of Christian children (devshirme) that Bayezit I (1389–1402) had instituted. Under Mehmet II (1451–1481) the devshirme became the recruiting mechanism for some of the most powerful figures in the empire. Agents went out into the villages to select Christian boys between the ages of eight and eighteen and escorted them to Istanbul. In the capital, the boys were tested for a variety of abilities. The most promising ten percent or so went sent for training to the palaces of Edirne and Istanbul, whereas the majority were assigned to Turkish farmers. Living with the families, they learned the Turkish language and the rudiments of Islam. When they became sufficiently acculturated, they were enrolled in the ranks of the Janissaries, where they received training in the use of muskets and artillery. The Janissaries owed supreme loyalty to the sultan. They were his personal slaves, and few retained any ties with their homelands.

The devshirme recruits who had been sent for palace instruction began a rigorous program of education and training of several years. They studied the Qur'an and the various religious sciences; became fluent in Arabic, Persian, and Turkish; and engaged in physical training such as wrestling, archery, and horsemanship. In addition, each trainee acquired a professional artistic skill like miniature painting or bookbinding. At the end of the program the candidates were subject to a second screening. The majority (probably about ninety percent) entered high-status positions in the sultan's household cavalry, administrative positions throughout the empire, or the profession of military engineer (for the all-important task of conducting siege operations). The elite ten percent who survived this second screening became the most powerful civilian and military officials in the empire. These included the governors, the highest officers of the army, the heads of departments in the central government, and the vizier, or chief minister to the sultan. Like the Janissaries, these officials were the personal slaves of the sultan.

By the early sixteenth century, the devshirme recruits had become the dominant element of the ruling class. They held the leading civilian and military offices and they comprised the most favored unit of the army, the musket-wielding Janissaries. The size of the Janissary corps rose from 6000 men at the end of Mehmet II's reign to 12,000 at the end of Suleyman's reign. The influence of the Turks, who had dominated Ottoman affairs in the early years, declined, but they remained a powerful force. They formed the bulk of the cavalry, which numbered as many as 50,000 in a single campaign (with many more in reserve) by the sixteenth century. The cavalrymen were known as *sipahis.* The Ottomans granted to a sipahi a *timar,* or the agricultural tax revenue derived from a specific region. The more important the sipahi was, the larger his timar. This correlation was not mere favoritism: A sipahi was responsible not only for his own military service, but also for perhaps several dozen troops in addition to their armor, tents, and supplies. The powerful Turkish sipahis continued to be the influential local lords in the countryside despite the growing authority of the devshirme in the cities.

One of the factors accounting for the dynamism of the Ottoman Empire during the fifteenth and sixteenth centuries was its merit-based system of administration.

The most powerful offices in the empire, whether in the cavalry or the devshirme system, were achieved through competence. The hereditary principle was certainly not absent among the Turks, for they were proud of their lineage, but it did not provide an automatic entrée into the ruling elite as it usually did in contemporary Europe. The most powerful posts in the empire were open to talent, and they were almost always held by men of proven ability. Moreover, the tension between the devshirme and the sipahis resulted in a balance that ensured both the sultan's security and the welfare of the peasants who lived on the timars: The devshirme officials, who themselves had been recruited from peasant families, set the policies that the sipahis had to follow with regard to the peasants who worked their land.

Bureaucratizing Islam

The Ottoman administration was the first Muslim government to develop a fully bureaucratic structure for the religious institutions of its society. From the Umayyad period (661–750) on, the ulama and the state maintained an uneasy relationship. The ulama mediated God's will to society through their jurisprudence, while the state granted society a reasonable degree of physical security in return for taxes. The ulama officially recognized the legitimacy of the government in return for a pledge of governmental nonintervention in the affairs of religion. The degree of mistrust between the ulama and their governments was often high. Governments were usually so despised for their corruption and brutality that the members of the ulama who did agree to serve as qadis when the state asked them to do so were frequently held in contempt by their fellow ulama, even though qadis were indispensable for the operation of the religious courts. The Mamlukes had made an unprecedented effort to control the religious institutions of their society. They attempted to gain influence with Sufi orders and madrasas by endowing their institutions, and they appointed qadis for all four schools of Islamic law (it had been customary to favor one school) so that none would be outside their system of patronage.

The Ottomans were even more systematic and thorough than the Mamlukes had been. They sought to control the religious establishment by creating an elaborate hierarchy of learned offices held by appointment. Although they did not succeed in making all important ulama state employees, their comprehensiveness was unmatched. Religious functionaries, from the highest-ranking specialist in the capital city to the lowliest preachers in the villages, were tied into the system. Lavish patronage of schools, hospitals, Sufi lodges, and mosques all over the empire facilitated the efforts to make local religious leaders dependent on the government. Many of the *waqfs* (religious endowments) throughout the empire were centralized under the administration of a new bureaucracy staffed by ulama.

The ulama who served the government were now powerful government officials. They possessed high status, honors, and privileges, and could pass their wealth and status to their children. Some of the ulama realized that the state was using Islam as a means to legitimize its own sovereignty and policies. They regarded government service as unethical. Most, however, rationalized such service as a way to standardize the norms of the Istanbul-based ulama throughout the entire empire. They eagerly sought the new opportunities.

The ruling elite were particularly concerned to monitor Sufi brotherhoods because the spiritual authority of the Sufi masters was a potential threat to the government's monopoly of power. Some of the orders, especially the Naqshbandiya, were not considered a threat because of their adherence to the norms of the Shari'a. The degree to which an order neglected the Shari'a was considered a barometer of its potential to threaten the government. Sufis considered spiritual authority to be higher than temporal authority (the government), and many of them regarded the Sufi engagement in spiritual communion to be higher than the emphasis on correct doctrine and ritual (which they associated with the ulama). Justice and morality were almost universal norms among the Sufis (the dervishes, as we have seen, defined "morality" in their own way), and they judged the worthiness of any government by the degree to which these two ideals were implemented.

Government officials knew that the discipline, obedience to the master, and organizational sophistication of the Sufi orders provided a potential source of worldly power to Sufi masters that could be mobilized whenever such a leader felt that justice and morality were being neglected. Even after Selim's defeat of the Safavids in 1514, Sufi-inspired rebellions continued to erupt in Anatolia. Suleyman was forced to alternate his campaigns of conquest with bloody suppressions of such revolts throughout his reign. In the middle decades of the seventeenth century, the ulama–government alliance engaged in several purges of Sufi orders during periods of economic hardship.

An intriguing exception to the enforcement of the Shari'a's norms was the case of the Bektashi Sufi movement, which was popular among the Janissaries. For the first century or so of the existence of the Janissary organization, the esprit de corps of its members was enhanced by a prohibition against marriage. The emotional needs of the Janissaries were sublimated through Sufi organizations, and the Bektashi order became the official order within the corps. The Bektashi movement was characterized by doctrines and practices (such as the use of wine in initiation ceremonies and belief in the trinity of God, Muhammad, and 'Ali) that would have scandalized most of the ulama. As a result, its members were tight lipped about their cult and publicly claimed to be Sunni.

On the other hand, the Bektashi order was well suited to facilitate the transition of rural Christian boys into an officially Islamic society. Reports from contemporary observers reveal that many Christian Balkan villagers could not explain the Eucharist or recite any prayers; in 1453, the Orthodox Church felt compelled to issue a condemnation of the practice of bowing to the sun and moon and addressing prayers to them. Boys from such backgrounds would not require intense indoctrination to enter an organization that was indifferent to the specifics of the Shari'a. Furthermore, the order taught that apparent contrasts between Christianity and Islam were due to metaphorical language used in both religions. Bektashi shaykhs taught that their mystical path was superior to any of the rituals and rules of the organized religions, including the Islam of the mosques and madrasas. Thus, many members of the Janissary corps found that, apart from the circumcision ceremony that awaited them upon their arrival from their home village into the capital, their transition into a Muslim society was quite painless.

The *Millet* System

For the first two centuries of their history, the Ottomans often incorporated non-Turks and non-Muslims into their enterprise. During that period the majority of the population in the empire (in both Rumelia and Anatolia) were Christian, and there were considerable numbers of Jews in some areas. By the turn of the sixteenth century, access to powerful civilian and military positions was largely closed to non-Muslims, but the government continued to cultivate good relations with its various religious communities. Like all governments of the day, the Ottoman administration was primarily interested in finances. Most aspects of government not directly associated with exploiting the wealth of empire were left to the subjects to organize as they wished. In the Ottoman context, that meant that the government's relations with non-Muslims would be guided by both custom and the Shari'a. The Ottoman administration integrated these guidelines in a unique manner that enabled the various religious communities to live together with the least possible friction while ensuring that the state treasury was the beneficiary of taxes paid by non-Muslims.

In the Ottoman Empire, all subjects were regarded as belonging to a certain religious community, or *millet.* Mehmet II began the practice of organizing the administration of the millets soon after the conquest of Constantinople. Originally, the official millets included only the Orthodox, Armenians, and Muslims, although the Jews were always treated as a de facto millet. The Ottomans eventually recognized as millets the communities of the Jacobites, Copts, and Maronites, as well. Each millet was allowed internal self-government according to its own laws and traditions, and each was directed by its own religious leader, who was responsible for civil as well as religious matters. In many ways, the millet system gave the non-Muslim religious leaders more power over their flocks than they had under previous regimes.

The most important non-Muslim millet was that of the Orthodox Church, which was by far the largest non-Muslim group in the empire. Its membership outnumbered even the Muslims until the incorporation of the Arab lands in the sixteenth century. The two largest ethnic groups among the Orthodox Christians were the Greeks and Slavs, but there were significant numbers of Arabs and other ethnic groups, as well. In fact, the inclusion of the various ethnic groups within the single millet remained a grievance for many of the Orthodox Slavs, because the Bulgarians and Serbs had maintained their own Slavic-language churches prior to the Ottoman conquest. In the single millet, they had to be subject to a Greek Orthodox administration, with deleterious consequences for their Slavic culture.

The fortunes of the Orthodox Church were decidedly different in Rumelia from what they were in Anatolia. In Anatolia the Orthodox Church was challenged by the Armenian Church, which the Orthodox regarded as heretical. The Armenians continued to thrive in the eastern and southern areas of the peninsula, but the Orthodox population of the central plateau gradually disappeared. In part, this decline was no doubt due to harassment by Turkish nomads, who raided Christian settlements whenever they could. The larger problem, however, seems to have been the difficulty of communicating with the patriarch in Constantinople after the Saljuqs took over Anatolia in the late eleventh century. It was difficult for the churches to recruit well-trained priests and to maintain their communal services. It became more and more difficult to maintain a Christian identity, and the poorer members of the church were tempted to seek aid from Muslim welfare institutions. As a result, the Orthodox community in those regions lost its cohesion and an individual Christian's gradual assimilation to Islam was not hindered by the many social constraints from family, friends, and church that prevailed in other areas.

In Rumelia, by contrast, the Orthodox population continued to thrive due to Ottoman recognition and an active, well-organized support network directed by the patriarch. Whereas Anatolia had suffered from repeated waves of incursions, warfare, and destruction over a period of four centuries, the Balkans were conquered in relatively short campaigns. Ottoman rulers rapidly incorporated the area into a well-organized and stable administrative system, for by now they disliked the predatory raiding of the gazis as much as anyone. Ottoman policy favored Christian nobles and churches as vehicles of Ottoman administration. In turn, at least until the late seventeenth century, Orthodox Christians openly expressed their preference for Ottoman administration to that of any Catholic power that coveted the Balkans, for they believed that they would suffer less religious persecution under the millet system than under Catholic rule.

The Catholic Church did not fare as well as the Orthodox Church did. Catholics were placed within the Armenian millet. This was a much more serious situation for Catholics than the merging of the Slavic and Greek Orthodox churches: Catholics regarded Armenians as heretics, and yet they were subject to the Armenian patriarch. This humiliation may have been a deliberate ploy on the part of the Ottomans, whose attitude toward the Catholic Church was one of suspicion and occasional hostility. The Ottoman attitude was largely a reaction to the hostility toward the Ottomans on the part of the Catholic nations of Venice, Hungary, and the Habsburg Empire (which included Spain and Austria during most of the sixteenth century). In the sixteenth century the Ottomans did develop close diplomatic ties with predominantly Catholic France, but France was a long distance away and shared certain foreign policy objectives with the Ottomans. The French and Ottomans cooperated diplomatically and militarily, and were both determined to make sure that the Habsburg rulers of Spain and Austria did not become dominant in Europe.

At the urging of the French Catholic king, also, Suleyman maintained diplomatic correspondence with an alliance of German Protestant princes who were fighting the Catholic Habsburg emperor, Charles V. He encouraged them and assured them of Ottoman support. Apart from his desire to harass Charles, Suleyman also seems to have had a genuine religious appreciation for the Protestant revolt because of the destruction of religious statuary and of images in stained glass windows that some of the Protestant groups practiced. The continuous Ottoman military threat directed against the Habsburgs between 1521 and 1555 forced the Habsburgs to grant concessions to the Protestants and was a factor in the final official Habsburg recognition of Protestantism. A common saying in the German-speaking lands of the time was *Der Türke ist der lutheranischen Glück* (the Turk is Lutheran good fortune).

The contrast between the Jewish experience in the Ottoman Empire and Christian Europe was striking. The growth of anti-Semitism in Europe brought increasing numbers of Jews to the empire during the fifteenth and sixteenth centuries. When Spain expelled its Jews in 1492, tens of thousands of refugees emigrated to Ottoman territories. Sultan Bayezit II issued proclamations throughout the empire, ordering his officials to welcome them. Some of the refugees achieved success quickly. A famous example is Joseph Hamon, who left Granada in 1493 and served Bayezit and Selim I as court physician for a quarter of a century. The immigration from Spain and Portugal was so great that the Sephardic Jews soon outnumbered their Ashkenazi coreligionists in the empire. Jews lived throughout the empire but were concentrated in Istanbul and Salonica (Thessaloniki), the two largest commercial port cities. They eventually became the majority population of Salonica, which was often referred to as "the Jewish city." It was also known as "La Madre de Israel" in recognition of its eminence as a center of Sephardic Jewish learning.

The millet system was a means by which the Ottomans could continue the traditional Muslim administrative practice of religious toleration toward Jews and Christians while simultaneously reaping financial advantage from them in the form of the religious head tax. Conversions to Islam did occur in the Balkans under Ottoman rule, but the evidence suggests that most were voluntary rather than the result of coercion.[2] The most dramatic example of large-scale conversion took place in Bosnia. Like the Croats, Slovenes, Serbs, and Bulgarians, most inhabitants of Bosnia were Slavic, descendants of the Slavs who migrated into the area in the seventh and eighth centuries. During the medieval period, the Slavs of the western half of the Balkans (the Croats and Slovenes) came under Habsburg influence and shared with their Austrian rulers the Catholic faith and the Latin alphabet. The Slavs in the eastern half of the peninsula (the Serbs and Bulgarians), however, gravitated to the Orthodox faith and used the Cyrillic alphabet, which had been developed by Byzantine missionaries. The Slavs in Bosnia, between these two regions, were in a frontier area where the Latin–Catholic culture competed with the Cyrillic–Orthodox culture. In these remote valleys there were few churches and even fewer priests, with the result that Bosniaks were even more notorious for their ignorance of the fundamentals of Christianity than other rural Balkan residents. The Bosniak nobility rapidly converted to Islam in the fifteenth century, taking advantage of the opportunities to hold high military and civil offices. Many villagers followed soon thereafter, with the Bektashi order particularly active in winning over converts. Bosnia and Albania became Bektashi strongholds.

The Economy

Agriculture was the foundation of the imperial economy. The conquest of Syria and Egypt in 1517 enhanced the value of this sector. The empire was nearly self-sufficient in the production of foodstuffs and made a profit from exporting grain to markets around the Mediterranean basin. The so-called "Columbian exchange"—the worldwide diffusion of plants and animals that took place after the European discovery of the western hemisphere—had a less pronounced effect on Ottoman society than it did in Europe, East Asia, and Africa, but it resulted in the introduction of some important products. The tomato entered the cuisine of the empire just as it did the other Mediterranean societies. Maize also made an impact, but it was valued as animal fodder, not as a staple of the human diet. Tobacco made its appearance in Istanbul about 1600 and spread rapidly throughout the empire. Men soon discovered the pleasure of smoking a hookah, or water pipe, in the coffee houses that had recently become fashionable.

Long-distance trade was an important supplement to agriculture. The Ottomans took over an area that had been a crossroads of commerce for millennia. Their first capital, Bursa, had been a terminus for the caravan route that brought raw silk from Iran to supply the European demand for that valuable commodity. Aleppo was a spice market for the trade route from Southeast Asia that ran through the Persian Gulf, while Cairo was the equivalent market on the Red Sea route. Istanbul, of course, was the preeminent market in the empire due to its size and its status as the capital city.

Much of the Ottoman interest in expanding into the Black Sea, Aegean Sea, and Mediterranean Sea stemmed from the desire to compete with the Venetians and Genoese, who had dominated those regions for centuries. The Genoese were particularly hard hit by the Ottoman conquest of Constantinople, for they had dominated the Black Sea trade since the thirteenth century. In 1484, the Ottomans placed a virtual prohibition on non-Ottoman shipping in the sea.

When the Portuguese entered the Indian Ocean after 1498, they did so with the intention of destroying Muslim commerce in the region. At first they were successful, as their aggressive attacks on Muslim shipping in the ocean caused the spice trade through the Red Sea to contract severely. The Ottomans conquered the Mamluke Empire just as the supply of spices coming into Cairo was starting to diminish due to the Portuguese blockade. In order to counter the Portuguese threat, the Ottomans seized Aden, on the southwestern coast of the Arabian Peninsula. Ottoman possession of this strategic port revived the Red Sea spice trade, and both the Ottomans and the Venetians benefitted. The Ottomans invested heavily to protect their trade routes from the Europeans. They fought the Portuguese in the Persian Gulf and along the African coast, and even sent ships, supplies, and soldiers to aid Muslims against the Portuguese on the Malabar Coast of India and on the island of Sumatra in Southeast Asia.

Ottoman officials valued international trade so highly that they granted foreign merchants a set of special privileges called *Capitulations.* These privileges were similar to the content of what we call diplomatic immunity today: They entailed exemption from Ottoman law and taxes. Special privileges had been granted to certain merchants from Italian city states in the fourteenth and fifteenth centuries, but the first major Capitulations were granted to the French in 1536, a year after France and the Ottoman Empire signed a formal alliance against the Habsburgs. In effect, the Capitulations bestowed upon the French merchant community in the Ottoman realm the status of a millet. In the sixteenth century, the Capitulations were reciprocal—Ottomans received them in France—but in later centuries, they proved to be instruments that enabled Europeans to gain important leverage in the Ottoman Empire.

Culture

The Ottomans always took pride in their origins as Central Asian Turks, but it had taken only a few decades for their culture to differ substantially from that of their nomadic ancestors. First at Bursa, then at Edirne, and finally at Istanbul, the Ottomans set about creating an imperial presence that would awe visitors and subjects alike. The most spectacular period of Ottoman cultural history began with Mehmet II's capture of Constantinople. The storied city had shrunk to a population of some 50,000 just before the conquest, and after the sack of the city it appears to have contained only 10,000 souls. Mehmet was determined to restore the city's stature as a great imperial capital, and he immediately began a program of repopulation and construction. He provided incentives for Christians, Jews, and Muslims alike to move to the city, and, when necessary, he forcibly settled his subjects in the capital.

Embellishment of the city was the greatest economic project in Ottoman history. It required the construction of schools, hospitals, baths, caravansaries, bazaars, and shops of all kinds. Mehmet II's reign alone witnessed the construction of over two hundred mosques, thirty-two public baths, and twenty-four schools. Engineers made repairs to the aqueducts, sewers, and other components of the city's infrastructure. Having turned the imposing, nine-hundred-year-old church, the Hagia Sofia, into the greatest mosque in the world, Mehmet soon commissioned the construction of a new mosque to rival it (it was destroyed by an earthquake in the eighteenth century).

Mehmet II also built two new palaces in the city, the most famous of which was the Topkapi. It began rising on 150 acres of land situated on the promontory overlooking the Bosporus Strait. Future sultans would continue to add on to it until it became one of the largest palace complexes in the world. The city that contained it was correspondingly large: By the end of Mehmet's reign in 1481, the population of Istanbul had risen to almost 100,000. By the end of Suleyman's reign in 1566, the city boasted 400,000–600,000 inhabitants, which was a population twice as large as either London or Paris could claim.

Mehmet II was a highly cultured ruler, even if many of his subjects found him to be arbitrary and cruel in his dealings with those who displeased him. A talented poet, he had eclectic cultural tastes. He gathered Italian humanists and Greek scholars at his court, and he ordered the Orthodox patriarch to write a credo of the Christian faith. He filled his palace library with works in Greek and Latin, and he commissioned Gentile Bellini to come from Venice to paint his portrait. Mehmet also recruited painters, astronomers, and mathematicians from Central Asia to his court.

Ottoman culture is most famous for its monumental architecture, and the greatest of the Ottoman architects was Sinan (1489–1588). A product of the devshirme, Sinan began as an officer in the artillery and then became a designer of military bridges and fortifications. He built his first nonmilitary building in 1539 and served as the chief imperial architect for the next forty years. He is credited with dozens of mosques and palaces as well as numerous public baths, tombs, madrasas, caravansaries, hospitals, aqueducts, and fountains.

Sinan's most famous works are the Suleymaniye mosque in Istanbul and the Selimiye mosque in Edirne. Using the Byzantine church as his inspiration, Sinan adapted the design to meet the needs of Muslim worship, which requires large open spaces for communal prayer. The huge central dome remained the focal point around which the design of the rest of the structure was developed, but he was able to reduce the bulk of the weight-bearing piers and buttresses, resulting in thinner walls that contained more and larger windows. The square-sided, domed mosque, punctuated with several pencil-shaped minarets, became the model for subsequent Ottoman religious architecture.

The Ottomans were also active in creating a new literary tradition. The Persian language had enjoyed an important role in the diplomatic correspondence and Sufi poetry of the Sultanate of Rum. As a result, even Osman's generation had been powerfully influenced by Persian literary motifs. The continuous migration of Persian-speaking bureaucrats and scholars into the Ottoman Empire consolidated the importance of Persian literature for Ottoman elites. Several of the sultans—most notably Selim I—were accomplished poets in Persian.

The Ottomans also used the Persian language for international correspondence, and under its influence they developed a new literary Turkish language that every bureaucrat was expected to be able to use. Ottoman Turkish was based on Turkish grammar, but its vocabulary was supplemented by Persian words and, like Persian, it used a modified version of the Arabic alphabet. After the conquest of the Arab lands by Selim and Suleyman, Arabic vocabulary became another important influence on Ottoman culture. By the second half of the sixteenth century, a majority of words in Ottoman poetry were Persian and Arabic loanwords.

Calligraphy continued to be a major form of the decorative arts under the Ottomans. It embellished manuscripts, monumental architecture, and objects as varied as bowls and swords. A major Ottoman innovation in calligraphy was the *tuğra,* a highly stylized signature or logo for the sultan. At the beginning of each reign, calligraphers would design the *tuğra,* which would then appear on all official documents and correspondence and on coins minted during the sultanate. By the time of Suleyman, the *tuğra* included the sultan's name, his father's name, and the phrase "ever-victorious": Suleyman Shah the son of Selim Shah Khan, ever victorious.

The writing of history flourished under the Ottomans. As early as the middle of the fifteenth century, sultans were commissioning histories of the dynasty, establishing a tradition of valuable historical writing that persisted for centuries. Major contributions were also made in cartography. The work of the admiral Piri Reis (d. 1553) is the most famous today. In 1513, he produced a map of the known world. Among his sources were several European maps showing the discoveries of Portuguese and Spanish mariners, including Columbus. His most important work was a remarkably detailed description of the natural features of the Mediterranean that contained 129 separate maps of the sea's basin.

Medicine and astronomy flourished in the sixteenth century. The Suleymaniye mosque complex included a madrasa complex that broke with tradition and emphasized medicine and mathematics over the religious sciences. Numerous hospitals were constructed all over the empire, in which physicians developed new surgery techniques and conducted original research in physiology and the treatment of disease.

The fields of mathematics and astronomy boasted some first-class intellects under the Ottomans. The leading astronomer under Mehmet was 'Ali Kuscu (d. 1474). 'Ali had directed a famous observatory in Samarqand and then moved to Tabriz to serve Uzun Hasan. Uzun, in an effort to impress Mehmet, sent 'Ali to Istanbul as his ambassador, but 'Ali was so impressed with Istanbul that he entered Mehmet's service. There he wrote a number of important works on mathematics.

The *tuğra*, or calligraphic seal, of Suleyman the Magnificent.

Taki al-Din Mehmet (1521–1585) was the greatest Ottoman astronomer of the sixteenth century. He made important corrections in existing astronomical tables and secured the construction of an observatory in Istanbul. The new edifice had hardly been completed, however, when it was razed in 1580 due to agitation on the part of the highest member of the ulama, the Shaykh al-Islam. Like some other members of the ulama, he identified astronomy with astrology, which he regarded as a violation of God's sovereignty. Unfortunately, the publicity surrounding the destruction of the observatory cast astronomy into disrepute, and thereafter little was accomplished in that discipline within the empire.

The razing of the observatory reflected a broader cultural retrenchment that began during the late sixteenth century. During the fourteenth and fifteenth centuries, Ottoman rulers annexed a wide variety of societies and were open to an equally wide variety of cultural influences. Mehmet II exemplified this period, inviting scholars from Central Asia and Italy to his court. During the sixteenth century, on the other hand, the campaigns against the Safavids and Shi'ite currents within the empire led to a suspicion of new ideas. The sultan's status as the guardian of the pilgrimage route to Mecca and the incorporation of ulama into the governmental hierarchy also militated against the appearance of sanctioning non-Islamic ideas and practices. The eager encounter with other cultures, characteristic of the fifteenth century, was replaced by a suspicion of new ideas in the seventeenth century. Not until the early eighteenth century did the elites begin to sample selected features of a neighboring culture again.

From Dominance to Parity

The reign of Suleyman I (1520–1566) was the culmination of an impressive revival and expansion of Ottoman might after Timur's crushing defeat of Bayezit I in 1402. Suleyman's power and the opulence of his court profoundly impressed contemporary Europeans, who called him Suleyman the Magnificent. No single European state would dare to attack his empire, and even coalitions of powers would think twice before doing so. The potential for further Ottoman expansion struck fear into the hearts of Europeans everywhere. The peoples of central Europe lived in constant fear of "the Terrible Turk," and even the rulers of powerful Spain, at the far end of the Mediterranean, were nervous about a possible invasion. Spain's Muslim minority fervently pleaded with the Ottomans to invade their country. Concentrated on the Mediterranean coast, the Muslims of Spain would have posed a critical security problem for Madrid in the event of such an attack.

During Suleyman's reign, however, the dynamic phase of Ottoman history came to an end. The momentum of the first half of the sixteenth century suddenly stalled during the great sultan's last few years, and his successors could never regain the momentum. One oft-noted feature of the period is that, with Suleyman's death, a period of almost two centuries of outstanding sultans (interrupted only by the civil war that followed Timur's defeat of Bayezit) came to an end, and a period of more than two centuries began during which all but one or two sultans were of inferior ability. A factor in the decline of the quality of leadership was a change in the training of Ottoman princes. Until the last quarter of the sixteenth century, princes of the dynasty were sent to the provinces for administrative experience. After Suleyman's death, they were confined to the palace instead. As a result, they not only failed to gain administrative experience, but they also were remarkably ignorant of any experience outside the highly artificial routines of the harem.

The limited experience of young sultans was not the only difference between the earlier period and the one after Suleyman. The first period was one of military expansion, when the most important trait of a sultan was military leadership, whereas the second period required the creativity to reorganize the empire's institutions and the determination and resourcefulness to implement the required changes in the face of determined opposition. Moreover, sultans faced enormous problems of inertia and inefficiency within the empire's vast bureaucratic structure, which was officially headed by the vizier. The demands on sultans and viziers alike had changed dramatically. The fact remains that the empire's leadership, whether focused on the sultan or generalized at the level of the ruling class, was not equal to the challenges facing the empire from the mid-sixteenth to mid-eighteenth centuries. By the end of the period, the empire had lost its preeminent position in Europe.

Strategic and Military Challenges

The most striking change that catches our attention is the abrupt end to territorial expansion. Suleyman's conquests brought the empire to the limits that its army could go on a campaign and return the same year. The campaigning season was normally from April to October in order to avoid the brutal winter weather and the prohibitive expenses that year-round provisioning would entail. This constraint forced the Ottomans to recognize limits to their sphere of activity. Taking terrain into account, Budapest and Lake Van were each a march of over 800 miles from Istanbul, and Baghdad was over 1000 miles. An army of 50,000–70,000 troops, complete with the tens of thousands of war horses and pack camels necessary for such a venture, could normally travel only twelve to fifteen miles per day. An expedition to Budapest or Lake Van would require four months just for the round-trip march, apart from any military action. It is suggestive that the only important annexations after Suleyman's death (of Cyprus in 1571 and of Crete, 1645–1669) were the result of naval operations, not long overland expeditions.

The end of the conquest phase was a serious matter because the entire administrative structure had been based on the assumption of territorial expansion. The military organization, civil administration, tax structure, and landholding system were all affected by the new development. Still, if the Ottoman elite had "only" been faced with reorganizing the system in order to deal with stable borders, they might have had the time and resources to make adjustments without wrenching changes. As often happens in real life, however, they were faced with a constellation of challenges simultaneously.

The cessation of territorial expansion took place during a period when both the empire and Europe faced rapid population growth and inflation. Population estimates are notoriously difficult to make for any region in the world in the sixteenth and seventeenth centuries, but it is clear that the population of Europe and the Ottoman Empire grew rapidly from the early sixteenth century to the early seventeenth century. During this same period, overall prices also increased. The experience of inflation in the Ottoman Empire occurred simultaneously with a similar phenomenon in Europe known as the Price Revolution, which is linked to the impact of a larger silver supply, both from domestic sources and from Spain's colonies in Latin America. Until recently, historians of the Ottoman Empire believed that Europe's increased silver supply and Ottoman inflation were closely linked in terms of cause and effect. The accepted explanation was that, when prices for commodities began skyrocketing in Europe, European merchants sought to purchase cheaper grains, metals, and wool from the Ottomans. The export of those commodities to Europe caused shortages of them in the Ottoman Empire, causing prices to rise there, as well. Today, economic historians agree that the export of commodities to Europe did feed inflationary flames, but that even more important for the rising prices were the debasement of Ottoman currency (the reduction of the silver content in coins) and the rising use of coins in the Ottoman economy.

The Ottoman administration was also undergoing disruptions due to its efforts to reorganize the army. In part, the need for military reform stemmed from the fact that inflation was making it impossible for many timar holders to equip their cavalrymen for combat. As a result, when imperial military campaigns were organized, the cavalry units would frequently be understaffed or poorly equipped. In addition, Ottoman military authorities were beginning to recognize that their army was losing its technological advantage in battle. Clashes with Austria in the late sixteenth and early seventeenth centuries demonstrated that European armies were rapidly shifting their resources to musket-carrying infantry, giving them an advantage over the relatively small Janissary corps. Ottoman cavalrymen found that their horses would not charge into the disciplined formations of European infantry and that the repeated discharge of thousands of European muskets produced a devastating effect upon horses and armored men alike. The Ottomans found themselves in the unaccustomed position of having fallen behind in both military technology and strategy.

To its credit, the government began to make changes in its military structure. Doing so, however, caused unforeseen problems for the system as a whole. Recruiting enough musketeers to match the Europeans could not be accomplished through the devshirme system, and so Muslim peasants began to be admitted into the army alongside the slave soldiers. Once the breach had been made in the devshirme system, ambitious Muslim families began asking why the devshirme should exist at all. It was gradually abandoned during the seventeenth century. From then on, military needs were filled by conscription of young men from Muslim families and civilian offices were filled by competition among leading families. The army began to increase the number of its infantrymen, expanding the number of soldiers in its Janissary corps from some 12,000 in 1570 to some 40,000 by the middle of the seventeenth century. By the beginning of the eighteenth century there were at least 80,000 on the rolls, although they were never mustered together at once.

While the infantry units were growing in size, the cavalry remained a large force. Sipahis, however, became caught between the pressures of rising prices and the government's need to pay cash to its professional foot soldiers. When a timar holder could not afford to fulfill his military duties, the government seized his property and turned it over to a government official or wealthy landowner as a tax farm. As a timar, the property's revenues had been used to equip cavalrymen, but as a tax farm its revenues were forwarded to the central government, minus any extra taxes the holder of the tax farm could collect. The system was obviously ripe for abuse, particularly since a tax farm was theoretically assigned to an individual for a specified period (usually three years, although tax farms later became hereditary). Since the administrator had no incentive to develop the property's value, he was tempted to squeeze out of it what he could in a short time.

These changes in military structure had major repercussions. Three are worth noting here. First, the transition from timars to tax farms came at the expense of public support of the regime. The low taxes that the Ottomans had levied in the fourteenth and fifteenth centuries were a major reason that the Balkan peasantry had acquiesced in Ottoman rule, but seventeenth-century peasants discovered that their standard of living was declining due to the avarice of the tax farmers. Starvation or eviction from the land was the fate of many families who could not meet the demands of rapacious tax farmers. Both Rumelia and Anatolia were affected, but peasant discontent in Rumelia, populated largely by Christians, was of particular importance in the long term. By the end of the eighteenth century, nationalist leaders would be able to take advantage of the discontent for their own purposes.

Second, the abandonment of the timar system reduced the number of loyal cavalrymen in rural areas. As a result, administrative and police authority declined in the countryside. Combined with the increasing resentment expressed by the peasant class, this development had serious consequences for centralized control. Until the last decade of the sixteenth century, rural revolts had been a recurring feature of Anatolian life, but the army had always been able to suppress them. Beginning in the 1590s, such revolts were far more difficult to contain. Between 1596 and 1608, the famous Jelali revolts produced a state of anarchy in large parts of western and central Anatolia. The earliest Jelali leaders were former cavalrymen who had been dispossessed of their livelihoods. The rebels looted villages, drove many peasants from their lands, and threatened to sack even the largest cities. The uprisings forced the government to incur the expense of establishing permanent garrisons of Janissary troops in the troubled regions. Sporadic Jelali revolts continued into the 1640s. By that time, the upheavals had led to disruptions in trade and agricultural production. The empire's population, which had been increasing for a century, began to decline.

A third consequence of the reforms was that the Janissary corps of the seventeenth and eighteenth centuries was quite different from the unit that had been formed of slaves. In the seventeenth century, the Janissaries who were assigned to provincial garrisons to keep the peace gradually melted into the local civilian population and became shopkeepers, butchers, and bakers while still retaining their membership on the military rolls. Many refused to report for service when needed in the wars against Austria, citing their responsibilities in their businesses. Unable to count on its own troops to report for duty, the central government had become stretched to the limit in order to fight external wars and suppress internal rebellions. It was forced to cede responsibility for local governance to landlords and merchants who, as local notables, carried out the functions of the state with or without the sanction of the central government. The Ottoman state was in the process of decentralization and fragmentation of authority precisely at the time when European rulers were centralizing control into their hands. The consequences of these opposing trends would be revealed in the eighteenth century.

Portrait of an Ottoman Gentleman

Turkish ethnicity was not a requirement for admission into the ranks of the Ottoman ruling elite, but a mastery of Ottoman culture and manners was. We can catch a glimpse of the Ottoman ethos in a description of one of the most powerful men in seventeenth-century Ottoman life, Melek Ahmed Pasha (1588–1662). Melek was a member of the Abkhazian ethnic group in the Caucasus. His father was an important military officer whose connections enabled him to find a sponsor who presented Melek to the court when Melek was fourteen. His talents proved to be worthy of the recommendation, and he eventually married Kaya Sultan, the daughter of Sultan Murat IV (ruled 1623–1640). He was governor in several sensitive posts, and he served as the empire's grand vizier in 1650. One of Melek's protégés, Evliya Çelebi, wrote this description of his patron, who had died several years earlier.

At no time did a falsehood issue from his lips. He spoke little and wept much and laughed sparingly. In his councils he never allowed idle talk and malicious gossip. But if a tasteful witticism was uttered in his presence, he would smile so broadly that you could see his teeth.

(Continued)

He was so scrupulous in his dress that he only wore garments sanctioned by religious law—various cotton stuffs, and those silken weaves and other splendid stuffs not forbidden by the Shari'a. And he was so clean and neat and elegant and refined, that he was famous among the viziers—his skirts were cleaner than the collars of his peers.

Indeed, Melek Pasha was clean-skirted (*i.e.*, chaste) in every respect, and was pure in every respect. He was very upright and pious, learned in religious sciences and active in carrying out religious prescriptions; he was virtuous and abstinent; a perfect *gazi* and brave vizier, the likes of Asaf son of Barakhya (the vizier of Solomon). . . . He was very skilled in archery, which is a Sunna of the Prophet, and in such sports as javelin throwing, swordplay, mace, and spear. And among his peers only Ipşir Pasha and Seydi Ahmet Pasha could rival him in horsemanship and cavalry exercises. Being a strong and courageous champion, he was also unexcelled in wrestling, familiar with seventy branches of that science: very few champions could bring his back to the ground. But sometimes he would have nice wrestling matches with his wife Kaya Sultan, for the propagation of the species. In the end he would overcome Kaya Sultan and bring her down. He engaged in this sort of "greatest jihad" forty-eight times a year—he did not indulge overmuch in sexual intercourse.

He read a good many books on the science of grammar; and was without equal in the science of canon law, particularly the laws of inheritance. He had by heart over 800 problems of the Shari'a and over 1000 prophetic Hadiths. Because he was inclined to the dervish path, he had on the tip of his tongue several thousand verses of the noble *Mesnevi* of Mevlana (Rumi) and the *Manevi* of Ibrahim Gülşeni, plus Persian and Turkish odes and mystical ghazels that he could recite at appropriate occasions.

In the science of calligraphy he . . . had been authorized by Sultan Murat IV to draw the illustrious *tuğra*, and under his tutelage he learned to draw it in a manner that rivaled the pens of Bihzad and Mani. Koca Nişancı Ankebut Ahmed Pasha, Nasuh-paşa-zade, Ömer Beg, and our head of chancellery Ginagı Efendi—all stood agape at Melek's *tuğra*.

Never did he accept bribes or allow others to accept them, nor did he get posts by means of bribery. Rather, he accepted dismissal from office. Of course, he did use to send some of the specialities of the regions he was governing, or some thoroughbred horses, as gifts to the imperial stirrup [the sultan] and to the viziers and deputies.

Source: Evliya Çelebi, *The Intimate Life of an Ottoman Statesman: Melek Ahmed Pasha (1588–1622): As Portrayed in Evliya Çelebi's Book of Travels (Seyahat-name)*. Translation and commentary by Robert Dankoff. Albany: State University of New York Press, 1991, 277–281.

Religious Unrest

The decline of central power became clear with the rise to prominence at the palace of religious reformers who never would have gained the ear of Suleyman or his predecessors. As the number of recruits of the devshirme system declined, important posts that had formerly been filled by slaves went to members of powerful Ottoman families instead. These families sought to improve their position both at court and in the provinces by creating coalitions to put pressure on the sultan and vizier to achieve a desired goal. Coalitions were particularly effective when they included Janissaries: In the seventeenth century, palace coalitions involving the Janissaries deposed and even killed sultans. As a result, sultans found it expedient to ally themselves with whatever interest groups could help them weather political storms. During the 1630s, a religious reform movement offered the young Murat IV (1623–1640) a welcome ally.

Murat inherited the throne at the age of twelve, after the deposition of the mentally ill Mustafa (1618), the deposition and murder of Osman II (1622), and the second deposition of Mustafa (1623). Murat's mother served as his regent during the 1620s, when wars with the Safavids were a constant drain on the treasury. The nearly constant warfare, inflation, and the Jelali revolts took their toll on the psyche of much of the population. In 1632, a Janissary revolt forced Murat to dismiss some of his highest officials and to execute another. The following year, a fire burned one-fifth of Istanbul. Social unrest was common. It was then that the religious reformers seized the opportunity to exert influence with the sultan.

The reformers were from among the lower-ranking members of the ulama. They were led by Kadizade ("Son of a Qadi") Mehmet Efendi, an influential mosque preacher. Because of his role, the movement came to be known as the Kadizadeli movement. Mehmet Efendi and his followers were concerned about a massive rise in the popularity of Sufism. This development was troubling for two major reasons: First, the reformers were hostile to Sufi practices that could not be justified by the Qur'an or the Sunna of the Prophet. The increased popularity of Sufism may well have been due to the need that people felt for a spiritual refuge in times of trouble, but to the Kadizadelis, the organizations themselves were a major cause of the troubles that the empire was suffering. The reformers condemned the use of music, rhythmic movements, and music in Sufi rituals, and they criticized the popular practice of visiting tombs of Sufi saints in order to obtain a blessing (*baraka*).

The second element of the Sufi movement that caused the Kadizadelis to be alarmed was that several popular Sufi leaders were taking over the pulpits of some of the major mosques. In the elaborate bureaucracy of the Ottoman Empire, men from the upper social classes dominated the higher echelons of the ranks of the ulama, much as the nobility dominated the ranks of the higher clergy in contemporary Christian Western Europe. The lower ulama knew that they would never be considered for the high religious offices in the government, and so they jealously guarded their access to the pulpits of the large congregational mosques. The competition of the Sufi leaders for these positions compounded a genuine religious difference with a social threat.

The Kadizadelis also noted that many Sufis drank coffee and smoked tobacco, activities that took place in coffee houses as well as in Sufi lodges. Coffee had been introduced to Istanbul from Yemen by 1555, and coffee houses soon followed. Tobacco came to the capital city from the Americas in 1601 (even before it was cultivated at Jamestown, in Virginia). By portraying coffee and tobacco in a negative light, the reformers cast Sufis into disrepute: Coffee and tobacco were reprehensible products on the grounds that they were mind-altering drugs; the practice of smoking tobacco could easily be blamed for the 1633

Istanbul fire; and the coffee houses were suspected of encouraging loitering, gossip, and illicit behavior.

For most of the period between 1633 and 1683, the Kadizadeli movement exercised influence on domestic policy. Mehmet Efendi convinced Murat IV that Sufi deviations had led to a weakened society, leaving the empire vulnerable to its foreign enemies, and that coffee houses were centers of sedition, where plots were hatched to overthrow the government. In 1633, Murat IV closed the coffee houses of Istanbul and made smoking a capital offense. During the remainder of the decade, thousands of Ottoman subjects were dismembered or impaled for the crime of smoking tobacco. After Murat died in 1640, the Kadizadelis continued to win favor at the palace. They managed to raze a Sufi lodge in 1651 and obtained a fatwa to ban music and dancing in Sufi ceremonies. When they tried to kill a Sufi leader in 1656, however, a new vizier banned their leaders.

Sufis had a respite from the reformers for only five years. In 1661, a plague killed thousands of people in Istanbul. In a desperate search for remedies, yet another vizier allowed the Kadizadelis to return to the palace. Sufis had to exercise caution for the next two decades until the Kadizadelis began to overreach again. They demanded that non-Muslims be forced to wear distinguishing clothing, be prohibited from producing and selling wine, and be prohibited from living in Istanbul. The sultan refused all of these demands, and patience with the group began to wane. In 1683, the Kadizadeli leader's prayers and exhortations at the siege of Vienna not only failed to win a victory for Ottoman troops, but were followed by a catastrophic loss. He was banished, and the Kadizadeli movement withered away.

The Tide Turns

Despite the turmoil of the seventeenth century, it was not clear for some time that the empire had actually been weakened compared to its rivals. During the first half of the seventeenth century, the Ottomans signed a treaty with their arch-enemy, the Safavid regime of Iran, and light skirmishes with Austria in western Hungary did not reveal major problems in the military's condition. It was only during the last quarter of the century that it became clear that the empire was no longer the dominant power that it once had been. Economic slumps and social unrest prompted the Ottoman vizier to attack Vienna in 1683 as a way of shaking the empire out of its malaise. The siege of the city was broken, however, by a coalition of European armies that came to Vienna's rescue, and the Ottoman army was routed. The Austrians quickly occupied Hungary and joined with Venice, Poland, and Russia in an alliance against the Ottomans. The empire had to fight in the Aegean, central Europe, and the northern coast of the Black Sea, and its resources were slowly ground down. In 1699, in the Treaty of Karlowitz, the Ottomans formally recognized the loss of Hungary and Transylvania to Austria. They ceded southern Greece and islands in the Aegean and the eastern coast of the Adriatic to Venice. Russia gained a foothold on the Black Sea. The Ottomans had lost their aura of invincibility, but everyone at the time realized that it had required a coalition of European powers sixteen years to force a treaty from them. The empire remained a dangerous foe throughout the first half of the eighteenth century. It defeated Russia's

Peter the Great in 1711, and although it lost to the Austrians in 1718, it defeated them in 1739.

Europe was obviously becoming more dynamic, and features of its culture began to intrigue many leading Ottomans. The most conspicuous borrowings from Europe during the 1720s and 1730s took place among the social elite, who became fascinated with European furniture styles, clothing fashions, and gardens. A reforming vizier acquired a printing press and announced sweeping military reforms patterned after European models. The proposed reforms, however, came to nothing at the time. The ulama forced the removal of the printing press, and the Janissaries, realizing that the reorganization, new weapons, and rigorous training programs would undermine their privileged position, used violence to force cancellation of the military reforms.[3]

The victory over Austria in 1739 seems to have calmed the unease among the Ottoman ruling class that the empire had lost its competitive ability. Reform movements that had been producing a momentum for change during the previous half-century were allowed to wither and die at the very time that European nations were developing new technologies and organizational techniques that would create a severe imbalance of power between them and the Ottomans. Although western and eastern Europe developed in quite different ways during the eighteenth century, both regions pulled ahead of the Ottomans in military and economic power by the mid-eighteenth century. The stage was set for a series of catastrophic setbacks for the Ottoman Empire beginning in the second half of the century.

The Arabian Peninsula

Islam appeared first in Mecca, in the Arabian Peninsula. The Prophet later established the seat of his Islamic state at Medina, some two hundred miles to the north (see Map 3.2). After the Prophet's death in 632, Medina served as the de facto capital of the Muslim world until 661, when the Umayyad dynasty began its rule at Damascus. Thereafter, despite the peninsula's location as the geographic center of the Dar al-Islam, large areas of its vast expanse were at the margins of economic and cultural developments that were taking place within Muslim society. Some of the peninsula's regions were so remote and so rarely visited that they became refuges for Muslims who rejected the decisions taken by the far larger Sunni and Twelver Shi'ite movements. On the other hand, a few cities were the object of heavy international traffic, either for religious or commercial reasons.

The Holy Cities

Mecca and Medina were obvious exceptions to generalizations about the remoteness of the peninsula. Both cities were located in the Hijaz, the plateau that slopes eastward from the northern half of the peninsula's Red Sea coastline. Mecca was the goal of the hajj, or pilgrimage, that each Muslim is expected to perform at least once if possible. Travel was so slow and dangerous until the twentieth century that only a tiny minority of Muslims were actually able to perform the hajj. Nevertheless,

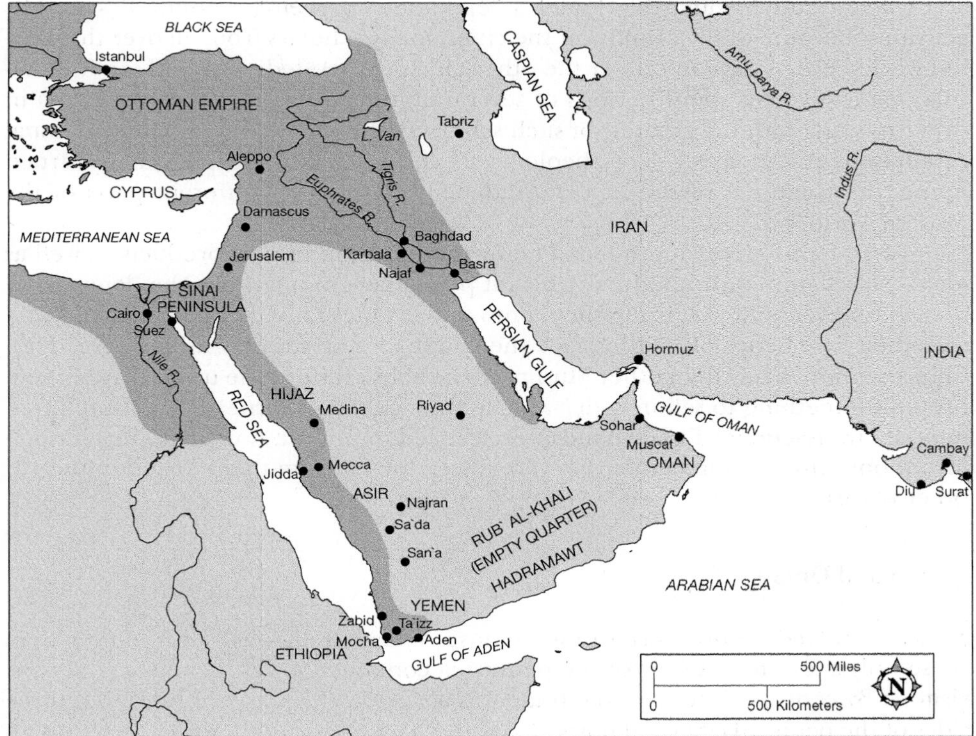

MAP 3.2 The Arabian Peninsula in the Mid-Sixteenth-Century.

tens of thousands of pilgrims arrived in Mecca each year, straining facilities and resources to the utmost. Medina, as the seat of the Prophet's government and his burial site, was usually included on the itinerary of pilgrims who performed the pilgrimage.

The hajj is not merely a ritual obligation. Especially for the faithful who live a long distance away, performing the pilgrimage is a deeply emotional, and occasionally life-changing, experience. The effect is felt immediately upon arriving at the boundaries of the sacred precinct around Mecca, when the pilgrim performs ritual ablutions and exchanges his or her clothing for the simple cloths required by the rituals. Having entered a state of sanctification, the pilgrim's spiritual antennae become much more sensitive than ever before. To touch the Ka'ba—previously only the imagined object of the direction of one's prayers—during the circumambulation of that venerable structure, to walk where the Prophet himself walked, and to stand where the Prophet preached his last sermon are simultaneously humbling and joyous experiences. The faithful are intensely aware that they are not only at the center of the Muslim world, but also at the very birthplace of the faith. It is unusual not to feel that one has encountered the holy in that place, or to leave without recommitting oneself to God's will.

Mecca and Medina developed a reputation for being centers of scholarly activities. Because of the sanctity of the cities, many scholars from all over the Muslim world chose to live in one or the other city for extended periods. Like Ibn Battuta, many pilgrims spent periods of several months to many years in the area in order to study with the greatest of such scholars, who had developed international reputations for their legal or theological expertise. As these pilgrims returned home, the teachings of the scholars radiated out to many different parts of the Muslim world.

Mecca and Medina were centers for the diffusion of new products as well as ideas. Merchants constituted a significant percentage of pilgrims. The demands of their business might well bring them onto trade routes flanking the peninsula, and thus they were better placed to make the hajj than most other Muslims were. They were also more likely than other Muslims to be able to afford the trip. Many of them brought something to sell in order to help finance their journey. As a result, international transactions of many kinds were carried out in the two cities. Techniques, inventions, information, and crops were disseminated from them to a multitude of other places.

Yemen and Oman

Mecca and Medina prospered only because of their religious status. Other than these holy sites, the interior of the peninsula contained no attractions for outside visitors. By contrast, international trade was active on the seas that bordered three sides of the peninsula. Several ports along the coasts were highly attractive to Indian Ocean merchants. Whereas most of the peninsula remained isolated from important cultural and economic developments, two regions located on corners of the peninsula—Yemen and Oman—played significant historical roles during our period.

Yemen

Yemen had been wealthy in pre-Islamic times, but the waning international demand for its incense left it to wither economically by the seventh century. Its precipitous mountain ranges and remote valleys provided refuges for two religious minorities that flourished for centuries. During the late ninth century, the Zaydi and Isma'ili movements became established in Yemen and have maintained a presence there ever since. The Zaydis became associated with the northern city of Sa'da, whereas the Isma'ilis found their strongest support in the central region between San'a and Ta'izz.

In 1174, Saladin, the ruler of Egypt, sent an army to conquer Yemen. His Ayyubid dynasty acquired all but the most inaccessible Zaydi regions of northern Yemen, but it left no lasting imprint in the country. The Ayyubids were distracted from Yemen by the third, fifth, and sixth Crusades, as well as by family quarrels. One of their governors in Yemen, 'Umar ibn al-Rasul, took advantage of Cairo's preoccupation with other matters. He became independent in 1228, inaugurating the two most flourishing centuries in Yemeni history during the Islamic period.

The Rasulid capital was in Ta'izz, but the dynasty placed a premium on developing the Red Sea coast as well as the port of Aden, on the southwestern tip of the peninsula. The Red Sea had long had a reputation as a dangerous region to sail, due to its many coral reefs and pirate dens. As a result, sailors on vessels that plied the Indian Ocean were reluctant to enter the sea. Aden, however, became a major port of call. Located at the entrance to the Red Sea, its distinguishing feature was a gray and black volcanic crater, ringed by red, jagged cliffs, which created one of the finest harbors in the world. Numerous ships docked there every year. Those carrying goods from the Indian Ocean basin unloaded their cargoes and replaced them with goods from Egypt. Other ships then took the goods that had been off-loaded at Aden and embarked on the risky voyage to Egypt.

Aden developed a reputation for handling the greatest and most lucrative trade in the world. It was the indispensable axis in the maritime trade of the western half of the Indian Ocean. The port linked Calicut, Cambay, and Hormuz with Kilwa and Mogadishu, as well as with Jidda, the city where pilgrims to Mecca disembarked. Aden offered travelers in the Indian Ocean banking services, transportation in every direction, and a remarkably wide variety of goods for sale. North of Aden, in a fertile and well-watered section of the Red Sea coast, the city of Zabid attracted a considerable number of wealthy merchants and became an international center of scholarship, especially in the field of Shafi'i law. It had so many schools that it came to be known as "the city of universities."

Rasulid power began slipping away during the first half of the fifteenth century, and Yemen became fragmented once again. The primary beneficiary of the changes were the Zaydis, who reasserted their power in the northern and central regions. The Rasulids were finally overthrown in 1454. Little more than four decades later, the Portuguese entered the Indian Ocean and a new era of struggle for Yemen began. Vasco da Gama sailed to India in 1498, and the Portuguese quickly seized control of numerous ports all along the ocean's rim.

Afonso de Albuquerque, who soon became governor of Portuguese possessions in India, sought to destroy Muslim commerce in the Indian Ocean. He placed a premium on seizing Aden. Albuquerque led an attack on the city in 1513 but failed to capture it. He then sailed into the Red Sea, hoping to make contact with Prester John, the king who, in the European imagination, would join forces with Europe to defeat Islam. Each generation had identified Prester John with a different region and monarch, much as each generation identified the Anti-Christ with a different individual or institution. Christians were convinced that Prester John's wealth and huge army would be decisive in extirpating Islam from the earth. Joining forces with him had been a major objective of Prince Henry the Navigator, who organized the series of Portuguese explorations along the western coast of Africa early in the fifteenth century that laid the foundation for da Gama's voyage.

Albuquerque identified Prester John with the king of Ethiopia. His discovery that the Ethiopian ruler was a mere chieftain and that his reputedly fabulous kingdom was actually a primitive and unstable society was disillusioning and disappointing. The Portuguese and Ethiopians did collaborate several times against Muslim forces in the Red Sea region, but their cultural differences resulted in a bitter split in 1634. The shattering of the Prester John myth brought an end to one of the most durable and motivating of medieval European collective fantasies. It also removed the major remaining reason that Europeans viewed the East with awe and respect. Henceforth, Europeans ventured into the Indian Ocean with the expectation that they could compete with anyone on at least an equal footing.

Upon annexing Syria, Egypt, and the Holy Cities in 1517, the Ottomans became a Red Sea power. They began to monitor the Yemeni coast to ensure that the Portuguese did not threaten it again. In 1538, when Suleyman captured Basra from the Safavids, he discovered that the Portuguese, having taken Hormuz in 1515, threatened every ship that entered or left the Persian Gulf. The Portuguese threat to the shipping of both the Red Sea and the Gulf placed the Ottomans in a vulnerable position. Suleyman ordered a fleet to be organized in the Red Sea. The ships set out from Suez and conquered the Red Sea coast of Yemen en route to Aden. At Aden, the sailors and soldiers launched a surprise attack against the local dynasty that controlled it. They succeeded where the Portuguese had failed, and secured Aden for their empire. Then the fleet sailed for Gujarat with the intention of capturing the Portuguese base at Diu. The fortress there, however, was impregnable, and the siege failed. The Ottomans and Portuguese engaged in several more conflicts in the Arabian Sea. Neither was able to destroy the other.

During the decades that the Ottomans were increasingly focused on Yemen as a security issue, a beverage from the region rapidly became an international sensation. Coffee, which grew on the well-watered mountain slopes of Yemen and Ethiopia, had been used since the mid-fifteenth century by Yemeni Sufis to help them stay awake during their evening devotions. The drink spread to Egypt and Mecca by the beginning of the sixteenth century, and Ottoman chronicles document that it was in Istanbul at least by 1555. Its use in the Holy Cities and in the larger urban centers of the Ottoman Empire provoked a fierce debate that lasted more than a century. Opposition to the drink was generated in part by its status as a stimulant: Some jurists saw an analogy with wine, the use of which is prohibited in Islam.

Perhaps even more problematic, however, was that the beverage came to be enjoyed as a social drink. Soon, coffee houses sprang up. The coffee house was a brand new secular institution, and its potential for mischief was the feature that was uppermost in the minds of some moralists. Restaurants did not exist at that time, and night life had been limited to the tavern, gambling house, or Sufi lodge. The convivial conversations, gossiping, board games, and live entertainment of coffee houses led many pious observers to conclude that the coffee house was the moral equivalent of the clearly disreputable tavern and gambling den. Moreover, it became clear that the coffee house could provide a setting for plots against the government, which was a major reason why Murat IV later closed coffee houses on pain of death. The establishments remained closed in the capital city for over forty years, to the anguish of many.

The use of coffee quickly spread to Europe. European demand for the product revived the Yemeni economy. Because the city of Mocha (Mukha) became the exclusive point of export for coffee, its name became forever associated with the beverage. Huge quantities of coffee were shipped to the warehouses of Cairo for distribution all over the Mediterranean and to northern Europe. Mocha became a fashionable and cosmopolitan city. English, French, Dutch, and Hindu merchants

The home of a wealthy seventeenth-century merchant in Mocha, Yemen.

competed with Yemenis in building fine homes that graced the otherwise bleak landscape around the city.

The Ottomans captured San'a in 1547, but they never had a secure hold on Yemen outside the major cities. The Zaydis fiercely resisted Ottoman attempts to expand. They even captured and ruled San'a and Aden temporarily. Because of them, Yemen developed a reputation as a graveyard for Ottoman soldiers. In 1598 a new, charismatic Zaydi Imam began a concerted effort to evict the Ottomans, and by 1631 the empire retained only a small area around Zabid. Istanbul soon ordered the evacuation of all Ottoman soldiers. For the next three centuries, Zaydi Imams were the effective power in the highlands of Yemen.

Zabid and Mocha, both on the coastal plain, continued to be important cities into the eighteenth century. Zabid played an important role in the diffusion of religious ideas throughout the Muslim world. Scholars from as far away as Southeast Asia and western China came to Zabid to study, and they took home with them ideas that transformed their societies. Mocha's coffee trade grew until it peaked in the period 1720–1740. By then, the Dutch realized that their control over several volcanic islands in Southeast Asia provided them with an ideal setting for growing duty-free coffee. Java soon replaced Yemen as the world's primary source of coffee and joined Mocha as a moniker for the beverage itself.

After the decline of Mocha and Zabid in the late eighteenth century, the interior of Yemen had almost no contact with the outside world until the second half of the twentieth century.

In stark contrast to the growing isolationism of the interior of Yemen, the southern rim of the Arabian Peninsula maintained active contact with all ports all around the Indian Ocean basin. Hadramawt, the eastern extension of modern Yemen, was engaged in international commerce from at least as early as 1000 B.C.E., when it was a major source of frankincense. During the period from the fifteenth through the eighteenth centuries, Hadramawti families migrated to East Africa, South Asia, and Southeast Asia in search of commercial opportunities. In each of the regions, individual Hadramawtis played important roles in commercial, political, or religious affairs.

Oman

International commerce thrived in the Persian Gulf. The history of the Gulf has been shaped by the fact that the Arabian coast is not as well suited to receive shipping as the Iranian coast. The water off the Arabian coast is shallow and littered with shoals and reefs. Fresh water is in short supply, and there are no natural harbors. For most of recorded history, the population of the interior was sparse and poor. Other than the pearls that local divers retrieved at great risk to their lives, the coast did not offer foreign merchants products they could not find more easily elsewhere. The Iranian coast, by contrast, had deep water, a few natural harbors, slightly better access to fresh water, and advanced societies in the interior that desired to engage in long-distance trade. A succession of wealthy trading cities appeared on the coast—or on islands just off the coast—in the Strait of Hormuz. By 1300 the dominant city was Hormuz, located on a remarkably barren, salt-encrusted island that had to have water brought from the mainland. Despite its lunar landscape, the city was wealthy and cosmopolitan, attracting merchants from all around the Indian Ocean basin.

During the thirteenth and fourteenth centuries, the rulers of Hormuz were Arabs from Oman. Oman, located just outside the Gulf, was oriented toward the Indian Ocean. It has been described as an island, for it is surrounded on three sides by the ocean and on the northwest by the Rub‘ al-Khali, or Empty Quarter. The Empty Quarter is the most formidable of all the deserts in Arabia. Its gigantic sand dunes and waterless wastes served for centuries as a defense shield for Oman against invasion from the interior. On the Omani coast, the port of Sohar was the most important until the fifteenth century, when Muscat began to eclipse it. Both were well situated to take advantage of the maritime traffic that plied the coastal waters between Hormuz and Aden.

Because Oman was isolated from the rest of the peninsula except by sea, it was attractive to the Ibadis, a religious minority that arrived in the middle of the eighth century. The Ibadis were the result of a development within the Kharijite group, which gained a reputation in the first Islamic century for regarding all Muslims who did not agree with them as infidels who deserved to be killed. Because of their intolerance and aggressiveness, the Kharijites were feared and hated by the majority of Muslims. One community of Kharijites in Basra, however, developed a theology and system of ethics that stressed coexistence with the larger Muslim community. They preferred to remain at arm's length from the corrupting influences of the majority culture rather than to provoke it. The Ibadis were one group within this moderate faction, deriving their name from one of their leaders, 'Abd Allah ibn Ibad. They sent missionaries as far afield as North Africa, Khorasan, Yemen, and Oman.

The Ibadis feared persecution as well as spiritual contamination by contact with sinners, and so they established themselves in the interior of Oman, away from the port cities. Individual Ibadis lived on the coast, but the ports were typically controlled by outsiders. The Ibadis became famous for their horse breeding. They supplied huge numbers of horses to India, especially to Delhi, after the thirteenth century. Hindu merchants set up holding pens in Muscat to ship the animals to India.

Oman's strategic location caught the attention of Albuquerque, who was determined that Portugal would control its coast. In 1507, he seized the important Omani port cities, and within a few years the Portuguese constructed the two picturesque forts that still stand high above Muscat's harbor. With the seizure of Hormuz in 1515, the Portuguese seemed to be in total control of the Gulf. The Ottomans, who captured Basra from the Safavids in 1538, made periodic attempts to evict the Portuguese, but their long imperial frontiers made too many demands on them to focus on their Iberian rivals. They sacked Portuguese-held Muscat twice, in 1551 and 1581, but did not secure it.

In 1624, Ibadi elders elected a new Imam who considered it his mission to evict the Portuguese from Oman. The Omanis captured Sohar in 1643 and Muscat in 1650, establishing Ibadi power on the coast for the first time. For the next several decades the Omanis were at war with the Portuguese at sea. They attacked the Portuguese on the Malabar Coast, on the Iranian coast, and in East Africa. In several East African ports they replaced the Portuguese as colonial powers.

This first attempt to create an Omani empire was not an economic success. Portuguese privateers and naval vessels harassed Omani shipping, and Muscat was not able to establish a profitable commercial network among its various holdings in Oman and East Africa. The Omanis were unable to establish a respectable reputation among international merchants due to the fact that they continued the practice of attacking and seizing ships that they had begun against the Portuguese decades earlier. Between 1680 and 1730, Oman developed an international reputation as a den of pirates.

In 1719, a dispute over succession to the Imamate resulted in the outbreak of vicious fighting among the tribes. Over the next thirty years, tens of thousands of Omanis died in a civil war. The chaos allowed Nadir Shah, the ruler of Iran, to occupy much of the Omani coast, including Muscat and Sohar. Ahmad ibn Sa'id became famous for his resistance against the Iranians and claimed the credit for their final expulsion in 1748. In the following year, Ahmad ibn Sa'id was elected Imam, and he began to consolidate power. He laid the foundations for a regional empire that flourished in the nineteenth century. His dynasty, the Al bu Sa'id, has continued to rule Oman to the present.

The Eurasian Steppes

Unlike the Ottomans, the Golden Horde was not able to recover from Timur's onslaught. During the 1390s, Timur systematically destroyed the trading cities of the steppe from the Black Sea to the Aral Sea. New Saray and Astrakhan were among those that he demolished. Long-distance trade was diverted permanently northward into Russia and southward into Iran. Moreover, the merchant and artisanal classes were shattered, with catastrophic results for cultural life and technology. Literature, art, and architecture never recovered, and the Horde lost its ability to manufacture firearms, just as its enemies were equipping themselves with them. In 1408 Moscow refused to pay tribute, and the Horde was unable to force it to do so. A new era had begun in Russia (see Map 3.3).

The Horde remained a dangerous force in Russia for several decades due to the quick-strike ability of its horse-mounted warriors, but it was never able to recover the territories it had lost. In the fourteenth century, the Horde had ruled over the Qipchaq steppe as well as Ukraine. It also exacted tribute from numerous Russian cities outside its area of direct control. By the fifteenth century, only the steppe remained, and even it was becoming threatened in the east by a cluster of Mongol–Turkish clans from Siberia. These were the Uzbeks, who migrated southward to the valley of the Syr Darya River during the first decades of the fifteenth century.

MAP 3.3 The Golden Horde and Its Successors.

The loss of tribute from the forested areas and the constriction of the steppe led to clashes among leading families regarding the distribution of resources. The Horde rapidly fragmented. During the 1430s and 1440s, it broke into four major independent khanates: the nomadic khanate of Sibir, which later gave its name to Siberia; the city-based khanates of Kazan and Astrakhan on the Volga; and the khanate of Crimea. The Horde itself was relegated to a nomadic existence west of the Volga. It gradually withered in importance until the Crimean khanate destroyed it in 1502. As the final destruction of the Horde suggests, the new khanates did not cooperate with each other. The Crimean khans, when they were not raiding Muscovy, consistently supported the Orthodox Muscovites against Muslim Astrakhan, and Astrakhan supported the Catholic Lithuanians against the Muscovites and the Crimeans.

The breakup of the Golden Horde coincided with the rise of Muscovy. A tribute-paying province of the Horde since the time of Batu, Muscovy had prospered during the thirteenth and fourteenth centuries. It took advantage of the warm relations between the Horde and the Byzantines to establish close commercial ties with Constantinople, and its capital of Moscow became the primary seat of the Orthodox Church in Russia. Its economy benefitted from Timur's destruction of the Horde's cities, for it lost rivals and gained the commerce that they had handled.

With the fragmentation of the Horde in first half of the fifteenth century, Muscovy no longer had to worry about domination by Tatars. Beginning with the reign of Ivan IV, "The Terrible" (1547–1584), Muscovy went on the offensive against them. It conquered and annexed Kazan and Astrakhan in 1552 and 1556, respectively. Ivan attacked Sibir in 1582, and it fell to Muscovy by 1600. Long-held grievances against the Tatars resulted in a Muscovite policy of expulsion of Tatars from cities, distribution of their land among Russian nobles and the Russian church, and colonization of the annexed regions by Russian peasants. Mosques were destroyed and Qur'an schools were closed. For the next two hundred years, many of the rural rebellions in Russia contained elements of Muslim anger and desperation. For the Russian elite, however, the instability was a small price to pay for removing the obstacles that had lain between them and expansion to the Pacific.

Of the four successor khanates, the one in the Crimea survived the longest. Founded about 1440, its history extended across more than three centuries. Like all the other khanates that broke away from the Horde, it retained almost no trace of its Mongol heritage. It was clearly a Qipchaq Turkish, or Tatar, society. Just over a decade after its founding, the Ottomans captured Constantinople and became a Black Sea power. The two Turkish societies worked out a modus vivendi that allowed them to cooperate rather than fight. The Ottoman sultan gained the right to confirm the choice of the Crimean khan and to use Crimean troops in his military campaigns, and the Crimeans enjoyed the protection and commercial advantages of the powerful Ottoman Empire. For the next two hundred years, tens of thousands of Crimean Tatars served as scouts, couriers, and raiders in Ottoman armies as far away as Hungary and Iran.

The khanate thrived on a mixture of agriculture and slave trading. Unlike the Golden Horde in its heyday, which worked out a tribute system with the cities of the eastern European steppes, the Crimean Tatars viewed such cities as fields where slaves could be harvested. Crimean slave raids penetrated as far as Vilnius and Moscow. As a result, the Qipchaq steppe, never densely populated, became a no-man's land where few dared to live. By the early sixteenth century, the only communities to be found there were self-governing villages along the Dnieper and Don rivers inhabited by Cossacks. *Cossack* is a Slavic derivation of the Turkish *kazakh,* which means "adventurer" or "free person." The term was originally applied to semi-independent groups of Tatars on these rivers, but by the end of the fifteenth century it was also applied to Slavic peasants who fled from serfdom in Poland, Lithuania, and Muscovy. The latter group eventually became exclusively identified with the term.

The Cossacks fished and hunted, engaged in limited agriculture, and raided neighboring territories. They owed allegiance to no government and could prove a threat to Tatars, Poland, and Muscovy alike. During the second half of the sixteenth century, several of the Cossack groups worked out arrangements with Poland and Muscovy to protect their frontiers from the Tatars. The decisive event that led to the cooperative relationships seems to have been a devastating Tatar raid on Moscow in 1570. After looting the city, the Tatars set it on fire. Thereafter, both Muscovy and the Polish nobility sought arrangements with the Cossacks, who began a systematic policy of raiding Tatar communities and intercepting Tatar raiding parties on their return from the north.

Because of its close contacts with the Ottoman Empire, the Crimean khanate became the most sedentary and Islamic of the Tatar khanates. Some of the Crimean khans became famous as poets and patrons of the arts. Islam permeated the majority culture: Property that had been consecrated to religious or charitable purposes (*waqf*s) amounted to one-fourth of all the land in the khanate. By 1783, the Crimea had 1500 mosques and a large number of religious scholars. From its earliest history, the khanate had a diverse population of Genoese, Iranians, Greeks, and Armenians in addition to its majority Turkish population. As in the Ottoman Empire, non-Muslims operated most trading, shipping, and banking enterprises.

During the seventeenth century, the balance of power shifted decisively away from the Tatars and toward the Russians. Under Peter the Great (1689–1725), Muscovy became known as Russia, and it began a military modernization program. Russia resumed the expansionist program that had made Muscovy so dynamic in the fifteenth and sixteenth centuries. It soon cowed Sweden, Lithuania, and Poland, and it was determined to extinguish the Muslim threat to the south and gain access to the Black Sea. The Russians also began to adopt agricultural techniques developed in northwestern Europe during the Middle Ages. The moldboard plow, larger plow teams, and new property concepts made cultivation of the steppe more practicable and investment in the region more attractive. The Cossack "screen" that had slowed the Tatar raids was now supplemented by the development of a Russian standing army, and the line of Russian settlement expanded inexorably southward.

The defeat of the Ottomans by the European alliance at the end of the seventeenth century and the resulting Treaty of Karlowitz were major blows to the Tatars. The Ottomans were forced to pledge that they and the Tatars would cease their raiding into Russia. The Tatars ignored the provision and continued their raids, but without Ottoman support they were not powerful enough to escape retribution for the raids or to impose tribute. As a result, their economy experienced a serious decline. Russia's expanding control of the steppe gradually exhausted the Khanate of Crimea, and Catherine the Great annexed it in 1783.

Conclusion

The Ottoman Empire brought a long period of stability to a wide arc of territory around the eastern half of the Mediterranean basin and the Black Sea. At its height, it brought prosperity and security to a remarkably diverse set of linguistic and religious groups. Its frontiers, bureaucratic structures, and artistic traditions remained powerful forces for centuries. In the seventeenth century, however, its inability to cope with an array of financial, demographic, and social challenges left its central government weakened. No longer able to protect the Balkan peasantry from rapacity and violence, the empire's legitimacy became vulnerable to challenges by Christian and nationalist creeds. The Ottoman loss at Vienna in 1683 showed that the empire was becoming more vulnerable to outside threats, as well. The Treaty of Karlowitz sixteen years later ended a period that had lasted three centuries, during which Europeans had to form a coalition to defeat the "Terrible Turk." During the eighteenth century, its neighbors regarded it merely as one of several powerful European states competing for resources.

The disintegration of the Golden Horde in the sixteenth century entailed the loss of a huge swath of the Muslim world. The loss may not have been significant culturally, because Timur's rampages through the steppe in the 1390s destroyed the Islamic institutions that had begun to flourish in the region's urban centers. The revival of the Horde after Timur's death never developed a momentum that suggested a renaissance of urban life. From a geopolitical standpoint, the collapse of the Horde was momentous. Just as the Ottomans and Mamlukes had blocked European expansion into the Muslim world through southwestern Asia, the Horde had confined Eastern European powers from expanding into the steppes. In the absence of the Horde, the way was open for Muscovy–Russia to expand eastward all the way to the Pacific and southward into the Muslim lands of the Crimea, the Caucasus, and Central Asia. The weakening of the Ottoman Empire and the disintegration of the Horde left many Muslim areas vulnerable to European intervention.

NOTES

1. The official name of the city during Ottoman times was Kostantiniye, but in colloquial speech, a variety of ethnic groups referred to the city by a term that evolved into *Istanbul.* The most widely accepted etymology for the name is that it derived from the phrase *eis tên polin,* which in the colloquial Greek language meant "to the city." Not until 1930, almost a decade after the collapse of the Ottoman Empire, was *Istanbul* used by the postal authority of the Republic of Turkey. Because the name was widely used for centuries in speech, however, it seems fitting to use it to refer to the city after 1453. Not only had the urban area that had once been the greatest capital city of the Christian world become the greatest capital city of the Muslim world, but it had also experienced an immediate economic, demographic, and cultural rebirth after Mehmet II's conquest.

2. See the discussion on the historiography on conversion in the Balkans in Dennis Hupchick, *The Balkans: From Constantinople to Communism* (New York: Palgrave, 2002), 151–156.
3. Francis Robinson makes a convincing argument that the opposition to the printing press in the eighteenth-century Ottoman Empire was due to its disruption of the personal manner in which knowledge was transmitted. Traditionally, Muslims had not assumed that the meaning of a text is self-evident; the purpose of the chain of transmission from scholar to scholar, and the significance of the *ijaza* that a successful student received, was to ensure that the author's meaning had in fact been conveyed in discussion. See Francis Robinson, "Technology and Religious Change: Islam and the Impact of Print," in *Modern Asian Studies* 27, 1 (1993): 229–251.

FURTHER READING

The Ottoman Empire

Barkey, Karen. *Bandits and Bureaucrats: The Ottoman Route to State Centralization.* Ithaca, New York: Cornell University Press, 1994.

Brummett, Palmira. *Ottoman Seapower and Levantine Diplomacy in the Age of Discovery.* Albany: State University of New York Press, 1994.

Hupchick, Dennis. *The Balkans: From Constantinople to Communism.* New York: Palgrave, 2002.

Imber, Colin. *The Ottoman Empire, 1330–1650: The Structure of Power.* Houndmills, U.K., and New York: Palgrave Macmillan, 2002.

Inalcik, Halil, Suraiya Faroqhi, Bruce McGowan, Donald Quataert, and Sevket Pamuk. *An Economic and Social History of the Ottoman Empire.* 2 vols. Cambridge, U.K.: Cambridge University Press, 1994.

Itzkowitz, Norman. *Ottoman Empire and Islamic Tradition.* New York: Alfred A. Knopf, 1972.

Murphey, Rhoades. *Ottoman Warfare 1500–1700.* New Brunswick, New Jersey: Rutgers University Press, 1999.

Pamuk, Sevket. *A Monetary History of the Ottoman Empire.* Cambridge, U.K., and New York: Cambridge University Press, 2000.

Pamuk, Sevket. "The Price Revolution in the Ottoman Empire Reconsidered." *International Journal of Middle East Studies* 33 (2001): 69–89.

Peirce, L. P. *The Imperial Harem. Women and Sovereignty in the Ottoman Empire.* New York: Oxford University Press, 1993.

Petry, Carl. *Protectors or Praetorians? The Last Great Mamluk Sultans and the Waning of Egypt as a Great Power.* Albany: State University of New York Press, 1994.

Robinson, Francis. " Technology and Religious Change in Islam and the Impact of Print," *Modern Asian Studies* 27 (1993): 229–251.

Zilfi, Madeline C. *The Politics of Piety: The Ottoman Ulema in the Postclassical Age (1600–1800).* Minneapolis: Bibliotheca Islamica, 1988.

The Arabian Peninsula

Bidwell, Robin L. *The Two Yemens.* Boulder, Colorado: Westview Press, 1983.

Hattox, Ralph S. *Coffee and Coffeehouses: The Origins of a Social Beverage in the Medieval Near East.* Seattle: Distributed by University of Washington Press, 1985.

Peters, F. E. *The Hajj: The Muslim Pilgrimage to Mecca and the Holy Places.* Princeton, New Jersey: Princeton University Press, 1994.

Risso, Patricia. *Oman & Muscat: An Early Modern History.* New York: St. Martin's Press, 1986.

Silverberg, Robert. *The Realm of Prester John.* Athens: Ohio University Press, 1972.

Wilkinson, John C. *The Imamate Tradition of Oman.* Cambridge, U.K.: Cambridge University Press, 1987.

The Eurasian Steppes

Halperin, Charles J. *Russia and the Golden Horde.* Bloomington: Indiana University Press, 1985.

Hartog, Leo de. *Russia and the Mongol Yoke: The History of the Russian Principalities and the Golden Horde, 1221–1502.* London and New York: British Academic Press and I. B. Tauris Publishers, 1996.

Khodarkovsky, Michael. *Russia's Steppe Frontier: The Making of a Colonial Empire, 1500–1800.* Bloomington and Indianapolis: Indiana University Press, 2002.

Yemelianova, Galina M. *Russia and Islam: A Historical Survey.* Houndmills, U.K., and New York: Palgrave, 2002.

the thirteenth century retained many familiar structures of life. Muslims continued to worship with minimal interference, they were allowed to retain their Shari'a court system, and they remained under the guidance of their market inspectors and qadis.

The tolerable living conditions confronted many Muslims with a dilemma. On the one hand, some of the most respected religious scholars taught that it was incumbent upon pious Muslims to perform *hijra* (emigrate) to Muslim-controlled territory in emulation of the Prophet's trek from heathen Mecca to Medina, and that it was a sin to remain in a land that was not under Muslim authority. On the other hand, the disruption of the wars and the flight of many Muslims had created a labor shortage in the newly conquered lands. King James offered economic inducements to discourage emigration, and Muslims who were willing to stay found ample opportunities for employment.

At first glance, the various Iberian kingdoms appear to have been pluralistic and harmonious. Alongside the Muslim population in the peninsula was a large, highly educated Jewish community. The Christian monarchs had a great stake in maintaining good relations with their non-Christian subjects due to the skills and knowledge that they possessed. In Aragon, the Mudejars were even known as the "Royal Treasure." They were allowed their own institutions as well as practices such as polygyny and the performance of the hajj to Mecca. In actuality, however, each kingdom contained parallel societies that harbored a great deal of mistrust toward each other. Mudejars found that, in spite of the royal decrees that were issued for their benefit, their lives became increasingly constrained by forces beyond the monarch's control. As the number of Christians in a given region reached a critical mass, conditions for the Mudejars often became intolerable. As Christian immigrants settled in Muslim-majority areas, the authority of Muslim market inspectors and qadis diminished, to be superseded by the jurisdiction of royal judges, bailiffs, magistrates, and bishops. Muslims who were under the feudal or legal jurisdiction of local Christian lords often had no appeal to the monarch. Kidnappers frequently seized them and held them for ransom or summarily sold them into slavery. Severe laws governed relations between the sexes of the two communities: A Christian woman who slept with a Muslim male was theoretically liable to being burned, and the man was subject to being drawn and quartered or burned. A Christian man who slept with a Muslim woman, on the other hand, was liable to no penalty at all, but the woman was invariably sold into slavery.

The Mudejars of Valencia may have faced the most difficult conditions, despite the intentions of King John. They were legally forbidden from emigrating, leaving them exposed to numerous types of repression. The Christian lower classes frequently rioted against the presence of the Mudejars, for they regarded them as threats to their economic well-being. At the time of the Black Death in the mid-fourteenth century, many Christians held the Mudejars to be responsible for the plague (a charge made against the Jews in other parts of Europe) and managed to enact restrictions on their ability to travel in an effort to limit their "poisonous" work. Several popes applied pressure on both the Aragonese and Castilian monarchs to convert their Mudejars. The Mudejars who did convert to Christianity, however, discovered that conversion solved no problems for them. Like the Muslim Arabs of the Umayyad period, many Christian lords were determined that they not lose the taxes or the forcible service that they could glean from members of the "protected" religion and refused to recognize their conversion. In addition, many of the so-called Old Christians were suspicious that the new converts were only pretending to have converted. The new converts were often called Christian Mudejars.

The Mudejars desperately tried to maintain their identity in the face of increasing pressures, but they found themselves in a position similar to that of their contemporaries, the Orthodox Christians of Turkish-dominated Anatolia. Both peoples experienced the loss of their cultural elites and of a strong institutional support structure. As a result, their identity and their numbers disintegrated in the face of a more aggressive culture. Many of the Muslim elites had fled Valencia at the time of the conquest, and most of the others who could afford to slip away to North Africa over the following generations did so. The Mudejar community gradually lost its scholars and natural leaders. By the middle of the fourteenth century, Arabic was still the spoken language of the majority in Valencia, but it was difficult to find Mudejars outside Valencia who could speak or read the language. In Castile and northern Aragon, a new religious literature began to evolve among Mudejars that came to be called Aljamiado. Used for translations of the Qur'an and for devotional literature, it was written in the Arabic script, but its vocabulary was that of the local Romance dialect. The loss of the Mudejars' linguistic identity was paralleled by the loss of their economic importance. As the Christian population increased in formerly Muslim territories, the new immigrants learned the skills that had originally made the Mudejars economically valuable, and the Muslims found their opportunities for gaining a livelihood increasingly limited. Gradually, Mudejars sank in status and were treated with derision by Christian society.

Granada

Neither the city of Granada nor the principality that shared its name had played a major role in Andalusian history prior to the thirteenth century. It had been a region of the second rank, always laboring in the shadow of Toledo, Cordoba, or Seville. For two and a half centuries after the fall of Seville and Cordoba, however, the principality of Granada became famous as the last redoubt of Muslim independence in the Iberian Peninsula. Most of Granada was barren and mountainous, but it managed to attain a surprising degree of prosperity. It traded sugar, figs, raisins, and almonds for the grain and olives that it imported from the Maghrib. Its manufactures—particularly its silk and ceramics—were also in high demand throughout North Africa as well as in sub-Saharan Ghana, where merchants were eager to trade gold for them.

In retrospect, it is easy to assume that Granadans must have been constantly preoccupied with the Christian threat from the north after the fall of Toledo in 1085. While there is no doubt that the fear of Christian conquest had to be in the back of everyone's mind after the eleventh century, the rulers knew that there were ways to keep the Christian powers at bay. Granada, like most of the other Muslim principalities of the time, occasionally allied with Christian powers against fellow Muslims. The principality even came to the aid of Castile in its decisive siege of Seville in 1248.

The disappearance of all the other Muslim principalities in the peninsula did not alter the fact that Granada continued to ally at certain times with Christians against Muslims and at other times with Muslims against Christians. Because of the power imbalance in the peninsula after 1248, Granada was contractually bound to pay a tribute to Castile. In order to assert its independence, however, its rulers occasionally refused to pay, incurring Castile's wrath. Granada would thereupon seek the assistance of the Marinid dynasty, which had replaced the Almohads in the Maghrib. When, on the other hand, the Marinids made unwanted demands, Granada sought the assistance of Christian Castile against the Muslim Marinids.

Although the rulers of Granada felt compelled to follow policies that maintained their independence from neighboring states, whether Christian or Muslim, their subjects were clearly influenced by the fact that their society had become isolated and vulnerable as the only Muslim principality on the northern shore of the Strait of Gibraltar. Their knowledge that several popes and many other Christian clerics called for crusades to eliminate Granada as a Muslim presence could only heighten their anxieties. As a result, Granada developed a more self-consciously Islamic and Arabized society than any that had been known in Andalus. Unlike the Mudejars, the Muslims of Granada spoke and wrote only in Arabic. Rulers zealously enforced Maliki law, and Muslims who were not conscientious adherents of ritual detail were subject to punishments. Whereas Jews were allowed to live and work in Granada, Christians were not. In stark contrast to most of the Muslim regimes of Andalus from the eighth to the thirteenth centuries, which had been a stimulating mixture of various races and creeds, Granada began expelling Christians as early as the twelfth century. By the thirteenth century, there is no evidence that any lived in the province.

The second half of the fourteenth century was the high point of Granada's history. Castile and Aragon became embroiled in a series of bloody wars with each other. The Marinid state in the Maghrib was in a state of decline and could not seriously threaten Granada. With Granada's three main rivals preoccupied, it was able to divert some of its wealth from its military forces to internal improvements. Much of the Alhambra palace complex, the most famous architectural monument of the Granadan era, was the work of Muhammad V (1354–1391), the ruler throughout most of this period. His court boasted the presence of several outstanding poets as well as that of two of the world's greatest historians of that era: Ibn Khaldun and Ibn al-Khatib.

We know remarkably little about Granada during the fifteenth century. After Ibn Khaldun and Ibn al-Khatib passed from the scene, no capable historian took their place. Our knowledge of the period derives largely from Arabic narrative poems and reports by Christians from Castile and Aragon. What is clear about Granadan society itself is that long-time rivalries among the great families became even more bitter and divisive. In foreign affairs, the balance of power in the region shifted decisively against Granada. The Marinid sultanate was no longer a factor in international affairs by the fifteenth century and was finally overthrown in 1465. For the first time, Granada was left without a potential ally in North Africa in the case of a crisis on its borders. Meanwhile, Aragon and Castile consolidated their power during the fifteenth century and became more stable and prosperous. In 1469, Ferdinand, the sixteen-year-old heir to the throne of Aragon, married Isabella, the princess of Castile. By 1479, Ferdinand and Isabella were the joint rulers of their respective kingdoms. Legally, Aragon and Castile remained separate kingdoms, but it is useful to begin the history of Spain from the union of the two crowns in 1479.

Moriscos

One of the problems the two young Christian monarchs faced was the growing tension between their Christian and Jewish communities. The dynamics of this conflict, as well as its denouement, foreshadowed that of the subsequent conflict between Christians and Muslims in Spain. Whereas most Mudejars were peasants, workmen, and artisans, Jews had long held positions in the Iberian Christian kingdoms as wealthy merchants, government administrators, and physicians. Their status as wealthy and influential non-Christians provoked the same intensity of anti-Semitism as was to be found in much of the rest of contemporary Europe. On the one hand, the monarchy and the nobility needed their skills and their wealth; on the other hand, many common people resented the high status enjoyed by some Jews. Crowds periodically vented their frustrations in riots. The most severe pogrom occurred in 1391, when mobs sacked the Jewish quarters of Toledo, Cordoba, Seville, Valencia, and Barcelona. Thousands of Jews were killed.

Out of fear of further persecution, many Jews converted to Christianity. These converts, known both as Marranos and Conversos, took advantage of the opportunities that the identity of "Christian" conferred on them. They enjoyed great success in gaining high offices in the municipal and royal governments as well as in the Church. The most spectacular case may well have been that of the rabbi of Burgos, Samuel Levi, who later became the bishop of the same city under the name Pablo de Santa Maria. The assimilation of Jews into Iberian Christian society was so successful that a government report of the mid-fifteenth century stated that almost all of the peninsula's Christian nobility had Converso relatives or ancestors. King Ferdinand himself had Jewish blood in his veins. Many of the "Old Christians," however, were jealous of the success of the "New Christians" and suspicious of their sincerity. They noted that many of them continued to live in the Jewish quarters of the cities, would not eat pork, stayed home on Saturday, and named their children after Old Testament figures. Some Conversos were even openly returning to the faith of their fathers.

The defection of a minority of Conversos back to Judaism was a threat to the position of genuine Jewish converts to Christianity. The issue only compounded Christian suspicions of the genuine Conversos and exacerbated Christian jealousy of the material success of many Conversos. There is evidence that influential Conversos at court and in the Church hierarchy pressed for the creation of the Inquisition to investigate the sincerity of New Christians in order to ferret out those who were likely to become apostates. Genuine Conversos felt that only by this process would their own position be secure. The Inquisition was created in 1478. Its leader was Tomas de Torquemada, himself a descendant of Conversos.

In 1492, the anti-Converso movement expanded into a hysteria against Jews in general. During the same year that Columbus sailed in the name of Queen Isabella, the crown demanded that the Jews of Spain choose between the options of baptism and expulsion. An estimated 50,000 Jews submitted to baptism, even though they knew that Conversos were subject to intense scrutiny and suspicion. Estimates of the number of Jews who refused baptism and went into exile range from 120,000 to more than 400,000. The Spanish monarchs pressured their neighbors to expel their Jews. Portugal complied in 1496, and Navarre followed in 1498. Perhaps 20,000 of the exiles died; some of the survivors found refuge in Italy or Greece, but the majority of them settled in the Muslim lands of North Africa, the Mamluke Empire, or the Ottoman Empire. An estimated 300,000 Conversos or descendants of Conversos remained in Spain. Despite continued persecution, they made major contributions to sixteenth-century Spanish culture, both secular and religious. Included among them were a novelist (Mateo Alemán), perhaps the greatest jurist of the age (the Dominican, Francisco de Vitoria), and a mystical saint who is probably better known today for having been immortalized in stone by Bernini than for her spiritual advice (Teresa of Avila).

In the fifteenth century, Mudejars did not elicit the popular fury among the general Christian population that Jews and Conversos did. Christian hostility was focused on Granada, instead. From 1431 on, Castilian rulers began seizing Granadan frontier towns. Tension between the two powers increased after the capture of Constantinople by the Ottomans in 1453. The pope insisted that a retaliatory blow should be struck for Christendom against the powers of Islam. With pressure rising for decisive action, many Christians in the peninsula began asking why Granada was still allowed to exist. In 1481, Granada launched a raid against Spain. This was only the latest in a series of hundreds of such attacks over the previous centuries, but it provided the pope with the pretext for a crusade. For more than a decade, the papacy and various European powers supplied Spain with arms and money for the final campaign to capture Granada.

Even in their hour of greatest peril, the great families of the last independent Muslim state in the peninsula could not maintain solidarity. The ruler of Granada fell out with his brother and his own son, and a civil war raged among the three family members even as Spanish forces closed in. The ruler's son, Abu 'Abd Allah (known in European romances as Boabdil), made a secret agreement that would allow him to gain control of Granada and then turn it over to Spain. He seized power but refused to surrender the city to Spain. After a huge Spanish army laid siege to Granada, Abu 'Abd Allah agreed to surrender the city in January 1492. He then went into exile in North Africa.

Granada, like the Iberian Muslim cities of the thirteenth century, was granted generous terms of surrender, including the possession of property and freedom of worship. Thousands of Muslim Granadans, however, chose to emigrate to the Maghrib rather than live under Christian rule. They would be glad they did: The expulsion of the Jews in the same year as the fall of Granada seems to have affected the perception of Mudejars by many Christians. A new sense of impatience at the failure of Muslims to convert to Christianity became palpable. In 1499, Archbishop Cisneros of Toledo dismissed the bishop who had been responsible for the sensitive treatment of Muslims in Granada. He assumed control of religious affairs in the province and immediately announced a policy of compulsory conversion of Muslims. He forcibly baptized 3000 Granadans on a single day, imprisoned many Muslims who refused to convert, and burned thousands of Arabic books. Granada responded with a major revolt that was quelled only in 1501.

In retaliation for the uprising, the monarchy issued a decree demanding that all Granadan Muslims choose between conversion and expulsion. In 1502, the court forced the small minority of Mudejars in Castile to make a similar choice. Local Christian authorities, already suffering economically from the expulsion of the Jews, often refused to allow Muslims to leave, forcing them to remain and be baptized. Satisfied with carrying out the formal requirements of the edict, the Spanish authorities pronounced that no Muslims remained in Granada or Castile. The great majority of the "converts," of course, continued to practice Islam secretly.

The authorities soon extended the provisions of the conversion decree to the rest of Spain. In Navarre, local Christians had enjoyed a history of good relations with their Muslim neighbors for centuries. The Muslims of Navarre were prosperous and continued to hold important positions in the army and government. In 1512, however, Spain annexed the country and Muslims began to suffer discrimination. By 1516, the Muslim community ceased to exist. In Aragon, the province of Valencia posed a difficult problem for the monarchy because Muslims composed an estimated one-third of the population even after three hundred years of Aragonese control. Valencia did not see large numbers of conversions to Christianity until after 1525.

Muslims who converted to Christianity were called Moriscos, or "little Moors." The term itself reveals that, even more than Conversos, they were not regarded as genuine Christians. In fact, many Moriscos made little pretense of having converted, for they deeply resented the flagrant violation of the promises of their original conquerors. Throughout the sixteenth century, their relations with the dominant Christian society were strained. They were subject to numerous strictures with regard to their dress, family life, and social institutions. Local courts often ignored illegal seizures of their property by Christians. The Inquisition punished Moriscos who were brought before it on charges of not eating pork. Ascetic Spanish monks who valued bodily dirt as a sign of spiritual purity were successful in closing the public baths that were integral to the Muslim hygienic regimen. In 1566, an edict demanded the surrender of all Arabic books and forbade women to wear a veil. The pressures in Granada became so intolerable that a massive revolt broke out in 1568. The army quelled it in late 1570 only with the aid of Austrian troops. King Philip II ordered all Granadan Moriscos dispersed throughout Castile. Although historians estimate that some 60,000–150,000 Moriscos managed to remain in the south, even larger numbers were dumped, homeless and unemployed, in the towns and villages of Castile.

The tensions between the parallel societies of Spain were heightened by developments within the Mediterranean basin. Spain's ambition to be the premier power in Europe and in the Mediterranean received several challenges during the sixteenth century. The Protestant Reformation, the machinations of the French monarchy, and the rapid expansion of the Ottoman Empire under Selim I and Suleyman made Spaniards nervous. The Ottomans were the most formidable threat. Selim conquered Egypt and Syria in 1517 and Suleyman attacked Habsburg Vienna in 1529. Meanwhile, the Ottomans were sending Janissaries, ships, and funds to support sailors in North Africa who were harassing Spanish shipping. The growing Ottoman involvement in the Maghrib was an intolerable threat to Spanish security.

Increasingly, Spanish Christians regarded the Moriscos as a potential fifth column who would thwart the unity of the country and collude with Spain's enemies. In fact, many Moriscos made no secret of the fact that they hoped that the Ottomans would sooner or later deliver them from oppression. Serious discussions concerning the prospects for expelling the Moriscos were held at the royal court in Madrid as early as 1582, but the obvious difficulties involved in such a project caused the plan to stall. Developments between 1588 and 1609, however, created the climate of opinion that made expulsion a viable political option: The defeat of the Armada by the English in 1588 was a grievous blow to the Spanish self-image; high taxes and currency devaluations led to acute economic problems by the early seventeenth century; and in 1609 the government was forced to sign a truce with the rebellious Dutch because of the near-bankruptcy of the treasury.

The Spanish king signed the royal decree ordering the expulsion of the Moriscos on the same day that he signed the truce with the Dutch. The expulsion was carried out in stages over a five-year period in order to avoid a sudden depletion of the labor force. Estimates of the number of Moriscos who were expelled range from 275,000 to 500,000. Most of them settled in Morocco, Algeria, and Tunisia, but they were not welcomed into economies that could not even support their own populations. Just as they had been regarded as Muslims in Spain, they were often called "Spanish Christians" in North Africa. Thousands died of exposure and malnutrition, and most of the first generation of refugees never fully assimilated into the local society. Had they known, they might have derived some satisfaction from learning that their departure entailed the loss of essential economic skills in Spain. The deportation contributed to the decline of the port city of Seville, agricultural disaster in the Ebro valley, and long-term economic stagnation in Valencia.

As late as the early eighteenth century, individuals were still being hauled before the Spanish Inquisition on charges of practicing Islam. For all practical purposes, however, Islam ended in Spain in 1614 after a nine-hundred-year presence in the peninsula. The influence of Arab–Islamic culture on Spanish place names, the language itself, art and architecture, and mores and customs was profound, although few Spaniards were willing to admit it until the late twentieth century. The dominant historiography portrayed the peninsula's history as Christian and Spanish, interrupted by an unfortunate and easily disregarded period of "Moorish" presence that was reclaimed by the Reconquista. Spanish historians are now making great strides in integrating the Muslim period into the continuum of the peninsula's history and making that history more intelligible and meaningful. What is still unclear is how the tragedy that befell the Jews and the Muslims could have been avoided, given the assumptions and prejudices of all the communities of the day.

The Maghrib

A heavy mist often envelops the Strait of Gibraltar, but when the sun breaks through, sailors enjoy the spectacle of the Rock of Gibraltar to the north and her sister peaks in North Africa—Jabal Acha and Jabal Musa—to the south. These European and African promontories are separated by only fourteen miles. To the ancient Greeks and Romans, they were the Pillars of Hercules and symbolized the edge of the world, beyond which a ship might simply fall into an abyss. The perception that danger lay in wait beyond the Pillars was not far-fetched. Heading west through the strait, sailors left an inland sea for the apparently boundless Atlantic, whose titanic waves could crush or flip a vessel designed for the Mediterranean.

Historically, the strait was a barrier only to east–west travel. It was a bridge, rather than an obstacle, to north–south relations. The migrations, cultural interchange, and maritime trade of the region served to reinforce that fact for centuries. The fifteenth century, however, reversed the relationship. Developments in shipbuilding and navigation enabled European navies to ply the waters of both the Mediterranean and the Atlantic with the same vessels, and the Atlantic became the theater for a vast enterprise of exploration. Simultaneously, relations between Iberian Christians and their Muslim neighbors in the Maghrib deteriorated, generating hostile attitudes on both sides of the strait that made communication and trade difficult. The strait became a cultural as well as a political boundary between Europe and Africa for the first time.

The Land

The Maghrib extends some 2500 miles from the western frontiers of Egypt to the Atlantic (see Map 4.2). Despite the region's enormous size, visitors throughout Muslim history have been struck by the cultural features shared by its constituent societies. Islamic institutions spread rapidly among the mixed Berber and Arab populations, and the Arabic language became the lingua franca. The economy was based on small-scale grain, fruit, and olive gardening; animal herding by pastoral peoples; a small textile manufacturing sector; and a thriving long-distance trade

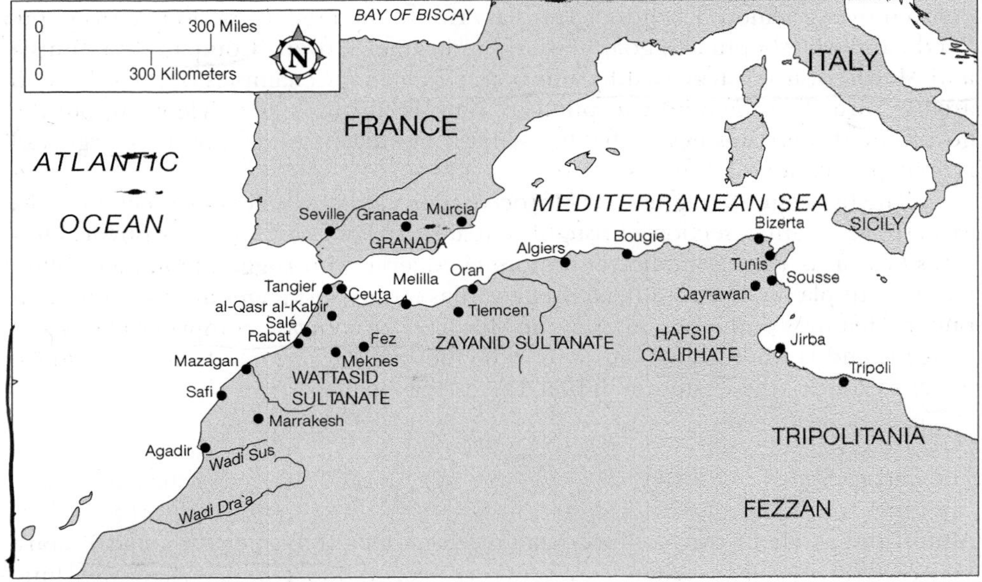

MAP 4.2 The Maghrib in the Early Sixteenth Century.

that linked the Mediterranean with sub-Saharan societies. In contrast to these culturally unifying elements, the Maghrib has been politically unified only a few times throughout history, and even then the actual area under centralized control was usually confined to the narrow coastal plain. Despite the overall pattern of uniformity, the Maghrib also exhibited distinctive regional traits.

The eastern Maghrib is known today as Libya, but historically, its three major regions were considered quite distinct. Cyrenaica, in the east, relied on a traditional economy of nomadic and seminomadic pastoralism. Tripolitania, in the west, benefitted from irrigated agriculture and boasted a region of dense juniper forests. Its chief port city of Tripoli lay on an extremely narrow plain, almost in the desert, and was the terminus of the shortest of all the trans-Saharan trade routes. It was a cosmopolitan city, attracting merchants and craftsmen from many ethnic groups. Fezzan was Libya's third major region. It was a constellation of oasis villages in the desert, some four hundred miles south of Tripoli. It grew cereals necessary for the survival of Tripoli and was a stopping point for trans-Saharan caravans.

Before the sixteenth century, Tripolitania was often regarded as the easternmost extension of the region known to Muslims as Ifriqiya, which extended northward to Tunis and westward to Bougie (modern Bejaia, Algeria). The central core of Ifriqiya became modern Tunisia. Olive gardens and wheat fields have covered the northern half of the Tunisian plain ever since Roman times. Tunis, despite its northerly location, enjoyed the benefits of the trans-Saharan trade. The agriculture and trade of this region allowed Ifriqiya to enjoy a generally prosperous—and occasionally spectacular—level of material life. As a result, it often had a powerful central government.

The central Maghrib, the area we know as Algeria today, extended from the region around Bougie to the vicinity of Tlemcen. Algeria's topography is characterized by an alternating series of mountain ranges and plains. As a result, it has never enjoyed the agricultural riches of Tunisia. Prior to the modern period, it was populated largely by shepherds, goat herders, and camel drovers. Compared to Tunisia and Morocco, it was less wealthy and boasted far fewer examples of great art and architecture. The splendid exception to the rule was the city of Tlemcen, but the government there was never able to establish significant control over its large and mobile population of nomads.

The far western Maghrib, or Morocco, is divided into an eastern section and a western, or Atlantic, section of roughly equal sizes. Eastern Morocco's physical features bear a strong resemblance to those of Algeria, with rugged mountains alternating with plains. The Middle and High Atlas mountain ranges are the dominant physical features of the region. Atlantic Morocco, by contrast, comprises plains and plateaus and is where the majority of the cities are. Governments always found it easier to control the western half than the eastern half.

The Berber States

Almost the whole of the Maghrib was united under the Berber Almohad Empire (1147–1269), which stretched from southern Morocco to Tripoli. When the Almohad regime collapsed, three major Berber successor states arose to fill the vacuum.

In the east, the Hafsid dynasty (1229–1569) was based in Tunis. The Hafsids had been loyal governors in Tunis for the Almohads and had ruled with little supervision during the first decades of the thirteenth century. After the fall of the Almohads, the Hafsid sultans claimed the title of caliph. The dynasty continued the long-standing maritime tradition of Tunisian states, importing timber from as far away as Scandinavia for its busy shipyards. It established commercial treaties with Italian city-states and would have done so with Aragon had it not been for the public outrage that followed Aragon's conquest of Valencia in 1236. Both Aragon and Tunis nevertheless maintained commercial contacts.

The Hafsid sultans were cultivated and civilized men who oversaw a sumptuous court. They commissioned the construction of many of the fine architectural monuments to be seen in Tunis today. Despite their claims to the caliphate, their actual concerns were decidedly secular and cosmopolitan. During the third quarter of the thirteenth century, in the immediate aftermath of the fall of most of the city-states of Andalus to the Reconquista, the caliphs permitted Dominican and Franciscan friars to preach Christianity to Muslims. They also employed Christian mercenary troops (largely from Aragon) in their army and palace guard.

The chief threat to the Hafsids was not Aragon or Castile, but rather the Marinid dynasty (1268–1465) based at Fez. Originally, the Marinids were a Berber pastoral tribe in southern Morocco. Later they became the chief factor in the collapse of Almohad power. In 1216, they began challenging Almohad authority and, despite a few setbacks, they seized one major city in Morocco after another until they captured the capital, Marrakesh, in 1269. The Marinids established their capital at Fez, but they did not attempt to centralize their administration in the Hafsid manner. True to their tribal orientation, they depended on allies to maintain stability in the provinces. Like the Hafsids, they employed Aragonese Christian mercenary troops, most of whom served in the cavalry.

Unlike the Almohads, the Marinids did not seize power in the cause of a particular religious doctrine. They were eager to establish their own legitimacy, however, and attempted to do so in a variety of ways. One was to exploit the sense of cultural and ethnic superiority that Arabs had traditionally expressed toward the Berbers. The Marinids made their court culture as "Arab" as possible, made a point of marrying daughters of prominent Arab leaders, and even contrived a family tree to establish their "descent" from a North Arabian tribe.

The Marinids also attempted to win popular support by their patronage of Sunni urban Islam. The violence and uncertainties of the thirteenth and fourteenth centuries spawned a myriad of popular religious movements in the Maghrib. Throughout the Maghrib, several individuals claimed to be the Mahdi, whom many Muslims expected to bring an end to history; others claimed to be the Shi'ite Twelfth Imam. Numerous revolts exploded in support of many of these pretenders. To combat these religious challenges, the Marinids invested huge sums and a public relations campaign in support of religious institutions. They built many madrasas, and—in contrast to the rest of the Muslim world—decreed that no madrasas could be supported by private religious endowments. They were contemptuous of the Hafsid claim to be at the head of a caliphate. In a gesture meant to insult the Hafsids, the Marinids recognized the figurehead Abbasid caliph of distant Mamluke Cairo, precisely because doing so entailed no obligations.

The buffer state between the Hafsids and the Marinids was the realm of the Zayanid dynasty (1236–1555) at Tlemcen. The Zayanid state was the weakest of the three. Its vulnerability and central location made it a constant target of Marinid and Hafsid ambitions. Algeria had few resources to covet, but Tlemcen was a glittering prize. It was situated inland on a fertile agricultural plain and was the terminus of trans-Saharan trade routes. It competed favorably with Tunis and Fez for the goods of sub-Saharan Africa and developed a large and prosperous mercantile class. Its proud citizens constructed elegant buildings, many of which still stand. Both the Marinids and the Hafsids captured Tlemcen at least once but could not retain control of it. The Zayanid state would have fallen permanently to one of its neighbors had it not been for the constant challenge of the other.

All three of the Maghribi states were affected by the tragic drama unfolding across the Strait of Gibraltar. Tens of thousands of refugees from Andalus poured into the Maghrib in the thirteenth century, triggered by the success of the Reconquista between 1236 and 1248. Andalusians in North Africa gained a reputation over the next several centuries for their architectural and administrative skills. The artistic influence of the Andalusian legacy is still visible today in the monumental buildings of Fez, Tlemcen, and Tunis constructed during this period. Andalusians introduced features of court etiquette and honed the diplomatic skills of Maghribi officials. They served as secretaries, financial advisers, and sometimes even as wazirs. Ibn Khaldun, the third-generation Andalusian historian born in Tunis, was typical in going from the service of one prince to another. The Andalusians' influence was felt with particular force in Tlemcen, which did not have the long ruling tradition of Tunisia or Morocco. Wherever Andalusians served, however, they remained outsiders and were vulnerable to the plotting of local families.

The power of all three dynasties relied on balancing the public support and revenues from the urban commercial populations with tribal allies in the countryside. These alliances constantly shifted as the fortunes and interests of the tribes fluctuated. As a result, the frontiers marking the three dynasties' areas of control were always in flux, as well. By the middle of the fourteenth century, the dynamism of all three dynasties had declined relative to that of the tribes for reasons that are not clear. The plague may have played a role, but we do not have detailed information on its impact in the Maghrib other than evidence that it struck the port cities. Whatever the reason, the nomads became a growing threat to the security of the trans-Saharan trade and to agriculture alike. The power of the dynasties was increasingly confined to the towns. In the areas where the state ceased to provide security, Sufi organizations became more important as a source of defense, spiritual solace, and material aid.

Sufism in the Maghrib was more provincial in some ways than in the eastern areas of the Muslim world. As a rule, the new orders that were spreading rapidly in the Dar al-Islam did not start making inroads into the Maghrib until the sixteenth century. Prior to that time, Maghribi Sufi organizations were based on the teachings of local Sufi teachers. They were more focused on ethical and ritual concerns than many in the east, and they were less likely to indulge in esoteric speculation. Precisely because of the emphasis that the shaykhs placed on personal integrity, the Sufi masters gained much stature among the local populations. As in other rural

areas of the Muslim world, shaykhs became mediators among tribes, and some even became the leaders of tribal coalitions, often in opposition to state regimes.

Even as Sufi leaders were becoming an alternative to the dynasties as local power brokers, another development was taking place in Morocco that would have powerful repercussions later: the reemergence of sharifian prestige. Throughout the Muslim world a descendant of the Prophet through his daughter Fatima and her husband ʿAli is known as a *sharif*. Among Sunnis and Shiʿites alike, sharifs have always been accorded great respect. Within Sunni communities they were frequently the local teachers, their counsel was always respected, and if they fell on hard times, the community made provision for them out of honor for the Prophet. In Morocco, one sharifian family, the Idrisid clan, was honored for having come to Morocco in the late eighth century, founding Fez, and creating a short-lived state. The Idrisids subsequently lost power, but their descendants remained members of a respected family in northern Morocco.

In the fourteenth and fifteenth centuries—simultaneously with the rise to prominence of rural Sufi shaykhs—sharifianism once again became a source of political capital. The Idrisids rose to prominence again, and other sharifian families arriving from Arabia during this period quickly became established within the social fabric of the Arab tribes because of their status as mediators. The reason for this phenomenon seems to be that the Marinid and Zayanid states continued to decline in effectiveness throughout the period. Nomads disrupted the trade routes of the western Sahara, damaging the economies of the Marinid and Zayanid states while inadvertently diverting the trade to Tunis and benefitting the Hafsid regime for a few decades after 1390. Sharifian and Sufi leaders alike gained status as the official rulers were increasingly unable to defend their subjects. Ominously, the weakening of central rule in North Africa was taking place during the period when the Iberian states of the Christian west and the Ottoman state of the Muslim east were in the early stages of becoming the dominant powers in the world.

Crusaders, Corsairs, and Janissaries

In the fifteenth century, Portugal became one of the most dynamic societies in Europe. It had long been a land of hard-scrabble farms and cattle herders, lost in the shadow of either Andalus or Castile. In the early fifteenth century, it was still tiny—it contained fewer than one million people, hardly more than sixteenth-century Istanbul—but it embarked upon a remarkable campaign of commercial and territorial expansion. It signaled its ambition in 1415 with an attack on the Moroccan port of Ceuta, sandwiched between the southern twin Pillars of Hercules. When the Portuguese army captured the city, it massacred the inhabitants. Even in the long history of the Reconquista, the massacre at Ceuta was a brutally shocking episode.

The violence may be understood in light of Portugal's goals. Ceuta was only the first objective in an ambitious, two-pronged plan to gain control of North African trade routes to the Indies and to link up with Prester John (whom Europeans now believed to be the monarch of Ethiopia) for a crusade against Islam. The Portuguese soon realized the difficulties involved in trying to control a corridor across North Africa, however. Instead, they began sailing down the western coast of Africa in search of a sea route to the Indies. Under the inspiration of Prince Henry the Navigator, Portuguese mariners began to improve their maps, charts, shipbuilding techniques, and navigational technology. Several of the advances (including the lateen sail, magnetic compass, and astrolabe) were direct borrowings from the Muslims. They enabled the Portuguese to venture out of the sight of land onto the fearsome Atlantic. By 1487, Bartolomeu Dias had rounded the southern tip of Africa, and in 1498, Vasco da Gama arrived in India using the sea route. From the Indian Ocean and the Red Sea, the naval commander Afonso de Albuquerque continued the quest to find Prester John during the early sixteenth century.

During their exploration of the Atlantic coast of Africa, the Portuguese wanted to acquire the gold of West Africa and establish bases in Morocco that would supply their fleet. They failed to capture Tangier in 1437, but over the next several decades, they saw more clearly how weak the Moroccan defenses actually were. Between 1458 and 1514, all the major ports of Morocco with the exception of Salé fell into Portuguese hands. Portuguese merchants established trading networks in the interior of the central and southern plains and gained a near-monopoly over the maritime trade. Exchanging clothing and metal products for slaves, gold, and ivory, Portugal siphoned the West African trade away from the Muslim markets of the Maghrib. By the end of the century, Lisbon's economy was booming, due in part to the fact that it was receiving West African goods without having to pay the middlemen and tax collectors of Maghribi ports on the Mediterranean. Once Albuquerque had secured most of the major ports of the Indian Ocean by 1515, the spice route to the Indies began to yield its riches. With these two developments in North Africa and the Indian Ocean, Portugal entered the ranks of the world's great commercial economies.

The early incursions of the Portuguese demonstrated the impotence of the Marinid government, causing many Moroccans to question the legitimacy of the dynasty's rule. A brutal revolt in Fez in 1465 ended the Marinid regime, but the Portuguese commercial domination of Morocco only intensified. The new Berber rulers of Morocco, the Wattasids, were more concerned about rival Arab tribes than about the Portuguese: They actually established a twenty-year truce with the Portuguese in order to be able to concentrate on fighting ambitious Arab chieftains. The truce required that they lift restrictions on trade with Europe. As a result, Christian merchants flooded into coastal and interior markets.

During the last several decades of Marinid rule, regional leaders had begun resisting the foreigners who were devastating Morocco. Sufi and sharifian leaders, in particular, began to fill the void of leadership. The massacre at Ceuta in 1415 provoked such outrage that tens of thousands of volunteers followed Sufi leaders in an unsuccessful attempt to retake the city. Sharifian nobles led the successful defense of Tangier in 1437. Wattasid inactivity against foreign intervention led to mounting frustration among many Moroccans. Eventually, a sharifian family in southern Morocco known as the Sa'dis began an alliance with Sufi leaders to unify Morocco against the Portuguese. Between 1510 and 1549, they slowly brought Morocco under their control as they gradually mastered the art of using the arquebus and artillery. First they dominated the various Berber and Arab tribes, and then they began putting pressure on the Portuguese themselves. Their capture of the

Portuguese fort at Agadir in 1541 forced the Portuguese crown to begin evacuating most of its other forts, as well. By 1551, Portugal retained only Ceuta, Tangier, and Mazagan (Al Jadida). The Sa'dis ruled Morocco for more than fifty years, and they demonstrated remarkable military and administrative acumen. Their success created a long-lasting expectation among most Moroccans that the ruler of the country should be from a sharifian family.

The fifteenth-century capture by outsiders of Moroccan port cities on the Atlantic was a harbinger of a similar fate for many Maghribi port cities on the Mediterranean in the sixteenth century. To the east of Morocco, Spain and the Ottoman Empire vied for control of North Africa's port cities. After Spain conquered Granada in 1492, it joined Portugal as a Moroccan power when it occupied the port of Melilla in 1497. The period between 1497 and 1505 witnessed serious attacks on the Spanish coast by North African Muslim raiders and the 1499 revolt by Granadan Muslims, who were protesting the forcible conversions ordered by Bishop Cisneros. In response to those threats, Spain decided upon a systematic occupation of the main ports of the Maghrib. The next six years revealed that a startling shift in the balance of power had taken place in the western Mediterranean from the days when the Marinids and the Hafsids could reasonably regard themselves as the equals of Castile and Aragon: Between 1505 and 1511, Spain easily occupied Oran, Bougie, Algiers, and Tripoli, as well as several smaller ports.

Unlike Portugal, which had an economic interest in North Africa, Spain's interest in capturing North African ports was only to reduce attacks on its shipping. Spain was much more interested in exploiting the New World and in establishing its supremacy in Italy. The effort it had to expend in North Africa was an annoying diversion. As a result, the Spaniards did not bother to secure the hinterland of the Maghribi ports that they captured, forcing the coastal garrisons to be dependent upon supplies from Spain, even for food. The territorial gap in the Spanish conquests—the Hafsid domain—now proved fateful. Spanish ships supplying Bougie and Tripoli had to run a gauntlet of Hafsid-sponsored corsairs in the Mediterranean.

Corsairs were at the center of a violent period of Mediterranean history. They shared characteristics with pirates and privateers. The term *pirate* is always a decidedly negative term and designates a robber in search of plunder who attacks from ships. The term *privateer* designates someone (or his ship) who, to all appearances, was a pirate, but who had an official commission (a *letter of marque*) from a government to attack ships belonging to an enemy nation. A government might find it useful to commission a privately owned and armed ship to take reprisals against another nation or, especially, to augment its navy during time of war. Although the crew members of privateers were not paid by the commissioning government, they were allowed to share in the plunder from captured vessels and were immune from prosecution by the commissioning government for their actions. The nations whose ships were attacked, of course, treated privateers as pirates. Moreover, privateers often found it difficult to give up their way of life after the termination of the letter of marque. They found it easy to segue into the life of a pirate and to become outlaws even among their own people.

Technically, a *corsair* was a privateer commissioned by a Muslim government. The Zayanids and Hafsids were among many North African and European ruling houses that commissioned privateers to enhance their naval capability. Some of the corsairs remained cooperative with their government, but others resisted attempts to control them. In the early sixteenth century, one group of corsairs established an independent base near Bougie and began making alliances with Berber tribes of the interior. The corsairs became so powerful that they threatened the security of both the Zayanids and the Hafsids. The two Muslim governments felt so vulnerable that they made alliances with Spain, their ostensible foe. In 1516, the corsairs captured Algiers from Spain with the support of the town's Andalusian population, which understandably supported a vigorous war against Spain. Refugees from Andalus in Tlemcen and Tunis also led factions that opposed their own regimes due to their governments' alliances with Spain.

The unrest in the central Maghrib occurred simultaneously with the Ottoman annexation of the Mamluke Empire, 1516–1517. The Ottomans, who were concerned about the recent Spanish activity in North Africa, began communications with the corsairs of Algiers. In 1525, they placed several thousand Janissaries, numerous ships, and large amounts of cash at the disposal of the corsairs in order to harass the Spanish. The corsairs, now working as privateers of the Ottomans, turned Algiers into a de facto Ottoman naval base. The city rapidly rose from obscurity to rank with the most powerful port cities on the Mediterranean.

For some five decades, the Ottomans and their corsair allies engaged in a major confrontation with Spain for possession of North African ports. Tunis changed hands five times between 1534 and 1574. In 1541, the Spanish demonstrated how threatened they felt by Algiers by launching an expedition that boasted 500 ships and 34,000 troops. Hernan Cortez, the recent hero in the war with the Aztecs, was an officer in the campaign. The huge force was destroyed by a storm before it reached Algiers, and the city remained the center of combined Ottoman and corsair activities against the Spanish.

Spanish-controlled Tripoli finally fell to corsairs in 1551 and became a major base for raids into Sicily and Italy. Malta, however, successfully resisted a major Ottoman expedition in 1565, denying Suleyman possession of a strategic harbor and a daunting array of fortresses. Six years later, a European naval alliance destroyed the Ottoman fleet at Lepanto, in the Gulf of Corinth. Although the battle showed that the Ottomans were not invincible, the battle settled nothing: The Ottomans replaced their fleet within two years. Perhaps the most disappointed group throughout this period was the community of Moriscos, and especially those of Granada. For two years the Granadan revolt of 1568–1570 held off the vaunted Spanish army without outside help. An Ottoman intervention during that time would have posed a lethal threat to the Spanish crown.

The far western Maghrib witnessed a contest between the Ottomans and the Sa'di dynasty. The Sa'dis, concerned about Ottoman expansion, sent an army of 30,000 soldiers to seize Tlemcen in 1551. Tlemcen's inhabitants threw the city gates open to the Moroccans: They hated the Spanish, were disgusted with their wavering Zayanid rulers, and distrusted the Ottomans. The Ottomans, however, captured the city within a few months and chased the Sa'dis back to Fez. They repeatedly threatened to invade Morocco, and the Sa'dis were so concerned about attacks from both the Portuguese and the Ottomans that they moved their capital from Fez to the more remote Marrakesh.

After 1578, the Sa'dis could breathe more easily. In that year, the young king of Portugal resolved to destroy Islam in Morocco. He led an army across the strait, where he was joined by Muhammad, a former Sa'di ruler who had been overthrown by his uncle two years earlier. The uncle, 'Abd al-Malik, met the combined foes at al-Qasr al-Kabir, where the invaders were utterly annihilated by the skilled Sa'di musketry corps. The Portuguese king and both Sa'di rivals were killed in the fighting (as a result, the conflict is popularly known as the "Battle of the Three Kings," as well as the "Battle of Alcazar"). A brother of 'Abd al-Malik, Ahmad al-Mansur, succeeded to the throne in Marrakesh.

The Sa'di victory convinced the Ottomans and the Portuguese that the costs of further campaigns in Morocco outweighed any possible gains. The Sa'dis, having intimidated Europeans and Ottomans alike, were given free rein to build up their power. They asserted their sharifian status as an alternative to the caliphal authority of the Ottomans and carved out a realm in northwestern Africa independent of Istanbul, Lisbon, and Madrid. With the hostile Ottomans in control of the rest of the North African coast, Ahmad al-Mansur realized that he had to base the Moroccan economy on trade between West Africa and Europe. In 1591, his army toppled the West African empire of Songhay and occupied the venerable city of Timbuktu. Gaining direct access to the gold of West Africa, the Sa'dis seemed ready to consolidate their power at the dawn of the seventeenth century.

The Regencies

The Ottomans and Spaniards finally agreed that their contest to keep each other out of North Africa was more expensive than it was worth. In 1580, they signed a truce that maintained the status quo in the Maghrib. Three years later, Spain annexed Portugal, including its remaining Moroccan ports of Ceuta, Tangier, and Mazagan. Over the next three centuries, Spain gradually relinquished all the port cities except Melilla and Ceuta.

Thus, during the last quarter of the sixteenth century, the bulk of the Maghrib was converted into a series of Ottoman provinces and an independent Morocco. Although local political disturbances continued to plague each region, the map of the area has remained remarkably stable for more than four centuries since then. Tripoli became the capital of a new dominion comprising Tripolitania and Fezzan. It eventually incorporated Cyrenaica, paving the way for modern Libya. The Ottomans created a new and powerful state in the central Maghrib, with its capital at the hitherto modest port of Algiers. As Algiers mushroomed in growth, Tlemcen declined to the status of a provincial town. The rise of Tripoli and Algiers left Tunis, in the middle, with a truncated version of the venerable old province of Ifriqiya.

The three Ottoman provinces of Algiers, Tunis, and Tripoli came to be known to Europeans as the Regencies. Throughout most of their history they were confined to their coastal regions, for they faced formidable opposition among the Berber and Arab tribes of the interior. Within their coastal communities they had to balance the power of their seafaring elite of corsairs with that of their Ottoman soldiers.

The Regencies were the bases of the Barbary corsairs. Their notoriety spread throughout Europe for the next two and one-half centuries. Their violence eventually drew even the Marines of the infant United States into action on "the shores of Tripoli" during the presidency of Thomas Jefferson. The threat they posed was real enough. Between the early sixteenth century and late eighteenth century, hundreds of thousands of Europeans were captured and enslaved for service in harems or in the galleys of the corsair ships; hundreds of thousands of others were held for ransom; and huge quantities of plunder were seized from merchant ships and coastal villages.[1]

Shipping in the Mediterranean was vulnerable to both corsairs and pirates. Most of the Muslim pirates were based in the Adriatic Sea, where they competed with Christian pirates. They would sometimes attack even the Ottoman fleet. The Muslim corsairs, by contrast, were funded by the ruling elites of the Regencies. The Regencies received a portion of the plunder that the corsairs seized. Corsairs usually sailed in squadrons, some of which were as large as fifteen to twenty ships. Tunis was the least active in the corsairing enterprise, whereas Algiers was the most active. Algiers, unlike Tunis and Tripoli, had little contact with overland trade routes, and so it relied on maritime trade and corsairing for its accumulation of wealth.

The corsairs were a menace to Europeans, and the suffering they caused was quite real. It is important, however, to place in historical perspective the accounts of corsairs that we find in European chronicles and literature, for the Europeans were not mere victims of privateers. Three factors are worth noting. First, during the period of greatest activity by the corsairs (the late sixteenth and early seventeenth centuries), the English monarchs were commissioning Francis Drake and other seamen to serve as privateers against the Spanish fleets. The Dutch, French, and Spanish courts were also commissioning privateers for activity against their rivals. Even the Knights of St. John on the island of Malta and privateers from other Christian islands and ports in the Mediterranean served the same function for Christian powers as did the corsairs for the Ottomans. Second, the taking of captives for slavery was a common practice among Europeans as well as corsairs. Catholics and Protestants sold each other into slavery after the battles of the Reformation, and Christian-manned ships frequently captured Muslims and sold them into slavery. Third, the "Barbary" corsairs—who are usually referred to as Berbers, Arabs, or Turks (Europeans often used *Turk* as a synonym for *Muslim* during the sixteenth and seventeenth centuries)—were often renegade Christians (European Christian adventurers who made a nominal conversion to Islam in order to serve in the corsair fleets). European visitors to Algiers regularly expressed their surprise to discover that renegades, primarily from Sicily and Corsica, were the most numerous group living in the town until the mid-seventeenth century. They were the "entrepreneurs" who rapidly transformed the sleepy fishing village into a thriving city whose vibrant market, luxurious suburbs, and numerous public baths made an immediate impact on all visitors.

The dominant role of the renegades in the corsair fleets and among the political and economic elite of the Regencies provides an insight into conditions in the societies bordering the Mediterranean during the sixteenth century. Many among the poor of Christian Europe realized that Muslim societies offered more opportunities for social mobility than their own rigidly stratified societies provided. The great Ottoman admiral Khayr al-Din (Hayrettin)—known as Barbarossa to the Europeans—was an inspiration to many: Born into a Turkish peasant family, he began his naval career as a corsair, but he earned a position as one of the most powerful men in the empire. Thousands of Europeans became corsairs, embarking upon careers that entailed raiding the ships and villages of their homelands. It was not unusual for them to raid their home village and to settle personal scores with enemies. Some eventually returned home and "reconverted" to Christianity, but most did not.

Istanbul never monitored the Regencies closely. Soon after the Ottomans acquired North Africa, the Jelali revolts provided evidence that the central government no longer had the capacity to control its provinces directly. The central authorities were compelled to focus their attention on the regions that possessed the greatest economic and strategic importance for the empire. Those areas lay around the eastern Mediterranean. By the second half of the seventeenth century, the three Regencies had all established a very tenuous relationship with Istanbul that suited the local elites. By 1689, the militia of Algiers was electing the leader of the Regency, and Algiers became, in effect, a military oligarchy. When, at the beginning of the eighteenth century, the political autonomy of Tunis was threatened by a military intervention from Algiers, the militia and notables of Tunis turned to one Husayn bin Ali, who reluctantly agreed to lead the resistance. His grudging involvement led to the creation of the Husaynid dynasty, which ruled Tunisia from 1705 until 1956 (although it was under French hegemony from 1881). Tripoli saw the installation of the Qaramanli dynasty, which ruled from 1711 until 1835.

The Hall of Justice in the Bardo Palace, Tunis, constructed in the late seventeenth century.

Alawite Morocco

In Morocco, the Sa'dis proved to be more vulnerable than most contemporary observers had anticipated. The great Ahmad al-Mansur (1578–1603), who came to power as a result of the Battle of the Three Kings, conquered Timbuktu and gained access to West African gold. With his new wealth, he constructed a palace in Marrakesh that rivaled any in the world. His government was organized on a bureaucratic basis and seemed to have overcome much of the area's endemic tribal divisiveness by possessing sharifian credentials. At his death in 1603, however, all three of his sons claimed the sharifian right to rule and contested the throne. For the next six decades, Morocco was engulfed in chaos. In addition to the civil war among Ahmad's sons, clashes took place among other sharifian leaders and Sufis, all of whom claimed the throne.

It was during this period of anarchy that the final expulsion of Moriscos from Spain took place, 1609–1614. Refugees settled all across the Maghrib and in the eastern Mediterranean. The Ottomans distributed agricultural land as far east as Syria for some of them. Several thousand settled in Salé, next door to Rabat, on the Atlantic coast of Morocco. There they created a self-governing community of corsairs that threatened any ship that sailed the Atlantic waters in an area bounded by Gibraltar, the Madeira Islands, and the Canary Islands. They even ventured as far north as Iceland and Ireland to attack European villages and ships.

At midcentury, a sharifian family from the region around Sijilmasa rose to prominence. Claiming descent from both the Prophet and his cousin and son-in-law 'Ali, it is known as the Alawite family. In 1666, an Alawite named Moulay ("My Master") Rashid took control of Fez. Using that city as a base, he conquered much of northern Morocco before his death in 1672. His brother Moulay Isma'il (ruled 1672–1727) established his capital at Meknes and continued the process of unifying Morocco. Realizing the instability of an army based on tribal alliances, he relied on a slave army that was replenished by raids into West Africa. It eventually attained a strength of 150,000 men and proved capable of conquering the rest of the country. Isma'il developed a well-deserved reputation for cruelty, but his reign brought unaccustomed prosperity to Morocco.

Rashid and Isma'il were the first two rulers of the Alawite dynasty, whose rule has lasted into the twenty-first century. Like the Sa'dis before them, they claimed legitimacy on the basis of their sharifian status and regarded themselves as caliphs with equal status to the sultan of Istanbul. Unlike the Sa'dis, they did not pursue the development of a bureaucratic apparatus to bring stability to the government. The weakness inherent in the sharifian claim was revealed at Isma'il's death, when all of his numerous sons (he is reputed to have sired more than 500 of them) could claim sharifian status. Until the end of the nineteenth century, ambitious sons of sultans had to contest with their brothers to become the sultan. Having won the throne, the new sultan found that the loyalties given to his father had evaporated and that he would have to reconquer the country before he could rule it. Even then, the effective rule of the government extended only to the plains, due to fierce resistance on the part of the Berbers of the massive Atlas mountain range. Later sultans placed more and more emphasis on their function as religious leader and granted the tribes a large degree of local autonomy. They contented themselves with investing local chiefs who were chosen or supported by local notables.

The Sudan

The geographical term for the vast region lying between the Sahara and the rain forests of central Africa is the Sudan (see Map 4.3). It extends from the Red Sea and Indian Ocean in the east to the Atlantic in the west. It is not to be confused with the modern country of Sudan, which forms only a part of the eastern section of the geographical Sudan. The Sudan is divided into two major zones, the *sahel* and the *savanna.* The sahel, which in Arabic means "shore" or "coast," is the transition zone from the desert into the plains farther south. Beginning at roughly 16 degrees latitude north of the equator (on a line extending roughly from the mouth of the Senegal River on the Atlantic to where the modern boundary between the countries of Ethiopia and Sudan meets the Red Sea), the sahel is a region of scrub grass and thorny acacias. Still further south, and receiving more rainfall, is the savanna. It, in turn, comprises two major regions: The northerly one is characterized by tall grass among the acacias, whereas in the south the acacias give way to broad-leafed trees.

The Sudan ends where the tropical rain forest begins. On the Atlantic coast, the northerly edge of the rain forest is in Guinea. The forested zone sweeps eastward from there for an average width of one hundred miles, except for the region of

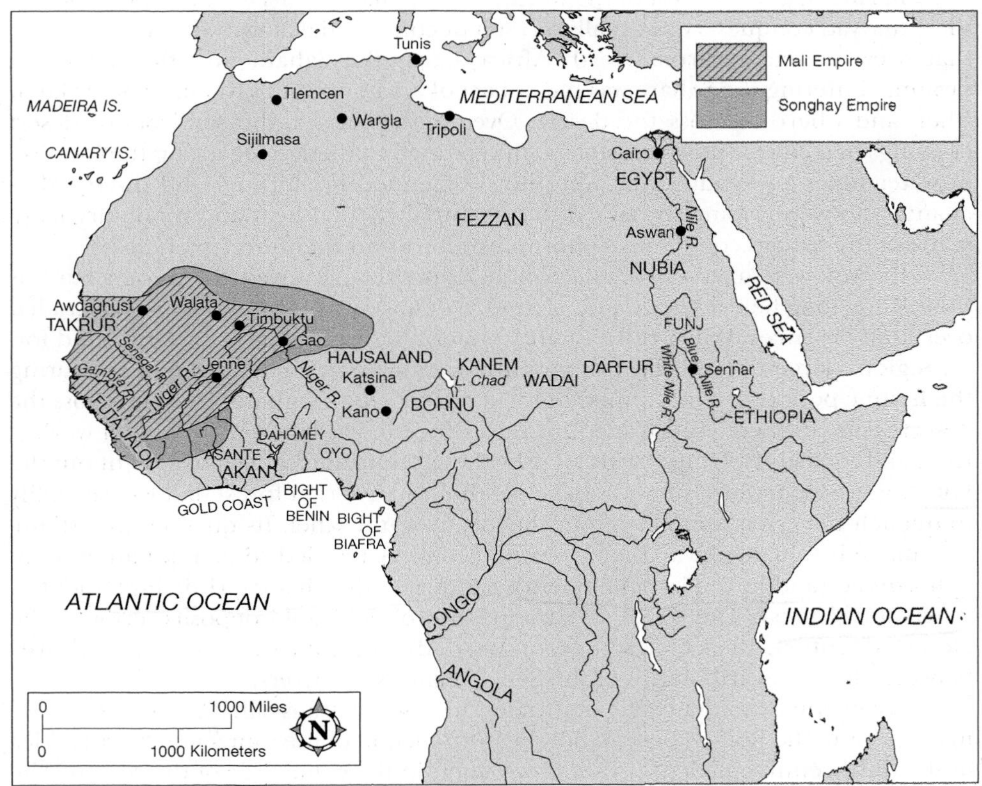

MAP 4.3 The Sudan, Fourteenth to Early Eighteenth Centuries.

modern Ghana, where the savanna interrupts it and extends all the way to the ocean. The Sudan was only lightly touched by Islam prior to the year 1400, but Islam eventually became the dominant religion in the area. During the period under review, two major themes dominate the history of the Sudan: Islamization and the intensification of the slave trade.

Trans-Saharan Trade

The Sahara is the largest and most extreme desert on earth. More than three thousand miles long and a thousand miles wide, it is larger than the United States. It has recorded the hottest temperature on earth (136 degrees), and some areas receive no measurable rainfall for years at a time. It is no surprise, then, that it posed a formidable barrier to the Arab conquests of the seventh and eighth centuries. The early Muslim zones of occupation in Africa were confined to the Mediterranean coastal plain and to the one pathway through the desert that could sustain an army—the Nile River. Even on the Nile, however, the Arabs were stopped in their tracks in the vicinity of Aswan by the Christian kingdom of Nubia. Nubia remained a barrier for several centuries, with the surprising result that Islam's introduction into sub-Saharan Africa occurred through the western and central Sahara rather than up the Nile.

In Africa, as in the rest of the world, the expansion of Islam after the period of the Umayyad conquests was usually a result of commercial activity. It was commerce that drew merchants from North Africa across the Sahara into the sahel and savanna. Entering the Sahara was the last act of amateurs, but savvy merchants knew when and where to cross the desert. Over the centuries, the survivors of desert crossings had contributed to a stock of life-saving knowledge regarding the location of water holes and routes that were not obliterated by shifting sand dunes. Merchants who were willing to hazard the potentially lethal heat and moon-dry landscape of the Sahara could make enormous returns on their investment.

In West Africa, south of the Sahara, a highly organized trading system was flourishing long before the Islamic period. Salt was one of the earliest goods traded over long distances. While this essential mineral was scarce in the savanna and forest regions, large deposits lay in the southern Sahara in ancient lake beds. During the Islamic period, salt was mined in huge quantities at Taghaza, halfway across the desert. The salt merchants traded for slaves (needed as laborers in the salt works), iron, and foodstuffs. Households all over the savanna and sahel also sought out the kola nut, whose bitter taste was not valued in its native rain forest, but whose ability to quench thirst was appreciated in the savanna and sahel. Its qualities as a stimulant made it valuable in a labor-intensive economy and led to its reputation as an aphrodisiac (and in the late nineteenth century as the characteristic ingredient in "cola" soft drinks). The southern savanna also offered gold deposits. Prior to the eleventh century, the chief source of West African gold was the highland area between the upper tributaries of the Senegal and Niger rivers.

Fragmentary evidence demonstrates that some trans-Saharan contacts were made prior to the Roman period, but the introduction of the camel into North Africa in the third century made possible a revolution in the commerce of the region. The Berbers of the desert fringes gradually took advantage of the opportunities that the camel presented both for trade and for raiding black West Africa. The surge in the scale of trans-Saharan commerce did not last long, because the western Roman Empire began to collapse in the fourth century. For several hundred years thereafter, neither North Africa nor Western Europe could afford West African goods. That situation changed by the eighth century, when Muslims were well established in the Maghrib and the Iberian Peninsula.

Initially, the major objective of North Africans was to acquire gold. The Umayyads of Damascus and the Abbasids of Baghdad were justly famous for the fine quality of their gold coins, but they had no gold supplies of their own. West Africa was one of several regions that supplied gold to both dynasties. Later, Europeans also came to depend upon West African gold. It is estimated that two-thirds of all the gold circulating in the Mediterranean area in the Middle Ages originated south of the Sahara.

The two major routes across the Sahara were the "western," leading from Sijilmasa to Awdaghust, and the "central," leading from Tunis to the bend in the Niger River. A third route connected Tripoli, via Fezzan, to Kanem, east of Lake Chad. The Tripoli–Kanem route was dominated by two major articles of commerce: Slaves from the south were exchanged for horses and armor from the north. Other routes connected West Africa with Egypt, but they were ephemeral due to the distance and insecurity of the various regions through which they had to pass.

The desert passage normally required about two months of travel. Resourceful merchants regarded the desert much as a sailor views the ocean: It was, indeed, a vast, empty region, but it was punctuated by a few islands (oases) where one could acquire provisions and recuperate after the rigors of travel. Given a trusty vessel (the camel) and a skilled navigator, one could make a comfortable living by transporting goods across it. Caravans from the north set out in winter because the horses that they brought to trade would not survive the summer heat. In addition to horses, Maghribi merchants also brought cargoes of dates, wheat, dried grapes, nuts, textiles, and manufactured goods of copper and silver. The camels and horses could go no farther than the Berber cities of Awdaghust, Walata, or Gao due to the danger of the tsetse fly. The cargo that was destined for southern markets was transferred to donkeys for the next leg of the trip. The remaining cargo was traded locally for slaves, ivory, indigo, leather, beeswax, and, especially, gold.

The Islamization of the Western and Central Sudan

The trans-Saharan trade introduced Islam into West Africa. Its first carriers were Berber merchants from Sijilmasa and Wargla. Muslim merchants rarely acted as missionaries. Rather, their status as international merchants made them influential, and Islam acquired a certain cachet as a result. Rulers valued the merchants' literacy and often employed them as scribes at court. The merchants' contacts in far-off, powerful countries made their services even more desirable. Local merchants who desired to participate in long-distance trade found that conversion to Islam facilitated their efforts, for it enabled them to socialize more freely with Muslim merchants in a wide variety of settings. Being Muslim also gave them access to Shari'a courts, where they enjoyed the benefits of numerous legal services, including the enforcement of contracts.

In towns, Muslims of all ethnic groups tended to live together, so as to be near the mosque, the Qur'an school, and the legal services of the qadi. They formed the cosmopolitan, outward-looking element in the trading societies. They tended to acquire prestige and power due to their travel and correspondence, which provided them with knowledge of what was happening elsewhere. By the eleventh century, Muslim merchants played an important role in towns in the kingdom of Takrur on the lower Senegal River, the kingdom of Ghana in the sahel, Gao on the Niger River, and Kanem, east of Lake Chad. The ruler of Takrur became Muslim in the eleventh century, and the rulers of Gao and Kanem became Muslim by the twelfth century.

In the West African countryside, educated ulama were exceedingly rare, but Muslim holy men became a feature of social life by the late eleventh century. Some of the most famous were from Takrur, where the ruler attempted to Islamize the entire population. These men were not highly educated ulama, but rather individuals who combined preaching with the teaching of rudimentary mystical practices, the making of amulets, and the treatment of disease with magico-medical procedures and applications. They proved to be as effective in their medical practice as the traditional healers, and their status in some cases was higher due to their ability to read and write. Although rural non-Muslims eagerly sought their healing and spiritual services, few converted to Islam, because traditional religious practices served their agricultural and hunting needs well.

The best-known phase of early West African Muslim history was the kingdom of Mali. In the thirteenth century, Mali's sphere of influence extended from the Atlantic in the west to Gao in the east, and from Awdaghust in the north to the gold fields of the Asante (Akan) peoples in the rain forest. More powerful than any West African dynasty that had preceded it, Mali prospered due to its agricultural resources on the Niger and its control of the gold fields. The city of Jenne (Djenne) became famous as a center of Islamic learning. Situated in the fertile "inland delta" region of the Niger River, where the Niger splits into several branches before resuming its single channel, Jenne was a prosperous and cosmopolitan city. The rulers of Mali were nominally Muslim, and they encouraged Muslim preachers who took their message eastward into Hausaland, where they introduced the rulers of Kano to Islam. As early as the second half of the thirteenth century, a ruler of Mali made the pilgrimage to Mecca, but the most famous instance of a Malian king making the hajj was that of Mansa Musa (ca. 1307–ca. 1336). When he passed through Cairo in 1324 en route to Mecca, he spent and otherwise distributed so much gold that his visit was discussed for generations afterward. Mansa Musa and his brother Mansa Sulayman (ca. 1341–1358) gained fame and respect among the Muslims of many lands for their construction of mosques and schools.

Despite its famous Muslim rulers, neither Mali nor any of the other West African states at this time was a "Muslim society," much less an "Islamic state." Mali's rulers were internationally recognized as professing Muslims and had warm relations with Muslim merchants and ulama, but visitors from North Africa or Egypt (including Ibn Battuta, who visited during the period of Mansa Sulayman's reign) were often shocked at what they considered to be the un-Islamic nature of Malian society. Even taking into consideration the visitors' ethnocentrism, it is clear that Islamic food prohibitions were ignored and that standards of modesty, especially for females, were strikingly different. Court ceremonials contained many pagan elements. In none of the West African societies was the Muslim population sufficiently large for Islamic law to take precedence over local custom.

Because traditional values and institutions were still dominant, Muslim rulers had to play a double role in order to maintain their power. In their dealings with other Muslim rulers and with Muslim traders, they acted as pious Muslims. When they interacted with most of their subjects, however, they carefully fulfilled their duties as divine kings. They patronized Muslim religious experts and their institutions, but also used the services of traditional priests, even at court. Polytheistic ritual and custom were too deeply embedded in Sudanic culture to ignore or flout.

Nevertheless, Islam granted an international legitimacy that rulers coveted. Caravans brought merchants and scholars, books, commercial credit, and other tangible benefits. By 1400, it probably would have been difficult for societies in the Sudan to conduct trade with the Maghrib without employing the commercial practice of the Shari'a. Thus, the typical Muslim ruler of West Africa from the thirteenth to the early eighteenth centuries attempted a compromise between the new culture and belief system of Islam and the ancient, persistent animism of the western Sudan.

In the 1450s, Portuguese efforts to reach the source of the gold trade began to bear fruit. When agents from Lisbon sailed up the Gambia and Senegal rivers and made direct contact with the Mali Empire, considerable commerce was redirected away from the Maghrib and toward the more accessible Atlantic coast. This diversion of commerce was among the final straws for the Marinid regime of Morocco, which fell in 1465. Meanwhile, Mali itself was coming under pressure. The city-state of Gao had broken free in the late fourteenth century, and by the mid-fifteenth century it was a growing challenge to Mali's hegemony in the area. Gao became the center of a kingdom dominated by the Songhay people. The Songhay Empire burst into prominence in the 1460s by conquering Timbuktu, which had eclipsed Jenne as the preeminent city of Islamic learning in the region. Timbuktu soon became better known outside the empire than the kingdom's political center at Gao.

The Songhay Empire destroyed Mali and became even larger than its illustrious predecessor. Under Askiya Muhammad (1493–1528) it continued to grow. Eventually, it extended from the basin of the Gambia River to Kano in Hausaland. Askiya Muhammad went beyond previous West African rulers in his patronage of Islam. Although he allowed traditional customs and practices in his court, his laws and policies were increasingly in accord with the Shari'a. His imperial venture was the most powerful and wide-ranging in sub-Saharan history before the colonial era.

Songhay, despite its dynamism, was also weakened by the Portuguese diversion of trade to the Atlantic. Its preeminent cities, Timbuktu and Gao, were east of the new trade routes, and their markets began to dry up. Then, in 1591, Ahmad al-Mansur, the Sa'di ruler of Morocco, attacked. Morocco's own caravan cities were suffering from the rerouting of the West African trade and had lost access to the gold fields. Al-Mansur daringly sent his army across the vast desert to attack Songhay, hoping to gain control of the trade routes himself. The Songhay army outnumbered the Moroccan force by perhaps nine to one, but it was armed only with traditional weapons. Al-Mansur's musketeers, by contrast, had already demonstrated their effectiveness thirteen years earlier at the Battle of the Three Kings. The Moroccans defeated Songhay easily and captured Timbuktu. The victory gave

Leo Africanus Describes Timbuktu

Al-Hasan ibn Muhammad al-Wazzan was born in Granada a few years before the principality fell to Spain. His family moved to Fez, where he became an emissary for the Wattasid ruler. In 1518, he was captured by a Spanish pirate, who presented him to Pope Leo X as a gift. Two years later, he was baptized and christened with a new, Latin, name: Leo Africanus. In 1527, Leo disappeared from the historical record. Some speculate that he remained in Europe; others think that he returned to the Maghrib.

Leo Africanus is best known for his Description of Africa, *which he wrote at the request of the Vatican. It apparently reflects his own experiences when he traveled as a diplomat for the ruler of Fez.*

The following extract is a description of Timbuktu at the time that the city was part of the Songhay Empire. The ruler whom Leo mentions was Askiya Muhammad (1493–1528), whose aversion to Jews is corroborated by other sources.

The name of this kingdom is a modern version of the name of a city that was built by a king named Mansa Sulayman in the year 610 A.H. (1213/1214 C.E.) about two miles from a branch of the Niger River. The city consists entirely of huts made of poles and mud and covered with thatched roofs. In the midst of the city stands a mosque constructed of stone and mortar by a master builder from Almeria, in Andalus. The same builder also constructed a large stone palace, which is where the king lives.

The city has numerous shops of artisans and merchants. Weavers of cotton cloth are particularly well-represented. Slave girls sell all the foodstuffs and fresh bread. The men wear fine black or blue cotton fabrics, some of which are imported from Europe by merchants from Berber territory. All the women here, except for the slaves, veil their faces.

The inhabitants of the city are quite wealthy, especially the foreigners among them. This explains why the present king has even given two of his daughters to two particularly wealthy brothers who are merchants. There are many wells with fresh, pure water. When the Niger floods, canals deliver water to the city. There is a great abundance of grain and livestock. The inhabitants consume much milk and butter, and there is much fruit. On the other hand, salt is in very short supply. It has to be brought in from Taghaza, 500 miles away. . . .

The king of Timbuktu is a mortal enemy of the Jews, which is why you will not find a single one anywhere in the kingdom. That is not all, however: If the king finds out that a Berber merchant has done business with Jews, participates with them in a trading company, or finances his business with Jewish credit, he arbitrarily confiscates all the merchant's goods. . . . He allows the victim as much gold as is required to return home.

The king provides patronage for many scholars, prayer leaders, and judges, for he esteems learned men. Many hand-written books from Barbary are sold, and sellers of books earn more from that source than from all their other goods combined. The people of Timbuktu use unrefined gold nuggets and gold coins as their standard currency, although for small purchases, they use cowries from Iran. . . .

SOURCE: The author's English translation of Dietrich Rauchenberger, *Johannes Leo der Afrikaner: Seine Beschreibung des Raumes zwischen Nil und Niger nach dem Urtext* (Wiesbaden, Germany: Harrassowitz, 1999), 275–283.

al-Mansur access to the gold fields, enabling him to begin his monumental construction projects in Marrakesh and elsewhere.

Far to the east of Mali, another early region of penetration for Islam was Kanem, on the eastern shores of Lake Chad. Its ruler was Muslim as early as the twelfth century. By 1250, several students from Kanem were studying in Cairo at al-Azhar mosque–university. In the fourteenth century, a military threat from a neighboring people forced a sizable proportion of the population of Kanem to migrate to the region southwest of Lake Chad. From then on, it was referred to as the kingdom of Bornu (Borno). Bornu reached its height of power and prestige during the period 1550–1700, when it cooperated with Tripoli to safeguard the caravan route between them. After the fall of Songhay to Morocco in 1591, Bornu was probably the most powerful state in black Africa. Culturally, its court was famous for the high standard of its legal and theological education. Militarily, it boasted a highly disciplined infantry armed with muskets and cavalry mounted on Barbary horses. The kingdom obtained the firearms and horses by trading slaves, which its raiders captured along its frontiers with the rain forests to the south.

Between Bornu and the eastern reaches of the Niger River lay Hausaland, a large region united only by a common language, Hausa. It was more isolated from the Maghrib than either Mali or Bornu, and did not engage in regular caravan trade until the mid-fifteenth century. Hausaland was not politically unified before the nineteenth century. Instead, it was characterized by a number of city-states that exercised influence over a radius of thirty to thirty-five miles from their city walls. The largest were Katsina and Kano. The evidence suggests that Islam first began to appear in Hausaland in the late fourteenth century. Whereas Islam entered the western Sudan by the mechanism of trade, it was introduced into Hausaland by preachers from Mali in the west and Bornu in the east. Both Katsina and Kano soon boasted rulers who, at different times, attempted to enforce the Shari'a. In each case, however, the strength of the traditional religions always doomed such efforts.

The Islamization of the Eastern Sudan

The upper (southern) Nile became progressively Arabized from the tenth century on. Nomads migrating up the river from Egypt sought additional grazing areas on the river's west bank, while miners and adventurers sought opportunities in the Eastern Desert between the river and the Red Sea. As early as the fourteenth century, Arabs arrived in the savanna region of the modern country of Sudan, at which point they began to migrate westward toward Kanem. In the fifteenth century, Nubia began fragmenting from internal stresses. An age of anarchy ensued, characterized by conflicts among local warlords. Taking advantage of the vacuum of power, a people known as the Funj (Fung) moved into the general vicinity of modern Khartoum at the beginning of the sixteenth century. We know little about the origins of the Funj, but the names of their rulers make it clear that they were already at least nominally Arabized and Islamized. They quickly seized control of the Nile valley for about three hundred miles in each direction from their capital at Sannar, which is about one hundred and fifty miles up the Blue Nile from Khartoum. The kingdom of the Funj exercised power on the upper Nile until the mid-eighteenth century.

Farther west, nomadic groups that claimed Arab descent—but appear to have been neither Arab nor Nubian in origin—set up powerful states in Dar Fur and Wadai in the mid-seventeenth century. Funj, Dar Fur, and Wadai all boasted rulers who professed to be Muslim, and Islam gained a major foothold in the eastern Sudan by the mid-seventeenth century due to their rule. Each of the leaders adopted the honorific traditionally used for a caliph: *amir al-mu'minin.* They also held religious scholars in high esteem and honored them with grants of land. Islam in this region, however, was quite underdeveloped compared with its West African counterpart. The paucity of cities, the difficulty of communication with the greater Muslim world, and the nomadic ethos of the region created conditions similar to those of Turkic western Asia. The people of the eastern Sudan adopted certain attractive features of Islam for use within a framework of traditional religions. The essence of Islam tended to be understood as obedience to the ruler rather than doctrinal or ritual correctness. Muslims from Arab lands were usually scandalized by discovering the central role of pork and beer in the diet.

The peoples of Funj, Dar Fur, and Wadai enjoyed enhanced security due to the rise of these states, but the economic systems of all three kingdoms were based on supplying slaves to Ottoman Egypt. In return for shipping the slaves, they obtained guns, horses, and armor, which made them even more efficient in acquiring slaves. Thus, the prosperity and security of each were bought at the cost of unending misery for their neighbors to the south. The areas that we know today as northern Cameroon, southern Chad, and the Central African Republic were targets of continual slave raids during the sixteenth, seventeenth, and eighteenth centuries.

The Intensification of the Slave Trade

Prior to the sixteenth century, the slave trade in West Africa was only one element of a thriving export trade that included gold, salt, and other goods. Slavery, nevertheless, was common. The typical slave had lost his or her status as a free person due to having become a war captive. Slavery was also a common punishment meted out by judicial tribunals. The continuous wars waged by such kingdoms as Mali and Songhay produced tens of thousands of slaves who were sold in local markets. The treatment of slaves in West Africa varied. In many places they became members of the households that acquired them, were given fictive family relationships, could marry nonslave members of the community, and might even inherit some of the family's assets. On the other hand, they might work in gold mines or on royal estates, where they endured brutal treatment.

Many West African war captives were sold to merchants for transport to the sahel or North Africa. In the sahel, and even in the desert, thousands of slaves were used to till the oases, mine salt, herd animals, and smelt copper. An even larger demand for slaves existed in the Mediterranean basin. As a result, slaves were among the "commodities" exchanged in the trans-Saharan trade. Most of the slaves who made the painful (and frequently fatal), two-month crossing of the Sahara were women and children, destined to become domestic servants or concubines. Reliable statistics related to the slave trade are impossible to obtain for any historical period, but no one disputes the assumption that thousands of slaves made the annual journey across the Sahara.

The dynamics of the slave trade began to change in the mid-fifteenth century with the arrival of the Portuguese off the Atlantic coast of Africa. As the Portuguese explored in the vicinity of the Gambia River, they realized that they were nearing the sources of the famed West African gold mines. As in Morocco, they attempted to gain what they wanted by force, but they had to change tactics due to the high death rate they suffered from malaria and yellow fever. They soon abandoned trying to penetrate the interior. Instead, they began to establish trading posts along the Atlantic coast. Eventually, these trading posts and forts dotted the coast for hundreds of miles. Their primary focus was the Gold Coast (modern Ghana), named for its proximity to the gold fields. The Portuguese traded European manufactured goods for gold, but they also became middlemen for trade among the various river deltas. The regional trade in slaves proved to be so lucrative that some traders who had gone in search of gold switched to full-time slave trading. In the sixteenth century, Dutch, English, Danish, and French traders arrived at the coastal slave markets. Many of them entered the regional slave trade, raising the demand for slaves.

Until the sixteenth century, coastal societies in West Africa had lagged a century or two behind the interior kingdoms of the western Sudan in the acquisition of technology and commodities from the Mediterranean. Now, however, maritime commerce conferred new wealth upon them, enabling them to purchase modern weapons and other European goods. The increasing demand for slaves made slave raiding an irresistible temptation for them. With the new gunpowder weapons, the coastal towns were able to overwhelm the peoples of the rain forests and southern savanna. Their large-scale raiding coincided with the appearance of Songhay and the Hausaland city-states, the period of Bornu's greatest strength, and the rise of Wadai, Dar Fur, and the Funj kingdom. All of these Muslim states engaged in slave raiding and the sale of war captives. Like the coastal towns, the interior Muslim states were becoming increasingly militarized. Their contacts with Ottoman merchants in Tunis, Tripoli, and Egypt provided them with Barbary horses, padded armor, and modern weapons. Their primary target populations for slave raids were precisely the same as those of raiders from the coastal cities. They attacked from the north while the coastal raiders attacked from the south. Thus, most victims of the slave trade came from the southern savanna and rain forests.

The demand for slaves increased even more at the beginning of the seventeenth century, when plantation colonies were established in the western hemisphere. Soon, the volume of the trans-Atlantic slave trade drew even with its trans-Saharan counterpart, which exported an annual average of 10,000 slaves. By the end of the seventeenth century, some 30,000–50,000 slaves were making the infamous "Middle Passage" across the Atlantic each year. By 1750, the annual volume was 70,000. In stark contrast to the trans-Saharan trade, the trans-Atlantic trade was primarily composed of adult or adolescent males, destined to work in the difficult conditions of the sugar cane, indigo, or rice plantations.

Slave markets appeared in ports all the way from Senegal to Angola. Four areas supplied the bulk of slaves. The busiest region extended from Gabon to Angola. Its ports supplied at least one-third of the slaves for the trans-Atlantic trade. Because Portugal dominated this stretch of the coast, most slaves from here were shipped to Brazil. The Bight of Benin—off the coast of modern Togo, Benin, and western Nigeria—was second only to the Congo as a source of slaves. It became known as the Slave Coast. The Bight of Biafra—off the coast of modern Cameroon and eastern Nigeria—was already a well-developed trading area before the arrival of the Europeans. It was not a major slave zone until after 1650, but in the eighteenth century it matched Benin, shipping more than one million slaves across the Atlantic. The Gold Coast, too, was late entering the slave trade. As late as 1700, its gold exports were greater in value than the entire Atlantic slave trade; by 1730, however, it was importing gold and paying for it by exporting slaves.

The busiest period of the trans-Atlantic slave trade was from about 1680 until about 1800. Estimates of the number of Africans who suffered the brutal experience range widely, but most historians in recent years agree that at least six million made the crossing during this time alone. Some four million were West Africans. Of these, the majority were from the rain forest and southern savanna. Some of the regions in these two areas suffered extensive depopulation, intense poverty, and misery. The coastal communities, by contrast, were almost immune from losses to the slave trade. They not only traded in slaves, but some of them actively engaged in slave raiding. They enjoyed considerable population increase and political development as a result of the Atlantic slave trade.

The Muslim states of the northern savanna engaged in slave raiding, but they also lost some of their population to the slave trade, a fact that accounts for the phenomenon of Muslim slaves in the United States. During the seventeenth and eighteenth centuries, many of the Muslim states were in an almost constant state of warfare. The Hausa city-states quarreled, Muslim rulers of Senegambia (the region embracing the basins of the Senegal and Gambia rivers) contested for supremacy, and non-Muslim states such as the Asante kingdom, Oyo, and Dahomey began to expand at the expense of their neighbors. These wars produced large numbers of captives—Muslim and non-Muslim—and led to a spectacular increase in the number of slaves available for domestic and export markets.

Islam in the Sudan

Before the eighteenth century, the Islamization of the Sudan made slow progress. Islam was more deeply rooted in the western Sudan than in the eastern section. In West Africa, it was characteristically an urban religion, associated with towns on long-distance trade routes. Commerce and artisanry provided the economic basis for urban Muslim communities that were able to support a body of scholars dedicated to the study and implementation of the Sharīʿa. Jenne on the Niger became the primary center of Islamic learning in the fourteenth and fifteenth centuries, but by the fifteenth century Timbuktu began to surpass it. Its Sankore Mosque, founded in the late fourteenth century, became the foremost institution of Islamic learning in the Sudan. During the second half of the sixteenth century, it reached the height of its influence when it offered the teaching of both Shafiʿi and Maliki law. The quality of its scholarship, combined with the diversity of opinions offered, granted it a higher level of prestige than any of the madrasas in the Maghrib, which taught only Maliki law.

The fall of Songhay to Morocco in 1591 was a setback in some ways to West African urban Islam. The era of great indigenous empires was over. Never again

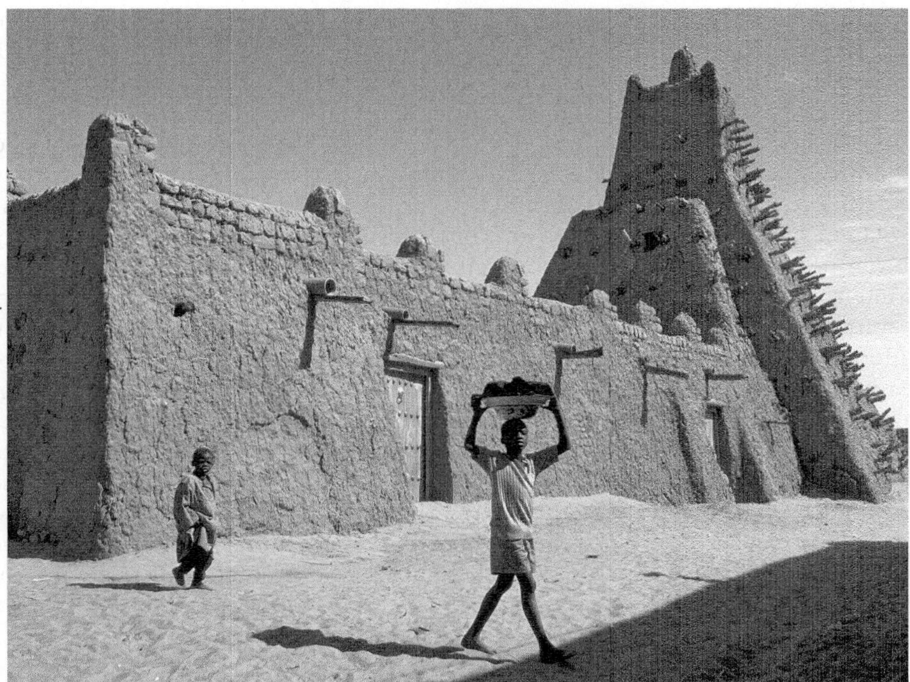

The Sankore Mosque in Timbuktu, a major seat of Islamic learning by the sixteenth century.

would West Africa experience a mighty ruler who could patronize Islamic scholarship and architecture on the scale that Mansa Musa or Askiya Muhammad had. Small states replaced the empires. Although they still engaged in the trans-Saharan trade, their markets were smaller. As the states became more insular and provincial, their rulers were less concerned than before to conform to Islamic values. In general, the ulama found it expedient to overlook the corruption and elements of un-Islamic practice that were characteristic of the regimes. They depended upon the patronage of the rulers, and did not risk offending them.

Even though the urban Muslim community was losing its vitality, Islam and literacy began to spread among the rural population in the seventeenth century. A major reason for that development was the appearance in the region from Senegambia to Hausaland of rural enclaves in which religious scholars studied the Qur'an, Hadith, and law. They served as nodes of literacy, which began to spread throughout rural West Africa for the first time. The communities in Hausaland were the most notable. They were founded by the Fulbe (Fulani) ethnic group, which had migrated into the region from the upper tributaries of the Senegal during the fifteenth century. They became respected for their agricultural success, excellent horsemanship, martial prowess, and Islamic scholarship. The increasing numbers of slaves being marketed in West Africa caused prices to fall, enabling the Fulbe to buy them cheaply and have them work the farms while they studied.

Several of these rural settlements developed into respected seats of learning. They often maintained a chilly relationship with nearby cities or towns, precisely because they regarded the urban areas (and their ulama) to be centers of vice.

By the dawn of the eighteenth century, the penetration of the rural areas of West Africa by religious communities such as these was beginning to have a noticeable impact on social relations. Peasants and pastoralists alike began interpreting their exploitation at the hands of rural landlords and urban-based rulers in terms of a violation of God's norms of justice. They considered the practice of Islam in the cities to be a debased form of the religion. The dynamic expression of Islam had shifted from the cities to rural strongholds.

In 1700, a protest movement began in what is now modern Guinea that foreshadowed fateful events in West Africa decades later. In Futa Jalon, a mountainous area in eastern Guinea that serves as sources for the Gambia, Senegal, and Niger rivers, prosperous Fulbe cattle herders sought relief from taxation and the threat of confiscation of their property by the Mandinka-speaking landowners of the region. They also demanded the freedom to establish mosques and schools. They expressed their grievances in Islamic and ethnic terms. For many years, their dissatisfaction was expressed primarily in sermons, but in 1725, they took military action and declared a jihad against their masters. By 1750, the Fulbe had overcome their rivals and they dominated the state. Their successful jihad would serve as a model for later reformers who would utterly transform West Africa in the nineteenth century.

Conclusion

As late as the thirteenth century, the Strait of Gibraltar served as a bridge between Europe and Africa and fostered cross-cultural exchanges. By the early seventeenth century, it had become instead a cultural barrier between Christian and Muslim societies. It separated two groups characterized by mutual hatred, xenophobia, and cultural stagnation. The stunning success of the Reconquista during 1236–1248 reduced Andalus to a single principality; the fall of Granada in 1492 ended the last independent Muslim state in the Iberian Peninsula; and the ethnic cleansing of Spain's Muslims between 1609 and 1614 destroyed the last remnants of Muslim society there.

Muslim culture on both sides of the Strait had been among the most creative in the world during the eleventh and twelfth centuries, but in the thirteenth century, it suffered a precipitous decline. Mudejars in the Iberian Peninsula struggled even to keep a tradition of learning alive until they were forcibly ejected. In the Maghrib, work in the sciences practically disappeared. Even the fields of jurisprudence and Sufi thought evolved separately from the currents in the rest of the Muslim world. The Maghrib had become isolated from its previous sources of inspiration. The threat of corsairs limited the number of European ships that entered Maghribi ports, and Maghribi merchants limited their own business activities to routes close to home. The rulers of the Regencies, who might have provided patronage for cultural production, were often from the same social background as their corsairs or Janissaries. They did not share the education and refinement characteristic of the Maghribi ruling elites of previous generations.

While Muslim societies in the Iberian Peninsula and the Maghrib were struggling—or disappearing—their counterparts in the Sudan were experiencing a period of dynamic growth. By the fifteenth century, several West African cities had become centers of Islamic learning. Timbuktu, in fact, developed into one of the greatest centers of scholarship in the Muslim world. Also in the fifteenth century, Islam ceased to be an exclusively urban phenomenon in West Africa and began to penetrate large areas of rural West Africa between Senegambia and Hausaland. It also expanded all along the sub-Saharan savanna. By the seventeenth century, Muslim-ruled states formed a continuous line from the Atlantic to the Red Sea.

Islam entered the savanna peacefully as the faith of merchants. For several centuries, it was primarily the religion of a merchant class that valued stability. By the middle of the eighteenth century, however, the religion's themes of justice and righteousness had been appropriated by rural groups in West Africa that sought to effect a major transformation of the existing social, political, and moral order. The region was about to witness a series of wars that combined religious fervor and a zeal for plunder in a manner that had not been seen in the Muslim world for centuries.

NOTE

1. Recent research suggests that "between 1530 and 1780 there were almost certainly a million and quite possibly as many as a million and a quarter white, European Christians enslaved by the Muslims of the Barbary Coast." See Robert C. Davis, *Christian Slaves, Muslim Masters: White Slavery in the Mediterranean, the Barbary Coast, and Italy, 1500–1800* (Basingstoke, U.K., and New York: Palgrave Macmillan, 2003), 23.

FURTHER READING

The Iberian Peninsula

Barcia, J. R., ed. *Américo Castro and the Meaning of Spanish Civilization.* Berkeley: University of California Press, 1976.

Boswell, John. *The Royal Treasure: Muslim Communities Under the Crown of Aragon in the Fourteenth Century.* New Haven, Connecticut: Yale University Press, 1977.

Burns, Robert J. *Medieval Colonialism: Postcrusade Exploitation of Islamic Valencia.* Princeton, New Jersey: Princeton University Press, 1975.

Chejne, Anwar. *Islam and the West: The Moriscos.* Albany: State University of New York Press, 1983.

Elliott, J. H. *Imperial Spain: 1469–1716.* New York: The New American Library, 1963.

Harvey, L. P. *Islamic Spain, 1250–1500.* Chicago: University of Chicago Press, 1990.

Harvey, L. P. *Muslims in Spain, 1500–1614.* Chicago and London: University of Chicago Press, 2005.

Perry, Mary Elizabeth. *The Handless Maiden: Moriscos and the Politics of Religion in Early Modern Spain.* Princeton, New Jersey, and Oxford, U.K.: Princeton University Press, 2005.

The Maghrib

Abun-Nasr. *A History of the Maghrib,* 3d ed. Cambridge, U.K.: Cambridge University Press, 1987.

Brett, Michael and Elizabeth Fentress. *The Berbers.* Oxford, U.K., and Cambridge, Massachusetts: Blackwell, 1996.

Cook, Weston F. *The Hundred Years War for Morocco: Gunpowder and the Military Revolution in the Early Modern Muslim World.* Boulder, Colorado: Westview Press, 1994.

Cornell, Vincent J. *Realm of the Saint: Power and Authority in Moroccan Sufism.* Austin: University of Texas Press, 1998.

Davis, Natalie Zemon. *Trickster Travels: A Sixteenth-Century Muslim Between Worlds.* New York: Hill and Wang, 2006.

Davis, Robert C. *Christian Slaves, Muslims Masters: White Slavery in the Mediterranean, the Barbary Coast, and Italy, 1500–1800.* Houndmills, U.K., and New York: Palgrave Macmillan, 2003.

Hess, Andrew. *The Forgotten Frontier: A History of the Sixteenth-Century Ibero-African Frontier.* Chicago: University of Chicago Press, 1978.

Julien, Charles-Andre. *History of North Africa.* Translated by John Petrie. New York: Praeger, 1970.

Laroui, Abdallah. *The History of the Maghrib: An Interpretive Essay.* Translated by Ralph Manheim. Princeton, New Jersey: Princeton University Press, 1977.

Oliver, Roland, and Anthony Atmore, eds. *The African Middle Ages, 1400–1800.* Cambridge, U.K., and New York: Cambridge University Press, 1981.

The Sudan

Ajaye, J. F. A., and Michael Crowder, eds. *History of West Africa,* 2d ed. Vol. 1. New York: Columbia University Press, 1976.

Diouf, Sylviane A. *Servants of Allah: African Muslims Enslaved in the Americas.* New York and London: New York University Press, 1998.

Hunwick, John, and Eve Troutt Powell, eds.*The African Diaspora in the Mediterranean Lands of Islam.* Princeton, New Jersey: Marcus Wiener Publishers, 2002.

Inikori, J. E., ed. *Forced Migration: The Impact of the Export Slave Trade on African Societies.* New York: Africana Publishing Company, 1982.

Insoll, Timothy. *The Archaeology of Sub-Saharan Africa.* Cambridge, U.K., and New York: Cambridge University Press, 2003.

July, Robert W. *Precolonial Africa.* New York: Charles Scribner's Sons, 1975.

Klein, Herbert S. *The Atlantic Slave Trade.* Cambridge, U.K.: Cambridge University Press, 1999.

Levtzion, Nehemiah, and Ronald Lee Pouwels, eds. *The History of Islam in Africa.* Athens, Ohio: Ohio University Press; Oxford, U.K.: James Currey; Cape Town, South Africa: David Philip, 2000.

Manning, Patrick. *Slavery and African Life: Occidental, Oriental and African Slave Trades.* Cambridge, U.K., and New York: Cambridge University Press, 1990.

Oliver, Roland, and Anthony Atmore, eds. *The African Middle Ages, 1400–1800.* Cambridge, U.K., and New York: Cambridge University Press, 1981.

CHAPTER 5

Central Asia and Iran

Central Asia and Iran formed the core region of Timur's empire. Long-distance trade routes linked them together as far back as history can record. They also shared elements of the Persian cultural tradition from at least as early as the Achaemenid Empire of the sixth century B.C.E. Within three centuries of the introduction of Islam, Central Asia and Iran became the most creative and productive region in the Muslim world for philosophy, mathematics, theology, Qur'anic exegesis, Sufi theory, linguistic studies, and art. As neighbors, they suffered equally during the numerous invasions and wars of the period that extended from the eleventh to the fourteenth centuries.

For three centuries after Timur, Central Asia and Iran once again played major roles in the economic and cultural life of the Muslim world. The ethnic and religious transformations in this region are among the most important developments in Muslim history during the period we are considering. After a spectacular revival of their fortunes, however, both areas began to experience a decline in wealth and security by the late seventeenth century. By the end of the eighteenth century, the economy, political structure, and cultural life of Central Asia and Iran had suffered catastrophic collapse.

Central Asia

The term *Central Asia* refers to a region surrounded by Iran, Russia, South Asia, and the populous regions of China (see Map 5.1). For the purposes of this book, *Central Asia* denotes the areas now occupied by Kazakhstan, Uzbekistan, Turkmenistan, Kyrgyzstan, Tajikistan, China's Xinjiang province, and the portion of Afghanistan that lies north of the Hindu Kush mountain range. Although the climate is similar throughout Central Asia—hot in summer, cold in winter, and little rainfall—nothing about its topographical features would lead a geographer to define it as a natural region. It has an identity for a negative reason rather than a positive one: For much of history it lay outside the effective control of the empires in Iran, India, China, and

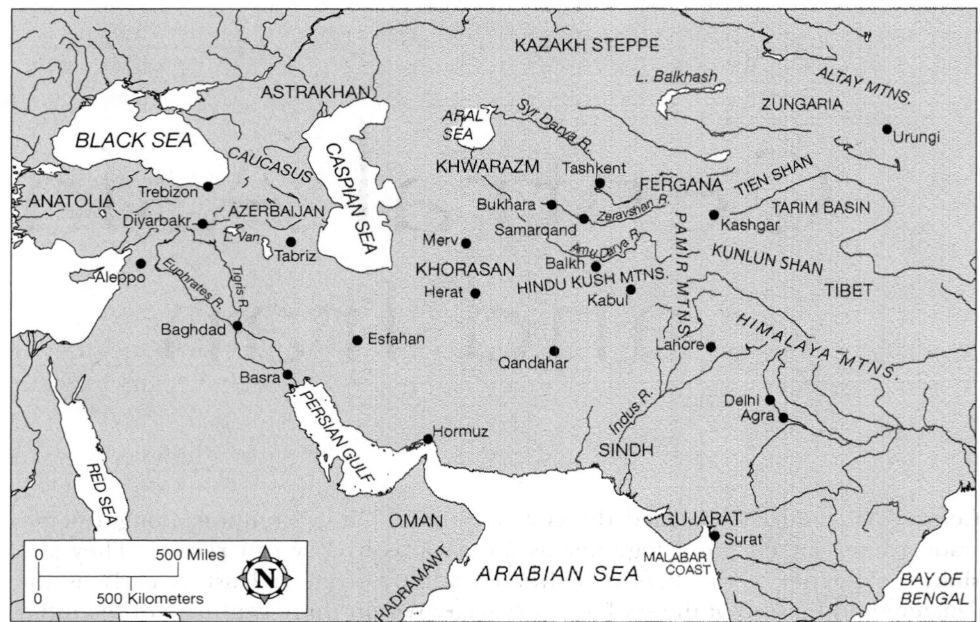

MAP 5.1 Central Asia and Southwest Asia.

Russia that bordered it. Throughout the centuries, the bulk of Central Asia's population was concentrated in the valleys of the Syr Darya, Amu Darya, and Zeravshan rivers. Agriculture was highly productive and commerce thrived. Away from the river valleys, pastoralists grazed their animals on such vegetation as they could find.

The outside world knows little about Central Asia today. The region's climate, topography, and remoteness from more famous empires in the past might suggest that Central Asia has always been a peripheral region. In fact, its location at the interstices of several large empires meant that it was at the crossroads of them all. Fed by oasis agriculture and situated on major long-distance trade routes that connected China with the Mediterranean and India with Russia, Central Asia attracted people from various cultures who became familiar with religions, languages, technologies, and arts different from their own. It became the locus for the diffusion of many elements of the various civilizations along its caravan roads, and it reaped the benefits of being an entrepôt for Eurasian trade. Under the Timurids and Uzbeks, its major cities were among the most beautiful and cosmopolitan in the world.

The Timurids

When Timur died in 1405, his four sons followed the Turkish custom of fighting each other to determine his successor. In 1407, the youngest, Shah Rukh (1407–1447), seized power in Herat. During the next two years, he secured Khorasan, Transoxiana, Khwarazm, and Fergana (on the upper Syr Darya River). Shah Rukh fought furiously to gain control of his father's empire, but his attempts to restore Timurid rule to Azerbaijan, western Iran, and Iraq were frustrated by the

Turkmen group known as the Black Sheep (Qara-Quyunlu). The Black Sheep had established themselves in Azerbaijan in the middle of the fourteenth century, but Timur's invasion had scattered them. In 1406, only a year after Timur's death, they regained Tabriz and proved too powerful for Shah Rukh to subdue. As a result, Shah Rukh relied upon an old ally of his father—the Turkmen of the White Sheep (Aq-Quyunlu) clans, who had long been established at Diyarbakr in eastern Anatolia—to harass the Black Sheep and keep them from posing a threat to Timurid positions in central Iran.

Shah Rukh was a skilled warrior, but he had no intention of emulating Timur's career of ceaseless military campaigns. He developed a reputation as a pious Muslim and a ruler who was concerned to improve the quality of urban life. He established his capital at Herat and granted to his seventeen-year-old son Ulugh Bey the city of Samarqand to rule. For almost four decades, Shah Rukh ruled over Khorasan and left Transoxiana practically autonomous under Ulugh Bey's direction. Jointly, these two men became as famous for their patronage of the arts and sciences as Timur is for his brutal conquests. In the fifteenth century, Herat, Samarqand, Bukhara, and Balkh (near modern Mazar-i Sharif) were among the most sophisticated in the world. Other than Cairo and Damascus, it is likely that only a handful of Chinese cities could compete with them in sheer cultural brilliance: No European city could yet compare with them. The major Central Asian cities benefitted from their location at the juncture of major long-distance trade routes and they were centers for the production of high-quality goods in the silk, cotton, leather, rug, jewelry, woodcarving, metal, and paper industries. Persian literature and poetry thrived, and Herat's calligraphers, painters, and manuscript illuminators won a reputation as the finest in the Muslim world. The city's school of Persian miniaturists became the standard for all subsequent work in the genre.

Under Ulugh Beg (1411–1449), the major cities of Transoxiana competed with Herat for cultural preeminence. Bukhara and Samarqand became more noted for architecture than painting, and for science and mathematics than literature. In contrast to his dour father, Ulugh Beg took pleasure in the talents of his court musicians and singers. He dabbled in philosophy, but was a competent astronomer and mathematician. He ordered the construction of a large observatory in Samarqand and invited the most prominent astronomers and mathematicians to it. During his reign, Samarqand was the site of the most advanced astronomical and mathematical research in the world. Ulugh and his scientific team developed the famous *Zij-i Gurgani*, which contained a catalog of visible stars together with tables of the planets and calendar calculations. It was translated into Latin in the mid-seventeenth century and used as far away as England.

Upon Shah Rukh's death in 1447, Ulugh Beg consolidated the rule of Herat and Balkh with that of Transoxiana, but his own son murdered him two years later. This act of patricide provoked a war among the Timurid princes. By 1451, Abu Sa'id, a nephew of Ulugh Beg, consolidated power over the cities that Ulugh Beg had united just before his death. Meanwhile, the Black Sheep and White Sheep began an intense competition with each other to control Azerbaijan, eastern Anatolia, Iraq, and western Iran. The White Sheep, under the leadership of Uzun Hasan (ruled 1453–1478), won the contest of the two Turkmen groups in 1467. They then began expanding eastward at the expense of their former allies, the

Timurids. In 1469, Abu Sa'id led an army to Azerbaijan to suppress the White Sheep, but the latter killed him and utterly routed his army.

Uzun Hasan now controlled the entire region from eastern Anatolia to Khorasan. He actively sought alliances with the Venetians as well as with the Christian rulers of Trebizon, who were descendants of the dynasty that ruled the Byzantine Empire during the First Crusade. Uzun's marriage in 1458 to Theodora Komnena (better known as Despina), the daughter of the emperor of Trebizon, committed him to defend Trebizon against the Ottomans. As we saw in Chapter 3, the Ottoman sultan, Mehmet II, considered Uzun to be a sufficiently serious threat to Ottoman aspirations that he led a major expedition against him in 1473 and defeated him decisively. The White Sheep remained a regional power for three more decades, but never again challenged the Ottomans.

Abu Sa'id's death in 1469 brought an end to the unity of Timurid rule. From that point on, the Timurid princes who governed the major cities of Central Asia jealously guarded their independence. The former empire became divided into tiny, weak principalities. The major Timurid cities were mutually hostile, held by relatives who feuded with each other. As slender as their resources might be, these petty princes continued the tradition of patronage of the arts that the first Timurids had begun, and their cities impressed visitors from any region who passed through them. The most prominent during this period was Herat. Its scholars made significant contributions in mathematics and medicine, and its artists integrated Chinese influences to mark a new departure in Timurid painting. Herat was also the home of two of the most famous poets of the age. Jami (1414–1492) wrote in Persian, and Nava'i (1441–1501) was the greatest figure in the emergence of Turki, or Chaghatay Turkish, as a literary language.

A century after Timur died, his descendants had become so divided and militarily weak that no one was surprised when an outside force saw an opportunity to pick them off one by one. During the first decade of the sixteenth century, Uzbeks began moving into Transoxiana and discovered that no Timurid could stand up to them without outside help. They began a new era in Central Asian history.

The Uzbek Khanate

The origin of the Uzbeks is unclear. Until recently, most scholars thought that they were the result of a schism within the Golden Horde; the dominant strain in the historiography of the subject now interprets their arrival on the Syr Darya as a southward migration from a homeland in Siberia. Soon after settling on the Syr Darya, they seem to have suffered a secession, and the breakaway group came to be known as the Kazakhs. The origin of the Kazakhs, however, is as uncertain as that of the Uzbeks. What most scholars agree on is that both groups traced their lineage back to Chinggis Khan, both were Turkicized Mongols, and that, whereas the Uzbeks settled along the lower Syr Darya, the Kazakhs moved eastward into northern Moghulistan, a region that came to be known as Zungaria.

Soon after their arrival on the frontier with Transoxiana, the Uzbeks inflicted a major defeat on Ulugh Bey early in his reign. They might well have conquered his domains had they not quarreled among themselves and become disorganized for several decades. Finally, in 1501, the Uzbek leader Muhammad Shaybani took advantage of a favorable conjunction of events: He had unified most of the Uzbek clans, and Ulugh Bey's successors were quarreling among themselves. Shaybani crossed the Syr Darya and attacked. He quickly seized Samarqand, and, over the next several years, he systematically conquered all of Transoxiana. He also took over much of Khorasan, including Herat.

Despite the ease with which Shaybani dispatched the various Timurid rulers, his ambitions were foiled by a twist of fate. His own conquests took place simultaneously with the meteoric career of Shah Isma'il of Iran, who created the Safavid Empire. Isma'il began conquering western Iran in 1501, the same year that Shaybani began his conquest of Transoxiana. Isma'il arrived in Khorasan in 1510 with the intention of annexing it. At Merv, the Savafid army defeated the Uzbeks, and Shaybani was killed in the fighting. Isma'il went on to capture Herat. Then, hoping to drive the Uzbeks out of Transoxiana, he offered an alliance with the sole surviving Timurid ruler, Babur of Fergana. Isma'il made the offer contingent upon Babur's conversion to Shi'ism. Babur was a Sunni who was deeply devoted to the Naqshbandi Sufi order, but he accepted the terms as a political necessity. A joint Timurid–Safavid campaign defeated the demoralized Uzbeks at Samarqand.

Babur ruled Transoxiana for two years, but his alliance with Isma'il turned out to be a Faustian bargain. He fulfilled his agreement with Isma'il by minting coins inscribed with the names of the Shi'ite Imams and ordering that sermons in the mosques be given in the name of Isma'il. The Sunnis of Transoxiana, however, suspected that worse was yet to come. They knew that Isma'il had forced the Sunnis in Iran to convert to Shi'ism, and they feared that they would soon be compelled to do so, as well. They protested violently against the policies. Important factions in Bukhara and Samarqand allied themselves with the Sunni Uzbeks, who attacked and forced Babur to flee to Kabul. The last of the Timurid rulers was now in exile south of the Hindu Kush.

The Uzbeks had regained Transoxiana from the Timurids, but they had lost Khorasan to the Safavids. They also lost the chance for a unified leadership when the charismatic Shaybani was killed. For the next seven decades, Uzbek clan leaders were content to remain in a loose confederation rather than see one of their peers become more powerful than the others. They were usually organized on the basis of confederations of nomadic clans, and the four or five most powerful clans established bases in cities. This was different from the tradition of the Horde, which ruled its tributary cities from rural encampments. The clans occasionally united in military expeditions to try to recover Herat and Merv from the Safavids, but they succeeded only in devastating the regions around those cities. The Safavid Shah Tahmasp, who succeeded his father Isma'il in 1524, concentrated his arsenal of artillery on the eastern plains against the Uzbeks rather than in the mountainous west against the more formidable Ottomans. The outgunned Uzbeks tried to avoid direct confrontation with the Safavid army and retreated quickly whenever it approached Khorasan.

In 1582, a descendant of Muhammad Shaybani named 'Abd Allah Khan united the Uzbeks again by forcing fellow clan leaders to submit to him. As a result, he was able to field an army with a more unified command structure than any other Uzbek force since the time of Shaybani himself. With it, he took advantage of turmoil within the Safavid empire and seized Khorasan in 1588. The Shaybanid period

(1582–1598) also witnessed the extension of Uzbek power into the Tarim basin and the central Kazakh steppe. Soon after 'Abd Allah's death in 1598, a rival clan of the Shaybanids, known as the Astrakhanids, seized power. For several decades they were organized into a confederation of two sub-khanates, one based at Bukhara and the other at Balkh. During the second half of the seventeenth century, the khanate was unified under a single Astrakhanid ruler who lived in Bukhara, but the clans still maintained a large degree of autonomy.

Despite the pastoral basis of the Uzbeks, the elites made great efforts to encourage the agricultural and commercial sectors of the economy. In order to promote wealth, they invested great sums in irrigation projects along the major rivers. They also facilitated long-distance trade by building new caravanserais and bridges. The Uzbeks' single greatest source of foreign earnings was the sale of horses. Central Asian horses were highly valued as far away as China and Russia, but their biggest market was India. Because of India's relative lack of good grazing pastures, it could not breed enough horses to keep the huge cavalry forces of its various rulers supplied. As a result, the trade in horses between South Asia and Central Asia was a major theme in Asian economic history until the late nineteenth century.

The cities of Transoxiana continued to flourish for over a century and a half under the Uzbek khanates. Like the Timurids, the Uzbeks patronized the arts, although there was a perceptible change in the nature of the patronage. Due to the growing influence of the Naqshbandi Sufi order on Uzbek rulers, the scientific and mathematical legacy inherited from the Timurid era was neglected at the expense of religious endowments. Because the Naqshbandiya were centered at Bukhara, that city soon gained preeminence over the others. Its libraries and artisans' shops were widely known, attracting scholars and potential buyers of fine art. Samarqand, Balkh, and Tashkent also thrived, enjoying the prestige and benefits of monumental mosques and madrasas. The most famous architectural legacy of this period is the Registan of Samarqand, a triad of madrasas facing a large square (see the photograph in the color plates). The oldest of the three monuments was commissioned by the Timurid Ulugh Bey, whereas the other two were built under the Astrakhanid dynasty between 1618 and 1660.

The flourishing life of the arts in the cities of Transoxiana stood in stark contrast to the fate of the cities of Khorasan. The numerous Uzbek campaigns of the sixteenth century against Herat, Merv, and other cities in Khorasan progressively impoverished the region. Herat suffered the greatest decline. The most splendid of the Timurid cities, it fell first to the Uzbeks, and then to the Safavids in 1510. In 1522, the greatest of the city's painters moved to the Safavid capital of Tabriz. Due to Herat's location in the extreme eastern part of the Safavid Empire, it was often unprotected against Uzbek attacks. It was brutally sacked twice, and rapidly declined.

During the second half of the seventeenth century, the wealth of Transoxiana began to shrink. The most tangible evidence of this development lay in the fields of architecture, painting, ceramics, and manuscript illumination, which experienced a dramatic decline in the production of noteworthy objects. More ominously for the ruling clans, independent Uzbek warlords began emerging in the horse-breeding centers of what is now northern Afghanistan, a symptom of the weakening of the power of the khan to control them. Much is obscure about the history of seventeenth- and eighteenth-century Central Asia, but it appears that the beginning of this economic decline was due in part to the global seventeenth-century economic crisis, which caused a slump in the trade in luxury goods. This economic slowdown did not persist, but when it ended, the volume of luxury goods traded through Central Asia had declined. By the late seventeenth century, the newly developed maritime routes dominated by Europeans had begun carrying more and more of the valuable luxury trade from Asia to Europe.

Market activity in Central Asian cities did not die. The east–west trade did not dry up completely, and the north–south trade through Transoxiana may even have increased. The Russians, who had long coveted the eastern goods that ended up in Astrakhan and Kazan, took over those cities of the old Golden Horde in the 1550s and established direct trading links with the Uzbeks and with commercial centers in India. The subsequent increase in the north–south trade, however, did not compensate the cities of Transoxiana for the decline in the profits of the east–west trade, for the north–south trade was in basic commodities rather than luxury goods, and therefore was not as profitable as the old trade pattern had been. Thus, during the second half of the seventeenth century, Central Asia still appeared to be a bustling trading center, but its wealth was slowly declining due to the changed nature of the goods that passed through its markets.[1]

By the early eighteenth century, the Uzbek khans of Bukhara and Balkh ruled in name only. Warlords competed with each other over declining resources, and old alliances fragmented. Nomadic Turkic newcomers were recruited to augment the manpower of local leaders. Violence became chronic, damaging both trade and agriculture. In 1740, the ruler of Iran, Nadir Shah, ended the Astrakhanid period. Having already replaced the Safavids as the ruler of Iran, he now subjugated Transoxiana. He ruled both Iran and Transoxiana until he was assassinated in 1747.

The Uzbek khanate was a new stage in the Turkicization of Transoxiana. Historically a region in which Persian culture had predominated, Transoxiana became increasingly populated by Turkic groups after the tenth century. Under the Turks, the Persian language continued to be widely used in belles lettres and as a chancery language for centuries, but its position was increasingly vulnerable due to the repeated waves of Turkish migrants into the area. By the late seventeenth century, the region was predominantly Turkish as far south as the northern arc of Khorasan (modern Turkmenistan). Although Persian speakers could still be found in Transoxiana and northern Khorasan, the "Persian frontier" had been pushed hundreds of miles south of the Amu Darya to roughly the northern borders of modern Iran, Afghanistan, and Tajikistan.

The Islamization of Central Asia

The period of Timurid and Uzbek rule marked an intensification and extension of the influence of Islam in Central Asia. The sedentary population of Transoxiana had been exposed to Islam for centuries, but pastoral populations were always less influenced by the formal doctrines and rituals of Islam than sedentary groups were. The Mongol invasions of the thirteenth century inaugurated an era of increased immigration by pastoral populations into Transoxiana. These new immigrants were overwhelmingly Turkic in language and culture. Most were also non-Muslim, and were potential recruits to Islam. The Yasavi and Kubraviya Sufi orders had engaged in active missionary work in Central Asia even before the invasion of Chinggis Khan, and the Kubraviya had been the instrument through which both Berke of the Golden Horde and Ghazan of the Il-khanate had converted to Islam. By the late fourteenth century, however, the most dynamic and ultimately the dominant tariqa in Central Asia was the Naqshbandi order.

Baha' al-Din Naqshband (d. 1389) of Bukhara came of age during the period when the Il-khanate collapsed and the Chaghatay khanate split. His importance lay not in the originality of his teaching—most of which he learned from his own pirs—but in his charisma and piety. He was able to unite a formerly disparate group of Sufis around a set of practices that included strict adherence to the Shari'a, rejection of music and dance, and the practice of a silent dhikr. Although some branches of the order continued to practice a vocal dhikr, the silent dhikr became a major distinguishing characteristic of the Naqshbandiya. It reinforced the order's stress on the importance of continuous devotion, for it enabled the devotee to repeat the name of God silently and perpetually, even when engaged in other activities.

As early as the reign of Timur, the Naqshbandiya gained a following among the merchants and artisans in Bukhara and Samarqand. Soon, the Naqshbandis were active among the rural population as well. Preachers and traders fanned out among the nomads of Timurid-ruled Transoxiana and among the Uzbeks north of the Syr Darya River. Naqshbandi traders were already in Kashgar and other cities of the Tarim Basin by the early sixteenth century. During the sixteenth and seventeenth centuries, Naqshbandi *khwajas* (pirs) extended their influence among the Uighurs, a Turkic people who had been settling in western China ever since the thirteenth century. By 1700, several khwajas had established thriving communities of Uighur disciples as far east as Gansu province (in the vicinity of the western terminus of the Great Wall, some 1500 miles from Kashgar). They also had followers among the Hui, the name applied to Muslims of central and eastern China, whose origins lay in the Muslim merchant communities that had existed for centuries along Silk Road and the Chinese coast. As a result of Naqshbandi activity, the Uighurs along the trade routes of the Tarim Basin became predominantly Muslim. The basin became a Muslim preserve between Tibet to the south and Mongolia to the north, both of which were Buddhist and shamanistic.

Naqshbandi leaders were famous for their political activism as well as for their missionary work. The order's insistence on a strict interpretation of the Shari'a brought it into conflict with the worldly ways of the Timurid ruling house during the fifteenth century. Naqshbandi leaders organized occasional mass protests in the streets, and Ulugh Bey attempted to pacify them by endowing madrasas and mosques in the larger cities. By the second half of the fifteenth century, Naqshbandi leaders were becoming prominent as spiritual advisors for several Timurid and Uzbek rulers who sought to enhance their standing among their subjects.

The acquisition of political influence on the part of Naqshbandi pirs happened at the time that pirs in many Sufi orders across the Muslim world were gaining enhanced stature in the eyes of their followers. Their disciples regarded them as more than mere teachers. They also considered them to be spiritual intermediaries between their disciples and God, and to have some degree of temporal authority, as well. In some orders, the actual mystic discipline was often submerged beneath the veneration of the pir. Because of their high prestige and perceived influence with God and with rulers, pirs were the recipients of gifts and bequests. Just as some ascetic monastic orders in medieval Europe eventually became wealthy due to the gifts and bequests that their admirers gave them, the Naqshbandiya of Central Asia became wealthy due to the awe and reverence that its leadership evoked. The order received religious endowments that included vast estates, artisanal workshops, and madrasas.

Despite the Naqshbandiya's growing wealth, its adherence to the Shari'a allowed it to escape some of the excesses characteristic of some of the other Sufi orders of the period. On the other hand, some of its khwajas became very powerful figures. The major Naqshbandi figure in the fifteenth century was Khwaja 'Ubayd Allah Ahrar (1404–1490). Khwaja Ahrar was a wealthy landowner when he became a pir, and his combination of economic wealth, spiritual charisma, and political ties with the Timurid elite enabled him to wield great power. His diplomatic efforts secured an agreement among Uzbek leaders not to intervene in Transoxiana during the Timurid civil war of 1449–1451, allowing Abu Sa'id to secure leadership of Transoxiana and Khorasan. Based in Samarqand, Khwaja Ahrar mediated numerous conflicts among warlords, served as an advocate for ordinary people who sought justice or tax relief at Timurid courts, continued the trend toward a uniform system of Naqshbandi doctrine and practice, and managed a far-flung and diversified set of economic interests that yielded a continuous stream of revenue into the order. His career created a model for subsequent Naqshbandi khwajas who sought to exercise political influence, either by advising dynastic rulers or by exercising political power themselves.

The Naqshbandiya thrived under the Uzbeks. Uzbek rulers enjoyed the prestige of lineal descent from Chinggis Khan, but so many of the Uzbek nobility shared in that status that no clan had an advantage in legitimacy. The successful leaders were the ones who worked out a symbiotic relationship with the Naqshbandi khwajas that allowed both to benefit. The warlords protected the khwajas, and the khwajas gave their blessing to the warlords. By the end of the sixteenth century, Naqshbandi khwajas served on the council that ratified the accession of a new khan.

Several Naqshbandi khwajas acquired sufficient political power to rule in their own right. During the 1520s, two sons of Khwaja Ahrar moved to Kashgar, in the Tarim Basin, which was under the control of the Chaghatay dynasty of Moghulistan. Over the next several generations, the influence of the Kashgari khwajas' descendants (who also became khwajas, due to the widespread assumption that spiritual authority was inherited) increased until they became governors in the region. During the seventeenth century, Naqshbandi khwajas went on missions to the east, to the region included in the modern provinces of Gansu, Ningxia, and Shaanxi. This was (and still is) the region in China with the largest concentration of the Hui people, or the Muslims of China whose first language was Chinese rather than a Central Asian language. It was the region where the major trade route between Mongolia and Tibet intersected with the legendary Silk Road, whose terminus was Chang'an (modern Xi'an, in Shaanxi province). Muslim traders from Central Asia had settled in this region over the centuries and had married Chinese women. Their children learned the Chinese language and culture of their mothers and the Islam of their fathers (see Map 5.2).

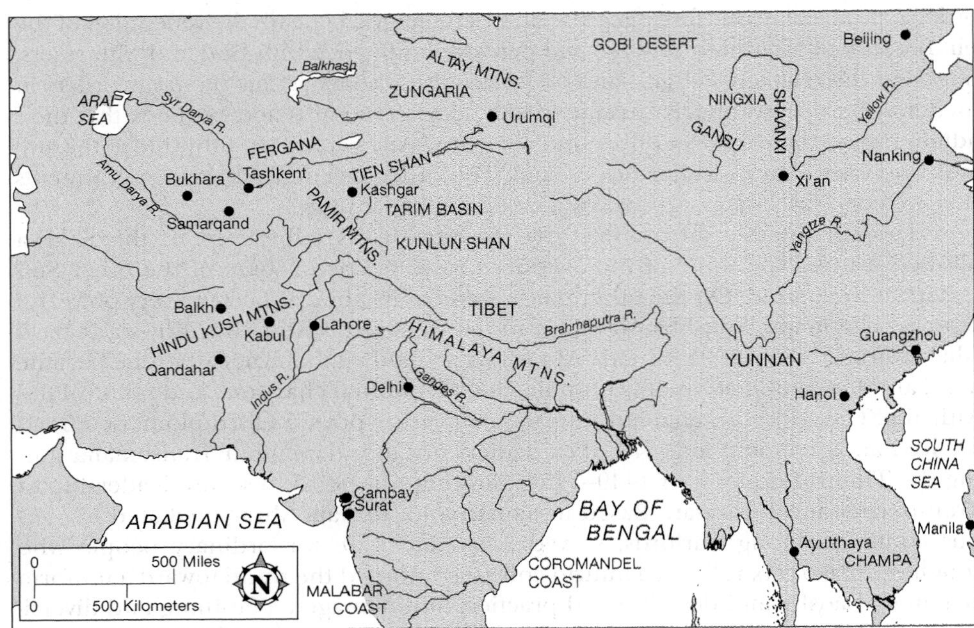

MAP 5.2 Central Asia and China.

The introduction of Naqshbandi ideas and organizational structures into the Hui population produced a schism within the community. Prior to the Naqshbandi arrival, the Hui had not possessed an organizational structure beyond their local mosque and had few contacts with the larger Muslim world. They spoke Chinese, and only the itinerant imams and teachers knew Arabic or Persian. Despite their remoteness from the centers of Islamic learning, they worked hard to stay faithful to the norms of the Hanafi law school, and they prided themselves on their attention to ritual detail. The Hui who joined the Naqshbandiya, by contrast, were suddenly thrust into an international organization that looked to a leadership centered far to the west, in Kashgar and Bukhara. They performed rituals that were puzzling to their friends and family who did not become Sufis, and they sought a mystical experience to complement the ritual activity performed at the mosque. They quickly learned that they were expected to read and learn texts that were written in Arabic and Persian, and that nothing of value could be written in Chinese. The Hui became polarized into two groups: the Gedimu (from *qadim,* meaning "old" in Arabic), who adhered to traditional Hui customs, and the Khufiya (meaning "secret" or "concealed"), who belonged to the Naqshbandiya.

In 1678, the Chaghatays, who gradually had become Islamized over the centuries, were overwhelmed by an invasion of a non-Muslim, Mongol people known as the Oirats. The Oirats were the western wing of the Mongols who had been expelled from China in 1368 by the Ming uprising. They had become established in Zungaria, or northern Moghulistan, the region north of the Tien Shan Mountains and south of the Altay Mountains. The khwajas of the Tarim Basin adapted immediately to their new masters and remained governors of their provinces.

The Ch'ing (Qing) dynasty that ruled China from Beijing after overthrowing the Ming dynasty in 1644 viewed the Oirats suspiciously, for good reason. Several times after the 1670s, the Oirats attempted to expand eastward at the expense of the Ch'ing. Finally, after yet another Oirat attack in the early 1750s, the Ch'ing emperor decided that it was time to settle the issue with the Mongols. The Chinese army pursued them in a series of battles throughout the decade. They finally destroyed the Oirat army and began a campaign of extermination that almost totally obliterated the population of one million. In 1759, China annexed the Tarim Basin and Zungaria, which today compose the province of Xinjiang. When the government sent agents into the Tarim Basin to collect taxes, the Naqshbandi khwajas of Kashgar refused to pay. The Chinese sent a military unit into Kashgar, forcing the khwajas to flee westward into Transoxiana. The Chinese conquest, combined with a smallpox epidemic, depopulated much of the Tarim. China annexed the basin in 1759, and although the government allowed Muslims to follow their religious practices, it developed a long-lasting suspicion of Naqshbandi khwajas.

Iran

The potential for a Sufi order to become a powerful political force was realized in the fourteenth and fifteenth centuries in regions as far apart as Morocco and Central Asia. The most fertile region for Sufi activity that combined explicit spiritual content with implicit political content was Iran. There, during the fourteenth and fifteenth centuries, several messianic movements arose that combined Sufi doctrines and practices with the expectation that the leader of the movement was the *mahdi.*

The concept of the mahdi arose during the second half of the first century of Islamic history, but the term was used in a variety of ways. Sunni Islamic history has witnessed the careers of several religio-political leaders who claimed to be the mahdi, and it is clear that they did not share a common conception of what the role should entail. Some Sunnis expected the mahdi to be a divinely appointed leader who would defeat the mundane forces of corruption and injustice in his generation, bringing a new order of purity and justice to history. Other Sunnis expected a divinely-appointed figure (Jesus was often mentioned) who would bring history as we know it to an end after a cataclysmic battle with the forces led by al-Dajjal, the Evil One.[2]

Among Shi'ites, the concept of the mahdi fused with the doctrine of the Imam. Devout Twelver Shi'ites expected the "hidden" Twelfth Imam to return from where God had kept him in "concealment" since the year 874. His role was to redeem history from its corruption and oppression and to institute an era characterized by goodness and justice. Isma'ili, or Sevener, Shi'ites—the Nizaris and Tayyibis—had confidence that their respective Imams would one day be recognized by the masses as the legitimate spiritual and temporal leader.

In the violent and chaotic decades after the collapse of the Il-khanid regime in 1335, several movements arose in Iran that offered security to their followers and a secret knowledge that explained the chaos that was whirling around them. They featured charismatic spiritual leaders who provided a vision of social justice and a new moral order that would replace the oppression and chaos of the present. Some of the movements were examples of what most Muslims called the *ghulat* ("exaggerators" or "extremists"), which usually entailed the belief in reincarnation and in the divinity of 'Ali. Most of them lasted only during the lifetime of their founder, or for a few generations. The Nizaris and Twelvers, on the other hand, had been in existence for six centuries or longer, and have survived to the present day.

The Nizaris Regroup

After the Hulagu's Conquest of Alamut in 1256, the Nizaris scattered throughout Syria, Iran, Central Asia, Afghanistan, and Sind.[3] According to Nizari tradition, a minor son of the last Lord of Alamut survived the Mongol catastrophe and became the new Imam. Out of fear of the Mongols and the petty rulers who came after them, he and his successors remained in hiding and were inaccessible to their followers for the next two hundred years. Communication among the various clusters of Nizari followers was difficult. As a result, local traditions developed independently of each other. The Syrian community was forced to acknowledge the political suzerainty of the Mamlukes, but in return it was allowed to retain its religious identity openly. Despite the continuing mistrust between the Mamlukes and Syrian Nizaris, their shared hatred of the Mongols enabled the two groups to cooperate several times to fight the Il-khans. In Mongol-dominated Iran and Central Asia, however, it was dangerous to be known as a Nizari. As a result, the Nizari communities there practiced *taqiya*—a religiously sanctioned concealment of one's true beliefs—usually in the guise of Sufis. Local spiritual leaders functioned as Sufi pirs and their followers appeared to be their Sufi *murshids*, or disciples. The Nizaris appeared to be but one of many Sufi groups during the pre-Safavid period that revered 'Ali, practiced contemplation and mystical exercises, and avidly read Rumi, Ibn al-'Arabi, Hafez, and numerous other Sufi poets and theorists.

The Nizaris found it easy to assume the guise of Sufis due to their mystical inclination, hierarchical religious organization, and genuine appreciation for the great figures in Sufi history. Moreover, after the split with the Fatimids in 1094, the Nizaris lost the earlier, distinctive Isma'ili obsession with cosmology and cyclical history. They could easily have been mistaken for a Sufi group of the fourteenth century because they focused on attaining the true spiritual reality of their Imam and they sought the inner, mystical meaning of the Qur'an and Shari'a, rather than remaining content with their literal meaning.

By the fifteenth century, however, the long-term practice of taqiya and the lack of a central Nizari authority had caused the Nizari community to decline in size. Numerous individual Nizaris lost their religious identity and became Sunnis, Twelver Shi'ites, or even—in Sindh—Hindus. About the year 1460, the Nizari Imam took the initiative to try to reverse this trend. He established his headquarters in the village of Anjudan, near Qum. Although still posing as a Sufi pir, he became accessible again to his followers. He also began a concerted effort to bring the widely scattered Nizari communities under his control. His agents visited the numerous towns and villages across Iran, Central Asia, and Sindh where Nizaris lived. They sought to reestablish the lines of communication between the Imam and his followers that had characterized the Alamut period. Due to the power and autonomy that local pirs had built up, the agents initially met with mixed success. By the beginning of the sixteenth century, their persistence had created a widespread network of communities that looked to Anjudan for guidance, enabling Nizari Shi'ism to survive and to harbor hopes of growth.

The Safavids: A Militant Sufi Order

While the Nizaris were still an underground movement, a Sufi movement began that ultimately claimed the leadership of Twelver Shi'ism and created a powerful empire. Shaykh Safi al-Din (1252–1334) of Ardabil gained a widespread reputation as a spiritual leader during his lifetime, which closely paralleled the Il-khanid era (1260–1335). Several important Il-khanid family members considered themselves Safi al-Din's disciples, and intellectuals at the cosmopolitan Il-khanid court admired him. Within a year of his death, the Il-khanid regime collapsed and Iran soon became divided into several petty kingdoms that constantly warred with each other. During this turbulent period, members of Safi al-Din's family not only maintained his organization (which is known as the Safavid order), but also engaged in active proselytism. Ardabil came under outside political control several times during the fourteenth and fifteenth centuries, but the Safavid organization remained intact due to its high quality of leadership.

During the Il-khanid period, the Safavid movement seems to have been a typical Sufi organization of the era, providing spiritual comfort and physical protection. Like many other Sufis, the Safavids did not attach much importance to labels such as "Sunni" and "Shi'ite." As noted in Chapter 2, many Sufis regarded 'Ali as a great hero (although not divine), and many Sufi orders traced their spiritual lineage back to him. Many non-Shi'ite Sufis also admired and revered the Shi'ite Imams as great saints of God. A person could admire and emulate 'Ali and the Imams without becoming a Shi'ite.

Our knowledge of early Safavid history is sketchy, hampered by scarce and conflicting evidence, but what can be affirmed is that, during the fifteenth century, the Safavid order became transformed into a militant messianic movement. The degree to which it incorporated elements normally associated with the ghulat is not clear due to the paucity of trustworthy evidence and to the inherent ambiguity of Sufi discourse itself, which, as we have seen, revels in the enigmatic and the ambiguous. It appears that the order made the transition to militant messianism about 1447. In that year, two descendants of Safi al-Din—Junayd and his uncle Ja'far—each claimed to be the sole, legitimate leader of the order. They clashed, and Ja'far gained control of the headquarters at Ardabil under the protection of the Black Sheep Turkic confederation, which dominated northern Iran and Azerbaijan at that time.

We do not know what Ja'far's teachings were, because it is with Junayd that the future of the movement lay. He fled westward and recruited followers from among pastoralists of eastern Anatolia and northern Syria. This area was not only a frontier where Ottoman and Mamluke interests were beginning to collide, but also the region where Uzun Hasan was building up his power. Uzun Hasan was the leader of the White Sheep confederation whom we have met before in his challenges to the Ottomans and the Timurids. Uzun was careful to patronize a wide variety of religious causes—Sunni, Twelver Shi'ite, and a variety of messianic ones—in his quest to build support. Junayd was fortunate to be looking for a patron at the moment when Uzun was looking for protégés. Uzun Hasan even arranged for his sister to marry Junayd as a sign of their alliance. The young couple soon had a son named Haydar.

Bolstered by the protection of the White Sheep, Junayd became an effective charismatic leader. His religious claims were combined with a call for jihad against Christian areas in the Caucasus and on the eastern shore of the Black Sea. His victories reinforced his charismatic claims, and he was able to deliver large amounts of plunder to his soldiers. As a result, he developed a large and enthusiastic following. In 1460, however, Junayd was killed when he attacked the Muslim ruler of Shirvan, a regional power some two hundred miles north of Ardabil.

At the time of Junayd's death, his son Haydar was too young to succeed him as the leader of his faction of the Safavids. Our knowledge of the era is so incomplete that we do not know who took Junayd's place during the next twenty years, but we do know that Uzun Hasan defeated his Black Sheep rivals in 1467 and took Ardabil from them. He thereby became the patron of the base of the order as well as of the group that Junayd had led. Just as he had made a marriage alliance with Junayd in order to maintain some leverage over a potentially disruptive religio-political movement, he also took care to make Haydar indebted to him. Haydar obtained a fine education at Uzun's court and then married Uzun's daughter by the Trebizon princess, Despina. He became the leader of the Safavids by 1480 at the latest, and he may have attained that position before Uzun died in 1478.

Haydar carried the Safavids to a higher degree of power than they had enjoyed before. He resumed the Caucasus campaigns that Junayd had begun, and he is credited with having devised a distinctive red headgear for his fighters. As a result, the Safavid fighters were soon known as the Qizilbash, or "Redheads." The Qizilbash regarded Haydar to be a special emissary from God, just as they had viewed his father. Haydar's success caused the White Sheep leaders who succeeded Uzun to become increasingly uneasy about the potential threat posed by the military successes of the Safavids. In 1488 the White Sheep joined a coalition of forces to defend Shirvan against the Safavids, and, like Junayd, Haydar was killed fighting the ruler of Shirvan.

The First Twelver Shi'ite Empire

The White Sheep leadership imprisoned Haydar's three sons for several years in order to deprive the Qizilbash of a leader around whom to rally. Only the youngest, Isma'il, survived to maturity. He was one year old when his father was killed in 1488. After his imprisonment at the hands of the White Sheep, his family's supporters spirited him away to hide him from the White Sheep. At first, he was taken to Fars, near the Persian Gulf, and then to Gilan, on the southwestern coast of the Caspian Sea. By 1494, both of his older brothers were dead. As a result, the community at Ardabil recognized Isma'il as its leader. In 1499, Isma'il left Gilan and returned to Ardabil with the goal of assuming his leadership position. The next year he raised an army, which he used to defeat the ruler of Shirvan, gaining some measure of revenge for the deaths of his father and paternal grandfather. He then attacked the White Sheep for their betrayal of his father, and captured Tabriz from them in 1501. It became his capital city, and it was there that he proclaimed himself shah, the title last used by the rulers of the Sasanian Empire (226–651 C.E.). He then began the conquest of the rest of Azerbaijan, eastern Anatolia, western Iran, and northern Iraq.

For several years, it appeared that Isma'il was content to rule over the former empire of Uzun Hasan, but in 1510 he abruptly turned to the east. In a series of ferocious battles, he conquered Khorasan. He overpowered the Uzbeks at Merv and killed Muhammad Shaybani. He then aided the Timurid ruler Babur in his attempt to reconquer Transoxiana from the Uzbeks. Shortly after Isma'il returned to Tabriz, a quarrel broke out between the Turkic and Iranian officers in the Safavid army that he had left in Transoxiana. The Uzbeks seized the opportunity of the quarrel to drive the Safavids south across the Amu Darya River and to send Babur fleeing to Kabul.

Isma'il impressed everyone who met him. His pedigree was impressive: He was a lineal descendant of Safi al-Din on his father's side and the grandson of Uzun and a Byzantine Christian princess through his mother. Other military and political leaders throughout history have accomplished great deeds at a young age, but even in that elite company Isma'il stands out. Our sources—Safavid and Ottoman chronicles, as well as reports from European visitors to the Safavid court—are in agreement that Isma'il was twelve when he began his military campaign and fourteen when he captured Tabriz and named himself shah. He was a teenager when he conquered the heart of his eventual empire, and by the age of twenty-three he was the ruler of a region that roughly corresponded to the Il-khanid realm. Like his father and grandfather, he was revered by his followers and regarded as greater than a mere mortal. His soldiers fought for him with zeal and fearlessness that amazed friend and foe alike. Unlike his father and grandfather, he left behind a corpus of writings, in the form of poetry. He wrote over two hundred poems in which he identifies himself with 'Ali, Alexander the Great, various Iranian epic heroes, Adam, and the long-awaited Hidden Imam. In several poems he claims to be God and demands the prostrations and absolute obedience due his divine status. Most of the poems appear to date from the first decade of Isma'il's rule—during the period of his conquests, when he was still a youth. As we have seen, Sufi poetry is replete with symbolism that is susceptible to multiple interpretations, but the claims that Isma'il repeatedly makes for himself are grander than most Sufi pirs made for themselves. Moreover, numerous inscriptions throughout his empire reiterate the claims that he had a divine nature.

European visitors who met Isma'il while he was still a teenager were awed by his bearing, native intelligence, wisdom, and skill at wrestling and archery. Isma'il was unquestionably a well-rounded prodigy. On the other hand, due to his incarceration as a child and his military life during his youth, Isma'il did not receive the quality of education that either his father or his son Tahmasp enjoyed. Moreover, the chronicles make oblique references to a group of seven advisors—or spiritual guides—who protected Isma'il in Gilan, returned him to Ardabil, and accompanied him during the first several years of his reign as shah. What role this shadowy group played in his military successes, poetic production, and administrative policy has yet to be clarified.

Shah Isma'il Describes Himself to His Followers

Hundreds of poems are credited to Isma'il under the pen name of Khata'i. Like other examples of mystical poetry, they are full of metaphors and symbols. Some of the symbols would be recognized by Muslims belonging to any number of mystical paths, whereas others would be specific to the Safavid group. In this one, Isma'il makes particularly strong claims for possessing a divine nature.

The sixth verse refers to Mim. Mim is one of the letters in the Arabic alphabet but here the allusion is almost certainly to its appearance as one of a handful of such letters that appear in the heading of several of the chapters in the Qur'an. The function of the letters is unknown, but their use has given rise to numerous theories. They are fruitful for mystics, for whom they have served as the start for meditations on the nature of God.

I am God's eye (or God Himself); come now, O blind man gone astray, to behold Truth (God).

I am that Absolute Doer of whom they speak. Sun and Moon are in my power.

My being is God's House, know it for certain. Prostration before me is incumbent on thee, in the morn and even.

Know for certain, that with the People of Recognition Heaven and Earth are all Truth. Do not stray!

The Garden of Sanctity has produced a fruit. How can it be plucked by a short-handed one?

If you wish to join Truth to Truth, (here is) God who has reached the stage of Mim.

The one of pure connections considers his own person. Suddenly Khata'i has come by a treasure.

SOURCE: V. Minorsky, "The Poetry of Shah Isma'il I," *Bulletin of the School of Oriental and African Studies,* 10 (1942): 1047a (poem 195). Reprinted with permission of Cambridge University Press.

One of the most important policy decisions that Isma'il ever made coincided with his assumption of the title of shah in 1501. Soon after capturing Tabriz, he announced that Twelver Shi'ism would be the official religion of his growing empire and that his subjects were required to profess it. All of our sources agree that Isma'il issued this edict and that his army forced Sunnis to curse the memory of the first three caliphs.[4] Many Iranians resisted the implementation of the policy, resulting in numerous casualties and much suffering. On the face of it, the account of the edict is astonishing and implausible. After all, for a decade following the proclamation, Isma'il wrote most of the poetry in which he makes claims for himself that would have been unacceptable to Twelver Shi'ites. He was actively trying to inspire his Qizilbash followers to believe that he had superhuman qualities, a claim that would have been blasphemous to Twelvers unless he were in fact the Hidden Imam. A second problem with the account is that it is hard to imagine the Qizilbash, whom Twelver Shi'ites regarded as heretics because they were ghulat, forcibly imposing Twelver Shi'ism upon Sunnis. The Qizilbash would have regarded doctrinal Twelver Shi'ism as bland, boring, and just plain wrong.

In all likelihood, the resolution to the paradoxes inherent in this account lies in the report that the Qizilbash forced Sunnis to curse the first three caliphs. It is certain that the unlettered Qizilbash did not require the conquered peoples to recite a formal catechism of Twelver Shi'ite beliefs. By forcing people to curse the first three caliphs, however, the soldiers would have made them imply that 'Ali should have been the first caliph, a conviction held by both the Qizilbash and the Twelver Shi'ites. Allegiance to 'Ali would have been the first step in the development of a national ideology that united the Iranians.

Isma'il's espousal of Twelver Shi'ism ran contrary to the claims that he made for himself in his poetry, but he wrote the poems in the Chaghatay Turkish dialect that Nava'i of Herat had pioneered, not in Persian. They were intended to motivate only the Turkish-speaking Qizilbash. Most of his followers would have been unaware of the differences between their beliefs and Twelver Shi'ism. Isma'il also needed the services of the talented Iranian administrative elites, however, who were repelled by the extreme doctrines of the Qizilbash. Twelver Shi'ism was much more acceptable to this educated, urban stratum, and for that reason Isma'il made claims (occasionally contradictory ones) regarding his place in the lineage of the Twelver Imams. An official religion of Twelver Shi'ism—deliberately left undefined at first so as not to confuse the Qizilbash—would have served to distinguish Isma'il's empire from that of his Ottoman neighbors to the west and that of his Uzbek neighbors to the east, facilitating his attempts to create a national identity and to mobilize his subjects to fight "heretics," or Sunnis.

Despite the forcible "conversion" of Iranians to Shi'ism, the Safavid Empire did not become a Twelver society in any meaningful sense for more than a century. A major reason for the time lag was the powerful influence that the Qizilbash wielded due to their overwhelming dominance of the armed forces. They were comfortable with the doctrine of reincarnation, the view of the ruler as superhuman, and a relaxed approach to the Shari'a. The Twelver Shi'ism of the urban ulama did not appeal to them.

A second major reason for the slowness of the transformation of Iran into a Shi'ite society was the dearth of Twelver scholars in the country. The chroniclers report that not a single Twelver Shi'ite authority could be found in the capital city at the time of the proclamation of the faith as the national religion. The new government had to recruit scholars and teachers from the traditionally Shi'ite city of Qum, and later, when southern Iraq was conquered, others were brought in from the holy cities of Najaf and Karbala. In later decades, Twelver ulama were recruited from Lebanon and Bahrain.

To many pastoralists in Anatolia, Syria, Iraq, and western Iran, Isma'il's meteoric rise to power was the fulfillment of the claims that his followers had been making for him. Moreover, much in the Safavid movement's ideology was familiar to them, for it had much in common with the teachings of the well-known Bektashi and Alevi groups of the region. Isma'il's spiritual gifts and his generosity in distributing the plunder of conquests were particularly attractive to pastoralists living in eastern Anatolia (under Ottoman rule) or Syria (under Mamluke rule), who were subject to imperial taxes and restrictions on their movements. After Isma'il's capture of Tabriz, fresh recruits flocked to his army from all over the region, fired with a zeal to reverse the effects of Ottoman and Mamluke policies. Isma'il welcomed some of them into his conquering army and sent others back into his opponents' empires in order to raid.

The loss at Chaldiran in 1514 was a major setback for the Safavid movement. Isma'il's ambitions to extend his influence into Anatolia were crushed, and the battle confirmed Ottoman hegemony there. The present border between Turkey and Iran is a legacy of Chaldiran: Despite subsequent gains and losses by both sides, the region around Lake Van consistently marked the frontier between the Ottomans and Safavids and between their successor states, as well. As a result, the Safavid Empire was not fated to control the heartland of Uzun Hasan's Turkmen state (the upper Tigris and Euphrates rivers) after all. Its capital, Tabriz, was suddenly transformed into a border city after the loss at Chaldiran, precariously close to the Ottoman frontier. The subsequent course of events would shift the center of gravity of the empire eastward, transforming the state's Turkish character into a Persian one.

The Apocalypse Postponed

The major geopolitical consequence of the battle of Chaldiran—the establishment of a frontier zone between the Safavids and their Ottoman neighbors—is fairly easy to identify. More difficult, and more intriguing, is ascertaining the impact of the battle on Isma'il and on the faith and beliefs of most of the Qizilbash. Isma'il's army had lost once before—against the Uzbeks—but only when Isma'il was a thousand miles from the battlefield. At Chaldiran, he was leading his army and yet the enemy won. What does it mean when God's emissary suffers a military defeat? Some chroniclers assert that, in the aftermath of the battle, Isma'il became despondent and remained so for the remaining decade of his life. A year or two after the battle, however, European ambassadors to Tabriz reported that his spirits seemed high. Moreover, we know that, during the next decade, Isma'il arranged alliances with numerous powerful chieftains, regardless of their religious affiliation, in an effort to secure stability in his realm and that he engaged in frequent correspondence with European rulers in an attempt to construct an anti-Ottoman alliance. The former efforts were more successful than the latter. Isma'il also introduced musket and artillery units into his army, although they were never on the scale of their Ottoman opponents.

The fact remains that Isma'il never again took the field to lead an army in person, either against the Ottomans or the Uzbeks, his only two rivals. It is understandable why he would not have wanted to face Ottoman artillery again, but it is less clear why he did not challenge the Uzbeks: They did not rely on artillery, and they controlled a wealthy region that historically had been within the zone of Persian cultural influence. We do not have access to the efforts by Isma'il or his Qizilbash followers to rationalize the catastrophe. The defeat at Chaldiran would not necessarily have disillusioned Isma'il's followers. Both his father and grandfather had been defeated and killed in battle without any apparent damage to their charisma or to the attraction of the Safavid cause. On the other hand, those two leaders had died as martyrs in the cause of ending "ordinary" history and ushering in an era that would embody God's will. Many thought that Isma'il had inaugurated the new age with his rapid conquests, but the decade between Chaldiran and Isma'il's death witnessed no tangible evidence of a transformation of history that would justify the passionate devotion of the Qizilbash to the Safavid cause. The nature of Qizilbash devotion, which combined elements of religious faith and the expectation of material gain, has yet to be fully understood.

In 1524, Isma'il died at the age of thirty-seven. This messianic figure who identified himself with God and the Hidden Imam was a heavy drinker, and the cause of his death was alcohol poisoning although, following in the tradition of Alexander the Great's devoted biographer, Isma'il's biographer carefully recorded the cause of death as a fever. The heir to the throne was Isma'il's ten-year-old son Tahmasp, who was not much younger than his father had been when he had created an empire. Tahmasp, however, inherited a powerful complex of Qizilbash military officers who also just happened to be the ambitious leaders of seven powerful tribes. Several of them hoped to use the opportunity of the regency of the young boy to advance their interests; the others were equally determined to prevent that from happening. Iran quickly succumbed to a decade of civil war among Qizilbash chieftains and, to a lesser extent, Persian-speaking notables. Tahmasp was officially the shah, but he was subject to the influence of a regent who had little power in the empire as a whole. Several times, Tahmasp was targeted for assassination by supporters of rival aspirants to the throne, but he survived to assume control in his own right in 1533.

Although Tahmasp did not possess the charisma of his father, he reigned successfully for over four decades (to 1576). He survived constant challenges from his own Turkmen elites and from repeated invasions by both the Ottomans and the Uzbeks of Transoxiana. In retrospect, his achievement was nothing less than remarkable. He managed to dominate his Turkmen opponents once he gained the throne. Between 1524 and 1538 he or his regent repelled five Uzbek invasions, and between 1533 and 1553 he survived four Ottoman invasions sent by Sultan Suleyman the Magnificent. These achievements were all the more remarkable in view of the fact that Safavid armies were always inferior in numbers to both the Ottomans and the Uzbeks. The Uzbeks could not stand up to the firepower of the new Safavid gunpowder units, but the Ottoman threat was acute. Suleyman temporarily captured Tabriz in 1534 and again in 1548. The Ottomans also captured Iraq during the 1534 campaign and held it permanently except for a short period in the seventeenth century. The Treaty of Amasya in 1555 brought a needed respite in the long conflict between the Ottomans and Safavids. The Safavids conceded the loss of Baghdad and certain areas of eastern Anatolia to the Ottomans, and Suleyman officially recognized Safavid sovereignty. Tahmasp and Suleyman even began to exchange courteous diplomatic notes.

The Ottoman wars had major consequences for the Safavids. One was the loss of Iraq, which was particularly disturbing, because it meant that Iranian pilgrims would find it difficult to travel to the holy cities of Najaf (the burial place of 'Ali) and Karbala (the burial place of Husayn, 'Ali's younger son and the Prophet's grandson). Another was that Tabriz had been demonstrated to be hopelessly vulnerable to Ottoman armies. Bowing to the inevitable, Tahmasp moved his capital at midcentury to Qazvin, almost three hundred miles to the east. The location of the new capital, situated on the Iranian plateau, meant that Persian influences would intensify at the Safavid court at the expense of Turkic influences.

In addition to warding off invasions, Tahmasp also engaged in campaigns of territorial expansion in the Caucasus. During the period 1540–1553, he waged four campaigns in that region and captured tens of thousands of Georgian, Circassian, and Armenian prisoners, most of whom were Christians. He placed many of the women in harems, including that of the royal court, whereas many of the male prisoners were incorporated into his army. Some were assigned to cavalry units; others were placed in infantry units and equipped with muskets and arquebuses.

After Tahmasp's death in 1576, a period of chaos set in that came close to destroying the dynasty. Like other Turkic groups before them, the Safavids believed that the right to rule was transmitted to all collateral members of the ruling family. As a result, rival Qizilbash groups had the opportunity to support different members of the Safavid family in order to achieve their political goals. During the resulting civil war, Qizilbash chieftains took advantage of the weakness at court to gain advantages over their rivals. Amid the confusion, both the Uzbeks and the Ottomans seized Safavid territory with impunity. A decade after the death of Tahmasp, almost half of the empire's territory was lost, and the civil war was making the survival of the empire highly questionable.

In 1587, Tahmasp's grandson 'Abbas (1587–1629) ascended the throne at the age of sixteen. The empire was at the nadir of its history, but 'Abbas proved to be one of his era's most gifted rulers. This multitalented teenager was primarily interested in recovering power for the royal court. He needed a counterweight to the destructive ambitions of the Qizilbash, and he found it among the descendants of the Georgians, Armenians, and Circassians whom Tahmasp had captured, as well as among others from those groups whom 'Abbas captured in his own campaigns. He reorganized the slave forces that he inherited and made them into a permanent army, answerable to the shah alone. He quickly developed a slave cavalry of 10,000 men, and eventually commanded 12,000 artillerymen and 12,000 musketeers. Using his new slave units (usually referred to as *ghulam*) as auxiliaries to his loyal Qizilbash, he quickly subdued the refractory elements of the Qizilbash, who were still fighting each other.

The structure of 'Abbas's new army resembled that of the Ottoman army, with its large cavalry unit largely composed of Turkmen and its nucleus of musket- and artillery-equipped infantry of slave soldiers from Christian areas. The ghulam infantry, however, never developed into as formidable a force as the Janissaries. The musket units were not as well trained, and artillery was never valued highly. Field artillery was not as useful to the Safavids as it was to other armies. To the west and north, the Zagros and Elburz mountain ranges and the rugged valleys of Azerbaijan provided a natural barrier to Ottoman penetration, but they also made the transport of artillery difficult for either army. To the northeast, the Uzbeks were in possession of inferior guns and thus did not provoke an arms race in gunpowder weapons. To the east, the Mughals were usually on friendly terms with the Safavids, and were, at any rate, at a safe remove: The Mughals were not likely to lug their own artillery into Iran.

Once ‘Abbas had united the Qizilbash with his slave army, he began recovering lands from the Uzbeks, Mughals, and Ottomans. He quickly regained Khorasan from the Uzbeks all the way to Herat. By 1603, he felt strong enough to challenge the Ottomans, who were severely limited in their capacity to respond due to the Jelali revolts. He recaptured Azerbaijan and campaigned strenuously in Georgia, although he could never control the region sufficiently to annex it. In 1622, he launched a lightning campaign against Qandahar, which had been surrendered to the Mughals in 1595 by a commander who was in disgrace with ‘Abbas. The city fell quickly to the Safavid army. After two decades of fighting the Ottomans, ‘Abbas even captured much of Iraq in 1623, although his successor lost those gains in 1638. Iran’s border with Iraq has remained remarkably stable since then.

Society

Safavid Iran (see Map 5.3) was one of the world’s great powers during the sixteenth and seventeenth centuries. It was located between two much larger Muslim powers: the Ottoman and Mughal empires. The Safavid realm contained a population of some six to ten million people, depending on the territories it controlled at a given time. Its population was comparable to contemporary England’s, but less than one-third that of the Ottoman Empire and less than one-tenth that of the Mughal Empire. Despite its comparatively small demographic resources, the Safavids managed to hold their own against their imperial rivals because of their formidable army and the great distance that Ottoman and Mughal armies had to travel to reach them.

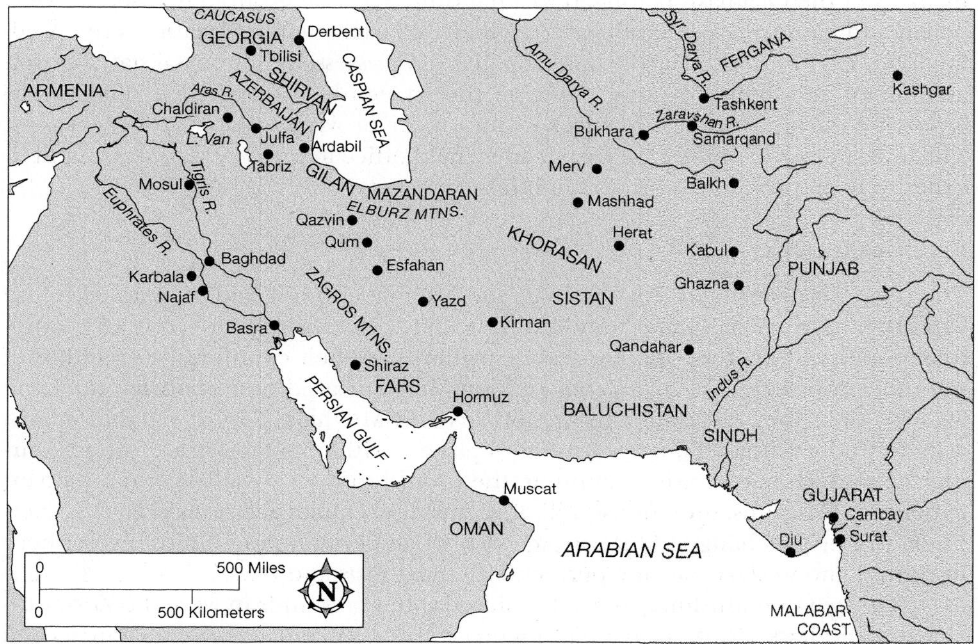

MAP 5.3 Safavid Iran.

Peasants and Herders

Peasants composed the vast majority of the population of Europe, China, the Ottoman Empire, and the Mughal Empire, but formed only slightly more than half the population of the Safavid Empire. The calamitous invasions of northern Iran that occurred from the eleventh through the sixteenth centuries transformed large areas from agricultural to pastoral pursuits. Iranian peasants were perpetually vulnerable to the depredations of nomads and the oppression of landlords. As a result, they suffered greatly during the period between the collapse of the Il-khanate and the reign of 'Abbas. Under 'Abbas, however, they enjoyed a respite from some of the greatest liabilities suffered by their fathers. 'Abbas began to bring large tracts of Iran under his direct ownership, and he used the revenue from them to pay for the high costs of his standing army. Thus, he had a vested interest in protecting the peasants from nomadic harassment. Throughout the seventeenth century, several rulers intervened on behalf of peasants against exploitation by local elites, and peasants enjoyed the cessation of wars and raids that had long disrupted the agriculture of northern Iran. Europeans visiting the Safavid Empire during this period reported the peasants to be well nourished and decently clothed, and compared their condition favorably with that of the peasants in the most fertile regions of Europe.

The Safavid Empire's pastoral subjects were almost as numerous as its peasants. This large reserve of horsemen provided a highly skilled and mobile military force that defended the empire's borders. Many were organized into tribes, which were groupings based at least nominally on kinship. Other types of groupings were possible, including temporary military or security arrangements. Isma'il's devoted followers included people who spoke Arabic, Kurdish, and Persian, but the vast majority of the Qizilbash belonged to a handful of Turkic groupings based in Azerbaijan and eastern Anatolia. Because of their "charter member" status as the original followers of Junayd, Haydar, and Isma'il, they possessed high social status as well as military and political power. During the sixteenth century, their chiefs were granted control of whole provinces in return for providing the shah with troops. The most powerful of the Qizilbash leaders held office in the central government in order to be in proximity to the shah himself.

Religious Groups

The religious diversity of the Ottoman and Mughal empires had no parallel in the Safavid Empire. The shahs' non-Muslim subjects composed a percentage of the total population that was incomparably smaller than their counterparts in either of the other two societies. On the whole, non-Muslims fared more poorly under the Safavids than they did under the Ottomans and Mughals. To understand Safavid religious policy, however, it is essential to place it within its historical context. During the period that we are examining, the Inquisition was in full operation, Spain expelled its Muslims, the English Bill of Rights disenfranchised non-Anglicans, New England Puritans hanged Quakers, and Christian communities almost everywhere in central and western Europe persecuted Anabaptists and Jews.

The two non-Muslim groups that suffered the most in Iran were the Zoroastrians and the Jews. Zoroastrians had incurred the stigma of polytheism during the Arab conquests of the seventh century and they were subject to periodic persecution thereafter. By the end of the Safavid period, almost no Zoroastrians were left in Iran. Most of the world's remaining Zoroastrians were by then known as Parsis (singular *Parsi,* a variant of *Farsi,* or *Persian*) and lived in Gujarat or the Malabar Coast.

Jews had resided in Iran ever since the period of the Achaemenid Empire. Although that empire's rulers allowed Jews to return to Jerusalem after the Babylonian Captivity of the sixth century B.C.E., most remained. Much later, several thousand Spanish Jews emigrated to Iran after their expulsion from Spain in 1492. On the whole, Iranian Jews were not as prosperous as those of the Ottoman Empire, but they fared well until the early seventeenth century. ʻAbbas was the first ruler of Iran in four centuries to force Jews to wear distinctive clothing. During the 1620s, he was persuaded by a Jewish convert to Islam that Jews were writing dangerous talismans against him. In retaliation, he forced the Jews of Esfahan to convert to Islam. Although ʻAbbas's successor allowed these Jews to return to Judaism, by midcentury the persecution of Jews became more intense and widespread throughout the empire. During the early eighteenth century, torture, starvation, and seizure of property became routine for Iranian Jews, who might well have disappeared as a community if the empire had not fallen in 1722.

Under ʻAbbas, Christians generally fared better than any religious community in Iran other than the Twelver Shiʻites themselves. Most of the empire's Christians lived in the northwest, in Armenia. They suffered considerably during the various wars between the Safavids and Ottomans because Armenia was the primary battleground of those wars, and both sides employed a scorched earth policy there to deprive the opponent of food and forage. ʻAbbas's campaigns during 1603–1605 were particularly horrifying in this regard, but the Armenians of Julfa won the sympathy of ʻAbbas. In part, ʻAbbas was motivated by the Armenians' having welcomed him into their city. Equally important, however, he hoped to exploit the commercial skills and contacts of the Armenian merchant community: Armenians had long been engaged in long-distance trade between Iran and its neighbors, and Armenians were well established on the Malabar Coast and in the Mughal court.

ʻAbbas decided to give the Armenian international merchants the responsibility for carrying out his plan to rejuvenate the Iranian economy on the strength of the export of silk. He transported the Julfans en masse to Esfahan, where he built a suburb for them called New Julfa. There the Armenians built a spectacular cathedral whose bells rang out across the city (a rarity in Muslim lands). Even though they were a pampered community by the norms of the day, ʻAbbas twice (in 1613 and 1621) extorted money from them and even demanded conversion to Islam, although the latter demand was not enforced.

Georgian Christians also fared relatively well under ʻAbbas. They were well regarded, perhaps enjoying a halo effect produced by the fact that thousands of Georgian converts to Islam served in the shah's standing army and held important civilian positions in the government. Not least in the popular imagination was the fact that Georgian women had an unrivaled reputation in Iran for beauty (thousands lived in harems throughout Iran, obtained by force, purchase, or consensual marriage). Like the Armenians, Georgian Christians enjoyed generous government loans and religious toleration. After the death of ʻAbbas in 1629, the position of both Armenians and Georgians became more vulnerable, however, and brutal persecution of both communities broke out several times during the remaining century of Safavid history.

It is useful to keep in mind that, despite recurrent Safavid persecution, the Armenians and the Georgians were each other's most consistent enemy. The Georgian Church was in close alliance with the Orthodox Church, whereas the Armenian Church was a Monophysite organization (like the Coptic Church of Egypt), which made it heretical in Orthodox eyes. Thus, hostility between the two groups raged unabated even when the Safavid court began persecuting them. Moreover, rivalry among factions within each church had a devastating impact on the cohesiveness and effectiveness of the major Christian groups in the country.

The capriciousness of Safavid religious policies is most clearly revealed in the regime's relations with its Hindu subjects, several thousand of whom made a comfortable living as moneylenders, money changers, and merchants. According to the tenets of the Qur'an and the Shari'a, most Hindus would qualify as idolaters and polytheists, whom Muslims should have fought until they became Muslims. Just as the Mughals did not follow that policy with their huge Hindu majority, neither did the early Safavids, with their tiny (and economically useful) Hindu minority. By the second half of the seventeenth century, Hindus, like other religious minorities, were beginning to experience harassment and persecution, although no more severely than Sunnis.

Like the Ottomans, European Christians, Georgians, and Armenians, the Safavids were most likely to exhibit consistent religious intolerance in their dealings with co-religionists whose beliefs and practices were perceived to be a threat to their own spiritual or physical well-being. Whereas the Ottomans frequently persecuted Shi'ites, Safavids frequently persecuted Sunnis. To be a Sunni implied a rejection of the central tenet of Shi'ism: the necessity of following a lineal descendant of the Prophet Muhammad (through the line of 'Ali) as the true spiritual and temporal leader of all Muslims. Thus, Sunnis implicitly rejected the legitimacy of the Safavid dynasty, which justified its seizure of power and its right to rule on its reputed lineal descent from Muhammad.

Isma'il and Tahmasp also engaged in severe persecution of the Nizaris. By this time, the latter were based at Anjudan, but they were still posing as Sufis. It is not clear why the two shahs included the Nizaris with the Sufi organizations that they regarded as security threats. Tahmasp, however, was so agitated by the Nizaris that he executed the Imam in 1574. In response to the persecution, the Nizari community began to practice taqiya as Twelver Shi'ites. The transition was successful, and Nizaris achieved an excellent relationship with 'Abbas. During his reign, the Nizari Imam even married a Safavid princess. Throughout the rest of Safavid history, the Nizari Imams continued to practice taqiya and simultaneously to work secretly to win over the allegiance of the Nizaris of the world who had not yet accepted their authority. By the end of the seventeenth century, the seat of the imamate had moved a few miles to the northeast of Anjudan, to Kahak. Almost all the Nizaris of Iran, Sindh, and Gujarat recognized Kahak as the center of their faith. Pilgrimage to the town became a goal of the faithful.

Women

In some ways, the roles of Safavid women resembled those of their Ottoman and Mughal counterparts. Most women from the elite social strata, for example, cultivated the arts of reading, calligraphy, and composing letters. Tahmasp's daughters were

A view of the Tien Shan range from Alma-Ata, Kazakhstan.

considered by their contemporaries to have been especially well educated. Several of the royal women, also, were active in patronizing monumental works of architecture, especially during the reign of 'Abbas I. Generosity in the funding of great works of architecture and charitable foundations, a high level of literacy, and a powerful influence on the ruler if he were one's husband or son are recurring features of women in the royal families of Muslim dynasties throughout history.

In other ways, however, Safavid women's behavior in the sixteenth century struck visitors as quite different from that of their counterparts in the Ottoman and Mughal empires. Ottoman and Mughal women—and urban, Persian-speaking, Muslim women in Iran—had been acculturated for centuries into the norms of the Shari'a. These guidelines granted women property rights that had no equal in contemporary Europe, but restricted their wardrobe options and tended to keep them secluded in the privacy of their homes (if their families could afford not to have them working). The Turkish-speaking Qizilbash, however, were pastoralists, and thus were accustomed to a high degree of interaction among males and females during both work and leisure activities. Their women commonly dressed in colorful garments, did not cover their faces, and enjoyed socializing in mixed female and male gatherings. Because the Qizilbash were the dominant political and social group in Iran during the sixteenth century, women in the early Safavid Empire were much more visible, both literally and metaphorically, than in other Muslim imperial courts.

Women played important political roles during the late sixteenth-century political crisis. Tahmasp's daughter Pari-Khan Khanum was one of his closest advisors and claimed the throne after his death. She contested for power with her brother Isma'il II (1576–1578) and was apparently involved in the plot that resulted in his murder two years later. She ruled for several weeks until her elder brother

Muhammad Khudabanda (1578–1587) arrived in Esfahan and became shah. Muhammad's wife was responsible for Pari-Khan Khanum's assassination, and she herself reigned for some seventeen months when Muhammad was disabled by eye problems. During that time, she took personal command of the army in a war against the Ottomans.

The growth of power for the court at Esfahan came at the expense of both the power of the Qizilbash and social opportunities for women. Shah 'Abbas instituted the seclusion of royal women, and the growing influence of Twelver ulama throughout the seventeenth century brought greater pressure for all women to adhere to the norms of the Shari'a. The climax of this process came during 1694–1695 in a series of royal edicts. These new rulings forbade women to linger in the streets and bazaars or to stroll in gardens or the streets with anyone other than their husbands. They were also forbidden to participate in public gatherings or to visit coffee houses. Women were ordered to cover their hair and bodies with an article of clothing that resembled today's chador, which covers everything but the face, hands, and feet. Officially, at least, conditions for Safavid women had changed profoundly since the sixteenth century. At the dawn of the eighteenth century, some European observers thought that the seclusion of women was even stricter in Iran than in the Arab regions of the Ottoman Empire, where women's movements were more restricted than in Anatolia or Rumelia.

The State

The Safavid shahs aspired to rule over a huge region that contained a large number of pastoral peoples. Their task can be contrasted with the opposite extreme: the ancient Egyptian pharaohs, who claimed the right to rule over the peasants of the Nile valley. The pharaohs needed only a small army to enforce their writ among farmers of the narrow Nile valley, whose fields and mud-brick villages were vulnerable to the demands of government tax collectors. Pastoralists, on the other hand, were highly mobile. Moreover, by virtue of their horse-riding skills and their need to protect their herds, their normal upbringing turned them into some of the most effective warriors in the world. Each grouping (tribe) of pastoralists competed for scarce resources with other such groupings and with urban populations. Scattered across almost a million square miles of territory, the tribes of the Safavid realm were a formidable force for any central power to control. Anyone who aspired to rule them would have to balance any concessions on the part of the tribes with incentives from the central government. Thus, Qizilbash leaders were not only military officers, but the equivalent of governors, as well. They were highly autonomous, and their provinces were considered to be their private property. The central government intervened only if it was not receiving its expected revenue.

As a result of the considerable autonomy that tribal leaders had in Safavid Iran, historians usually regard the Safavid government to have been less centralized than the Ottoman or Mughal. Some historians cannot even bring themselves to speak of a Safavid state. That seems extreme, because the Safavid government boasted a complex bureaucracy and it obtained enough revenue to build some of the greatest architectural monuments in history. It is true that the Safavid government did not evolve quickly. Isma'il had begun the process by staffing his military with the Qizilbash Turks and his fledgling administration with Persian-speakers, usually called Tajiks. Tahmasp was preoccupied throughout his half-century reign with finding ways to keep independent-minded chieftains in line. He took a tentative step toward diluting the military monopoly of the Qizilbash when he began incorporating the Circassian, Armenian, and—especially—Georgian prisoners of war into his army, as we saw previously. ʻAbbas built upon that base, creating a regular standing army composed largely of Georgians. The new cavalry and gunpowder units were able to crush the quarreling Qizilbash, and the Georgian units became the pillar of ʻAbbas's power.

Safavid rulers were wary of the Qizilbash for reasons other than their tribal fractiousness, as well. The same religious zeal that had brought the Safavids to power could also bring them down. Periodically, the rulers had to engage in suppressing messianic movements that challenged the legitimacy of the shah. The fear of competing religious movements led the shahs to be suspicious of all Sufi groups, because of the potential of their leaders to claim spiritual and political legitimacy and the potential of the Sufi membership to constitute a formidable army. Both Isma'il and Tahmasp occasionally persecuted non-Qizilbash Sufis because of their loyalty to their own pir rather than to the shah. Many Sufis emigrated from Iran to South Asia during this period, seeking a less oppressive regime.

Both the fractiousness of the Qizilbash and the potential threat of their religious enthusiasm confronted ʻAbbas when he ascended the throne in 1587. During his first four years as shah, he was preoccupied with reasserting royal control over them. Their internecine conflicts had raged ever since Tahmasp's death in 1576, leaving Iran in chaos. The Uzbeks and Ottomans seized the opportunity to occupy large tracts of Iranian territory. As a result, ʻAbbas began to regard the Qizilbash to be as much of a liability as an asset. Then, in 1591, an event occurred that forced him to take drastic action. The year 1591 was the turn of the millennium on the Islamic calendar, and many people all across the Muslim world expected that God would demonstrate his control of history by intervening in a dramatic manner. Some expected the arrival of the Mahdi, while others hoped at least for a radical improvement in social conditions and the implementation of justice. These expectations were at the heart of a plot within one of the popular Sufi orders in Iran—the Nuqtavi—to overthrow ʻAbbas and place the pir of the order on the throne. The Nuqtavi order was a classic example of ghulat: It taught reincarnation, and it made little distinction between God and Adam or Muhammad. Its doctrines were popular among many of the Qizilbash, who, like the members of many mystical orders of the day, frequently belonged to more than one such organization.

ʻAbbas learned of the planned uprising just before it was scheduled to take place and ordered its leaders arrested and executed. The incident awoke ʻAbbas to the implicit political threat that Sufi pirs posed to the authority of the state. He began a campaign to break the potential political threat of Sufism in his empire. The persecution of Sufism extended to the ranks of the Qizilbash, where spiritual guides were purged. ʻAbbas no longer allowed the Qizilbash to be in attendance at the court or to serve in his personal bodyguard. Court chroniclers continued to refer to the shah as *murshid-i kamil* ("Ultimate Mystical Guide") and to the Qizilbash as Sufis, but the usage was perfunctory and sentimental and not descriptive of any actual relationship. Qizilbash leaders continued to serve as important military and administrative leaders, but the special relationship was over.

'Abbas and subsequent shahs maintained vigilance against Sufi orders, Sufi rituals, and individual Sufis. Sufism and Twelver Shi'ism, which for centuries had coexisted and cross-fertilized, became increasingly distinct, and many of their adherents became mistrustful and hostile toward each other. Some of the ulama supported the court's suspicion of the mystical orders. During the remainder of the century, the campaign to fight Sufi groups was led by ulama. They tarred all Sufis with the brush of ghulat, and even prominent ulama who valued sober and intellectually sophisticated versions of Islamic mysticism soon ran the risk of persecution.

As a result of 'Abbas's skill and ruthlessness, the Safavid state attained an unprecedented degree of stability during the early seventeenth century. He developed a powerful permanent standing army, gained leverage over the Qizilbash, forced many Sufi orders to go underground, and had the loyalty of a mature Twelver Shi'ite religious establishment. At the time of his ascension to the throne in 1587, the Safavid entity still retained many features of its origins as a tribal confederation under the leadership of a Safavid pir; by the end of 'Abbas's reign in 1629, the government had been transformed into a powerful, sophisticated, and wealthy enterprise.

The Decline of Tariqa Sufism

The ulama who were recruited into Safavid service from other countries chafed for decades at the influence of groups that they considered to be ghulat, including the Qizilbash. They were determined to enforce the observance of the Shari'a and to ban doctrines such as the divinity of the shah and the transmigration of the soul. Thus, when 'Abbas I began his persecution of messianic groups, many of the ulama joined forces with him. 'Abbas distrusted Sufi orders because of their potential as breeding grounds for religious enthusiasm that might threaten the stability of the dynasty. The actual religious practices of apolitical Sufis had not been the target of his campaign—he had a lifelong interest in mystical practices and frequently consulted ulama who found Sufi meditative practices and interpretive techniques to be useful in their own devotional lives. He had even sought spiritual guidance from the Nuqtavi pir who subsequently tried to overthrow him in 1591. The militant, Shari'a-minded ulama, however, equated mystical thought and practice with the ghulat. In their quest to purify Safavid society and to establish acceptable norms for Twelver rituals and doctrines, they were determined to eliminate religious practices that they considered heretical.

The seventeenth-century campaign in Iran against Sufism was one more stage in the centuries-long struggle between Shari'a-minded ulama and mystically oriented personalities. The opponents of Sufism resented the claims of mystics to be spiritual authorities. Members of the ulama, who had undergone many years of rigorous academic work, were contemptuous of the self-taught Sufis who claimed to be able to lead novices into the presence of God. Many were also resentful of those among their fellow ulama who asserted that the life of the Shari'a was incomplete without a mystical experience. Moreover, many Shi'ite ulama sensed that the master–novice relationship characteristic of Sufism was essentially incompatible with the relationship between the Hidden Imam and the believer. If a Sufi looked to his master for spiritual guidance, did that not challenge the spiritual authority of the Imam? In an effort to restore the doctrine of the centrality of the Hidden Imam, it was necessary to extirpate Sufism, root and branch. The fact that a victory in that effort would benefit the Shari'a-minded ulama in both status and wealth was an added bonus.

The campaign against Sufi orders was brutal. With the power of the royal court and army allied with the antimystical ulama, Sufi orders did not stand a chance. Many Sufis fled to neighboring regions, especially India. Some orders went underground in an attempt to survive. The campaign against mysticism caused a conflict even within the community of the mujtahids, or highest-ranking ulama. Some of the ulama found both mysticism and Sufi philosophy attractive, and they fought a rear-guard action against the reformers. The most prominent was the brilliant and politically well-connected Mulla Sadra (d. 1640), who was associated with the so-called School of Esfahan. The School of Esfahan continued the tradition of the "Illuminationist" school founded by al-Suhrawardi al-Maqtul (d. 1191). Al-Suhrawardi was a philosopher who had mastered the spectrum of Greek philosophy. Rejecting the rationalist and empirically grounded Aristotelian tradition, he favored the idealism and mystical orientation of Pythagoras and Plato. He acknowledged the value of the rational mind, but he argued that mystical knowledge (*'irfan*) was even more important. In order to obtain wisdom it was necessary to develop both the rational and intuitive aspects of the mind.

Mulla Sadra acknowledged the need to acquire a deep knowledge of the Shari'a and to follow it scrupulously and wholeheartedly, but he also insisted on the reciprocal relationship of formal knowledge and experience. The complete religious life requires the mystical vision or illumination that comes only after fasting, self-denial, and mystical practices. Mulla Sadra's corpus of writings was a brilliant synthesis of the Illuminationist tradition and Twelver Shi'ism. It provided the philosophical underpinnings for Shi'ite 'irfan. The legalistic mujtahids continued to rail against 'irfan, but it survived even within the halls of the madrasas. Students who wished to take "tutorials" in the theory and practice of mysticism were usually allowed to do so, as long as it was not part of the official curriculum of the madrasas, and as long as the instruction remained on an individual basis. 'Irfan continues to be viewed with suspicion by the majority of the highest spiritual authorities in Shi'ism. On the other hand, equally influential authorities, such as the Ayatollah Khomeini (d. 1989), have been ardent practitioners of it.

Mystical thought in Iran thus continued within circles of the elite classes, but organized Sufism among the lower classes declined dramatically under the combined assault of the throne and the Shari'a-minded ulama. The near-demise of the tariqas was an ignoble fate for these organizations, which had been a vehicle for the survival of Shi'ism in Iran during the period of the Mongols and their chaotic aftermath. The changed conditions of the seventeenth century put organized, institutional Sufism under suspicion of being potentially heretical and treasonous. The development reflected a major change in Safavid religious life: Whereas mystical experiences were the characteristic religious expression of the first century of the Safavid state, the ulama of the second century increasingly linked religious expression to the exposition of texts.

court throughout Safavid history. As Isma'il and Tahmasp employed more and more Persian-speaking bureaucrats in their administrations, however, the Persian language and culture became increasingly influential, particularly since the Persian language was already the predominant language of diplomacy in the eastern Muslim world. Persian was the language of poets and the educated middle class. It became the vehicle of diplomatic correspondence, belles lettres, and history.

Tahmasp's transfer of the capital from majority-Turkish Azerbaijan to Qazvin signaled a growing identification of the Safavid court with its Iranian territory. In 1590, 'Abbas made this identification complete when he moved the capital from Qazvin to Esfahan.[5] Esfahan had served as the administrative center for the Saljuqs over five hundred years earlier and already boasted one of the most impressive mosques in the world: the Masjid-e Jami'. 'Abbas was determined to build upon that legacy and turn the city into an imperial capital. His project became the greatest example of urban design and planning in the Muslim world since the creation of Baghdad in the eighth century. Esfahan became a large and impressive capital city that supported 20,000 court functionaries of all levels. It was so beautiful and offered so many opportunities for wealth, culture, power, and entertainment that it became common for Iranians to say *Esfahan nesf-e jahan*: "Esfahan is half the world."

At the center of the city, 'Abbas laid out the Maydan-e Shah, a large square (today known as the Maydan-e Imam). The open space measures 1600 by 540 feet, or about the size of twenty football fields. It was intended to serve as a market, polo ground, and general entertainment venue for jugglers, magicians, and games. At its southern end is the royal mosque, the Masjid-e Shah, decorated with brilliant enameled tiles. At the eastern end is the Masjid-e Shaykh Lotfollah, the mosque that 'Abbas used for his private devotions. On the west is the 'Ali Qapu, which served as an audience hall and from whose balcony the shah could watch polo games or other entertainment taking place in the square. On the north is a monumental arched gateway that leads to the enormous royal bazaar. During the Safavid period, a person could leave the Maydan-e Shah and follow the Chahar Bagh, an avenue that led to the summer palace. Over two miles long, it was lined with gardens and lavish residences, and was decorated with basins, fountains, and rows of trees. 'Abbas obviously meant for the new additions to the city not only to impress subjects and foreigners alike, but also to provide for his own enjoyment. As it turned out, military campaigns kept him far from his capital for all but three years of the last three decades of his reign.

Safavid cultural excellence was not limited to monumental architecture. The art of bookmaking achieved its zenith there, and Europeans valued Safavid ceramics as highly as they did the products of China. Perhaps most famous, however, was the art of painting. In 1522, the great Timurid painter of Herat, Bihzad, relocated to Tabriz when his pupil, Tahmasp, was recalled home by his father the shah. Bihzad became the head of the royal workshop. Unlike the Arabs, for whom painting always posed at least a potential violation of the prohibition of idolatry, the Iranians prized paintings. They took particular delight in miniatures and also excelled in manuscript illumination. The Tabriz school produced an illustrated edition of the eleventh-century epic poem the *Shah-nameh* that is considered one of the world's greatest masterpieces of illuminated manuscript art. 'Abbas encouraged the paintings of such nonreligious themes as battles, hunts, and life at the royal court.

The citadel at Herat, built on the site of a fort erected by Alexander the Great.

Whereas the Safavids continued the Timurid tradition in the arts, we do not have evidence that they followed its lead in the sciences. They produced some excellent maps and astrolabes, but they are not known for important work in such fields as astronomy, mathematics, optics, or medicine. The reasons for those lacunae are unknown. On the other hand, some of their intellectuals produced impressive work of lasting value in philosophical theology.

The End of an Empire

The achievement of Shah 'Abbas can be appreciated by comparing the stability of the regime before and after his reign. In contrast to the two long civil wars that occurred between Isma'il's death in 1524 and the accession of 'Abbas in 1587, the transfer of power from shah to shah occurred peacefully all four times between the death of 'Abbas in 1629 and the end of the empire in 1722. 'Abbas had devised a formula that allowed the ghulam, Qizilbash, ulama, and wealthy merchants to have a stake in the perpetuation of the Safavid monarchy. This was particularly significant in light of the fact that the theory of the shah as a mahdi had fallen into disuse. Iranians had come to look upon their ruler in much the same way that Ottomans did.

Another major, and welcome, difference in Safavid history between the sixteenth and seventeenth centuries was that, in contrast to the repeated invasions by Uzbeks and Ottomans that Tahmasp had to face, the empire was subject to no external threat for several decades after 1639. In that year, the Safavids and Ottomans signed the Treaty of Zuhab after the Ottomans invaded and captured Baghdad the previous year. By the terms of the treaty, the two parties agreed to a frontier that closely reflects today's Iran–Iraq border. The two countries never fought again, and the Ottomans encouraged the transshipment of Iranian silk across Iraq and Syria to the Mediterranean. In fact, for the remainder of the century after the death of ʻAbbas in 1629, the history of Safavid Iran was undisturbed by cataclysms. The country's lack of outside threats did not mean that life was secure: Everyone in the world during that era had to experience occasional famines and plagues. Compared to most other large societies in the world, however, Iran seems to have been fortunate.

The avoidance of major catastrophes did not mean that all was serene within the empire. Economic hardships occurred, particularly in conjunction with the periodic famines. As a way of distracting the people's attention from their hardships, the administration embarked upon its occasional persecutions of religious minorities, much as imperial Russia did two centuries later when it encouraged pogroms against Jews. The campaign against Sufism continued and may have reached its peak in the 1690s. In 1709, the Afghan Ghilzai tribe revolted and seized Qandahar, a city that had been under Safavid control for several decades after alternating between Safavid and Mughal occupation. In 1716, a rival Afghan tribe, the Abdali, captured Herat from the Safavids. Four years later, in 1720, revolts flared all over the empire: the northwest, southwest, and northeast.

Historians do not yet know enough about Safavid history to say with confidence why the breakdown in security occurred in the early eighteenth century, transforming Iran from one of the safest places to travel to one of the most dangerous. The most curious episode occurred during 1721–1722, when a member of the new ruling family in Qandahar, Mahmud Ghilzai, led an army into eastern Iran. He could not capture Kirman or Yazd, but that did not deter him from advancing to Esfahan. There, in the spring of 1722, his tribal levies of some 18,000 troops crushed the Safavid army of at least some 40,000 troops and laid siege to the capital. The subsequent siege lasted from April to October, causing incalculable suffering. Starvation drove victims to cannibalism and the consumption of human excrement. Typhus and cholera ran rampant. Some 80,000–100,000 people died from hunger and disease. When the Afghan army finally took the city, it burned major buildings, including libraries and the royal archives.

The Safavid shah became a puppet of the Afghan regime. The Ottomans and Russians took advantage of the confusion in the empire to partition the region between the Black Sea and the Caspian Sea. By 1724, Iran was divided at least four ways by Afghans, Ottomans, Russians, and forces still loyal to the Safavids. The loyalists were centered on Mashhad in northeastern Iran, where Nadir Afshar, a member of one of the great Qizilbash tribes, maintained his base. Nadir gradually built up his power, and in 1730 he captured Esfahan from the Afghans. He installed a Safavid prince on the throne but made all the important decisions himself. In 1736, having grown impatient in the role of protector of a titular shah, he deposed the last Safavid ruler and declared himself Nadir Shah.

Nadir Shah (1688–1747) proved to be a remarkably talented military leader. He reconquered western and northern Iran as far as Tabriz. Then he moved east and captured Qandahar, Ghazna, Kabul, and Lahore. In 1739, he plundered the

Mughal capital of Delhi. He also annexed Uzbek lands on the Amu Darya River and occupied Oman between 1736 and 1744. Nadir's leadership abilities began slipping in the 1740s, when he began showing signs of mental instability. He treated his troops in an increasingly brutal fashion until 1747, when his own Afshar tribesmen murdered him out of fear for their lives.

The period between the fall of the Safavids in 1722 and Nadir's assassination in 1747 was important for Twelver Shi'ites and Nizaris alike. Two and a half centuries after Isma'il began the transformation of Iran into a Twelver Shi'ite society, Nadir attempted to unravel that history overnight. Not particularly interested in the finer points of religious doctrine, he was quite interested in two consequences of the integral relationship of Shi'ism to the Iranian monarchy. First, since he could not claim Safavid lineage, his position as ruler would always be challenged by supporters of Safavid family members. Second, the Shi'ite identity of Iran had made the country a pariah state in the eyes of the Ottomans and Uzbeks, with whom it would be useful to have good diplomatic relations. Nadir announced that he wanted Shi'ism to lose its separate identity and be recognized simply as a fifth school (*madhhab*) of Sunni law. When the Shi'ite ulama resisted, he persecuted them and seized much of the property that they administered.

Due to Nadir's relentless attacks on Twelver ulama, many of them moved to Iraq. The most prominent of them taught at Karbala and Najaf, the preeminent centers of learning in the Shi'ite world. Living and teaching in Ottoman territory, these scholars were careful not to antagonize their Sunni rulers, but they continued to provide their followers in Iran with spiritual leadership. The eighteenth century turned out to be a notable one for Twelver organizational history, as we shall see in Chapter 8.

By the early eighteenth century, the Nizaris discovered that their long period of practicing taqiya had taken a heavy toll on their community. Many Iranian Nizaris assimilated into the Twelver society to which their parents had only pretended to belong. By the end of the Safavid regime in 1722, the Nizaris in Iran were outnumbered by those in Sindh and Gujarat. Kahak's remoteness from Sindh and Gujarat became a major problem due to the chaos that engulfed Iran after the fall of Esfahan to the Afghans. Nizari pilgrims from South Asia who set out for Kahak were frequently robbed and killed. Many were dissuaded from making the trip, and the financial condition of the Imamate deteriorated as a result. In the 1740s, the Imam moved to Kirman province so that his South Asian followers would not have so far to travel in order to meet with him. In post-Safavid Kirman, the circumstances of the Nizari leadership vastly improved. The Imam now felt safe enough to allow his followers to abandon taqiya. In addition, the number of pilgrims arriving from South Asia increased dramatically, restoring the financial stability of the Nizari organization.

Nadir's death in 1747 marks a turning point in Iran's history. With his heavy hand gone, Iran collapsed into a paroxysm of civil war that lasted sixteen years. His death also led directly to a division of the historic Iranian cultural area that has endured to the present. One of Nadir's most trusted followers, a young Afghan named Ahmad Abdali, returned to western Afghanistan with his troops when Nadir died. There he was named paramount chief of the Afghan warlords, and he adopted the name Ahmad Durrani (from a phrase meaning "Pearl of Pearls"). Durrani

(1747–1772) began the process of creating Afghanistan, which had never been united before. Herat, Qandahar, Kabul, and Balkh all came under his control. He and his son even controlled Khorasan until the 1790s. Iran regained Khorasan but would never again count Herat or Qandahar among its possessions.

Conclusion

Of the new Islamic groups that emerged in Iran during the fourteenth and fifteenth centuries, one of the most influential was the Safavid movement. Its importance lay not in its doctrines and practices—which in any case did not last long in their original form—but in the fact that the order was responsible for creating an empire. The consequences of this development were immense: The creation of the Safavid Empire entailed the forcible conversion of Sunni Muslims to Shi'ism, and the transformation of Iran into a Shi'ite society exacerbated natural rivalries between it and its Sunni neighbors to the east and west. Ironically, the government of the Safavid Empire eventually became implacably hostile to Sufi orders, and by the late seventeenth century, the empire created by Sufis was the region in the Muslim world where a visitor would have to look the hardest to find a Sufi.

The period from Timur to Nadir Shah witnessed profound developments in Central Asia and Iran. Historically, Central Asia was a Persian cultural area, but most of it became Turkicized during this time. Numerous Turkic confederations entered the region, and a few were so influential that they became immortalized in the names of the countries where they predominated. The massive immigration of pagan Turks posed a potential threat to the Islamic heritage of Central Asia, but active missionary work by the Yasavi, Kubravi, and Naqshbandi Sufi orders resulted in widespread Islamization among the new arrivals. Some of the urban ulama criticized the syncretistic admixture of shamanism and Islam practiced by many of the Turks, but others were confident that the Islamic elements would eventually triumph. The spread of Islam among the Turks was good news to Central Asian Muslims, but developments in the economic and cultural history of the era were not. The region's wealth slowly ebbed, and its cultural production faded accordingly. Central Asian cities that had once been the envy of contemporaries on the opposite side of the globe had faded into obscurity by the close of the eighteenth century.

During the period that Persian Central Asia became Turkicized, the Turkish religious movement that led Iran became Persianized. The Safavid leadership of Iran increasingly adopted Timurid cultural elements, culminating in the striking grandeur of reborn Esfahan. Under the Safavids, Iran assumed the geographic shape that we identify with it today. Under their leadership, also, Iran became an almost exclusively Shi'ite state for the first time in its history. The Safavids declared Twelver Shi'ism to be Iran's state religion during the process of carving out an empire. As a result, Sunni and Shi'ite identities became embroiled in the imperial rivalries and competing ambitions of Safavid Iran, the Ottoman Empire, and the Uzbek khanate. The hostilities and mutual suspicion that developed between Sunnis and Shi'ites of that era have not completely dissipated to this day.

NOTES

1. For an introduction to the historiography of the controversy regarding the Central Asian economy during the seventeenth and eighteenth centuries, see Jos J. L. Gommans, *The Rise of the Indo-Afghan Empire c. 1710–1780* (Leiden, Netherlands; New York; and Köln, Germany: E. J. Brill, 1995), 1–6. For a more detailed treatment, see S. A. M. Adshead, *Central Asia in World History* (New York: St. Martin's Press, 1993), 178–186 and 198–201.
2. An excellent treatment of Muslim views of the end of times is David Cook, *Studies in Muslim Apocalyptic* (Princeton, New Jersey: Darwin Press, Inc., 2002).
3. This survey of Nizari history relies exclusively on Farhad Daftary, *The Ismailis: Their History and Doctrines* (Cambridge, U.K.: Cambridge University Press, 1990), 435–500, *passim.*
4. Shi'ites believe that 'Ali should have been the successor, or caliph, to the Prophet as the leader of the Muslims, but he did not become caliph until after three other men had served in that position. As a result, Shi'ites have traditionally held the first three caliphs in contempt for having usurped the rightful place of 'Ali.
5. The traditional date for the development of Esfahan as the Safavid capital is 1598, but Stephen Blake makes a convincing case for the earlier date. See his "Shah 'Abbas and the Transfer of the Safavid Capital from Qazvin to Isfahan," in Andrew J. Newman, ed., *Society and Culture in the Early Modern Middle East: Studies on Iran in the Safavid Period* (Leiden, Netherlands, and Boston: E. J. Brill, 2003), 145–164.

FURTHER READING

Central Asia

Adshead, S. A. M. *Central Asia in World History.* New York: St. Martin's Press, 1993.

Allworth, Edward A. *The Modern Uzbeks: From the Fourteenth Century to the Present: A Cultural History.* Stanford, California: Hoover Institution Press, Stanford University, 1990.

DeWeese, Devin. *Islamization and Native Religion in the Golden Horde: Baba Tukles and Conversion to Islam in Historical and Epic Tradition.* University Park, Pennsylvania: Pennsylvania State University Press, 1994.

Fletcher, Joseph. *Studies on Chinese and Islamic Inner Asia.* Edited by Beatrice Forbes Manz. Brookfield, Vermont: Variorum, 1995.

Levi, Scott C. *The Indian Diaspora in Central Asia and Its Trade, 1550–1900.* Leiden, Netherlands, and Boston: Brill Academic Publishers, 2002.

Lipman, Jonathan N. *Familiar Strangers: A History of Muslims in Northwest China.* Seattle and London: University of Washington Press, 1997.

McChesney, R. D. *Waqf in Cental Asia: Four Hundred Years in the History of a Muslim Shrine, 1480–1889.* Princeton, New Jersey: Princeton University Press, 1991.

Sengupta, Anita. *The Formation of the Uzbek Nation-State: A Study in Transition.* Lanham, Maryland: Lexington Books, 2003.

Soucek, Svat. *A History of Inner Asia.* Cambridge, U.K.: Cambridge University Press, 2000.

Starr, S. Frederick, ed. *Xinjiang: China's Muslim Borderland.* Armonk, New York: M. E. Sharpe, 2004.

Iran

Arjomand, Said Amir. *The Shadow of God on Earth and the Hidden Imam.* Chicago: University of Chicago Press, 1984.

Babaie, Sussan, Kathryn Babayan, Ina Baghdiantz-McCabe, and Massumeh Farhad. *Slaves of the Shah: New Elites of Safavid Iran.* London and New York: I. B. Tauris, 2004.

Babayan, Kathryn. *Mystics, Monarchs, and Messiahs: Cultural Landscapes of Early Modern Iran.* Cambridge, Massachusetts, and London: Distributed for the Center for Middle Eastern Studies of Harvard University by Harvard University Press, 2002.

Bashir, Shahzad. *Messianic Hopes and Mystical Visions: The Nurbakhshiya Between Medieval and Modern Islam.* Columbia, S.C.: University of South Carolina Press, 2003.

Blake, Stephen P. *Half the World: The Social Architecture of Safavid Isfahan, 1590–1722.* Costa Mesa, California: Mazda Publishers, 1999.

Floor, Willem. *Safavid Government Institutions.* Costa Mesa, California: Mazda Publishers, Inc., 2001.

Foran, John. *Fragile Resistance: Social Transformation in Iran from 1500 to the Revolution.* Boulder, Colorado: Westview Press, 1993.

Garthwaite, Gene R. *The Persians.* Malden, Massachusetts: Blackwell, 2005.

Ghougassian, Vazken S. *The Emergence of the Armenian Diocese of New Julfa in the Seventeenth Century.* Atlanta, Georgia: Scholars' Press, 1998.

Matthee, Rudolph P. *The Politics of Trade in Safavid Iran: Silk for Silver, 1600–1730.* Cambridge, U.K., and New York: Cambridge University Press, 1999.

Mazzaoui, Michel M., ed. *Safavid Iran and Her Neighbors.* Salt Lake City: University of Utah Press, 2003.

Melville, Charles, ed. *Safavid Persia: The History and Politics of an Islamic Society.* London and New York: I. B. Taurus & Co., Ltd, 1996.

Newman, Andrew. *Safavid Iran: Rebirth of a Persian Empire.* London and New York: I. B. Tauris, 2006.

Petrushevskii, I. P. *Islam in Iran.* Translated by Hubert Evans. Albany: State University of New York Press, 1985.

Stierlin, Henri. *Islamic Art and Architecture from Isfahan to the Taj Mahal.* London: Thames & Hudson, 2002.

Turner, Colin. *Islam without Allah? The Rise of Religious Externalism in Safavid Iran.* Richmond, U.K.: Curzon, 2000.

Woods, John E.. *The Aqquyunlu: Clan, Confederation, Empire.* Rev. and expanded ed. Salt Lake City: University of Utah Press, 1999.

Chapter 6

South Asia

The subcontinent of South Asia provoked awe and wonder in the minds of the peoples of southwestern Asia. *Al-Hind* was a land of fabulous wealth and strange customs that seamen, travelers, and merchants longed to visit. For the first few centuries of Muslim history, the sheer distance that one would have to travel from the major centers of Islamic culture to reach South Asia contributed to the sense that the region was exotic and alien. Until the thirteenth century, few Muslims inhabited South Asia other than in the Indus River valley and along the Malabar Coast, the regions closest to the Muslim heartlands. These areas were isolated from the rest of South Asia by a large, harsh desert and a steep escarpment, respectively.

Newcomers to South Asia from the Arabic-speaking world or Iran sometimes found it difficult to interact with Hindus. Hinduism—a catch-all term for a wide variety of religious expressions indigenous to South Asia—was at odds in many ways with the doctrines and practices that the ulama of Arab and Iranian societies had come to accept as the essentials of Islam. Equally problematic were modes of social interaction prescribed by the caste system of South Asia. Members of each caste and subcaste were taught that they had specific duties to perform and certain activities to avoid in order to earn a higher existence when reincarnated. The prescribed behavior included detailed regulations regarding how to relate to people not belonging to one's caste. It was easy for a newcomer to offend—and be offended by—Hindus without knowing what behavior or words had triggered the misunderstanding.

Despite the difficulties, Muslims and Hindus learned to coexist. The social elites discovered that they shared many important values, and it was not uncommon for wealthy Muslim merchants to socialize with high-caste Brahmins, who found ways not to be ritually defiled by contact with them. At the other end of the social scale, Muslim and Hindu peasants visited each other's shrines and celebrated each other's religious festivals. The nature of the political leadership played a great role in shaping the patterns of Muslim–Hindu interaction.

South Asia After the Delhi Sultanate

Because of the initial physical and cultural obstacles to the spread of Islam in South Asia, it would have been no surprise if Islam had failed to leave an imprint there. In fact, however, the Delhi Sultanate was only the first of numerous Muslim-ruled states that proliferated across the subcontinent after the thirteenth century. The royal courts of these states attracted Muslim soldiers, scholars, artists, and holy men as a magnet attracts iron filings. Immigrants came from all parts of the Muslim world in quest of patronage. The soldiers, scholars, artists, and holy men produced lasting effects on South Asian society.

Southern and Central South Asia

The Deccan Plateau is a major topographical feature of South Asia, constituting most of the peninsular section. The Narmada River is the traditional boundary between the plateau and the central plains. The Satpura mountain range immediately south of the river marks the beginning of the plateau, which is bounded on the west and east by the Western and Eastern Ghats, two mountain ranges that separate the plateau from the coastal regions of the peninsula. For seven hundred miles, the Western Ghats loom as the backdrop to the peninsula's narrow western Malabar Coast. The mountain peaks there range in height from 3000 to 8000 feet. The Deccan slopes gently eastward from the Western Ghats to the Eastern Ghats, which range in height from 2000 to 4000 feet. Whereas the Western Ghats give the appearance of a uniform line of cliffs and peaks, the Eastern Ghats are composed of disconnected masses of hills. They descend to the Coromandel Coast on the eastern side of the peninsula.

The Deccan was the site of the most vibrant Muslim presence in South Asia between Timur's sack of Delhi in 1398 and the rise of the Mughal Empire. In the 1330s, sections of the Deccan began breaking away from Delhi's rule, and soon most of the plateau was consolidated into two kingdoms. The northern one was the Muslim Bahmani kingdom, named after its founder, 'Ala' al-Din Bahman Shah. The southern kingdom was Vijayanagar, ruled by Hindus.

The Bahmani kingdom was founded in 1347, as the Mongol polities in Iran, Russia, and Central Asia were breaking up into chaos and the plague was sweeping across Eurasia north of the Himalayas. As a Muslim-ruled state, the Bahmani kingdom offered Turks and Iranians fleeing the violence of the post-Il-khanate period a new chance for a career. The kingdom needed the services of skilled military officers, civilian bureaucrats, and religious specialists. The Iranians became dominant. Soon, their culture created a Persianate cast to the Bahmani court, which used the Persian language as its vehicle of literature and diplomacy. The kingdom's capital was in Gulbarga until 1424, when it was moved to Bidar.

The Bahmani kingdom developed a high level of cosmopolitan culture. When it exchanged ambassadors with Sultan Mehmet II (1451–1481) of Istanbul, it became the first state in the subcontinent to exchange ambassadors with the Ottomans. Governing a Muslim-ruled state with a majority Hindu population, its rulers worked hard to achieve a modus vivendi with their subjects. The kingdom engaged in bloody wars with its major rival, the Hindu kingdom of Vijayanagar, but the two states were not enemies for religious reasons. Both tolerated adherents of other faiths and they shared a remarkably similar culture. The real problem was their mutual desire to dominate the rich agricultural region of Raicha that lay between them south of the Krishna River. The Bahmani kingdom also had to struggle against several Muslim-ruled states—especially Malwa and Gujarat—over territorial issues.

Internally, the Bahmani court suffered from tension between the "Foreigners" and the "Deccanis." The Foreigners were the Turkish and Iranian immigrants, whereas the Decannis included several groups. Among their number were descendants of early Arab traders in the area, Turks (the majority of whom were soldiers) who had immigrated during the period of Delhi's rule, descendants of Abyssinian (Ethiopian) slaves, local converts to Islam, and Hindus. The Deccanis were jealous of the success of the newly arrived Muslims from the west. They were also perturbed that active recruitment of Iranians continued: The court even dispatched ships to bring them to the kingdom. Ominously, the military ranks were dominated by Deccanis of Turkish descent, whose loyalty became increasingly problematic. Between 1484 and 1525, four provinces—Ahmadnagar, Bijapur, Golkonda, and Berar—broke away under Deccani leadership, leaving the capital city of Bidar only a fragment of its former territory to rule (see Map 6.1). From 1525, this remnant of the Bahmani kingdom was known as Bidar.

During the sixteenth century, the most powerful of the five successor states of the Bahmani kingdom were Bijapur, Golkonda, and Ahmadnagar. All three were much more powerful than Berar and Bidar, which were landlocked. The three larger states were officially Shi'ite for most of their history. Because they were rivals, they formed shifting patterns of alliances with—and against—each other and Vijayanagar. The two smaller Muslim states survived by siding with the dominant alliance at any given time. All five cultivated a Persianate court culture and, as a result, suffered from continuing Foreigner–Deccani tensions and occasional violence.

Bijapur was situated on a flat and barren plain, but it possessed great natural resources. It controlled a prosperous section of the Arabian Sea coastline. It also secured Raicha, the rich agricultural area over which the Bahmani kingdom and Vijayanagar had fought. Its founder was Yusuf 'Adil Shah, a Turkmen from Anatolia. In his youth, Yusuf became a follower of the Safavid leader Junayd, the grandfather of Shah Isma'il I. Migrating to the Deccan, he became governor of Bijapur under the Bahmanis, but declared his independence in 1489. When Isma'il I declared Twelver Shi'ism to be the religion of his Safavid Empire, 'Adil Shah did so, as well.

During the first century of its existence, Bijapur's official religion alternated between Shi'ism and Sunnism with each generation. By the 1580s, its rulers were consistently Shi'ite, although one of them was so heterodox in his rituals that many of his contemporaries thought he was a Hindu. Close maritime links developed between Bijapur and Iran despite aggressive attempts by the Portuguese after 1498 to control the entire commerce of the Indian Ocean. In 1510, the Portuguese seized Bijapur's major port of Goa and turned it into their headquarters in Asia. The loss was not devastating to Bijapur, because the kingdom was able to develop smaller ports farther north. Relations with Iran continued uninterrupted. By the seventeenth century, Bijapur had developed into a city of several hundred thousand inhabitants that was adorned with impressive works of monumental architecture.

Golkonda was founded by a descendant of the founder of the Black Sheep Turkmen clan of western Iran. Unlike Bijapur, which maintained ports on the Arabian

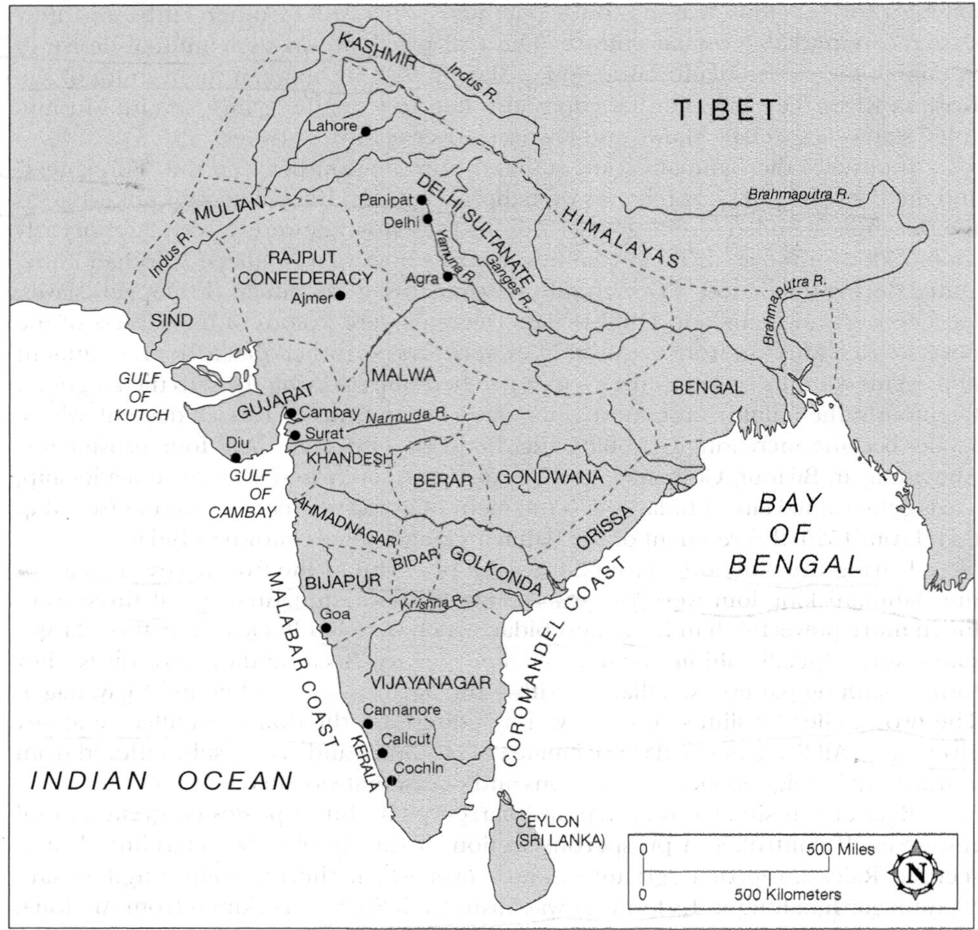

MAP 6.1 South Asia at the End of the Fifteenth Century.

Sea, Golkonda had ports on the Bay of Bengal. The inland city of Golkonda (modern Hyderabad) was famous as a source of diamonds. It was perhaps the wealthiest city in the subcontinent during the fifteenth and sixteenth centuries. Because of its wealth and its Shi'ite court, it attracted numerous Iranian immigrants.

Ahmadnagar, the third of the great Muslim Deccan states, was founded by the son of a converted Hindu Brahmin (the highest caste) in 1490. The dynasty became Shi'ite in 1538. The sultanate was distinctive in that its "Foreigner" and "Deccani" factions exhausted each other by the end of the sixteenth century through constant fighting, and they were replaced by Marathas and Ethiopians. The Marathas were Hindus who spoke the Marathi language. We will hear more about them later. The Ethiopians, or *Habshis,* were brought in as slaves, but, like military slaves in some regions, many had gained their freedom and attained high office. One notable example of a freed Habshi was Malik Ambar, who became the power behind the throne in Ahmadnagar from about 1600 until his death in 1626. He served as regent for the sultan, even when the latter attained his majority, and was the undisputed authority in both civil and military affairs. He led the successful military defense of the sultanate against repeated Mughal aggression. Of his 50,000 troops, some 10,000 were Habshis.

To the north of the successor states of the Bahmani kingdom lay still more Muslim-ruled kingdoms. Khandesh, the northernmost of the Deccan states, emerged in the 1380s. North of the Deccan, Gujarat gradually became independent of Delhi between 1390 and 1401. Gujarat's cities were important centers for textile production, and its ports were important entrepôts for commodities from South Asia and Southeast Asia that were destined for East Africa and the Mediterranean. The textile-manufacturing center of Ahmadabad and the port of Cambay (Khambat) became world-famous in the fifteenth and sixteenth centuries. Cambay ranked with Aden, Hormuz, and Melaka as one of the chief ports of the Indian Ocean in the early sixteenth century.

To the east of Gujarat lay Malwa, which rejected Delhi's control in 1401. Founded by an Afghan noble, it lay in a barren region but thrived on the taxes it imposed on the transit trade connecting Gujarat with the interior. Its rulers also launched raids into surrounding regions in pursuit of plunder to supplement its meager natural resources.

Hundreds of miles to the east of Malwa, in the delta of the Ganges (Ganga) River, lay Bengal, which seceded from the Delhi Sultanate in the 1350s. Turks dominated it for most of the next two centuries. Due to the shifting course of the Ganges, the rulers had to move the capital several times, so no single city became identified as the seat of government. As in the other Muslim states, Persian language and culture dominated the Bengal court despite the Turkish background of most of the rulers. Bengal's ample supply of water produced an environment strikingly different from those of most of the other Muslim-ruled states. It exported rice and sugar, but was even more famous for its cotton textiles. The region had exported cotton products at least as early as the tenth century. By the sixteenth century, it was attracting Portuguese, Dutch, and English merchants, who exchanged silver for fine-quality cloth.

The Indo-Gangetic Plain

The power base of the Delhi Sultanate had been the 1500-mile-long arc of the Indus and Ganges river valleys that was known as the Indo-Gangetic plain. Its relatively flat terrain facilitated the movement of armies, and its productive, irrigation-based agricultural economy generated lucrative tax revenues. Timur's destruction of Delhi was so thorough, however, that for three years after he left, the city was almost uninhabited. A member of the Tughluq dynasty attempted a revival of power in 1401, but the weak effort lasted only to 1413, when a Turk overthrew the regime. The new government was dominated by the Sayyid dynasty, which was also short lived. In 1451, the Sayyids were overthrown by an Afghan who had served in the Sayyid army and administration. The new ruler founded the Lodi dynasty, which ruled Delhi until 1526. During this period, thousands of Afghan peasant–herdsmen and adventurer–soldiers migrated into the Indo-Gangetic plain. Afghans supplanted Turks and Iranians to become the most powerful and widely dispersed foreign Muslim group in the region. Many settled on the land as local lords who controlled the majority Hindu peasantry. Afghan warlords dominated the Punjab and conquered existing states on the Ganges, including Bengal. The Lodi government was able to co-opt some of them and expanded Delhi's control once again. By the early sixteenth century, the dynasty ruled the area from the Punjab to Bihar in the east.

The Lodis had reinvigorated Delhi, but they faced formidable challenges. Fellow Afghans in Bengal refused to cooperate with them and the Rajputs—a Hindu warrior class in Rajasthan—began to challenge their authority. The last of the Lodis, Ibrahim (1517–1526), was unable to command the allegiance of the warlords who had served his father, and soon found himself confronted with unrest both in Bihar and Lahore.

Islam in South Asia

South Asia was on the periphery of the Muslim world until the thirteenth century. For several centuries after the creation of the Delhi Sultanate, the subcontinent attracted tens of thousands of Muslim migrants, but Islam became the majority religion in only a few regions. Overall, South Asia did not become as Islamized as Iran or Andalus. Like the Balkans, it bore the distinct impress of Muslim rule, but most of its inhabitants retained their earlier religious identity. Although Islam has never become the religion of the majority of the population of South Asia, the region's huge overall population has meant that the absolute number of Muslims there became very large indeed—today South Asia contains more Muslims than any comparable land area in the world.

Patterns of Muslim Influence

Muslim traders began appearing along the Malabar Coast of western India soon after the Prophet's death in 632. The coast—especially its southern extension, known as Kerala—had long been a staging area for Arab and Iranian traders because of its location in the Indian Ocean. The cyclical movements of the monsoon winds dictated that any commerce across the width of the ocean include a layover on the southwestern coast of South Asia. After the rise of Islam, most of the merchants and sailors from the Persian Gulf region were Muslims. Their frequent business dealings along the Malabar Coast resulted in the creation of a Muslim community in Kerala that was an extension of the societies ringing the Persian Gulf. The community maintained close contacts with the Gulf thanks to the sea route, whereas its contacts with the interior of the Deccan were limited due to the formidable Western Ghats. The Muslims of the coast were usually under the political dominance of Hindu princes. Members of the Hindu and Muslim communities developed a symbiotic relationship in which the merchants relied upon the security provided by the rulers, and the rulers benefitted from the wealth and overseas contacts provided by the merchants.

In contrast to the peaceful growth of Muslim settlement of the Malabar Coast, most of the rest of South Asia experienced the first arrival of Muslims in the form of violent conquests. By 715, Arab armies had conquered Sindh and Multan, in the lower and middle Indus River valley, respectively. These areas were situated on overland trade routes linking South Asia with Iran. The Muslim community of this area began to lose its Arabic character in the early eleventh century when Mahmud of Ghazna led plundering expeditions into the Punjab and Gujarat. Mahmud was of Turkish background, but he admired and cultivated Persian language and culture. Eventually, Mahmud took possession of most of the Punjab and the Indus valley. His dynasty, the Ghaznavids, established Lahore as a major Muslim city.

During the late twelfth century, the Ghurid clan from Afghanistan seized power from the Ghaznavids. The Ghurids expanded their rule down the Ganges as far as Bihar. The Delhi Sultanate replaced the Ghurids in the early thirteenth century and extended Muslim influence into the Deccan and Bengal. As we have seen, the Delhi Sultanate did not retain its dominance over the subcontinent for long, but its many successor states maintained Muslim rule over a vast area. The result of this legacy was that, from the early eleventh century until the waning of the Mughal Empire in the eighteenth century, the dominant political and military figures of the Indo-Gangetic plain and of the Deccan were of Turkish or Afghan origin but they patronized Persian culture at court.

These conquests were only the latest in a long series of destructive invasions of South Asia. The Sanskritic culture itself came into the subcontinent during the second millennium B.C.E. by means of military invasions. The Muslim invasions, however, are better documented and more recent. As a result, they are seared into the historical memory of Muslims and Hindus alike. To the former, the invasions were heroic episodes of military glory and religious duty in which the true faith was extended to pagans. To the latter, they were brutal assaults that resulted in cultural humiliation, physical destruction, and mass suffering. Centuries later, they still touch a raw nerve and are occasionally exploited by Hindu politicians.

Recent research demonstrates that both perspectives require modification. The early raids of Mahmud of Ghazna into Gujarat were, indeed, vicious and rapacious. Mahmud conducted a public relations campaign with the Muslim world, portraying the incursions as expressions of jihad, but they are hard to explain as other than murderous looting. Mahmud's conquest of the Punjab was a more complicated process in which the inevitable violence of invasion was mitigated by policies to stabilize the economy and work out a modus vivendi with the local population. Subsequent Muslim invasions into most of South Asia followed a similar pattern. The period of conquest was characterized by murder, rape, kidnapping, and looting. Some Hindu temples were not only razed, but replaced by mosques. Subsequently, however, Hindus resumed a routine of life similar to what they had experienced prior to invasion.

This pattern of violent destruction, followed by a return to normalcy, was characteristic not only of Muslim invasions, but also of the wars among regional Hindu rulers. Triumphant Hindu generals destroyed temples that were devoted to the particular gods or goddesses associated with the previous ruler's regime. The practice was a way of delegitimizing the former regime. A similar policy was followed by most Muslim conquerors. Temples not associated with the royal cult were not molested. Moreover, Muslim rulers often repaired Hindu temples and even financed the construction of new ones.[1]

Muslim conquerors rarely attempted forcible conversion to Islam except when a ruler felt that the profession of Islam by a local leader would result in the pacification of a troubled area. Muhammad ibn Tughluq, the Sultan of Delhi who is known for his toleration of all religions, forcibly converted several rulers in the Deccan in an effort to consolidate his rule there. Numerous reports survive of forcible conversions of tribal leaders in what is now the Northwest Frontier Province of Pakistan. Once a hostile territory became a revenue-paying province, however, the overwhelming majority of Muslim rulers in South Asia followed a laissez-faire religious policy. Only rarely did any of them even impose the head tax and land tax on non-Muslims that were stipulated in the Shariʿa. Although the tax records of these regimes refer to such taxes, they are almost always instances of using the terminology of the Shariʿa for a tax that both Muslims and Hindus paid.

Because the subject of this book is the worldwide Muslim community, discussions focus on religious affiliation more than on ethnic identity. It is important, however, to be aware that the Indian chroniclers who wrote at the time of the Muslim invasions referred to the invaders as Turks or Afghans, not Muslims. The events were not viewed by the victims as attempts to eradicate their religion, but rather as yet another instance of the martial Turk or Afghan at war. Thus, in the context of world history, the Muslim invasions of India were Turkish and Afghan invasions, just as the Christian (and explicitly Christianizing) conquests of Mexico and Peru were Spanish, and the Christian colonizing of Massachusetts was English.

The degree of Islamization varied widely in the areas under Muslim rule. Muslims ruled the middle and lower Indus River valley continuously after the early eighth century, and so the indigenous population had many centuries to respond to inducements to convert to join the dominant social class. Perhaps an even more important factor was that Hinduism had never been well established there, and Buddhism had been weakened by Hindu persecution in the seventh century. In the basins of the upper and middle Yamuna and Ganges rivers, however, Islam made little impact, even though Muslim regimes were based in this north-central area of the subcontinent almost continuously from the early thirteenth century through the eighteenth century. In this densely populated region, Hinduism and its patterns of social organization were deeply entrenched. Strong social ties, patterned behavior, and peer pressure reinforced traditional rituals and doctrines.

South Asian Sufism

Sufism became the majority expression of Islam in South Asia as it did in most areas of the Muslim world after the fifteenth century. Numerous orders made their appearance. By the seventeenth century, the Qadiriya, Naqshbandiya, and Shattariya had large followings, but the two most popular were the Suhrawardiya and the Chishtiya. Both entered South Asia at the end of the twelfth century. The founder of the Chishtiya, Muʿin al-Din Chishti, was born in Chisht, near Herat, but in 1193 he moved to Ajmer, where he died. As a result, the Chishti order is usually considered to be the most "Indian" of the major orders of the subcontinent. The tomb (*dargah*) of Muʿin al-Din Chishti at Ajmer and that of his successor, Nizam al-Din Awliya, in Delhi became major pilgrimage sites for both Hindus and Muslims.

The Chishtiya scandalized members of the Qadiriya and Naqshbandiya because of their practice of *sama*ʿ (musical session) and *raqs* (dancing) during their dhikr. They were enthusiastic advocates of Ibn al-ʿArabi's concept of the Unity of Being, the doctrine that all Reality is an expression of the Being of God. Many other Sufis were influenced by the Unity of Being, but the Chishtiya were the most consistently identified with it. The early Chishtis developed a reputation for asceticism and avoided royal courts and courtly affairs. By the mid-fourteenth century, however, Chishti saints in the Deccan were siding with the court of the Bahmani kingdom because of a shared hostility toward Muhammad ibn Tughluq, the ruler of Delhi. Within a short time, Chishti devotees in that region, at least, were in agreement with many other Sufis that pirs had an important political role. They were the true sovereigns of this world who had delegated political sovereignty to kings in order to free themselves for purely spiritual concerns. The Bahmani king built a dargah in Bidar for the Chishti saint who had brought him to power, and it became a major object of pilgrimage in the Deccan.

Sufism in South Asia received a boost in the sixteenth and seventeenth centuries as a result of the repeated waves of persecution that the Safavid regime directed against Iranian Sufis. Leading pirs and lowly disciples alike fled from Iran to the subcontinent, where the Muslim courts were Persian-speaking. Several major pirs migrated to the Deccan, where the Twelver Shiʿite courts usually welcomed them in order to enhance their own spiritual legitimacy.

It was once thought that Sufis played an active role in the conversion of South Asians to Islam by means of preaching and teaching. That idea has been modified in recent years. Research has shown that some Sufis did engage in active proselytizing in the subcontinent, just as they did in Central Asia. Far more Sufis, however, regarded Hindus to be beyond hope of salvation and had no interest in trying to convert them. It now seems more accurate to say that Sufis played an important, but indirect, role in the spread of Islam in South Asia. Many Hindus were attracted to Sufi pirs due to their reputation as healers, miracle-workers, and exorcists. They did not go to the pir in order to learn the highly demanding spiritual exercises that he taught his inner circle of disciples. Rather, they went in the hope of gaining a spiritual benefit, just as they would seek help from a *saddhu,* or Hindu holy man. They took some token gift, and the pir or his assistants blessed the supplicants or provided an amulet in the form of a piece of paper etched with the names of God or a verse from the Qur'an.

As in other parts of the Muslim world, the spiritual power of the khanaqa did not fade away with the death of the pir. His dargah became the object of pilgrimage and the site of festivals and prayers. One of his direct descendants would typically become the administrator of the shrine. He was known in South Asia as a *pirzada.* As the saint's proxy, he possessed the *baraka* (blessings, or presence of God) of the saint. The tomb-shrines became the primary means by which many peasants came to experience Islam. For illiterate peasants who lacked convenient access to a mosque and who certainly could not read the Qur'an, dargahs provided the space where they could encounter the mystery and mercy of God as mediated by the pirzada.

Most of the supplicants who sought favors from a pir or pirzada were women. While visiting a shrine they would hear the songs of worship that the murshids sang, which drew upon local religious vocabulary and local styles of verse and music. Back home they would hum a few of the verses while doing household chores or sing them as lullabies to their children. The amulets, the poetry, and the general veneration in which the pirs were held provided the children with impressions of Islam. As they grew up, they assimilated these ideas into their own families' patterns of worship. It was common for people of any faith to visit both the dargah and the Hindu temple, as well as to participate in both Muslim and Hindu festivals. Few peasants thought of Islam or Hinduism as exclusive religious systems, but rather viewed them as spiritual traditions that contained techniques for drawing upon supernatural assistance in solving problems or enhancing one's position in the world.[2]

An Isma'ili Revival

In the aftermath of Hulagu's destruction of the Nizari organization centered on Alamut, some Nizaris stayed in Iran and struggled to survive in a hostile environment. Others migrated hundreds or even thousands of miles to escape persecution. Many settled in the towns and villages of Sindh and Gujarat. Their experience in those regions laid the foundation for today's community of Khoja Muslims. Meanwhile, members of a rival branch of Isma'ilism known as Tayyibi Islam were also seeking a haven from persecution. Based in Yemen, large numbers of the group migrated to Gujarat, where a branch of their organization had existed since the late eleventh century. The Tayyibis of Gujarat evolved into today's community of Bohra Muslims. Thus, as Isma'ilis found life increasingly unsustainable in the region from Yemen to Iran, many sought refuge on the western fringes of South Asia, where most of them are found today.

Nizaris (Khojas)

Nizaris ↓ Khojas

Of the Nizaris who fled their villages when Hulagu destroyed Alamut in 1256, a considerable number migrated to Sindh. The area was under the rule of an independent dynasty and was inhabited by both Muslims and followers of Indic (Hindu) religious practices. Very little is known about the history of the Nizaris in Sindh for the next several centuries. All that is certain is that several outstanding spiritual teachers kept the community intact. Whether they engaged in active proselytization is unclear, but by the fourteenth century, the community had begun to gain adherents from the local population. The Nizaris were especially successful in winning followers among the Lohanas, a lineage group known for its trading activities. The Lohanas of Sindh used the word *khwaja* as a respectful form of address for each other, and the practice carried over into the Nizari community. Over time, this title became a distinctive characteristic of the Nizaris of the area. Thus, the Nizaris of Sindh came to be known as Khojas. By the mid-sixteenth century, the Khojas outnumbered the Nizaris of Iran.

Like Nizari groups everywhere between the fall of Alamut and the establishment of Nizari headquarters at Anjudan, the Khojas developed doctrines and practices independently of the Imam in Iran. In fact, the Khojas splintered into several groups. Some became closely identified with Sunnism, others with Twelver Shi'ism, and still others assimilated local Indic concepts. The Khoja group that is most widely known today (the followers of the Aga Khan) developed a doctrine called the *Satpanth,* or "true path." The Satpanth bore the stamp of Nizari assimilation into Indic religious traditions. Achieving the true path enabled converts to be liberated from the cycles of rebirth and to attain salvation in Paradise. The Qur'an was considered to be the last of the Vedas (the sacred scriptures of Hinduism), which abrogated the older ones. 'Ali, the first Imam, was the anticipated tenth avatar (incarnation) of Krishna. His essence continued in his successor Imams. Whereas Sunnis and Twelver Shi'ites supplement the Qur'an with a collection of accounts regarding the Prophet's sayings and model behavior called the Hadith, the primary devotional literature for the Khojas is a body of literature called the Ginans. Apparently composed by early Khoja pirs, the Ginans are hymnlike poems that began as oral traditions and were only later recorded in writing. Other Khoja practices that set the early community apart from Sunnis and Twelver Shi'ites were a prohibition on widow remarriage, a limitation of inheritance to males, and a substitution of three daily ritual prayers recited in the Gujarati language for the five Arabic-language prayers of the salat.

During the second half of the sixteenth century, the Khojas of Sindh began suffering from Sunni persecution. Many fled to Gujarat, which the Mughals conquered in the early 1570s. The Mughals introduced a policy of religious toleration, allowing the Khojas to thrive under their rule. The leaders of the Khoja community soon established contacts with the Imam in Andujan. By the seventeenth century, the Khoja community no longer had a pir. Instead, the Imam appointed a special representative for the community who relayed communication between the Imam and his followers. Ties between the Khojas and the Imam became even stronger after the latter's transfer to Kirman in the eighteenth century.

Tayyibis (Bohras)

Tayyibi Isma'ilis were rivals of the Nizaris. Whereas the Nizaris had broken from the Fatimids of Egypt in 1094, the Tayyibis seceded from the Fatimids in 1130, soon after the murder of al-Amir, the Fatimid caliph-Imam. They acquired their name due to their insistence that al-Amir's toddler son, Tayyib, should have succeeded to the throne after his father's murder. Al-Amir's cousin al-Hafiz seized it instead, and his descendants ruled Egypt until the end of the Fatimid line four decades later. Fearing for Tayyib's life, the boy's supporters spirited him away to Yemen.

The Isma'ili leaders of Yemen formally adopted Tayyib's cause and rejected the authority of Cairo. Moreover, the Isma'ili community in Gujarat, which had been established by Fatimid missionaries from Yemen in the 1060s, also accepted Tayyib as their Imam at this time. Tayyib lived incognito in Yemen. His followers gained their spiritual guidance from the Imam's *da'i mutlaq,* or "chief missionary." Tayyibis believe that Tayyib's son inherited the Imamate from him and that the line has continued to the present day. None of the Imams has ever made himself known, and yet his followers have been convinced that the Imam's physical presence is necessary to sustain the very existence of the world. Technically, he is not in seclusion, but rather lives among his people in the world, perhaps as a successful corporate executive or as a fishmonger in some poverty-stricken village. The public face of the

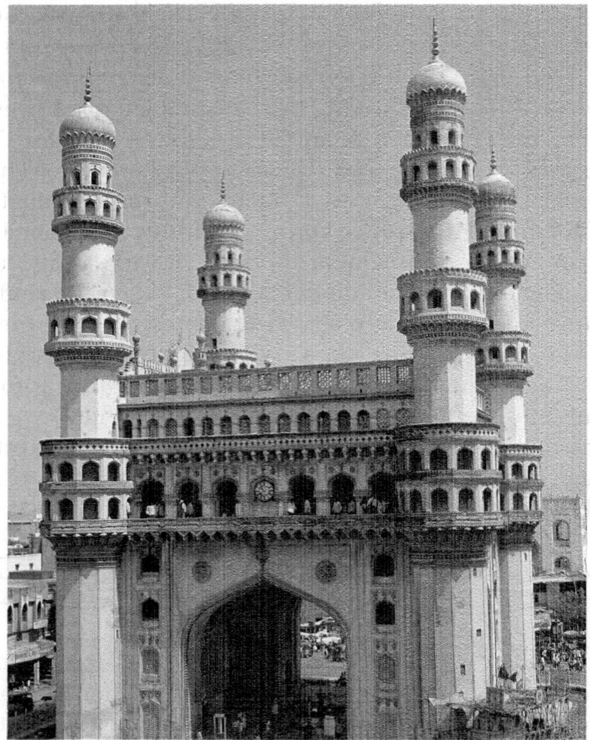

The Charminar in Hyderabad, a mosque built by Muhammad Qutb Shah in 1591 when a plague lifted. The prayer space for the mosque is on the top floor

Imam continues to be the da'i mutlaq, who commands the absolute obedience of the faithful. Unlike Nizaris, Tayyibis retained a large corpus of Fatimid writings on cosmology, the nature of history, and spiritual discipline, and have thus remained closer in doctrine and practice to the Fatimid tradition.

In Yemen, the Tayyibis struggled almost continuously with the Zaydis, who slowly gained the upper hand in a contest for territory. The Tayyibi community in the region lost its dynamism and began to shrink. Meanwhile, their co-religionists in Gujarat made numerous conversions among a Hindu merchant caste. As a result, they gradually became known as Bohras, from a Gujarati term for "merchant." They prospered in the international maritime trade until 1298, when Gujarat was conquered by the Delhi Sultanate. Because of persecution, most Tayyibis began to practice taqiya in the form of Sunnism. Later, under the Sultanate of Gujarat, they suffered even more intense persecution. Well over half the community converted definitively to Sunnism in the first half of the fifteenth century.

By the mid-sixteenth century, the Tayyibis of Yemen were trapped between a newly aggressive Zaydi campaign in the highlands and the Ottoman occupation of the Yemeni lowlands that had begun in 1538. The situation became desperate, because moving to Gujarat was not a viable option given the need to practice taqiya there. Fortunately for the movement, the Mughal conquest of Gujarat occurred before disaster struck in Yemen. The da'i mutlaq moved the Tayyibi headquarters to Gujarat at the very time that Khojas from Sindh were coming into the province to escape persecution. Under the Mughal policy of religious toleration, the Bohras resumed practicing their religion openly.

In Gujarat, the Bohras thrived economically and their community began to grow again. The cessation of persecution, however, allowed differences within the community to burst into the open. As early as 1589, the Bohras experienced a major controversy over the issue of succession to the office of da'i mutlaq. A minority seceded from the main group and became known as the Sulaymani Bohras. Their new da'i mutlaq soon relocated their base of operations to the region around Najran, in the Arabian Peninsula. The larger, original, group has been known as the Da'udi Bohras since the secession. Another succession dispute within the Da'udi Bohras resulted in the creation of the 'Aliya Bohras in 1624. The Da'udi and 'Aliya groups have remained based in Gujarat. Even after four centuries, doctrinal and ritual differences among the three groups are trifling. The original schisms were triggered only by disagreements over which person should inherit the mantle of the da'i mutlaq.

The Timurids in South Asia: The Mughals

The descendants of Timur cultivated a dazzling cultural life in Central Asia during the fifteenth century. Unfortunately for their dynasty, their political exploits at that time did not match their cultural achievements. They were ousted from their thrones one by one, and the last Timurid—Babur—was not able to retain Transoxiana even with the help of Shah Isma'il's army. Among Babur's many exemplary traits, however, were persistence and creativity. He soon turned his ambitions and energy toward South Asia. His remarkable career there laid the foundation for the Timurids' greatest achievement: the Mughal Empire.

The Mughals (Moghuls) referred to themselves as the *Gurkani,* a word that derives from *gurkan,* a Persianized form of the Mongolian word *kuragan,* meaning "son-in-law." Timur appropriated the term as an honorific title. His greatest regret was that he could not claim descent from Chinggis Khan. He made up for his deficiency by marrying not merely one, but two, Chinggisid princesses. He was thus a "son-in-law" of the great conqueror twice over (albeit several generations removed). Babur and his descendants, always proud of their Timurid lineage, continued to use the title. Many Arabic- and Persian-speaking contemporaries, however, referred to them as "Mongols" (*al-mughul*), and the name has stuck.

The Formation of the Mughal Empire

Babur was born in 1483 in Fergana (Farghana), a large valley in the eastern extremity of what is now Uzbekistan. Fergana is effectively enclosed by the precipitous mountain ranges that tower over it on the east, north, and south. It contains the headwaters of the Syr Darya River, and its fertile soil has supported a large population for centuries. Babur's father was the Timurid ruler of Fergana, and his mother could trace her ancestry to Chinggis Khan. Babur thus had a notable pedigree as a fifth-generation descendant of Timur and a thirteenth-generation descendant of Chinggis Khan. Like his contemporary, the Safavid ruler Shah Isma'il, he was a remarkably gifted individual. Best known for his military and administrative achievements, he was also a writer of considerable ability. His autobiography—the *Babur-nameh*—reveals him to have been cultured, witty, gregarious, insatiably curious, and possessed of a keen eye for the beauty of nature.

In Timurid fashion, Babur's father had regarded himself eligible to rule any part of Timur's domain, and he spent his life trying to gain control of Transoxiana. Babur followed in his footsteps, fighting fellow Timurids for their holdings. He managed to capture Samarqand from one of them, but then the Uzbeks invaded Transoxiana and his forces were overwhelmed. In subsequent battles with them he lost both Samarqand and Fergana. In desperation, he captured Kabul in 1504 and turned it into his base. From there he watched as the Uzbeks captured Herat, the last remaining Timurid realm, in 1507.

In 1510, Shah Isma'il appeared in Khorasan with his army, having conquered the rest of Iran. Isma'il respected the Timurid lineage but distrusted the Uzbeks. He offered Babur an alliance to reconquer Transoxiana if he would rule the region as a Shi'ite. The stipulation ran counter to Babur's inclinations: He was a devoted follower of the Naqshbandi order, which was hostile to Shi'ism. On the other hand, he saw the alliance as his last chance to claim the patrimony of his ancestors. He donned the red headgear of the Qizilbash and joined Isma'il in a war against the Uzbeks. After the Timurid and Safavid armies conquered Transoxiana, Babur honored his agreement with Isma'il. His implementation of Shi'ite practices, however, alienated his Sunni subjects. When they revolted in 1512, the Uzbeks reestablished their control over the region.

Defeated for a second time by the Uzbeks, Babur had to retreat to Kabul. He now realized that what he considered his natural destiny—ruling over Timur's empire—was out of the question for the foreseeable future. Transoxiana to the north and Khorasan to the west were divided between the Uzbeks and Safavids, each of which was too powerful for him to challenge. Kabul was inadequate for his ambitions, however, and so he began exploring other possibilities for imperial rule. To the east lay only towering mountain peaks and remote canyons, but to the south the way was open to wealthy agricultural and commercial regions. He soon began raiding the environs of Qandahar and then ranged across the Khyber Pass into the Punjab. He reorganized his army, developing an effective corps of musketry and artillery that supplemented the cavalry corps.

In 1522, Babur felt strong enough to attack Qandahar itself, and he captured it. In 1526, he followed the Khyber Pass and ventured into the vicinity of Delhi. There, far from home and surrounded by formidable enemies, he won a series of military victories that made him famous. At Panipat, fifty miles north of Delhi, his small army of some 12,000 met Ibrahim Lodi's much larger army that included one hundred war elephants. Babur's use of artillery unnerved the elephants and Afghan soldiers alike, and his cavalry's wheeling tactics routed the enemy. After his victory at Panipat, Babur was challenged by the charismatic leader of the large Hindu Rajput confederacy. Again facing overwhelming odds, Babur defeated the Rajputs in 1527. He followed that victory with a crushing defeat of the huge army of Ibrahim Lodi's

Babur, Horticulturist

Babur was the quintessential Timurid ruler: He was a brilliant military commander, polished writer, skilled translator, Sufi adept, and connoisseur possessed of an insatiable curiosity. His autobiography is fascinating for its revelations of its author's interests. This selection is drawn from his account of his expedition of conquest into northern India, or Hindustan. He confesses that he did not like many features of Hindustan—its climate, people, and architecture—but he did find much about the flora and fauna that captivated him. It is easy to imagine that the military commander of an invading army would be single-mindedly focused on the pressing issues of keeping his army fed and prepared for battle. Babur, as we know, took care of business with regard to his military aims, but, as this selection reveals, he was also a man upon whom nothing was lost.

There are some marvelous flowers in Hindustan. One is the hibiscus, which some Hindustanis call *gudhal.* It is not a shrub but a tree with stems. It is somewhat taller than the red rose, and its color is deeper than the pomegranate flower. It is as large as a red rose. The red rose blossoms all at once after budding, but when the hibiscus blossoms, from the middle of the petals yet another slender stalk is formed, as long as a finger, from which still more hibiscus petals open. The result is a double, fairly amazing flower. The flowers look beautiful in color on the tree but do not last long. They blossom and fade within a day. They bloom well and plentifully during the four months of monsoon and often throughout most of the year. Despite their profusion they have no odor.

Another flower is the oleander, which occurs in both white and red. It has five petals like the peach blossom. The red oleander bears a resemblance to the peach blossom, but the oleander blooms with fourteen or fifteen flowers in one place, so that from a distance it looks like one big flower. The bush is larger than the red rose. The red oleander has a faint but agreeable smell. It too blooms beautifully and abundantly during the monsoon and can be found throughout most of the year.

The screw pine is another. It has a delicate scent. Whereas musk has the disadvantage of being dry, this could be called "wet musk." In addition to the plant's having a strange appearance, the flowers can be from one-and-a-half to two spans long. The long leaves are like those of the reed and have spines. When compressed like a bud, the outer leaves are spiny and greenish and the inner leaves soft and white. Nestled among the inner leaves are things like in the middle of a flower, and the good scent comes from there. When it first comes up, before it develops a stalk, it resembles the male reed bush. The leaves are flattish and spiny. The stalk is extremely unharmonious. The roots are always exposed.

Then there is the jasmine. The white variety is called champa. It is larger and has a more pronounced fragrance than the jasmine in our country.

SOURCE: Babur, *The Baburnama: Memoirs of Babur, Prince and Emperor.* Translated, edited, and annotated by Wheeler M. Thackston. Washington, D.C.: Freer Gallery of Art: Arthur M. Sackler Gallery, Smithsonian Institution; New York: Oxford University Press, 1996: 347–348.

brother, Mahmud, near Lucknow in 1529. Babur, whose reputation was in tatters in 1512, was now master of the Indo-Gangetic plain as well as eastern Afghanistan.

A few months after Babur secured his new realm, his son Humayun fell critically ill. In a formal ceremony, Babur asked God to take his own life in exchange for Humayun's. Humayun recovered, whereupon Babur fell ill, dying in 1530 at the age of forty-seven. It soon became evident that Babur's bargain with God had been a poor one. Humayun lacked many of the qualities of leadership that his father possessed. His apparent weaknesses elicited challenges from within his own military as well as from the Afghans who had retreated down the Ganges valley after their defeat at the hands of Babur. Humayun missed several opportunities to consolidate his power, primarily due to his indulgence in wine and opium, which he took simultaneously.

In 1539, an Afghan army led by Sher Khan Sur defeated Humayun, who fled to the Punjab. There he found that even his own brothers in Lahore and Qandahar were plotting against him. He wandered aimlessly in Sindh for several years, his career apparently at an end. Then, in 1544, he sought refuge in Herat, in Safavid territory. During his stay there, he received an invitation from Tahmasp to come to his court at Qazvin.

Tahmasp made Humayun an offer similar to the one their fathers had agreed upon thirty years earlier: Safavid military aid would be at the Timurid prince's disposal on condition of his acceptance of Shi'ism. Contradictory accounts leave us in the dark regarding what actually happened at the meeting, but it seems that, after a tense confrontation that threatened the lives of all in the Timurid party, Humayun conceded just enough to win Tahmasp's help without making him subservient to the Safavid emperor. Humayun returned to Qandahar with several thousand Safavid troops to begin winning back his kingdom. He captured Qandahar without difficulty, but he had to capture Kabul three times from his brother before it was secure. He could then turn his attention to the regions that his father had conquered two decades earlier.

Sher Khan Sur, who adopted the title Sher Shah Sur after defeating Humayun, had quickly taken control of the Punjab, Kashmir, and the entire Ganges valley. In addition to his military achievements, he instituted innovative and constructive reforms in taxation and administration. He also began negotiations with the Ottoman sultan Suleyman I to create an alliance to crush the Safavids between them. Sher Shah Sur's considerable accomplishments over a short period of time suggest that he was well on his way to creating an impressive state in South Asia. In 1545, however, he was killed in battle. Eight years later, a treaty among his successors divided the Indo-Gangetic plain into four Afghan-dominated mini-states. The creation of the four small states was a godsend to Humayun. He attacked immediately, before any of their rulers could begin to recombine them. By the summer of 1555, both Lahore and Delhi were once again under his control. Just as Humayun could begin to feel satisfaction that he had proven his detractors wrong about his abilities, however, he fell down a stone staircase after smoking opium, suffering a fatal concussion. He was succeeded by his twelve-year-old son, Akbar.

Akbar (1556–1605) was a charismatic leader of the stature of Isma'il, Babur, and Sher Shah Sur. Due to his age, regents made the important decisions in his name for the first five years of his reign. During this period, the army scored quick victories in the Punjab, Rajasthan, Malwa, and the central Ganges valley. Akbar himself took the throne in 1561 and continued the remarkable series of Mughal conquests. During the 1560s, he completed the subjugation of Rajasthan; in the 1570s, he secured control of Gujarat, Bihar, and much of Bengal; and during the 1580s, he annexed Kashmir and Sind. During the 1590s, he subdued the Indus delta, Khandesh, part of Ahmadnagar, and Berar. Of all his campaigning, Akbar's experience in Bengal was the most frustrating. The region's Afghan warlords fought ferociously, and the rain forests and delta terrain caused great logistical problems for the huge Mughal army. Akbar fought off and on in Bengal until he died in 1605.

The empire's frontiers remained relatively stable during the half-century after Akbar's death. Akbar's son Jahangir (1605–1627) stated that his goal was to conquer the Timurid homeland of Transoxiana, but nothing came of that plan. His armies subjugated the parts of Bengal that were still not under Mughal control. In 1616, he captured much of Ahmadnagar, but that sultanate's Habshi regent, Malik Ambar, initiated a brilliant guerilla war against the Mughal army, inflicting severe damage on it. The heavy-handed Mughal military presence also provoked Maratha resistance. Marathas had served along with Habshis in Ahmadnagar's military, and one, Shahji Bhosle, came from a particularly distinguished family, his father having served as Malik Ambar's most trusted assistant. Shahji inherited his father's estate and served as an officer in Malik's army. After Malik Ambar's death in 1626, the Mughals began making inroads into Ahmadnagar, and even captured the young sultan in 1633. At that point, Shahji intervened, installing another young member of the royal dynasty of Ahmadnagar to replace the captured sultan, and Shahji himself filled the role that the Habshi regents had served for over three decades. Shahji led the Maratha resistance to the Mughals for the next three years before Ahmadnagar was finally divided by the Mughals and Bijapur. His legacy of anti-Mughal guerilla activity remained alive, however. As we shall see, it would prove to be a major element in the destruction of Mughal control over the Deccan by the end of the century.

It was Jahangir's son Shah Jahan (1627–1658) who finally defeated and formally annexed Ahmadnagar in 1636 after killing the last member of the ruling dynasty. Guerilla warfare by the Marathas continued, but the stationing of the Mughal army in the kingdom did force Bijapur and Golkonda—cities that were more vulnerable to the Mughal armies than elusive guerilla fighters were—to pay tribute. In 1646, Shah Jahan attempted to fulfill the long-time Mughal ambition to conquer Transoxiana. As his army encountered the Uzbeks in the frontier area beyond Kabul, however, the campaign bogged down. The Mughals had an overwhelming advantage in firepower, but their opponents had learned from their confrontations with the Safavids not to charge into the face of artillery and musket fire. The Uzbek light cavalry avoided the gunpowder units and harassed the heavy calvary of the Mughals. The campaign could not advance beyond Balkh (near modern Mazar-e Sharif) in northern Afghanistan, where the Mughal horses ran out of grazing area as winter closed in. Shah Jahan's army was forced to retreat, and it suffered thousands of casualties on the way back to Kabul. At enormous expense in treasure and lives, the Mughals had managed to extend their frontier about forty miles.

Shah Jahan's son Aurangzeb (1658–1707) devoted the bulk of his career to military campaigns. His primary focus was the Deccan, where he conquered Bijapur and Golkonda during the period 1685–1687. Both kingdoms suffered massive damage as a result of particularly brutal campaigns. The large and impressive city of Bijapur was practically destroyed. Aurangzeb extended the Mughal frontier almost to the tip of the peninsula, but his actual progress ended in 1687. For the remaining two decades of his life, he was embroiled in suppressing revolts, most of which were led by Marathas. He was in the field, living in a tent, for almost the entire period, neglecting events that were causing his nobles to become restive.

The Mughals ruled the most powerful state to have emerged in South Asia for a millennium and a half. They never related to another South Asian kingdom as an equal. Rather, they regarded all other states in the region merely as potential future provinces of the Mughal Empire. The Mughals commanded a formidable military machine and their conquests appear to have vindicated their self-confidence and arrogance. What is often overlooked about the Mughal military victories is that many of them were achieved only with the utmost determination. Babur's series of victories was achieved against dramatic odds in manpower, they were hard fought, and each victory could easily have been a loss. From Akbar's reign through that of Aurangzeb, the Mughals commanded large armies that boasted tens of thousands of cavalrymen in addition to archery units, artillery, and musketry. Nevertheless, the Mughals' opponents also had large armies, fought fiercely, and provided no easy victories. Even Akbar could not subdue his opponents in the rain forests and marshes of Bengal. Jahangir, Shah Jahan, and Aurangzeb all encountered military frustrations. As long as the Mughals fought in the Indo-Gangetic plain, they had the advantage over their opponents, but in the Deccan, Bengal, and Afghanistan, they reached the limits of their expansion.

A striking illustration of the limits of Mughal power was the history of Qandahar from the late sixteenth through the early eighteenth centuries. Qandahar was a major agricultural and commercial center, and possession of it was important for protecting communications with Kabul and for keeping open the route to Central Asia. Nevertheless, the Mughals had to contest the Safavids for it, and were not as successful as their rivals. The Safavids, who had less than one-tenth the population of the Mughals, occupied the city for most of the period from 1558 to 1709.

Within their sphere of influence, the Mughals considered the Uzbeks and Safavids to be their only rivals. Relations with the Uzbeks were hostile due to the long-standing dream of the Mughals to reclaim their homeland from the Uzbek usurpers. Commercial relations, however, remained open, and trade flowed freely between the two powers. The Safavids and Mughals clashed over Qandahar, which lay on their mutual frontier, but their relations were usually proper and, occasionally, even cordial. "Ambivalent" might be the best description of their attitude toward each other. Until the 1630s, native Persian-speakers formed a large contingent within the Mughal nobility and administration, and they maintained close ties with their families in Iran. Both the Mughal and Safavid courts were Persianate in language and culture.

Although Jahangir and Shah 'Abbas never met, they established a cordial diplomatic relationship and frequently exchanged letters, embassies, and gifts. Jahangir esteemed the Persian aesthetic and was married to an Iranian woman, Nur Jahan. She and several of her relatives were powerful forces at the Mughal court. Because of the close relationship that Jahangir had developed with 'Abbas, he was shocked by ‘Abbas's recapture of Qandahar in 1622 (Akbar had seized it in 1595 while ‘Abbas was desperately trying to gain control of his Qizilbash). ‘Abbas dismissed the event as a mere affair of state that should not affect their personal relationship. During the reign of Shah Jahan, relations with the Safavids became more distant, not least because Shah Jahan made it clear that he wanted to recapture Qandahar, extend his rule over Central Asia, and annex the Shi‘ite states in the Deccan.

Society

Mughal = big

The Mughal Empire (see Map 6.2) had the largest population in the world after China. Scholars estimate that in 1600, the empire contained sixty to one hundred million people, and that by 1700, following Aurangzeb's conquests, it may have contained 150 million inhabitants. The Ottoman Empire (twenty-five to thirty million) and the Safavid Empire (six to eight million) paled in comparison, while the combined population of all the countries of Europe west of Poland amounted to approximately seventy million in 1600 and eighty-five million in 1700.

The empire was a study in diversity. It encompassed a wide variety of climatic zones—from the deserts of Sindh to the rain forests of Bengal—and of topographical features—from the Himalayas to rice paddies—while its people spoke a thousand languages and dialects. The vast majority of the population adhered to what we call Hinduism, a term that encompasses a staggering variety of religious doctrines and practices. The caste system that is so intimately bound with Hinduism produced a much more rigidly stratified social structure than was found in the lands to the west, where Islam had developed. Research into the mutual interaction of the caste system and Islam is in its infancy, but the evidence suggests that Islam's insistence on spiritual equality did little if anything to break down social inequalities. Low-caste Hindus who converted to Islam were embraced neither by the ruling Muslim elite nor by high-caste Hindus who converted to Islam. Formal caste distinctions did not continue to identify a person who converted to Islam, but social distinctions continued to be sharply defined.

Slavery was a common feature in South Asia before and after the arrival of Muslims. Until the late sixteenth century, slaves were most commonly obtained as part of the plunder of conquest: The wives and children of defeated soldiers could expect to become slaves for the rest of their lives. Akbar ended this practice, and from his reign on, most slaves—the vast majority of whom were of South Asian origin—were purchased. Although the Delhi Sultanate and some of its successor states used slave soldiers, the Mughals did not. We also have little evidence that slaves were used for agricultural purposes. Mughal slavery in South Asia was overwhelmingly found in the home or palace. Slaves performed a wide variety of functions, from the most menial and degrading to the most sophisticated. They served as maids, servants, guards, business agents, advisors, and tutors. A powerful nobleman might have hundreds of domestic slaves; an emperor would have thousands. Many of the female slaves were concubines who lived in the *zanana* (women's quarters) of the palace. Some of the numbers are amazing: Akbar's zanana was home to 5000 women and Aurangzeb's contained 2000. Although many relatives lived in the zanana, these numbers clearly suggest the presence of many slave concubines.

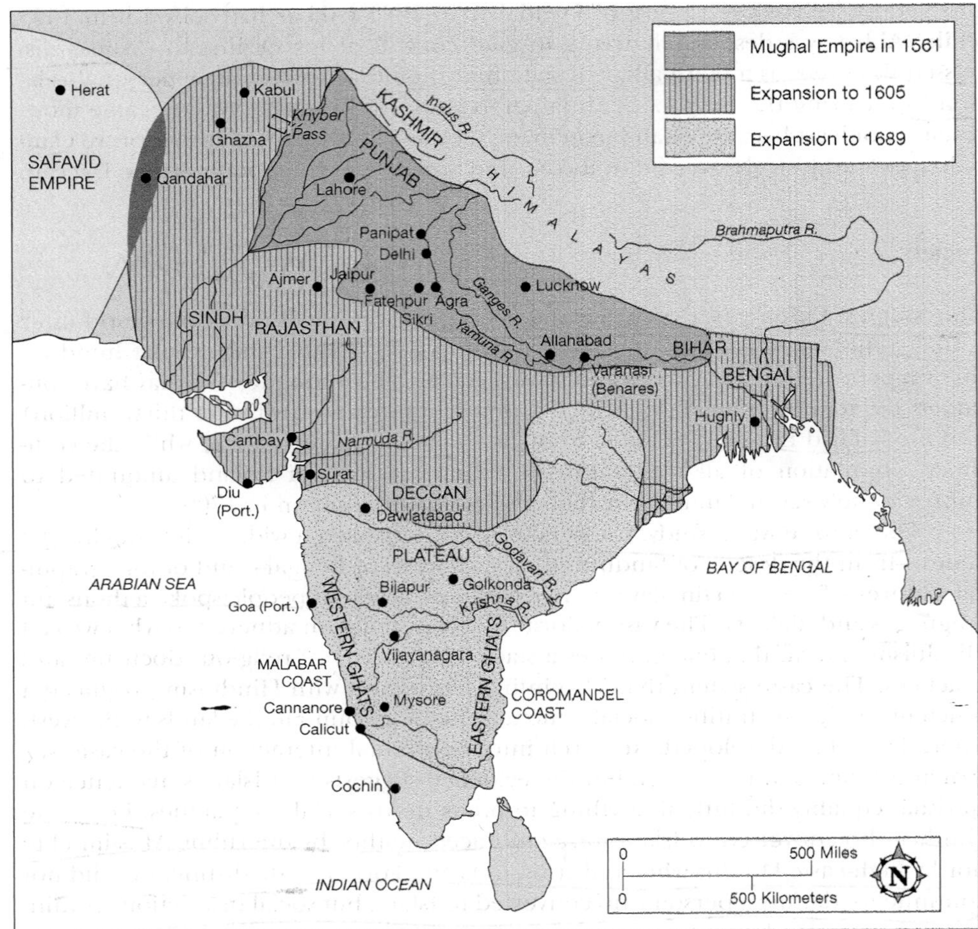

MAP 6.2 South Asia under the Mughals.

Women's roles in the Mughal Empire were similar to those of contemporary Ottoman society and the last few decades of Safavid society. Women in elite families were ordinarily secluded, both in the sense of wearing a veil and of being confined within the women's quarters of the home. (In South Asia, the seclusion of women is known as *purdah.*) As in other Muslim societies, lower-income women were much less likely to practice purdah. Many of them worked outside the home in artisanal occupations or in the fields as peasants.

Women in the royal household were typically highly educated and sophisticated as well as wealthy. Many of them were patrons of the arts. Women in Shah Jahan's family commissioned some of the most impressive construction projects of the new capital city that he built: The city's two enormous bazaars and six congregational mosques were the result of the beneficence of ladies in the royal court. Whereas in most of the Muslim world, women were a tiny minority of mosque attendees, in India they were usually prohibited from entering a mosque at all. We do not know if the ladies who built the congregational mosques were welcome to pray in them.

Indian society has always been complex and riven with paradoxes. The Mughal period was no different in that regard. The same culture that practiced purdah and prohibited women from entering mosques also featured women who served as warriors. Paintings by both Hindu and Muslim artists during the Mughal era contain scenes in which women are hunting, playing polo, and engaging in warfare. Shah Jahan and other South Asian rulers recruited armed women warriors, and by the end of the eighteenth century, the Nizam of Hyderabad (the ruler of a Mughal successor state in the Deccan) controlled a corps of 2000 female soldiers who guarded the zanana and escorted members of the zanana when traveling. During the eighteenth century, women even commanded military units in battle.[3]

The State

The size and complexity of South Asian society required the Mughals to be creative and flexible in their approach to governing. The splendor of their court was dazzling, but their power was more apparent than real. They found it necessary constantly to renegotiate the terms of the bargain they had struck with the elites of the realm. The system worked as long as the rulers were at least tacitly aware that their power rested on the consent of the elites. When the central government began acting unilaterally, the central government's effective power collapsed.

The *Mansabdari* System

Mughal administrators, like those in the Delhi Sultanate, had to deal with the complexities of operating a Muslim government in a society that was overwhelmingly non-Muslim. They adapted the Timurid model of government (which combined Persian and Mongol elements) to the complex South Asian environment. At the center, four ministers reported to the emperor. They were responsible for finance, the army, judicial and religious issues, and the royal household. A division of labor also existed at the provincial level, where a governor, who reported directly to the emperor, was responsible for security and military affairs. He shared power with a revenue official who reported to the revenue minister; a military paymaster who reported to the military minister; and a religious official who reported to the minister for religious affairs.

Superimposed over this framework was yet another flow chart of responsibility known as the *mansabdari* system. Royal princes, provincial governors, and powerful warlords were assigned a graded position (*mansab*) that designated how many troops they were responsible for providing to the emperor when he demanded them. During Akbar's later years, there were almost two thousand of these *mansabdars*, who were responsible for over 140,000 heavy cavalry, in addition to war horses, war elephants, and both mounted and foot musketeers. Many of them were responsible for providing only a few troops, but a few were obligated to command and outfit as many as 7000 soldiers each.

A mansabdar was granted a *jagir* to finance his military obligation. A jagir was the right to collect the taxes of a specified region, which could be as small as a few fields or as large as a whole governate. Jagirs were assigned by the imperial revenue minister, and each mansabdar received a new jagir every few years so that he would not be able to establish a power base in a given area. Seven-eighths of the empire's taxable land was assigned as jagirs; one-eighth was reserved for the emperor.

At first glance, the jagir appears similar to the Ottoman timar, but it was quite different. The Ottoman government awarded timars to the tens of thousands of cavalrymen in the sultan's army. Jagirs were handed out to only a few hundred great nobles, with the result that the Mughal government's reach did not extend as deeply into its society as the Ottoman government's did into its own. On the other hand, the degree of centralization in the Mughal Empire was considerably more advanced than that of the Safavid Empire until the period of 'Abbas, when the Safavid ruler consolidated considerable power.

Unlike the Ottomans and the later Safavids, the Mughals did not have a corps of military slaves to balance the power of free soldiers. Thus, the emperors had to satisfy the political and economic ambitions of mansabdars by granting them an honorable degree of autonomy as well as an income that was commensurate with their status. The vast majority of the subcontinent's warlords discovered that participation in the mansabdari system provided them with as many rewards as they had enjoyed prior to having been conquered by the Mughals. The system was open to Hindus as well as Muslims, and to native Muslims as well as Timurids, Turks, Iranians, Uzbeks, and Afghans.

Despite the apparently uniform administrative system of the empire, the central government actually maintained a variety of relationships with its constituent parts. Akbar and his immediate successors did not try to be consistent in every instance. For example, they granted some of the Hindu Rajput nobles and warlords more autonomy than other notables enjoyed because of an unusual premium that Rajput culture placed on status and dignity. On the other hand, emperors had to be able to assert their authority over all nobles in order to maintain stability. Much of the system's equilibrium actually depended on the personality of the emperor himself and the degree to which he won both the respect and the loyalty of the great nobles of the realm.

Even this sophisticated and powerful imperial system faced many problems, however. A drought in one region might render the jagirs of a large number of mansabdars worthless. A period of rapid conquest might bring many new mansabdars into the system, but the conditions in the newly conquered area might become dangerous and unproductive due to continuing warfare. As a result, there would be more mansabdars than viable jagirs. The practice of periodically transferring jagirs was to the advantage of the emperor, but it was a nuisance for nobles, who resisted its enforcement. The terms of the relationship between a mansabdar and the emperor were constantly being renegotiated—and occasionally resisted—by the empire's elites.

Even more problematic for the empire's stability was the fact that, at the local level, traditional notables known as *zamindars* wielded considerable power. A zamindar was typically a large landowner and was the head of the dominant family in a large village or cluster of smaller villages. His wealth and kin connections, combined with his position at the apex of traditional lines of authority in a hierarchical society, endowed him with a great deal of influence. His actual power derived from his command of local military forces. In the Indo-Gangetic plain, the peasants had a tradition of being heavily armed and of honing their martial skills. Many of them, like their Swiss, Scot, and Irish contemporaries, left their villages to become mercenaries. Whether they left or stayed at home, they frequently found short-term or long-term employment as soldiers in local or regional private armies. Zamindars thus had a large pool of soldiers from which they could draw. Constant skirmishing took place as mansabdars attempted to collect more revenue than zamindars wanted them to, or as provincial governors attempted to fulfill their duty of providing security by disarming zamindars.

Establishing Imperial Legitimacy

No single city embodied the notion of the "imperial center" for the Mughals the way that London did for Akbar's contemporary Elizabeth of England (1558–1603) or the Paris–Versailles axis did for Aurangzeb's contemporary Louis XIV (1643–1715). The Mughals moved their capital even more frequently than the Safavids did, enabling several cities in the Indo-Gangetic plain to reflect the huge imperial investment in monumental architecture. Upon becoming emperor in 1561, Akbar established his headquarters at Agra. The city remained his capital until 1571, when he built Fatehpur Sikri a vast imperial center twenty-five miles west of Agra.

In 1585, Akbar transferred his headquarters once again. This time he moved to Lahore in order to be closer to Afghanistan. 'Abdullah Khan Uzbek had been successful in provoking Afghan tribes to challenge the Mughal regime at Kabul. By 1598 (when 'Abdullah Khan died), Akbar felt that he had secured his Afghan frontier, and so he moved his capital back to Agra. His son Jahangir (1605–1627) retained Agra as his capital, but Jahangir's son Shah Jahan (1627–1658) built a new imperial city in the 1640s in an open space near the ruined city of Delhi. This fabulous new city of palaces, mosques, and gardens became known as Shahjahanabad ("Shah Jahan's City"). Today it is known as Old Delhi. (New Delhi was built by the British in the early twentieth century.)

Mughal rulers could not establish their political legitimacy in the same manner as Ottoman, Safavid, and Uzbek rulers. By the mid-sixteenth century, the Safavids and Uzbeks ruled populations that were largely Muslim, and the Ottomans enjoyed the support of at least a large minority of Muslims. Because Muslim religious leaders could influence public opinion toward the government, the rulers carefully cultivated relations with them (or destroyed them, as the Safavids did with many Sufi leaders). Rulers had to adjust their claims as conditions changed, but they knew that appeals to religious legitimacy were effective. European rulers of the seventeenth century such as James I of England and Louis XIV of France attempted a similar course in their almost exclusively Christian societies by claiming a "divine right" to rule. Likewise, Chinese emperors claimed the "Mandate of Heaven."

The Mughal Empire, however, had a large non-Muslim majority of at least eighty per cent. Non-Muslims were not impressed by a ruler's title of caliph, his boast of a lineage that derived from the Prophet or his Companions, or claims that he possessed special insight into the meaning of the Qur'an. As a result, the early Mughal court made few appeals to religion, and its rulers faced the constant challenge of how to persuade their subjects to be loyal to them. They knew that many of their subjects were asking themselves, "By what right do the Mughals rule other than through the exercise of sheer force?"

Muslim regimes in South Asia prior to the Mughals made little or no formal distinction between Muslims and non-Muslims. Although the Shari'a required that non-Muslims pay a head tax, Muslim rulers in South Asia had rarely imposed it. Babur (1526–1530) and Humayun (1530–1539, 1555–1556) were both devout Muslims and followed the teaching of Sufi pirs (Babur identified with the Naqshbandiya, and Humayun followed the Shattariya). Both rulers, however, spent their entire careers leading military campaigns and never had to develop an ideology for the regime. Akbar (1556–1605) began his career as a devout Muslim, but he quickly made it clear that his government would not support the Islam of the ulama. Subsequent Mughal rulers had to decide whether they would accept, modify, or reject Akbar's policy.

Akbar began his reign as a pious follower of a Chishti saint. When the saint's prophecy of the birth of Jahangir was fulfilled, Akbar dedicated an enormous palace–mosque complex as a memorial to the pir near his dargah at Fatehpur Sikri. During his early years in Fatehpur Sikri, Akbar demonstrated his devotion by sweeping the floor of the great mosque and serving as its prayer leader. During the 1570s, however, Akbar's natural inquisitiveness and impatience with dogma led to a dramatic change in his religious orientation. The first signs of his disaffection with Shari'a-based Islam appeared several years after he began inviting Muslim scholars to the palace to discuss theological topics. Akbar was the only Mughal ruler who was illiterate (some scholars suspect that he had dyslexia), but all who met him were impressed by his intelligence and his learning, which he picked up from having books read to him and from engaging in discussions. He enjoyed—and actively participated in—philosophical and theological discussions.

To Akbar's disappointment, the palace seminars often degenerated into bitter arguments and charges of heresy being hurled by one scholar at another. He was disillusioned by these scenes. He was searching for Truth, both to satisfy his own quest for meaning and to find a universal religion that all his subjects could share. He began inviting scholars of other religions to the discussions, including representatives of Hinduism, Jainism, Zoroastrianism, and Judaism. In 1579, he invited Jesuits from the Portuguese enclave at Goa to come to his palace, and they became prominent members of the seminar.

As a result of the court discussions, Akbar became increasingly convinced that all the religions possessed only a partial understanding of the spiritual realm. He concluded that to patronize any one of them would be unjustifiable, since to do so would inevitably splinter his subjects into factions. With the help of Abu al-Fazl (a Shi'ite Iranian émigré and Akbar's closest advisor and confidante), Akbar began developing a new religious path. Inspired in part by al-Suhrawardi's theory of Illuminationism, the religion was called the *din-i ilahi,* or Divine Religion.

The new faith taught that the emperor was divinely illumined to be the leader of his people. Akbar now claimed to be the Perfect Man, a venerable Sufi concept that suggested he had attained spiritual fulfillment in his quest for the presence of God. He also declared that, when disagreements arose over a point of interpretation within any religion, religious authorities should bring the issue to him for resolution. Akbar himself worshiped the sun four times a day and made a sacred fire the center of further devotions. He began each day by appearing at a window of his palace as the sun rose, and the crowd that had gathered outside would greet him by prostrating before him.

Akbar never promulgated the Divine Religion widely, and he certainly did not attempt to impose it on his subjects. Outsiders viewed it as an ersatz Sufi order or even an attempt to capture the aura of Twelver Shi'ism. It echoed Sufi concepts in its portrayal of Akbar as pir and Perfect Man, and it suggested Shi'ite influences by its exaltation of Akbar as the enlightened Imam. The new "path" was intended for the elite of society. A large number of the Mughal nobility—perhaps even a majority of them—applied to be Akbar's disciples, and in their initiation ceremonies they vowed their willingness to sacrifice their lives, wealth, and honor for him.

Despite the self-promoting aspects of his new faith, Akbar seems to have made a genuine effort to formulate an official ideology that conveyed the message that the emperor was a spiritual leader whose wise guidance promoted the well-being of the entire realm. He asserted that reason should be the basis for determining religious truth, and he sought to instill the idea that ethics, rather than doctrine or ritual, should be at the heart of religious concerns. He made it known that he had begun to abstain from meat consumption, sexual intercourse, and—perhaps even more surprising in a Mughal ruler—the drinking of alcohol.

Akbar openly demonstrated his break with Islam not only by his worship of the sun, but also by terminating government sponsorship of caravans and flotillas for the hajj, a practice that had begun with the capture of Gujarat in 1574. He formally abolished the head tax on non-Muslims and the taxes on Hindu pilgrims. He also banned child marriage and forbade Hindu girls from converting to Islam as a condition of marriage. Rather than enforcing the Shari'a's ban on the construction and repair of temples, he contributed financially to the construction of Hindu temples, as well as to hospitals and caravanserais.

Pious Muslims were bitterly opposed to Akbar for these policies. Some of the initiatives were clearly heretical, but the ulama had the additional grievance that the new policies deprived them of authority. Akbar had asserted his sole sovereignty—both temporal and spiritual—and had made it clear that he would be the arbiter of the meaning of the Shari'a. Some Muslims were also upset that non-Muslims continued to be treated as the equals of Muslims. They felt that, with the establishment of a major Muslim-ruled state, the secondary status of non-Muslims should be enforced.

The Economy

For centuries, outsiders viewed South Asia as a source of fabulous wealth. The subcontinent was almost economically self-sufficient: It needed to import only precious metals, war horses, and certain spices. For the rest of the world, it was a major source of such valuable commodities as pepper, saffron, sugar, indigo (a word that derives from the Greek word that signified *Indian dye*), and silk and cotton textiles.

Prior to the sixteenth century, commerce in South Asia took place across vast distances despite a large number of independent states and frequent wars. Merchants, however, knew that business could be even better if their caravan agents did not have to pay numerous tariffs and bribes as they crossed frontiers, suffer exposure to raids by highwaymen, change currency frequently, and encounter a wide variety of road conditions. The reign of Sher Shah Sur (1539–1545), who chased Humayun out of Delhi in 1539, marked a major step forward in the economic history of the subcontinent. The Afghan brought about several reforms that had a lasting impact. He introduced the rupiya (rupee) coin, which gained wide distribution throughout the subcontinent; improved the system of crop taxes by making them regular rather than arbitrary; and began construction of a network of roads. The Grand Trunk Road lay at the center of this transportation system, extending from the Khyber Pass to Bengal.

The Mughal conquests that began in the second half of the sixteenth century resulted in unprecedented internal commercial ties within South Asia and allowed Sher Shah Sur's reforms to have an impact over a wide area. The annexations linked Bengal, Gujarat, Delhi, the Punjab, and Kabul. The Mughals' trade policy was to encourage overland trade with the Safavids and even with their old nemesis, the Uzbeks. They placed no frontier restrictions on the trade that connected the subcontinent with Iran and Central Asia. The Mughals allowed merchants from all nations to trade in their ports and to travel and live freely within the empire. This freedom of movement stood in stark contrast to the situation in China, where foreigners were tightly controlled by imperial officers, and in Japan, where foreigners were excluded after 1639.

The Mughals also recognized the importance of the maritime trade on their coasts. If the Mughals had come to power earlier in the sixteenth century, they might have clashed with the Portuguese. The Portuguese conquered Goa on the Malabar Coast and established Hughly in Bengal, intending to control all commerce on both sides of the subcontinent. By the time the Mughals arrived on both coasts, however, Portuguese power had declined dramatically. The Sa'dis of Morocco defeated the Portuguese army during the same decade that Akbar conquered Gujarat, and shortly thereafter, Spain annexed Portugal. In 1633, the Mughal army expelled the last Portuguese soldiers from Hughly.

As Portuguese power waned in the central Indian Ocean, English, Dutch, and French activity increased. These Europeans found that Cambay was no longer the major port of the subcontinent, as it had been during the previous three centuries. The channel into Cambay's harbor had been gradually silting up throughout the sixteenth century, and it finally became impossible for larger ships to berth at the city's wharves. Surat, located closer to the open sea, displaced Cambay as the major port in the subcontinent by the last quarter of the sixteenth century.

The vast overland trade network that the Mughals controlled now linked up with the maritime networks of the Dutch, English, and French companies to bring unprecedented economic prosperity to most of the subcontinent. The volume of South Asian exports bound directly for Europe increased dramatically during the seventeenth century, especially the cotton textiles that the English East India Company bought.

Although the volume of Mughal trade with Europe was growing, the subcontinent's most important markets remained Iran, Central Asia, and the lands that bordered the Indian Ocean. Many of the commodities that were traded in the seventeenth century were familiar to long-time customers. Saffron, sugar, and indigo continued to be important, and cotton textiles grew in importance during the Mughal period. Gujarat had a reputation for making cheap, coarse textiles, and the Coromandel Coast and Bengal were noted for their high-quality fabrics.

Because of new developments taking place in the global trading networks, the pattern of exports from South Asia experienced some significant changes in the seventeenth century. One was the introduction of tobacco cultivation. Only a few years after Captain John Smith helped to establish tobacco as a cash crop in Virginia, the "weed" became an important export from the Mughal Empire. Another was a precipitous decline in the export of black pepper. For centuries, this spice had been grown almost exclusively on the Malabar Coast, but by the seventeenth century, Sumatra had displaced the Malabar Coast as the major producing region. A third change was that the Coromandel Coast became a major source for slaves. The Dutch East India Company began acquiring slaves there after 1635 and exported tens of thousands of them to other regions in the Indian Ocean basin.

The Mughals themselves were particularly interested in the importation of war horses. The subcontinent's climate and relative dearth of good grazing grounds required that thousands of horses be imported every year to supply the vast Mughal cavalry. Some came from the Arabian Peninsula, but most came from Safavid and Uzbek territories. The Mughal palace kitchens also stimulated a rise in the imports of spices from Southeast Asia, and Mughal nostalgia for Central Asia caused the ruling elites to import large quantities of melons, dried apricots, almonds, and carpets from there.

The largest economic project undertaken by the Mughals was the transformation of eastern Bengal into a major rice-growing region. Western Bengal had been settled for centuries and was predominantly Hindu. Eastern Bengal was a heavily forested region that lay beyond the influence of Sanskritic civilization. Shah Jahan initiated a policy that encouraged the clearing of the jungles in eastern Bengal, but the major effort had to wait until the 1660s, after piracy had been eliminated from the major estuaries. Aurangzeb's administration awarded tax-free grants of land to individuals who brought forested areas into rice cultivation. These grantees, in turn, recruited peasants to clear-cut the forest and cultivate rice.

The grantees were also obligated to build a temple or mosque for the cultivators. Since most of the agents were Muslims, they tended to build mosques for their workers and appointed Chishti pirs to be the supervisors of the mosques. The cultivators, most of whom followed local, animistic, religions, were drawn to the spiritual gifts of the pirs. Despite a Mughal ban on proselytizing the non-Muslims in the region, eastern Bengal became heavily Islamized. The Islamization of eastern Bengal is one of the most impressive testimonials that history offers to illustrate the spiritual charisma of Sufi pirs.

The development of eastern Bengal dates from this Mughal initiative. The region's population grew enormously, and Islam became the primary religion. The region's economy boomed, for rice and sugar cane were produced on a commercial scale, and large quantities of both were exported. The profit made on these crops supplemented the wealth that was generated from the export of the world-famous Bengali silk and fine cotton textiles.

Merchants from around the world came to the subcontinent during the Mughal period, and South Asian merchants fanned out across the continent and the Indian Ocean to facilitate the marketing of South Asian agricultural and manufactured goods. South Asian merchants and financiers were to be found in the ports of any size all around the Indian Ocean. Thousands of them—Muslim and Hindu—lived and worked in Iran and Central Asia during the seventeenth century. They provided services as money changers, lenders, and financiers. Others were in the retail or wholesale trade. Many other South Asian businessmen made their way as far north as Astrakhan and Moscow during the early seventeenth century. These businessmen enjoyed the same competitive advantages and edge in expertise as their Venetian counterparts had when their services had been in demand throughout Europe during the fourteenth and fifteenth centuries.

Culture

South Asia contains a large number of distinctive regional cultures, but the notable aspect of Mughal elite society was the prominent role that Persian cultural elements played in it. For several hundred years, Persian culture streamed into South Asia by way of the Delhi Sultanate, the Deccan kingdoms, Gujarat, and Bengal. Under the Mughals, the Persian language, literary themes, and motifs in the visual arts became even more influential. This development coincided with the dominance of Persian culture among the Uzbeks and Safavids and the high regard that Persian culture enjoyed in the Ottoman Empire. The result was that the ruling elites from Bengal to the Balkans shared similar tastes in manners and customs, styles of dress, literature, and the visual arts. During the seventeenth century, educated individuals in Dhaka, Delhi, and Lahore could value the same art, enjoy the same poetry, and adhere to the same values as their peers in Bukhara, Esfahan, and Istanbul.

As an educated Timurid, Babur was fluent in both Persian and Chaghatay Turkish. His grandson Akbar designated Persian to be the official language of the Mughal court, and Persian became not only the language of imperial recordkeeping and correspondence, but also of belles lettres. Akbar encouraged the immigration of Persian-speaking intellectuals, who came largely from the Safavid and Uzbek realms. Many of them were attracted by the greater wealth of the Mughal Empire. Others were Sunnis, Sufis, or Zoroastrians threatened by the unsettled political conditions of the Safavid empire during the second half of the sixteenth century or the increasing restrictions on cultural creativity in Central Asia under the rule of Abdullah Khan Uzbek.

In 1590, Akbar commissioned the *Babur-nameh* to be translated from Chaghatay into Persian, and the *Mahabharata,* the great Hindu epic, to be translated from Sanskrit into Persian. Under Akbar and Jahangir, Iranian philosophy, especially the works of al-Suhrawardi, became a major focus of study. South Asian Sufism, already more strongly influenced by the Iranian schools of thought than by the Arab world, now became even more heavily Persianized than before. Numerous commentaries were written on the work of the great Sufi masters who wrote in Persian, especially thirteenth-century Rumi and fifteenth-century Jami. Persian culture was at its height during the reign of Jahangir (1605–1627), when the emperor's wife, the Iranian Nur Jahan, exercised enormous power, both directly and through members of her family who were prominent at court.

Shah Jahan, Jahangir's son (but not Nur Jahan's son), resented the influence of the Iranians and began recruiting Central Asians in their place. During the reign of Shah Jahan's son Aurangzeb (1658–1707), Central Asians came to dominate the court. Persian culture continued to have a powerful influe Aurangzeb's conquest of the Deccan in the 1680s, many of the c Deccan were absorbed into the court culture at Delhi. They b their Dakani language, which had developed over the previous t hybrid of Persian and local Deccan languages. Its intelligibility to s European languages in the Indo-Gangetic plain, combined with i simplicity, facilitated its rapid transformation into the lingua franca the region. During the eighteenth century, the language was increa Urdu, and it became the vehicle for a remarkable literary flowering. I became the official language of modern Pakistan.

The use of the Persian language was, on the whole, restricted to the elites of South Asia. It must be noted, however, that the language had a much greater impact than that bald fact might indicate, for two major reasons. First, Hindus as well as Muslims used the language. Especially in the north, many upper-caste Hindus read Persian, just as some Muslims read Hindi. The use of Persian as the official language of government no doubt spurred many Hindus to learn the language, but many cultured Hindus learned it simply because they and their Muslim counterparts often shared the same arts and learning. Many Hindus in business and finance used Persian because it was the language of commerce in the region that extended from the Punjab to the Syr Darya River in the north and to the Zagros Mountains in the west.

The second reason for the influence of Persian is that, like many other languages of the Indo-Gangetic plain, it is an Indo-European language. Since it shares features of grammar and vocabulary with many dialects spoken in northern India, it is easy to learn for anyone who speaks those languages. It eventually exercised a profound influence on the Bengali, Marathi, Pushtu, Sindhi, Baluchi, and Kashmiri languages. Each of them came to be written in the Persian alphabet (itself a slightly altered form of the Arabic alphabet), and each borrowed heavily from Persian vocabulary. It appears that the use of Persian among Muslims in the Deccan kingdoms and among Muslims and Hindus of the Mughal Empire made South Asia the center of Persian culture in the early seventeenth century. Assuming similar literacy rates in Iran and South Asia, the huge population of the latter would have ensured that far more people used Persian in South Asia than in Iran.[4]

Among tourists to South Asia, the Mughals are even more famous for their patronage of monumental building and miniature painting than for their literature. It is worth noting that, whereas the most famous Ottoman and Safavid buildings are mosques, the Mughals are known for their forts, palaces, imperial cities, gardens, and tombs. The architectural works that Akbar commissioned, such as those of the complex at Fatehpur Sikri, tend to reflect traditional indigenous styles. Jahangir was less interested in architecture than in miniature paintings and imperial gardens. Like all the Mughal emperors, he loved the beautiful valleys of Kashmir, where he built some particularly noteworthy gardens.

Shah Jahan was the greatest of the Mughal patrons of architecture. He is famous for having commissioned the imperial city of Shahjahanabad, the Red Fort at Delhi, and the Peacock Throne. The Peacock Throne required seven years to design and build. It was inlaid with rubies, diamonds, pearls, and emeralds. Above its canopy stood the peacock that gave the throne its name. The bird's body was made of gold inlaid with precious stones and its tail was made largely of sapphires.

The *dargah* of Hazrat Nizamuddin Aulia, the founder of the Chishti Sufi order in Delhi.

As remarkable as these commissions were, Shah Jahan is most famous for the Taj Mahal, a tomb he commissioned for his wife Arjumand Banu Begam, a niece of Nur Jahan. She is better known by her nickname, Mumtaz Mahal ("Beloved of the Palace"). Mumtaz Mahal died in childbirth in 1631, bearing the couple's fourteenth child in nineteen years of marriage (only seven lived past infancy). Like most royal marriages, it had been arranged purely for political reasons. Unlike most such marriages, it was characterized by deep and abiding affection: Shah Jahan and Mumtaz Mahal were inseparable companions after their marriage in 1612. Her death was a crushing blow to him, and he vowed to build a monument worthy of her. He brought in skilled artisans from all over the Persianate world to construct a forty-two-acre garden tomb in the Central Asian tradition. The mausoleum was placed in the middle, flanked by a guest house and a mosque. Shah Jahan expected pilgrims to visit the tomb, which would eventually house his body as well as that of his wife.

We have little information regarding advances made in the fields of the natural sciences and mathematics during the Mughal period. Little research has been done in these areas. It appears that, although Mughal emperors provided patronage for literature, art, and architecture, none after Babur was interested in the sciences. The astronomer of the Mughal period about whom we are best informed was Sawai Jai Singh (1688–1743), who inherited the rule of one of the most powerful mansabs in Rajasthan in 1700 at the age of twelve. After the death of Aurangzeb in 1707, he accumulated power so skillfully that, by the mid-1720s, he became autonomous without having clashed with Delhi. He was so powerful that it was commonly said that he owned all the land between Delhi and Surat.

Jai Singh, a Hindu, was intellectually precocious as a youth, and he continued his passionate curiosity about astronomy throughout his life. He was disturbed by discrepancies between the planetary and lunar tables that he possessed (from both the Sanskritic tradition and the Timurid tradition of Ulugh Bey), on the one hand, and the findings of continuing observations, on the other. He launched a massive project to improve astronomical knowledge: He built libraries, constructed observatories at five different cities in order to compare data, personally designed instruments to measure time and angles, and assembled teams of astronomers that included Hindus, Muslims, and Jesuit missionaries from Portugal. The observatory at Jaipur remains almost intact and is an impressive monument to Jai Singh's commitment to science. Also impressive was Jai Singh's determination to tap into the astronomical knowledge accumulated in Europe. Unfortunately, his European contacts were the Portuguese of Goa, with whom he made arrangements to send a delegation to Lisbon. The group remained in Portugal throughout the year 1729, but it remained unaware of the heliocentric theory that had become dominant in northern Europe. Because of the hostility of the Catholic Church of the period toward the heliocentric theory, members of the delegation never had access to the works of Copernicus, Galileo, Kepler, or Newton.

Islam gained numerous adherents in South Asia during the Mughal period. In addition, the large-scale immigration of Sufis from Iran and Central Asia expanded the offerings in what was already a wide spectrum of spiritual paths from which South Asian Muslims could choose. The most important order introduced during this time was the Naqshbandiya, brought to Delhi from Kabul in the 1590s by Khwaja Muhammad Baqi Billah. One of his disciples was Ahmad Sirhindi (1563–1624), who in turn became a famous khwaja. Sirhindi continued the Naqshbandi emphasis on balancing the mystical experience with the requirements of the Shari'a, cautioning Sufis against becoming "intoxicated" by their experiences. He also tried to reinterpret Ibn al-'Arabi's doctrine of the "Unity of Being"—which underlay almost all Sufi movements of the period—in a way that did not infringe on the traditional doctrine of God's unity.

Sirhindi was widely admired, but no one held him in higher esteem than himself. A considerable number of his followers believed that he was in the line of "renewers" whom Muslims believed were sent by God at the beginning of each Islamic century to reform Islam. Sirhindi himself believed that he was not merely the eleventh century's renewer, but the renewer of the entire second Islamic millennium, which began in 1591 C.E. Although he conceded that prophecy had come to an end with Muhammad, he claimed that certain individuals (including himself) had direct experience of divine inspiration and possessed prophetic qualities. His extravagant claims for himself provoked such a hostile reaction from other members of the ulama that Jahangir was compelled to imprison him during 1619–1620 to allow passions to cool.

The growing number of Sufi orders provided South Asian Muslims with increased opportunities to develop the inward, spiritual life. Those opportunities, however, came at the expense of the creation of new ideas regarding the broader role of Islam within the empire. When Akbar began devising his universal religion, he was, in effect, challenging the ulama to demonstrate how Islamic institutions should function in a largely Hindu empire ruled by a Muslim dynasty. Rather than confront the problem, Muslim religious leaders tended either to retreat from society into their mystical path or simply to charge Mughal rulers with heresy or apostasy. Despite Sirhindi's reputation today as an activist who sought to influence court policy in the tradition of Central Asian khwajas, he actually exerted few efforts in that direction and had no discernible political influence on Mughal emperors.[5]

Neither Sirhindi nor any other seventeenth-century religious leader devoted serious efforts to the problem of reconciling Islamic ideals to Mughal realities. As a result, emperors lurched from one religious policy to another. Jahangir maintained Akbar's policy of treating all religions alike. Like his contemporary Shah 'Abbas, who was largely ignoring the royal cult established by Isma'il (and from which Tahmasp had distanced himself), Jahangir gradually abandoned the royal cult established by Akbar. He ruled without reference to Islam. Shah Jahan, in contrast, reactivated the ban on the construction or repair of churches and temples, and he ordered that recently built temples in the Hindu holy city of Benares be razed. Unlike Akbar and Jahangir, he publicly participated in Islamic festivals and stressed their importance.

The End of Imperial Rule

After a century of existence, the Mughal Empire in the 1650s was wealthy and powerful. Its achievements had been legion. Its conquests had unified such widely scattered territories as Bengal, Gujarat, and Kabul; brought them under a uniform revenue system; and granted them a relative degree of stability and peace. The integration of these regions generated a long period of economic growth. The pattern of South Asia's commercial relations with the outside world sheltered it from the seventeenth-century economic crisis that affected Europe, the Ottomans, and the Safavids. The new capital city of Shahjahanabad was an impressive symbol of imperial glory. Even pious critics of the regime grudgingly conceded that reforms were occurring that gave more centrality to Islamic themes. The imperial ruling class could justifiably expect the next century to be even better.

Rather than consolidating its rule, however, the Mughal dynasty entered upon a period in which its power unraveled. It is a saga that still intrigues historians—and must have confounded contemporaries—for by outward appearances, the empire seemed to prosper. The territorial and demographic size of the empire greatly increased by 1689 and the economy in most areas continued to grow. Ominously, though, the dynasty itself was not able to solve challenges to its authority that in the past it would have handled easily. Local and provincial leaders, accustomed to the give-and-take of challenge and compromise with the Mughals, now found that when they resisted the financial or military demands of the Mughals, they got away with their defiance.

The Reign of Aurangzeb

The empire's problems began with a civil war that erupted when Shah Jahan seemed to be dying in 1657. Years earlier, Shah Jahan had made it clear that his eldest and favorite son, Dara Shukoh, was his choice to be his successor. Now, however, the four sons that Mumtaz Mahal had borne for him began to contest for the throne. Two of the brothers dominated the struggle. Dara Shukoh was an intellectual. He was a master of languages, philosophy, and religions, and he appreciated fine music and art. He developed a high regard for Hinduism and translated the Upanishads into Persian. His chief challenger was his youngest brother, Aurangzeb. Aurangzeb's personality stood in sharp contrast to that of Dara Shukoh, for he was an ascetic and scrupulous observer of Islamic ritual. His intense piety and his contempt for music and art may have led Dara Shukoh to underestimate him, for he was no religious hermit: He combined great military and administrative abilities with high ambitions, and he seems to have considered the prospect of Dara Shukoh's accession to the throne to be a catastrophe for Islam.

The civil war among the brothers lasted from 1657 to 1661. Shah Jahan temporarily threw the ambitions of his sons into question by recovering from his "terminal" illness, but they had too much invested in the war to allow him to regain the throne. In 1658, Aurangzeb imprisoned him in a fortress near the Taj Mahal. For the remaining eight years of his life, he could see, but was never allowed to visit, the shrine that he had commissioned for his beloved wife. By 1661, Aurangzeb had defeated and killed his brothers. He took the title *Alamgir,* which, like *Jahangir,* means "world-seizer."

Aurangzeb (1658–1707) felt a sense of responsibility to rule the empire in accordance with the will of God. His affiliation with the Naqshbandiya had reinforced his disdain for the universalist and inclusive nature of the Mughal regime's ideology. He was also hostile to both Sikhism[6] and Shi'ism, apparently viewing both as intolerable threats to Sunni Islam. Although previous Mughal rulers had coexisted with Sikhs, Aurangzeb began a systematic attack on them in the Punjab, where most of them lived. The ruthless wars created a long-lasting hatred of Muslims by Sikhs.

Aurangzeb's most famous conquests were in the Deccan. In the 1670s his authority was challenged by a talented young Maratha named Shivaji, who was the son of Shahji Bhosle, the noble who had led the last formal resistance to the Mughal capture of Ahmadnagar in the 1630s. Shivaji inherited the charisma and ability of his father and grandfather, and he led disaffected Marathas to throw off Mughal rule, creating an avowedly Hindu kingdom that extended from Surat to Goa. After it became clear that Shivaji could not be coaxed back into the Mughal Empire, Aurangzeb went to war. He had a dual purpose in doing so. The main objective of defeating Shivaji was complemented by a desire to annex Golkonda and Bijapur. The two kingdoms were still wealthy, but they had become militarily weak. Any Mughal leader might well have coveted them; Aurangzeb had additional motives: Both of these Shi'ite kingdoms had recently installed Brahmins (high-caste Hindus) as chief ministers, exacerbating Aurangzeb's loathing of them. In addition, Shivaji had sought an alliance with Golkonda against Delhi, and Aurangzeb used that as a pretext to attack both Golkonda and Bijapur.

In an effort to rally the Muslims of the empire behind him in what would undoubtedly be a long and expensive war, Aurangzeb announced changes in governmental religious policy. He enforced the Shari'a-mandated head tax on non-Muslims, and he taxed Hindus who went to their own religious festivals. Perhaps most shocking to other members of the ruling family, he prohibited the consumption of wine and opium. Aurangzeb could be utterly ruthless in the execution of his policies, but we should note that some of his attempts to implement Islamic principles actually benefited non-Muslims. Although he imposed the head tax on non-Muslims, he also abolished a number of taxes *not* authorized by the Shari'a that had fallen primarily on Hindus. Although he destroyed some Hindu temples, he authorized the construction of a few Hindu temples for political reasons and occasionally gave land grants to Brahmins. On the whole, however, there can be no doubt that many non-Muslims became disaffected from the regime because of his policies. The disaffection was noticed not so much among the elites as among the urban masses, who were harassed and abused by collectors of the head tax.

The Mughal army defeated Shivaji and took control of the major Maratha cities. Shivaji and his successors, however, continued to conduct guerilla warfare against the Mughal army. Aurangzeb could never be certain that he exercised control in the region, and he had to station large numbers of troops in it. Meanwhile, between 1685 and 1687, Aurangzeb conducted a scorched-earth policy against Golkonda and Bijapur. His army devastated the two kingdoms in an orgy of destruction, looting, and rape. No one—including his family members, leading ulama, and generals—could dissuade him from wreaking devastation. He also ignored protests and appeals from Esfahan. The Mughal–Safavid relationship, which had been correct and occasionally warm despite genuine competition, became unremittingly hostile due to Aurangzeb's anti-Shi'ite policies. There were no diplomatic missions between the Mughals and the last two Safavid emperors (1666–1722).

By 1689, Aurangzeb had annexed the ruins of Golkonda and Bijapur and had destroyed the Maratha state. The Mughal leader was at the peak of his career, and, at least on the map, he had re-created the boundaries of Muhammad ibn Tughluq of the Delhi Sultanate: Aurangzeb claimed to be the master of the region from Kabul in the north to a line just above Calicut in the south. Like Ibn Tughluq, too, he had overreached himself by venturing deep into the Deccan. Although he campaigned constantly in the Deccan after 1681, he could not return to Delhi in triumph. Numerous rebellions began breaking out all over the empire, but they were especially severe in the Maratha areas. Aurangzeb lived in military field camps between 1689 and 1706, when he sought rest in the city of Ahmadnagar. He died there the following year at the age of 88.

Collapse

Upon Aurangzeb's death, a war of succession broke out. Before it was over, two of his sons and three of his grandsons were dead. His eldest son, sixty-four-year-old Bahadur Shah, succeeded to the throne in 1707. He faced unrest all over his empire, and his treasury was depleted. He tried to win over disaffected Hindus by repealing the discriminatory measures enacted by Aurangzeb, but that gesture hardly mattered: His chief rivals were fellow Muslims. After his death in 1712, two more wars of succession took place before 1720.

None of Aurangzeb's successors, once having achieved the throne, could quell the provincial revolts that had begun during Aurangzeb's reign. Provincial and local forces became more and more autonomous until they could act without referring to Delhi. Sikhs in the Punjab broke free from Mughal control in 1708. A Maratha state quickly reemerged, and other states south of Delhi were autonomous soon after 1710. The weakness of the Mughal dynasty was so evident that Nadir Shah of Iran, having deposed the last puppet Safavid ruler, attacked Delhi in 1739. His troops sacked the city and returned to Mashhad with a treasure trove, including the Peacock Throne, the symbol of Mughal authority and might. Delhi had not experienced a trauma on the scale of Nadir Shah's attack since Timur Lang's atrocities two and one-half centuries earlier. Judging from the written accounts from the period, the inhabitants of northern India viewed it as a cataclysm.

Encouraged by the ease and thoroughness of Nadir Shah's victory, the Marathas began expanding their influence from the Western Ghats northward until they controlled the region almost to the valley of the Ganges. From the opposite side of the Punjab, another in a long series of Afghan incursions into India began. This time was different, however: The leader of the military campaigns was not a mere military adventurer, but the first ruler of Afghanistan, Ahmad Shah Durrani. Durrani made major changes in the map of India. For many centuries, the Kabul valley had been under Indian influence, and it was a major outpost of Mughal power. When Durrani united it with Qandahar and Herat, it became part of Afghanistan, and it has remained so to this day. A much more temporary victory in India was Durrani's acquisition of the entire Indus valley in 1749, including the Punjab as far east as Lahore and the length of the river to the Arabian Sea. He attacked Delhi three times, in 1748, 1757, and 1760. After capturing the city in 1757, he forced a treaty from the hapless Mughal ruler. Although Mughal "emperors" remained in Delhi for another century, their writ barely extended beyond the walls of the city.

The fragmentation of the empire occurred with stunning rapidity. Whereas the contemporary Ottoman system survived even while suffering simultaneous blows from a severe economic crisis, internal revolts, and external attacks from international military alliances, the Mughal system collapsed from within, at the very height of its territorial expansion and economic health. It was moribund even before Delhi suffered the attack from Nadir Shah.

The rapid collapse of the empire's power was the outcome of a long-term shift in power from the center to the periphery of the empire. The Mughals had ruled by co-opting the few thousand warlords into a system that offered wealth and the prestige of being affiliated with a dazzling imperial court. The governors and other mansabdars found it to their advantage to cooperate with the court in order to suppress ambitious and powerful zamindars, whose authority was limited to the local level. Zamindars could command surprising power due to the large numbers of armed peasants in many areas, but they were no match for concerted imperial power.

By the end of the seventeenth century, two developments converged to doom this system. One, ironically, was economic success. The Mughals had developed a well-integrated domestic economy at the very time that world demand was growing for South Asian products. Peasants, money lenders, financiers, artisans, merchants, and zamindars all benefited. Vast amounts of wealth accumulated at the local level, and new alliances formed among social groups to try to expand and protect that wealth. The zamindars were at the center of such alliances, and they became wealthier, better organized, and more experienced than before. Their armed forces became formidable challenges to mansabdars.

The growing wealth and power of the zamindars coincided with the second development, which was Aurangzeb's opening of the Pandora's box of the Deccan. The Deccan wars caused a great financial drain on the mansabdars who had to supply the troops for over two decades of continual warfare. When they tried to extort more tribute from zamindars, the latter had become able to resist effectively. The central government, which normally would have sided with the mansabdars, was too distracted by the Deccan campaigns to respond. Without assistance from Delhi, governors began to formulate their own policies for dealing with local challenges. Inevitably, such chances entailed a smaller amount of revenue being sent to the imperial capital. When Delhi objected, governors and zamindars found common cause. One by one, the provinces became autonomous, until the Mughal emperor had no empire.

Despite the collapse of Mughal power, the imperial legacy lived on. The aura of power and legitimacy possessed by the Mughals was one that all of their successors wished to share. Few of the new states had a natural legitimacy of their own that allowed them to rule over their own people unchallenged, much less to exert hegemony over the other new states. Provincial rulers found that it was in their interest to continue the fiction of Mughal authority, despite the lack of actual power at Delhi. Even Sikhs and Marathas sought the Mughal imprimatur. Thus, throughout the eighteenth century, many South Asian provincial rulers went through the motions of obtaining an honorary "office" in the ceremonial court at Delhi in order to share in the aura of the "emperor." They offered only token financial tribute to Delhi, and their deference was only perfunctory. Most of their own subjects, of course, never realized that their rulers were engaged in a shadow play.

By the middle of the eighteenth century, South Asia had fragmented into a number of autonomous and ambitious states. Among the most powerful were Durrani's Afghan empire, the Maratha confederacy, Bengal, Hyderabad (the new name for Golkonda), and Mysore. The Mughal court retained enormous prestige, but it exercised power only in the vicinity of Delhi. The new states were highly competitive, and the century witnessed a correspondingly high level of violence as a result.

A noteworthy feature of the political relationships in South Asia during the eighteenth century was their nonsectarian nature. Today it is easy to assume that Hindu states that broke free from Mughal control would have engaged in religious wars with Delhi and other Muslim states. There were, indeed, Muslim and Hindu religious leaders who urged their rulers to act in the name of their religion against people of other faiths. In fact, however, little violence took place that can be identified as having religious roots. Maratha rulers abandoned the ideal of a Hindu empire and were satisfied to rule the country in the name of the emperor, fully content to act and behave like other Mughal nobles. Nizam al-Mulk, the Muslim ruler of Hyderabad, did not intervene when Marathas encroached on Delhi's territory, and the Mughal emperor encouraged Maratha expansion in the Deccan that came at the expense of Nizam.

Despite the numerous wars of the eighteenth century, the cultural life of South Asia entered a vibrant period compared with the reign of Aurangzeb. The new states competed culturally as well as militarily, as they strove to develop sophisticated capital cities. Numerous South Asian rulers—rather than a single emperor—offered patronage to intellectuals, poets, and artists. By the middle of the eighteenth century, religious leaders were becoming active in reform movements, poets were producing a huge body of literature in the new Urdu language, painters were experimenting with new themes, and architects were designing new palaces and mosques for the glory of South Asia's new rulers. The ominous feature of the fragmentation of political and military power that had made the cultural efflorescence possible was that South Asia had become vulnerable to the ambitions of outside powers. The greatest threat came from an unlikely source: a joint-stock European company.

Conclusion

Timur's destruction of Delhi in 1398 did not diminish the Muslim presence in South Asia. For more than three centuries after Timur's orgy of looting and murder, Muslim-ruled states became the norm in the region. From the western Punjab to eastern Bengal and from Kashmir to the Deccan, most of the population were subjects of Muslim sovereigns. During this period, large numbers of Muslim immigrants poured into South Asia. Many of them came from Iran and Central Asia. They brought with them the Persian language and Irano-Timurid administrative practices and artistic styles. Long after the Mughal Empire had lost its effective power, the Timurid legacy was still evident in the arts, architecture, and languages of the region. The empire's grandeur and its vision that the subcontinent's disparate regions should be united under one rule sparked the imagination of many of South Asia's inhabitants.

Islam spread widely throughout South Asia during the three and one-half centuries under examination in this section. Enormous numbers of people came into contact with pirs at their khanaqas or dargahs and with qadis at their courts of law. They adopted features of the Islamic tradition that met their immediate needs and they integrated their new practices into their preexisting worldview. As a result, it was common in South Asia to witness "Hindus" attending Muslim shrines and festivals, and "Muslims" attending Hindu shrines and festivals.

The varieties of Islamic expression were more diverse in South Asia than in Iran or the Ottoman Empire. The Mughals, unlike the Safavids and Ottomans, did not attempt to impose state control of Islam and did not develop the elaborate bureaucracies that regulated religious life in the other two empires. The Deccan, which was only lightly touched by Mughal rule, continued to be predominantly Shi'ite.

Profound social differences also separated the Muslims of South Asia. Even within the Sunni community, the languages and cultural artifacts of the Punjab were strikingly different from those of, say, Bengal. Deep social cleavages separated wealthy Muslims from the poor, and sharifs insisted that non-sharifs pay them homage. One of the great ironies of South Asian history is that the regions where the most dramatic Islamization occurred—East Bengal and the western regions of modern Pakistan—lay on the fringes of Muslim rule in the subcontinent, where government rule was weak. The regions in the Delhi–Agra axis—the heart of Mughal power—were, by contrast, only lightly Islamized.

Mughal power collapsed simultaneously with the Safavid Empire and while the Ottoman Empire was in a century-long diminution of central power. In each case the central government lost the advantage that it had enjoyed over regional elites within its respective empire. The contrast between the decline of central authority in these states and the increased power of central governments in contemporary Europe is striking. Each of the Muslim empires had its own unique set of circumstances, and yet the simultaneous weakening of all three governments raises provocative questions about the possibility of a general crisis affecting the huge area from Delhi to Istanbul. Answers to those questions are inconclusive at this point. All that is certain is that the decline in central government power rendered the areas vulnerable to future outside interference.

NOTES

1. See Richard M. Eaton, "Temple Desecration and Indo-Muslim States," in *Beyond Turk and Hindu: Rethinking Religious Identities in Islamicate South Asia,* eds. David Gilmartin and Bruce B. Lawrence (Gainesville: University Press of Florida, 2000), 246–281.
2. This section on the role of the dargah in the gradual spread of Islam in much of South Asia is based on Richard M. Eaton's study, "Sufi Folk Literature and the Expansion of Indian Islam," in his *Essays on Islam and Indian History* (New York: Oxford University Press, 2001), 189–199.
3. See Gavin R. G. Hambly's article, "Armed Women Retainers in the Zananas of Indo-Muslim Rulers: The Case of Bibi Fatima," in his *Women in the Medieval Islamic World* (New York: St. Martin's Press, 1998), 429–467.
4. Juan R. I. Cole, "Iranian Culture and South Asia, 1500–1900," in Nikki R. Keddie and Rudi Matthee, eds., *Iran and the Surrounding World: Interactions in Culture and Cultural Politics* (Seattle and London: University of Washington Press, 2002), 18.
5. See Yohanan Friedmann, *Shaykh Ahmad Sirhindi: An Outline of His Thought and a Study of His Image in the Eyes of Posterity* (New Delhi: Oxford University Press, 2000).
6. Sikhism is a religion that has been rooted in the Punjab since its founding in the fifteenth century by Nanak (ca. 1469–1538). It shares elements of its faith with both Islam and Hinduism: Sikhism is monotheistic, and the believer's highest aspiration is to be absorbed into God. Salvation is not the achievement of paradise after death, but rather the loss of personal identity in a union with God. This can be achieved only by constant meditation on God; to be distracted by the things of this world only prolongs the round of rebirths that karma inflicts on humanity.

FURTHER READING

South Asia after the Delhi Sultanate

Alam, Muzaffar. *The Languages of Political Islam: India, 1200–1800.* Chicago and London: University of Chicago Press, 2004.

Eaton, Richard M. *A Social History of the Deccan, 1300–1761: Eight Indian Lives.* The New Cambridge History of India. I, 8. Cambridge, U.K., and New York: Cambridge University Press, 2005.

Lal, Kishori Saran. *Twilight of the Sultanate.* New York: Asia Publishing House, 1963.

Michell, George, and Mark Zebrowski. *Architecture and Art of the Deccan Sultanates.* The New Cambridge History of India. I, 7. Cambridge, U.K., and New York: Cambridge University Press, 1999.

Rizvi, Saiyid Athar Abbas. *A Socio-Intellectual History of the Isna 'Ashari Shi'is in India.* Canberra, Australia: Munshiram Manoharlal Publishers Pvt. Ltd., 1986.

Roy, Atul Chandra. *History of Bengal: Turko–Afghan Period.* New Delhi: Kalyani Publishers, 1986.

Islam in South Asia

Asani, Ali S. *Ecstasy and Enlightenment: The Ismaili Devotional Literature of South Asia.* London and New York: I. B. Tauris, 2002.

Bayly, Susan. *Saints, Goddesses and Kings: Muslims and Christians in South Indian Society 1700–1900.* Cambridge, U.K., and New York: Cambridge University Press, 1989.

Blank, Jonah. *Mullahs on the Mainframe: Islam and Modernity among the Daudi Bohras.* Chicago and London: University of Chicago Press, 2001.

Daftary, Farhad. *The Ismā'īlīs: Their History and Doctrines.* Cambridge, U.K., and New York: Cambridge University Press, 1990.

Eaton, Richard M. *Essays on Islam and Indian History.* New Delhi and Oxford, U.K.: Oxford University Press, 2001.

Eaton, Richard M. *The Rise of Islam and the Bengal Frontier, 1204–1760.* Berkeley, Los Angeles, London: University of California Press, 1993.

Eaton, Richard M. *The Sufis of Bijapur, 1300–1700: Social Roles of Sufis in Medieval India.* Princeton, New Jersey: Princeton University Press, 1978.

The South Asian Timurids: The Mughals

Alam, Muzaffar. *The Crisis of Empire in Mughal North India: Awadh and the Punjab, 1707–48.* Delhi and New York: Oxford University Press, 1986.

Bayly, C. A. *Indian Society and the Making of the British Empire.* Cambridge, U.K., and New York: Cambridge University Press, 1988.

Dale, Stephen F. *The Garden of the Eight Paradises: Babur and the Culture of Empire in Central Asia, Afghanistan and India.* Leiden, Netherlands, and Boston: Brill Academic Publishers, 2004.

Dale, Stephen Frederic. *Indian Merchants and Eurasian Trade, 1600–1750.* Cambridge Studies in Islamic Civilization. Cambridge, U.K.: Cambridge University Press, 1994.

Gommans, Jos, J. L. *The Rise of the Indo-Afghan Empire c. 1710–1780.* Leiden, Netherlands, and New York: E. J. Brill, 1995.

Gommans, Jos, J. L., and Dirk H. A. Kolff, eds. *Warfare and Weaponry in South Asia, 1000–1800.* New Delhi and New York: Oxford University Press, 2001.

Hintze, Andrea. *The Mughal Empire and its Decline.* Aldershot, U.K., and Brookfield, Vermont: Ashgate, 1997.

Richards, John F. *The Mughal Empire.* Cambridge, U.K.: Cambridge University Press, 1993.

Streusand, Douglas E. *The Formation of the Mughal Empire.* Delhi and New York: Oxford University Press, 1989.

motives for assuming a Muslim identity. Nevertheless, it is reasonable to agree with scholars who suggest that at least some non-Muslims in port cities around the Indian Ocean concluded that visiting Muslim merchants had two advantages over them. One was the universality of their religion. Adherents of traditional religions typically worshiped spirits that were known locally but were not recognized in other regions. Once away from their homes, such people were beyond the range of familiar spirits and at the mercy of spirits that could be manipulated by their enemies. Islam offered universally recognized values and a deity who was always available. Regardless of where a Muslim went, he would remain in a predictable, moral world in which God would protect him from evil spirits. The other advantage that Muslim merchants possessed was that their trading partners thousands of miles away shared the same Islamic legal and moral system that they followed. Contracts and bills of credit were worth much more when moral and legal systems existed to reinforce mutual trust and respect. The universal qualities of Islam may well have played a major theme in the spread of the religion in commercial cities.

By the fifteenth century, the Indian Ocean was ringed with settlements whose economies were dominated by Muslims. These towns were linked by ties of economic interdependence, possessed sophisticated commercial and maritime techniques, and accepted Islamic religious and legal precepts. On the other hand, they were small and commanded practically no navy. Prior to the sixteenth century, they had no reason to develop a maritime military power because the commercial routes were threatened only by the occasional pirate. Maintenance of the economic network worked to the advantage of everyone in the region.

The East Coast of Africa

Islam came into the Horn of Africa (Ethiopia, Eritrea, Djibouti, and Somalia) and East Africa (Kenya, Uganda, and Tanzania) by way of the sea (see Map 7.1). The region's commercial economy was oriented to the Indian Ocean and maintained contacts with the Persian Gulf as well as with the interior of its own continent. As in West Africa, traders—rather than soldiers—introduced Islam into the area. No major Muslim state emerged in this area during the period we are studying. Like the Greek city-states two millennia earlier, the Muslim city-states prospered for a time, but they proved to be highly vulnerable when a major foreign state sent its military forces into the area.

Berbera and the Land of the Zanj

Arab geographers referred to the coastline north of Mogadishu as Berbera, and they called the region south of that city the Land of the Zanj (*zanj* means "black"). Eastern Africa exhibits a variety of land forms and climate. The entire Horn of Africa and the coastline of southern Tanzania are largely arid, whereas the coastline that Kenya and northern Tanzania share is green and fertile. The coastal plain of Kenya and Tanzania is quite narrow and rises to the west in a series of plateaus. Where the rainfall is adequate, the coasts and the highlands support woodlands, but the rain forests of West and Central Africa do not extend

MAP 7.1 Western Indian Ocean and East Africa.

into East Africa. East Africa was not blessed with a wealth of natural resources. Its main products were ebony and mangrove timber, coconut oil, tortoise shell (used to make combs), ambergris that had washed up on shore, and, particularly, ivory. Trade in slaves was a minor segment of the economy south of Ethiopia until the eighteenth century.

Romans describe well-established commercial links between eastern Africa and southern Arabia during the early Christian era, but no known documents record anything about the region south of Ethiopia during the first few centuries of the Islamic period. Only archaeological excavations testify that Muslim communities began to appear along the Ethiopian coast of the Red Sea in the eighth and ninth centuries and that a mosque was built as far south as the Lamu archipelago by the ninth century. Historians assume that the trade between Africa and southern Arabia continued during this period. Merchants from Muslim lands who wished to trade with the residents of eastern Africa could send vessels on winter's northerly monsoon as far south as Kilwa, and the southeasterly monsoon could bring them back in summer.

Mogadishu was founded in the tenth century. By the twelfth century, many nomads in the Horn of Africa had become Muslim. Islam spread widely among the nomadic tribes of the interior of the Horn. The highly mobile nature of the pastoral societies there facilitated the faith's dispersal, and the trade routes that ran from the Horn to the interior of the continent attracted Muslim merchants. By the thirteenth century, Islam was the majority religion on the Harar plateau, and the city of Harar had become a regional center of Islamic scholarship.

Archaeological evidence suggests that groups of Bantu-speaking people began settling the coastal regions from Mogadishu south to Kilwa during the first or second century C.E. and became the dominant ethnic group by the early Islamic era. Over the next several centuries, these immigrants developed a distinctive culture and language that came to be called Swahili (from the Arabic word *sahel,* meaning "coast"). They spoke a patois that was based on Bantu grammatical structure but borrowed heavily from the vocabulary of indigenous languages and from traders who visited from lands across the sea. They also became predominantly Muslim.

After the tenth century, Arab travelers describe a thriving trade in the region, and they report a growing number of prominent Muslims in the towns. A large number of them were the descendants of earlier generations of Arab merchants who settled in the region and sought mates (both wives and concubines) among the local, largely Bantu, population. Their offspring possessed the high status of the Muslim merchant class as well as the kin network of local families.

By the thirteenth century, the Muslim element of the population was the dominant social group along the coast. It included the most powerful rulers as well as many of the prominent merchants, large landowners, and craftsmen. A striking feature of Muslim life along the East African coast was that it was confined to the narrow coastal plain. South of Somalia, every mosque and Muslim tomb that remains from the period prior to the nineteenth century is located within a few minutes' walk from the shoreline.

During the twelfth or thirteenth century, the city–states of Mogadishu and Kilwa emerged as the most powerful political units in eastern Africa. Both were ruled by Muslims. Kilwa thrived due to its control of the gold trade that had its origins on the upper Zambezi River. In the fourteenth century, Ibn Battuta visited both Mogadishu and Kilwa. Kilwa was the more prosperous of the two cities, but Mogadishu had a Shari'a court. The court, like those in Egypt and the Sunni regions of Yemen, administered law according to the rules of the Shafi'i school. The law court was, in fact, worth noting, for by all accounts, the other Muslim cities along the coast had no ulama in them. Until the mid-sixteenth century, when Lamu became a center for religious studies, students as far south as Kilwa who wanted to study the Qur'an, Hadith, or the Shari'a had to travel to Mogadishu, Yemen, or Egypt to find qualified instructors.

By the end of the fifteenth century, some thirty Muslim cities dotted the East African coast from Mogadishu to Kilwa. Most were only nominally Muslim, for their inhabitants had little or no access to religious instruction. On the whole, they were geared more toward commerce than war, although quarrels did break out. To the north, in the Horn of Africa, a much different history was being played out. There, Muslim settlements were established well inland in both Somalia and Ethiopia. In the early fourteenth century, the Christian Ethiopian kingdom and Muslim rulers were encroaching on territories that the other claimed, and almost constant fighting occurred in the region until the late sixteenth century.

The Impact of Imperialism

European merchants paid premium prices for the products of the Indian Ocean basin when they bought them in the Mamluke ports of Egypt and Syria. A new era opened in 1498, when Vasco da Gama rounded the Cape of Good Hope and entered the harbor of Calicut on India's Malabar Coast. Six years after Columbus mistakenly thought he had arrived in the Indies by sailing west, da Gama finally achieved the Iberian dream of reaching India by sailing east. The event marked the beginning of an era of great opportunity for Europeans—first the Portuguese, and later the English and Dutch—who eagerly sought the spices and other commodities of the East.

The Indian Ocean was the theater in which European imperialism—as opposed to colonialism—conducted its dress rehearsal for the more famous nineteenth-century version. In the Indian Ocean of the sixteenth and seventeenth centuries, we see the attempts of novices. The Portuguese government could never dissociate its economic goals from that of a religious crusade, and the Dutch and English governments tried to obtain economic gains on the cheap by leaving the dirty work in the hands of chartered private companies. Both approaches had their distinct limitations, which gradually became apparent back home. By the late nineteenth century, European governments regarded imperialism to be a matter of national security strategy. It was an exclusively secular affair of the state, too important to be delegated to a particular business group.

Da Gama visited many ports along the East African coast in April 1498. He was surprised and angered to find Muslims in so many commercial cities and to discover that Muslims were the leading merchants in the region. Despite the ethnic differences between these Muslims and the Muslims he had encountered in the Maghrib, he called them *Moros,* or Moors. At Malindi, da Gama hired a Muslim pilot who knew the way to Calicut. Da Gama's voyage to Calicut accomplished little other than offending the port's Hindu ruler.

A second Portuguese fleet, under the leadership of Pedro Cabral, made an even worse impression in Calicut. Its visit provoked a violent uprising in the city, with the result that da Gama returned in 1502 with twenty ships to exact revenge on the city. En route to India, he secured control of the sea lanes along the eastern coast of Africa. Since the region was dotted by small city-states, he found them easy to subjugate. He forced all the cities between the mouth of the Zambezi River and Kilwa to pay tribute. Throughout the rest of his voyage he employed indiscriminate violence against local shipping interests, particularly when Muslims appeared to be involved. This voyage began a period of more than a century of staggering violence that the Portuguese directed against Muslims of the Indian Ocean. In the course of the campaign, the Portuguese regularly bombarded cities without cause and massacred hapless fishermen. They captured every ship they suspected of being owned or manned by Muslims. After plundering the ship, they either decapitated and mutilated the crew and passengers or burned the ships along with the passengers and crew.

The Portuguese practiced unrestrained violence because they were continuing the crusade against Islam that they had begun in the Maghrib. Since they had not found Prester John in North Africa, they hoped to discover him in the Indian Ocean. With his help and the wealth derived from control of the spice trade, they would be able to extirpate Islam root and branch. In the meantime, they occasionally looted coastal towns and periodically bombarded them in order to force them to pay tribute. All ships not flying the Portuguese flag were liable to be destroyed. Trade along the East African coast diminished, and the wealth of the coastal cities declined precipitously. The one exception was Malindi, which allied itself with the Portuguese in order to compete with its more powerful rival, Mombasa. It served as an independent supply and repair port for the Portuguese fleet.

In 1517, the Portuguese attacked and burned cities along the Somali coast of the Gulf of Aden. In the same year, the Ottomans defeated the Mamlukes and annexed their empire. From that point on, the Ottomans and Portuguese tried to contain each other without having to engage in a costly conflict. A major arena of conflict for them was the coast of Ethiopia. During the 1530s, Muslim sultanates in Somalia and in the southern and eastern regions of what is now Ethiopia (especially at Harar) began capturing Ethiopian territory. Portugal's entry into the region had made it a potential ally of Christian Ethiopia, and in 1543, the two powers formed an alliance that defeated a coalition of local Muslims and the Ottomans. Ethiopia thereupon recovered most of the territory it had lost. The Ottomans continued to patrol the area, with the result that Muslim influence increased along the coast of the Red Sea and Gulf of Aden, although it declined in the interior of Ethiopia.

During the first fifteen years of the sixteenth century, the Portuguese engaged in a frenetic campaign to establish military bases on the eastern and northern rims of the Indian Ocean basin in order to control the trade of the region. For many decades, they did not do so in East Africa, where they were satisfied to maintain access to the port at Malindi. The economy of the African coast did not interest them, and they did not want to sustain the expenses that maintaining a garrison in a port city would entail. By the 1580s, however, their violent policy toward local shipping had provoked a reaction in kind from local residents. The Portuguese began to suffer an increasing number of attacks on their own ships, which they condemned as piracy. The combination of local attacks and the growing threat from the Ottomans forced them to consider the establishment of a military presence along the coast. They attacked and captured Mombasa, at that time the largest of the cities along the coast. In 1593 they consolidated their presence in the city by completing the construction of Fort Jesus, the most imposing citadel in all of Africa.

Portugal's dominance of Indian Ocean trade was gradually reduced by the Dutch and the English, but it was Oman that delivered the coup de grâce. Throughout the second half of the seventeenth century, the Omanis developed a fleet that was able to compete with the finest of the Portuguese ships. Using it with skillful effect, they gradually pushed the Portuguese out of Oman and much of eastern Africa. At the invitation of the inhabitants of Mombasa, Oman laid siege to the city during 1696–1698 and finally captured Fort Jesus. When the fort fell, Portugal lost all the territory that it had possessed north of Cape Delgado. The Omanis quickly revealed that they were liberating Mombasa from Portuguese control only for the purpose of incorporating it into their own nascent imperial project. Despite suffering a catastrophic civil war during the first half of the eighteenth century, the Omanis continued to expand their influence along the East African coast. In particular, they secured control of Pemba and Zanzibar, which became the jewels of their nineteenth-century mini-empire.

Kerala

The southwestern coast of India has been known by a variety of names. In modern history, the region from around Mumbai (Bombay) south to Goa has been known as the Konkan Coast and the region south of Goa to the tip of the peninsula has been called Malabar. During the period that we are examining, the term *Malabar* was often used to refer to the entire coast up to the head of the Gulf of Khambat (Cambay). The term *Kerala* was used to denote the section of Malabar that lay south of Goa (modern Malabar). Even more confusing is the fact that after India became independent of British colonial rule, the new government created a state named Kerala that encompasses only the southern half of historic Kerala. In this chapter, we will use the older meaning of the terms: *Malabar* will denote the entire southwestern coast, whereas *Kerala* will denote the region of the coast lying south of Goa.

The Land of Pepper

The northern section of the Malabar Coast is semiarid, but Kerala is well watered by the monsoons. As a result of abundant rainfall, Kerala is covered with evergreen forests and boasts numerous rivers. Rice is the staple of the diet. The narrow coastal plain is bounded by the Western Ghats, a steep escarpment that extends parallel to the Arabian Sea for over seven hundred miles, making communication with the interior of the subcontinent difficult. Because of this natural barrier, Kerala's contacts with the political and cultural developments of the interior were limited. By contrast, communication with Southeast Asia, Arabia, and East Africa was relatively easy. Even the Roman Empire had trading contacts with Kerala. The region became famous in Christian lore as the legendary destination of St. Thomas, one of the Twelve Apostles, who was said to have been martyred there.

Kerala became heavily involved in the Indian Ocean trade. Its forests provided hard wood, which was valued for lumber, and aromatic woods, which masked disagreeable odors and served a number of symbolic functions in religious rituals. Ginger, cardamom, and cinnamon also grew there, but Kerala was particularly renowned for its black pepper. As a result, it was known for centuries as "the land of pepper." In addition to supplying its own high-demand commodities, Kerala lay at the midpoint of the voyage between the Strait of Melaka and East Africa. It was a natural point for goods to be delivered from all around the Indian Ocean basin and then redistributed to specific markets. Cochin, Calicut (Kozhikode), Cannanore, and Goa became flourishing ports in Kerala that competed for trade with Cambay, located on the northern end of the Malabar Coast.

Jews, Nestorian Christians, and Arabs established settlements in Kerala in pre-Islamic times, but the region's history during the early Islamic period is as obscure as that of eastern Africa. The coast's Arab population may have become rapidly Islamized after the spread of Islam out of Arabia, but the first actual evidence of a Muslim presence there comes from the ninth century. As a consequence of Kerala's close contacts with the Arabic-speaking lands, its Muslim communities maintained a culture that was noticeably distinct from that of the Muslim Turkish–Persian sultanates of Lahore, Delhi, and the Deccan. Preserving Arabic as their primary language, they also preferred the Shafi'i school of law, in contrast to the Hanafi school used by the Turks.

In the fourteenth century, Ibn Battuta reported meeting Muslims in every port he visited along the Malabar Coast. They included Arabs from all around the Arabian Peninsula and from Baghdad, as well as Iranians from Qazvin. The largest settlement of foreign merchants, especially Arab Muslims, was at Calicut. Calicut became an important port through the sheer force of will of its Hindu ruler, whose title was *zamorin*. The city had no natural harbor, forcing sailors to cast anchor three miles offshore and unload their cargoes onto small boats. Despite the inconvenience—a dramatic contrast with the fine natural port at Goa—Ibn Battuta discovered that Calicut attracted a large number of merchants from all around the Indian Ocean and even from China.

Politically, most of Kerala was divided among a number of independent Hindu rulers. The wealth that poured through Calicut established the Zamorin as the most powerful of them. Goa's superb harbor made it irresistible to the landlocked kingdoms in the Deccan. From 1347 to 1489, the Muslim-ruled Bahmani kingdom and its great rival, Hindu-ruled Vijayanagar, contested for control of it. In 1489, Bijapur seceded from the Bahmani kingdom and took Goa with it.

Although Kerala and the part of the Deccan that lay south of the Bahmani kingdom were ruled by Hindus, many communities of foreign Muslim traders were scattered throughout the Hindu states. They exercised considerable political influence on their rulers due to their commercial contacts and diplomatic skills. By the end of the fifteenth century, tens of thousands of local inhabitants had adopted Muslim identities. They are known to history as Mappilas (Moplahs), a name that derives from an early term of respect in the region. Their society was to be transformed forever by the Portuguese invasion.

The Impact of Imperialism

Vasco da Gama's arrival at Calicut in 1498 was the culmination of over sixty years of Portuguese efforts to establish a route to India by sailing around the southern tip of Africa. After all those decades of exploration, the Portuguese were strangely unprepared when they finally arrived in India. As had happened when they explored the East African coast, they were surprised and outraged to find "Moors" dominating the commerce in general and the spice trade in particular. Da Gama's visit to Calicut was a harbinger of the future relations between the Portuguese and Indian Ocean settlements. Da Gama offended the Zamorin by presenting him with cheap trinkets instead of the luxury goods to which the ruler was accustomed. He also antagonized the local community by kidnapping several residents to take back as trophies to his king. Perhaps most surprisingly, this veteran seaman who was proud of his ability to take the measure of men came away from Calicut with the assumption that the Zamorin, a Hindu, was a Christian.

Subsequent Portuguese expeditions into the Indian Ocean had two primary purposes. One was to secure control of critical choke points around the Indian Ocean basin that would enable Portugal to control the spice trade (see Map 7.2). The other was to obliterate the Muslims both as a religious community and as commercial competition. Despite rivalries among Portuguese commanders and the hostility of most of the cities they entered, the overwhelming superiority of their vessels and firepower enabled them to seize all the cities that they targeted except Aden. On the Malabar Coast, Afonso de Albuquerque captured Cochin and Goa. Bijapur retook Goa from the Portuguese, but Albuquerque launched another attack in 1510 and captured it again. This time he systematically massacred 6000 Muslim men, women, and children over a period of four days. The Portuguese subsequently established forts at Cannanore and Calicut, although the one at Calicut was abandoned after two decades. Goa's harbor was so superior to the others along the coast that it became the headquarters for the Portuguese on the Malabar Coast.

The Portuguese seized Hormuz in 1515, but their failure to capture Aden meant that the goal of controlling all the choke points in the Indian Ocean would not be achieved. Trade between Southeast Asia and Egypt resumed by midcentury, to the satisfaction of the inhabitants of both regions. For the Mappilas, the failure of the Portuguese to obtain all of their goals was of little consolation. Unlike East

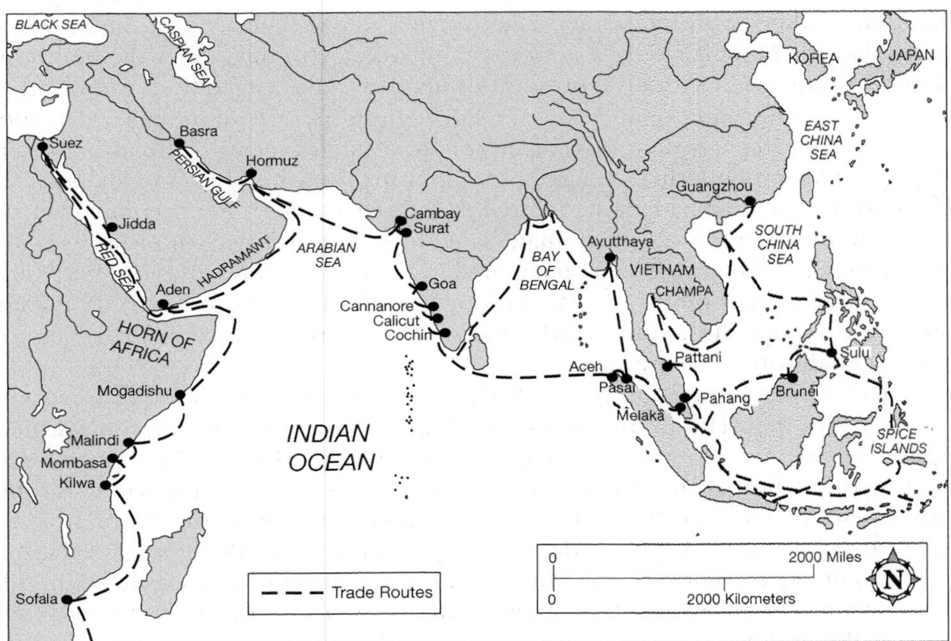

MAP 7.2 Indian Ocean Trade Routes.

Africa, Kerala was dotted with Portuguese forts, and the Europeans closely monitored developments along the coast. Kerala attracted Portuguese attention because of its large population of Muslims and its role as a source of luxury goods. The Portuguese made a concerted effort to gain control of the coastal commerce and to exclude Muslim merchants. They began with a monopoly on pepper and ginger, and then extended their control to all spices and rice. They systematically burned cities and mosques in the area, killed pilgrims performing the hajj to Mecca, and insulted Islam and the Prophet.

As if these pressures were not enough, the global pepper industry experienced a major structural change. By the second half of the sixteenth century, Kerala's role as the source of black pepper for southwestern Asia and Europe was being challenged by Sumatra, where the plant could be grown more cheaply. By the middle of the seventeenth century, the advantages enjoyed by Southeast Asia resulted in a startling turn of events: Consumers in the land of pepper were importing black pepper from Sumatra.

The Portuguese crusade against Islam in the Maghrib ended during the late sixteenth century with the loss at the Battle of the Three Kings. The crusade in Kerala lasted much longer, even though the Portuguese had lost their sovereignty to Spain. Portuguese attacks in Kerala provoked a response in kind from the Muslims, who interpreted their fight against the Portuguese to be an expression of jihad. In the Shari'a, one of the two major functions of jihad is to defend Islam against hostile aggression. The Portuguese had made it clear that they intended to destroy Islam, and thus the Muslim defensive response was obligatory from the standpoint of Islamic law. The treatises on jihad, however, assumed that a Muslim ruler would be in charge to coordinate activities, and they assumed that the emergency situation would be only temporary. They did not prepare believers for the situation in Kerala: The Mappilas were a minority population, typically under the authority of Hindu rulers. Thus, their expression of jihad could not take the form of organized, state-led warfare. In addition, the Portuguese crusade was not a single expedition, but a campaign that was waged for more than a century. Jihad in Kerala began as a form of guerilla warfare, and it eventually evolved into suicidal attacks. The tradition of jihad had always exalted the martyr (*shahid*), but becoming a martyr had never been the object of jihad. The object was to survive in order to enjoy victory, glory, and plunder. What happened in Kerala was quite different, for a veritable cult of martyrdom arose. Martyrdom became the ideal to which a believer could aspire, and the rewards and benefits of martyrdom became the object of poems and devotional literature.

The desperate reaction by the Mappilas to attempted genocide exacerbated relations with their Hindu neighbors. The Muslim community had become armed and defensive, and many Muslims increasingly interpreted any social slight or economic exploitation at the hands of Hindus to be a threat as serious as that of the Portuguese. In addition, some Hindu rulers cooperated with the Portuguese in order to survive, provoking the Mappilas to greater hostility. By the end of the sixteenth century, the harmonious Muslim–Hindu relations characteristic of the fifteenth century had deteriorated into mutual suspicion and occasional violence.

In the middle of the seventeenth century, the Dutch began evicting the Portuguese from Kerala. By 1663, they had removed them from all their forts south of

Goa. The Hindus and Muslims of the area welcomed this development and initially viewed the Dutch as allies against the Portuguese. The Dutch soon disabused them of their illusions, as they tried to enforce their own monopoly over the spice trade in the area. Muslim resistance in Kerala simply changed its target from the Portuguese to the Dutch. By the middle of the eighteenth century, Muslim society in northern Kerala was widely known throughout the Indian Ocean basin for its militance and religious zeal. Three centuries of struggle for religious and economic survival against the Portuguese and Dutch imperialists and Hindu landowners and merchants had conditioned many Muslims there to be xenophobic and to regard social conflict as having religious implications.

Southeast Asia

Southeast Asia encompasses the modern countries of Myanmar (Burma), Thailand, Laos, Cambodia, Vietnam, Malaysia, Singapore, Brunei, the Philippines, Indonesia, and Papua New Guinea (see Map 7.3). The region lies astride the sea route linking the western Indian Ocean with China. Seafarers making the passage between the Indian Ocean and the South China Sea are forced to employ one of two narrow straits: the Strait of Melaka (Malacca) or the Sunda Strait. Throughout history, it was more convenient for most mariners engaged in long-distance trade across the Indian Ocean to use the Strait of Melaka. The Sunda Strait was used only when piracy or war rendered the more northerly passage too dangerous to enter. Southeast Asia also contains the famed Spice Islands, or Maluku (the Moluccas). For centuries, these islands were the world's preeminent source of nutmeg, cloves, and mace.

Because of Southeast Asia's strategic location and spices, Muslim merchants from Arabia, Iran, and South Asia visited the area and established residence in several locations. From these small bases, Islam then spread to other areas in the region. Although Islam was historically late in coming to Southeast Asia, it became one of the three dominant religions in the area. Today Indonesia is by far the most populous Muslim country in the world.

The Malayo–Polynesian Lands

Southeast Asia has a tropical climate. Before the modern exploitation of its timber, almost the entire region was covered in dense forests. On the mainland, human settlement is concentrated in the broad alluvial plains and fertile deltas of large rivers. These regions support intensive rice agriculture and large numbers of people. Southeast Asia also boasts the largest number of islands in the world. The Philippines has 7000 islands, strung along a north–south axis of 1000 miles. Most are very tiny, but about 500 are a square mile or more in area. Indonesia has 13,667 islands spread across some 3000 miles. The vast majority are too small to be inhabited, but the largest, Sumatra, is 1000 miles long. Most of the islands feature a mountainous interior and a swampy coast. The major exception is Java, whose interior plateau allowed the growth of inland cities. On the other islands, settlements were usually established in the coastal areas that were suitable for rice agriculture.

The Portuguese Sack of Mombasa, 1505

In 1505, Grand-Captain Francisco d'Almeida led a Portuguese fleet of fourteen large men-of-war and six caravels around the Cape of Good Hope. The expedition's objective was to subdue and loot the port cities of the Swahili coast. The fleet rounded the Cape of Good Hope on June 20 and entered the harbor of Kilwa on July 22. The Portuguese easily overwhelmed the city's resistance and plundered its wealth. The fleet then sailed to Mombasa, some sixty leagues (180 nautical miles) to the north. It arrived there on August 13, 1505. The following extract is from an account of the pillaging of Mombasa that is believed to have been written by Hans Mayr, a German sailor in the service of the Portuguese.

Mombasa is a very large town and lies on an island from one and a half to two leagues round. The town is built on rocks on the higher part of the island and has no walls on the side of the sea; but on the land side it is protected by a wall as high as the fortress. The houses are of the same type as those of Kilwa: some of them are three storeyed and all are plastered with lime. The streets are very narrow, so that two people cannot walk abreast in them: all the houses have stone seats in front of them, which made the streets yet narrower.

The Grand-Captain met with the other captains and decided to burn the town that evening and to enter it the following morning. . . . Once the fire was started it raged all night long, and many houses collapsed and a large quantity of goods was destroyed. For from this town trade is carried on with Sofala and with Cambay by sea. There were three ships from Cambay and even these did not escape the fury of the attack. . . .

The Grand-Captain ordered that the town should be sacked and that each man should carry off to his ship whatever he found: so that at the end there would be a division of the spoil, each man to receive a twentieth of what he found. The same rule was made for gold, silver, and pearls. Then everyone started to plunder the town and to search the houses, forcing open the doors with axes and iron bars. . . . A large quantity of rich silk and gold embroidered clothes was seized, and carpets also. . . .

On the morning of the 16th they again plundered the town, but because the men were tired from fighting and from lack of sleep, much wealth was left behind apart from what each man took for himself. They also carried away provisions, rice, honey, butter, maize, countless camels and a large number of cattle, and even two elephants. . . . There were many prisoners, and white women among them and children, and also some merchants from Cambay. . . .

The King of Mombasa wrote the following letter to the King of Malindi: May God's blessing be upon you, Sayyid Ali! This is to inform you that a great lord has passed through the town, burning it and laying it waste. He came to the town in such strength and was of such cruelty, that he spared neither man nor woman, old nor young, nay not even the smallest child. Not even those who fled escaped from his fury. He not only killed and burnt men but even the birds of the heavens were shot down. The stench of the corpses is so great in the town that I dare not go there; nor can I ascertain nor estimate what wealth they have taken from the town. I give you these sad news for your own safety.

Source: G. S. P. Freeman-Grenville, *The East African Coast: Select Documents from the First to the Earlier Nineteenth Century*. Oxford: The Clarendon Press, 1962, pp. 108–111.

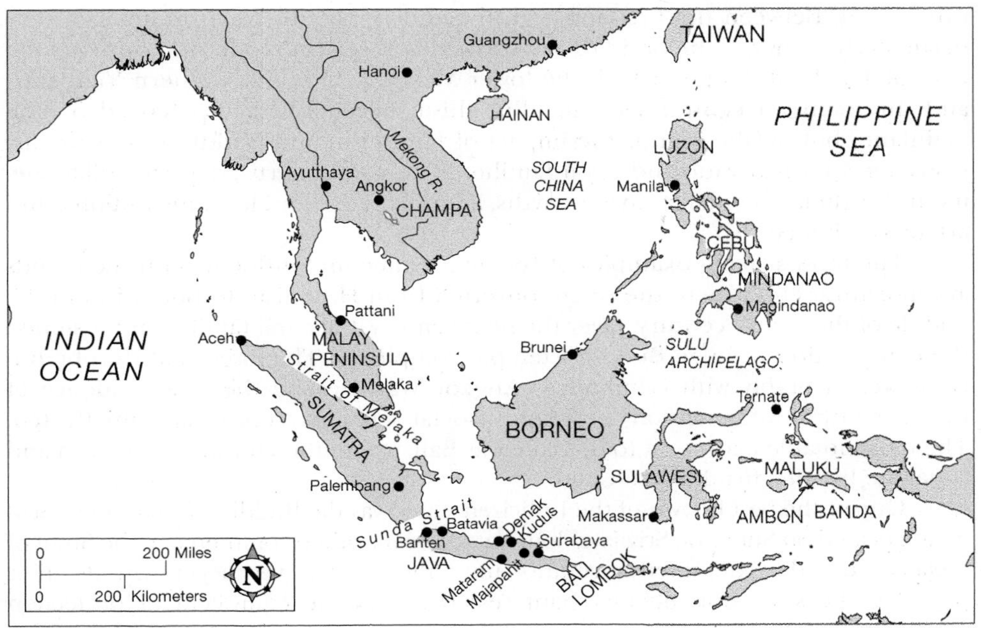

MAP 7.3 Southeast Asia.

One of the most striking differences between the mainland of Southeast Asia, on the one hand, and the Indonesian and Philippine archipelagos, on the other, is that the latter are volcanically active whereas the former is not. Most of the islands were formed from volcanic eruptions, and dozens of their volcanoes are still active. The view of the mountains from the sea can be striking, for some of them rise to altitudes well above 12,000 feet, towering over their low-lying plains or plateaus. Despite the tropical heat of the region, these peaks are snow-capped all year long. The periodic deposit of volcanic ash on the level areas of Java and a few other islands over a period of thousands of years has created some spectacularly productive agricultural areas.

In the areas that developed large Muslim populations—the Malay Peninsula, central and western Indonesia, and the southern Philippines—hundreds of languages are spoken, all deriving from the Malayo–Polynesian family of languages. The Malayo–Polynesian peoples have been great seafarers for thousands of years. Some of them made their way westward across the open sea to settle Madagascar (5000 miles away); others sailed to the east and settled South Pacific islands as far away as Easter Island. Malayo–Polynesian settlements thus extended across a swath of the globe that was 10,000 miles wide.

At least as early as the beginning of the Christian era, commercial interests linked Southeast Asia with South Asia, China, and the Roman Empire. During the Roman period, the most valued products from Southeast Asia were aromatic woods, camphor, and lacquer. Over the next several centuries, the region's spices became widely known and prized. These commercial contacts opened Southeast Asia to foreign cultural influences. Its relations with South Asia proved most decisive in this regard. Between the first and eighth centuries, South Asian influences were particularly strong in the basin of the Irrawaddy River (in modern Myanmar), the Gulf of Thailand, Java and Bali, the lower Mekong River (in southern Vietnam), and the plains of central Vietnam. Buddhism became widely practiced on the mainland, but on the islands the impact of Hinduism and Buddhism was usually restricted to aristocratic and royal families. The royal courts adapted Indian elements for their calendar, coinage, myths, administrative and legal institutions, and art and architecture.

The most striking examples of Indian architectural influences on the islands are in central Java, where the ruler converted from Hinduism to Buddhism in the middle of the eighth century. Over the next century, the royal family commissioned the construction of huge Buddhist temple complexes. The largest, at Borobudur, compares favorably with Cambodia's Angkor Wat. Despite the clear evidence of Indian cultural influence on the islands, social relations were usually unaffected. The most notable exception to this rule was Bali, where the Hindu caste system and ritual life became firmly established.

One of the best known of the Indicized states was the Buddhist kingdom of Srivijaya. Located on Sumatra, Srivijaya dominated the maritime commerce of the Strait of Melaka from the late seventh century until the early eleventh century. Its ships patrolled the strait, forcing merchant vessels to pay the equivalent of protection money. In the eleventh century, the south Indian kingdom of Chola sacked the Srivijayan capital of Palembang. Thereafter, the kingdom never regained its former strength, although its trade with China continued to be important for another century.

As Srivijaya declined, another kingdom in Southeast Asia rose to prominence. Known to history as Majapahit, it was located far to the southeast of Srivijaya in eastern Java. Its wealth was originally based on the rice cultivation of Java's fertile volcanic soil. By the twelfth century, it made the strategic decision to control the spice trade of the region. Southeast Asia's spice harvest had become an increasingly important segment of its exports. Its cloves, nutmeg, and mace—all of which were produced in the cluster of islands known as Maluku—were in particular demand. The clove is the dried flower bud of an evergreen tree that, until the late sixteenth century, was found only on Ternate and four other small islands in northern Maluku. Nutmeg is the seed of yet another evergreen tree that, until the late eighteenth century, grew only on the tiny cluster of islands known as Banda in southern Maluku. Mace is the dried outer covering of the nutmeg fruit. In response to the increasing value of Maluku's products, Majapahit established a monopoly over the external trade of spices. By virtue of its increasing wealth, the kingdom gradually extended its control westward to Sumatra itself, filling the vacuum of power left by Srivijaya. Its golden age was the second half of the fourteenth century, when it sent embassies to China and the major states on the mainland of Southeast Asia. Its elite culture was a syncretistic mixture of Hinduism and Buddhism.

The Lure of the Spice Islands

Although Muslims did not establish a significant presence in Southeast Asia until the fifteenth century, Muslim merchants and sailors from the Red Sea, Persian Gulf, and Indian coasts were frequent visitors to the region long before then. Many passed through Southeast Asia on their way to Guangzhou (Canton) in the eighth and ninth centuries. Many other Muslim merchants lived in Guangzhou, part of a large community of foreign merchants there. They purchased goods that arrived in Guangzhou's markets from inland China and then shipped them to markets in the western Indian Ocean. This arrangement lasted until 879, when a xenophobic reaction resulted in the massacre or expulsion of almost all foreign merchants from the city. Many of the surviving Muslims resettled in Southeast Asia. Some settled in or around Srivijaya, where they continued to engage in international trade. In their new home, they served as middlemen for Chinese and Southeast Asian products. Others gained high posts in the Srivijayan court. Individual Muslims continued to play important roles in the strait after the collapse of Srivijaya due to their commercial contacts and practical skills. Marco Polo, visiting northern Sumatra in 1292, encountered Muslims who served as advisors to the ruler whose court he visited there.

Scattered evidence—usually in the form of tombstones—demonstrates that, as early as the eleventh century, indigenous Muslims lived in the predominantly Hindu kingdom of Champa in what is now southern Vietnam. Others lived in Brunei, the Malay Peninsula, and the Sulu archipelago in the fourteenth century. The most tantalizing discoveries are tombstones from eastern Java that suggest that some members of the elite families in the Hindu–Buddhist state of Majapahit were Muslim when that state was at the pinnacle of its influence in the 1350s. Muslims also began returning to China under the Sung dynasty (960–1279). Many Muslims in eastern and central China intermarried with local Chinese women and adapted to the local culture. They were the genesis of the indigenous Chinese Muslim community that later came to be called the Hui.

In the 1360s and 1370s, thousands of Muslim refugees arrived in Southeast Asia from China in an eerie replication of the ninth-century Muslim flight from Guangzhou. The stimulus for the exodus was the fall of the Mongol Yuan dynasty in 1368 and its replacement by the Ming dynasty. The Muslims of China had developed a good working relationship with the Mongols, who had subjugated China during the thirteenth century. The ethnic Chinese, by contrast, did not bother to conceal their contempt for their conquerors, whom they regarded as barbarians. As a result, the Mongols regarded the Chinese as security threats. When possible, they used ethnic groups other than the Chinese to staff their bureaucratic posts. Marco Polo is the most famous example of these civil servants who combined the possession of mercantile skills with a lack of local family ties. Numerous Muslims, as well, staffed customs posts, served as tax collectors, and filled other positions that kept the empire functioning. When the Ming dynasty overthrew the Mongols in 1368, many Muslims—both foreign and indigenous—were killed or expelled on the grounds that they had been collaborators with the detested Mongols. Many of them resettled in Southeast Asia, on the trade routes that had led their ancestors to China in the first place.

Still, Muslims might have remained a tiny, isolated minority in Southeast Asia had it not been for one of the great developments in world economic history: the spice trade of the period from the fourteenth through the seventeenth centuries. In the aftermath of the demographic shock caused by the plague in the mid-fourteenth century, Europe and China grew rapidly in population. Their demand for imported luxuries grew even more rapidly. Spices, especially peppers, were in particularly high demand. Of all the condiments, pepper was the cheapest and most widely used. Merchants sold ten times more pepper than all the other spices combined, and Kerala could no longer supply the voracious demand for it. As a result, entrepreneurs introduced the pepper tree to Sumatra by the early fifteenth century, and international merchants became more interested in the Malay archipelago than ever.

The bulk of Maluku's spice harvest was exported to China prior to the late fifteenth century. This trade intensified in the early part of the fifteenth century, during a period highlighted by a series of voyages led by Zheng He (Cheng Ho). Between 1405 and 1433, Zheng, a Chinese Muslim eunuch, led six maritime expeditions for the Ming government. The ships and fleets were huge. Some of the ships had a displacement of 1500 tons (da Gama's ships at the end of that century were 300 tons). One of the fleets was an armada of sixty-two ships, with 27,000 people on board. The voyages were extensive: Zheng He's ships visited Hormuz, Aden, and the eastern coast of Africa. In Southeast Asia, Zheng extended offers of protection to port cities in return for "gifts" (tribute) to the Ming emperor. He also destroyed several pirates' nests in the region of the Strait of Melaka.

The precise objectives of the expensive Chinese voyages across the Indian Ocean remain among history's great mysteries. The expeditions were discontinued in 1433, when advisors persuaded the emperor that the voyages' benefits did not justify their costs. In a remarkable change of policy, the Ming dynasty soon entered upon a formal policy of isolationism, forbidding its Chinese subjects (even fishermen and merchants) from embarking upon private ventures. Foreign visitors were prohibited from entering China's ports other than Guangzhou. Despite the edict, foreign trade continued on a large scale due to smuggling and lack of enforcement of the ban by local officials.

The quarter-century period of Zheng He's expeditions witnessed the growth of several port cities in Southeast Asia. This growth seems to be related to close ties that developed between the port cities and China. Brunei, Sulu, Manila, Ayutthaya (in Thailand, which was known as *Siam* until recently), and cities in Cambodia, Champa, and Java began to offer tribute and exchanged envoys with China. Of particular note is Melaka, located on the Malay Peninsula side of the strait that shares its name. Melaka had been a sleepy fishing village until the volume of maritime traffic through the strait increased at the beginning of the fifteenth century. The port offered fair trading practices and reliable docking and warehousing facilities. In 1405, Zheng He blessed it with a declaration of protection. The Chinese admiral made good on his promise, docking there several times and destroying pirates that hindered trade in the strait.

Within a few years, Melaka became a major international port. It was strictly an entrepôt, for it had no goods of its own to export and had to import all of its food supplies. Sometime during the first third of the fifteenth century, the ruler of Melaka adopted Islam and even began missionary work on behalf of his faith. At midcentury, one of his successors began to conquer towns on both sides of the strait in order to gain control of their food products and gold. By the 1470s, the city controlled the main population centers along the strait and had grown into the largest city in Southeast Asia. Its population of 100,000–200,000 was comparable to contemporary

Paris and London. Due to its location on the strait and its efficiency as a port, shippers from numerous countries chose to collect their cargoes there rather than going all the way to Java or Maluku. Melaka had joined Aden, Hormuz, and the cities of the Malabar Coast among the elite group of entrepôts in the Indian Ocean.

The northern coast of Java lay on the route between Melaka and Maluku. As traffic on the route increased, Chinese, Indian, Malay, and Arab Muslims began to settle in Javanese port cities. Little is known about the early history of these communities except that some of them were led by Muslims of foreign origin and others were led by indigenous Muslims. Still other Muslims made their way to Maluku itself, where rulers on several islands had become Muslim by the mid-fifteenth century. Within a few decades, the most powerful of these rulers, at Ternate, was underwriting successful missionary campaigns in the southern Philippines, especially on the island of Mindanao.

Thus, by the beginning of the sixteenth century, Muslims could be found throughout the extent of the archipelago. Muslims ruled Sulu, much of Maluku, and most of the cities along the northern coast of Java and along the Strait of Melaka. These thriving port cities were beginning to challenge the dominance of the older, agrarian-based cities on the interior of the islands. The most dramatic example of the struggle was in Java, where the coastal cities were engaged in periodic warfare with Majapahit.

The Impact of Imperialism

The spice trade was the source of fantastic wealth for some communities and individuals all along the trade routes from the source of production to the final markets. During the sixteenth century, four European nations made a concerted effort to establish some degree of control of the trade at its source. Within thirteen years of Vasco da Gama's entry into the Indian Ocean, the Portuguese secured control of Melaka and were preparing to penetrate the inner islands. Soon the Spanish, Dutch, and English had entered the area as well, using techniques of overwhelming force and monopoly commerce to achieve their ends. By 1650, Europeans had gained control of the important ports and products of the region.

The Portuguese and Spanish

The distribution system that evolved over the centuries to transport goods from one end of the Indian Ocean to the other was a marvel of international cooperation. Merchants at both ends of the ocean could count on staying in business even though their goods were shipped across thousands of miles and through the hands of numerous middlemen, who used a bewildering array of languages, currencies, and systems of weights and measures. No council governed the trade, and no navy patrolled the sea lanes to protect the commerce.

As the Portuguese attempted to bring the spice trade under their control, they found that these features of the commercial network worked to their advantage. Since goods were routed to a few entrepôts, the Portuguese could exploit their military technology to establish permanent bases at these crucial choke points. The most important one for their purposes was Melaka, since it lay beside the strait through which all the spice trade usually passed. The Portuguese made a reconnaissance voyage to Melaka as early as 1509, a year before they secured Goa. They discovered that the city–state was experiencing unrest and was vulnerable to attack. In part, the city's problems were due to corruption and instability within the government itself, and in part to resistance from the cities that it had subjugated along the coasts of the strait. The Portuguese resolved to attack.

As soon as Albuquerque retook Goa from Bijapur in 1510, he converted its harbor into the staging area for an expedition to Melaka. In 1511, Albuquerque set out for Melaka with nineteen ships. His fleet destroyed much of the city in a naval bombardment, and then his soldiers captured what was left. The Portuguese quickly discovered the location of clove and nutmeg production and sailed to Maluku. They seized Ternate from its Muslim ruler and established a base at Ambon. Maluku subsequently became the focus of intense Portuguese efforts to control the spice trade and to spread Catholicism.

Soon after the capture of Melaka, Albuquerque turned his attention to Aden, which he attacked in 1513 but failed to win. He captured Hormuz in 1515. Except for Aden, the Portuguese had obtained their objectives by 1515. They occupied Melaka, Goa, and Hormuz, and soon controlled the entire coast of Kerala. The plan that had looked so good on paper, however, did not work out in practice. The Portuguese quickly learned that Melaka was dependent on outside sources for food and that they would have to trade with, or fight, traditional suppliers to maintain the flow of provisions. Because the city was so far from Portugal and any Portuguese naval base, the city was chronically short of money and manpower.

Portuguese expectations suffered another blow when it became clear that the conquest of Melaka disrupted the organization of the trading system. The biggest miscalculation of the Europeans turned out to be their assumption that Melaka was essential to the spice trade. When spice vendors discovered that the Portuguese demanded spices at lower-than-market prices, they simply developed other trade routes. Those who had traditionally sold to Chinese and Japanese merchants abandoned Melaka and took their products to Brunei and Sulu instead. Those who intended to ship goods to Aden transported their cargoes by caravan across the Malay Peninsula or through the Sunda Strait and up the southwestern coast of Sumatra. Melaka began to wither away.

Portuguese ambitions to destroy the Muslim-dominated trade from the Indian Ocean into the Mediterranean failed. Their naval dominance in the Indian Ocean did allow them to divert a third of the spice trade around the Cape of Good Hope over the next two decades, thus denying the Mamluke regime significant customs revenue, but demand for the products of the Indian Ocean basin (which included dyes and cotton and silk goods as well as spices) grew rapidly. Due to the new routes that avoided Portuguese control, the spice markets of Cairo and Aleppo (under Ottoman control after 1517) were once again bustling as early as the 1530s.

The Portuguese intended the conquest of Melaka to deliver a serious blow to Islam as well as to lead to control of Indian Ocean trade routes. One of the great ironies in history is that, in the immediate aftermath of the fall of Melaka, the Islamization of Southeast Asia accelerated. Muslim merchants and teachers who fled Melaka established bases along the new trade routes that rapidly developed. The dynamism of Brunei and Sulu, combined with the increasing volume of international trade along the southwestern coast of Sumatra, led to the introduction or intensification of Islam in those areas.

In the vicinity of the Strait of Melaka and Sunda Strait, anti-Portuguese sentiment led to the adoption of Islam as an ideological symbol of resistance. The rise of Aceh (Acheh, Atjeh) is the clearest example. The rulers of Aceh appear to have become Muslim in the mid-fourteenth century, but they were minor players in regional politics for two centuries. After the fall of Melaka, they became more important. As the Portuguese began intervening in the affairs of other ports on the strait, rulers in the area supported the sultan of Aceh in his drive to unite the northeast Sumatran coast into a force that could resist the Portuguese. From the 1520s into the mid-seventeenth century, Aceh was a serious military threat to the Portuguese position at Melaka. In addition, merchants in Aceh demonstrated that they could send their cargo ships to the Red Sea directly across the Indian Ocean without having to stop over on the Portuguese-dominated Malabar Coast.

Major changes were also taking place in Java. The Muslim cities on the northern coast of Java were fighting Majapahit even before the Portuguese entered the region. In 1528, they defeated the Hindu city. Some five decades later, a new Muslim kingdom of Mataram arose in its place, with its capital near the present site of Yogyakarta. Mataram's economic base lay in the same rich rice-growing region that had supported Borobudur. Despite the profession of Islam by its rulers, the kingdom continued to patronize the arts and manners of the local Indicized culture.

Western Java had resisted the encroachments of the Muslim cities on the northern coast for years, but that changed in the 1520s. When the Portuguese attempted to establish an alliance with a Hindu kingdom in the Sunda Strait, Sumatran and Javanese rulers cooperated to create the Muslim port city of Banten on Java's west coast. The new city soon extended its authority to the rich pepper-growing districts of southern Sumatra. Whereas Aceh sent its pepper westward, Banten supplied the China market.

Farther east, Brunei and Sulu became busier ports after the fall of Melaka as Chinese and Japanese merchants came to these ports to purchase spices. The ruler of Brunei soon converted to Islam. He acquired a reputation for sponsoring Islamic missionary activity in the Philippine Islands. This missionary activity replaced the efforts that had previously been conducted from Ternate, which by then had fallen to the Portuguese. The accumulation of missionary work in the Philippines paid off with the rise of Muslim political power in the islands. By midcentury, Muslim rulers were ruling in cities as far apart as Magindanao (on the island of Mindanao) and Manila (far to the north on the island of Luzon).

By the middle of the sixteenth century, Portugal's investment in Indian Ocean enterprises had stalled. It was apparent that the Portuguese navy would never be able to achieve a monopoly over the region's trade and that it was more cost-effective simply to maintain a handful of bases to protect the nation's merchant marine. By this time, too, many Portuguese merchants and seamen had become aware of the potential wealth to be achieved in the trans-Atlantic slave trade. They were more interested in the potential profits to be made at the mouth of the Congo and in Brazil than in Southeast Asia. Portuguese influence in Maluku declined after 1550, and the government abandoned Ternate in 1575. Thereafter, Catholic priests who remained in the area could not rely on the support and protection of the Portuguese government. A handful of Portuguese military and civilian personnel remained in Maluku, but Portuguese activity in the Indian Ocean centered on Kerala thereafter.

As Portugal was cutting back its activity in Southeast Asia, Spain entered the region. Ferdinand Magellan was a Portuguese nobleman who had served for a decade in the Portuguese navy's Indian Ocean fleet, but a plot against him cost him the support of the king. Magellan then offered his services to Spain, instead. He proposed a circumnavigation of the globe. Setting sail with five ships in September 1519, he survived a storm-tossed voyage around the tip of South America, periods without wind for his sails in the Pacific, and bouts of scurvy and ravenous hunger, only to be killed in a skirmish with inhabitants of the southern Philippines in April 1521. One of his navigators led the sole surviving ship back to Seville in September 1522.

The Spanish sent three further expeditions to the Philippines, but they all met disaster. The fifth voyage to the islands, commissioned by Philip II, established the first permanent Spanish settlement in the Philippines in 1565, on the island of Cebu. Due to the settlement's success, the archipelago was christened the Philippines in honor of the king. The Spanish were aghast to find a large Muslim presence in the region. Like the Portuguese, they called the Muslims *Moros,* or Moors. The use of the term has continued to the present, although it obscures more than it clarifies. Muslims of the region are separated by three major and ten minor ethnolinguistic groups and are scattered across hundreds of islands. They have been ruled by local chiefs who have jealously guarded their powers against each other.

The establishment of Spanish control over the Philippines took place during the height of the fierce clash between the Ottomans and Spanish for control of the Maghrib. As a result, Madrid's policy in the archipelago was driven by an obsession to convert the peoples of the region to Catholicism and to extirpate Islam. In 1571, an expedition destroyed the Muslim sultanate at Manila and replaced it with a Spanish settlement. In 1578, another expedition burned the mosque in Brunei. By the end of the century, the coastal areas of the northern and central Philippines were largely under Spanish control. The numerous Muslim societies of Sulu and Mindanao, on the other hand, succeeded in thwarting Spanish efforts to subdue them until the late nineteenth century.

The Dutch and English

In 1587, the Dutch gained their de facto independence from Spain after four decades of brutal fighting. More war would be required in the seventeenth century to secure a peace treaty and full independence, but the Dutch wasted no time in establishing a global trade network. Their merchant marine was already the primary supplier of sea transport in the North Atlantic. Over the course of the next century, Dutch mariners dominated the globe, just as the Portuguese had in the sixteenth. Every bit as courageous and brutal as the Portuguese, they possessed better guns and ships, and their organization and financial backing were superior to those of the Portuguese.

After the Spanish annexation of Portugal in 1580, the Iberians jointly dominated Southeast Asia. The Dutch, however, were confident that their seafaring skills would enable them to displace their former masters in the islands. The first Dutch expedition to Southeast Asia set sail in 1595 and made port at Banten the following year. The commercial success of that voyage triggered intense competition among Dutch merchants, and many companies sent ships to the Indies. Spice prices quickly plummeted. In an effort to reduce the risks of open competition, several Dutch companies merged in 1602 as the United East India Company (Verenigde Oost-Indische Compagnie, or VOC). The government granted it a legal monopoly over the spice trade in return for helping to fight the enemies of the Netherlands. The VOC possessed quasi-sovereign power to conclude treaties, build fortresses, and wage war in the vast area east of the Cape of Good Hope and west of the Strait of Magellan.

The VOC's strategy was different from that of the Portuguese. Rather than attempting to capture the entrepôts of the Indian Ocean trade, it was interested solely in controlling the source of the spice trade. In 1605, the VOC went to the very center of Maluku and captured Ambon from the few Portuguese remaining there. The company normally did not sponsor missionary activity, but its antipathy toward the Portuguese caused it to make an exception in this case. It expelled the Portuguese Catholic priests and began applying pressure to encourage local Catholics to convert to Calvinism. Although Ambon was perfectly located to monitor spice production in Maluku, it was not the ideal location for a company headquarters. In 1619, the company chose Jakarta, which had the best harbor on Java and was well sited for access to the Strait of Melaka. The VOC overthrew the ruling Muslim prince and renamed the city Batavia. Batavia became the VOC headquarters in the east, outfitted with offices, warehouses, and ship repair facilities.

The Dutch attempt to dominate the spice trade was quickly challenged by yet another European power. English merchants arrived at Banten in 1600. For twenty years, they competed with the Dutch for control of the spice trade. They obtained monopolistic treaties with rulers of various islands—sometimes through negotiations and sometimes through force—and attacked ships that were not under their flag. Their activity in the Sunda Strait intercepted the non-European ships that were taking spices to the Red Sea. As a result, by the 1620s, Istanbul was having to import its pepper and other spices from western European merchants. Although the English made a small profit, twenty years of vicious competition with the Dutch finally forced the English to concede their defeat, and they redirected their attention to India. The English East India Company maintained only a token presence in Banten thereafter, conceding Southeast Asia to the VOC.

Achieving the Dutch goal of monopolizing the spice trade in the islands was facilitated by the dispersal of local political and military power among a large number of islands. Since all the local rulers were relatively weak, even the rise of a powerful local ruler did not necessarily jeopardize the Dutch position. For example, in 1605—the same year that the Dutch took over Ambon—the ruler of the port of Makassar, on the southwestern tip of the island of Sulawesi, converted to Islam. Makassar had become prosperous due to its export of rice, rather than spices, and its ruler was ambitious. Using a combination of military campaigns and diplomacy, he and his successors gained the submission of most areas on Sulawesi by 1640. During this period, Makassar's rulers were so defiant of Dutch monopolistic intentions that they allowed Portuguese merchants and mercenaries—men who had previously been personae non gratae in the region—to reside in Sulawesi. Despite Makassar's dynamism, the VOC was able to contain it by making alliances with local states whose rulers were more fearful of Makassar than of the Dutch.

The reaction of Makassar's neighbors was characteristic of local rulers. Despite frequent demands for a combined jihad against the Dutch, individual rulers were unwilling to allow a rival to become the leader of an anti-VOC coalition for fear of his gaining an advantage over them and perhaps even annexing their realms. The Dutch, after all, simply wanted a monopoly over trade; they signed a contract to purchase a ruler's stock of spices and paid him a negotiated price in silver. The drawback was that the ruler was not permitted to negotiate a better deal with a competitor to the Dutch. The rivalries among the islands allowed the VOC to consolidate its power in the islands relatively easily. Even when the Dutch used genocidal measures, neighboring states did not band together to stop them. The first major instance of massive blood-letting was during the period 1620–1623, when the VOC declared a monopoly over the nutmeg and mace trade on Banda. When the islanders resisted, the Dutch utterly exterminated them.

The only two regional powers that could pose a significant challenge to the VOC in the seventeenth century were Mataram and Aceh. The Dutch did not try to subdue Aceh until the late nineteenth century, but Mataram was an early threat because of its proximity to Batavia. During the fifty years after its founding in the 1570s, it expanded to control all of central and eastern Java, as well as the island of Madura on the northern coast. In 1628 and 1629, Mataram attacked Batavia, but it had to withdraw both times without capturing the city. From then on, the two rival powers worked out a modus vivendi. Batavia needed to buy rice and timber from Mataram, and Mataram occasionally sought Batavia's assistance against rebels and local rivals. The price for Mataram of such assistance was the cession of land to the Dutch, which was a factor in the progressive weakening of the Muslim kingdom.

The Appeal of a Universal Faith

The period of commercial intensification and European intervention witnessed a religious transformation in Southeast Asia. Several of the great world religions made major gains during this time. On the mainland, Buddhism and Confucianism achieved their final geographical consolidation. Islam spread rapidly in the Malay Peninsula and Indonesia after the Portuguese captured Melaka. Catholic Christianity made rapid gains in the Philippines and in central Indonesia as a result of intensive missionary work by Spanish and Portuguese priests. Of the great religions in the region, only Hinduism declined, perhaps because its identity was so closely bound up with that of India. Only in Bali and surrounding small islands did local variants of Hinduism continue to flourish.

During the period that Islam spread among the islands of the various archipelagoes, it also made gains on the mainland of Southeast Asia. Small communities of

Prayer niche (*mihrab*) of the Kilwa mosque, built in the twelfth or thirteenth century.

Muslims had existed in several of the mainland ports since at least the ninth century, but they began to grow in the late fifteenth century. During the seventeenth century, the Muslim presence became particularly noticeable in Cambodia, Thailand, and the kingdom of Champa, which was located in what is now southern Vietnam. Just as the population of Champa's Muslims, known as Cham, reached a critical mass, the kingdom of Vietnam, which lay to the north, annexed Champa. The Confucian-dominated court of Vietnam began a major persecution of the Cham, most of whom fled to Cambodia. From there they became dispersed throughout the region.

Factors in the Spread of Islam

Prior to the sixteenth century, most Muslims in Southeast Asia were concentrated in a handful of cities. After 1511, many port cities throughout the region received the thousands of Muslim merchants, teachers, and artisans who fled the Portuguese conquest of Melaka. Their diffusion served to create bases from which Islam could penetrate the hinterland of their new homes. The growth of the Muslim community coincided with intensive Christian missionary activities. From the mid-sixteenth to the mid-seventeenth centuries, both Islam and Christianity became solidly entrenched in the region. Historians estimate that, by 1700, half the population of the islands and of the Malay peninsula adhered to one or the other of the two religions.

Another way that Islam spread was through war. Islam's introduction into the islands was peaceful, but the traditional, chronic warfare among the states in the region made it almost inevitable that religion would become a factor in the conflicts. The most striking example of this phenomenon involved Makassar on Sulawesi. Makassar's ruler, who converted to Islam in 1605, forced his defeated rivals on Sulawesi to declare a formal conversion to Islam. Soon, most of Sulawesi had become nominally Muslim.

A third factor in the spread of Islam was its use as a symbol of resistance to subjugation. The Portuguese and Spanish came into the area with the explicit intention of waging holy war against the region's Muslims. The Portuguese were particularly brutal against Muslims in Melaka, Banten, and Ternate. As Portuguese momentum slowed, the Spanish took their place. During the period 1580–1660, Spanish Catholic missionary work extended south from Luzon to Mindanao, northern Sulawesi, and Maluku in an explicit attempt to defeat Islam in the cause of Christianity. In the regions of the most intense conflict, local inhabitants were under intense pressure to choose between the two faiths. Missionaries preached the need for salvation, merchants favored fellow believers, and armed men made implicit or explicit threats. The Europeans made it clear that the conflict was between two international religious alliances, one of Christians and one of Muslims. In the face of such pressure, many Indonesians felt it advisable to convert to one or the other faith.

Muslim resistance to Christian aggression led to notable instances of pan-Islamic cooperation during the second half of the sixteenth century. From as early as 1538, when the Ottoman Empire tried to capture Diu from the Portuguese, Muslims around the Indian Ocean basin slowly gained an appreciation for the efforts of the Ottoman Empire to thwart the Portuguese attempt to gain a monopoly over the shipping of the region. In 1566, the sultan of Aceh sent a petition to Istanbul, requesting military aid against the Portuguese. Two years later, Sultan Selim II dispatched two ships with a cargo of artillery as well as several dozen gunners and military engineers. The two rulers also opened diplomatic relations with each other.

Interregional Muslim cooperation against Portuguese aggression also involved Muslim states in the Deccan. An alliance of Bijapur, Golkonda, and Ahmadnagar attacked Portuguese Goa in 1570, but failed. Golkonda then formed an anti-Portuguese alliance with Aceh, supplying arms and men for its assaults on Portuguese-held Melaka. The involvement of the Ottomans and Indian Muslims in conflict against the Portuguese stimulated a spirit of pan-Islamic solidarity in the Indian Ocean that generated a spirit of confidence and a sense of momentum for several decades.

Variations on a Theme

Despite the wave of conversions to Islam and the heightened self-consciousness of Muslim identity in the region, visitors to the islands—Muslims and Christians alike—remarked that Muslims in the islands were different from those they had observed in the cities of North Africa and southwestern Asia. That was hardly surprising, since the region was a frontier for Islam, and new converts rarely can make an abrupt change in their patterns of worship and life routines. In the Malay archipelago, the difficulties were even greater than for, say, monotheists of southwestern Asia and North Africa who converted to Islam. In the islands, the bulk of the population was attuned to a mystically inclined polytheism, and the elites in many of the islands were heavily Indicized. It should be remembered, too, that in a few areas, such as on Sulawesi, some communities that were defeated in warfare were forced to convert formally to Islam. Members of these communities would certainly have resisted any radical change in behavior. If visitors judged local Islam by their example, they would, indeed, have been puzzled.

Many new converts did, in fact, make important changes in their lives that enabled them to call themselves Muslim. They began using Islamic forms of salutation, and some modified their wardrobe. The practice of circumcision was already common on many of the islands, and thus its adoption as a Muslim identity marker was not the major cultural shift that it was in many other societies. On some of the islands, in fact, both males and females had traditionally undergone circumcision, a feature that is usually associated with the Nile River valley and the Horn of Africa, where the Shafi'i school of the Shari'a prevails. The Shafi'i school was the only one of the four major legal traditions in which many jurists argued that both male and female circumcision are obligatory. The earliest Muslims to the region were Shafi'is, and they were gratified to discover that, on some of the islands, both men and women were already following a practice converts in many other cultures were reluctant to accept. Thus, a local customary rite was given new prominence and a new Islamic interpretation.

Judging by the anecdotal evidence of recorded observations by visitors to the islands, it may be said that most new Muslims renounced pork, but fewer gave up alcohol. Much more powerful emotions attended the adoption of Islamic funerary rites and dietary practices. The cremation of corpses was a widespread practice in the archipelago prior to the advent of Islam. The Shari'a, however, requires that Muslims be buried in the ground, facing Mecca. For islanders who believed that the funeral pyre's flames had a purifying effect on the corpse, the switch to burial—which entailed the decomposition of the body—was a major concession to their new religion.

The spread of both Islam and Christianity in the archipelago had an impact on the social roles of women. Information about women during the period under review is scarce, but it is clear that, traditionally, women had served the important function of spirit medium and ritual healer. Islam and Christianity not only limited acceptable worship to a single deity who was referred to as male, but religious leadership was also dominated by males. Catholicism's priesthood was an exclusively male preserve, and women could achieve leadership positions only within the cloistered world of the convent. Within Islam the roles were not as rigidly delineated: Males might seek guidance from highly respected female Sufis and Hadith scholars, and women could be Qur'an reciters and spiritual advisers to other women. On the other hand, all public leadership positions at mosques were restricted to males. Ulama who were educated in Islam's heartland expected women to dress more modestly than before and to play a less public role.

The introduction of the two monotheistic religions sparked a backlash among some women. Women led resistance to the introduction of Christianity in the Philippines and against Islam in Lombok and Sulawesi. Despite the resistance, the new gender norms became dominant. Women's clothing became more modest (by the 1650s, some women in Makassar were entirely covered from head to foot, but that was an isolated case in Southeast Asia). Women's opportunities for religious leadership declined as male Catholic priests monopolized Christian leadership positions in the Philippines and as the growing number of ulama in Southeast Asia allowed no women into their ranks.

Opportunities for women in other than religious roles also disappeared. On both the mainland and in the islands, numerous females had ruled in the pre-Islamic and early Islamic periods, either as regents or in their own right. In early seventeenth-century Mataram, women armed with pikes and muskets guarded the

the region's first universal history and first book on comparative religions, and he made useful criticisms of local Sufi interpretations of Ibn al-'Arabi's doctrine of the "Oneness of Being," providing as a corrective the standard interpretations of that doctrine that were prevalent in the Arab world. On the other hand, al-Raniri did not just criticize local Sufis for their version of Ibn al-'Arabi's theory; he persuaded the sultan to kill them as apostates and to burn their books.

The exchange of scholars between Aceh and the Arab world was not merely in a west-to-east direction. Several scholars from Sumatra went to Arabia to study. A few stayed and were numbered among the outstanding teachers in the Holy Cities at whose feet students from all over the world studied. Others returned to Southeast Asia. One of the most famous who returned was 'Abd al-Ra'uf al-Sinkili (ca. 1615–ca. 1693). After studying for nineteen years in Arabia, al-Sinkili returned to Aceh about 1661. Like al-Raniri, he was a prolific scholar and was concerned with correcting what he considered to be errors in doctrine and practice. He was particularly concerned about insisting that the practice of the Sufi path required fulfillment of the obligations of the Shari'a. His main difference from al-Raniri was that his reform efforts were implemented by reason and personal example rather than coercion.

By contrast with Aceh, Java possessed the most developed Indicized court culture of any of the Southeast Asian societies that accepted Islam. Prior to the advent of Islam, Indic culture was most closely identified with the courts of the interior of the island. The Muslim-ruled states of the northern coast that sprang up in the late fifteenth century were on the periphery of that culture and were considered less developed. That status began to change after the coastal cities defeated Majapahit in 1528. Thereafter, they began attracting many of the island's most talented artists and craftsmen, and the rulers of the coastal cities and the new Muslim kingdom of Mataram (in central Java) commissioned works in the Indic tradition. Mosques and shrines incorporated the great wooden pillars that support the traditional Javanese pavilion as well as the brickwork and ornamentation characteristic of the architecture of Majapahit.

Java's differences with Aceh extend to that of ethos. Whereas dramatic performances were repugnant to the Arab-influenced Muslims of Aceh, the *wayang,* or shadow play, continued as popular as before in Muslim Java. Worship of the Goddess of the Southern Ocean continued to be the most important spiritual force in the lives of many Javanese in the central section of the island. Eastern and central Java are also famous for the ongoing strength of *kejawan,* or "Javanism," even today, after five centuries of diffusion of Islam on the island. Kejawan connotes a specific spiritual discipline that stresses the control of passions, a refusal to become beguiled by wealth, and the quest for enlightenment. It stresses living in harmony with nature and with people, and suggests a general lack of concern for the legalistic issues associated with a strict interpretation of the Shari'a. The persistence of kejawan is not due to some innate character trait among the Javanese of the eastern half of the island. It derives in some part, at least, from policies of the rulers of Mataram. Although they were nominally Muslim, they did not brook criticism from ulama. Dutch accounts of the seventeenth century report that the kings of Mataram killed as many as 5000 members of the ulama who insisted on the implementation of the Shari'a.

A page from the *Chronicles of Java,* a late-seventeenth-century account of the history of Mataram. The script is Old Javanese.

A Loss of Dynamism

One of the great ironies of Southeast Asian history is that, whereas a major objective of Portuguese activity in the region had been to eradicate Islam, the actual effect of Portuguese policies was to stimulate the spread of Islam throughout the Malay archipelago. Conversely, although the Dutch VOC followed a secular policy and was unconcerned about religious issues unless they affected profits, its policies were instrumental in dealing a devastating blow to the vitality of Islamic life in the archipelago.

The dispersal of Muslims throughout the islands occurred during the early part of the sixteenth century. The period of the most rapid growth of Islam was from the mid-sixteenth century to the mid-seventeenth century. This was also the period of the greatest demand by the world market for the products of the region. Muslim merchants and rulers became wealthy, and their contacts with the outside Muslim world thousands of miles away were evidence of their dynamism. Many residents of the islands found compelling reasons to adopt a Muslim identity. Motives were different—and mixed—in each case, but the new religion offered a superior spiritual experience to some, an ideological challenge to the Portuguese to others, and a way to participate in the material benefits of a global commercial community to still others.

The economic boom disappeared by the middle of the seventeenth century. Between 1635 and 1641, the Tokugawa shogunate closed off Japan from the world, forcing Japanese merchants resident in Southeast Asia to return home. In the 1640s, Chinese demand for Southeast Asian commodities began to wane due to the growing economic crisis of the period. In the same period, Europeans discovered other products in the Indian Ocean—notably Indian fabrics and indigo—that interested them as much as spices had. In 1640, spices and pepper constituted the vast bulk of European cargoes shipped from the Indian Ocean, but by 1700 they were a small fraction of such cargoes.

In order to cope with the declining demand for Southeast Asian products, the Dutch took decisive action. Having already gained absolute control over the nutmeg and mace trade, the VOC progressively monopolized the trade in cloves between 1640 and 1653. In 1641, the VOC captured Melaka—the last major presence of the Portuguese in the region—and settled Cape Town in 1652 in order to control the shipping lanes around Africa. By 1658, the VOC controlled most of Ceylon (modern Sri Lanka), the source of most of the world's cinnamon. In 1683, the Dutch began planting groves of clove trees on Ambon. When the trees were mature and began producing, the VOC destroyed all the clove trees on Ternate and other northern islands. The islanders, outraged by the destruction of their trees, fought back. The Dutch massacred them in large numbers. Previously independent cities, such as Makassar and Banten, were subjugated by the VOC when they continued to resist signing contracts for monopolies.

The Dutch fixed the prices that the VOC paid to growers at minimum levels. All Asian intermediary traders and ports were eliminated from a share in the profits. By the second half of the seventeenth century, the company was able to sell spices in Europe at about seventeen times the price for which it had bought them in Maluku, with none of the profit passing into Asian hands. In their single-minded fixation on making profits, the Dutch effected several important changes in the patterns of trade in the Indian Ocean. They introduced the cultivation of coffee into Ceylon and took Ceylon's traditional product of cinnamon to plantations in Southeast

Asia. They also introduced the cultivation of coffee, sugar, and tobacco into Southeast Asia. For the previous three centuries, most coffee had been grown in Yemen and Ethiopia, but the Dutch introduced coffee into Java in 1696. The first harvest was delivered in 1718. Dutch techniques to market their "Java" were so successful that Yemen's share of the world's coffee production declined rapidly in the eighteenth century.

The impact of Dutch policy on Muslim-ruled states was profound. As late as 1600, merchants and rulers of most port cities in Southeast Asia interacted as equals with Europeans, but by 1700 the situation had been dramatically transformed. The wealthy merchant class of the region was shrinking rapidly. In many regions, local farmers switched from cash crops to staples due to the low prices that the Dutch were paying for spices. Visitors to the region commented on the impoverishment of formerly wealthy cities such as Banten, where the inhabitants had begun to weave their own coarse cloth because they could no longer afford fine Indian fabrics. The immense cities of Southeast Asia lost population and wealth after the mid-seventeenth century: Melaka, Makassar, and Banten lost three-fourths of their inhabitants. Cities such as Banten and Makassar, which had been among the most cosmopolitan and dynamic cities in the region, stagnated and exhibited little interest in the ideas and technology of the outside world.

Under the new Dutch mercantile system, local rulers could be autonomous only if they were inland, out of the reach of Dutch gunboats. The disadvantage of being inland was that it left local culture at least somewhat closed off from developments in the world at large. The establishment of VOC headquarters at Batavia had the long-term effect of closing off Javanese society from the larger Muslim world. As Mataram gradually lost control of its port cities to the Dutch in the second half of the seventeenth century, its communication with developments in the larger Muslim world became intermittent and indirect. Javanese of the interior remained Muslim, but during the eighteenth century they were only vaguely aware of the major developments taking place in the Muslim world as a whole.

As Southeast Asia's contacts with the outside world declined, its religious dynamism subsided. Because the crusading Portuguese were no longer a threat to local Muslims, Islam no longer served the ideological function of providing a unifying and oppositional identity to a hostile enemy. The decline in wealth of the regional economy provided fewer opportunities for religious scholars from the larger Muslim world to find patronage in the islands. There were no more reformers with the stature of al-Raniri to persuade local communities that the old spirit cults were a threat to the welfare of the Muslim community. Thus, it was easy for many Muslims to assume that abstention from pork and the presence of a mosque made a community Islamic even though—as numerous observers bear witness—mosque attendance throughout the region was sporadic at best. The evidence we have suggests that, at the beginning of the eighteenth century, only Aceh and Banten had Shari'a courts. The presence or absence of Shari'a courts usually serves as a barometer of Islamic practice: In a society without qadis to rule on matters of Islamic law, the provisions regarding criminal law, real estate issues, contracts, marriage, inheritance, and divorce are unenforceable. If many urban Muslims had only a marginal grasp of the basics of their faith, villagers could hardly begin to understand Islam's strict monotheism and its accompanying ethic and rituals. For most of the people, Islam assumed a variety of meanings that enabled them to cope with their world of demons and spirits, nights of impenetrable darkness, and diseases without cures.

The economic stagnation of the seventeenth century eventually led to the disintegration of the largest Muslim state and to a major outbreak of ethnic violence that continues to echo today. Mataram, the major Muslim state in the islands, suffered a major blow when the Dutch established monopolies with the kingdom's vassal port cities on the northern coast of Java. The VOC paid less money than before for the export crops and redirected customs revenue from Mataram to Batavia. The kingdom's revenues plummeted, and even a radical rise in the taxes imposed on the country's peasants could not make up for the shortfall. The central government began to experience paralyzing schisms as members of the royal family competed for their share of the ever-shrinking resources. Formerly lucrative positions in the kingdom could no longer support the lavish standard of living that the princes required, and so rivals fought to achieve the throne, which alone could satisfy their material desires. Princes frequently requested military aid from the VOC on behalf of their cause. Almost constant violence racked the kingdom during the last quarter of the seventeenth century and throughout first half of the eighteenth century.

The internecine violence in Mataram coincided with a crisis for the VOC. Although the earliest Chinese immigrants into Batavia had been wealthy or skilled, by 1740, thousands of unskilled Chinese laborers had migrated into Batavia and western Java in hopes of finding employment. Many remained unemployed, and substantial numbers of them joined criminal gangs in order to survive. The situation became so dangerous that the Dutch enacted immigration quotas and required newcomers to produce permits. The regulations were easily bypassed, and so the VOC announced that illegal immigrants would be deported. Rumors swept the Chinese community that the Europeans were going to arrest them and dump them at sea. Already angry and despairing, thousands created an armed band that attacked Batavia. Inside the city walls, the Europeans panicked. Suspecting that the Chinese who lived in the city would help the attackers, the Europeans massacred them; contemporary Dutch chroniclers estimated that 10,000 Chinese were murdered.

Many of the city's surviving Chinese and remnants of the attacking mob fled to the east, where they joined up with other Chinese in coastal cities and with Javanese peasants from the interior who had lost their land due to high taxes and low prices for their crops. The Chinese and Javanese joined forces and, in a manner that echoes the Jelali Revolts in the Ottoman Empire a century earlier, they began attacking estates, towns, and VOC-held forts. Anyone of any ethnic group who was wealthy became a target. The rebel forces were huge, with armies of more than 20,000 men equipped with artillery besieging the VOC's forts. The king of Mataram was inclined to aid the rebels, because he saw a chance to end the rule of the VOC once and for all. He helped them capture one Dutch fort, but when the rebels attacked his own capital, he reversed course and sought the aid of the VOC. Other members of the royal family continued to side with the rebels, supplying them with resources. The disciplined firepower of the Dutch gradually began to have its effect, and the army of the VOC—staffed largely by Javanese—began turning the tide against the rebels. Property owners of all ethnic groups flocked to the VOC's forts for safety, and support for the rebels waned. The rebellion was largely quelled by late 1743.

During the rebellion, the VOC required economic concessions from the king and the property owners in return for its military help, and so the war actually enabled it to acquire valuable rights to taxes, tolls, and other revenues throughout the eastern half of the island. The concessions that the king of Mataram made to the VOC were unacceptable to some of the nobility of his kingdom, and yet another civil war broke out in 1746 within the kingdom. It raged for nine years before officials of the VOC helped to negotiate the Treaty of Giyanti, which divided the kingdom. One branch of the royal family maintained its royal court at Surakarta, and the other built its palace complex at Yogyakarta, some thirty-five miles away. As had happened so many times before in the islands, the local rulers had played into the hands of the Dutch: The Europeans were pleased to see Mataram split into two small kingdoms that could not challenge the power of the VOC.

Conclusion

Prior to the fifteenth century, the process of the introduction of Islam into the Indian Ocean littoral bore striking similarities to the spread of Islam in West Africa. In both cases, the Muslims who introduced their monotheistic faith to their communities lived in societies dominated by polytheistic and animistic religions. These Muslims were not warriors, but rather merchants and holy men. Unlike the West African case, Muslim merchants in many of the small states of the Indian Ocean basin became political rulers. They usually intermarried with local families, became members of the elite social stratum, and established new cultural syntheses. Islam spread as more and more merchants in the region realized the universal features of the new religion.

The fifteenth and sixteenth centuries witnessed a commercial revolution in the Indian Ocean. The intensification of the spice trade monetized many local economies for the first time, capital accumulated, and cities grew rapidly. The economic growth of the period would have been sufficient to induce major social, political, and cultural changes, but whatever indigenous developments were underway in that regard were quickly preempted by the violent intrusion of the Portuguese and Spaniards. These two European powers were obsessively focused on the dual goals of controlling commerce in the region and destroying Islam. The Portuguese did not expend much effort to extirpate Islam in East Africa, but they made a concerted effort to do so in Kerala and Southeast Asia. Likewise, the Spaniards massacred or evicted all Muslims that they could in the Philippines, Sulu, and Brunei.

The Portuguese crusade in Indonesia had the opposite effect from what was intended. Islam spread rapidly throughout the islands as a result of the flight of Muslim refugees from the Strait of Melaka and Maluku. Moreover, many inhabitants of the region adopted a nominal Muslim identity as they saw their Muslim neighbors justifying their defensive war against the outsiders with the concepts of justice and divinely sanctioned war by God's people against the enemies of God. Outside Indonesia, the Iberian crusaders accomplished some of their objectives. Some historians believe that the brutal Portuguese and Spanish military campaigns were all that prevented Kerala and the Philippines from eventually joining Indonesia in the rank of Muslim majority societies.

As destructive as the sixteenth-century Portuguese and Spanish campaigns had been on the Muslims of the Indian Ocean, they paled in comparison with the effects of developments in the second half of the seventeenth century. The seventeenth-century global commercial crisis, combined with the slowing of demand from Japan, the Ottoman Empire, post-Safavid Iran, and the Mughal court, would have forced some readjustments in the region's economy. Dutch policy preempted any such readjustments. The VOC had no quarrel with Islam. Its monopolistic economic policies, nevertheless, had devastating effects on the economies of the Indian Ocean. It used violent methods to compel compliance with the monopolies, paid artificially low prices to producers, and excluded indigenous merchants from participating in international commerce. As a result, local economies withered, the cosmopolitan cities of the region became provincial and culturally isolated, and the knowledge and practice of Islam remained in a state of arrested development for over a century.

FURTHER READING

A Muslim Lake

Boxer, C. R. *The Portuguese Seaborne Empire 1415–1825.* London: Hutchinson & Company, 1969.

Chaudhuri, K. N. *Asia Before Europe: Economy and Civilisation of the Indian Ocean from the Rise of Islam to 1750.* Cambridge, U.K.: Cambridge University Press, 1990.

Chaudhuri, K. N. *Trade and Civilisation in the Indian Ocean: An Economic History from the Rise of Islam to 1750.* Cambridge, U.K.: Cambridge University Press, 1985.

Das Gupta, Ashin and M. N. Pearson, eds. *India and the Indian Ocean, 1500–1800.* New York and Calcutta: Oxford University Press, 1987.

Kearney, Milo. *The Indian Ocean in World History.* New York: Routledge, 2004.

The East Coast of Africa

Beachey, R.W. *A History of East Africa, 1592–1902.* London: I. B. Tauris & Co., 1995.

Hiskett, Mervyn. *The Course of Islam in Africa.* Edinburgh, Scotland: Edinburgh University Press, 1994.

Horton, Mark and John Middleton. *The Swahili: The Social Landscape of a Mercantile Society.* Oxford, U.K., and Malden, Massachusetts: Blackwell Publishers, 2000.

Insoll, Timothy. *The Archaeology of Sub-Saharan Africa.* Cambridge, U.K., and New York: Cambridge University Press, 2003.

Levtzion, Nehemiah and Randall L. Pouwells, eds. *The History of Islam in Africa.* Athens: Ohio University Press; Oxford, U.K.: James Currey; Cape Town, South Africa: David Philip, 2000.

Maxon, Robert M. *East Africa: An Introductory History.* Morgantown: West Virginia University Press, 1994.

Nurse, Derek and Thomas Spear. *The Swahili: Reconstructing the History and Language of an African Society.* Philadelphia: University of Pennsylvania Press, 1985.

Pearson, Michael N. *Port Cities and Intruders. The Swahili Coast, India, and Portugal in the Early Modern Era.* Baltimore and London: The Johns Hopkins University Press, 1998.

Kerala

Bayly, Susan. *Saints, Goddesses and Kings: Muslims and Christians in South Indian Society 1700–1900.* Cambridge, U.K., and New York: Cambridge University Press, 1989.

Dale, Stephen Frederic.*Islamic Society on the South Asian Frontier: The Mappilas of Malabar, 1498–1922.* Oxford, U.K: Clarendon Press; New York: Oxford University Press, 1980.

Miller, Roland E. *Mappila Muslims of Kerala: A Study in Islamic Trends.* Madras, India: Orient Longman, 1976.

Southeast Asia

Azra, Azyumardi. *The Origins of Islamic Reformism in Southeast Asia: Networks of Malay–Indonesian and Middle Eastern 'Ulamā' in the Seventeenth and Eighteenth Centuries.* Crows Nest, New South Wales, Australia: Asian Studies Association of Australia in association with Allen & Unwin; Honolulu: University of Hawai'i Press, 2004.

Chaudhuri, K. N. *Asia Before Europe: Economy and Civilisation of the Indian Ocean from the Rise of Islam to 1750.* Cambridge, U.K.: Cambridge University Press, 1990.

Chaudhuri, K. N. *Trade and Civilisation in the Indian Ocean: An Economic History from the Rise of Islam to 1750.* Cambridge, U.K: Cambridge University Press, 1985.

Gordon, Alijah, ed. *The Propagation of Islam in the Indonesian–Malay Archipelago.* Kuala Lumpur: Malaysian Sociological Research Institute, 2001.

Hadi, Amirul. *Islam and State in Sumatra: A Study of Seventeenth-Century Aceh.* Leiden, Netherlands, and Boston: Brill, 2004.

Hooker, M. B. *Islam in South-East Asia.* Leiden, Netherlands: Brill, 1983.

Reid, Anthony. *Southeast Asia in the Age of Commerce, 1450–1680.* 2 vols. New Haven, Connecticut: Yale University Press, 1988, 1993.

Reid, Anthony. "Islamization and Christianization in Southeast Asia: The Critical Phase, 1550–1650." In *Southeast Asia in the Early Modern Era: Trade, Power, and Belief,* ed. Anthony Reid, pp. 151–138. Ithaca, New York, and London: Cornell University Press, 1993.

Ricklefs, M. C. *A History of Modern Indonesia Since c. 1300,* 3d ed. Stanford, California: Stanford University Press, 2001.

Riddell, Peter G. *Islam and the Malay-Indonesian World: Transmission and Responses.* Honolulu: University of Hawai'i Press, 2001.

Shaffer, Lynda Norene. *Maritime Southeast Asia to 1500.* Armonk, New York, and London: M. E. Sharpe, 1996.

Tarling, Nicholas, ed. *The Cambridge History of Southeast Asia.* Vol. 2, *1500–1800.* Cambridge, U.K.: Cambridge University Press, 1992.

PART THREE

The World Turned Upside Down, 1750–Present

From the sixteenth to the early eighteenth centuries, the Ottoman, Safavid, and Mughal empires constituted a formidable bloc of Muslim states that extended from southeastern Europe to Bengal. The presence of these empires represented a dramatic achievement by the Muslim world in the aftermath of the destruction wrought by the Mongols and Timur Lang: Islam spread across much of Africa and Asia, and a trio of mutually competitive, Muslim-ruled states arose that were universally recognized to be as powerful and sophisticated as any others in the world.

Then, in the early eighteenth century, the Safavid and Mughal empires collapsed, and several European states rapidly eclipsed the Ottoman Empire in military effectiveness. The Ottoman government lasted until 1923, but only because Britain and France prevented Russia from destroying it much earlier. The extraordinary conjunction of political and military failure by the three greatest Muslim powers of the era coincided with the beginning of a period during which European nations gradually conquered the vast majority of the Muslim world. By 1920, in the aftermath of World War I, fully ninety-eight percent of the world's Muslims lived under foreign, non-Muslim rule.

Until recently, the failure of the major Muslim states and the advent of European imperialism were central themes in the Western historiography of the Muslim world. Western historians assumed that, because Muslim political and economic power had declined, the only significant developments during the period were those introduced by Europeans. Islamic religious life received hardly any attention from historians, who assumed that Islam had become stagnant and moribund. Recent research has drastically revised that interpretation. It is now clear that both Shi'ism and Sunnism underwent major changes in the eighteenth century. Of particular importance was the emergence of a Sunni reform movement at the beginning of the eighteenth century that has continued to unfold in successive waves.

Much of what is happening in the Muslim world today is incomprehensible without understanding the stages of this movement.

The eighteenth century was a watershed in Muslim history. Two features are of particular importance for our treatment of the period since that time. One is that Islamic civilization came to an end during that century. For the millennium prior to the eighteenth century, it is possible to speak of an Islamic civilization, in spite of the notorious slipperiness of the term *civilization.* The widespread use of the Arabic and Persian languages by the educated class, the universality of the Shari'a, and a common knowledge of numerous works in the sciences, literature, philosophy, and mysticism provided the cultured elites throughout the expanding Muslim world with the degree of cultural coherence normally associated with only a single nation.

The necessary conditions for nurturing Islamic civilization began to disappear in the eighteenth century. The provincial powers that took the place of the great empires did not patronize elite culture to the degree that princely courts of the past had done. As a result, the Arabic- and Persian-based elite culture was transformed by indigenous popular cultures. Even more devastating was the advent of imperialism, which drastically modified traditional Islamic institutions of all types—social, economic, and political. Notably, the new schools of the age of imperialism emphasized European and vernacular languages at the expense of Persian and Arabic, making international Islamic communication more difficult.

The other major change that took place in the eighteenth century was the emergence of a challenge to a fundamental element of the normative Islamic world view. Underlying the bulk of the works of jurisprudence that are conventionally referred to as the Shari'a is the assumption that the world is bifurcated into two qualitatively distinct zones. The *Dar al-Islam,* or "Abode of Islam," comprised the areas that Muslims ruled. At least theoretically, that was where the Shari'a was implemented. The *Dar al-Kufr* was the "Abode of Unbelief," ruled by non-Muslims. Since non-Muslims used a system of law other than the Shari'a, the ulama taught that it was impossible to be a Muslim in the Dar al-Kufr. A synonym for the Dar al-Kufr was the *Dar al-Harb* (the "Abode of War"), because of the widespread assumption that God expected His people to conduct jihad against the Dar al-Kufr until the Dar al-Islam encompassed the entire world.

Muslims found it increasingly difficult to accommodate this model of the world with their experience. In the eighteenth century, the army of the English East India Company conquered much of India, and the Dutch began to transform their monopoly of trade over the Indonesian archipelago into a system of colonial rule. In the nineteenth century, huge populations of Muslims came under the control of non-Muslims. Imperialist regimes were careful not to interfere with matters of worship, but the jurisdiction of Shari'a courts was gradually confined to personal and family affairs. New technologies, school curricula, and clothing fashions replaced traditional ones. Scrupulous Muslims were concerned: Did they still live in the Dar al-Islam, or were they now in the Dar al-Kufr? Can a person live an authentically Islamic life under a government dominated by non-Muslims? The subjection of almost the entire Dar al-Islam to non-Muslim rule was a world turned upside down, and many people were profoundly disoriented.

It is impossible to understand the spiritual distress of many Muslims during the nineteenth and twentieth centuries without coming to terms with the difficulty of

The Court of the Lions of the Alhambra palace, Granada. The most admired sections of the Alhambra date from the reign of Muhammad V (1354–1391), a century before Granada's capture by Spain.

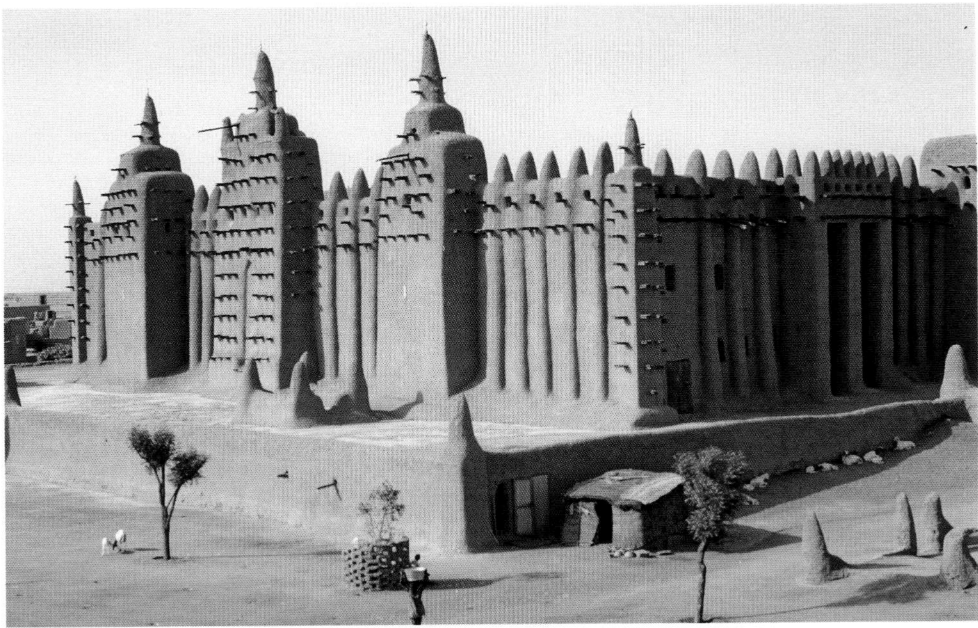

The Jenne Mosque of Mali. The structure is made of mud brick. The primary task of the palm trunks that project from the sides is to support the workers who replaster the exterior each spring.

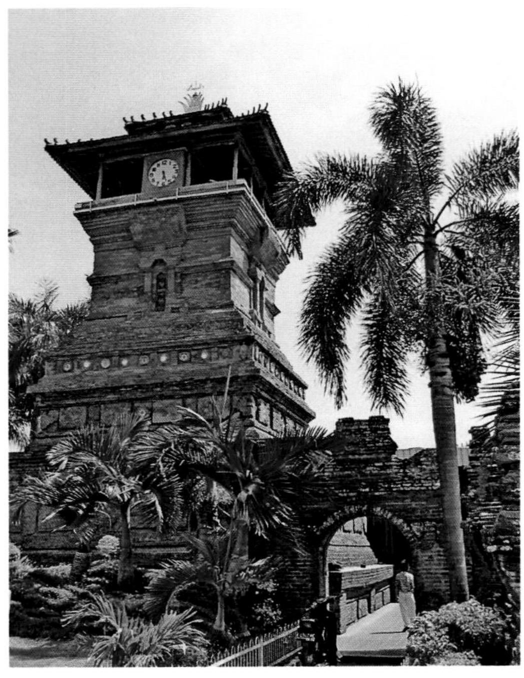

The minaret of the mosque at Kudus, Java. Dating from the early sixteenth century, it takes its inspiration from watchtowers of fortified Hindu temples.

The mosque at Talok Manok, Thailand. Constructed about 1769, the mosque contains no nails and is held together instead by interlocking pieces of timber. Its design incorporates Thai, Malay, and Chinese elements.

reconciling the status of being a colonial subject with the fundamental assumption that the world is divided into a Dar al-Islam and a Dar al-Kufr. The inner turmoil of Muslims was analogous to that of European Christians whose model of the universe was challenged by Copernicus's proposal of a sun-centered cosmos. The acceptance of the heliocentric model required not only the belief that the rising and setting of the sun were optical illusions, but also the abandonment of millennia-old assumptions that conditions and processes on earth differed from those in the heavens. These differences had provided explanations for mundane puzzles, such as the fact that raindrops fall rather than rise, as well as for more exalted issues, such as why heaven was located beyond the realm of the stars and hell was located at the center of the earth. The geocentric and heliocentric models were as incompatible for their metaphysical implications as they were for their basic structure.

The concept of the Dar al-Islam conveys the assurance that, even when corruption and oppression are the order of the day, God is ultimately in control and His objectives will be accomplished. The Dar al-Kufr, on the other hand, is utter chaos, and nothing of permanent value can be found there. This model of the division of the world into good and evil domains is profoundly appealing to many people—it has parallels in many cultures and religions—and it has proved to be far more durable than the era of imperialism that first challenged it. Many Muslim activists attribute the weakness of Muslim nations in the world today to the fact that the Dar al-Islam no longer exists because of the prevalence of un-Islamic laws and habits that derive from the West. Their mission is to restore the Dar al-Islam, and to reverse the condition of a world turned upside down.

CHRONOLOGY

1730–1762	Career of Shah Wali Allah of India
1744–1773	Career of Muhammad Ibn ‘Abd al-Wahhab
1757	Battle of Plassey
1774	Treaty of Kuchuk Kaynarja
1780–1817	Career of Uthman dan Fodio
1800–1859	Russian conquest of the Caucasus
1839–1876	*Tanzimat* period in the Ottoman Empire
1857	Revolt against British policies in India
1865–1882	Russian conquest of Central Asia south of Kazakhstan
1867	Founding of the Deoband madrasa
1873–1903	Aceh War
1875	Founding of Muhammadan Anglo–Oriental College at Aligarh
1875–1920	Era of “the New Imperialism”
1878	Congress of Berlin resolves Balkan issues
1889–1905	Career of Muhammad ‘Abduh
1906–1911	Iranian constitutional movement
1908	“Young Turk” revolution in the Ottoman Empire
1914–1918	World War I
1915	Gandhi moves back to India from South Africa
1917	Balfour Declaration
1919–1947	Career of Huda Sha‘rawi
1924	Declaration of Turkish republic and the abolition of the caliphate
1928–1949	Career of Hasan al-Banna
1932–1979	Career of Abu’l A‘la Mawdudi
1937–1945	World War II (from the Japanese attack on Shanghai and Nanjing)
1947	Indian and Palestinian partitions
1952–1970	Career of Jamal ‘Abd al-Nasir
1954–1965	Sayyid Qutb’s imprisonment
1967	Six-Day (June) War
1978–1979	Iranian Revolution
1979–1989	Soviet occupation of Afghanistan
1981	Assassination of Anwar Sadat
1990–1991	Gulf War to force Iraq out of Kuwait
2001	Al-Qa‘ida’s attacks on New York and Washington
2003	American invasion of Iraq to remove Saddam Husayn (Hussein)

Chapter 8

Reform and Renewal, 1750–1875

The early eighteenth-century change in fortunes of the Mughal, Safavid, and Ottoman empires entailed a seismic shift in the international balance of power. Two of the empires disappeared from the international scene, whereas the other lost much of its leverage to accomplish its foreign-policy goals. In contrast to the failure of the civil bureaucracies and military forces, Islamic doctrines, practices, and institutions became more vibrant during this period. The eighteenth and nineteenth centuries witnessed major developments in both Shi'ite and Sunni Islam. Twelver Shi'ism developed the institutional hierarchies and the Muharram rituals with which we are familiar today. Sunnism experienced numerous movements of Islamic reform and renewal. Most of the religious developments within both branches of Islam were the result of patient work by scholars and contemplatives, but because violence gains more notice than works of patience, the most well known were the work of men who sought to enforce their programs on others by force.

The period under review is also when the first significant loss of Muslim territory to foreign, non-Muslim rulers began. Most notable were foreign acquisitions in South Asia, Central Asia, and Southeast Asia. Ottoman and Iranian governments began to implement reforms that were intended to enable them to avoid succumbing to European powers themselves, but their initiatives came to little. Political reformers were handicapped by domestic opponents who fought hard to protect their vested interests and by European economic power and threats of military intervention that severely circumscribed their freedom of action. Governmental reformers merely delayed the inevitable.

Developments within Twelver Shi'ism

The institutions, doctrines, and rituals of Twelver Shi'ism continued to evolve during the eighteenth century. A major impetus to change came in the form of back-to-back political crises. The collapse of meaningful Safavid authority in 1722 shattered the system of court patronage that had always supported the leading ulama, and the accession to power of Nadir Shah in 1736 brought to the throne an autocrat who was virulently anti-Shi'ite. Many of the leading Iranian religious scholars fled to the Shi'ite holy centers of Iraq. Beyond the reach of Nadir Shah and having to devise their own means of financial support, these ulama engaged in a bitter and often violent internecine struggle to define their status in society. Meanwhile, in the chaos and that plagued Iran, the Shi'ite masses brought to maturity the observance of ta'ziye, the single most defining ritual of Twelver Shi'ism. By the late eighteenth century, it had largely assumed the form that we know today.

The Growth of Mujtahid Authority

By the middle of the seventeenth century, the Iranian Shi'ite religious establishment had finally become a powerful and self-confident institution. For a century and a half, shahs had recruited ulama from abroad, but the first few generations labored under handicaps. Many of them were Arabic speakers in a Persian-speaking land; the bulk of the population was not familiar with the formal doctrines of Twelver Shi'ism;

and the powerful Qizilbash leaders were able to block many reforms that the ulama attempted to implement. Over the years, however, the shahs granted the more eminent ulama large tracts of land, enabling their descendants (religious scholars themselves) to become wealthy landowners. Their political influence rose as the power of the Qizilbash declined. By the late seventeenth century, the ulama were prepared to assert their religious authority.

The four successors of Shah 'Abbas (1587–1629) did not possess his imposing and imperious personality. Moreover, their love of wine compromised their authority in the eyes of the ulama. During the latter half of the seventeenth century, the more powerful ulama began laying the groundwork for their eventual claim of spiritual supremacy over the shah. They had to overcome the fact that the shah still retained the aura of being the highest religious figure in the empire. Even though he no longer made explicit claims of religious leadership, the Safavid official genealogy claimed that the shah was a descendant of the seventh Imam.

The ulama were no longer willing to acknowledge the Safavid claim of an exalted pedigree. Descent from an Imam granted a person only the respect due the family of the Prophet—it was not a sufficient condition for religious leadership. Moreover, the ulama developed the doctrine that Isma'il I (1501–1524) had been only a sign of the coming of the Hidden (Twelfth) Imam rather than having been the Hidden Imam himself (much less an incarnation of the deity). After the death of 'Abbas I in 1629, the ulama began challenging some of the decisions of shahs. In the 1690s, leading religious scholars began issuing directives to the rulers, including a ban on wine drinking (at least where the ulama could see it).

Although Twelver ulama could agree among themselves that their spiritual authority exceeded that of the shah, they were sharply divided over several issues. Apart from the clash over the acceptability of mysticism that we examined in Chapter 5, the most serious division was the Akhbari–Usuli controversy. This arose during the reign of 'Abbas I and grew in intensity until the late eighteenth century. It had its roots in the rise to prominence of mujtahids in the thirteenth century. By that time, Twelver Shi'ites generally agreed that the Hidden Imam was the only legitimate religious authority and that he communicated his will to his community by means of dreams and visions granted to the most learned and pious scholars—the mujtahids. Mujtahids had successfully completed a long and rigorous course of study in law, philosophy, and Qur'an. They were qualified to exercise their own rational judgment in the administration of justice and in the arbitration of disputes. Shi'ite scholars had traditionally given more precedence to the use of reason in the formulation of doctrines and legal decisions than Sunnis had. The majority would not regard as valid any legal decisions or doctrines derived from the Hadith passed down by the Prophet and the Imams that contradicted what was derived from rational principles.

During the reign of 'Abbas I, some members of the ulama began to challenge the doctrine that mujtahids should have a monopoly on religious judgments. This group, known as the Akhbaris (from *akhbar,* or "reports," referring to the Hadith), argued that when an individual religious scholar made a ruling on legal, moral, or ritual affairs, he was obligated to adhere to the literal interpretation of the Hadith. His reasoning powers and erudition could not trump the plain meaning of the written record. Mulla Sadra, whose status as a great philosopher might cause us to assume that he disagreed with the Akhbaris, supported them because of his conviction that God grants all true believers access to truth by means of illumination. Akhbaris asserted that all Shi'ites were capable of understanding the Qur'an and Hadith if they used their own reason and the spiritual insights they derived from prayer and ritual. They need not accord special respect to the ruling of a mujtahid.

The clerics who asserted that mujtahids were needed to interpret the foundations of the faith were known as Usulis (from *usul,* meaning "sources" or "foundations"). Many Usulis adopted their position on the controversy due to their hostility to Sufism. They were contemptuous of people who claimed spiritual authority without having mastered the rigorous curriculum of the madrasa. They asserted that ordinary believers below the rank of mujtahid were not competent to interpret the faith. It was incumbent on pious Muslims to select a scholar who had been deemed capable of exercising ijtihad and model their behavior on his legal rulings. Usulis did not assert that mujtahids were infallible—they explicitly stated that each generation must seek new mujtahids to follow, for the decisions of the previous generation were not necessarily valid for all time.

During the late seventeenth century, the Akhbari school of thought became the dominant position in the schools and mosques of the shrine cities of southern Iraq, but Usulism remained preeminent in the great centers of learning in Iran. The crises caused by the fall of the Safavids in 1722 and the accession to power of Nadir Shah in 1736 stimulated many of the leading ulama to migrate to Iraq. The infusion of talent transformed Karbala, and then Najaf, into the premier centers of Shi'ite scholarship. The religious leaders were beyond the reach of Iranian rulers and the

Ottoman central government alike: From 1747 to 1831, Baghdad was governed only indirectly by Istanbul through the medium of a mamluk class of governors. The governors wielded little power outside the walls of Baghdad and were not greatly worried about the influence of the Shi'ite ulama, because only a few Iraqis outside of the shrine cities were Shi'ite during the eighteenth century. The growth of the Shi'ite community into Iraq's largest population group was a development of the nineteenth and early twentieth centuries, when Sunni Arab tribes migrated from the Arabian Peninsula into southern Iraq and only then assumed a Shi'ite loyalty.

Usuli Iranian immigrants had more to fear from the local Akhbari community than from the Ottomans or Nadir Shah. Akhbaris regarded Usulis as ritually unclean, and in some cases they violently assaulted anyone who possessed Usuli literature. In self-defense, the Usulis mounted a counterattack and became the dominant community during the last quarter of the eighteenth century. Key figures in the triumph of the Usulis were two leading scholars of Karbala: Vahid Bihbahani (1705–1792) and his son 'Ali. Vahid made the use of ijtihad obligatory for jurists and declared any Shi'ite who refused to accept the Usuli position to be an infidel. He enlisted the aid of urban gangs to inflict corporal, and even capital, punishment on those who disagreed with him. He and 'Ali combined their war against Akhbarism with a campaign against mysticism. They banned the teachings of the School of Esfahan, and 'Ali pursued Sufis with such intensity that he was known as "the Sufi-slayer."

The Usuli-Akhbari debate was not merely theological: It also had implications for the status of scholars. Those who argued for the primacy of the Hadith were making a case for egalitarianism among the religious scholars, because a large number of them could make rulings based on the literal interpretation of the Hadith. Those who stressed the importance of reason were making a case for a hierarchy of scholars, since some would be able to wield logic and evidence better than the others. Thus, the Usuli triumph had important repercussions. Religious scholars and society at large began evaluating scholars on the basis not only of their piety but also of their reasoning skills. As a result, a hierarchy of scholars began to develop on an informal and tacit basis. A highly respected scholar came to be referred to as a *hojjat al-islam* ("proof of Islam"). Among this group of highly respected scholars, a particularly outstanding one might be referred to as an *ayatollah* ("sign of God"). Since there was no longer a Safavid shah who claimed religious authority, the religious elites developed an even higher status than they had possessed before. The fusion of religious and political authority characteristic of Safavid society was now replaced by a separation of religion and politics. The dominant Twelver perspective reverted to the pre-Safavid attitude that, in the absence of the Hidden Imam, politics and worldly affairs were of little value and should even be shunned.

Twelver Ritual Life

One of the most important rituals for Muslims is that of pilgrimage. For all Muslims, the hajj in Mecca is theoretically the most important, but historically it has been impossible for most to perform, due to the distance and expense of the trip. The fact that the cities of Mecca and Medina fell under Ottoman control in 1517, soon after the creation of the Safavid Empire, made the performance of the hajj even more problematic for Safavid subjects. On the other hand, the shrines of deeply spiritual men and women were usually within a reasonable distance of any Muslim. As sites that were believed to be capable of dispensing grace, they often served as objects of pilgrimage for Sunnis and Shi'ites alike.

For Twelver Shi'ites, the most spiritual figures in history after the Prophet himself are the Imams. Medina is the burial site for four of them (Hasan, the second Imam; 'Ali Zayn al-'Abidin, the fourth; Muhammad al-Baqir, the fifth; and Ja'far al-Sadiq, the sixth). The other seven who died are buried in either Iraq or Iran, and the majority of Iranians were within a reasonable pilgrimage distance of at least one of them. The largest number were in Iraq: 'Ali (the first Imam) is buried in Najaf; Husayn (the third Imam) is buried in Karbala; Musa al-Kazim (the seventh Imam) and Muhammad al-Jawad (the ninth Imam) are buried in Baghdad; and 'Ali al-Hadi (the tenth Imam) and Hasan al-'Askari (the eleventh Imam) are buried in Samarra. The fierce wars that the Safavids fought against the Ottomans over Iraq were motivated as much by the desire to control these shrines as they were to control the agricultural wealth of Iraq. Isma'il I had conquered Iraq, but the youthful Tahmasp lost it to Suleyman in 1534. 'Abbas I reconquered it in 1624, but the Ottomans reclaimed it permanently in 1638.

Most Iranian Muslims made frequent pilgrimages to the shrines of Sufi saints until the seventeenth century, when the growing awareness of Twelver doctrine and the destruction of Sufi tariqas and shrines gained momentum. Since Iraq was under the control of the hostile Ottoman Empire for most of Safavid history, making a pilgrimage to the Iraqi shrines was difficult. As a result, the shrine of 'Ali al-Rida (the eighth Imam) in Mashhad became more important to Safavid subjects than it might otherwise have been. 'Abbas I performed a pilgrimage to it and provided it with a huge endowment that made it into a spectacular shrine. It became the largest, the most visited, and the most beautiful of the shrines of the Imams. Mashhad was the capital of Nadir Shah, and he continued to beautify the city's shrine, despite his opposition to Shi'ism itself. During the chaos that followed the violent death of Nadir Shah, a visit to Mashhad became even more important to the emotional life of Iranian Shi'ites. Much as Chaucer's pilgrims sought comfort, reassurance, and protection from the plague by visiting the shrine of Thomas Becket at Canterbury, times of crisis stimulated Shi'ites to throng to the shrine of Imam 'Ali al-Rida at Mashhad even more frequently than usual.

The eighteenth century also witnessed the emergence of the modern form of the distinctive rituals that commemorate the martyrdom of Imam Husayn in 680. The first evidence that we have of the public observance of Husayn's tragic death dates from the reign of the Buyid dynasty in Baghdad during the tenth century, but the rituals associated with Ashura evolved over a period of many centuries. Husayn was killed on the tenth (*'Ashura*) of Muharram, the first month of the Islamic calendar. Ashura is observed throughout the Muslim world. Among Sunnis, it is a minor holy day of repentance and is often observed by fasting, but among Twelver Shi'ites, it is the most important religious festival of the year.

Among Shi'ites, the commemoration of Ashura gradually came to fill the first ten days of the month. In our own era, crowds typically spend all ten days listening to prayers, recitations from the Qur'an, sermons, and poetic descriptions of the lives and deaths of the major characters involved in the tragedy. The narratives portray the loving family and devoted followers being attacked in the desert before they can arrive at their destination. Cut off from the river, the children begin to die of dehydration. Husayn, the model father, tries to carry his young son to the water. Before he can reach the river, however, troops sent by the Umayyad dynasty murder both of them and most of the other members of the party, as well. In some versions of the story, the soldiers carry Husayn's severed head to Damascus as a trophy for the evil Umayyad caliph. En route to the capital city, the head converts infidels and even a lion, but not the Umayyads.

The mourning during Ashura climaxes on the tenth day. By the late sixteenth century, the final day featured a display of effigies of the bodies of the various victims of the massacre. Many members of the audience, already weeping, would begin to beat their chests with their hands or even to cut their flesh with knives, swords, or metal-tipped whips, in order to share in Husayn's suffering. Ashura's theatrical element evolved throughout the seventeenth and, especially, the eighteenth centuries. By the late eighteenth century, the battle and, particularly, the deaths of each member of Husayn's family became the subject of a dramatic reenactment known as *ta'ziye.* It is the only indigenous form of dramatic art in the Muslim world.

These dramatic reenactments are not practiced in all Twelver communities. In South Asia, Shi'ite memorials of Husayn's death have remained at the level of parades and pageants. There, the term *ta'ziye* usually denotes replicas of Husayn's tomb that are painstakingly constructed and paraded through towns during Ashura. The reasons why the dramatic form of the ta'ziye arose are unknown, but its emergence in eighteenth-century Iran suggests that it was linked to the collapse of the Safavid Empire. As we have seen repeatedly, the insecurity that results from the collapse of central political authority often stimulates the emergence of new organizations, rituals, and ad hoc religious and political leadership as people attempt to bring security and meaning to their lives.

The long-established narrative rituals of Ashura remind the listening audience of the abandonment of Husayn by the inhabitants of Kufa, who had asked him to come to their city to deliver them from the Umayyads. Central to the Shi'ite world view is the tragedy of Husayn's avoidable death, which precluded the inauguration of a just and righteous order in the world. Ashura allows Shi'ites to repent of their own share in the collective guilt that caused Husayn's suffering and to hope that their sins will be forgiven. Shi'ites express their remorse in different ways. In Iran, where the plays have been performed for almost three centuries, members of the audience weep and cry out, expressing their sorrow and repentance. In South Asia, where the dramas are not performed, male Shi'ites typically cut or flog themselves during their ta'ziye processions, sometimes drawing copious amounts of blood. The reasons for this difference in the expression of grief and guilt are not fully understood, but it is noteworthy that accounts of Iranian rituals prior to the eighteenth century describe acts of self-mutilation. Such shedding of one's own blood has been rare in Iran since then. The familiar dynamics of theater seem to be at work here: Members of the audience at a dramatic form of ta'ziye momentarily suspend their emotional distance and feel that they are part of the action on the stage or arena, and they experience their catharsis through a deep emotional experience. In lieu of this experience, many Shi'ites feel the need to shed their own blood to express their

Participants in a *ta'ziye* in Iraq prepare to enter the arena.

remorse and devotion. In southern Lebanon and Iraq, the dramatic form of ta'ziye was introduced relatively recently, due to both countries' having been part of the Ottoman Empire. In both instances, self-mutilation continues to exist alongside the drama as an atavistic remnant of earlier patterns of ritual observance.

Sunni Reform Movements

Sunnis as well as Shi'ites actively reshaped their traditions during the eighteenth and nineteenth centuries. During this period, Sunni activists from Southeast Asia to North Africa achieved widespread agreement regarding the elements of a reform program. It echoed features of the demands made in the seventeenth century by al-Raniri and al-Sinkili in Aceh, the Kadizadelis in Istanbul, and al-Sirhindi in Delhi. What distinguished the later period was that, whereas the earlier movements remained confined to local circles of devotees, mass movements developed when the same themes were raised again in the eighteenth century.

The Sunni reforms of the period are notable for two major features. One is that the most influential leaders of the movements felt fully qualified to make independent judgments. If the "gate of ijtihad" had in fact been closed, they were determined to reopen it. They felt that the traditional method of studying the Shari'a, which emphasized a close examination of works of jurisprudence and of commentaries on those works, had removed vitality and meaning from the law. They wanted to return to the sources that the original formulators of the Shari'a had used in the first centuries of Islamic history: the Qur'an and Hadith. By careful examination of

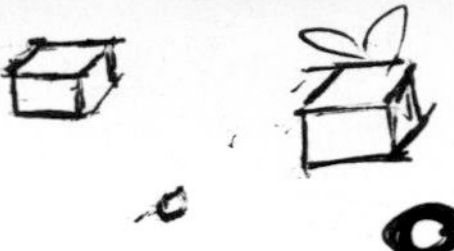

the original sources of the faith, they argued, Muslims could recapture the dynamism and authenticity of the first generation of Islam.

The other salient feature of the Sunni reform movements of this era is a renewed emphasis on a duty that is theoretically incumbent upon each Muslim: commanding the good and forbidding the evil (*al-amr bi al-ma'ruf wa al-nahy 'an al-munkar*). This duty, which is mentioned in the Qur'an, had been interpreted and applied in various ways through the centuries. Implementing it necessarily entails confronting people about their behavior, and few individuals are grateful for being told, even in a tactful way, that they are breaking God's law. Like people everywhere, many Muslims found ways to avoid confronting their neighbors when they saw them violating ritual or ethical norms.

The eighteenth-century reformers were men who felt a keen sense of responsibility for carrying out God's will. Just as ijtihad itself was a responsibility as well as a right, enforcing proper conduct in others was a responsibility that could not be evaded. Reformers felt obligated to preach what they believed to be God's will and to eliminate religious and social practices that were contrary to God's will. Some believed that rational argument and spiritual example would suffice to transform their communities; others felt that they had no recourse but to use compulsion to bring about a righteous society.

A Search for First Principles

The Sunni reform movements had their inspiration in the Arabian Peninsula. By the eighteenth century, the madrasas of Zabid, San'a, Mecca, and Medina were attracting increasing numbers of students from West Africa, China, Southeast Asia, and other regions where Islam had become firmly established by that time. As a result, the scholars who taught in the madrasas were becoming aware of how varied the practice of Islam was in different regions of the world. Once they had become conscious of how differently Muslims lived and worshiped abroad, they began to view the religious practices in their own localities through different lenses. Previously, they simply shrugged at religious practices in the peninsula that could not be supported by scripture. Now, in the context of the collapse of two of the great Muslim empires and the challenges facing the third, some of the scholars developed the conviction that Islam was in a state of crisis.

Advocates of reform could, and did, identify a number of problems that needed to be rectified, but most reformers could agree that both the veneration of living holy men and the rituals performed at the tombs of deceased holy men were frequently indistinguishable from worship of the men in question. Criticism of these practices became the core of most of the reform programs of the era. Such criticism was a major departure for Muslim religious leaders. Ibn Taymiya, the fourteenth-century Syrian intellectual who was persecuted by Mamluke authorities for his criticism of saint veneration and shrine visits, was one of only a handful of religious authorities who had spoken out against the practices prior to the eighteenth century. Throughout Muslim history, the bulk of the ulama had been sympathetic both to the reverence for saints and to the undertaking of pilgrimage to their tombs. Scholars who interpreted the Shari'a on points relating to these topics had

usually given worshipers the benefit of the doubt and simply urged them not to slip into patently idolatrous practices at tombs. The veneration of saints and devotional services at their tombs were practiced all over the Muslim world in the eighteenth century, just as they were in most of the Christian world.

The reformers were quite aware that Islamic tradition upheld the two practices (as well as other customs that they opposed). What makes their work so remarkable is the boldness and certitude with which they fought the practices. Within a culture that frequently associated innovation with heresy, they broke continuity with almost a millennium of tradition in methods for determining Islamic law. In the early tenth century, most Sunni religious scholars had agreed on the use of four sources for determining Islamic law: the Qur'an, Hadith, analogy, and consensus. They first searched the Qur'an and Hadith to try to find an answer to a problem. Then, if necessary, they used analogies with other cases of jurisprudence in order to arrive at a decision. Finally, when a ruling was supported by a consensus of religious scholars, it was considered to have become part of the Shari'a.

Eighteenth-century reformers asserted that the use of analogy and consensus had degraded original Islamic principles by integrating pre-Islamic practices, and they insisted that the only two acceptable guides for behavior were the Qur'an and Hadith. This meant that scholars would have to abandon *taqlid* (uncritical acceptance of the decisions of previous jurists) and begin to exercise ijtihad. Regardless of just how closed the "gate of ijtihad" had ever been,[1] the reformers were determined to force it wide open.

The reformers were not only breaking with Sunni tradition, but they were also moving in the opposite direction of that of their Shi'ite contemporaries: Whereas the Shi'ite Usulis won a victory for rationalism over Hadith-centered methods, Sunnis tended to be critical of reason-based approaches to religious issues and to shift the focus to the Hadith. Likewise, whereas Shi'ite ulama encouraged visits to the shrines of Imams and allowed the development of the Iranian ta'ziyeh, a major theme of Sunni reformers was a bitter criticism of shrine visits and any form of drama. Finally, whereas most Shi'ites opposed Sufism, only a few Sunni reformers did so. In fact, this was a period of growth for Sufi orders in the Sunni world. Most Sunni reform efforts took place at the initiative of Sufi shaykhs and through the agency of Sufi orders. As a result of the diverging trends between Sunnis and Shi'ites, relations between the two groups deteriorated during this period.

The innovation of the reform-minded scholars in the Arabian madrasas was that they spent less time teaching the texts of jurisprudence—or they abandoned them altogether—and engaged in a close study of the Qur'an and Hadith. To appreciate how radical their revision was, it is useful to survey the typical educational path of a madrasa student. The two major divisions of formal education in the Muslim world were the *kuttab* and the *madrasa.* The kuttab was a primary school where young children learned to recite the Qur'an. The actual skills taught in a kuttab varied from region to region and from instructor to instructor. In many regions, memorization of long passages of the Qur'an was the sole objective, and some prodigies committed the entire book to memory after eight or nine years. Since a mastery of classical Arabic was not the objective of the kuttab, students commonly did not understand the meaning of much that they had memorized. Some kuttabs did introduce pupils to functional literacy in Arabic, but most children who learned to read and write did so in their own home or in the home of a private tutor.

A small percentage of students continued their education beyond the kuttab, either with a tutor or at a madrasa. Tutors could teach medicine, astronomy, alchemy, literature, or a variety of other subjects. Madrasas, by contrast, specialized in the study of the Shari'a. They had no fixed curriculum. By the thirteenth and fourteenth centuries, fewer and fewer madrasas offered instruction in Qur'anic exegesis or Hadith studies, since most scholars assumed that those sources had been sufficiently mined in the process of creating the Shari'a. By that time, the focus of study shifted toward a close reading of works of jurisprudence and of commentaries on those works.

Students came to a madrasa not to earn a degree from the institution, but rather to study with a particular scholar. At the conclusion of the course of study, the instructor would present the student with a certificate (*ijaza*) attesting to the student's mastery of the meaning of one or more texts. The point was not to mine the text for new meanings, but to pass along the author's original meaning in a chain of transmission, much as Sufi masters passed along a method of spiritual discipline. The working assumption was that the meaning of a text could not be acquired by reading it on one's own, but only by hearing an exposition of its meaning by the instructor and by engaging in formal, dialectical arguments regarding its logical implications.

For a handful of scholars to shift the course of study in their classes from the works of jurisprudence to the Qur'an and Hadith might have been as inconsequential as Ibn Taymiya's criticism of shrine visits had it not been for the fact that these scholars taught in madrasas that were located conveniently for pilgrims making the hajj. Young scholars and pious pilgrims sought the insights of scholars living in Mecca and Medina as early as the first generation of Islamic history, and the rise of Zabid and San'a as intellectual centers under the Rasulid dynasty (1228–1454) made the Hijaz–Yemen axis a powerful magnet for scholars. The fact that these schools were at the heart of the international network of scholarship is important, but perhaps even more important was the psychological effect of studying in conjunction with the pilgrimage. During this era of religious and political crisis, combining the pilgrimage with a serious study of the religious sciences in the Arabian Peninsula could have an explosive impact on the psyche. The performance of the hajj itself is a profoundly emotional experience for the faithful and commonly results in a renewed sense of purpose and responsibility. Pilgrims who joined a madrasa began a period that might last a year or twenty years, studying with other seekers who came from all over the vast region that extended from Senegal to Maluku. In casual conversations with each other, they developed a new awareness of how varied what people called "Islam" was. They became more critical of their own tradition, and sought authoritative guides to the proper way of living a life acceptable to God. To many pilgrim–students, the provincial and idiosyncratic features of their own religious practice became clear as they studied with the reformers. They resolved to return home to be a leavening agent for what they believed to be the timeless and universal truths of Islam.

One such pilgrim–scholar became the central figure in the South Asian Sunni reform movement, Shah Wali Allah (1703–1762) of Delhi.[2] His father was a famous religious scholar and a pir within the Naqshbandi order. Wali Allah followed in his father's footsteps. An intellectual and spiritual prodigy, he became an instructor in a madrasa and a Sufi pir while still a young man. Despite his achievements at that age, the turning point in his life occurred in 1731, when he went on the hajj. He was gone for over a year, studying with leading Naqshbandi scholars in Medina and Zabid. His sojourn in Arabia transformed his career.

Wali Allah returned to Delhi with a passion for reform that gripped him for the remainder of his life. The interrelated issues of tomb visitations and veneration of saints became a major focus for him. Many Indian Muslims not only visited the tombs of Muslim saints; they also attended the festivals of their Hindu neighbors and followed Hindu social practices that violated the Shari'a, such as denying women the right of inheritance and denying widows the right to remarry. Many Indians who adopted a Muslim identity incorporated elements of Islam that supplemented familiar customs and did not clash with local mores. In many cases they were exposed to only the forms of Islam that the pirzada of the local dargah happened to share with them. They saw no contradiction in continuing to follow many of the traditions of their ancestors.

Wali Allah, on the other hand, conceived of Islam as a universal religion with norms that should be upheld everywhere. He set for himself an enormous task that consumed the remainder of his life. He sought to eradicate unscriptural practices, to overcome the divisions among the four schools of law, and to bridge the chasms that separated mystics from theologians and the literate from the illiterate (but not to establish harmonious relations with Shi'ites, against whom he wrote bitter invectives). Wali Allah invested prodigious energy into creating a new synthesis for the Muslims of his age, based on the Qur'an and Hadith. He made original contributions in both Arabic and Persian on a wide variety of topics, and these writings were disseminated all over the Muslim world. His independence of mind is revealed in that he translated the Qur'an into Persian, persisting in the face of bitter criticism from many ulama, who argued the traditional doctrine that the Qur'an can exist only in the original Arabic. Subsequently, his sons translated the Qur'an into Urdu. Muslims debated the point whether the translations were in fact the Qur'an or only paraphrases of it, but the important point was that the meaning of the Qur'an had become available to vast numbers of people who did not understand Arabic. From this point on, non-Arabs could study the Qur'an and interpret it for themselves. They were no longer dependent on scholars who were fluent in Arabic.

Numerous other scholars worked quietly and assiduously in the manner of Shah Wali Allah. Two North African reformers who were also inspired by their experiences in Arabia should be noted due to their lasting influence. Ahmad al-Tijani (1737–1815) was born in southern Algeria and studied in Fez. He joined several Sufi orders and then embarked upon the hajj in 1772. He remained in the Hijaz for almost a decade, engaged in meditation and Sufi exercises. He returned to Fez in 1782, convinced that God had chosen him to be the leader of a new order, the Tijaniya. In an unusual move, al-Tijani obligated his disciples to break ties with other orders and to be a member only of the Tijaniya. Like many of the other reformers of the era, Tijani opposed the veneration of shaykhs and tomb visitations. He died in Fez, where, in an ironic twist, his tomb became a popular shrine that attracted huge numbers of pilgrims each year.

Ahmad ibn Idris (1750/60–1837) was born in Morocco but never returned after he left for the hajj in 1799. He settled in Egypt for a time and then returned to Mecca in 1818. He became a popular teacher there, but he stirred up such fierce jealousies among the ulama of Mecca that he had to flee for his life to Yemen in 1827. He disapproved of saint veneration and tomb visitations, rejected music and dancing during Sufi meetings, and opposed an exclusive allegiance to any particular school of the Shari'a. Like Wali Allah, he was convinced that the way to overcome the divisions of the schools of law was by a sole reliance on the Qur'an and Hadith.

Ahmad ibn Idris's charisma and profound ideas attracted several impressive personalities into his entourage who subsequently founded their own tariqas. One is worth noting here, since we will be referring to his tariqa in later discussions. He was Muhammad ibn 'Ali al-Sanusi (1787–1859), who left the Arabian Peninsula after his master's death and settled in Cyrenaica (eastern Libya) in 1843. He subsequently founded a ribat, or Sufi lodge, deep in the Libyan desert. His teachings remained very similar to those of Ibn Idris, particularly his doctrine that the object of meditation was not to identify with God (a goal that could compromise the doctrine of monotheism) but with the Prophet. He is most famous for ministering to the nomads of the Sahara. He built large compounds in tribal areas that included a mosque, a school, cells for meditation, and a guest block for the use of travelers and caravans.

Jihad Movements

Most reformers attempted to bring about change through their teaching, preaching, writings, and personal example. For a variety of reasons, other reformers chose to use force. Most who did so justified their use of violence by claiming to be involved in a jihad against evil-doers. Already engaged in a reform effort that required major breaks with traditional religious practices, militant reformers also had to redefine the traditional meaning of jihad in order to employ it against fellow Muslims.

According to the Shari'a, a jihad is an armed struggle (1) to fight a foe who has refused to accept a formal demand to convert or (2) to protect Islam against an aggressive attack. The former circumstance imposes a collective obligation upon the Muslim community that someone—not everyone—be engaged in the jihad, and it requires that a Muslim ruler initiate and lead the jihad. The defensive jihad is an individual responsibility: No Muslim can claim exemption from it on the grounds that someone else is fighting. The defensive jihad does not require the leadership of a Muslim ruler, but rather can be leaderless.

The concept of jihad appears in the Qur'an and was elaborated over the centuries by jurists who were developing the Shari'a. The rules governing jihad were quite elaborate, and some of the details varied from one madhhab to another. All of the madhhabs assumed that a jihad was a matter of Muslims fighting non-Muslims, but we have seen that rulers of Muslim states would sometimes exploit the notion of jihad to provide a rationale for a war against other Muslim rulers. Often they could point to sectarian differences—such as the conflict between Shi'ism and Sunnism—or to a policy or a statement that could be construed as a threat, and hence a threat to "Islam" that justified war. As a rule, they used the concept whenever it suited the purposes of their own interests.

The eighteenth- and nineteenth-century reformers who engaged in jihad in order to implement their programs directed their jihads against fellow Muslims. Their violent attacks entailed serious injuries, deaths, and the destruction of property. Because many onlookers reacted with shock to the violence, the men who declared jihad had to develop arguments for their unusual application of the concept. They justified the violence on the grounds that the targets of their attack were heretics or apostates who were precluding the implementation of true Islam throughout society. In that sense, they argued, the jihad was a defense of Islam.

Arabia

Today the best-known *mujahid* (one who engages in jihad) of the eighteenth century is Muhammad ibn 'Abd al-Wahhab (1702/3–1791/2). He is of interest for several reasons. First, his jihad was conducted at the very heart of the Muslim world, whereas most of the renewal efforts of this era were in regions where Islamic influence had not been felt for long or where Muslims were a minority group. Second, he attacked Sufism as a scourge rather than using its structures and ideas to carry out reform. Third, the Wahhabis are a controversial force in the Muslim world today, and scholars debate the extent to which their current ideas reflect those of their founder.[3]

Born near modern Riyad (Riyadh) in the Arabian Peninsula, Ibn 'Abd al-Wahhab was the same age as Shah Wali Allah. He was the son of a qadi and the grandson of a mufti. He studied in the Holy Cities and in Basra, and he shared in the revulsion that some of his teachers felt toward certain religious practices that were common among the Muslims of central Arabia, including the visitation of saints' tombs, the veneration of natural wonders such as springs and unusual rock formations, and the wearing of amulets to ward off evil. Ibn 'Abd al-Wahhab also criticized the tradition that had exalted Muhammad to a status that, in some cases, approximated the status of Jesus among Christians. Ibn 'Abd al-Wahhab insisted that Muhammad had been an ordinary man who should not be worshiped and whose grave should not be revered. Muslims should not ask Muhammad to intercede on someone's behalf with God.

By nature sensitive and scrupulous, Ibn 'Abd al-Wahhab could not tolerate such practices in himself or in those around him. He was utterly possessed by a vision of the absolute oneness and sovereignty of God (*tawhid*), and so he opposed anything that appeared to be claiming authority separate from God. In fact, his followers have always called themselves *muwahhidun,* or Unitarians, not Wahhabis. Like many other labels that have become standard, the term *Wahhabism* was originally a moniker pinned on the tradition by its critics.

At first glance, Ibn 'Abd al-Wahhab's program did not look much different from that of Shah Wali Allah and numerous other Sunni reformers of the era. Its major distinction was its unwillingness to compromise or to take the time to persuade and educate fellow Muslims that certain rituals performed by many Muslims for centuries were not sanctioned by the Qur'an or the Hadith. Ibn 'Abd al-Wahhab called anyone who engaged in those acts a polytheist, who was a valid target of jihad. Under his definitions of Islam and polytheism, most people who called themselves Muslims fell into the category of polytheists, and true Muslims had an obligation to raid and even kill them. Like Shah Wali Allah and many other Sunni reformers of the era, Ibn 'Abd al-Wahhab was hostile toward Shi'ism, but unlike his

Indian counterpart, he developed an equal hostility toward Sufism, which he accused of fostering the practices that he had come to oppose. He associated Sufism with saint and tomb worship; the notion that Muhammad had been the Perfect Man; and the use of tobacco, drugs, and music.

As a young man, Ibn 'Abd al-Wahhab began challenging Muslim practices in central Arabia, but he was chased out of several towns after he offended prominent individuals. In 1744 he allied with the ruler of the town of Dir'iya, Muhammad ibn Sa'ud. This alliance combined the fierce, self-righteous ideology of the Wahhabis with the fighting power of one of the peninsula's most powerful and ambitious chieftains. The result was a series of quick and decisive victories and the spread of Ibn 'Abd al-Wahhab's influence throughout much of central Arabia. In 1773 Ibn 'Abd al-Wahhab stepped aside from his position as political advisor and devoted the remaining nineteen years of his long life to religious scholarship and teaching.

After Ibn 'Abd al-Wahhab's retirement from political life, the Sa'udi political and military machine continued to gain its religious legitimacy from enforcing Wahhabi teachings. The Sa'udis' frequent military campaigns were always carried out in the name of jihad. They raided Muslim settlements, plundering all of the movable property and killing many of the victims. The raids were deadlier than traditional bedouin raids, which had usually avoided killing for fear of triggering a blood feud.

After the capture of Riyad in 1773, the Sa'udis began advancing in all directions. In 1802 they captured Karbala, destroyed much of the mausoleum of Husayn on the grounds that it was an idolatrous Shi'ite shrine, and massacred thousands of Karbala's citizens. Southern Iraq continued to be a rich field for Sa'udi raiding for several more years. The Sa'udis captured Mecca in spring 1803, but held it for only three months before disease among their troops forced them to withdraw. In 1805 they captured Medina, and in the following year they recaptured Mecca. During the period 1808–1810, the Sa'udis plundered and destroyed villages as far north as the environs of Aleppo and Damascus, but the major cities were too well fortified for them even to attempt besieging them. By 1810 they controlled almost the entire Arabian Peninsula. They were in direct control of the northern two-thirds of the peninsula, and they received tribute from the rulers of Muscat, Yemen, and Hadramawt. The peninsula, however, turned out to be the Sa'udis' limit of expansion. Their form of plundering required them to be able to melt quickly back into the desert when they encountered modern armies such as were being developed in Egypt, Anatolia, and Iran.

The Ottomans had never seriously tried to control central Arabia before this period, but the Sa'udi raids on Iraq and the capture of the Holy Cities caused tremendous loss of face for the Ottoman ruling family. In 1811, the Ottoman sultan ordered the governor of Egypt, Muhammad 'Ali, to send an army to destroy the Sa'udis. For seven years, the Egyptian army methodically pursued the Sa'udis and finally destroyed their capital at Dir'iya. In 1824, a surviving Sa'udi prince, Turki, established a base of power at Riyad, which has remained associated with Sa'udi power to this day. As long as the Egyptians remained in occupation of northern Arabia, Turki fought for survival against them and fellow Arabian chieftains. When the Egyptians evacuated Arabia in 1840, Turki's son Faysal began expanding his power. He established a second Sa'udi state by 1843 in central and eastern Arabia that enforced Wahhabi doctrines. He did not try to recapture Mecca and Medina, and he did not threaten its neighbors to the north. When he died in 1865, his sons fought each other, and the state splintered. Two decades later, in 1887, the Rashidi tribe captured Riyad, and it appeared that Sa'udi power was finished. In 1893, the head of the family settled in Kuwait under the protection of its ruler.

The Wahhabi movement is notable for its intolerance of ritual observances that differ from its own. Its members took very seriously the stricture to "command the good and forbid the wrong" as they understood the categories of *good* and *wrong*. The Wahhabi propensity to fight Muslims who differed from them was a major difference from the movement associated with Shah Wali Allah, which used education and persuasion to try to change people's behavior. Ibn 'Abd al-Wahhab has frequently been compared to the seventh-century Kharijites, who gained notoriety for killing Muslims who adhered to doctrines or rituals different from their own. The Kharijites even killed pious Muslims who differed from their own position on a single point: The degree of deviation from what the Kharijites considered true Islam did not matter. Among Muslims who assumed that the practice of Islam could legitimately range over a continuum of doctrines and rituals, *Wahhabi* joined *Kharijite* as a term of opprobrium.

When the Wahhabi–Sa'udi alliance moved against the Holy Cities a decade after Ibn 'Abd al-Wahhabi's death, it deliberately provoked a war with the Ottomans. Wahhabi leaders justified the war against the Muslim empire on the grounds that the Ottomans failed to provide adequate security for pilgrims to the region and allowed a wide range of un-Islamic practices. The Wahhabis called their war against the Ottoman forces a jihad, justifying their use of that term by appealing to arguments in selected passages from the work of Ibn Taymiya, the mujtahid of the Mamluke era discussed in Chapter 2. Ibn Taymiya argued that war by the Mamlukes against the Mongol Il-khanid regime of Ghazan (1295–1304) was an obligatory jihad on the grounds that the Il-khanids were infidels. Ghazan, said Ibn Taymiya, claimed to have converted to Islam, but he continued to adhere to elements of Mongol customary law. Since Ghazan did not fully implement the Shari'a, Ibn Taymiya declared him to be an infidel against whom a jihad should be waged. Likewise, the Wahhabis argued, although the Ottoman sultan claimed to be a Muslim, his failure to enforce the Shari'a caused him to forfeit his right to rule. This Wahhabi doctrine that Muslim rulers should be overthrown for failing to enforce the Shari'a has persisted into the twenty-first century.

China

About a decade after Shah Wali Allah performed the hajj, another Naqshbandi embarked upon his own pilgrimage. Ma Mingxin lived in Gansu province in China. Like Shah Wali Allah, Ma Mingxin returned home with the intention of beginning a reform movement that would purify his society. Despite his good intentions, his efforts had tragic, unintended consequences. His reforms produced a deep schism within the Naqshbandi community in Gansu and led to the development of a lasting suspicion of his followers on the part of a group of Chinese government officials. The result was a series of violent episodes that have haunted the history of the Chinese Muslim community.

Ma Mingxin spent twenty years in Arabia. For most of that time he was a student at several Naqshbandi zawiyas, especially the important center in Zabid. Ma shared the typical reformer's revulsion toward shrine visits and the veneration of saints. In addition, at Zabid, he was persuaded by some of the leading Naqshbandis to adopt the practice of the spoken dhikr in place of the more characteristic Naqshbandi practice of the silent dhikr. After twenty years in Arabia, Ma Mingxin left for home. His arrival in Gansu occurred only two years after the Chinese government had seized Xinjiang from the Oirats and had chased rebellious Naqshbandi khwajas into Central Asia.

The returning pilgrim wasted no time in implementing his reforms. He and his followers began criticizing other Chinese Muslims for their assimilation into Chinese culture. They opposed such practices as the use of incense, the veneration of saints, tomb visitation, and the retention of traditional Chinese burial practices. Ma's group also insisted on the requirement of using the vocal dhikr. Their dhikr was often accompanied by rhythmic swaying, hand movements, and even ecstatic dancing to the accompaniment of music. Because Ma's proposed reforms were so different from traditional Naqshbandi practices in Gansu, they were called the New Teaching.

Ma became an itinerant preacher, and he went on missions throughout Gansu, the Tarim Basin, and Zungaria. His efforts to reform Islamic practice in central and western China elicited hostility from both the traditional Muslim leaders and Ch'ing authorities. Adherents of the Old Teaching and the New Teaching went beyond arguing to actual fighting, and the violence became so frequent and severe that the state intervened. Ma's opponents, who usually represented the more powerful families, were able to turn the authorities against Ma. The Ch'ing authorities, already wary of the Naqshbandiya due to their recent clash with the khwajas of the Tarim Basin, were quick to react to disturbances that cast doubt on their ability or legitimacy to rule. Ch'ing officials arrested Ma in 1781, and when his followers rebelled in support of him, Ma was executed. The New Teaching had become identified by imperial authorities with opposition to imperial rule. For the next century, Chinese officials were highly suspicious of any Muslim religious leader who favored the New Teaching.

The Hui were careful to maintain correct relations with their government for the next several decades. Unlike some of the Muslims of the Tarim Basin, the Hui considered themselves to be Chinese, and only a few extremists considered the government in Beijing to be illegitimate. Over the years, however, the Hui and their non-Muslim neighbors became a classic case of living together separately. The elite, Confucian-based ethic of the court regarded all other ways of life to be immoral and foreign, and nonelites were offended by a people who judged pork and beer to be illicit foods. The stereotype of the Hui held by many non-Muslim Chinese was that they were dirty, immoral, and violent. The self-identity of the Hui, on the other hand, was codified in the phrase *qing zhen,* which suggests *purity* and *truth.* They believed that their ideals of bodily cleanliness, fidelity to the Shari'a, and monotheism were superior to the values of the surrounding culture. Indeed, foreign Muslims who visited China remarked that the Hui adhered more scrupulously to Islamic dietary regulations than was common in the Arab world.[4]

Misunderstandings and mutual suspicions continued to grow during the first half of the nineteenth century. The schism between the adherents of the Old Teaching and those of the New Teaching persisted, and the cultural gap widened between the Hui and their non-Muslim neighbors. Then, at midcentury, China suffered catastrophic upheavals. The massive Taiping Rebellion (1851–1864) in southeastern China, which killed twenty to thirty million people, was followed by the Nien Rebellion (1853–1868) in central China, during which millions more died. Both rebellions were led by Han peasants against the government. The violence was on such a colossal scale that reports about it spread all over the country. Unfortunately, much of the information was composed of hearsay, rumor, and conspiracy theories. Not knowing why the violence was occurring, peasants in central China became frightened and mistrustful. As a precaution, communities formed militias in the event that trouble came their way. Unfortunately, in regions where Muslims and non-Muslims lived, people were segregated by religion affiliation. Thus, the Muslims and non-Muslims typically formed their own militias. It was all quite natural, but given preexisting suspicions, these militias and their makeshift forts appeared to be provocative to their neighbors.

Violence began between Hui and their non-Muslim neighbors in Yunnan province in 1855, when non-Muslims, having exhausted their own gold and silver mines, tried to evict Muslims from theirs. Seven years later, a major war broke out in Shaanxi when Muslims and non-Muslims argued over the price of a bamboo pole. Refugees from Shaanxi fled to Gansu and Ningxia, where they claimed that the Ch'ing government was planning to exterminate all Hui in China. Since Gansu and Ningxia composed the area that was the center of the New Teaching, many Muslims feared a renewed campaign of government terror against them, and they attacked government forces.

This massive wave of hysterical fighting, which lasted from 1862 until 1873, is known as the Great Rebellion. Like the other rebellions of the period, it had no single cause. Many people participated simply for self-preservation, rather than to accomplish a goal. Although part of the Hui community was loyal to the government, the Shaanxi refugees and most followers of the New Teaching fought the government. The Great Rebellion concluded the series of major upheavals in China that lasted from 1851 to 1873, during which an estimated sixty million people died. The Muslim rebellion resulted in the disappearance of ninety-five percent of the one million Muslims who had lived in Shaanxi prior to the war. The government tried—and nearly succeeded—in exterminating all followers of the New Teaching in Gansu and Ningxia. Tens of thousands of Hui refugees fled to Xinjiang and across the Pamirs into what are today Kyrgyzstan and Kazakhstan, where they settled permanently.

Southeast Asia

In Southeast Asia, a jihad movement developed first not in Java or Aceh, but in the region of Minangkabau, located on the middle third of the southwestern coast of Sumatra. During the heyday of the Spice Island trade, Minangkabau was a source of gold. Thus, even though it was not on the Strait of Melaka, it attracted shipping from all over the Indian Ocean and East Asia. Muslims were reported to be among its residents in the sixteenth century. By the 1780s, the supply of gold was dwindling, but other products from the region—salt, coffee, and textiles—were increasingly in demand. Whereas the gold supplies had been controlled by the local aristocracy, the new products were produced by peasants and distributed by merchants who had no ties to the social elites.

As these changes were taking place in Minangkabau's economy, a new group of Muslims began to appear in the region, a group that was particularly noteworthy due to its impact throughout the Indian Ocean during the eighteenth and nineteenth centuries. For reasons that are not yet clear, the number of people emigrating from Hadramawt (located in extreme southeastern Yemen) began to increase after the middle of the eighteenth century. Many of these were *sayyid*s (a synonym of *sharif*s, or descendants of the Prophet). They moved throughout the Indian Ocean basin, from East Africa to Malaya. In Southeast Asia, they settled in numerous port cities of the mainland and the archipelago. Because of their pedigree, they were much desired as husbands for women of high status, and they rapidly assimilated into the power elite. Some actually became rulers of city–states, whereas others served as qadis, envoys, and advisors. By the end of the eighteenth century, many ruling families in the western half of the island chain had sayyid blood. Several Hadramawtis made their way to Minangkabau, where they opened Islamic schools. Promoting a strict adherence to the Shari'a, the immigrants sparked a reform movement within the older Muslim community of Minangkabau during the 1780s.

In 1803, several pilgrims from Minangkabau performed the hajj only a few months after the Wahhabis captured Mecca. Perhaps inspired by the dynamism of the Wahhabi movement, they assumed leadership of the ongoing Minangkabau reform movement when they returned home. Under their leadership, it became known as the Padri Movement. Members of the Padri Movement called for stricter adherence to the Shari'a and attacked such obvious targets as gambling, cockfighting, and the use of opium and alcohol. They also criticized features of Minangkabau's famous matrilineal social system, in which all ancestral property was inherited by women. Local dowry customs, marriage rites, inheritance rules, and patterns of domestic residence were all products of this system, and all were contrary to elements of the Shari'a. The Muslim reformers were particularly incensed by the claim of divinity made by the royal family of Minangkabau. One surprising feature of the Padri Movement that seems incongruous with its Wahhabi inspiration was that its leaders did not criticize the veneration of saints or holy places.

The leaders of the Padri Movement declared a jihad against the royal family and their aristocratic allies. Their main support came from the members of the social classes that were involved in the new export trade, who resented the taxes and confiscations to which the aristocracy subjected them. In 1815, the rebels murdered most of the royal family and seized control of the greater part of Minangkabau. The surviving members of the royal family and several of the notables met with Dutch officials and asked them to take control of the region in return for eradicating the rebels. Due to the Dutch preoccupation with a war on Java, little progress was made against the Padri leaders for several years, but in 1830 the colonial authorities were able to shift troops from Java to Sumatra. By 1838, they had destroyed the Padri Movement and were in control of the region. In an ironic twist, the jihad that had begun as an effort to implement the authority of the Shari'a in Minangkabau proved instead to be the catalyst that precipitated colonial rule in the region. Nevertheless, all contemporary observers agreed that the movement brought about a deeper Islamization of Minangkabau society.

West Africa

Almost simultaneously with the outbreak of the Padri Movement, a jihad broke out in West Africa that began a permanent transformation of the region. The Fulbe-speaking community that spread out from Senegal across a vast swath of West Africa during the sixteenth and seventeenth centuries was destined to become the instrument of major changes. By the late eighteenth century, the Fulbe were well versed in Islam and had produced several serious religious scholars. In many places in West Africa, they had never been fully accepted by long-established ethnic groups. Outnumbered and sensitive to slights and perceived exploitation, they began to accentuate their Muslim identity. They stressed Islamic themes of justice and righteousness, and they were impatient with the behavior of their neighbors, non-Muslim and nominal Muslim alike. In Chapter 4, we saw that one group of Fulbe fought a jihad in Guinea between 1725 and 1750 that produced a new state. In the 1770s, another jihad led to Fulbe domination along the Senegal. These wars were precursors of three major Fulbe jihads in the nineteenth century.

In Hausaland, the northern region of modern Nigeria, a well-educated Fulbe scholar and preacher named Uthman dan Fodio (1754–1817) began an itinerant preaching ministry during the 1780s. For more than a decade, he called upon Muslims to follow Qur'anic prescriptions regarding food prohibitions and modesty, and he preached against dancing and the use of music. He made a special point of criticizing the deeply embedded customs of divination, the use of magic, and the veneration of rocks and trees. In contrast to most other major reformers of the era, he defended the practice of visits to shrines as well as the belief that holy men perform miracles.

If Dan Fodio had remained focused on issues of ritual purity, he would have been little noticed by the Hausa political elites of his city–state, Gobir. He attracted their attention when he criticized the enslaving of Muslims by Muslim chiefs and the failure of rulers to enforce the Shari'a. In 1794, Gobir's ruler, Yunfa, threatened Dan Fodio, whereupon the latter's preaching and writing began to take a more adversarial tone. Dan Fodio moved out of Yunfa's territory, but in 1804, Yunfa attacked his settlement, killing several of Dan Fodio's followers. In response, Dan Fodio declared a jihad against him and the rulers of any Hausa city–states who were not enforcing the Shari'a. Like the jihad of Ibn 'Abd al-Wahhab, Dan Fodio's campaign was directed against rulers who regarded themselves as Muslims and whose advisers were ulama.

The call for the jihad touched a chord of widespread resentment against Hausa rulers, and Dan Fodio attracted numerous followers. By 1808 his forces captured Gobir, and in the following year he created a new capital, Sokoto. The new Sokoto Caliphate sprawled over a huge area between the lower Niger River and Lake Chad. Rather than being a centralized empire, it was composed of a large number of semi-autonomous states nominally subordinate to Sokoto. Dan Fodio held the title of caliph, but after 1810 he interpreted that role to be the spiritual teacher of the people of the region. He turned administrative responsibilities over to his brother Abdullah and son Muhammad Bello. They remained the most important political figures in the caliphate until their deaths in 1837 and 1842, respectively. Dan Fodio's daughter, Nan Asma'u, was as highly educated as her father, uncle, and brother, and became famous for her efforts to spread literacy among the women of Hausaland. She wrote poetry in Hausa and Arabic as well as in the local Fulbe dialect of Fulfulde.

Uthman dan Fodio Declares a Jihad

This selection contains extracts from the manifesto issued by Uthman dan Fodio (rendered Ibn Fudi here) justifying the declaration of jihad against Hausa rulers. Notice his arrogation of the title Commander of the Faithful, or Caliph. This was the title given to the successors of the Prophet Muhammad. Uthman does not justify his use of the title, but expects Muslims to submit to his caliphal authority. Note also that some of the clauses are obligations that Muslims owe to God, whereas others are crimes that the Hausa rulers have committed.

In the name of God, the Merciful, the Compassionate. May God bless our master Muhammad, with his family and his companions, and welcome [them] with greetings.

Praise be to God who has bestowed upon us his dispensation of Islam and guided us by our lord and master Muhammad, on whom from God the Exalted be most gracious blessings and noble salutation.

After which, this is a dispatch from Ibn Fudi, the Commander of the Faithful, Uthman, to all the folk of the Sudan, and to whomso God wills of the brethren in the (Hausa) States; it is a dispatch advantageous in the present times. Thus speak I, and success comes of God.

Know then, my brethren, that the commanding of righteousness is obligatory by assent and that the prohibition of evil is obligatory by assent, and that hijra from the land of the heathen is obligatory by assent.

And that the appointment of the Commander of the Faithful is obligatory by assent and that obedience to him and to all his deputies is obligatory by assent and that the waging of jihad is obligatory by assent.

And that by assent the status of a town is the status of its ruler: If he be Muslim, the town belongs to Islam, but if he be heathen, the town is a town of heathendom from which hijra is obligatory.

And that to make war upon the heathen king who will not say "There is no god but Allah" on account of the custom of his town and who makes no profession of Islam, is obligatory by assent, and that to take the government from him is obligatory by assent.

And that to make war upon the king who is an apostate—who has not abandoned the religion of Islam as far as the profession of it is concerned, but who mingles the observances of Islam with the observances of heathendom, like the kings of Hausaland for the most part—is also obligatory by assent, and that to take the government from him is obligatory by assent.

And that to make war upon backsliding Muslims who do not own allegiance to any of the Emirs of the Faithful is obligatory by assent, if they be summoned to give allegiance and they refuse, until they enter into allegiance.

And that the anathematizing of Muslims on a pretext of heretical observances is unlawful by assent, and that the anathematizing of Muslims for disobedience is unlawful by assent, and that residence in enemy territory is unlawful by assent.

And that to make war upon the Muslims who are residing in Muslim territory is unlawful by assent, and that wrongfully to devour their property is unlawful by assent, and that to enslave the freeborn among the Muslims is unlawful by assent.

(Continued)

And that to make war upon the heathen to whom peace has been granted is unlawful by assent; wrongfully to devour their property is unlawful by assent, and to enslave them is unlawful by assent.

SOURCE: A. D. H. Bivar, "The Wathiqat Ahl Al-Sudan: A Manifesto of the Fulani Jihad." *Journal of African History*, 2, No. 2 (1962): 239–241.

Sokoto became the model for many West African Muslims who were dismayed by the disparity between what they considered to be the norms of Islam and the actual practice of self-proclaimed Muslim rulers. One of Sokoto's admirers was another Fulbe, Seku Ahmadu (1773–1845), who preached in the inland delta of the Niger River, a region known as Masina. Seku Ahmadu launched his own jihad in 1818. Unlike Dan Fodio, whose jihad was underlain by the ethnic differences between Fulbe rebels and Hausa rulers, Seku Ahmadu attacked Fulbe leaders, whom he charged with heresy. He captured several cities in Masina—notably the venerable city of Jenne—and founded a new capital city of Hamdullahi (a variant of the Arabic phrase meaning "God be praised"). Masina was much more centralized than Sokoto, and it became known as a strict enforcer of the Shari'a. Mosques and Qur'anic schools were established in every village, and each governor set up his own council of ulama, which served as his advisory council. The land of non-Muslims was declared state land, and non-Muslims were degraded to a status akin to that of serfs. As Seku Ahmadu consolidated his power, his state became a rival of Sokoto for influence in the Niger River valley, but Hamdullahi's prestige declined after his death in 1845. Non-Islamic festivals were once again celebrated at the court, and a rift developed between succeeding rulers and important religious scholars. Some religious leaders even questioned the legitimacy of the dynasty to rule.

The final major jihad in nineteenth-century West Africa was led by another Fulbe, al-Hajj Umar Tal (c. 1797–1864), a native of Senegal. As a young man, he went to Guinea for advanced study and then gained his title of al-Hajj by going on pilgrimage in 1828. The title, always a badge of honor, was particularly unusual in West Africa and distinguished him from the other leaders of the Fulbe jihads. He studied for two years in Mecca and then moved to Sokoto, where he spent the period 1831–1838. During the course of those years, he enjoyed a close relationship with Muhammad Bello and developed a reputation as a great scholar, a powerful preacher, and an outstanding military leader. Returning to Guinea, he began cultivating a reputation as an advocate for transforming West Africa into a society that adhered to the Shari'a.

Al-Hajj Umar's decade-long career of conducting jihads began in 1852. His methods differed from those of Dan Fodio and Seku Ahmadu in two major respects. First, whereas the previous jihad leaders had conducted campaigns to transform their own societies, al-Hajj Umar recruited Fulbe warriors to overthrow regimes in other regions. Second, Dan Fodio and Seku Ahmadu regarded a person's Sufi membership to be a personal decision, but al-Hajj Umar was an aggressive Tijani Sufi, who forced Muslims to join the Tijaniya.

During the period 1852–1862, al-Hajj Umar brought under his control a region that extended for more than a thousand miles, from the middle Senegal River valley almost to Timbuktu. He began by defeating a non-Muslim ruler to the east of Guinea and then took over the middle and upper valley of the Muslim-dominated Senegal River and its tributaries. He then laid siege to the large non-Muslim city of Segu and captured it after an epic battle in February 1861. Muslims all over West Africa and North Africa heralded the conquest as a major advance for the cause of Islam.

Al-Hajj could not feel complete satisfaction over his victory. He was angry at the ruler of Hamdullahi, the grandson of Seku Ahmadu, who had refused to join al-Hajj in the war against Segu. In fact, it was quite clear that Hamdullahi had been actively cooperating with Segu in recent years. In al-Hajj's mind, that meant that the ruler of Hamdullahi was an apostate; al-Hajj launched an attack on Hamdullahi, in which massive armies of Muslims fought each other, and tens of thousands died. The grotesque blood-letting led to the formation of an alliance of Muslims and non-Muslims in the region who feared that it was only a matter of time before they would be killed by al-Hajj. The leaders of Timbuktu took the lead in the alliance. They attacked Segu and killed al-Hajj, who was hiding in a cave. Members of al-Hajj's family subsequently managed to regain control of several cities in the region, but they became rivals of each other and fought continuous wars for the next twenty years. The region of Masina, which had been a prosperous agricultural region prior to al-Hajj's conquest of Segu, was devastated.

The period of the great West African jihads (1804–1864) yielded a mixed legacy (see Map 8.1). There is no doubt that this was the period during which Islam became firmly rooted in the region. The almost continuous warfare broke up the old religious and social structures in many areas. Massacres, slave-raiding, and the destruction of the symbols and meeting houses of the traditional religions destroyed the old order. Many individuals who became nominal Muslims during this period out of compulsion or desperation eventually developed into active and productive Muslims. As a result, the French and British discovered that much of this region was operating under a fully functioning Islamic legal system when they carved it up into imperial territories later in the nineteenth century and early twentieth century.

The price that the inhabitants of West Africa had to pay for this period of Islamization was very high. Each of the three jihad states had begun as attempts to embody the highest spiritual ideals, but they evolved into unpopular despotisms, wracked by succession disputes and factional rivalries. By the time that al-Hajj Umar's campaign captured Segu, it was little more than a looting expedition. Even the governors that al-Hajj placed in control of the major cities ruled by terror and seized property arbitrarily. Al-Hajj's campaign against Masina was met with revulsion by Muslims and non-Muslims alike in West Africa. The call to jihad had begun to sound like a call for plunder, murder, and famine. The Masina campaign discredited the jihad ideal, and subsequent calls for jihad in West Africa met with a limited following, even against invading European armies later in the century. It was abundantly clear in the aftermath of Masina that the successor states to al-Hajj Umar's jihad had as their purpose the pursuit of Fulbe privilege and power rather than the strengthening of Islam. The systems of Islamic law and the charitable organizations that became established in West Africa were created largely by private initiative, not by the Islamic states for whose creation so many people gave their lives.

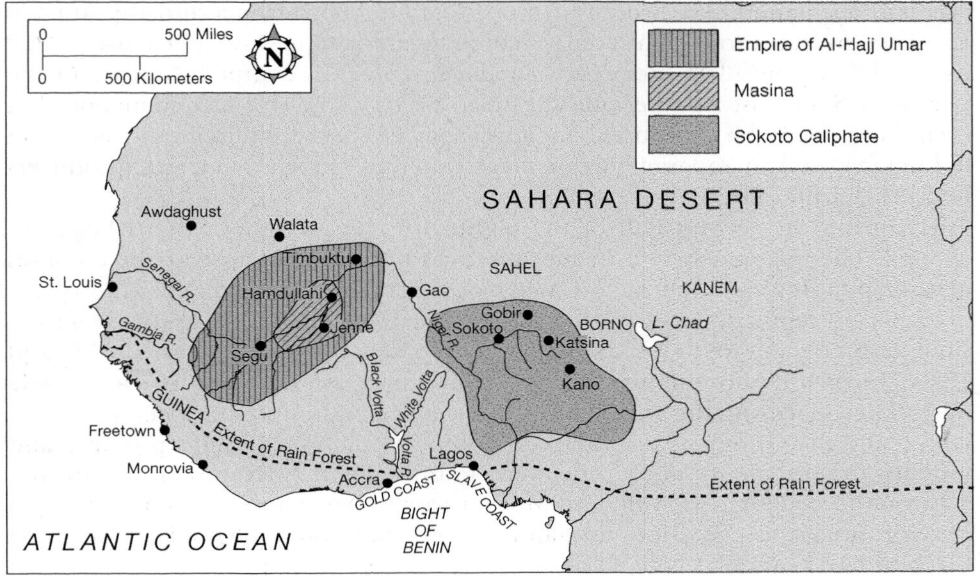

MAP 8.1 West African Jihad States.

Perhaps the greatest tragedy of the era was the ironic outcome of one of Dan Fodio's major themes. Dan Fodio's had been particularly disturbed that the elites of Gobir made no distinction between Muslims and non-Muslims when they bought slaves, and yet the jihad campaigns of the nineteenth century resulted in the enslavement of more Muslims than ever before. Prior to the nineteenth century, most of the victims of the slave trade in West Africa came from the largely non-Muslim frontier zones between the savannah and the coastal cities, and Muslims from the savannah had been among the most active raiders. Beginning with Sokoto's wars of expansion, however, losers (many of whom were Muslims) were enslaved on a major scale. The jihads of Dan Fodio and Muhammad Bello enslaved tens of thousands of Hausa and Yoruba Muslims. Many were exploited in Sokoto; others were shipped to Brazil. When the British occupied Sokoto in the early twentieth century, one-fourth of the state's roughly ten million people were slaves. Masina created slave villages populated by war captives, and at least half of the state's population were slaves. Al-Hajj Umar conquered huge areas of the western Sudan in the process of conducting his jihad. Regardless of what religious identity the victims of the wars claimed to be, al-Hajj's warriors regarded them as non-Muslims in order to justify the jihad and to enslave them. Although slavery and slave-raiding had existed in West Africa for centuries, neither had ever reached the scale they achieved in the nineteenth century.

European Intervention and Annexation

In the fifteenth century, European explorers set sail in quest of the fabled riches of the East. Some of them unexpectedly stumbled across the Americas, and it was there that subsequent generations of Europeans established colonial empires. The original destination, Asia, received much less attention. China and the Mughal Empire were too formidable even to contemplate conquering, and Japan sealed itself off from outside visitors early in the seventeenth century. Kerala and the islands of Southeast Asia became the main arena of European domination, but even there—with the exception of Spanish activities in the Philippines—the object was not to create an imperial bureaucracy but to force, at gunpoint, local producers to trade at artificially low prices.

During the second half of the eighteenth century, this pattern began to change. The colonial system in the Americas began to collapse as the colonies became populous and self-reliant. When they decided that the mercantile system of taxes and regulations was too onerous to bear any longer, it was nearly impossible to force them to do so. Many gained their independence between 1781 and 1830. Meanwhile, a dramatic shift in the European assessment of Africa and Asia was taking place. At the same time that the Mughal and Safavid empires collapsed and the Ottomans lost their aura of invincibility, economic, political, and military developments in Europe were granting both private companies and states unprecedented power. The Muslim world began to experience the first wave of foreign interventions and annexations that would plague it for the next two hundred years.

South Asia

The vacuum of power left by the gradual disintegration of the Mughal Empire was filled by several ambitious Indian rulers and by a newcomer, the English East India Company. In 1600, five years after the Dutch government chartered the VOC, the English government created the English East India Company. Its purpose, like that of the VOC, was to make large profits for its shareholders and to enhance the power of the government that created it. The English company's efforts to share in the trade of the Indian Ocean met violent resistance from the Dutch and the Portuguese. In 1622, having suffered dozens of casualties in clashes with the Dutch, the East India company abandoned its efforts to establish a base at Banten in northwestern Java. In a fortunate turn of events for the company, that was the same year that its ships helped the Safavid ruler Shah 'Abbas drive the Portuguese from Hormuz, an act that provided the company its entrée into the Iranian silk trade.

Meanwhile, the East India Company was negotiating the rights to establish a presence on the coasts of India. After some initial difficulties, it obtained the right from the Mughals to establish fortified trading centers at Bombay on the Malabar Coast and at Calcutta in Bengal. It also created a base at Madras on the Coromandel Coast, an area which the Mughals did not claim. Because of the constant threat from the Dutch and Portuguese at sea, and the possibility of attack by bandits and rogue armies on land, the company hired European and Indian mercenaries to provide protection at each of its major bases.

During the early eighteenth century, the company became embroiled in the frequent conflicts among successor states to the Mughal Empire. Its directors realized that the new, post-Mughal circumstances could work to the company's advantage if they succeeded in playing off one regional state against another and offered their own business and military services for sale to those same states. The company's three bases in India worked independently in this regard. The agents at Madras and Calcutta were more active than those at Bombay, who had to exercise caution due to their proximity to the powerful Maratha Confederation, a loose alliance of five Maratha states that controlled most of central and northern India during the second half of the eighteenth century.

The company's branch at Calcutta proved to be particularly aggressive in regional intrigues. In 1757, at the Battle of Plassey, Calcutta's army defeated the much larger army of the Nawab of Bengal. In the aftermath of the battle, the company's agents took over the reins of power from the Nawab. By 1765, they ruled over Bihar as well as Bengal. Many of the company's representatives in Bengal became fantastically wealthy in the aftermath of Plassey. It soon became clear that they had done so by confiscating property, granting themselves tax farms, and pocketing tax revenues. By the early 1770s, the corruption of the company's agents and directors had bankrupted the company in spite of the enormous amounts of revenues that it handled. The resulting scandal forced the British Parliament to become involved. During the 1770s and 1780s, Parliament passed laws that brought the company's policies under governmental oversight.

Parliament explicitly stated that conquest and any extension of dominion in India were "repugnant" to Britain, but over the next several decades, the company found it expedient to conquer vast areas of the subcontinent (see Map 8.2). Its allies frequently asked for protection against rivals, its own borders needed to be defended, and commercial and military interests in London exerted strong pressure to gain their objectives. Each conquest, in turn, produced a longer border that required protection against new, potentially hostile, neighbors. Between 1802 and 1818, the British subdued the Maratha Confederation. In 1803, the company conquered Delhi but allowed the Mughal emperor to retain his title and reign over the area within the confines of the Red Fort. During the 1840s, the British fought a series of bloody wars to gain the Indus River valley and the Punjab from the Sikhs, but lost an entire 16,000-man army in an attempt to gain control over Afghanistan. By 1850, the company was the only significant military power in India. It ruled roughly one-third of the subcontinent directly. The rest of the subcontinent was composed of several hundred "princely states" whose *rajas* ("princes") and *maharajas* ("great princes") were willing to collaborate in a system of indirect rule by accepting British advisors at their courts.

The East India Company's domination of India brought about profound changes for the people of the region. The introduction of the concept of private land ownership, intended as a reform that would make Indian agriculture more profitable, produced much the same effect as the Enclosure Acts of England had over the course of the previous century: Numerous small farmers were expelled from the land that their families had tilled for centuries. The British also set up entirely new systems of courts and procedures of justice, replaced existing taxes with new ones, and established a government monopoly over the collection and sale of salt. In 1835, the company replaced Persian with English as the medium of instruction in company schools and public administration.

The British viewed India as a vast market for the products of their industrializing economy, and so they removed obstacles to the importation of British manufactured goods. The result was that, by 1833, the entire Bengali textile industry, once the envy of the world, was in ruins. Millions of Indian craftsmen became unemployed and desperate for a means of livelihood. Indians also faced a new challenge to their religious beliefs. The English East India Company had initially resisted the entreaties of Christian missionaries to come to India, but after 1813 it progressively loosened restrictions on their activity. Missionary schools and social services served valuable functions, but many individual missionaries could not refrain from making acerbic, public criticisms of Hinduism and Islam. Some Hindus and Muslims feared that the missions' activities were part of a plot by the Company to convert them.

Indians responded in a variety of ways to the changing circumstances. Muslims were particularly incensed by the new legal system, which came at the expense of the administration of the Shari'a. One prominent critic was Shah 'Abd al-'Aziz (1746–1824) of Delhi, Shah Wali Allah's most prominent son. In response to the new legal procedures, he declared that the areas of northern India under British rule no longer belonged to the Dar al-Islam, but rather to the Dar al-Harb. His declaration had little effect other than to ease the conscience of those who lived under British rule.

Some Muslims took a more activist approach. One example was Sayyid Ahmad Barelwi. Born in 1786, he was a disciple of Shah 'Abd al-'Aziz. In the tradition of Shah Wali Allah, he was primarily concerned with internal Islamic affairs, but he was also troubled by the growth of the military and political hegemony of the British in India. He promised to free the Indo–Gangetic plain from the rule of Christians, but he never challenged the East India Company directly. Instead, he sought to reform the practice of Islam in preparation for creating a genuinely Islamic state. A practicing Sufi himself, Sayyid Ahmad echoed themes that reformers were urging all over the Muslim world. He rejected the notion of the intercession of saints and he condemned pilgrimage to Hindu holy places and participation in Hindu festivals. He moved from Oudh to the Punjab in order to create a militant, Shari'a-observing society, but his ambitions collided with those of the Sikhs of the region. He clashed with them several times and was killed in battle in 1831.

By midcentury, even Indians who had not been particularly concerned about British occupation of South Asia began to sense how dramatically their lives were changing as a result of foreign control. During the 1850s, misgivings about the new schools and increased missionary activity were exacerbated by several incidents that alienated important sections of the Indian population. The growing tension and suspicion exploded in 1857 within the ranks of the heretofore loyal Hindu and Muslim troops of the Bengal army. Soldiers had to bite off the end of the paper cartridge of their new Enfield rifled musket, and they discovered that the waterproofing coating that covered the paper contained grease. Rumors swept among the Hindus that the grease was from cows; Muslims suspected that it was lard from pigs. When British officers humiliated and discharged troops who refused to use the new cartridges, a mutiny broke out in Meerut, near Delhi. The mutiny, in turn, was the spark that led to the most vicious war India has suffered in recorded history. Large areas in north-central India—particularly the regions dominated by the cities of Delhi, Lucknow, and Kanpur (Cawnpore)—were lost to the British for a considerable period of time.

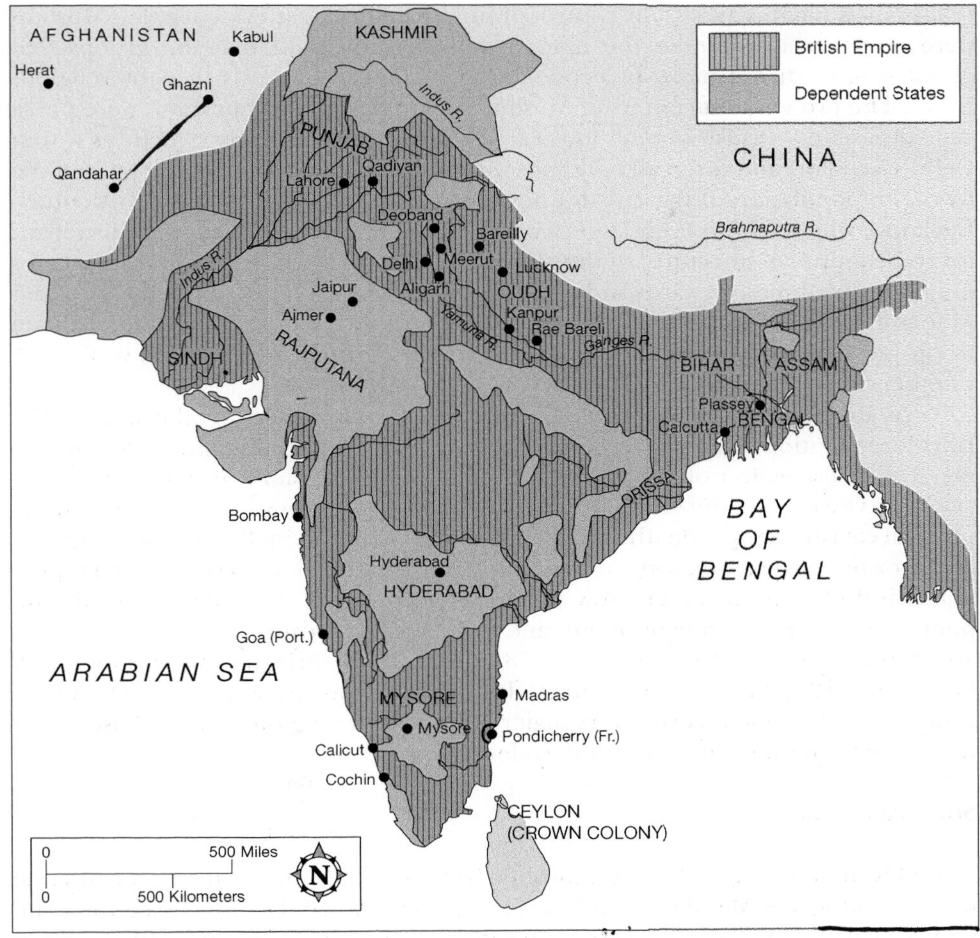

MAP 8.2 India under the British.

The revolt was not a unified movement, but rather a large number of uncoordinated uprisings by a bewildering variety of competing interest groups. Meanwhile, many Indians even in the core region of the revolt openly sided with the British. For a year and a half, the British and the rebels engaged in unspeakable atrocities and wanton murder against each other, and tens of thousands of noncombatants died. The Mughal emperor's sons were murdered in cold blood by a British officer, and the emperor was exiled to Burma. In 1858, several months before the revolt was quelled, the British government dissolved the English East India Company and took full responsibility for ruling India. India had become too important to the economy of Great Britain to allow it to slip away. A Viceroy would henceforth rule in India, and in London a Secretary of State for India sat on the Cabinet.

The war was a profound shock to the British, who were convinced that Indians should be grateful to them for bringing them the blessings of modern civilization. Influential British government ministers were convinced that the war had proved that Islam was a threat to their control of India, despite clear evidence that Muslims were no more involved in the uprising than Hindus and that the groups that rebelled were driven more by economic and political interests than by religious issues. The two greatest centers of Muslim culture, Delhi and Lucknow, were physically devastated. British demolition teams destroyed most of the structures within Delhi's Red Fort and razed all buildings within a quarter of a mile of the walls of the fort. The population of the city did not recover its prewar level for half a century. Lucknow, which was an even larger city than Delhi, was famous among Europeans for its beautiful architecture. In the aftermath of the war, a corridor over four miles long and five hundred yards wide was cleared through the heart of the city, and wide avenues were carved out through other neighborhoods in order to facilitate troop movements. Everything that lay in the path of the new avenues was razed, whether house, tomb, or mosque.

As shocked as the British were, Indians were traumatized by the scale of the British retribution. Many believed that the destruction in Delhi and Lucknow presaged the destruction of the entire culture of India. Muslims, in particular, were anxious. The exile of the Mughal emperor was a psychic blow that compounded the physical catastrophes of death and property loss. Weak and ineffectual in reality, the emperor had been a link with an imperial Muslim past and was a symbol of a potential revival of Muslim power. Now there was no pretense of independent Muslim political power in the subcontinent, and there was no prospect of it in the foreseeable future. The cataclysm of 1857–1858 (known to the British as the Sepoy Rebellion or the 1857 Mutiny and to many Indians today as the First National War of Independence) loomed over every major political and religious policy decision that was made in the subcontinent for decades to come.

Southeast Asia

The VOC had originally been established to monopolize the distribution and sale of the products of Maluku, popularly known as the Spice Islands. Once the company's headquarters were established at Batavia, however, company officials naturally took an increasing interest in the affairs of Java. By the eighteenth century, the growing profitability of the tea and coffee plantations on Java led to a general retrenchment of VOC activities outside of Java. This process accelerated after 1770, when Pierre Poivre, the governor of French-ruled Mauritius, smuggled clove, mace, and nutmeg plants out of Maluku and began cultivating them on his island. (Poivre's name is rendered "Peter Pepper" into English, and his exploit inspired the "Peter Piper" tongue-twister.) Meanwhile, the 1755 settlement of the chronic conflict between the major Javanese sultanates, Yogyakarta and Surakarta, contributed to the growth of the overall economy of the island. Agricultural productivity and population both grew. In Java, the population is estimated to have tripled from 1.5 million in 1750 to 4.5 million in 1815.

Despite the positive developments for the VOC on Java, the company declined during the second half of the eighteenth century. Its activities in the Indian Ocean and China were becoming less profitable due to increased international competition; its officials were engaged in financial corruption; and it lost seventy percent of its assets during the Anglo–Dutch War of 1780–1784. After 1792, the

Netherlands could not avoid becoming entangled in the wars of the French Revolution and suffered a French invasion in 1794. From then until 1813, it was a protectorate of France. Britain took advantage of the new situation: In the name of fighting France, British forces began seizing Dutch territories such as Capetown and Melaka (1795) and Ceylon (1796).

The loss of these territories bankrupted the VOC. The Dutch government dissolved it in 1800 and took possession of its remaining holdings in Southeast Asia. These territories, too, became targets of the British. In 1811, British military forces sent by the English East India Company captured Batavia and Dutch plantations in Maluku. Stanford Raffles, the new governor of Batavia, began reorganizing the administrative apparatus with the expectation of long-term British control of the region despite a lack of interest in the project from London.

In 1815, Mt. Tambora, on the island of Sumbawa, produced the greatest volcanic eruption in the world since the destruction of Santorini (Thera), near Crete, in 1645 B.C.E. The explosion killed 10,000 people outright, and almost 100,000 people died shortly thereafter from cholera and famine. The eruption column was twenty-eight miles high, and climatologists believe that the debris and gases that it carried aloft were the major cause of the "year without a summer" in 1816, in which snow and frost occurred throughout the year in western Europe and as far south as Virginia in the United States.

Tambora's main explosion occurred in April 1815, and the volcano continued to belch until July. In the meantime, in June, Napoleon was defeated at Waterloo. The Napoleonic wars were over, and the Congress of Vienna concluded its work. By the terms of its treaty, the British returned Batavia and Melaka to the Dutch, but they kept Capetown and Ceylon, which were of strategic value for protecting the route to India. Stanford Raffles was willing to concede Batavia, but he was outraged that London had even contemplated returning Melaka, due to the strategic importance of the strait that it controlled. In 1819, on his own initiative, he negotiated a treaty with a Malay sultan that granted the island of Singapore to Britain.

Raffles's maverick diplomacy prompted some of his superiors in London to reassess British interests in Southeast Asia. Since the early seventeenth century, the British had had little interest in the Indonesian archipelago. Their only major outpost in the region was Fort Marlborough at Benkulen (Bengkulu), on southwestern Sumatra, in the middle of a pepper-growing region. By the early nineteenth century, Britain's interest in the region had declined due to the availability of spices elsewhere. On the other hand, East India Company officials such as Raffles were aware of the need that the company had for a secure trade route between India and China.

In the new international balance of power that followed Waterloo, both the British and the Dutch realized the need to define their relative spheres of influence in Southeast Asia (see Map 8.3). They signed the Treaty of London in 1824, according to which the British would have a sphere of influence in the Malay Peninsula in return for Dutch paramountcy in the archipelago. Britain exchanged Fort Marlborough for Melaka. The British recognized all of what we know today as Indonesia to be a Dutch sphere of influence except for Aceh, which remained independent. Thus, for the first time in history, a boundary ran the length of the Strait of Melaka, separating the Malay Peninsula from the Malaysian archipelago.

The British interest in the Malay Peninsula lay in its ports. Little was known of its interior due to the region's nearly impenetrable rain forests. By the 1840s, tin was discovered in the interior, but even then, the port cities remained Britain's priority due to the need to establish coaling stations for the nation's new steam-powered ships. Most local rulers—the most powerful of whom were Malay Muslim sultans—remained practically autonomous. The Malay-dominated areas of Kelantan (extreme northeastern Malaysia), Pattani (now in southern Thailand), and Kedah (extreme northwestern Malaysia) on the west coast were distinctly Islamic in atmosphere and were famous for the number and quality of their religious instructors. By contrast, the so-called Straits Settlements of Singapore, Melaka, and Penang were strategic, cosmopolitan ports that required more careful oversight. In those cities, the British learned to delegate most important tasks to Chinese merchants and revenue farmers, who maintained networks with their kin and partners in China and throughout Southeast Asia.

Unlike the British, Dutch government officials were eager to become directly involved in the administration and economic development of their sphere of influence. They did not hesitate to become involved in suppressing the Padri Movement even though they were not able to commit their full resources to it for several years due to their involvement in the catastrophic Java War (1825–1830). The roots of the Java War lay in developments that had taken place in central Java during the first two decades of the nineteenth century. Both the Dutch and British administrators of Java of that time tried to defray the costs of the Napoleonic Wars at the expense of the Javanese. Both groups annexed lands held by Yogyakarta, depriving many Javanese officials of their livelihood. Both also raised tolls and customs duties and forced peasants to work on lands that had been rented out to Europeans and Chinese as cash-crop plantations.

During the early 1820s, a poor rice harvest, a cholera epidemic, a rise in the number of marauding gangs, and a volcano eruption were interpreted by many people as signs that the sultan of Yogyakarta had lost his right to rule. One of his sons, Prince Dipanagara, had experienced a vision as early as 1805 in which the Goddess of the Southern Seas had promised that he would become the eventual ruler of his father's kingdom. During the crises of the early 1820s, he began making contacts with village leaders, Muslim teachers, and palace officials, identifying himself with the powerful Javanese theme of the Just Prince who would end chaos and restore harmony and tranquillity. In 1825, when the Dutch tried to arrest him, he declared war. During the early stages of the war, the peasants and Muslim leaders were overwhelmingly in support of Dipanagara, whereas aristocrats were evenly divided. As the war progressed, however, many Muslim leaders became disillusioned with the un-Islamic values of the prince's retinue, with the result that they withdrew from the coalition. Other participants withdrew their support when the rebels conducted wholesale massacres of Chinese. Disease and famine killed tens of thousands of people. The Dutch finally captured Dipanagara in 1830 and sent him into exile. Over 200,000 people had died in the war, including half the population of Yogyakarta.

At the conclusion of the Java War, the Dutch began a systematic effort to organize and exploit the economic resources of Java. They began their own version of the traditional Javanese tax system whereby farmers paid their taxes in crops that were then exported through government monopolies. Under what the Dutch

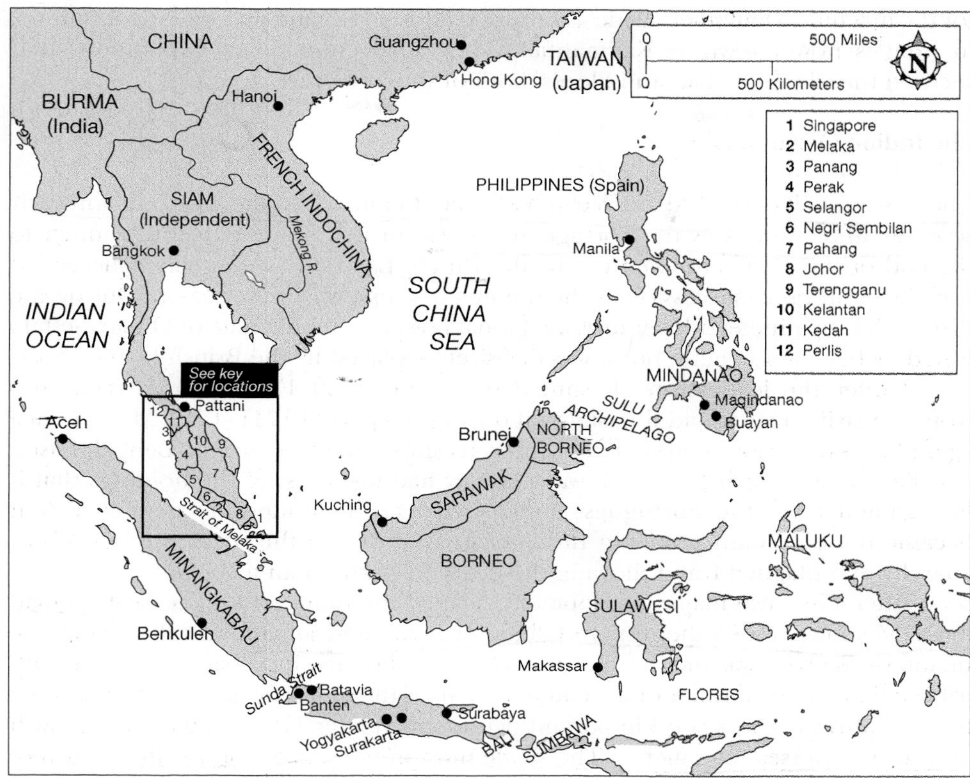

MAP 8.3 Southeast Asia under Imperialism.

called the Cultivation System, farmers were compelled to set aside a section of their farms to grow export crops. They had to pay their taxes in specified amounts of sugar, coffee, tea, tobacco, or indigo. Any surplus they raised had to be sold to the government at fixed prices. By midcentury, the profits that the government made from selling its crops accounted for one-third of the state revenues of the Netherlands. The Cultivation System was phased out in 1870, as laissez-faire economic theory spread from Britain to the Netherlands.

Both the VOC and the Dutch government became involved in the affairs of the Indonesian archipelago in order to make a profit, not to administer a territorial empire. As a result, large areas of the island chain were initially of no concern to either enterprise. The large island of Borneo was the largest of the areas that the Dutch had not made an effort to secure before midcentury. In 1840, an English adventurer named James Brooke entered the service of the sultan of Brunei and helped him suppress a challenge to his rule. As a reward, the sultan appointed Brooke as governor of Kuching, on the northwestern coast of Borneo. Over the next quarter of a century, Brooke expanded the area under his personal rule, even at the expense of the sultan's holdings. He called his kingdom Sarawak. The rapid expansion of Sarawak alarmed the Dutch, who now became more conscious of the strategic need to secure their hold over regions other than Java. During the 1840s, for the first time, Dutchmen made a concerted effort to expand into the rest of Borneo, in what is now known as Kalimantan. They also sent military expeditions that secured the islands of Bali and Flores, both of which lie east of Java.

The Indian Ocean Basin

The western half of the Indian Ocean had been dominated in the sixteenth and early seventeenth centuries by the Portuguese, and from the mid-seventeenth century to the end of the eighteenth century by the Dutch. Later, two other states succeeded each other in rapid succession as the dominant sea power in the region. During the first half of the nineteenth century, a regional power—the sultanate of Oman—established its hegemony there, but it was decisively replaced by the British by the 1860s.

Under the leadership of Ahmad ibn Sa'id (1749–1783), Oman recovered from the civil war that had devastated it during the period 1711–1749. Muscat once again became a major commercial center. Its ships sailed to Batavia, Bengal, Basra, and East Africa. During the civil war, the city had lost most of the holdings that it had gained from the Portuguese in East Africa, but under the new dynasty it became the dominant power in the Persian Gulf due to the recurring periods of anarchy that plagued Iran following the death of Nadir Shah in 1747.

After 1785, two major developments shaped the future of Oman. First, Ahmad ibn Sa'id's sons divided the responsibilities for Imam and sultan. A result was that the Imam, whose base was the interior oasis of Nizwa, became increasingly involved with tribal politics in the interior of the country, whereas the sultan focused on the maritime trade of Muscat. The second important development after 1785 was the rapid growth of Muscat's overseas commerce. The single most important reason for the growth of trade was a higher demand for slaves on France's Indian Ocean islands of Mauritius and Réunion. The closest source of slaves for the islands' spice plantations was East Africa. The French began negotiations with Muscat to use its contacts to facilitate the acquisition of slaves, and the sultans were more than happy to oblige. Zanzibar, which had been a minor slave market, became a major slave market for the first time.

The major Omani figure of the nineteenth century was Sultan Sayyid Sa'id (1807–1856). Recognizing the political and commercial possibilities in the Swahili ports, he moved to regain the control of these areas that Oman had exercised a century earlier. By 1837, several years of fierce warfare allowed him to rule all the coastal towns from Cape Delgado to southern Somalia. Recognizing the economic potential of the area, he moved the seat of his government from Muscat to Zanzibar in 1840.

Sayyid Sa'id's consolidation of the various Swahili ports stimulated economic activity in the region. In the agricultural sector, he introduced the cultivation of cloves to Zanzibar and neighboring Pemba, where immigrants from Oman were soon directing large and profitable plantations that were worked by slaves. East African cloves became a major competitor to the Dutch clove production in the East Indies. This spice became a major export in East Africa's international commerce, which blossomed during this period. With the demand for ivory and slaves also escalating, the trade between the coast and the East African interior intensified. Swahili and Arab merchants organized caravans that carried cloth, wire, beads, and guns to be traded primarily for ivory and slaves, but also for rubber, millet, and coconuts.

The increased economic opportunities stimulated immigration into the region. Sayyid Sa'id encouraged Khoja and Bohra merchants from Gujarat to immigrate, and he granted them religious freedom. They continued to play a salient role in the region's economy until the last third of the twentieth century. Sunni Arabs from Hadramawt also arrived in significant numbers. Most possessed minimal skills, but others were religious scholars who were lured by the new mosques and schools that merchants and plantation owners had built by virtue of their newly gained wealth. East African Muslims finally had access to local centers of Islamic education. Qadis were now available to administer the Shari'a, and the Hadramawti scholars translated a large body of devotional materials from Arabic into Swahili for those who would not have the chance to become fluent in Arabic. It was during this period that modern Swahili became heavily Arabized and that the influence of Islam began to be felt beyond the immediate coastline.

Sayyid Sa'id's accomplishments were a success story from the Omani perspective, but they were not always a boon for the indigenous people. The sultan funneled the import and export trade through Zanzibar at the expense of the other ports, which declined. Arab immigrants did not assimilate into local Swahili society and gave the distinct impression that they viewed the Swahili population with disdain. Thousands of slaves were required to work on the new plantations, and hundreds of thousands of slaves were seized in the interior of Africa to satisfy the growing demand for them. The armed caravans that began frequenting the trails to the interior wrought havoc in the region: Slave traders in the caravans encouraged villagers to go to war on one another in order to enslave each other. By the 1840s, all the inhabitants in the vast region between Lake Victoria and Lake Malawi feared for their lives and freedom. For several decades, villages were burned, people who resisted being captured were butchered, fields were abandoned, and vast numbers were forced to make the arduous trek to the coast to be sold into slavery.

When Sayyid Sa'id died in 1856, his sons quarreled over who should succeed him. Great Britain offered to mediate the quarrel, and the result was a division of the Omani empire in 1861. One brother acquired Zanzibar and its East African dependencies, and the other received Muscat and Oman. Because Zanzibar was the wealthier of the two areas, its ruler agreed to pay an annual subsidy to Muscat and Oman.

Britain was an acceptable mediator in the dispute because of a long history of Omani–British relations. In the first decade of the nineteenth century, Britain had become concerned about the growing French–Omani friendship that was based on Oman's role as a middleman in supplying slaves to French-owned Mauritius. Britain threatened to cut off Oman's trade with India if it did not break diplomatic relations with France. When Oman complied with the demand, Britain became its ally.

British interests soon took on a wider scope in the western half of the Indian Ocean. By the end of the eighteenth century, several tribes along the Arab side of the Persian Gulf—particularly those of the fearsome confederation led by the Qasimi tribe—had acquired a reputation for attacking ships in the Gulf. Due to their exploits, the coastline that extended for a little more than three hundred miles westward from the Strait of Hormuz came to be known as the Pirate Coast. In 1819, the English East India Company, with Oman's consent, destroyed the ships of the Qasimi fleet. The following year, the company's directors from Bombay began signing truces, or treaties, with the major tribes along the Gulf coast of the peninsula. The

British and the Arab tribes found that, by cooperating, they could satisfy their own interests. The British promised mediation and protection services, while the Arabs agreed to stop attacking international shipping and to stop the local slave trade. Because of the various treaties that the tribal shaykhs signed with Britain, the former Pirate Coast came to be known as the Trucial Coast, and the various tribal entities were known as the Trucial States. (These were the six components of the modern United Arab Emirates that faced the Persian Gulf; the seventh emirate, al-Fujayrah, faces the Gulf of Oman.) Britain also began signing similar treaties with the leaders of Bahrain, Qatar, and Kuwait. British interests in the peninsula were secured when the Bombay office of the East India Company seized Aden in 1839.

The Caucasus and Central Asia

Large swaths of Muslim-majority areas in the Caucasus Isthmus and Central Asia came under Russian control during the eighteenth and nineteenth centuries. The process began during the reign of Peter the Great (1689–1725), who was trying to overcome Russia's physical isolation. When he came to the throne, Russia lacked access to the Baltic Sea and Black Sea, and its southern frontiers were defined by the towering Caucasus Mountains and the hostile Safavid territories along the western coast of the Caspian Sea. Peter gained access to the Baltic Sea at the expense of the Swedes, but he could not dislodge the Ottomans from the northern coast of the Black Sea. He then turned to the Caucasus in order to secure a commercial route to Iran and the rest of southwestern Asia. The Afghan destruction of the Safavids in 1722 gave Peter the opportunity he had been seeking. In the vacuum of power that developed after the fall of Esfahan, Peter seized territories all along the western and southern coasts of the Caspian Sea. These proved to be only temporary gains that he lost to Iran's Nadir Shah when the latter consolidated power in Mashhad in the 1730s. Peter's only lasting achievement in the region was to establish fortresses at the mouth of the Terek River, which follows the northern edge of the Caucasus Mountains and flows eastward into the Caspian Sea. Over the next several decades, more fortresses, which were garrisoned by Cossacks, were built all along the Terek. The annexation of Crimea in 1783 opened the way for a further extension of the forts, and by 1832, the Cossack Line extended all the way from the Caspian Sea to the Sea of Azov. The security promised by the forts stimulated the immigration of large numbers of Russian colonists into the region along the Terek during the late eighteenth century.

While the Russians were building forts and colonizing the Terek valley, they were also cementing relations with Georgia, which lay to the south of the Caucasus Mountains. Both Russia and Georgia identified with the Orthodox Church, and after centuries of knowing little about each other, both had reasons for drawing together more closely. At the same time that the Russians were wanting to extend their influence into the region south of the Caucasus Mountains (Transcaucasia), Georgians were becoming desperate for aid from outside powers. Georgians had a proud history, and they wistfully recalled a great medieval Georgian kingdom that had dominated Transcaucasia prior to the depredations of the Mongols. Over the centuries after that catastrophe, their country had become a devastated battleground between the Ottomans and Safavids.

After the collapse of the Safavids, conditions did not improve for Georgia. In the absence of central authority, Turkish tribes in Transcaucasia began a fratricidal warfare that was as devastating for farmers and city folk as any of the conflicts between the Ottomans and Safavids. The Georgian king began negotiations with Russia for military protection, but the clear signs that Georgia was seeking Russian aid led to an Iranian military expedition against Tbilisi in 1795. The city was sacked, thousands of people were butchered, and thousands of others were taken away into slavery.

The atrocity at Tbilisi provoked calls on both sides of the Caucasus for Russia to come to Georgia's aid. In 1800, the Russians did so on their own terms: Rather than allying with Georgia, Russia annexed the country, murdering the Georgian ruling family in the process. In 1804, Russia moved south of Georgia to annex the Iranian territories of Armenia and Azerbaijan. Russian expansion provoked two fierce wars with Iran, but in 1828, Tehran was forced to agree to a common border along the Aras River, which to this day remains the northwestern border of Iran (see Map 8.4).

By claiming responsibility for regions in Transcaucasia, the Russians set themselves a daunting task. A physical obstacle to Russia's line of communications with Transcaucasia was one of the greatest mountain ranges in the world. The Caucasus Mountains extend for over seven hundred miles, and only narrow coastal plains separate them from the Black Sea to the west and the Caspian Sea to the east. The range is more imposing than any in Europe: It contains seventeen peaks that are higher than Mont Blanc, the highest point in the Alps.

Another obstacle that thwarted Russian plans in Transcaucasia for several decades was the large number of autonomous societies in the mountains and foothills of the northern slopes of the mountains. The Caucasus Isthmus was inhabited by a greater variety of ethnic groups than any other region of comparable size in the world. The ancestors of these groups had migrated into the hills, ravines, and mountains in order to escape the grasp of central authority. They were suspicious of outsiders, and most were determined to preserve their autonomy. Because of the difficult terrain, the various groups had developed separate identities and allegiances. As the Russians moved to consolidate their hold on the region, they inevitably provoked a reaction from the local inhabitants. To compound the antagonism, many of the communities on the flanks and northern slopes of the Caucasus mountain range were at least nominally Muslim. In many cases, therefore, economic, social, and political differences became exacerbated by religious ones.

The Russian effort to secure control of the region between the Caspian Sea and Black Sea required over six decades of fierce fighting. On the eastern coast of the Black Sea, the Circassians (Cherkess) fought fiercely against Russian efforts to secure the area. The Circassians had combined Christian and animistic elements during the period in which the Egyptian Mamlukes obtained their slave boys from the region (to 1517). As the Ottomans annexed the area in the late sixteenth century, most Circassians slowly lost their Christian identity and began combining Islamic and animistic elements. Neither Christianity nor Islam was ever the primary identity marker for Circassians, and many Circassian families included Muslim, Christian, and animistic members who encountered no problems relating to each other.

Religion, therefore, played only a secondary role in Circassian resistance to Russian encroachment during the late eighteenth and nineteenth centuries. The conflict was, nonetheless, extremely bitter. From the 1820s on, the Russians sent

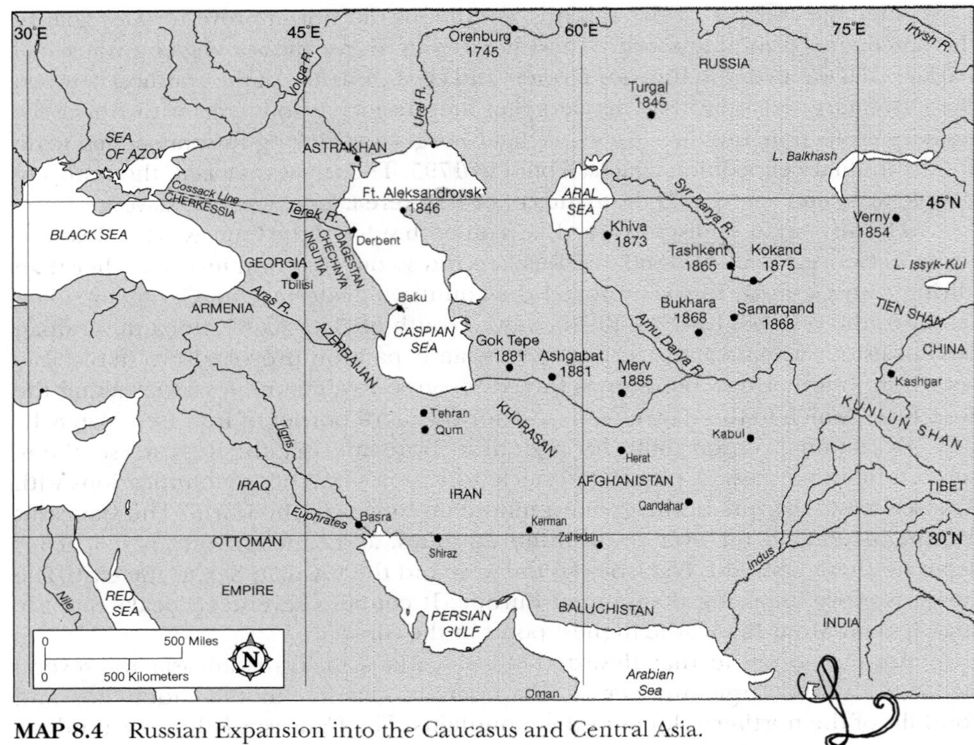

MAP 8.4 Russian Expansion into the Caucasus and Central Asia.

several expeditions into the area, and they frequently employed a scorched-earth policy. After their humiliating defeat in the Crimean War (1853–1856), the Russians were determined to take firm control of Circassian territory. During the period 1861–1864, their ruthless policy made it clear that Circassians would have to flee or be exterminated. Many, in fact, were murdered, and an estimated 800,000–1,000,000 fled for their lives into Ottoman territories.

In the eastern half of the Caucasus range, the Dagestanis and Chechens fought the most famous war against Russian expansion. The coastal plain of Dagestan, which had been captured by Arab forces of the Umayyad dynasty in the eighth century, was known for producing outstanding scholars of the Arabic language and religious studies. The city of Derbent was a cosmopolitan center of scholarship and international trade. Despite its role as a regional seat of government for the Safavid dynasty, Sunni Islam and Arabic culture predominated over Shiʿism and Persian influences. Due to trade and the work of missionaries, the Dagestani hill country also became Islamized over the centuries.

Chechnya and Ingushetia lay west of Dagestan on the northern slopes of the Caucasus Mountains. Like Dagestan, they encompassed a variety of land forms. They extended southward from the rich agricultural valley of the Terek River into heavily forested foothills, and then rose into remote mountain valleys that lay at altitudes of several thousands of feet. Missionaries from Dagestan introduced Islam into the area in the second half of the sixteenth century, but Islamic beliefs and rituals became

widely accepted there only in the eighteenth century. Visitors to the region during the last quarter of the eighteenth century reported that Chechens (who call themselves Nokhchi) and Ingush blended Islamic practices with traditional animistic elements in a colorful syncretism.

The Ingush reacted sullenly to the Russian colonization of the Terek plain and to Russian military forays into the Causasus Mountains en route to Transcaucasia; the Dagestanis and Chechens resisted fiercely. The Russians responded with military expeditions that only increased the ferocity of the resistance. In 1817, Russia began to wage a war of mass terror and genocide in its efforts to subdue Dagestan and Chechnya. Naqshbandi Sufi shaykhs led the most effective resistance. The most famous of the shaykhs was the Dagestani Imam Shamil, who frustrated the Russians in Chechnya from 1834 until his capture in 1859. His brilliant resistance made him an admired and legendary figure even in Christian Europe. The war in the Caucasus lasted half a century, and Russia had as many 200,000 troops in the field at one time. Tens of thousands on both sides lost their lives.

In addition to the Caucasus, the Russians wanted to gain control of Central Asia. For centuries, Central Asia was known to Russians as the source of precious goods that came to them through Mongol middlemen. When, in the sixteenth century, Muscovy annexed Astrakhan and Kazan, Russians began dealing directly with the Central Asian entrepôts. Commerce with the Central Asian oasis cities was hazardous, however. Both major routes—across the Kazakh steppe and between the Caspian Sea and the Aral Sea—were vulnerable to nomadic raiders. Every Russian heard tales of Russians who had been captured and sold into slavery by Central Asians. During the 1730s, in order to protect themselves against Kazakh raids, the Russians constructed the famous Orenburg Line, a series of forty-six forts and twice that many fortified outposts along the Ural River.

The Kazakh steppe offered both a route to the commercial cities of the south and potential agricultural wealth. Russia's wars with the Ottoman Empire, Iran, and the peoples of the Caucasus delayed any meaningful expansion into the steppe until after 1830, when non-Kazakh nomads attacked the Kazakhs from both the east and the west. The attacks were so severe that the Kazakhs were forced to request Russian military assistance against their enemies. The Russians obliged by erecting forts in the region. Moscow then used the forts as bases to annex Kazakhstan between the 1840s and the 1860s. The Russian conquest of Kazakhstan was significant not just for the expansion of Russian territory, but also for its role as a catalyst for the Islamization of the Kazakh people. The Kazakhs, who had been little influenced by Islam prior to the eighteenth century, sought help in their struggle against Russia from the Muslim cities of Transoxiana. They acquired little effective military aid from the ancient centers of Islamic culture, but they did receive religious guidance. The war of conquest by Christian Russia quickly generated a powerful self-conscious Islamic identity among many Kazakhs who were new to Islam, but who came to interpret the war as a religious one as much as a territorial one.

Russia secured the Caucasus in 1859 and annexed the whole of Kazakhstan by the early 1860s. Troops that were not required for the subsequent Circassian campaign were then sent to the Syr Darya River in order to conquer Transoxiana. Not having to fight in rugged mountains or to chase highly mobile nomads, the Russian army made quick work of the urban oasis settlements. It captured Tashkent in 1865, Bukhara and Samarqand in 1868, Kiva in 1873, and Kokand in 1875.

North Africa

North Africa was the section of the Muslim world most familiar to many Europeans because of its location on the southern shores of the Mediterranean. The region had been the setting of the monumental power struggle between Habsburg Spain and the Ottoman Empire during the sixteenth century, and it was the base for the corsairs who plagued European shipping for centuries. Due to the weakening of central power in Istanbul, the Regencies had achieved a de facto autonomy within the Ottoman Empire by the eighteenth century. Simultaneously, the hostility that Europeans and North Africans had developed for each other during the heyday of the corsairing period, the Reconquista, and the Ottoman–Hapsburg conflict gradually diminished. The only remaining irritant was that of the corsairs, but the frequency of their actions was abating: European navies became more adept at neutralizing their attacks, and the rulers of the Regencies began restricting the activities of corsairs in exchange for protection money paid by European shippers. As a result, the volume of trade between North Africa and Europe began to rise during the eighteenth century. North Africa resumed its former role as a source of grain, wool, and hides for Europe. The Napoleonic wars of the period 1800–1815 enhanced these commercial links, for the British needed meat for their sailors docking at Malta, and their French enemies bought North African grain to supply their armies.

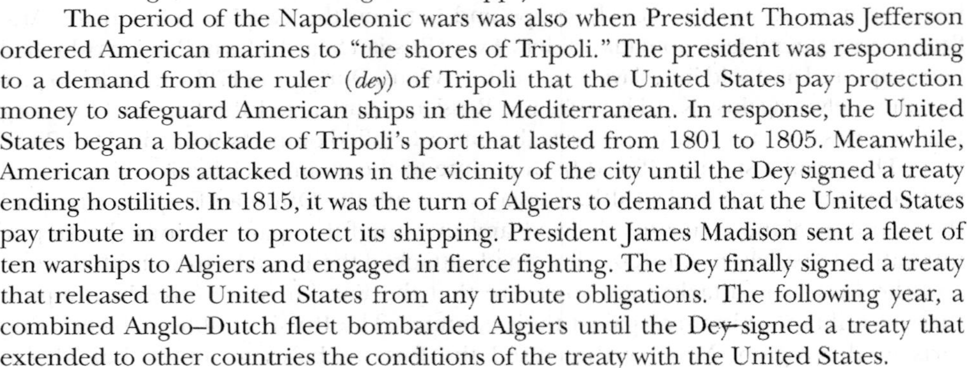

The period of the Napoleonic wars was also when President Thomas Jefferson ordered American marines to "the shores of Tripoli." The president was responding to a demand from the ruler (*dey*) of Tripoli that the United States pay protection money to safeguard American ships in the Mediterranean. In response, the United States began a blockade of Tripoli's port that lasted from 1801 to 1805. Meanwhile, American troops attacked towns in the vicinity of the city until the Dey signed a treaty ending hostilities. In 1815, it was the turn of Algiers to demand that the United States pay tribute in order to protect its shipping. President James Madison sent a fleet of ten warships to Algiers and engaged in fierce fighting. The Dey finally signed a treaty that released the United States from any tribute obligations. The following year, a combined Anglo–Dutch fleet bombarded Algiers until the Dey signed a treaty that extended to other countries the conditions of the treaty with the United States.

In the aftermath of the Napoleonic wars, European merchants and bankers became active in North African markets. They invested in businesses and lent money to the governments of the Regencies and Morocco. Some of the middlemen were unscrupulous, and both European and North African governments occasionally discovered that they had not received goods or services for which they had paid. The governments pressed each other to pay the debts that were owed them by their respective citizens. In Algiers, a dispute over a debt had major consequences. The Dey of Algiers, irritated by the inaction of the French government to enforce a debt that a French citizen owed the Dey, struck the French ambassador with a fly swatter. Gallic pride demanded satisfaction, and France began a three-year-long blockade of the port of Algiers. In 1830, the autocratic and incompetent French king, Charles X, was under severe pressure from his bourgeoisie to liberalize the government. He sensed an opportunity to distract his subjects' attention with an attack on Algiers. The invasion resulted in the occupation of Algiers, but Charles was overthrown within days of his success by Louis Philippe.

Louis Philippe's bourgeois regime had not been responsible for the invasion of Algiers, but the representatives of business interests argued that a peremptory withdrawal from the city would be rash and imprudent before economic opportunities were explored. As time passed, French military actions in the region provoked resistance to the occupation. Soon, a full-scale revolt erupted, led by the shaykh of the Qadiriya Sufi order in the region. His son 'Abd al-Qadir al-Jaza'iri (1807–1883) took over the leadership of the resistance in 1831. He was so successful that, by 1839, an army of 100,000 French troops was still unable to quell the uprising. 'Abd al-Qadir created an autonomous state in eastern Morocco and western Algeria from which to launch attacks on the French forces. Not until France forced the Moroccan sultan to put pressure on 'Abd al-Qadir was the revolt suppressed in 1847. 'Abd al-Qadir was detained in France for four years, but was treated respectfully because of his own humanitarian treatment of French prisoners of war during the revolt. The emperor, Napoleon III, allowed him to move to the Ottoman Empire in 1851. In 1855, after living for several years near Istanbul, he moved to Damascus, where he became a prominent religious leader.

The Algerian revolt resulted in immense property destruction and thousands of casualties among the French and their new subjects. The French seized upon the revolt as a pretext for confiscating the desirable agricultural land of Algeria. European colonists from Italy, Greece, Malta, and Spain moved to Algeria to make a new life. In 1848, the French legislature agreed to classify Algeria as an integral part of France rather than as a colony.

Meanwhile, in 1835, when the Ottomans finally realized that the French were intent upon a war of conquest in Algeria, the sultan sent an army to secure Tripoli from the same fate. He replaced the last member of the Qaramanli dynasty, which had ruled since 1711, with his own governor. The other nominally Ottoman provinces in North Africa, Egypt and Tunis, were modernizing quickly in an attempt to escape domination by either the Ottomans or the Europeans. They soon found that their sovereignty could be as effectively undermined by outside intervention as by invasion. Under the remarkable Muhammad 'Ali (1805–1849), Egypt attempted an ambitious set of military, industrial, and agricultural reforms. By the 1830s, in fact, Muhammad 'Ali seized Syria from the Ottoman Empire and invaded the Anatolian heartland. Britain was so concerned about Egypt's threat to Ottoman and European interests that in 1840 it sent troops to Syria to force Egypt's army out, and it forced Muhammad 'Ali to disband the system of state monopolies that financed his program.

During the 1860s, Muhammad 'Ali's grandson Isma'il embarked upon a massive program of investment in order to modernize Egypt. His grandest achievement was the opening of the Suez Canal in 1869. Isma'il, however, became a victim of his own poor judgment and of the era's aggressive and corrupt investment bankers. He borrowed so much that he could not meet the obligations of his loan payments. In 1875, in order to stave off bankruptcy, he reluctantly sold his shares in the Suez Canal to the British government. The following year, the British and French forced him to create an international finance commission to manage Egypt's revenues. Thereafter, the commission, rather than the government, made the decisions about how the government's revenues were to be spent. It made the payment of the foreign debt the highest priority.

The international commission that controlled Egypt's finances was modeled after one that had been created seven years earlier for Tunis. Like Egypt, Tunis had wanted to modernize its country in order to be able to fend off both the Ottomans and the Europeans. It had to borrow to invest in military improvements, and by the 1860s, payment on the debt was consuming half the annual revenue of the state. In 1869, Italy, Britain, and France forced Tunis to submit to an international debt commission that seized control of the government's revenues.

Both Egypt and Tunis also had to suffer the indignity of having their laws flouted by foreigners. Both countries experienced large-scale European immigration in the 1860s and 1870s. The immigrants demanded the continued implementation of the terms of the sixteenth-century Capitulations treaties that Europeans had negotiated with the Ottoman Empire so that they would not have to pay tariffs or be subject to local legal systems. European governments forced Egypt and Tunis to set up a system of Mixed Courts, composed of local and European judges, to hear cases involving Europeans. To the anger of local residents, Europeans almost always received a more lenient sentence for a given crime than would those who could not claim European citizenship or protection. In the mid-1870s, Tunisians and Egyptians were aware that they had lost their de facto sovereignty to Europeans.

Governmental Responses to External Threats

It was clear to Europeans of the late eighteenth and early nineteenth centuries that their nations were rapidly eclipsing the military and technological abilities of the Ottoman Empire and Iran. Even Russia, whose economic and political systems lagged behind those of Western Europe, was clearly more powerful than either of the Muslim nations by the end of the eighteenth century. Nevertheless, this unprecedented disparity of power, which seemed self-evident to Europeans, was a matter of concern for only some Ottoman and Iranian officials. Those who desired radical and immediate reforms felt an acute sense of urgency, for Russia, the most aggressively expansionist European state during the first half of the nineteenth century, shared frontiers with both countries. The reformers would discover that sometimes their most intractable obstacles were their own countrymen.

The Ottoman Empire

At the midpoint of the eighteenth century, many leading Ottomans could convince themselves that the military defeats and territorial losses that characterized the period 1683–1718 had been only a temporary setback and that the empire's place in the world order was once again secure. During the decades after those awful years, the empire recovered territory from Russia, easily defeated Austria, and fought a bloody war with Iran's Nadir Shah that concluded with a reaffirmation of the seventeenth-century border with Iran. Moreover, the empire was by then the dominant power in the Muslim world, if only by default: Nadir Shah's sack of Delhi in 1739 demonstrated the weakness of the Mughal Empire, and his own assassination in 1747 threw Iran into chaos. The years between 1744 and 1768 were free of external threats. Ottoman imports and exports were increasing, and agricultural production was adequate for the standards of the era.

Despite the halcyon quality of the era, some Ottoman officials were aware that the empire had developed serious problems. Palace officials fretted that provincial notables were growing increasingly autonomous and insolent, but as long as even partial taxes were paid, the central government was loath to engage in a confrontation with local representatives. Top military officers fumed that the Janissaries had become ineffective and unreliable as a result of their having been allowed to start families and to open private businesses. The Janissaries were poorly trained, and they often refused to report for duty. They were fiercely protective of their privileges, and they murdered viziers and sultans who attempted military reforms. As a result, the military leadership was increasingly forced to rely on the Ottoman and Crimean cavalry units and less on the infantry units of the Janissaries.

The Ottoman failure to keep pace with developments in Europe proved disastrous. The time had long passed when the Ottomans and a rival such as the Safavid Empire or Spain simply competed for an outlying parcel of real estate like Georgia or Tunis. Russia was no longer a mere rival, but a mortal enemy, determined to dominate—if not destroy—the Ottoman Empire. In 1768, Polish Catholics, France, and the Crimean Tatars persuaded the Ottomans to attack Russia in order to contain Catherine the Great's aggressive expansionism. The Russians soundly defeated the Ottomans in a war that lasted from 1768 to 1772. In the Treaty of Kuchuk Kaynarja (Küçük Kaynarca) of 1774, Russia finally obtained its long-sought warm-water port by annexing a narrow foothold on the north shore of the Black Sea. It gained the right for all of its ships to sail in the Black Sea and for its commercial vessels to pass through the straits between the Black Sea and the Aegean Sea. Russia also claimed the right to intervene at the Ottoman court on behalf of the Orthodox subjects of the sultan.

As humiliating as the Treaty of Kuchuk Kaynarja was for the Ottomans, it would have been much more costly had Austria, Prussia, and other European powers not intervened to prevent the Russians from annexing outright the swath of Ottoman territories from Romania to the Crimea that their troops had occupied. Ottoman weakness had been exposed for all to see, and for the next century, the empire was regarded as the "Sick Man of Europe." During that period, central and western European diplomats were preoccupied with the so-called Eastern Question: the fate of the Ottoman Empire. Russia's ambitions to obtain control of the straits posed the real possibility of the dissolution of the Ottoman realm. None of the European states wanted Russia—or any other competitor—to gain the leverage that control of the straits and the eastern Mediterranean would entail. Knowing that the Ottomans were no longer a military threat to themselves, they preferred to leave them where they were rather than to upset the European balance of power.

Thus, whereas Russia was possessed of a burning desire to administer a mercy killing to the Sick Man and inherit the choicest parts of his estate, several European countries agreed to keep him alive until conditions were propitious for their own interests. They did not object to the occasional amputation of the Sick Man's limbs, and so they allowed Russia to wield the axe on selected Ottoman territories. Russia annexed the Crimea in 1783 and subsequently annexed additional territories around the northern coast of the Black Sea. Russia also intervened in uprisings in the Balkans, where Ottoman central authority had disappeared entirely. Christian and Muslim peasants alike revolted in desperation against plundering Janissaries and barons who acted like Mafiosi. In 1815, Russia forced the Ottomans to grant autonomy to Serbia and Romania—although the two provinces remained officially part of the empire—and Russians became the most influential political agents in the two provinces.

When a war for Greek independence broke out in 1821, many Europeans expressed sympathy for Greek nationalist aspirations because the Neoclassical and Greek Revival movements had prepared the ground for a romantic and idealistic interpretation of the Greek heritage. Few, if any, of the Europeans understood that the ideals and images that they held of the region bore no relationship to what actually existed in the nineteenth century. Greeks killed an estimated 15,000 of the 40,000 Muslims in the Peloponnesus during the first few months of the revolt, provoking reprisals from the Ottomans that resulted in the deaths of thousands of Greeks. European powers intervened when the Greeks started to lose, and by 1829, the combined European military units had forced the Ottomans to recognize Greek independence. Greece was now independent, but it was not the glorious enterprise that the nationalists had envisioned: The victorious Europeans installed a German monarch over the new kingdom, which contained fewer than half the number of Greeks still living in the Ottoman Empire.

Sometimes the European powers were determined to prevent one another from taking Ottoman territory. When the French Directory sent Napoleon to conquer Egypt from the Ottomans in 1798, the British were sufficiently concerned about protecting the route to India that they helped the Ottomans expel the French army. Even more impressive was the effort made by France and Britain (along with more modest contributions from other European states) to ally with the Ottomans during the Crimean War of 1853–1856 when it became clear that Russia intended to capture Istanbul and the straits. Each side lost 250,000 men during the conflict. Due to the bitter rivalries of the European powers, the Ottoman ruling elites were given a reprieve to introduce reforms in an effort to save the empire.

For half a century after Kuchuk Kaynarja, several sultans, viziers, and military officers tried to bring about reforms. The twin pillars of most of the reform programs were centralization and modernization. The increased autonomy of the provincial notables had come at the expense of the authority and revenue of the central government. The loss of power at the center made the empire more vulnerable to foreign aggression, and every time a local baron abused the villagers under his authority, it was the empire that forfeited the peasants' loyalty. Centralization was required for the survival of the empire, and it required the development of a more rationally organized government bureaucracy and a better-equipped and organized military.

The ineffectiveness of the Janissaries against modern infantry formations, combined with the loss of the vast manpower reserves of the Crimea, required a total overhaul of military tactics and strategy. Still, the Janissaries fiercely resisted any changes, sensing correctly that their privileged position would be lost if the army were reorganized. Some members of the ulama also resisted change, on the grounds that the proposed innovations would entail the adoption of infidel customs in the place of traditions practiced by generations of Muslims. Opponents of reform were aided in their cause by the blow to the sultan's prestige that resulted from Napoleon's invasion of Egypt (1798) and the Wahhabi capture of Mecca and Medina (1803). During the first decade of the nineteenth century, the Janissaries and their supporters murdered two sultans and one vizier in their efforts to maintain the status quo.

Mahmut II (1808–1839) witnessed the murders of his two predecessors and barely escaped death himself as a prince. He quietly and patiently bided his time as he placed loyal supporters in positions of military and religious authority. Then, in 1826, he announced that the Janissaries would have to adjust to a new military reorganization. When they revolted, he ordered his pre-positioned artillery units to fire upon their barracks in the capital until all the Janissaries were dead. Janissaries in the rest of the empire were also killed, and the Bektashi Sufi order, which had been closely identified with the Janissaries, was declared illegal.

Mahmut had long hoped that the elimination of the Janissaries would enable him to implement desperately needed reforms. First, however, he had to confront the Greek rebellion, which was supported by European powers, and then, throughout the 1830s, he had to contend with an invasion by his nominal Egyptian vassal, Muhammad 'Ali. Just before his death in 1839, Mahmut commissioned an edict that was issued posthumously in the same year. It was the first in a series of reforms that are collectively called the *Tanzimat*, or "reorganization," that spanned the period 1839–1876. The government reorganized the military and built railroads and telegraph lines. Reformers planned a new, secular educational system. Equally important was the emergence of a new understanding of the nature of law and a new concept of individual identity. Previously, the millets had possessed their own sets of laws that were assumed to derive indirectly from God, and the sultan claimed the right to issue regulations known as the qanun. Under the Tanzimat, laws were issued by special commissions composed of graduates of secular European schools and the empire's new technical schools. Henceforth, all Ottoman subjects were to be treated equally under the law, with equal rights and responsibilities, regardless of millet. Although members of the millets could continue administering their own laws, legal cases between members of different millets were removed from Shari'a courts and assigned to a new system of secular courts.

Efforts to implement the Tanzimat were hindered by internal opponents. After the death of Mahmut II, the program was in the hands of bureaucrats in the vizier's office who wanted to centralize power but to weaken the power of the sultan, who was usually more conservative than the reform-minded technocrats in the vizier's office. In response, supporters of the sultan often worked at cross purposes to the vizier's office, thwarting many initiatives. Almost all provincial notables whose families had benefited from the decentralization of state power over the previous two centuries also resisted the overall centralizing thrust of the program.

The ulama were divided in their response to the Tanzimat. Some of the most important architects of the new educational system were graduates of madrasas who had subsequently gained a modern education as well. Most of the ulama, however, were antagonistic to the new judicial and educational plans. They controlled the primary schools and did not allow any changes in them. They did not oppose the creation of new secondary schools that taught modern subjects such as advanced mathematics, foreign languages, chemistry, and biology, because they thought that their influence would be limited to the training of a few specialists. They also did not reform the madrasas of the empire—the reforms in the Hijaz and Yemen that focused on the Qur'an and Hadith were contrary to the policies of the leading ulama and succeeded only because they were so distant from the major cities. On the whole, the Ottoman ulama followed a path that increasingly marginalized their influence on the debates regarding the major issues of the era.

Ottoman efforts to reform were also hindered by external challenges. European powers refused to rescind the Capitulations, which allowed European manufactured products to destroy thousands of jobs of artisans. The Ottomans also confronted the challenge of housing and feeding more than one million Muslim refugees who fled the territories that Russia conquered during the period of the Tanzimat. During and immediately after the Crimean War (1853–1856), Russia evicted the bulk of the Crimean Tatars. Over 300,000 refugees fled to Ottoman territories, where many thousands died in miserable camps before the survivors could be settled. The Russian conquest of the Caucasus resulted in even more refugees. Untold thousands of Dagestanis and Chechens north of the Caucasus and Turks south of the Caucasus were evicted. In 1864, on the Black Sea coast of the Caucasus, the Russians herded the survivors of their genocidal campaign onto ships sent by the Ottomans. Stripped by the Russians of all their possessions, hundreds of thousands of these wretches died in Ottoman camps in Black Sea ports. By 1865, one-tenth of the population of Anatolia was composed of refugees from areas Russia had recently conquered.

By the 1870s, the aura of the Tanzimat had diminished. Some sectors of the empire's population prospered during the period, but these were primarily the non-Muslim commercial groups in Anatolia that established links with Europe. By obtaining the sponsorship of a European business or diplomat, Christian subjects of the empire enjoyed the privileges of the Capitulations, which granted them exemption from the empire's laws and tariffs. This gave them a tremendous economic advantage over their Muslim competitors. After more than thirty years, the lofty goals of the Tanzimat had not been translated into significant improvements in the lives of most Muslims and non-Muslims. The debt was increasing due to a taxation system that had never been able to finance the new programs. Bureaucrats in the vizier's office were widely perceived to be acting arbitrarily and for the sake of building up their own power. Muslims complained that the granting of increased legal rights to the empire's Christians had only emboldened them to demand still more concessions. The Russian threat appeared to be as severe as ever.

In 1871, the rising discontent within the empire emboldened Sultan Abdulaziz II (1861–1876) to wrest control from the vizier's office, and he began to exercise the power that he had been denied under the Tanzimat. His extravagance and reckless borrowing sent the economy into a tailspin. Even many of his erstwhile supporters began to look for alternatives to the traditional forms of Ottoman rule. By 1875, several political reform movements had arisen, searching for a way to maintain an Ottoman identity while creating a government that would address the needs of the people.

Iran

The second half of the eighteenth century was a low point in the history of Iran. The bulk of the period can be divided into three sixteen-year periods. Nadir Shah's assassination in 1747 plunged Iran into a civil war that lasted until 1763. The two dominant forces in the conflict were the Persian-speaking Zand tribe and the Turkish-speaking Qajar tribe, which had been one of the seven major tribes of the Qizilbash confederation. The war ended when the Zand managed to bring all of Iran under their control except Khorasan, which was under the control of Ahmad Shah Durrani of Afghanistan. Much of Iran now began to enjoy a relatively peaceful interlude under the leadership of Karim Khan Zand (1763–1779), who established his capital at Shiraz.

At Karim Khan's death in 1779, anarchy erupted again. The Zand princes fought each other to secure the throne, giving the Qajars another chance to compete. One of the Qajars, Aga Muhammad Khan, won a series of decisive military victories during the 1780s and established his base at Tehran in 1786. From there, he directed a conquest of the Iranian plateau, Khorasan, and Azerbaijan. He secured the boundaries of modern Iran by early 1795. Late in the same year, he attacked Georgia and ordered the infamous sack of the Georgian capital of Tbilisi that triggered the annexation of Georgia by Russia. In 1796, he claimed the title of shah, thereby inaugurating the Qajar dynasty in Iran (1796–1925).

Aga Muhammad Khan's career was eerily similar to that of Nadir Shah. He was a brilliant military leader, but his growing rage and cruelty exceeded the acceptable bounds even of his era, which tolerated arbitrary and repressive actions by rulers. The first major episode of his rage was the gouging out of the eyes of thousands of the males of the city of Kirman in 1794. The sack of Tbilisi in 1795 was characterized by unusually gruesome atrocities. Like Nadir, Aga Muhammad became too dangerous to tolerate. During his second invasion of Georgia in 1797, two of his servants quarreled in his presence. Annoyed, Aga Muhammad announced that they would be executed the next day for their indiscretion. That night, the servants, whom Aga Muhammad had not bothered to shackle, killed him instead.

The Qajar dynasty (1796–1925) came to power in Iran at an inauspicious time in both foreign and domestic affairs. In foreign affairs, Russia was poised to mount its all-out expansionist campaign south of the Caucasus Mountains, a region that had been a Safavid sphere of influence. Iran tried to defend Transcaucasia from the Russians, but bloody conflicts ended in two treaties in 1813 and 1828 that settled Russian paramountcy north of the Aras River. The treaties also forced Iran to grant Russia generous economic concessions and extraterritoriality (the exemption of Russian nationals from Iranian legal jurisdiction while in Iran). As a result, Russian merchants and officials acquired enormous power in the country.

The British became concerned about Russian dominance in northern Iran, fearing Russian inroads into Iran and Afghanistan that would threaten the East India Company's interests in India. At first, the British offered to help Iran against Russia, but promises of cooperation turned to conflict in 1837–1838, when the Qajar shah attempted to recover Herat during a period of turmoil in Afghanistan. To the Iranians, Herat was an integral part of their empire. Historically, ethnically, and culturally, Herat had been part of the Persian sphere of influence until Ahmad Durrani made it part of his Afghan empire in the mid-eighteenth century. The British, however, took seriously the old adage that "Herat is the key to India," and they sent troops to help break the Iranian siege. Subsequently, the British carefully monitored Iranian actions both in Afghanistan and in the Persian Gulf.

In domestic affairs, the Qajars also faced formidable challenges. They were not as powerful as their Ottoman counterparts. When Mahmut II destroyed the Janissaries in 1826, he and subsequent sultans had a significant degree of latitude for introducing changes due to the bureaucratization of religious institutions that previous generations of rulers had instituted. Casual visitors to Iran might well think that the Qajar shahs, too, commanded enormous power from their capital in Tehran. They reveled in lavish palaces, fine clothes, and all the trappings of royal splendor. They owned all lands not under the control of religious institutions, military commanders, or court favorites. Theoretically, their power for making and enforcing policy was unlimited. In practice, however, the shahs were quite weak. They lacked the large standing armies and complex bureaucracies of rival rulers. Their military was still largely composed of tribal levies, and their governors came from the ranks of the country's most powerful families. Dependent on good relations with the tribes and large landowners, shahs relied on their skills of persuasion and manipulation rather than on force.

The triumph of the Usuli faction of the Shi'ite ulama over the Akhbari school also entailed serious problems for the new dynasty. The Qajar legacy of having been one of the Qizilbash tribes did not provide political capital in an era when mujtahids were viewed as representatives of the Hidden Imam. By the Qajar

Imam Shamil, the leader of the resistance to Russian advances in the Caucasus during the mid-nineteenth century.

period, Shi'ism no longer had an integral connection with the monarchy, and the development of a hierarchy within the ranks of the mujtahids endowed the most prominent among them with a stature and authority that a mere shah could no longer hope to match. The ancient Shi'ite assumption that temporal authority was illegitimate if not under the direction of the Imam was once again a latent undercurrent of Iranian national life. It held the potential to pose a mortal challenge to a regime.

Throughout the Qajar era, the authority of the ulama increased relative to that of the shah. The ulama combined material wealth with spiritual authority. They administered huge religious endowments as well as almost all the schools and charitable organizations in the country. They collected and allocated the use of the *zakat* (religious tax). They presided over Shari'a courts, which followed time-honored methods, unlike the government courts, which were characterized by the arbitrary decisions of governors according to the needs of the state at a given time. The homes of the ulama, along with mosques, were sites where refugees from secular authority could obtain *bast,* or sanctuary. Overall, the state and the Twelver Shi'ite religious establishment coexisted in a state of tension, each with its own sources of authority.

The Qajars enacted few reforms compared with the Ottoman Empire. Their inactivity seems not to have been due solely to calculations of resistance from the mujtahids and provincial magnates. None of the Qajar shahs seemed to grasp the need for, or requirements for, a reform program to counter the growing threats to their nation's economic and political security. A few princes, government ministers, and intellectuals realized the need for changes in military organization, technology, and education, but those who initiated changes died at an early age, either of natural causes or at the hands of conspirators. Their reforms were usually reversed, and remarkably little in the way of modern infrastructure was built. Iran did obtain the telegraph during the 1860s, but it built few roads and constructed no railroads. The most significant reforms were undertaken for the military. The early Qajar shahs inherited a military the majority of whose warriors were tribal horsemen who were obligated to serve only a few months out of the year. By midcentury, the need for a permanent standing army was becoming clear, and foreign advisors were brought in to train and equip infantry recruits. The only modern school the government built, the Dar al-Fonun, opened in 1852 in Tehran. Patterned after the French military academy at St. Cyr, it taught engineering, mathematics, and foreign languages to military officers.

The Qajars faced two major periods of instability during the first three-quarters of the nineteenth century. One was the decade of the 1840s, which is important for two religious developments. The first was the rise of the Babi/Baha'i movement. It emerged against the backdrop of traditional Shi'ite millennial expectations. Twelver Shi'ites had looked for the return of the Hidden Imam ever since his disappearance in the year 874 (260 on the Islamic calendar), and by the early nineteenth century, many expected that he would return in triumph after an absence of a millennium. This expectation reached a feverish pitch among a group of Shi'ites who predicted that he would return in 1844 (1260 on the Islamic calendar). Several events transpired in the years leading up to 1844 that appeared to be portents of the End of Days. First were the military defeats at the hands of Russia in the Caucasus (1828) and Britain at Herat (1838), as well as major outbreaks of plague, cholera, and famine in the 1830s. The economy was also beginning to sputter. The rapid growth of imports of cheap European manufactured goods caused many craftsmen to lose their jobs, and a devaluation of the Iranian currency led to explosive inflation. Then, in 1843, Ottoman troops brutally suppressed a rebellion in the Shi'ite shrine city of Karbala, in Iraq, killing 5000 people in one day. When the Qajar Shah Muhammad (1834–1848) did not respond militarily to this brutal act of the hated Sunni enemy, Iranian Shi'ites were left with a feeling of helpless outrage.

In May 1844, a young merchant from Shiraz, Sayyid 'Ali Muhammad, made the startling announcement that he was the *bab*. Of Arabic origin, this term means "gate" or "door," but in Shi'ism it connotes someone with special access to the Hidden Imam. Shortly thereafter, he claimed to be the Hidden Imam himself. He proclaimed the need for a new order, preaching against the wealthy landowners for their greed and oppression and against the mujtahids for their extravagant life styles and their preoccupation with theological trivialities. He denounced European merchants, who flaunted their privileges in the faces of Iranians. He prophesied that, even though he was the Hidden Imam, God would soon manifest an even greater figure to the world.

For the next eight years, Iran was thrown into turmoil. Groups all over the country flocked to the Bab's standard, and many appropriated the movement for their own ends. The royal family, wealthy landowners, and higher clergy were all unnerved by the Bab's movement. The Bab was arrested in 1847, convicted of heresy, and executed in 1850. In 1852, after an attempt on the life of the new ruler, Nasir al-Din Shah (1848–1896), the Babis were ruthlessly persecuted. Thousands were killed, and thousands others fled the country. One of the émigrés, Baha'ullah, fled to Baghdad, where, in 1863, he announced to a group of admirers that he was the figure whom the Bab had prophesied would follow him. Four years later, in Edirne, he sent letters to several national rulers, announcing his identity. Until his death in 1892, he laid the foundations for the modern Baha'i faith, which teaches the unity of all religions and the universal brotherhood of man. Neither Baha'is nor Muslims consider the religion to be Islamic.

Simultaneously with the rise of the Babi movement, the Nizari leadership moved from Iran to India. The Nizari Imams had a cordial relationship with Fath 'Ali Shah, the second Qajar shah. Fath 'Ali Shah (1797–1834) appointed the Nizari Imam, Hasan 'Ali Shah, to be governor of Qum and arranged for one of his own many daughters to marry the Imam. It was at this time that the Imam's followers began calling the Imam by the honorific title, Aga Khan. In 1835, the next shah, Muhammad (1834–1848), appointed the Aga Khan to be governor of Kirman. Soon thereafter, for reasons that are now obscure, relations soured between the Aga Khan and the shah, and their military forces fought each other. In 1841, the Aga Khan fled to Afghanistan with a large retinue. At Qandahar he made contact with the British Indian army, which was then engaged in its ill-fated First Afghan War. After the British were forced to retreat to India, the Aga Khan lent his cavalry to help the British secure Sindh. The British rewarded the Aga Khan with an annual pension and tried to help him return to Iran. This diplomatic effort had the misfortune to take place during the early stages of the Bab's movement, when Iranian authorities were not keen to welcome back someone whom they viewed as a potential source of discord.

When the repatriation efforts failed, the Aga Khan settled permanently in Bombay in 1848. Many Khojas there had long recognized him and his ancestors as the titular leaders of their community, but the Khoja community had remained autonomous. The Khojas had been without the leadership of a pir for centuries, and a variety of doctrines and practices had developed within the group. These ranged from clearly Sunni Muslim practices to clearly Hindu ones. Now, as the Aga Khan was in position to provide leadership, the process of creating an organized community proved to be difficult. Several dissident groups arose, challenging the Aga Khan's policies and his authority. They brought lawsuits against him in the British-controlled courts of Bombay. The courts recognized the Aga Khan's claims to head an Isma'ili community, his right to all customary Khoja dues, and his claim to be a lineal descendant of the Nizaris of the Alamut period. The modern history of the Khojas dates from this period, and all subsequent Imams have been known as the Aga Khan.

Whereas the disturbances of the 1840s arose from internal causes, the second period of instability (the 1860s and 1870s) for the Qajar monarchy was a reaction to growing foreign intervention in Iranian affairs. After the 1828 treaty that settled the Aras River boundary, relations between Iran and Russia were chilly but proper. During the 1860s, however, Iranian anxieties regarding Russian intentions began rising again as Russia conquered the Central Asian principalities of Tashkent, Kokand, Bukhara, and Samarqand between 1865 and 1868. It was clear that Russia intended to expand even farther south, into the large region around Merv (the modern country of Turkmenistan). Historically an Iranian cultural region, Turkish speakers had replaced Persian speakers in the area over the previous centuries, but Iranians had to wonder whether adjacent Iranian territory was in Russia's sights. The Iranian prime minister hoped that he could counter the potential Russian threat by involving Britain in Iran's affairs. He thought that Iran could modernize and simultaneously have its territorial integrity protected by offering British capitalists opportunities for profitable investment.

In 1872, the prime minister offered Baron Julius de Reuter (a naturalized British subject who had founded the Reuters news agency) the exclusive right to construct and operate railways and to exploit Iran's mineral resources for seventy years; to operate Iran's customs, to exploit the national forests, and to build Iran's dams, wells, and canals for twenty-four years; and to have first option should Iran create a national bank. In effect, Reuter was offered most of the Iranian economy. When Iranians learned of the concession, they demonstrated in the streets. Russia was furious that the beneficiary was a British subject rather than a Russian one, and threatened retaliation. Even the British government was lukewarm in its support of the concession because many British business interests were outraged that they were shut out of a chance to make a profit in Iran. Due to the political pressure, the shah withdrew the concession, but Reuter was awarded the right to establish the Imperial Bank of Persia as consolation. The fiasco inaugurated a period of political infighting and economic corruption within the government.

all of Africa and most of the economically attractive regions of Asia. The era of the New Imperialism provided the circumstances for further elaboration of the new developments within Islam.

NOTES

1. See Chapter 2 for a discussion of "the closing of the gate of *ijtihad*."
2. Shah Wali Allah was not a ruler, despite the *Shah* in his name. All three words are respectful titles that his followers gave him. *Shah* is an honorific that Sufis had begun to award to revered *pirs* by the fourteenth century, and *Wali Allah* means "friend of God," which was a common title for Sufis to give to particularly holy *pirs*. Shah Wali Allah's birth name was Ahmad ibn 'Abd al-Rahim.
3. Natana J. DeLong-Bas has argued that modern Wahhabism is quite different from the teachings of Ibn 'Abd al-Wahhab himself. See her *Wahhabi Islam: From Revival and Reform to Global Jihad* (New York: Oxford University Press, 2004).
4. Gladney, Dru C. *Muslim Chinese: Ethnic Nationalism in the People's Republic*. Cambridge, Massachusetts: Council on East Asian Studies, Harvard University: Distributed by Harvard University Press, 1991, 1996.

FURTHER READING

Developments Within Twelver Shi'ism

Arjomand, Said Amir. *The Shadow of God and the Hidden Imam: Religion, Political Order, and Societal Change in Shi'ite Iran from the Beginning to 1890*. Chicago: University of Chicago Press, 1984.

Cole, Juan. *Sacred Space and Holy War: The Politics, Culture and History of Shi'ite Islam*. London and New York: I. B. Taurus Publishers, 2002.

Momen, Moojan. *An Introduction to Shi'i Islam: The History and Doctrines of Twelver Shi'ism*. New Haven, Connecticut: Yale University Press, 1985.

Newman, Andrew J., ed. *Society and Culture in the Early Modern Middle East: Studies on Iran in the Safavid Period*. Leiden, Netherlands, and Boston: Brill, 2003.

Stewart, Devin. "The Genesis of the Akhbārī Revival." In *Safavid Iran and Her Neighbors*, ed. Michel Mazzaoui, pp. 169–194. Salt Lake City: University of Utah Press, 2003.

Sunni Reform Movements

Baljon, J. M. S. *Religion and Thought of Shāh Walī Allāh Dihlawī 1703–1762*. Leiden, Netherlands: Brill, 1986.

Cook, Michael. *Forbidding Wrong in Islam: An Introduction*. Cambridge, U.K.: Cambridge University Press, 2003

Kim, Ho-dong. *Holy War in China: The Muslim Rebellion and State in Chinese Central Asia, 1864–1977*. Stanford, California: Stanford University Press, 2004.

Levtzion, Nehemia and John O. Voll, eds. *Eighteenth-Century Renewal and Reform in Islam*. Syracuse, New York: Syracuse University Press, 1987.

Lipman, Jonathan N. *Familiar Strangers: A History of Muslims in Northwest China*. Seattle and London: University of Washington Press, 1997.

Lovejoy, Paul E. *Transformations in Slavery: A History of Slavery in Africa*, 2d ed. Cambridge, U.K.: Cambridge University Press, 2000.

Reis, João José. *Slave Rebellion in Brazil: The Muslim Uprising of 1835 in Bahia.* Trans. by Arthur Brakel. Baltimore and London: Johns Hopkins University Press, 1993.

Ricklefs, M. C. *A History of Modern Indonesia Since c. 1200,* 3d ed. Stanford, California: Stanford University Press, 2001.

Robinson, David. *The Holy War of Umar Tal: The Western Sudan in the Mid-Nineteenth Century.* Oxford, U.K.: Clarendon Press, 1985.

Vassiliev, Alexei. *The History of Saudi Arabia.* London: Saqi Books, 2000.

Voll, John Obert. *Islam: Continuity and Change in the Modern World,* 2d ed. Syracuse, New York: Syracuse University Press, 1994.

European Intervention and Annexation

Allworth, Edward, ed. *Central Asia: 120 Years of Russian Rule.* Durham, North Carolina, and London: Duke University Press, 1989.

Baddeley, John F. *The Russian Conquest of the Caucasus.* With a new foreword by Moshe Gammer. Richmond, U.K.: The Curzon Press, 1999.

Broxup, Marie Bennigsen, ed. *The North Caucasus Barrier: The Russian Advance towards the Muslim World.* London: Hurst & Company, 1992.

Dalrymple, William. *The Last Mughal: The Fall of a Dynasty: Delhi, 1857.* New York: Alfred A. Knopf, 2007.

Hardy, Peter. *The Muslims of British India.* London: Cambridge University Press, 1972.

Inikori, J. E., ed. *Forced Migration: The Impact of the Export Slave Trade on African Societies.* New York: Africana Publishing Company, 1982

Kanya-Forstner, A. S. *The Conquest of the Western Sudan: A Study in French Military Imperialism.* Cambridge, U.K.: Cambridge University Press, 1969.

Levtzion, Nehemiah and Ronald Lee Pouwels, eds. *The History of Islam in Africa.* Athens: Ohio University Press; Oxford, U.K.: James Currey; Cape Town, South Africa: David Philip, 2000.

Manning, Patrick. *Slavery and African Life.* Cambridge, U.K., and New York: Cambridge University Press, 1990.

Maxon, Robert M. *East Africa: An Introductory History,* 2d ed. Morgantown: West Virginia University Press, 1994.

Metcalf, Thomas R. *The Aftermath of Revolt: India, 1857–1870.* Princeton, New Jersey: Princeton University Press, 1964.

Oldenburg, Veena Taiwar. *The Making of Colonial Lucknow, 1856–1877.* Princeton, New Jersey: Princeton University Press, 1984.

Pouwels, Randall L. *Horn and Crescent: Cultural Change and Traditional Islam on the East African Coast, 800–1900.* Cambridge, U.K., and New York: Cambridge University Press, 1987.

Zelkina, Anna. *In Quest for God and Freedom: The Sufi Response to the Russian Advance in the North Caucasus.* New York: New York University Press, 2000.

Governmental Responses to External Threats

Algar, Hamid. *Religion and State in Iran, 1785–1906: The Role of the Ulama in the Qajar Period.* Berkeley: University of California Press, 1980.

Amanat, Abbas. *Pivot of the Universe: Nasir al-Din Shah Qajar and the Iranian Monarchy, 1831–1896.* Berkeley: University of California Press, 1997.

Berkes, Niyazi. *The Development of Secularism in Turkey.* Montreal: McGill University Press, 1964.

Findley, Carter. *Bureaucratic Reform in the Ottoman Empire: The Sublime Porte 1789–1922.* Princeton, New Jersey: Princeton University Press, 1980.

Inalcik, Halil with Donald Quataert, eds. *An Economic and Social History of the Ottoman Empire, 1300–1914.* Cambridge, U.K., and New York: Cambridge University Press, 1994.

Lambton, Ann K. S. *Qājār Persia.* Austin: University of Texas Press, 1987.

McCarthy, Justin. *The Ottoman Turks: An Introductory History to 1923.* London and New York: Longman, 1997.

Naff, Thomas and Roger Owen, eds. *Studies in Eighteenth Century Islamic History.* Carbondale and Edwardsville: Southern Illinois University Press, 1977.

Quataert, Donald. *The Ottoman Empire, 1700–1922.* Cambridge, U.K.: Cambridge University Press, 2000.

CHAPTER 9

The Loss of Sovereignty: 1875–1920

Over the course of little more than a century, Europeans radically revised their assessment of the Muslim world. Until the mid-eighteenth century, Europeans had regarded the great Muslim states with awe and a certain degree of fear, but by the late nineteenth century, Europeans stood in awe of no Muslim state. By the latter period, in fact, Europeans who visited the Muslim world did so to experience a quaint and exotic locale, filled with strange and wonderful curiosities. The genre of the travel book was flourishing, as was the new leisure activity of tourism; books and tours that featured any region within the Muslim world were sure to attract an eager audience. Increasingly aware that Europe was, in fact, more powerful than the Dar al-Islam, Muslims took consolation in the claim that they at least had a spiritual advantage over the crass materialism of the West.

The Muslim perception of spiritual superiority was of little value when, in the last quarter of the nineteenth century, Europe suddenly began the process of completing the takeover of almost the entire Muslim world. Armies invaded every part of the African continent and most regions of Muslim Asia. Suddenly, the pressing issue of the day was how to react to political rule by non-Muslim foreigners. The new imperialist regimes produced a bewildering array of unfamiliar challenges to traditional material culture and moral values.

Muslims were not passive victims of the onslaught that afflicted them. In most cases, they fought bloody wars before being overwhelmed. Thereafter, they sought ways to come to terms with the new regimes. The responses of local Muslims were determined by an array of factors that included geographical features, local traditions, social organization, current international conditions, and the economic and military resources at their disposal. They created political, religious, and social organizations that enabled them to express a wide array of reactions to the new order, from uncritical acceptance to passive hostility.

European Imperialism, 1875–1914

During the last quarter of the nineteenth century, several European countries—and eventually the United States and Japan—engaged in a frantic and desperate effort to acquire overseas territories. As we saw in the previous chapter, major imperial conquests had already taken place: During the pre-1875 period, the British conquest of South Asia, the Dutch expansion out of Java, the Russian expeditions in the Caucasus and Central Asia, and the French campaign to subdue Algeria involved major wars that killed hundreds of thousands of people, created well over one million refugees, and transferred sovereignty over enormous areas of the Muslim world to Europeans. Numerous other, smaller areas had been seized by European countries during the century, often simply to serve as coaling stations for their new, steam-powered fleets. What distinguished the conquests undertaken toward the end of the century were their unprecedented scope and intensity.

For several decades after the 1820s, many Europeans assumed that the era of empire was over. The independence movements in the former English and Spanish colonies raised serious questions about the value and cost of the colonial enterprise. Colonies were increasingly viewed as a political headache, for it was now clear that ungrateful colonists would eventually reject the helping hand of the mother country and demand self-rule. The economic potential of colonies was also in question, for the increasing replacement of mercantilism by capitalism meant that colonial economies could no longer be controlled to the advantage of the mother country.

The conquests of Muslim territory in the pre-1875 era did not alter this view. Russia's massive human and material investment in southward and eastward expansion was overland, a fact that caused many observers to regard it as analogous to the simultaneous westward expansion of the United States. The architects of both programs of conquest usually spoke in terms of "nation-building" rather than of the occupation of foreign soil. The conquest of South Asia by the armies of the English East India Company was accomplished under the watchful eye of the British government during the period 1757–1856, but most contemporary British subjects regarded the military campaigns largely as a matter for stockholders, not a British imperial venture. The French seizure of Algeria and the Dutch government's mercantilist initiatives in the East Indies were the primary exceptions to the general trend of creating colonies on the old pattern, and both were frequently explained away as atavistic anomalies. By midcentury, the doctrines of free-market capitalism were taking hold in Western Europe, and most government ministers wanted to avoid the expenses and policy dilemmas entailed by the conquest, occupation, and administration of foreign territories.

The period between 1875 and 1914 is notable because, in fact, several industrializing countries did engage in a frenzy of overseas territorial seizure on an enormous scale. By the end of that period, all of Africa except Liberia and Ethiopia was under European control, and all of Asia was under some form of European hegemony except for Japan, Siam (Thailand), and the Turkish and Arab provinces of the Ottoman Empire.

The Balkans

The era that we are considering is known for the division of Africa and Asia, but we need to preface that account with a glance at the near-total loss of Ottoman territories in Europe, a process that was happening simultaneously with the events on the two other continents. For a century after the Treaty of Kuchuk Kaynarja (1774), the Ottoman Empire had existed largely on the sufferance of the more powerful European states. Only competition and mistrust among the Europeans prevented the empire's dismemberment: France and Britain, in particular, foresaw threats to their own economic and strategic interests in southwest Asia if Russia were to cause the breakup of the Ottoman realm. By the end of the third quarter of the nineteenth century, the spread of nationalist ideas to minority communities within the empire provided Russia with the tool it needed to weaken the Ottoman grip on the straits between the Black Sea and Aegean Sea.

During the 1870s, Russian consuls and agents promoted pan-Slavism (the presumed cultural unity of all the Slavic peoples) as a means of securing their nation's interests in the Balkans at the expense of Austria and the Ottomans. Serbia was particularly passionate about the idea, seeing in pan-Slavism a means to re-create its medieval empire. The Ottomans played into the Serbs' hands by failing to reform the administration of most of their holdings in the region. In 1875, a rebellion broke out in Bosnia against the chronic grievances of the previous two centuries: rapacious landlords and high taxes. Muslim and Christian peasants alike joined the revolt, but Serbia chose the occasion to intervene for its own purposes, and its soldiers began to attack and kill Muslim villagers. When the Ottoman army responded and almost obliterated the Serbian army, European governments intervened, demanding Ottoman concessions to the rebels.

Meanwhile, trouble broke out in Bulgaria. This was the one region in the Balkans where Tanzimat reformers had made meaningful administrative reforms, but not in time to stem the tide of pan-Slavism among sections of the middle class. In 1876, nationalist rebels murdered one hundred or more innocent Muslim villagers. The Ottoman army, preoccupied in Bosnia, used poorly trained, Muslim Bulgarian irregular troops to quash the rebellion. The irregulars, many of whom had either suffered at the rebels' hands or had heard rumors of maltreatment of Muslims, took their revenge against the Christian rebels. A massacre ensued, during which an estimated 15,000 civilians were killed.

In Europe, newspapers and politicians denounced these "Bulgarian horrors." Russia was emboldened to declare war against the Ottomans in 1877. As its army moved into the Balkans in early 1878, Bulgarian Christians joined with the Russian soldiers in massacring a quarter of a million Bulgarian Muslims. Half a million Muslim refugees fled toward Istanbul with the retreating Ottoman army. In contrast to the reaction to the Bulgarian horrors, the death or displacement of three-quarters of a million Bulgarian Muslim civilians did not elicit sympathy from Europe.

Russia forced the sultan to sign a treaty in March 1878, but its terms were so favorable to Russia that Britain, Germany, and Austria were convinced that it had unacceptably altered the European balance of power. Led by Britain, these three nations forced Russia to meet with them at the Congress of Berlin later in the spring of 1878. The diplomats at this conference demarcated the borders for an autonomous Bulgaria; awarded Bosnia and Herzegovina to Austria for an indefinite period of occupation and administration; granted independence to Montenegro, Romania, and Serbia; and awarded Russia former Ottoman territories in eastern Anatolia. A few weeks later, the Ottoman government signed an agreement that granted Britain the island of Cyprus in return for aid against any further Russian aggression.

The Congress of Berlin deprived the Ottoman Empire of the vast majority of its sizable European territory and population. This region, which had been called Rumelia, had been the heart of the empire at the height of Ottoman glory, more valued than Anatolia. As shocking as the loss of Rumelia was, an even more pressing concern was the fact that Istanbul, already teeming with refugees from the Crimea, the Caucasus, and Central Asia, was now swollen with hundreds of thousands of additional angry and frightened displaced persons from the Balkans. The course of the last few decades of Ottoman history is incomprehensible without an awareness that the leaders of the empire lived under the constant threat of the loss of additional territory to European Christian nations and the subsequent expulsion of Turks and other Muslims.

North and West Africa

Tunisia and Egypt were the first Muslim societies to become victims of what is known as the "Scramble for Africa." In the previous chapter we saw that, during the second half of the nineteenth century, thousands of Europeans settled in the two countries, particularly in the great port cities of Tunis and Alexandria. The rulers of the countries became so deeply in debt to European banks that their budgets came under the control of European auditors (Tunisia in 1869 and Egypt in 1876). The auditors refused to allow state revenues to be used for any purpose until debts to foreign bondholders were paid. In the case of Egypt, the debt swallowed over sixty percent of annual state revenue. The reallocation of Egyptian and Tunisian state revenue to the bank accounts of bondholders caused shortfalls in the state budget. Employees were paid erratically if at all, and investment in public works dropped sharply in those countries.

As European population and investment in Tunis and Alexandria reached a critical mass, consuls and activists within the immigrant communities of the two cities began competing with each other for dominance. The two largest immigrant groups in Tunis were Italian and French. Italy had been unified as a country only in the 1860s, and its leaders hoped to achieve great-power status for their country by seizing Tunisia as a colony. Tunisia also seemed a natural target for Rome due to the fact that Italians formed the single largest expatriate community there. Despite Italian ambitions, France pre-empted Italy in 1881 by declaring Tunisia to be a protectorate of its own.

Meanwhile, in 1879, European consuls in Egypt managed to replace the ruler, Isma'il with a more compliant one, triggering an angry response from the public and the army. A powerful political movement arose that opposed European control of the country and called for the creation of a national assembly that

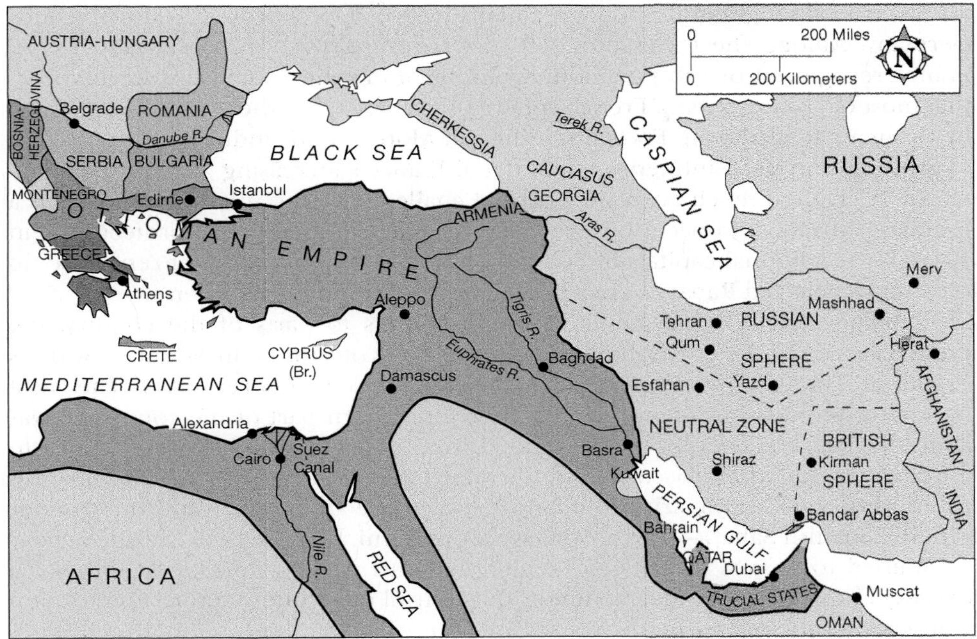

MAP 9.1 Ottoman Losses in Rumelia, 1878, and the 1907 Anglo-Russian Partition of Iran.

would manage the country's own finances. The new Egyptian assertiveness caused France and Britain to worry that the movement would produce a nationalist government that would refuse to pay its debts and restrict international access to the Suez Canal.

When Egyptian military forces began reinforcing coastal forts in the spring of 1882, the British government decided to act. In June, its fleet bombarded the city of Alexandria, and its army invaded Egypt. After three months of bitter fighting, the Egyptian army surrendered. British Prime Minister William Gladstone, whose career to that point had been based on a rejection of imperialism, assured his citizens that this was a temporary occupation. The British claimed to be serving as trustees for the Ottomans—still the de jure authority in Egypt in spite of two centuries of de facto Egyptian autonomy—and asserted that they would leave the country as soon as they restored order and financial solvency. As it turned out, the British kept troops in Egypt until 1956.

In the far western Maghrib, no European power had threatened Morocco in the three centuries since the Battle of the Three Kings in 1578. Then, during the second half of the nineteenth century, European economic and diplomatic interests in the country multiplied. Spain, Britain, and France were the most active, but it was the emergence of Germany as an aggressive actor on the international scene that forced the issue of which country would occupy Morocco. In the 1890s, Kaiser Wilhelm II began to alarm the rest of Europe by his efforts to assert German military supremacy on both land and sea. By 1904, Britain and France had become so concerned about German ambitions that they set aside their traditional rivalry and settled several long-standing disagreements in order to coordinate efforts against Germany. Among the issues they settled were the fates of Morocco and Egypt. France recognized British paramountcy in Egypt in return for British recognition that most of Morocco was a French sphere of influence. Neither subsequent efforts by Germany to challenge French standing in Morocco nor indigenous opposition to growing European influence could derail France's increasing grip on the country. In 1911, the French army used a local challenge to the sultan's authority as a pretext to invade and occupy Morocco. France declared a formal protectorate in 1912. The traditional capitals of Fez and Marrakesh were hotbeds of resistance, so the French selected Rabat as their protectorate's new political center.

Acknowledging long-standing Spanish claims to parts of the country, the French agreed to the creation of a small Spanish protectorate in Morocco, with its capital at Tétouan. The Spanish zone was composed of three parts. The most important was a strip of land in the extreme northern part of the country. It was about thirty-five miles wide and extended from the Atlantic coast to the Algerian border. It included Morocco's entire Mediterranean coast. The other two Spanish zones were the Tarfaya strip—the land between the Dra'a River and the frontier with the Spanish Sahara—and an enclave around Ifni. Because both European powers wanted to possess the city of Tangier, its status was left unresolved for over a decade. Finally, in 1926, it came under the control of an international commission composed of the representatives of several countries.

Both the Spanish and the French encountered stiff resistance to their efforts to secure control of their respective protectorates. Fierce Berber resistance in the Rif Mountains of northern Morocco bedeviled both European powers, and the Berbers of the Atlas Mountains fought with equal ferocity, preventing the French from enforcing their writ much beyond the plains in the central and southern parts of the country. Not until the mid-1920s did either power feel secure in its control of the territories that it claimed.

As France was occupying Morocco, Italy began an invasion of Libya. Italy had not overcome its bitter disappointment at losing Tunisia to France in 1881. After Britain occupied Egypt in 1882, Libya was the only remaining North African territory in the eastern Mediterranean. Some Italians wanted to occupy Libya because the possession of overseas territories had become a status symbol for great powers; others wanted an Italian-ruled territory where Italian emigrants could settle. Emigration out of Italy was on a massive scale during the several decades prior to World War I: During the first decade of the twentieth century, the exodus averaged over 600,000 persons annually. Many among the ruling elite reasoned that if Italy possessed Libya, its citizens could move to a "fourth shore" of their homeland rather than having to go to a foreign country.

The Italians invaded Libya in late 1911, anticipating an easy victory. Their expeditionary force of 60,000 was opposed by only 7000 Ottoman troops. What they had not counted on was the resistance of the Libyans themselves. During the yearlong conquest, the Italians lost almost 4000 dead and more than 4000 wounded. The Ottoman government finally ceded Libya in a treaty that was signed in October 1912, but Italy was unable to control much territory beyond the coast until after World War I.

In West Africa, Europeans rarely ventured into the interior during four centuries of sailing along the coast en route to the Indian Ocean. Prior to the nineteenth century, European trade in the area was restricted almost exclusively to the exchange of manufactured goods for slaves in port cities. Britain, France, and the United States banned the importation of slaves into their territories in the early nineteenth century, but they did not cease trading with West Africa. By that time, European technology had devised ways to use vegetable oils for industrial purposes and for use in the manufacture of soap. West Africa, a major source of ground nuts (peanuts) and palm and palm kernel oil, thus became valuable for agricultural products rather than for slaves.

The French maintained trading posts on the lower Senegal River, hoping to tap into the trade of the interior of West Africa, whereas British merchants focused on establishing secure trading centers on the coast. By 1861, the trade in the delta of the Niger River had become so valued by the British government that it declared the port of Lagos to be a crown colony. Thereafter, the British began a concerted campaign to establish trading monopolies in other ports along the West African coast.

Some French imperialists dreamed of an African empire that would rival British holdings in India. They had little concrete knowledge of the economic potential of the interior of West Africa, but they were mesmerized by the prospect of capturing fabled Timbuktu. By midcentury, however, the West African jihad movements had become a widely publicized phenomenon, and it was clear that major fighting would be required for France to acquire such an empire. Military officers in the Senegal River valley wanted to embark upon a campaign of conquest against al-Hajj Umar as early as the 1850s, but Paris was not prepared to invest the required financial or human resources into such a campaign. In 1857, a French expedition and al-Hajj Umar's army skirmished on the upper Senegal River but, when each recognized how powerful the other was, they avoided further clashes.

For more than two decades, the French remained immobile, torn between desiring a large West African empire and not wanting to repeat the nightmare of the Algerian revolt under 'Abd al-Qadir (1831–1847). In 1879, the French government decided to begin constructing a trans-Saharan railroad in the expectation that it would yield commercial benefits. Military officers in Senegal considered such a project to be a license to begin the conquest of West Africa, assuming that security needed to be guaranteed for the railway. Between 1879 and 1898, French army units often acted without orders—or even contrary to orders—and conquered the vast majority of the interior of West Africa.

The success of the French campaigns owed much to fortuitous timing. One advantage was that military technology had changed rapidly in the years after 1860, and Europeans were soon equipped with repeating rifles, machine guns, and light artillery, and they were able to travel up the rivers in steamboats rather than have to rely on sails or oars. Another was that al-Hajj Umar's empire had splintered into rival petty states. The only major opponent the French armies faced was Samori Ture, who built a well-organized state for the Malinke people during the 1870s in what is now eastern Guinea and southern Mali. He was finally defeated and captured in 1898.

French expansion in West Africa caused the British government to fear that its merchants might be shut out of the trade beyond the coastal regions. Imitating the French policy of entering West Africa via the Senegal River, in 1891 British military units began penetrating the interior of West Africa by means of the Niger

River and rivers in the Gold Coast (Ghana). Indigenous merchants and chiefs fought hard to keep their autonomy, but the British punished resistance and rebellions by the destruction of entire villages and the exile of leaders. In Hausaland, the British struggled to subdue Sokoto during 1900–1903. In 1902, they took the territory belonging to Bornu that lay on the southwestern coast of Lake Chad. The French, who had supported Bornu in its fight against the British, took Bornu's territory that lay on the other three sides of the lake. France claimed suzerainty of areas to the north of Sokoto, but pacification of the region was not complete until the 1920s.

The Western Indian Ocean

Throughout the nineteenth century, Britain became increasingly involved in the affairs of Zanzibar and Muscat. After 1856, the British consul in Zanzibar became the effective power, relegating the sultan to figurehead status. The sultan did not realize his loss of authority until 1873, when the consul demanded that he stop temporizing on the issue of outlawing slave exports from Zanzibar. When the sultan failed to issue a ban on the practice, the consul ordered gunboats to fire on the palace. Slave exports ceased.

Because the Portuguese in Mozambique were not interested in expanding their control beyond existing frontiers, British officials thought that they would have the luxury of time in consolidating their control over East Africa. Germany's chancellor, Bismarck, surprised and embarrassed them in 1885 when he declared a protectorate over Tanganyika (modern Tanzania), the region that lay across the channel from Zanzibar. Over the course of the next decade, Germany and Britain engaged in negotiations that determined boundaries between their respective holdings over the interior of East Africa. Due to the rise in tensions, Britain considered it expedient to declare a protectorate over Zanzibar and Pemba in 1890, formalizing the de facto power that it already exercised there. The country now known as Kenya was declared part of the British sphere of influence. For its first thirty years under British control, it was known as the East Africa Protectorate or British East Africa.

As the Germans occupied Tanganyika, the Italians and French began to probe the Horn of Africa. In 1885, Italy laid claim to the Eritrean coast, and France occupied French Somaliland (now Djibouti). In response, the British declared a protectorate over the Somalis who lived in the vicinity of Berbera, on the Gulf of Aden. Subsequently, the Italians embarked upon a disastrous invasion of Ethiopia. Their humiliating rout at the Battle of Adowa in 1896 allowed Ethiopia to share with Liberia the distinction of being one of the only two countries in Africa not seized by Europeans before World War I. By way of compensation, the Italians signed a treaty with the British in 1896 that allowed them to declare a protectorate over the southern half of Somalia.

The frenetic activity in West Africa, East Africa, and the Horn provoked anxiety in London regarding the security of the British position in Egypt. British officials assumed that the European armies in Africa—the French at Lake Chad and Djibouti, the Belgians in the Congo, the Germans in Tanganyika, and the Italians in Eritrea and Italian Somaliland—would not stop conquering until there was nothing left unclaimed. In 1894, wanting to protect the sources of the Nile from falling into the hands of a rival, Britain declared a protectorate over Uganda and began preparing for the conquest of Sudan.

Sudan had been claimed by Egypt since Muhammad 'Ali's armies conquered parts of it in the 1820s. Attempts by the Egyptian government to increase its control of Sudan in the 1870s backfired, provoking numerous revolts instead. In 1879, a Sudanese named Muhammad Ahmad proclaimed himself to be the Mahdi and declared a jihad against the govenment's authority. When the British conquered Egypt in 1882, they inherited the rebellion. Realizing that they needed to devote all their resources toward the consolidation of power in Egypt, they tried to evacuate their citizens and Egyptian army units from the Sudan. The effort was botched, and the British suffered the humiliation of losing a considerable number of soldiers while fighting rearguard skirmishes with the Mahdi. They abandoned Sudan to its fate while they established a stable administration in Cairo. By the mid-1890s, the British were sufficiently secure in their position in Egypt to attempt the conquest of the Sudan, which had meantime passed under the rule of the Mahdi's successor, the Khalifa ("caliph"). In 1898, a joint Egyptian–British army crushed the Khalifa's forces at Omdurman, near Khartoum. Rather than rejoining Sudan to Egypt, the British created a separate administration for the new possession.

During the 1880s, as East Africa and the Horn were being carved up by the Germans, British, French, and Italians (see Map 9.2), several powers began contesting for primacy in the Persian Gulf. Russia made no secret that it hoped to push through Iran to establish a presence there; the Ottomans established a garrison of troops in Qatar; and Britain was determined to maintain the relations that it had established with the Trucial States. In 1891, Britain persuaded the sultan of Muscat to sign a secret treaty in which the sultan promised not to enter into any agreement or even correspondence with any other European power, and not to allow a representative of another European government to reside in his territory. Although Muscat was not a formal British protectorate, it functioned as a de facto protectorate for several decades. Britain's interest was the harbor of Muscat, and not the interior of Oman, where Ibadi elders selected an Imam who maintained only very strained relations with the sultan of Muscat. The de facto division between Muscat and Oman lasted until 1957.

After persuading Muscat's sultan to sign the secret treaty, Britain obtained the signatures of the rulers of the Trucial States to almost identical agreements in 1892. During the years prior to the outbreak of World War I in 1914, the British signed similar treaties with the rulers of Kuwait, Bahrain, and Qatar. London's representatives also signed additional agreements with these Arab states that granted the British the first option on oil concessions should petroleum be discovered in their territories.

Central Asia and Iran

Readers of Rudyard Kipling's *Kim* (1901) are familiar with the phenomenon of the Great Game: the competition—rife with skullduggery and intrigue—between Britain and Russia for influence in Central Asia and Iran. Between the 1850s and

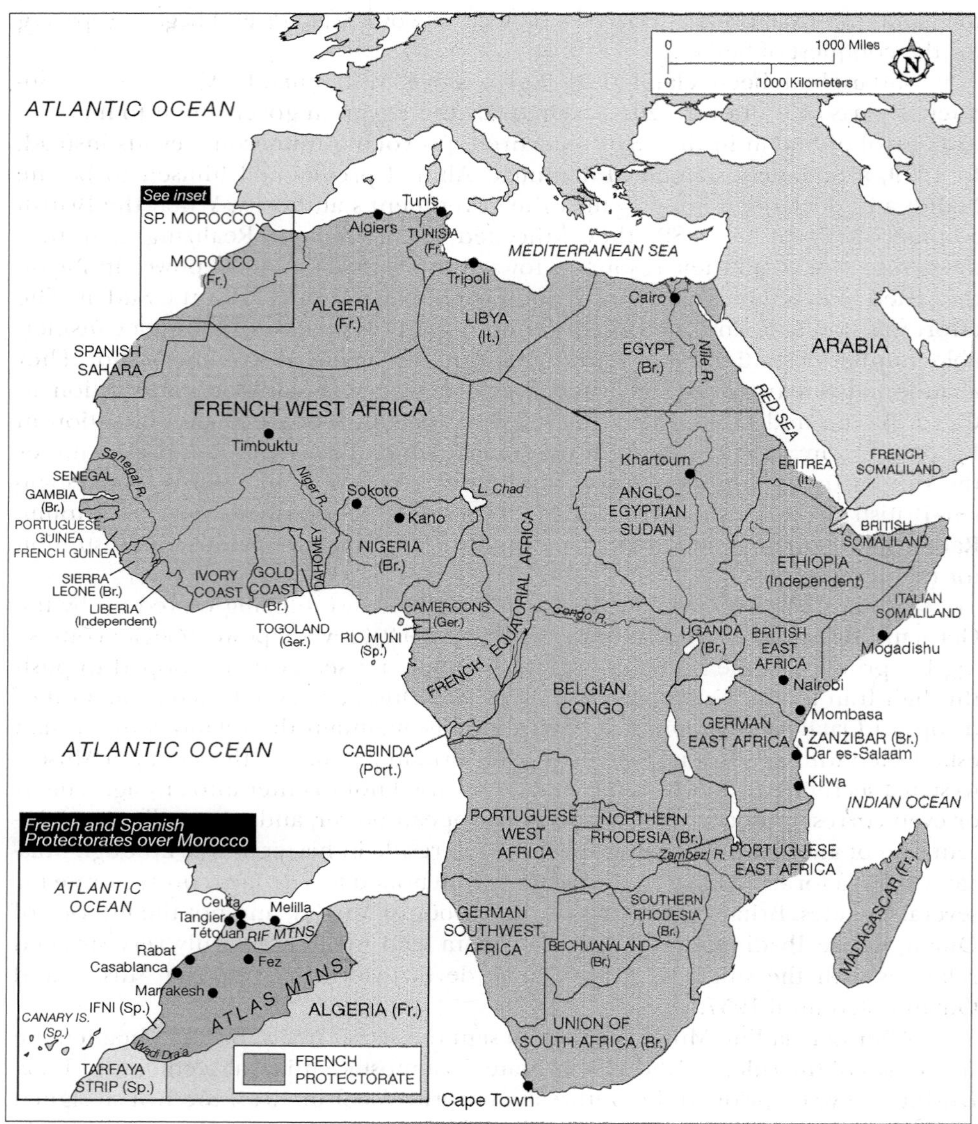

MAP 9.2 Imperialism in Africa.

1907, tensions between the two European powers escalated as each increasingly viewed the other as a threat to its own geopolitical interests. Beginning with the Crimean War (1853–1856), Russia became convinced that Britain was spitefully obstructing St. Petersburg's goals of gaining territory from the Ottoman Empire. Whereas the central and western European powers were satisfied that the 1878 Congress of Berlin had preserved the European balance of power, Russia regarded it as a back-stabbing plot that the British engineered to rob Russia of its hard-won territory. From the British point of view, Russia's annexation of Central Asia and its attempts to gain dominance in Tehran were potentially lethal threats to Britain's possessions in India and its influence in the Persian Gulf. For several important decades, events in Afghanistan and Iran were played out in the shadow of the Great Game, indelibly shaping the character of both countries.

From an economic perspective, Russian officials achieved their major policy objectives in Central Asia when they captured the three major khanates of Khiva, Bukhara, and Tashkent between 1867 and 1875. They knew that further expansion would yield little in the way of economic benefit, but rising international tensions altered their calculation. Russia retaliated for the Congress of Berlin by threatening the British position in South Asia. A few months after the conference, St. Petersburg sent a consul to Kabul without prior authorization from the Afghan government, and the amir was cowed into accepting his presence. The bold move alarmed the British, who had no diplomatic presence in the Afghan capital. They demanded equal representation. The amir's response was not as prompt as the British expected, and they interpreted the delay as a refusal. They invaded Afghanistan and forced the amir into exile. His successor was compelled to sign a treaty in 1879 in which he ceded the city of Quetta, the Khyber Pass, and other territories to the British, and he agreed that the British would control Afghanistan's foreign affairs.

The Russian plan had backfired, extending the string of diplomatic defeats that Russia had suffered at the hands of the British. Rumors began to circulate that St. Petersburg was planning war with Britain. The top generals in the tsar's army were eager to invade India, but the civilian leadership seems to have wanted only to threaten an invasion in order to keep Britain from again thwarting Russian designs in the Balkans. The Russian government began a campaign to seize the desolate plains south of the wealthy Central Asian oases that they already possessed. By establishing military bases and railroads in that region, they would be able to threaten Herat and the easily traveled path south of the Hindu Kush into India.

In 1879, a Russian army marched into the region that is now the country of Turkmenistan. No major military foe opposed them there, for the area was divided into a number of fiefdoms ruled by mutually hostile warlords. The Russians' first objective was the immense, fortified compound of Gek (Geok) Tepe, just west of Ashgabat (Ashkhabad). Gek Tepe was a mud fortress, surrounded by three miles of eighteen-foot-high walls. Russian overconfidence and misjudgments led to a humiliating defeat, and the Russian soldiers had to flee for their lives. Two years later, another Russian army appeared before the fort, determined to exact revenge. Some 40,000 civilians sought refuge in the fort, which was defended by 10,000 troops. This time, the Russians approached their task methodically, employing an intense artillery barrage and a mine under the walls to force an entry. An estimated 8000 Turkmen died inside the walls of the fort. When the survivors fled, the Russians chased down and massacred 6000 more.

In 1885, in a direct challenge to the British, Russia annexed the city of Merv and then pushed 150 miles south toward Herat. Newspapers in Europe and in the United States predicted that war was imminent between the two powers. In spite of the prevailing war fever, the British and Russians agreed to try to avoid further crises by forming a joint commission to determine the northern boundary of Afghanistan. By 1887, they signed a treaty that fixed the boundary as it now stands.

The delineation of the boundary was strictly a Russian–British affair—the Afghan amir was not allowed a voice in the surveying process. Six years later, the British unilaterally decided on the location of the border between British India and Afghanistan. The border, known as the Durand Line after the surveyor who marked it, cut through the main concentration of the Pashtun ethnic group, leaving half on each side of the line. The line was so arbitrary that it sometimes even divided villages from their fields. It became the cause for many conflicts between Pashtuns and the British Indian army, and it continues to plague relations between Afghanistan and Pakistan in the twenty-first century.

When Afghanistan signed agreements with China (1896) and Iran (1905), its borders were fixed for the first time in history. Rather than providing an impetus for development as a modern nation, the borders seem to have had the effect of sealing the nation off from outside influences. Previously, Afghanistan had been a crossroads of international commerce and ideas, but throughout most of the twentieth century, the country was one of the most isolated in the world.

Southeast Asia

For several decades after signing the 1824 Treaty of London, Britain and the Netherlands remained satisfied with their division of the Strait of Melaka. That began to change in the 1850s, when increased commercial activity by French and American merchant ships in East and Southeast Asia made both of them nervous. Then, the opening of the Suez Canal in 1869 promised to transform the dynamics of the entire Indian Ocean. Both Britain and the Netherlands were concerned that another industrialized nation might try to establish a presence at Aceh, at the head of the strait. The treaty of 1824 had specified that Aceh should remain outside the sphere of influence of either Britain or the Netherlands, but in 1871, the two nations signed a treaty that allowed the Dutch to assume control over the sultanate.

By the time of the 1871 treaty, the Dutch had expanded their control over most of southeastern Sumatra and were already pressing on Aceh's frontiers. After the treaty was signed, the sultan of Aceh sought American help against a possible Dutch invasion. To preempt American aid, the Dutch attacked Aceh, expecting a rapid victory. Their confidence was misplaced. Aceh fought a skillful guerilla war, forcing the Dutch to fight for thirty years (1873–1903). By the time the conflict ended in 1903, the Dutch had lost 15,000 soldiers and the Acehnese had lost at least 25,000.

The high cost of the Aceh War in human and material resources convinced the Dutch that they needed to protect their investment in the archipelago by not allowing other outside powers to lay claim to any of the islands. During the last phase of the war, they began to conquer the outlying islands in the Indonesian archipelago, completing the formation of the Netherlands Indies. The last territory acquired was Irian Jaya, or western New Guinea, which was claimed during 1919–1920.

Like the Dutch in Sumatra, the British in Malaysia eventually felt compelled to expand their control over regions that bordered their possessions. The decision was made reluctantly: In the 1820s, expansion was the farthest thing from the mind of officials in London. They had hoped to keep their expenses and commitments to a minimum by assuming control of the Straits Settlements while leaving the Muslim sultans of the other Malay states to keep order in their realms. Their goal was upset by the discovery of vast deposits of tin in the states in the western half of the peninsula. The opportunity for wealth prompted the immigration of tens of thousands of outsiders, mainly Chinese miners and merchants. Conditions in the mining towns resembled the Wild West atmosphere of some American mining towns of the same period. Fighting and near-anarchy prevailed, creating a sense of insecurity among the residents of the Straits Settlements. Beginning in the mid-1860s, merchants and European tin miners began to demand British government intervention.

The British Colonial Office, which was responsible for the Settlements after 1867, was initially reluctant to intervene in the sultanates, but by 1873 it changed policy. The damage to commerce in the region, coupled with the potential threat of foreign intervention, persuaded the Colonial Secretary to order the governor of the Straits Settlements to begin appointing British officers as Residents to the courts of Malay sultans. By the spring of 1874, the unstable sultanates of Perak, Selangor, and Negri Sembilan had accepted the Residents on the assurance that the advisors would only give advice.

Contrary to the sultans' expectations, the Residents quickly became the effective rulers of the sultanates. They controlled taxes and state expenditures as well as all policies except those affecting Islam and Malay customs. Any resistance on the part of the sultans resulted in their exile. Pahang was forced to accept a Resident in 1888, and in 1896, it and the other three sultanates were placed under a unified administration called the Federated Malay States (FMS). In 1909, Britain and the king of Siam (Thailand) signed an agreement whereby Siam renounced its former claims of sovereignty over the Muslim states of Kedah, Kelantan, Perlis, and Terengganu. Britain thereafter designated them to be individual British protectorates. In 1914, Britain forced the sultan of Johor to accept a Resident. Johor and the four former Thai states were ruled in much the same way as the FMS except that each had its own individual administration. Collectively, they were known as the Unfederated Malay States.

Meanwhile, on the northern coast of Borneo, the Muslim Sultanate of Brunei was the victim of continuing territorial expansion on the part of the Brooke dynasty of Sarawak to its west and of British timber companies to its east. In 1888, the sultan voluntarily accepted for his sultanate the status of a British protectorate in order to preclude further territorial losses. Sarawak also became a protectorate at that time. Neither the sultan nor the Brooke family had to accept a British Resident.

During the period in which the Dutch and British claimed the last independent states in Indonesia and Malaya, the Spanish lost the Philippines. Spain had not made control of the entire archipelago a high priority. After it failed to subjugate the Muslim sultanates of the large southern island of Mindanao and of the Sulu archipelago in the sixteenth century, a state of "no peace, no war" characterized relations between Manila and the sultanates for almost three centuries. The Spanish and the Muslims of Sulu and southwestern Mindanao periodically skirmished with each other, but they also engaged in commerce with each other on an increasing scale. The two major rival sultanates in Mindanao—Magindanao and Buayan—occasionally even allied with the Spanish against each other.

In the eighteenth century, the Spanish naval policy of interdicting ships that sailed between Mindanao and China began to weaken the sultanate of Magindanao, whose capital was located on the site of the modern city of Cotabato. The use of steam gunboats after 1846 accelerated Spain's advantage, enabling it to take over the sultanate in 1861 in a bloodless coup. It was another thirty years before the Spanish were able to occupy Buayan, which was upriver from Magindanao. Several minor sultanates on Mindanao remained outside Spanish control. The Sulu Sultanate also resisted Spain's centuries-long attempts to annex it for almost three centuries, but the Spanish navy managed to wrest the northeastern section of the archipelago from its sultan in the 1870s. The newly captured territories were placed under military occupation, but they were not incorporated into the civilian administration of the Philippines.

During the 1890s, nationalist sentiment was building in the Philippines, and Spain narrowly averted a major revolt in 1896. Then, in 1898, Spain's rule over the Philippines was challenged by the United States. During the Spanish–American War, American military leaders proclaimed to the Filipinos that they had come to their islands in order to deliver them from "Spanish tyranny." Persuading Filipino nationalists to join their military campaign, the Americans invaded Luzon. The joint military actions made quick work of the Spanish. Expecting American diplomatic recognition, the Filipinos were shocked to learn in December 1898 that Spain had been forced to sell the islands to the United States. The Filipinos, reeling from what they considered to be a betrayal, revolted against the Americans. The war lasted from 1899 to 1902 and was characterized by vicious fighting and atrocities on both sides. Over 200,000 Filipinos died from fighting, famine, and disease, and over 4000 American soldiers died. Even after the war was officially over, occasional revolts flared throughout the island chain. The most determined resistance took place in the Muslim regions of the south, whose inhabitants were violently opposed to American plans to incorporate their lands into an overwhelmingly Christian Philippines.

Imperial Rule

The impact of imperial rule varied from territory to territory. The British usually preferred a form of indirect rule, whereby a British "advisor" was present to direct overall policy but allowed a considerable degree of autonomy to an indigenous governor. This policy tended to cost the home government less than direct rule did. It also entailed fewer risks of implementing policies that would provoke political unrest by violating local customs. Local conditions dictated the extent to which direct or indirect rule could be implemented. When the British conquered the Sokoto Caliphate, the traditional Islamic institutions that implemented the Shari'a made their work very easy. In eastern and southern Nigeria, by contrast, British administrators had to construct new mechanisms of authority and implement direct rule.

The French usually preferred forms of direct rule. They almost always rationalized their imperial ventures as a *mission civilisatrice* ("civilizing mission") that required direct rule in order to build the schools and other institutions that would enable the indigenous population to absorb French culture. Due to lack of funding and sufficient staff members, little assimilation into French culture actually took place. Only a tiny percentage of subjects attended French schools, and noncitizens had no political rights to protect them from arbitrary arrest and imprisonment.

The American and Dutch imperial ventures combined elements of direct and indirect rule. Americans in the Philippines claimed that their policy of deposing dynastic rulers and instituting direct rule would inculcate traits of individualism and self-reliance in their new subjects. In practice, the policy was never implemented uniformly. In the Muslim south, only the former sultanates of Magindanao and Buayan collaborated with the Americans. In most of the other Muslim areas, local administration remained in the hands of the local elites, as it had under the Spanish. By the end of the first decade of imperial rule, the Americans were beginning to hand over significant authority to Filipinos all over the archipelago.

The Netherlands Indies was scattered throughout thousands of islands and had been obtained piecemeal over a period of four hundred years. The Dutch were utter pragmatists, employing a variety of relationships with the hundreds of local rulers in their imperial possessions. Some were under Dutch direct control, but far more were examples of the "native state" that had agreed to accept Dutch hegemony in return for a greater or lesser degree of local autonomy.

North Africa and Central Asia (along with a few British colonies in sub-Saharan Africa) were among a handful of special cases in the imperial venture that were genuine settler colonies. After 1848, European settlers in Algeria had all the rights and privileges of Frenchmen who lived in mainland France, including representation in the national assembly. Muslims, by contrast, were denied citizenship. With only a few exceptions, Algerian Muslim children were typically denied access to French schooling and were offered training only in agriculture and crafts. French justices of the peace began to operate in place of qadis in some areas, and all litigation involving immovable property was removed from the jurisdiction of qadis. The number of Muslim courts in Algeria was reduced by two-thirds from 1870 to 1890. At the beginning of the twentieth century, European colonists in Algeria comprised one-eighth of the total population of four million, but they owned five-eighths of the wealth.

Russia sought to enforce its political control in Central Asia without necessarily destroying local political administration. The khanates of Bukhara and Khiva retained a large degree of autonomy. In the Kazakh steppes, the Kazakh ruling class was given a privileged status in order to placate it while the region became the focus of a carefully planned colonization project. Between 1891 and 1914, more than one million Russian and Ukrainian colonists settled on the steppes. Other Slavic settlers moved into other parts of Central Asia and the Caucasus.

The imperial impact in most areas has been long-lasting, despite an average period of rule of only seven or eight decades. A major legacy has been the borders that the imperial powers drew. The example of the Durand Line in Afghanistan was repeated hundreds of times. Peoples that shared languages and other cultural features were separated from each other by political boundaries. The new borders shattered affinity groups and disrupted trade routes. Local economies often suffered as a result.

Perversely, the same boundaries that fractured affinity groups also enclosed radically different societies within the same polity. Groups with different languages, religions, and means of subsistence were lumped together and were expected to live together, even if they had a history of hostile relations. As many as 200 or 300 different political groupings might be contained within a single new colony. Two of the most egregious examples were the British protectorates of Nigeria and Sudan. The boundaries drawn for these two possessions had never existed before in history, and they enclosed predominantly Muslim groups in the north of each country with predominantly Christian and animist groups in the south. The religious differences were overlain by linguistic differences and stark contrasts in subsistence patterns, ranging from those who were primarily nomadic savannah dwellers to the inhabitants of rain forests.

The imperial powers invested considerable sums in their new possessions. They built railroads, urban public transport, highways, port facilities, telegraph and telephone networks, and electrical systems, usually for the first time. Even where such infrastructure had already begun appearing prior to formal occupation, the pace of investment typically accelerated after a protectorate was declared, because investors assumed that the security of their property would be guaranteed under European rule. The telegraph and the railways brought immediate benefits to many of the local inhabitants, but the benefits of electric power and telephone service were so costly that their use was restricted to a tiny elite in the imperial possessions. Not accessible even to many rural Americans until the second third of the twentieth century, they are still unavailable to hundreds of millions of people in Africa and Asia.

In spite of the benefits that much of the new infrastructure brought to the territories as a whole, the great bulk of the investment was designed to benefit foreign investors, not the local population. Railway travel, which subject peoples took advantage of without hesitation, is a good example. Railroads were owned by foreigners or the imperial governments, and were laid out with two major objectives: to get raw materials to ports for export and to facilitate troop movements. Although they offered the subject peoples occasional convenience, their routes were not designed to enhance the common welfare by tying the various parts of the country together or to facilitate the natural movements of the local populations.

Improvements to irrigation systems were another major investment that imperial powers announced with great fanfare. Dams and canals did boost agricultural production, but they were built for the cultivation of cash crops that were valued by the imperial power, not for the cultivation of essential foodstuffs that the local populations needed. Local landlords who cooperated with the imperial power grew wealthy. Peasants, on the other hand, often found that they were forced to work harder than before and that they suffered a declining standard of living due to higher taxes and a reduced amount of locally grown food.

Some colonial planners did hope to raise the standard of living of their wards, but it was impossible for any but the richest imperial administration to plan and implement meaningful programs of economic development. Most areas were so devoid of natural resources or indigenous wealth that they could not provide enough revenue to support even such basic administrative services as policing. This plight was particularly striking in the savannah and sahel regions of Africa. Even when colonial administrations attempted to implement humanitarian reforms, the results could be unexpected and disastrous. The most illuminating example was the

French and British abolition of slavery in most of their possessions in West and East Africa during the decade prior to the outbreak of World War I. Half the population in some areas was slave, and the economies were dependent upon their labor. Emancipation meant that crops were not harvested, with the result that large numbers of people starved to death. No governments provided the freed slaves an economic basis to support their freedom, forcing many of them to become squatters. Clashes with property owners were inevitable.

Investments in colonies sometimes brought about significant transformations as local economies became tied into the world market. Rubber trees, for example, were native to Southeast Asia, but the varieties found there were distinctly inferior to those of Brazil. In 1888, British officials introduced the Brazilian variety into Malaya, and the Dutch introduced it into Sumatra in 1900. Within a generation, Southeast Asia was producing most of the world's rubber. Cocoa, native to the Americas, became a major cash crop in West Africa. The introduction of the railroad into Central Asia made possible the cultivation there of American upland cotton for the Russian market: By 1911, cotton occupied a quarter of the arable land of Central Asia, and the region was supplying half the total needs of Russia's cotton textile industry.

New crops were not the only transforming feature of the economies. The growth of exports and the expansion of government services required vast reserves of manpower. Sometimes these were available locally, but in some cases workers were brought in from other countries. Malaya was one of the more dramatic examples: Due to the demand for workers in the tin mines and the new rubber plantations, vast numbers of workers were recruited in India, Ceylon, the Netherlands Indies, and, especially, China. As in the Philippines and the Netherlands Indies, Chinese merchant networks recruited Chinese workers from their homelands and exercised a dominant role in the commerce of several of the Malay states. By the end of the nineteenth century, Malay speakers constituted barely half of the population in the Federated Malay States.

Encounters with Tradition

The imperialist juggernaut generated shock waves throughout the Muslim world. At the beginning of the twentieth century, most Muslims were subject to imperial, non-Muslim masters, and the few remaining independent Muslim states were in danger of falling under European control. In previous eras, members of the ulama had advised Muslims who fell under non-Muslim rule to flee to a Muslim-ruled land. That option had always been economically impractical for the vast majority of settled peoples, but it was even less of an option when all the neighboring countries had been conquered by non-Muslims, too. In the protectorates and the independent states alike, groups of reformers arose to try to preserve their societies from being overwhelmed by outside influences. Almost without exception, they looked to the past for inspiration as they charted a course for the future. Each group had its own set of priorities that it sought to justify by finding antecedents in a particular element of the Islamic legacy. Because each group believed that it represented the essence of Islam, vehement disagreements were common.

The new organizations tended to fall into one of two general groups. One tended to stress political and social issues, whereas the other emphasized moral and spiritual issues. As a result, this section of the chapter makes a distinction between "movements of political and social reform" and "movements of religious reform and renewal." Few of the participants in these movements would have found the distinction meaningful (although a growing number were beginning to accept a Western concept of religion as a matter of the conscience). The purpose of doing so here is to recognize that certain groups made their priority the modernization of governmental and educational structures, whereas others made their priority the deepening of piety and the strengthening of moral virtue.

Movements of Political and Social Reform

Many Muslim reformers devoted their lives to the strengthening of governmental and social institutions. The Ottoman Empire and Qajar Iran were still independent during the most frantic period of imperialism during the last quarter of the nineteenth century, but they were in danger of falling under European dominance. Both countries had experienced various reforms prior to 1875, but the challenges that arose during the period 1875–1914 forced a new generation to exert its energies in an effort to save the nations from succumbing to the imperial powers.

In regions where Europeans or Americans already ruled, it became clear that continued armed resistance against the invaders would be suicidal due to the overwhelming power that recent developments in military technology had granted to the industrialized nations. Some activists, realizing that a single protectorate could not resist alone, hoped to unify the Muslim world against imperialism in a movement known as Pan-Islam. Some of Pan-Islam's leading advocates hoped that a coalition of Muslim nations, armed with modern weapons, could successfully confront the imperial powers on their own terms. Other opponents of imperialism attempted to mobilize opposition to imperialism only in their own country, and in a nonviolent manner. These nationalist movements were the forerunners of the larger and better-organized nationalist movements that proliferated after World War I. A third group of activists in the protectorates shifted the focus away from resistance (although not necessarily abandoning it) and toward cultural renewal. Their priority was modernization, especially of educational systems.

State Reform

The period 1875–1914 was one of almost constant crisis for the Ottoman Empire. Muslim and Christian subjects alike were disillusioned with the Tanzimat reforms that the vizier's office had promulgated, but Sultan Abdulaziz II's evisceration of the vizier's power in 1871 had simply exchanged an ineffective administration for a profligate and reckless one. Then the disastrous conflicts in the Balkans began in 1875. In May 1876, when the Bulgarian conflict reached its horrific stage, reformers were convinced that they had no option but to remove Abdulaziz II. Unfortunately, his successor was incapacitated by paranoia and alcoholism, and so the activist bureaucrats replaced him after only four months with Abdulhamit II (1876–1909).

In December 1876, the reformers promulgated the first constitution in the Muslim world, and an Ottoman parliament met for the first time in April 1877. The Ottoman constitution predated those in many European countries, but the timing of its appearance could hardly have been worse. The liberal ideas that lay at its base were derived from European political thought, and it was precisely Europeans who were criticizing and attacking the empire during the 1876–1878 period. To many Ottomans, it seemed that Europe was about to have political mastery over the empire as well as economic advantages. In addition, many Ottomans were uneasy about the manifest substitution of a secular legal framework for the Shari'a. The Tanzimat was secular, as well, but its provisions could be rationalized as supplements to the Shari'a-based structure of the empire. The new constitution had unequivocally transformed the empire into a secular state. As the Ottoman war effort against Russia went badly, Abdulhamit II was able to exploit the widespread lack of support for the constitution to his benefit. In February 1878, he dissolved parliament and ceased to rule according to the constitution, claiming that the new administrative structure had weakened the Ottomans in the face of efficient Russian absolutism.

The empire was in dire straits, having lost major sources of revenue in the Balkans, caring for half a million refugees from the Balkans, and facing the costs of the war and the indemnities for it that Russia demanded. Treasury officials discovered that eighty percent of the budget was allocated to debt repayment. The government sought an agreement with foreign creditors, and in 1881 it created the Ottoman Public Debt Administration, which assumed control of state revenues. This international body had the authority to collect taxes, allocate state revenues, and pay the government's creditors.

Thus, in 1881, the treasury of the empire and the treasuries of two of its nominal provinces, Tunis and Egypt, were under the control of foreigners. Like Tunis and Egypt, the Ottoman government remained bound to the terms of the sixteenth-century economic privileges known as the Capitulations, which the empire had begun awarding in the sixteenth century to encourage trade with European powers. The Capitulations exempted foreigners from paying tariffs and from being subject to Ottoman law. The Ottomans had granted the concessions when the Ottoman Empire was more powerful than any European state. By the late nineteenth century, when the empire needed protection from powerful capitalist economies, the Capitulations subjected the Ottoman economy and judicial system to the whims of Europeans, who refused to renegotiate the treaties.

Abdulhamit II was reactionary politically, but he realized the need to modernize the empire's infrastructure. He invested in railroads and telegraph systems, and he enacted reforms in education and the judiciary. He searched for a European ally to replace France and Britain—the Ottomans viewed these two countries, which had been the dominant foreign influences during the Tanzimat era, with increasing hostility as they began to seize Ottoman territories in North Africa. Germany offered to supplant them, and Abdulhamit developed close relations with Kaiser Wilhelm II (1888–1918). Germany quickly became the single largest investor in the empire.

Abdulhamit's absolutism provoked opposition. Intellectuals, civil servants, and military officers formed a variety of groups within the empire itself and among communities of exiles living in Europe. Some were most concerned to implement a democratic, constitutional administration, whereas others placed a higher priority on technological modernization. Ultimately, the most important of the opposition groups proved to be the Committee of Union and Progress (CUP), formed in 1889. Its founders were students at the military–medical academy, but the group appealed to a wide variety of people who wanted to be free of European intervention and yet desired to emulate European technology, political organization, and cultural values.

As leader of the Ottoman Empire, Abdulhamit was in possession of a variety of resources to counter his critics. One that he hoped would resonate with the majority of his Muslim subjects was the title of *caliph.* Ottoman sultans included the honorific of caliph in their long list of titles, but the claim had not been emphasized since the early sixteenth century. During first two or three centuries of Muslim history, the title had implied that the caliph was the symbolic head of the entire Sunni community. As the Muslim world became politically fragmented by the year 950, however, the claim had a hollow ring, and it became simply another title that any ambitious Muslim ruler would add to his list of honorifics. Then, during the 1860s, the Turks of Central Asia appealed to Istanbul for help against the Russian conquests. In response, Abdulaziz II (1861–1875) began to refer to his status as the caliph, implying that he was in some sense a spokesman and advocate for all Muslims in the world. There was, in fact, no competing potentate who could challenge his claim. Later, during the ferocious conflicts of 1875–1878 in the Balkans, Muslims in India expressed their concern for the safety of "the caliph" and even donated huge sums of money to help the Ottoman cause. Thereafter, Abdulhamit II wielded the title frequently, and he threatened to mobilize the whole Muslim world against the French and British if they appropriated any more of his territory. He also hoped to cultivate the loyalty of his own subjects by shifting the terms of debate from his abrogation of a modern, European-style constitution to the fact that he shared the title once held by the successors of the Prophet.

A palpable change took place during this period in the Ottoman government's relations with its minority subjects. For centuries, European visitors to the empire had been surprised to discover the degree of toleration that the government granted to its numerous linguistic and religious groups. Although Ottoman Muslims were convinced that they were superior to non-Muslims and required non-Muslims to pay a special tax, non-Muslims were not persecuted or subject to a policy of harassment. No European government prior to the French Revolution was even remotely as tolerant of religious minorities as the Ottoman state was.

During the nineteenth century, as the empire came increasingly under European pressure, xenophobia began to manifest itself, and during the last quarter of the century, some Ottoman Muslims began to express outright hostility toward non-Muslims. Causes for the change in attitude began accumulating from midcentury: Between the early 1850s and the late 1860s, the Russians expelled Crimean Muslims during and after the Crimean War, expelled and killed Muslims of Circassia and the Caucasus, and brutally conquered Muslim Central Asia. Over one million survivors of these conflicts entered the Ottoman Empire as homeless and starving refugees, with horror stories of those who had been killed in their homelands. During this same time, the British brutally suppressed the 1857 Indian uprising and blamed Muslims for starting and directing it.

The Tanzimat's declaration of the intention to grant equal legal rights to the empire's own Christians seemed asymmetrical to many Ottoman Muslims in light of how Britain and Russia were treating Muslims, and many were convinced that legal equality for non-Muslims was in direct violation of the Shari'a. In 1875–1878, Ottoman Muslims were furious at what they considered the hypocrisy of Europeans, as the latter condemned Muslim massacres of Christians but ignored Christian massacres of Muslims. They also had to confront the needs of an additional half-million Muslim refugees from the Balkan wars who were desperate, angry, and demanding revenge. Then, in 1881–1882, the French seized Tunis, and the British invaded and occupied Egypt.

The Christian group that suffered the brunt of Muslim frustration was the Armenian millet. That was ironic, because historically, this millet had the best relations with the Ottoman elites of all the non-Muslim groups. Their merchants, craftsmen, and translators had maintained close relations with the palace, and as late as the turn of the twentieth century, Armenians continued to hold important posts in the Ottoman government. During the nineteenth century, the Armenian community in the large coastal cities of western Anatolia enjoyed increased economic prosperity, rapidly rising educational levels, and a new political awareness.

The period that seemed to portend a glorious future for Armenians ended with horror. The precise reasons for the Armenian massacres of the 1890s are unknown, but historians have identified several factors that helped to shape the context for them. One was an echo of the undercurrent of anti-Semitism that was sweeping Western Europe at the same time. Just as many European Christians resented the success that newly emancipated Jews were experiencing, many Ottoman Muslims resented the contrast between the improving conditions for Armenians and the worldwide decline in the conditions for Muslims. Another factor was the Ottoman–Russian war of the late 1870s, when groups of Armenians in eastern Anatolia aided the Russian army and some moved to Russia when the Russian army withdrew from Ottoman territory. Russia was the Ottomans' arch-enemy, and the revelation that groups of Armenians on the eastern frontier were betraying the empire on behalf of Russia cast a cloud over the deliberations of Abdulhamit's government. A third factor was a handful of Armenian extremists who demanded autonomy or even independence for Armenians in the empire. They began a campaign of assassinations of Ottoman officials and of random public bombings. A fourth element in the background to the massacres was the sultan himself, who was never averse to using force to respond to threats to his power or the empire's integrity. Having lost the vast bulk of his Balkan holdings to Christian nationalists, he was suspicious of Armenian intentions and was determined not to allow yet another Christian group to shrink the empire by seceding.

In 1894, when Armenian peasants in eastern Anatolia defended themselves against attacks by Kurdish brigands, Ottoman forces responded to the clashes by massacring thousands of Armenian peasants, not the Kurds. Then, on two occasions in 1895 and 1896, peaceful demonstrations by Armenian political radicals in Constantinople were followed by government-led massacres of Armenians in numerous locations throughout Anatolia. Most historians who have studied the three incidents conclude that the Ottoman government killed between 100,000 and 300,000 of its own Armenian subjects. The vast majority of the victims were not political radicals and never knew why they were being slaughtered. The massacres did not provoke intervention from outside powers, but these massacres joined the Bulgarian Horrors in the consciousness of Europeans, deepening their aversion toward the Ottoman state.

As the twentieth century dawned, opposition toward the sultan continued to grow, both within the empire and among Ottoman associations in Europe. The best-organized group was the Committee of Union and Progress (CUP), which was based in cells of military officers stationed in garrisons from Syria to Macedonia. In 1908, members of the CUP led a coup d'état and forced Abdulhamit to reinstate the constitution of 1876. The following year, they removed Abdulhamit and became the power behind his successor, who served as a mere figurehead. The coup was greeted with demonstrations of relief and joy by Muslims and non-Muslims alike. The defunct constitution had been so idealized for thirty years that multitudes who knew nothing of its content were convinced that it would magically make possible the fulfillment of their dreams, whatever they were. They were to be quickly disillusioned.

The Young Turks, as the members of the CUP were called, had aspired to modernize their country following European models. Their long-standing admiration for European technology and political systems quickly turned to anger, however. Expecting to win European approval for their overthrow of a despot, the CUP instead had to confront a series of hostile acts from European nations. Shortly after the 1908 coup, Austria annexed Bosnia and Herzegovina, which it had administered since 1878 but which were technically still Ottoman territories. In 1911, Italy invaded Libya, and during 1912–1913, a coalition composed of Serbia, Greece, Bulgaria, and Montenegro attacked their former Ottoman masters in an attempt to gain more territory from them. By 1913, the only European territory remaining in Ottoman hands lay to the east of Edirne.

In the face of this series of dangers, the CUP began to centralize its power with a vengeance. Moreover, it gradually began to cultivate a Turkish identity for the remaining parts of the empire, even though large sections of the population, notably the Arabs, were non-Turkish. The CUP's single-minded and heavy-handed approach toward governing began to alienate important provincial elites. By 1914, as a major war loomed in Europe, the CUP had forfeited much of the loyalty it desperately needed.

Iran, like the Ottoman Empire, struggled during the decades after 1875 to avoid collapsing under the pressure of European economic and military superiority. It was even less equipped to do so than the Ottomans. Throughout the nineteenth century, Iran lagged behind the Ottoman Empire in its exposure to modern developments in technology, science, politics, and military reform. Moreover, in 1879, Shah Naser al-Din (1848–1896) was so impressed by the Cossack troops that he saw during a visit to Russia that he requested the creation of a Cossack Brigade in Tehran, whose officers would be Russians. This well-trained and well-paid military force became an effective channel through which St. Petersburg could exert its influence.

Iran's chronic shortage of revenue led its ministers to offer numerous concessions to foreign firms, as happened with the Reuter concession of 1872. In return for a cash payment, rent, and a share of the profits, more and more foreigners were granted monopolies over various sectors of the economy. Most were on a small scale, but in 1890, news of a concession on the scale of the Reuter monopoly was leaked to the public. This one was considered even worse: Whereas the Reuter concession had planned to create new capital improvements in the country, this one granted a fifty-year monopoly to a British subject for the production, sale, and export of all Iranian tobacco. Thus, rather than creating a new national infrastructure, it would have hurt the existing economic interests of farmers, shopkeepers, and export merchants. A wide array of groups, from secular reformers and members of the ulama to the shah's wives, joined together to lead what became the first successful mass political opposition movement in modern Iranian history. Violent protests and a highly successful boycott of tobacco products forced the cancellation of the concession.

Any hopes that this display of public anger would halt the granting of concessions were soon dashed. Concessions continued to be plentiful, with Russians receiving the largest number. The most important was the petroleum concession granted to an Australian, William D'Arcy, in 1901. D'Arcy was given exclusive rights to the exploitation of gas and petroleum reserves for sixty years in central and southern Iran. The company struck oil in 1908, leading to the creation of the Anglo–Persian Oil Company the following year. The British navy was in the process of switching from coal-powered engines to oil-burning engines at the time, but the United Kingdom had no petroleum reserves of its own. In 1914, for reasons of national security, Parliament supported the cabinet's proposal to purchase a controlling interest in Anglo–Persian in order to guarantee an oil supply for the nation. Fortunately for the British, this occurred eleven days before the assassination of Archduke Franz Ferdinand, which began the countdown to the outbreak of the Great War.

The ineptitude and corruption of the Iranian government during the first few years of the twentieth century were too obvious to ignore. Antigovernment sentiment became widespread again, and a major opposition movement erupted in late 1905. During the winter of 1905–1906, numerous members of the ulama, merchants from the bazaar, and secular intellectuals united in a protest that took on the dimensions of a national movement. They demanded the establishment of a representative assembly, and some began advocating the writing of a constitution. The Qajar shah, shaken by the huge movement, agreed to the creation of a *majlis,* or assembly.

The Iranian constitutional movement faced impossible odds. Its Ottoman counterpart had the advantages of access to European sources of constitutional thought, powerful support in the government, and a strong secular impulse, and it still failed. Iranian intellectuals were much further removed from European thought, and the constitutional movement was a popular protest that was opposed by the most powerful forces in the government. Perhaps most critically, the coalition that demanded a constitution contained a large number of religious clerics who belatedly realized that a constitutional system might well be incompatible with some of their prerogatives and religious assumptions alike.

The Majlis opened in October 1906. One of its first measures was to name a committee to write a Fundamental Law. It soon became clear that the constitutional impulse had its roots in the popular anger against foreign exploitation of the country: The major focus of the Fundamental Law, which was based on the Belgian constitution, was to subject the shah and his ministers to the oversight of the Majlis, particularly in matters of treaties and foreign loans. The document also guaranteed equality before the law for people of all religions, and, like British law, it provided freedom of speech and press as long as blasphemy was not committed. The Majlis committed itself to provide public education for all children.

The constitutional movement had an electric impact on Iranian society. All over the country, volunteer associations, city councils, newspapers, and literary and revolutionary societies appeared. Newspapers and political organizations expressed a wide range of political opinion, including Marxism. In spite of the growing reservations of some members of the ulama, who were beginning to realize that their role would be diminished in a constitutional system, the possibilities for Iranian political development were wide open.

We will never know what would have happened if Iran had been able to develop without interference, though. In 1907, Russia and Britain brought an end to the Great Game. Britain had become more concerned about Germany's massive naval project than Russia's intentions in Asia, whereas Russia needed to recover from its defeat in the 1904–1905 Russo–Japanese war and the political and economic damage caused by the Revolution of 1905. The two powers signed a treaty settling their differences in Asia. The treaty, known as the Anglo–Russian Convention of 1907, included a partition of Iran, regarding which no Iranian official was consulted. The Russians claimed a sphere of influence in northern Iran, including most major cities. The British moved troops into southeastern Iran, and the central section of the country remained a neutral zone between the two great powers.

Tsar Nicholas II, who was in the process of eviscerating the parliament that liberals had demanded as a condition of bringing the Revolution of 1905 to a close, sided with the shah in his own resistance to a parliament. In June 1908, the shah ordered his Cossack Brigade against the Majlis, and the building was almost destroyed by artillery fire. Several leading constitutionalists were executed, and others fled the country. When the shah's inept rule almost caused the nation to collapse, Russia and Britain allowed the constitutionalists to regain power in 1909. The new government, determined to turn its back on traditional Qajar fiscal measures, invited an American economic delegation to help it organize its finances. The financial reforms proved to be so successful that the British and Russians feared that Iran might attempt to become independent of them. Threatening military violence, they closed the Majlis in December 1911. The constitutional revolution was over. Under the watchful eyes of the British and the Russians, a weak shah and a conservative cabinet tried to act as though they were managing a sovereign country.

Educational Reform

One of the most significant developments in the history of the modern Muslim world was the introduction of schools patterned after Western models. Rulers and private individuals alike recognized that the challenge of European technological, economic, and military power required Muslim nations to develop educational systems that would enable their own people to compete with the foreigners. Many of them began a deliberate policy of imitating Western models of curriculum and organization in the expectation that their own societies would be transformed.

It is useful to bear in mind that the curriculum, organization, and purpose of elementary, secondary, and university education in mid-nineteenth-century Europe and the United States bore little similarity to what we know today. Elementary and secondary education were only then becoming responsibilities of the state in those regions, and universities were undergoing wrenching changes in their curriculum and identity. The study of Latin and Greek texts remained the heart of the curriculum of the most prestigious European and American universities until the second half of the nineteenth century, but the centrality of the classics was under attack: The intellectual excitement generated by the Scientific Revolution and Enlightenment had cultivated a growing attention to mathematics, experimental inquiry, and political theory during the eighteenth century. More and more texts began to appear in the vernacular rather than in Latin, and the study of modern languages began to challenge the dominance of Latin and Greek. Courses in "moral philosophy" (an examination of ethics based upon reason and natural law) became more popular than courses in Christian doctrine. The slow accumulation of these changes led almost imperceptibly to a rearrangement of priorities at universities and to a change in the very definition of a college education. Universities had become places for the discovery of knowledge, rather than merely the transmission of knowledge. The new type of university, appearing simultaneously with the Industrial Revolution, capitalism, and political liberalism, became a major factor in the rapid growth in power of the nations of the north Atlantic.

During the period when Europeans and Americans were beginning to make major changes in their educational institutions, the structure and purpose of Muslim education remained largely as it had been for centuries. As in premodern Europe, education in the Muslim world was viewed as a philanthropic enterprise. With the exception of specialized palace schools, the major schools were funded by religious endowments granted by wealthy individuals. Some madrasas, as we saw in Chapter 8, began to revise their approach to the study of the Shari'a, but they continued to play the same role that they had for centuries. Independent of the state, they nevertheless provided the state with a cadre of socially prominent men who had been rigorously trained in memorization and scholastic argument, and whose character had been shaped by exposure to the finest values of the Islamic heritage. The ulama who were products of the madrasa were assumed to be competent not only to serve as imams of major mosques and teachers in madrasas, but also to meet the demands of a variety of civilian posts in the state administration. The need for specialists (such as military engineers) was satisfied by the existence of palace schools and state-funded technical schools.

As Muslim rulers became aware of the growing disparity of power between Europe and their own societies, they realized that they could not rely on the madrasas to provide them with the professionals required to create and staff a modern army and navy, an industrial infrastructure, and a government bureaucracy. As a result, they embarked upon a crash program to create schools based on European models. Muhammad 'Ali of Egypt (1805–1849) and Mahmut II of the Ottoman Empire (1808–1839) were the first to do so. The impetus for their action was the need to train officers for their armed forces. Both sent student delegations to Europe to learn modern languages (especially French) and modern academic subjects. The plan was to translate European textbooks into Arabic or Ottoman Turkish for use at the schools and then for the European-trained students to take over the operation of the schools. Muhammad ʿAli established technical schools that trained military officers, military engineers, military doctors, and translators. The schools were created hastily, and they were not part of an overall educational system. No modern primary or secondary schools were created that would have prepared students for the professional institutions. These did not appear until the reign of Ismaʿil (1863–1879), who also created a state-funded teacher education college.

The Ottoman government established a modern medical college in 1827 that used French as the language of instruction, and it created numerous technical and professional schools for its army and navy. Over the decades, these schools gradually provided an educated, professional elite that served the civilian sector, as well. The goal of the Tanzimat reformers to create a full system of secular primary and secondary schools was thwarted by chronic budget shortages and opposition from the ulama, but by 1900 the state had opened a university. Even more numerous than these government-funded schools were schools that were founded by Europeans and Americans. Most were established by missionary groups, but some were created by diplomats and merchants for the children of expatriate communities. Many still exist. Among the most influential were the Syrian Protestant College (now American University in Beirut) in Lebanon and Robert College in Istanbul, both founded in the 1860s. St. Joseph University in Beirut began as a college of medicine in 1881, and then added engineering and law by 1913; the American University in Cairo opened its doors as a secondary school in 1920 but rapidly added college-level courses. All of these were founded by missionaries except Robert College, which began at the initiative of a businessman.

In addition to the new state-funded schools and the private schools that were established by European and American interests were Western-style schools set up by private Muslim groups. Perhaps the largest private-initiative Muslim movement was an educational reform movement that arose in the Russian Empire during the last quarter of the nineteenth century. It was known as Jadidism (from the Arabic word *jadid,* meaning "new") because of the movement's focus on the teaching of Arabic by means of a new phonetic method. Jadidism was prominent among the Turkic Muslim communities of the Crimea, the Volga River, Transcaucasia, the Kazakh steppe, and Transoxiana. Because each of those regions had different conditions and needs, the content and concerns of Jadidism varied slightly from region to region, but all of the branches of the movement included the new method of teaching Arabic, a commitment to the notion of progress, and the creation of schools with a modern curriculum. Its proponents established publishing houses and opened bookstores to disseminate their ideas. They also tried, unsuccessfully, to develop a form of literary Turkish that all Turkic peoples of Russia could use. Among the most prominent leaders of Jadidism were Ismaʿil Gasprinskii of the Crimea (1851–1914) and Mahmud Behbudi (1874–1919) of Samarqand.

The central focus of Jadidism was to improve formal education, but it was also a cultural reform movement that sought to improve public morality and eliminate superstitions from the practice of Islam. It was not a nationalist movement. Its adherents voiced no demands for separation from Russia or even for self-government. It defended a modernist interpretation of Islam against what its adherents considered to be obscurantist ulama on one side and the hostile attacks of Russian Orthodox Christianity on the other.

In India, a major contribution to higher education was the opening in 1875 of the Muhammadan Anglo–Oriental College, known today as Aligarh Muslim University. The founder of the college was Sayyid Ahmad Khan (1817–1898), a member of the wealthy landholding social class whose ancestors had held important positions within the Mughal Empire and the Naqshbandi Sufi order. He was an employee of the East India Company when the revolt of 1857 occurred. That event, coupled with his own first-hand experience of visiting Europe in 1869–1870, convinced him that Muslims had to master Western techniques and learning in order to compete in the modern world.

Sayyid Ahmad Khan knew that Islamic civilization had once been unsurpassed in the world. Now, he felt, the culture of Indian Muslims had deteriorated to such a profound degree that Muslims had no choice but to be tutored by the British. When he visited England, he pronounced himself to be embarrassed by the disparity between the levels of culture in Europe and in India. He was convinced that, for Muslims to be qualified to hold positions in the British-dominated government of India, they would have to be educated in schools with a Western curriculum. Sayyid Ahmad explicitly used Cambridge University as a model for the organization and curriculum of his new college, and he decreed that its language of instruction would be English. He proclaimed that he wanted Indian Muslims to be able to obtain an English education without the Christianity that was still a part of most English schools' curricula.

The new, Western-inspired schools became the primary source of recruits for government service from Morocco to Indonesia. Imperial powers were in a dilemma. On the one hand, they required technocrats, clerks, and lower-level bureaucrats, but on the other, imperial officials were acutely aware of the risks they ran in operating such schools: Graduates from the schools would be equipped with the concepts and skills that would enable them to challenge the legitimacy of imperial rule. The British, for example, deliberately limited the number of public secondary schools in Egypt to the point that fewer than one hundred students graduated annually from them as late as 1900. British officials also fought the attempts to create the privately funded Egyptian University, which finally opened its doors in 1908.

The administrators of madrasas also felt pressure to introduce elements of a Western-style curriculum into their schools. They almost uniformly rejected the idea, however, because of the fear that doing so would be an admission that Islamic culture was inferior to Western culture. Thereafter, as a result, a madrasa education prepared a man for little other than to be a teacher in a madrasa or the imam of a mosque. Two parallel systems of education existed side by side in most of the Sunni Muslim world: One offered a Western curriculum—perhaps with an optional class in religion—and the other offered a religious curriculum with little or no instruction in science, mathematics, philosophy, history, or geography. Because madrasas remained largely unchanged, their students had few skills that qualified them for government service. This situation became aggravated as rulers—whether Muslim or imperialist—issued new regulations and established new courts for their needs. The new courts and their procedures relegated the judicial services of the ulama solely to the scope of family law: marriage, divorce, and inheritance.

The ulama had once been the most highly respected group in society. Most began life with the advantage of belonging to the ranks of the social elites, and they acquired the added luster of having mastered a rigorous curriculum exclusively devoted to the religious sciences. By the dawn of the twentieth century, the situation had changed. The social elites tended to send their sons to Western schools due to the much greater career opportunities they offered. The ulama increasingly came from the ranks of the middle or lower social classes, for whom a madrasa education still retained a high status. The lack of knowledge about the modern world that most of the ulama demonstrated, combined with their lower social status, created a palpable divide between them and the social elites.

Their plight may be illustrated by the contrast posed by their contemporaries, the Christian clergy of Europe and the United States. The clergy in the major Christian denominations attended a university and then a theological seminary. They could attract corporate executives and scientists to their congregations because they shared a common world view derived from their modern education, and they could demonstrate their competence in their professional specialization, just as their peers in business and science could. The ulama, on the other hand, could not carry on a conversation very long with members of the new Muslim professional classes. A fissure had emerged among the educated classes of society that would lead to serious problems in the future. Meanwhile, the status of the ulama remained high among the majority of Muslims, and was perhaps at an all-time high: The economic and political disruptions of imperialism had demoralized and frightened many people. They sought comfort and assurances from their religious leaders. The vast majority were illiterate, and so the narrow frame of learning of their imams did not trouble them.

Pan-Islam

A popular response to the assault of imperialism on the Muslim world was *Pan-Islam*. It became widespread during the same era that Pan-Slavism, Pan-Germanism, and Pan-Hellenism were inspirational ideals for other groups of people. Just as the European analogues of Pan-Islam could celebrate and exploit religious values without being religious movements themselves, so Pan-Islam has had only an incidental relationship with religious revivalism or religious reform. Unlike its European counterparts, Pan-Islam is still a factor on the international scene.

References to Pan-Islam, or transnational Muslim unity, began among the Young Ottomans in the 1860s. Its most famous advocate, however, was not an Ottoman, but rather an Iranian who pretended to be an Afghan. Jamal al-Din al-Afghani (1838–1897) was one of the more remarkable figures of his age. He was a highly charismatic figure who traveled widely throughout the world. He spent extended periods of time in Afghanistan, India, Anatolia, Egypt, the Hijaz, France, England, and Russia. Afghani became a political radical after visiting Afghanistan and India during—or immediately after—the 1857 Indian revolt. He became a hostile critic of both the British and the corrupt and incompetent rulers that held sway in the Muslim world. He wanted to become an agent of change, mobilizing Muslims to oppose both the British and corrupt indigenous rulers with force. For him to succeed, he would have to overcome two handicaps. One was the reputation he developed as a young man of being a free thinker and even a heretic. In fact, at no time in Afghani's adult life does he appear to have been a pious man who was concerned with spirituality or with scrupulous regard for adherence to the Shari'a. The other obstacle was that, as a native of predominantly Shi'ite Iran, he would be viewed with suspicion in the predominantly Sunni Turkish, Arab, Afghan, and Indian regions.

In order to overcome the first handicap, Afghani couched his message in terms of Muslim unity. He did not urge a return to the Qur'an and Hadith, as the revivalists did, and he did not reach out to the ulama, most of whom he despised. He insisted, rather, on the need to resist the West and to strengthen the Muslim world against outside attack and internal corruption. He taught that Islam, rightly understood, was the instrument that could defeat the West. Islam, he argued, was compatible with reason, freedom of thought, and modern science and technology. Afghani finessed his Iranian origin by claiming that he was an Afghan, not an Iranian. Because the overwhelming majority of Afghans were Sunnis, Muslims everywhere assumed that Afghani himself was a Sunni. The new identity was a convenient disguise, because most Afghans spoke a dialect of Persian, Afghani's native language.

At first, Afghani urged Muslims to rise against both their local, corrupt Muslim rulers and against the imperial powers that ruled their country. Over time, he began to realize that opposition to imperialism would require a coalition of Muslim powers. Because he knew that he would have to harness the power of Muslim states, and not just the masses, he softened his criticism of Muslim rulers. He even attempted to become a political advisor to Shah Naser al-Din of Iran (1848–1896) and Sultan Abdulhamit II of the Ottoman Empire (1876–1909), two rulers whom he held in contempt. In the end, though, his impatience led to his undoing. He could not refrain from criticizing Naser al-Din, whose court expelled him from Iran. He moved to the court of Abdulhamit II in 1892, where he developed his message that the Muslim world needed a universal caliph to preside over a pan-Islamic society. He argued that the Ottoman sultan was the only possible choice for that role. Unfortunately for Afghani, he could not conceal his disgust with Abdulhamit, and he was forced to live under house arrest under his Ottoman "host." In 1896, apparently at Afghani's instigation, one of his disciples assassinated Naser al-Din. A year later, Afghani died of cancer, alone.

In his commitment to modernizing the Muslim world, Afghani resembled Sayyid Ahmad Khan, who founded the university at Aligarh, but the two men were worlds apart politically and temperamentally. Sayyid Ahmad freely admitted Indian backwardness and believed that it was in the Indians' best interest to learn from the British as a pupil would from a tutor. He devoted his life to an internally consistent intellectual struggle to accommodate the Indian Muslim experience to the modern world. Afghani, by contrast, was a man of action who adopted a variety of poses to provoke fellow Muslims to action. His writings contain a diverse set of attitudes and arguments, making it difficult to systematize his thought but making it easy for Muslims with a wide range of commitments to claim him as an inspiration.

Afghani was genuinely enraged by Sayyid Ahmad's deferential attitude toward the British, and he wrote a blistering attack on Sayyid Ahmad in late 1880 or early 1881 entitled "The Refutation of the Materialists." It is his most famous essay, and his rhetorical devices make it appear that he is a devout Muslim, defending Islam against an atheistic naturalist. Two years later, in 1883, Afghani wrote an article in a French journal—one unlikely to be read by Muslims—in which he unambiguously argues that all religions, including Islam, are hostile to philosophy and science, which seek to free the mind from the shackles of religion. This essay caused the eminent French skeptic Ernest Renan to believe that Afghani was a kindred spirit.

Afghani has continued to influence generations of young Muslims who are frustrated with the political, economic, and military weakness of the Muslim world. Many among the ulama continue to distrust his ideas, but he is highly popular among groups of Muslims who seek to modernize and strengthen their societies without Westernizing them. His legacy stresses the quest to identify historical precedents that legitimize borrowings from modern, Western culture. For Afghani and his disciples, the West poses a dilemma. On the one hand, it is a threat to one's society and religious tradition, and yet it is the source of the technology, science, philosophy, and education that are needed to repel it.

Early Nationalist and Communal Movements

Afghani's message evolved into Pan-Islam after he became convinced that local efforts could not succeed against modern imperial armies. Other anti-imperialist Muslims channeled their energies into nationalist or communal movements instead, although some nationalist and communal movements exploited pan-Islamic appeal when it served their purposes.

Nationalism was a nineteenth-century phenomenon in Europe that reconceptualized the notion of identity. People all over the world had traditionally answered the question, "Who are you?" by identifying themselves as members of a family, the subjects of a ruler, the inhabitants of a village or region, the speakers of a language, or the adherents of a particular religion. After the French Revolution, most Europeans gradually became convinced that their identity was that of a member of a *nation,* a group of people who shared common characteristics—especially language—and a common historical experience. The political objective of nationalism was usually to create a *nation–state:* a government representing the nation, with its own distinctive geographical boundaries.

When Europeans subsequently carved up the rest of the globe during the era of imperialism, they took with them both their technology and their assumptions. They surveyed their new possessions, drew boundaries, and gave names to places (such as *Libya*) and peoples (such as *Libyans*). Often, as in the case of Libya, the names of the places and peoples bore no relation to terms that the inhabitants themselves used. In some cases, the notion of national identity took root easily, because it reinforced existing concepts. Egypt is an example. Many Egyptians along the Nile valley already thought of themselves as distinct from the peoples south of Aswan and the peoples east or west of the Nile. The political content of nationalism was also very useful: If a nation should have its own nation–state based on the principle of self-determination, then imperialism was a violation of the very principles that Europeans cherished so strongly at home. Nationalist movements possessed the moral high ground in their struggle for self-determination and independence.

Whereas nationalism sought an identity in a nation, and Pan-Islam sought an identity in a supranational group, *communalism* was the expression of a search for

Al-Afghani on Faith and Reason

The selection included here comes from the 1883 article discussed in the text that Jamal al-Din al-Afghani wrote in response to an earlier article by Ernst Renan. In his letter, Afghani refers to an alleged instance of persecution of philosophers by the caliph al-Hadi. He cites the fifteenth-century Egyptian scholar al-Suyuti as his source. The reference to al-Hadi's alleged purge is puzzling. We have no record of the caliph's having ordered such a thing, and he is unlikely to have done so: He ruled for only a few months during 785–786, and his reign occurred during a period that was much earlier than the era when ulama perceived philosophy to be a threat to Islam. Philosophers did encounter growing—but nonlethal—difficulties from the late ninth century on.

It is permissible . . . to ask oneself why Arab civilization, after having thrown such a live light on the world, suddenly became extinguished; why this torch has not been relit since; and why the Arab world still remains buried in profound darkness.

Here the responsibility of the Muslim religion appears complete. It is clear that wherever it became established, this religion tried to stifle the sciences and it was marvelously served in its designs by despotism.

Al-Suyuti tells that the Caliph al-Hadi put to death in Baghdad 5000 philosophers in order to destroy sciences in the Muslim countries down to their roots. Admitting that this historian exaggerated the number of victims, it remains nonetheless established that this persecution took place, and it is a bloody stain for the history of a religion as it is for the history of a people. I could find in the past of the Christian religion analogous facts. Religions, by whatever names they are called, all resemble each other. No agreement and no reconciliation are possible between these religions and philosophy. Religion imposes on man its faith and its belief, whereas philosophy frees him of it totally or in part. How could one therefore hope that they would agree with each other? When the Christian religion, under the most modest and seductive forms, entered Athens and Alexandria, which were, as everyone knows, the two principal centers of science and philosophy, after becoming solidly established in these two cities its first concern was to put aside real science and philosophy, trying to stifle both under the bushes of theological discussions, to explain the inexplicable mysteries of the Trinity, the Incarnation, and Transubstantiation.

It will always be thus. Whenever religion will have the upper hand, it will eliminate philosophy; and the contrary happens when it is philosophy that reigns as sovereign mistress. So long as humanity exists, the struggle will not case between dogma and free investigation, between religion and philosophy; a desperate struggle in which, I fear, the triumph will not be for free thought, because the masses dislike reason, and its teachings are only understood by some intelligences of the elite, and because, also, science, however beautiful it is, does not completely satisfy humanity, which thirsts for the ideal and which likes to exist in dark and distant regions that the philosophers and scholars can neither perceive nor explore.

SOURCE: Nikki R. Keddie, *An Islamic Response to Imperialism: Political and Religious Writings of Sayyid Jamāl ad-Dīn "al-Afghānī"* (Berkeley and Los Angeles: University of California Press, 1983), 187.

identity in a subnational loyalty. It is the assumption that the religious community is a social and political entity as well as a spiritual association. Communalism entails the conviction that the members of a religious group possess specific interests in common and will act politically to protect those interests. This sense of identity worked in opposition to nationalism, for it denied the claim that individuals' shared national characteristics—such as language and common historical experience—transcended other differences. Well-organized nationalist and communal groups emerged only after World War I, but Egypt and India produced several prototypes prior to the war. The Egyptian organizations that emerged before the war were eclipsed in 1919 by a new movement as the dynamic force of Egyptian nationalism, so we will focus on the two organizations that shaped the pattern of Indian independence.

The Indian National Congress was established in 1885 by an Englishman sympathetic to the difficulties that Indian businessmen were having in communicating their wishes to British government officials. For three decades it remained an organization for business and landowning elites from all major religious groups in the country. During that period, Indian independence did not appear among its goals. Instead, Congress focused on the expansion of the elective principle in provincial legislative councils (most members of which were appointed by the British government) and greater Indianization of the administration. Congress attracted several talented Muslims to its membership. The most notable of its early Muslim members was Muhammad Ali Jinnah (1876–1948), who was from a Khoja family in Karachi. Jinnah gained his law degree in London during the 1890s and settled in Bombay after returning to India. He joined Congress in 1906. Jinnah's brilliant legal mind and ability to work with Indians of many religious backgrounds soon convinced the leading Hindus of Congress that he might well be the individual who would eventually lead a united India to independence.

Many other Muslims were wary of Congress. Sayyid Ahmad Khan opposed the work of Congress when it became clear that it was seeking a representative government for India. He was convinced that the interests of Hindus and Muslims were so opposed that they constituted two separate nations. He was afraid that national elections would consign Muslims, who formed twenty-five to thirty percent of India's population, to inferior status. He urged fellow Muslims to boycott elections and to deal directly with the British instead, securing positions of power by appointment.

Sayyid Ahmad was in a minority of Muslims in his cultural ideas, but he spoke for a growing number of Muslims in his political sensitivities. Rifts between Muslims and Hindus were gradually widening during this period. All knowledgeable observers—British, Muslim, and Hindu—agreed that the wealthy and well-educated Hindu merchant class had no counterpart among the Muslims. This middle class was achieving success in gaining important positions of influence in the economy and politics of India. Moreover, a dynamic Hindu renaissance was underway that made many Muslims anxious. A few Hindu extremists proclaimed the goal of a Hindu-dominated India in which Muslims would be subservient, and some began campaigns to protect cows from being slaughtered.

The major issue that unnerved Muslims toward the end of the century was a campaign by Hindus that challenged Urdu's newly won dominance in northern India. Urdu was employed primarily as a vehicle for poetry until the early nineteenth century, but the British decree of 1837 that terminated the use of Persian for administrative purposes provided Urdu's champions with an opportunity to extend its reach. It soon became the language of government in Bihar, Awadh (Oudh), the North-West Province (Agra), and Punjab. Both Hindu and Muslim bureaucrats used it. During the 1860s, leaders of the Hindu renaissance advocated replacing Urdu with Hindi, which was a form of the same vernacular. Whereas Urdu was written in a modified version of the Arabic script, the Hindi script and loan words were derived from Sanskrit. The debate over the relative merits of the two languages raged among Hindu and Muslim bureaucrats in provincial governments and in the press. Hindi managed to gain equal status with Urdu as the language of official business in Bihar in 1881 and the United Provinces (Awadh and Agra) in 1900. By that time, the struggle over the languages had definitively associated Urdu with Muslims and Hindi with Hindus.

In 1906, Britain announced that it would increase the representative element in the legislative councils of India. A delegation of wealthy, concerned Muslims, led by the Aga Khan, called on the Viceroy to request that Muslims be represented in the councils in proportions greater than their percentage of the population. The Viceroy promised to aid them, and the Morley–Minto Reforms of 1909 included a provision for separate Muslim electorates. From this point onward, the British recognized the rights of Muslims as a distinct community, a provision that would complicate Muslim–Hindu relations in coming decades.

Meanwhile, a small group of Muslims began to organize for political influence. In December 1906, a few months after the Aga Khan's delegation met with the Viceroy, a group of wealthy Muslim landlords and merchants announced the formation of a Muslim political organization called the All-India Muslim League. The creation of the Muslim League was a major break with the tradition of Muslim political quietism that Sayyid Ahmad had advised. The League's platform called for it to act aggressively to safeguard Muslim interests within the framework of loyalty to British rule. The League was an explicitly communal organization, which operated on Sayyid Ahmad's assumption that Hindus and Muslims constituted two separate nations. It stood in sharp contrast to Congress, which advocated a multireligious, multiethnic India.

Within a few years, circumstances challenged the League's loyalty to the British Empire. In 1911, the British revoked their 1905 decision to partition Bengal. Many Muslims had been pleased by the 1905 partition, for it created a Muslim-majority East Bengal. Hindus, on the other hand, had been overwhelmingly against it. They began a boycott of British goods, and some extremists used bombs against government officials. The British finally yielded to the agitators, revoking the partition. The revocation angered and disillusioned Muslims, for it meant the loss of administrative posts and political influence for Muslims. Muslim anger at the British about-face was exacerbated during the Balkan Wars of 1912–1913, when it appeared to them that European Christian powers were trying to crush the Ottoman Empire and destroy the caliphate. The League gained an important new member in 1913, when Muhammad Ali Jinnah was persuaded to join. He agreed to do so with the proviso that his membership would not conflict with his Congress activities or with his vision for the wider national interests of India.

Jamal al-Din al-Afghani, a pioneer in the Pan-Islam movement.

Movements of Religious Reform and Renewal

The imperialist wars and administrations of the second half of the nineteenth century triggered a wave of explicitly religious movements as well as political agitation. Themes from the previous century continued to be important in most of the new Islamic movements, but a change in tone was evident: Whereas the earlier reform movements were provoked by a sense of responsibility for having allowed Muslim institutions to decline or even collapse, many of the new movements arose out of a sense of responsibility for having allowed alien, non-Muslim forces to seize control of the levers of power within Muslim societies. The large-scale violence of the imperial venture had been traumatic, but its psychological impact was exacerbated by the imposition of foreign, non-Muslim regimes. Uncertainty and fear were rife, and people—particularly in urban centers—needed reassurance that normal life could go on under the new circumstances.

Muslims of South Asia were the first to address the impact of imperialism in a systematic fashion. All around them were the architectural reminders of the era of Mughal glory, when a Muslim regime had dominated the subcontinent. Actual Mughal political power had disintegrated by the mid-eighteenth century, but the continued presence of a Mughal emperor in Delhi and the persistence of

Mughal traditions in numerous petty courts throughout India had mitigated the true impact of the expansion of British power during the century prior to the 1857 uprising.

The ruthlessness with which the British suppressed the rebellion in 1857–1858 brought the reality of foreign rule into sharp focus. The Mughal emperor was exiled, and many of the symbols of his rule were destroyed. For the previous century, the Mughal emperor had possessed almost no power outside his palace complex, and yet the reaction to the abolition of his office among many Indian Muslims was similar to the reaction among many Sunni Muslims to the destruction of the thirteenth-century Abbasid caliphate, whose symbolic power was likewise much greater than its effective power. In both cases, the destruction of a symbol of Muslim political and spiritual power caused a profound psychological shock even though the actual impact of the destruction was negligible on the practical affairs of Muslims who lived outside the capital city.

In the aftermath of the revolt, Hindus and Muslims alike began to seek alternatives to active resistance to British rule. Although some of the ulama urged Muslims to "perform hijra" (to leave the land of infidel rule as the Prophet had done when he left Mecca for Medina), most of the ulama went to considerable effort to convince the British that they were not disloyal. At the same time, many of them sought to create a parallel society to the one dominated by British rulers and military forces. Even though the reins of political power were held by non-Muslims, the creation of new social institutions would enable Muslims to live a life that conformed to the tenets of Islam. The role played by these Muslim activists was similar to that of the Sufis who, in the thirteenth and fourteenth centuries, created communities and institutions for the millions who were affected by the invasions of the Mongols and Timur Lang.

Recapturing the True Faith

A major theme of the late nineteenth century reform movements was the one that had formed the core of the reforms of the previous century and a half: the quest for the essence of the faith. It is significant that the most important of the new movements took place outside the Indian metropolitan areas. British vengeance for the revolt had shattered the two great cities of Delhi and Lucknow, and large British garrisons were stationed there. The reformers preferred to set up their organizations in provincial towns with sizable Muslim populations. The first major reform movement began in 1867 at Deoband, some ninety miles northeast of Delhi. Here, the purpose was to create a new type of madrasa. At first glance, the new school appeared simply to be in the tradition of the modern reformist emphasis on the study of the Qur'an and Hadith, and it included courses on logic and Hanafi law. It offered nothing in the modern sciences or the English language, and so its graduates could aspire only to obtain positions in other madrasas or major mosques, or to fill the few positions available for Muslim scholars in government service.

In spite of the continuity of subject offerings, Deoband's organization was a major innovation in the seven-century history of the madrasa. The new school had its own library run by a professional staff; it offered a fixed curriculum that was punctuated with a schedule of exams; it depended on fund-raising campaigns rather than a religious endowment granted by individual; and it was under the leadership of a bureaucratic administrative hierarchy rather than the executor of an endowment. The Deoband madrasa was devoted to the goal of providing religious and moral guidance to Muslims who lived under alien, non-Muslim rule. It achieved that goal both directly and indirectly. Its direct influence lay in the noninstructional work of the scholars at the school who issued immense numbers of fatwas in response to requests from individuals for religious and moral guidance. Its indirect influence lay in the graduation of numerous young ulama who were committed to the goals of the reform movement of the previous century. The school's founders claimed the mantle of the tradition of Shah Wali Allah. They were among the leading Sufis of their era, but they were highly critical of the intercessory roles of the pirzadas at shrines. The Deobandis taught that each believer had an individual responsibility to follow the teachings of the Qur'an and Hadith and not to seek blessings at a shrine to substitute for that responsibility.

The Deobandis acknowledged that the British held political power in India, but they encouraged Muslims to cultivate an attitude of moral and spiritual superiority to their rulers. They maintained correct relations with the British because they wanted to fill whatever religious positions came open in the government, but they did not socialize with them. They eagerly engaged in the interconfessional debates that were a characteristic feature of the last quarter of the nineteenth century in India: Christian, Sunni, Shi'ite, and Hindu spokesmen would often meet together in public debates to argue for the supremacy of their own tradition, and then each community would proclaim that it had won. Fair-minded observers often commented that the Deobandis always acquitted themselves very well. They continued their pugnacious attitude toward Shi'ites and Hindus beyond the debating platform, refusing to pray with Shi'ites and refusing all social contact with Hindus.

The Deoband madrasa played a major role in the continuing development of Urdu as the language of learning for South Asian Muslims. Deoband, which arose just as the debate over the languages began, employed Urdu as its language of instruction and publication. Deobandis eagerly accepted the printing press in order to distribute their publications and fatwas widely. The use of Urdu in devotional books, Hadith collections, and translations of the Qur'an gave a major boost to the language's popularity among Muslims. The use of Urdu was not limited to the Sunni community of India. Shi'ites also used it, and the Bohras switched from Gujarati to Urdu. The Khojas retained Gujarati even though they played an important role in the Muslim League.

The school at Deoband rapidly achieved fame all across the Muslim world. It soon ranked with al-Azhar in Cairo as one of the two premier Sunni madrasas in the world. It made such a positive impression on Sunnis throughout South Asia that an informal system of affiliated colleges gradually emerged. By the end of the nineteenth century, several dozen of them were scattered over northern India. On the occasion of the school's centennial, an estimated 10,000 such schools existed.

Some critics pointed out two problems with the proliferation of Deobandi-affiliated schools. One was that it was impossible to staff so many schools with instructors who could maintain the justly famous philosophical rigor of the traditional madrasa. The result was that the quality of the intellectual experience at many so-called madrasas was little more than that of old-fashioned, elementary-level, Qur'an schools (*kuttabs*). The other problem with the "daughter" schools of Deoband was that their curriculum never adjusted to changing social conditions. They did almost nothing to prepare the students to participate in the modern world.

A rival group of Sunni ulama engaged in bitter debates with the Deobandis. Called Ahl-i Hadith ("People of the Hadith"), they derided the claims of Deoband to be the heir of Shah Wali Allah. They claimed that legacy for themselves on the grounds that, whereas Deoband insisted on adherence to the Hanafi school as a practical matter, Ahl-i Hadith rejected all four of the law schools in favor of seeking guidance from only the Qur'an and Hadith. They also criticized Deoband's practice of Sufi meditation and discipline, for they argued that there was no way to protect oneself from what they considered to be the corruptions of Sufism other than to abandon Sufism altogether.

In contrast to the Deoband group, which attracted followers from a wide variety of social backgrounds (with a notably large number from less prosperous families), members of Ahl-i Hadith typically came from the landholding elite. Some historians interpret their open hostility to British rule and their vehement criticisms of other Muslims to be expressions of their bitter frustration at not being able to hold the high offices that would have been theirs within a Muslim regime. Their Muslim opponents, such as the Deobandis, responded to their attacks in kind, branding them "Wahhabis" because of their virulent attitude toward Sufism and their denunciations of fellow Muslims. Members of Ahl-i Hadith vigorously protested the label because of the political problems it entailed for them. The label, coupled with their rejection of the legitimacy of British rule, caused British intelligence officers to monitor them until the 1890s for fear that they were planning a jihad.

A third reform group, Ahl-i Sunna wa Jama'a, arose in reaction to both the Deobandis and Ahl-i Hadith. Unlike the first two groups, which coalesced around groups of intellectuals, this one was centered on the charismatic figure of Ahmad Riza Khan Barelwi (Barelvi). It may be useful at this point to caution against confusing him with Sayyid Ahmad Barelwi (1786–1831), the reformer who led a jihad against Sikhs in the Punjab during the first half of the nineteenth century (discussed in Chapter 8). Sayyid Ahmad was from the town of Rae Bareli on the middle Ganges, whereas Ahmad Riza Khan was from Bareilly, about two hundred miles to the northwest. During the 1880s, Ahmad Riza (1856–1921) attracted the group that called themselves Ahl-i Sunna wa Jama'a, which can be rendered "The People of the Way (of the Prophet) and the Community." To outsiders, they have been known as Barelwis (Barelvis) from the beginning, and that name is now much better known than their formal identification.

Ahmad Riza Khan insisted on the need to adhere scrupulously to the Hanafi law school while preserving the rites of the shrine complex. Whereas the Deobandis and Ahl-i Hadith condemned the emphasis on mediation and intercession associated with the dargah complex as a reprehensible innovation, Ahmad turned the tables on them. On the grounds that the concept of the intercession of pirs had been approved by the vast majority of ulama for centuries, he argued that it had thereby become an integral part of Islam. Thus, to reject the practice after so many centuries during which the consensus of pious scholars had accepted it was itself a reprehensible innovation. Ahmad wrote vehement denunciations of both the Deobandis and Ahl-i Hadith, but he was particularly incensed by the latter group, since it was in favor of dispensing with the schools of law. He accused both groups of unbelief.

These three groups captured devoted followings, and all three continue to wield enormous power among the Muslims of South Asia today. All three made emulation of the Prophet's life the central theme of their programs. The Deobandis and Ahl-i Hadith turned to the Hadith for accounts of the Prophet's behavior and extra-Qur'anic teachings. The Barelwis, too, revered the Hadith, but their approach to piety was more strongly marked by a doctrine developed within certain Sufi groups that meditated on the "light of Muhammad." According to this doctrine, the Prophet was created from God's light prior to the creation of the world. The world, in fact, had been created for Muhammad. While Ahmad did not equate Muhammad with God, he did say that the Prophet is not "other than God." He told his followers that they could claim any attribute for Muhammad other than divinity. Ahmad placed a heavy stress on the intercessory role of the Prophet, and he encouraged his followers to celebrate the Prophet's birthday, a festival that the Deobandis and Ahl-i Hadith disapproved of on the grounds that it compromised the unity of God.

Modernism

The Deobandis, Ahl-i Hadith, and Barelwis focused exclusively on currents within the Islamic legacy to legitimize their programs. Another trend of thought among their contemporaries drew its inspiration from both the Islamic legacy and European intellectual movements. It is often called Islamic modernism. One example of Islamic modernism was the Aligarh Movement of Sayyid Ahmad Khan, whom we have met as the founder of the Muhammad Anglo–Oriental College in Aligarh. Today, Sayyid Ahmad is famous primarily for his college, but during his lifetime he was even better known for the theological framework that he created. He was a religious man who genuinely believed that Islam, rightly understood, anticipated and incorporated the findings of science and rigorous philosophy. He believed that the purity of original Islam had become corrupted and weakened by the accumulation of superstition and paganism. Purged of these accretions, Islam would be revealed as the exemplar of both spirituality and intellect.

Sayyid Ahmad spent decades formulating an Islamic theology that demonstrated the unity of God within the context of rational thought and the findings of modern science. As a youth, Sayyid Ahmad had been educated in the tradition of Mughal nobles rather than in a madrasa. Because he had a broader view of what constitutes education than did most of the ulama, his midlife program of self-education included not only Qur'anic commentaries, Hadith studies, and Islamic law, but also the Muslim philosophers of the Abbasid period, whose Greek-influenced works were later condemned by most ulama. He also studied modern science and European thought. As a result of his studies, he became one of the first Indians to reject the geocentric model of the universe, at about the same time that the Catholic Church formally did so (1860). Sayyid Ahmad came to believe that nature operates according to natural laws, a conclusion radically at variance with the Sunni position developed in the tenth century that argued that God creates each moment by an act of will. His study of the development of Islamic thought caused him to conclude that religious thought develops historically in response to changing conditions. This, too, seemed heretical to most Sunni ulama.

The new theology and the new university that Sayyid Ahmad Khan left as his legacy won for him a devoted following among a sector of India's small Muslim middle class. Those same innovations, coupled with his political cooperation with the British, generated deep opposition to him among other Muslims. To them, he appeared to be too deferential to the British and to be betraying Islam. Deobandis, Ahl-i Hadith, and Barelwis considered him a heretic, whereas Jamal al-Din al-Afghani—who agreed with Sayyid Ahmad on the need to close the technological and scientific gap with Europe—found his open admiration of the British to be an affront to Muslim dignity.

As Sayyid Ahmad Khan's influence was peaking, a related set of ideas was being articulated by a movement centered in Syria and Egypt that is called the *salafiya*.[1] The term derives from the phrase *al-salaf al-salih,* meaning "the pious ancestors," the first few generations of Muslims. The movement sought to distinguish between the essential doctrines of Islam (found in the Qur'an and Hadith) and the laws and social teachings that have been extrapolated from them through the centuries. The *salafi*s (the late nineteenth- and early twentieth-century scholars who were part of the movement) believed that true Islam confirms the results of pure reason and is compatible with science. For them, the essentials of Islam are simple and self-evident. They include belief in God, the finality of Muhammad's prophethood, moral responsibility, and God's judgment of our actions. The Shari'a and any moral code, on the other hand, are interpretations of these essentials that are valid only for a particular time and place. When circumstances change, interpretations of the essentials must change, as well. In the modern world of the late nineteenth and early twentieth centuries, Muslims were under an obligation to reexamine the essentials and to apply them to the new conditions.

Perhaps the most famous salafi was Muhammad 'Abduh (1849–1905) of Egypt. He was a student at the great madrasa of al-Azhar in Cairo when Jamal al-Din al-Afghani came to Egypt in 1872. He studied Islamic philosophy under Afghani and followed him into exile when the British occupied Egypt in 1882. He soon became disenchanted with Afghani's obsession with revolution and moved to Beirut, where he taught theology. He convinced the British that he was interested only in reforming the practice of Islam, and they allowed him to return to Egypt in 1889. He became a judge, and in 1897 he published his most famous work, *The Theology of Unity.* In 1899 he became the mufti of Egypt, and in the remaining six years of his life he was a trusted and admired advisor to the British High Commissioner of Egypt. He reformed the Egyptian Shari'a courts, founded a college for qadis, and began a massive commentary on the Qur'an that he was unable to complete before he died in 1905.

By asserting the need to exercise ijtihad, the salafis challenged the authority of the official ulama, which was based on the ulama's knowledge and perpetuation of the vast corpus of texts that constituted the Shari'a. By advocating the need to incorporate modern subjects into the schools, the salafis also implied that the traditional religious education of the official ulama was inadequate for the new era. Prominent salafis who were in a position to effect change, as 'Abduh was, were bitterly attacked by the traditional ulama, the group that, until World War I, tended to include the wealthiest and best-connected religious officials. In Egypt, the British protected salafis from legal action, but in Ottoman Syria the ulama sometimes harassed them quite severely.

In the Netherlands Indies, Islamic modernism rapidly developed a mass following that was unparalleled elsewhere in the Muslim world. Its rise coincided with a period rife with political upheavals in Asia: Within a span of little more than a decade, Spain was evicted from the Philippines (1898) after an occupation of more than three centuries; Japan defeated China (1895) and Russia (1905); Iran and the Ottoman Empire attempted constitutional experiments (1906 and 1908, respectively); and the Chinese Revolution toppled the Ch'ing dynasty (1911). Each of these events was a major phenomenon; their occurrence in rapid succession inspired many Indonesians to hope that they would no longer be merely reacting to Dutch actions, but rather creating their own history.

The period of the upheavals (1895–1911) was one of stress in the Netherlands Indies. The Dutch finally quelled the revolt in Aceh in 1903. By that time, numerous voices had arisen in the Netherlands demanding a change in policy from exploiting the Indies to bringing them humanitarian reforms. Thus was born the so-called Ethical Policy, which was an effort to invest in education, health, and economic development. The program featured some genuine benefits, but they were unevenly distributed throughout the islands, and many were not nearly as evident as the burden of the increased taxes that the general population had to pay to fund the program. The heavier taxes came at an inopportune time, for the population of the islands increased dramatically throughout the nineteenth century. (By 1900, Java's population had increased to twenty-five million from some five million in 1800.) With more mouths to feed, families had less money available for taxes. There was also considerable economic hardship within the indigenous population of urban laborers and small businessmen. These groups were feeling the sting of competition from tens of thousands of Chinese laborers and entrepreneurs who had flooded into the region during the last quarter of the nineteenth century.

A mass movement arose in 1912 in central Java that was called *Sarekat Islam* ("Islamic League"). Although nominally Islamic, its leaders were not steeped in religious studies. They were, rather, a group of small businessmen, particularly in the batik industry, who had been hurt by local Chinese competition. Sarekat Islam began as a mutual aid society for these Muslim businessmen, but its appeal was not limited to this class alone. Because of its critique of Chinese economic power and its call for political autonomy, it attracted members from a variety of social classes and from both rural and urban areas. Some historians, in fact, have pointed out that its major significance was in overcoming the isolation of the village. Its growth was so rapid that, by 1919, the organization had attracted the loyalty of between half a million and two million members in almost one hundred branches throughout the archipelago.

Although Sarekat Islam's combination of appeals to justice, economic prosperity, political autonomy, and Islamic reform helped it to attract a massive following, the same wide range of goals proved to be its undoing. By 1919, Marxists became influential in the organization, as they realized its potential to sway the masses. Internal dissensions began to fray the group, and local chapters split with each other over the question of whether the priority should be Islam or communism. When communists began a revolt against the Dutch in the mid-1920s, Sarekat Islam became guilty by association in the eyes of the authorities, and even its noncommunist membership was persecuted. The organization quickly disappeared as a viable movement.

Another organization appeared almost simultaneously with Sarekat Islam that was more explicitly religious in nature, and it has remained a powerful force down to the present. Called Muhammadiya, it also arose in central Java, in Yogyakarta. It focused its attention on education, health care, and aid to the poor within the context of Islamic reform. It did not concern itself with formal politics, and thus did not attract Marxists and did not alarm the Dutch.

Muhammadiya reflected the urban, middle-class values of the milieu in which it arose, echoing the work of Sayyid Ahmad Khan and 'Abduh. Its leaders combined Western organizational methods with an unambiguously Islamic orientation that continued the reformist tradition of emphasizing the study of the Qur'an and Hadith, discouraging grave site visitation and mysticism, and encouraging greater adherence to formal obligations. Muhammadiya was particularly known for the schools that it established. All followed a curriculum that combined Western subjects with religious instruction based on a study of Arabic and Qur'anic exegesis. Some even used Dutch as the medium of instruction. Muhammadiya also created youth and women's organizations, clinics, and other social service agencies.

Because Muhammadiya was more narrowly focused on religion, education, and social services than was Sarekat Islam, it grew much more slowly. It began to expand rapidly only during the 1920s. When Sareket Islam was taken over by Marxists, many of its members left it to join Muhammadiya. The organization gained additional strength in the mid-1920s when it established branches in Minangkabau, on Sumatra, where a powerful Islamic modernist movement was rising.

Messianism

Some Muslims reacted to the dislocations of the late nineteenth century by developing messianic hopes. Throughout history, many Sunni Muslims have looked forward to the coming of the Mahdi, the redeemer that God is expected to send at the end of history in order to inaugurate an era of justice in a world now filled with injustice and tyranny. As within Christianity, Muslim messianic movements have proven to be particularly resonant at the turn of a century or millennium. The end of the thirteenth century on the Islamic calendar came in November 1882, a month that fell in a period marked by messianic expectation in several regions of the Muslim world.

Messianic sentiment in the Netherlands Indies was the culmination of a century of Islamic activism in Java. One expression of that activism was the new role of an institution called the *pesantren*. In pre-Islamic Java, pesantrens had been rural monasteries of various Hindu–Buddhist traditions. As Islam began to spread slowly across the island, they were adapted to Islamic purposes by holy men who provided religious instruction or healing to pilgrims and seekers. During the nineteenth century, many of the pesantrens became boarding schools where students worked at manual labor and learned religious lessons by rote. As more and more Javanese became aware of the reform movements in the larger Muslim world and desired to provide a wholesome education for their children that was unsullied by imperialistic influences, they sent their children to pesantrens to study the Qur'an and Hadith and to engage in farm labor.

By the middle of the nineteenth century, pesantrens acquired a reputation for teaching the duty of jihad against the Dutch and the collaborating Javanese aristocratic rulers. The government was shaken by several violent attacks whose participants claimed to be involved in jihad. After the opening of the Suez Canal in 1869, the number of hajjis from Java began to increase due to the larger number of ships that now entered the Red Sea. During the 1870s, Dutch officials claimed that they had identified a number of hajjis who subsequently took up residence at pesantrens to foment an Islamic revolution. In western Java, the Dutch recorded several instances of individuals who claimed to be the Mahdi or the Just Ruler of Indonesian tradition.

The year 1882 came and went without any major incident, but tension rose palpably after the 1883 eruption of Krakatoa (Krakatau), a volcano in the Sunda Strait. Although Krakatoa's explosion was not as great as Tambora's in 1815, it was a colossal outburst that was heard 2500 miles away. Its tsunami generated waves one hundred feet high that killed over 36,000 people in western Java and southern Sumatra. Many Muslim preachers pointed to it as a sign that the Mahdi's arrival was imminent. Simultaneously, a major agricultural crisis struck Java. A blight struck both the coffee and sugar sectors, and foreign competition dealt an additional blow to sugar producers. Agricultural unemployment soared. Many people interpreted the crisis as God's punishment for allowing infidels to rule. In 1888, a major religious revolt broke out in western Java in the expectation that the Mahdi would intervene. The Dutch suppressed it only after a ruthless campaign. The violence of the revolt and of the ongoing war in Aceh convinced many Javanese that an alternative to armed conflict needed to be found. Over the next thirty years, some of them began to develop political tactics such as rallies, journalism, and mass organizations, including Sarekat Islam.

The Aceh War of 1873–1903 had the unintended consequence of creating a more conscious Islamic identity among Acehnese. Late-nineteenth-century observers noted with amazement that they saw remarkably little evidence even in Aceh and the Muslim Malayan port cities that Shari'a courts functioned or that rulers led public celebrations of Islamic rituals. In spite of the militant, sixteenth-century assertion of Islam in Aceh against the Portuguese and the seventeenth-century reforming work of al-Raniri and al-Sinkili, Islam remained a nominal identity for most Acehnese. The war changed that. The Dutch entered the conflict confident that they could crush all local power centers and rule directly, rather than having to negotiate arrangements for the exercise of indirect rule. By the early 1880s, the army finally destroyed the power of all the traditional chiefs, but activist members of the ulama (notably sayyids from Hadramawt) arose to fill their place. The conflict then became reinterpreted by the Acehnese. No longer was it merely a war to defend their homes; rather, it was a jihad against an aggressive infidel.

Once the war evolved into a jihad, influential Dutch officials wanted to end the war and work out an arrangement for Acehnese autonomy. At that point, geologists discovered petroleum in Sumatra. The Dutch then had a concrete material interest in the region, not just a geopolitical one, and so they dropped the autonomy proposal. The war continued for another twenty years. The Dutch belatedly sought out local notables with whom they could make suitable power-sharing arrangements. By 1903, the Dutch managed to create a fairly stable government in Aceh, but some ulama carried out resistance for another decade. Many Acehnese never recognized Dutch authority. Occasionally, an individual would conduct a suicidal attack on Dutch officials, convinced that he would go to paradise when he was killed in retaliation.

The best-known Muslim messianic movement of the period took place on the upper Nile, where the British invasion of Egypt in 1882 presented opponents of Egyptian rule in Sudan with an opportunity to revolt. The most famous of the rebels was Muhammad Ahmad ibn 'Abd Allah (c. 1841–1884). Muhammad Ahmad had developed a reputation for ascetic holiness since childhood, and by the late 1870s, he attracted disciples who revered him as a source of spiritual guidance. In 1881, Muhammad Ahmad sent letters to the notables of Sudan announcing that he was the Mahdi. He announced that he had come to establish the Sunna of the Prophet and to lead the community of true Muslims. He considered his coming to be a harbinger of the end of history. During 1882, the Mahdi began a series of successful military engagements against the Egyptian governor-general's army. His growing number of victories gave credence to his claim to be the representative of God. Tens of thousands of fighters joined his army. They did so for a variety of reasons: Some genuinely believed in his status as the Mahdi; others were angry at the loss of the slave trade; and the bulk of the troops were nomads who had a visceral hatred of any bureaucratic government.

Le Petit Journal

ADMINISTRATION

5 CENT. SUPPLÉMENT ILLUSTRÉ 5 CENT.

ABONNEMENTS

22me Année — Numéro 1.096

DIMANCHE 19 NOVEMBRE 1911

LA FRANCE VA POUVOIR PORTER LIBREMENT AU MAROC LA CIVILISATION LA RICHESSE ET LA PAIX

Although cynical about each other's motives, Europeans could always rationalize their own imperalist policies. Here, a French journal promises that its nation's occupation of Morocco would usher in an era of peace, prosperity, and civilization.

London tried to avoid involvement in Sudan while consolidating power in Egypt, but it could not avoid sending military forces into the region to evacuate Egyptian and British personnel. The Mahdi annihilated the poorly organized British armies that came up against him in 1883 and early 1884. He then set up his headquarters at Omdurman, on the west side of the Nile across from Khartoum. He took modest steps toward creating a new state: He minted fine gold coins and replaced Egyptian taxes with some authorized by the Shari'a. Other reforms, and any plans he had for extending his rule over other regions of the Muslim world, were cut short by his illness and death in June 1885.

The Mahdi's long-time confidante, 'Abd Allah ibn Muhammad, became the preeminent figure in a triumvirate of *khalifa*s ("deputies" or "successors") that succeeded the Mahdi. His period of rule (1885–1898) was a dizzying series of military clashes with Sudanese rebels—including several individuals who claimed to be the Mahdi himself—and neighboring states, including Ethiopia and British-ruled Egypt. The Khalifa gradually assumed total power and began to rule as an autocrat, and he even imposed new taxes and dues that were not consistent with the Shari'a. In 1898–1899, the British invaded Sudan in order to secure the area from rival Europeans. In a rapid series of battles, their military technology and organization easily defeated and killed the Khalifa. They then absorbed Sudan into their empire.

British Somalia was the scene of some of the fiercest resistance that imperial powers confronted in Africa. The key figure there was Muhammad ibn 'Abd Allah Hasan (1864–1920), a religious scholar and Sufi leader who preached against the use of stimulants such as tobacco, coffee, and qat (leaves from a brushy tree in Yemen and the Horn that contain a variety of amphetamine) as well as the veneration of holy men. He conveyed much of his message through the medium of poetry, a technique that attracted thousands of followers who would have ignored him otherwise.

Profoundly disturbed by the invasion of Christian forces, Muhammad ibn 'Abd Allah Hasan raised a revolt against the British in 1899. His claim to be the Mahdi proved to be a powerful recruiting tool, and his army eventually contained 15,000 warriors. He managed to fight off British expeditions four times before working out an agreement with the Italians to settle in their sphere of Somalia in 1905. He resumed the fight against the British in 1908 and fought until his death a short time after his stronghold fell in 1920. Among the British, the Mahdi's indefatigable resistance earned him the unflattering nickname of the "Mad Mullah."

Another messianic movement arose during this period in India. Unlike the examples just discussed, this movement was peaceful and has lasted to the present. The Ahmadiya movement was inspired by Mirza Ghulam Ahmad (c. 1835–1908), who grew up in the city of Qadiyan in the Punjab. Always a meditative and religiously sensitive young man, he published a four-volume work during the early 1880s that claimed a special spiritual standing for himself. His teachings proved to be quite popular, and by 1886 he was engaging in the public religious debates that had become a characteristic of the era. In 1889, he announced that he had begun to receive communications from God. He later explained, too, that God had merged Ghulam Ahmad's identity with that of Jesus and sent him to earth to serve as the Mahdi.

Ghulam Ahmad's claims for himself stirred up deep passions that were similar to the hostile reaction to the Bab in Iran half a century earlier. Had it not been for the presence of the British administration and military forces, Ghulam Ahmad might well have suffered the martyr's fate of the Bab. Because of intervention by the authorities, he remained grateful for British religious toleration throughout his life. His critics, led by Deobandis, accused him of flouting the doctrine that Muhammad was the seal of the prophets, and they declared him an apostate. Ghulam Ahmad clarified his claim, pointing out that he was not denying that Muhammad was the seal—or the greatest—of the prophets. He did not claim to be the law-giving type of prophet that Muhammad had been, but was simply claiming that every generation required continuing revelation from God. He also reaffirmed that the Qur'an was eternally valid and will never be superseded.

The controversy did not abate, and eventually Ghulam Ahmad declared his critics to be heretics themselves for not recognizing his claims. He ordered his followers not to pray with nonmembers and not to marry into families of nonmembers. Thus, in part because of the actions of their critics and in part due to their own policies, the Ahmadiya quickly became set apart from both the Sunni and Shi'ite communities. Considering themselves to be the only true Muslims, they became active in missionary work all over the world and have distributed Qur'ans more widely than any other Muslim group. They made considerable inroads in Africa and Southeast Asia. In the Arab world, where the status of Muhammad was jealously protected, the only place that they were able to establish a base was in Haifa (in 1931, during the period of the British mandate of Palestine).

After Ghulam Ahmad's death in 1908, the continuing hostility toward the Ahmadiya caused a growing rift within the organization itself. In 1914, it split into two groups. The smaller one, based in Lahore, downplayed the prophetic claims of its founder and tried to accommodate itself with the Sunni community. Its members refer to Ghulam Ahmad simply as a uniquely inspired spiritual teacher. The larger group, based in Qadyan, continued to revere him as the Mahdi. The members of this group, the Qadiyanis, are the best-known Ahmadi group today. Their leaders possess the title of the Mahdi.

World War One

By 1914, international and domestic tensions were running high in Europe. Photographs of the last few years prior to 1914 do not reveal this fact as dramatically as art and music do: This was the era in which the Cubism of Braque and Picasso replaced Impressionism, and Stravinsky's *Rite of Spring* (1913) produced a riot within a Parisian ballet audience, most of whose members were expecting the lush harmonies and steady rhythms of such works as Tchaikovsky's *The Nutcracker* (1892). Nationalist rivalries, a major arms race, economic strains, labor unrest, and the anger of frustrated women's rights activists were only a few of the factors that produced a palpable sense of imminent catastrophe. The popular genre of "invasion literature," exemplified by H. G. Wells's *War of the Worlds* (1898) and numerous works by William Le Queux, notably *The Great War in England in 1897* (1894) and *The Invasion of 1910* (1906), reflected a generalized anxiety regarding an imminent conflagration. The rulers of the leading nations organized international alliances in anticipation of just such a clash—some leaders hoped to avert conflict, whereas others sought allies in a war that they desired.

The spark that ignited the highly volatile powder flashed in the new Balkan states that had been carved out of the Ottoman Empire in 1878. Intoxicated by dreams of glory and power, none were content with their borders. They began demanding territory from each other and threatening to use force to get it. Their mutual rivalries and competing claims entangled Austria and Russia, as well: Serbia aspired to annex swaths of Austrian territory where millions of Slavs lived, thereby making a mortal enemy of the Austrian government in Vienna. Russia, the greatest of the Slavic countries, felt that its long-standing interests in the straits between the Black Sea and the Aegean Sea compelled it to block Austrian expansion in the Balkans and to aid Serbian national aspirations. In June 1914, a troubled and tubercular young Serb named Gavrilo Princip murdered the presumptive heir to the Austrian throne, Franz Ferdinand, in Sarajevo, the capital of the former Ottoman province of Bosnia–Herzegovina. When Austria retaliated by threatening to take over the government of Serbia, Russia mobilized its troops. The prewar alliance system then clicked into motion, just as it had been designed to do. Europeans entered the war enthusiastically, even though millions were unable to explain precisely how the sad incident in Sarajevo affected them personally

World War I was, in fact, a war with worldwide involvement. Millions of Muslims were involved, directly or indirectly. The Ottoman Empire was a major actor in the war, and its territory suffered extensively from major combat operations in Iraq, Syria, and Anatolia. Even in areas that were not directly involved in the war, untold millions of people were caught up in the war because the imperial European powers deployed huge numbers of the inhabitants of their protectorates to the front lines of the war as soldiers and laborers. France sent 300,000 of its African subjects to the front, and North African troops under French command suffered the first German gas attack in April 1915. The British transported more than one million Indians alone to Europe, Iraq, and Egypt. For the peoples of the world empires, the war was not merely an item in the news.

The war began in August 1914 as a strictly European affair. The Ottoman cabinet favored neutrality for the first three months, but in October a faction within the CUP ordered a naval attack on the Russian fleet. The Ottoman Empire had begun its last war. It was now an ally of Germany and Austria–Hungary and an enemy of Russia, Britain, and France. The gamble could be rationalized at the time: Russia and her allies Britain and France had all taken territory from the Ottomans and were thus enemies, whereas Germany had been unfailingly helpful over the previous two decades. Moreover, the Germans had overwhelmed the Russian army at the start of the war and were driving it back into the Russian interior. The Pan-Turk faction within the CUP believed that this was an opportune time to strike at Russia in the Caucasus and lead a campaign that would unite the Turkic peoples from the Balkans to China under the leadership of Istanbul. The CUP then demanded of the sultan to call upon the Muslims of the world to enter into a jihad to support the Ottomans. Thus, the CUP, which had been so contemptuous of Abdulhamit's claim to be the caliph, now sought to benefit from the religious aura of that same title.

Germany sent advisors and troops to aid the Ottomans, who acquitted themselves particularly well at Gallipoli, the slender peninsula that forms the northern shore of the Dardanelles. From January 1915 to January 1916, they held a large

British expeditionary force at bay until it was forced to withdraw after suffering over 140,000 casualties. (The Ottomans suffered even more.) They also routed the British-led Indian army in several battles in Iraq. The campaigns against Russia, by contrast, were poorly executed, and the Ottomans suffered tens of thousands of unnecessary casualties.

The British position in Egypt was aided by the Arab Revolt, which was made famous in the West by T. E. Lawrence ("Lawrence of Arabia"). The revolt was organized by the Ottoman governor of the Hijaz, the Sharif Husayn, who studiedly ignored the sultan's call for jihad against the British. Husayn hoped to become the ruler of the Arab lands of the Ottoman Empire, and he thought that he had obtained British agreement to the plan in the Husayn–McMahon Correspondence of 1915–1916. Once he thought that he and the British understood each other, he sent his forces north. They fought their way to Damascus in late 1918, and the official British history of the war credited the Arab forces with tying up 30,000 Ottoman troops that the British did not have to engage. In October 1918, the Ottomans collapsed under the strain of fighting on several fronts at once.

The most notorious feature of the war in the Ottoman theater was the annihilation of hundreds of thousands of Armenians. Most historians today agree that the number of dead was in the range of 600,000 to one million. Beginning in early 1915, Ottoman troops forced Armenian villagers from their homes in central and eastern Anatolia and herded them south into the Syrian desert. En route, many died of exposure and many others were murdered. A century later, the episode still produces furious controversy: Angry Armenians insist that the deaths were the goal of a genocidal policy orchestrated by the state, whereas defensive Turks insist that they were an inadvertent result of a simple relocation policy that went awry. Serious historians suggest that the reality was much more complex than partisans on either side want to admit. It is harder to conclude that a formal program of genocide was implemented against the Armenians than it was in the case of the Nazi genocide of Jews for two main reasons: There is no "paper trail" comparable to the documentation of the Nazi policy, nor is there oral testimony from among the thousands of participants who would have been required to execute such a policy, in contrast to the numerous testimonies from German soldiers and policemen who spoke of following orders to kill. On the other hand, even the Austrian and German diplomats in the Ottoman Empire, who were Ottoman allies during the war, were unequivocally convinced that Enver Pasha, a member of the ruling triumvirate within the CUP, had decided to eradicate the empire's Armenian population. It is also clear that the organizers of the deportations knew that the absence of railroads in the Armenian region would require the deportees to walk for weeks or months through desolate mountain ranges and deserts without adequate supplies of food, water, or shelter from the elements. There was no prospect that the deportations as they were carried out could have been accomplished without a large number of casualties. A consensus is growing that a handful of powerful men within the Ottoman government wanted to be rid of the empire's remaining Armenian population; many Ottoman military and civilian officers refused on principle to implement the deportations; wartime conditions in Anatolia and Syria had produced hardships and food shortages among all the inhabitants of the region, exacerbating the normal hazards of moving large numbers of people through the area on foot; and deportees were murdered both by local tribesmen and by some of the very soldiers who were escorting them, for unknown reasons. Wartime hysteria, decades-old ethnic rivalries, ineptitude, economic hardship, and the sheer brutality of certain individuals were all factors in the horrors of 1915 and 1916. Historians still cannot agree on the relative weight to assign to each element.[2]

In Russia, the early course of the war was a huge relief for government officials, who had feared that their Turkic Muslim subjects would be sympathetic to their fellow Turks of the Ottoman Empire. They were relieved when the Tatars of the Volga region remained determined to assimilate to Russian nationality. Several Russian Muslim conferences and proclamations made unambiguous statements of loyalty to the Russian cause, and many Tatars volunteered to fight the Ottomans. Nevertheless, as the war dragged on, it became clear that the Muslims of Russia had a diverse set of perspectives on the war. Azeris, who were caught in the shatter zone between Ottoman and Russian armies, tended to support the Ottomans against the Russians and Armenians, and Russian officials in Crimea began to suspect the loyalty of the Crimean Tatars.

The Muslims of Russian Central Asia were far removed from the fighting. Any pro-Ottoman sentiment was muted, but there was also little pro-Russian sentiment. A few Kyrgyz and Kazakh nomads volunteered for cavalry service; otherwise, Central Asians just wanted to ignore the war. The war came anyway. As the conflict took its toll on the country's economy, the government began to draw more on the resources of Central Asia. It requisitioned horses and other livestock and levied exceptional taxes.

Then, in the summer of 1916, the tsar issued a decree requiring half a million Central Asians to serve in various military auxiliary units behind the front lines. The accumulated grievances of Central Asians against colonization erupted in a revolt. The first resistance was in the urbanized areas of Fergana and Samarqand, and it was quickly suppressed. The following month, a much larger and widespread revolt erupted among the nomads from Khiva to the frontier with Siberia. The most lethal fighting took place in what is now the extreme eastern corner of Kyrgyzstan, where Kazakh and Kyrgyz nomads were still seething over having been forced off their lands by Russian settlers around Lake Issyk-Kul. They killed more than 3000 Russian settlers and destroyed all the immigrant settlements. When the Russian army and settlers counterattacked, the results were devastating to Muslims of all ethnic groups. The Kazakhs and Kyrgyz were singled out, but lynch mobs imperiled the lives of any non-European in their path. Hundreds of thousands were killed, and hundreds of thousands fled into permanent exile in Xinjiang. Russian historians estimate that the decline in the Muslim population of Russian Central Asia was at least 300,000 people and may have exceeded one million.

The following year, the February and October revolutions radically altered Russia's government. The former replaced the tsar with a liberal government, and the latter replaced the liberals with Lenin's communist Bolsheviks. Between the two events, the country's Muslims held a series of conferences in which they debated the course of action for Muslims in postimperial Russia. The delegates represented a wide political spectrum, but they agreed to oppose separatism. They voted to support a unified Russian state whose federal system would guarantee a degree of political, cultural, and national autonomy for non-Russian peoples.

When the Bolsheviks seized power in October 1917, they hoped to win over Russia's Muslims on the basis of their decrees regarding ending the war, redistributing land and wealth, and recognizing the equality of all the nationalities of Russia. Leading Bolsheviks also claimed that there was no conflict between communism and Islam, and they promised to preserve the Shari'a courts. Significant numbers of Tatar Muslims, particularly those who had been involved in the Jadid movement, embraced communism. For a while, it seemed to many of them that Russia's Muslims were in the vanguard of a future pan-Islamic revolution against Western imperialism. Many Chechens and Dagestanis fought on the Bolshevik side during the civil war that followed the October revolution.

Nevertheless, armed resistance to the new Soviet government was common in other Muslim areas. Serious fighting took place in the Crimea, Kokand, Khiva, and Bukhara. Those regions were secured by the central government by 1921, although revolts continued in Central Asia until 1928. Ferocious reprisals followed the fighting in the Crimea, where 60,000–70,000 Muslims were executed. On the international front, by contrast, the Bolsheviks extended a welcome to Muslim leaders of anti-imperialist resistance movements. They were invited to the Soviet Union for conferences, education, and training.

The Iranian government did not join either side in World War I, but the combatants refused to allow the country to escape sharing in the war's agony. Britain maintained its military presence in the country, primarily to protect its petroleum interests in the southwest, an area not awarded to Britain in the 1907 partition agreement with Russia. Meanwhile, the Ottomans and Russians conducted a scorched-earth war against each other in Iran's Azerbaijan province. German agents worked among Iran's various tribes, encouraging them to attack the British and Russians, and many Iranian nationalists were pro-German due to their hostility toward Russia and Britain. Famine was widespread.

Even when the fighting on its borders waned toward the end of the war, Iran remained in chaos. The Bolsheviks withdrew Russian troops from the country, partly out of a reluctance to honor any commitments that the tsar had made and partly because they needed them in the civil war that was ravaging the Soviet Union. The British were now the only major foreign presence in Iran, but their forces were impossibly undermanned. They began paying the salaries of the troops of the Cossack Brigade, the only other professional force in the country. A group of Iranians insisted that they be allowed to submit a demand for sovereignty before the peace conference that met at Versailles during the first half of 1919, but Britain refused to allow them to attend. In August of that year, Britain signed a secret agreement with pro-British Iranian cabinet officials that would have given Britain control of Iran's finances and armed forces. News of the agreement was leaked, and it gave rise to angry separatist movements in the north. The Soviet Union was alarmed about the implications of the agreement for its own security, and it sent troops back into northern Iran. The international outcry, combined with the pressures of Britain's other imperial crises, forced the British to begin evacuating their military forces from Iran. By late 1920, it appeared that Britain was in no position to enforce its will on Iran, but the possibility that Iran could simply disintegrate from outside pressure and internal upheaval was very real.

The war set the stage for the final settlement of Ottoman territory. For over a century prior to the war, Russia, France, and Britain had been suspicious of each other's ambitions regarding the fate of the empire. It was only their common fear of Germany that had made them unlikely allies in World War I. Soon after the war began, they agreed that it was time to administer euthanasia to the Sick Man of Europe. They decided that, at the conclusion of the war, Russia would receive the straits between the Balkans and Anatolia as well as Istanbul itself. The French would exercise direct control of a strip of the Syrian coast and maintain a sphere of influence in the Syrian interior, whereas Britain would take direct control of Baghdad and Basra while maintaining a sphere of influence in the region extending from what is now the Israeli coast into northern Iraq.

Meanwhile, the British were negotiating other territorial deals. The agreement made with the Sharif Husayn was one of several statements issued to various Arab groups. Moreover, in early November 1917, the British issued the Balfour Declaration to the Zionist movement, which had the goal of creating a national home for Jews. The declaration was worded in such a way that it actually committed London to very little. It promised support for "the establishment in Palestine of a National Home for the Jewish people, . . . it being clearly understood that nothing shall be done which may prejudice the civil and religious rights of existing non-Jewish communities in Palestine. . . . " Nevertheless, the Zionists were elated, for they believed that they had Great Power backing for their project. The various territorial agreements made during the war regarding the dispensation of Ottoman territory were incompatible with each other. By the end of the war, it was clear that only a few of the commitments could be honored.

Because of the complexities of the war, several treaties were required to settle the main issues. The most famous one, forged at Versailles, dealt with European affairs. The territories of the Ottoman Empire were treated in several other conferences. In April 1920, members of the supreme council of the Allies met at San Remo on the Italian Riviera to award control of the Arab world between Iran and the Mediterranean to France and Britain. This conference made decisions that were later formally ratified by the new League of Nations, calling the territories "mandates" instead of "colonies" due to the negative connotation that the latter term had acquired over the years. France took possession of Syria, while Britain took Palestine and Iraq. Borders for these territories, which had never existed before, were determined over the next few years. France subsequently carved Lebanon out of Syria, removing from Syrian control the important ports of Tripoli, Sidon, and Tyre. The disposition of the territory ignored all the wartime pledges made to the Arabs; the pledge made to the Zionist movement was incorporated into Britain's mandate over Palestine, where, although Arabs outnumbered Jews ten to one, the British agreed to cooperate with the Zionists to create a Jewish homeland.

In August 1920, delegates who were responsible for settling the affairs of the Ottoman theater of the war finally completed their deliberations. These delegates, who met in the Paris suburb of Sèvres, completed their work more than a year after the signing of the Treaty of Versailles. Called the Treaty of Sèvres, it partitioned Anatolia into several fragments. The straits and Istanbul itself, which had been promised to Russia during the war, were placed under international control instead—the new Soviet Union refused to recognize the wartime agreements that the tsar had made, and Britain and France were not willing to negotiate with the new communist state even if it had claimed the territories. In response to heavy lobbying by Greek diplomats, the treaty awarded to Greece the last remaining Ottoman foothold in Europe around Edirne as well as the province of Smyrna (Izmir) on the Aegean coast. It granted the Dodecanese (a group of twelve Aegean islands, including Rhodes and Kos) to Italy. The treaty's map also designated two areas in eastern Anatolia as possible sites for future states for the Armenians and the Kurds, but those two peoples were left to negotiate—or fight—with each other and the Ottomans over the issue. The remainder of Anatolia was left for the Ottomans were to administer, although Italian and French troops occupied areas in the peninsula's southwestern and south-central regions, respectively, where their leaders hoped to obtain concessions.

Conclusion

The subjection of almost the entire Muslim world to non-Muslim rule by 1920 was a blow to both the dignity and the worldview of many Muslims. Not only was the experience of imperialism humiliating, but it also posed the same questions that the thirteenth-century conquest of most of the Muslim world by Christian Iberians and pagan Mongols had raised: Why did God allow this to happen to followers of His final revelation? What should be the Muslim response? The questions were particularly vexing in light of the historical knowledge that only a few generations earlier, Muslims had ruled some of the most powerful empires in the world.

The numerous organizations and societies that arose during this period in the Sunni world reveal in graphic form the need that millions of people felt for belonging to a group that formulated meaningful answers to the most pressing questions of the era. Some felt that it was their duty as good Muslims to adopt as much of Europe's technology and learning as possible; others rejected everything that was distinctively European as infidel; and most wound up somewhere on the spectrum between those two extreme positions.

In some Sunni regions, the intensity of the cultivation of pious behavior is striking. Many new mosques arose, the number of hajjis increased enormously, and the printing and distribution of religious books became a huge industry, in spite of high rates of illiteracy. Enormous efforts were directed toward the identification of the authentic spirit of Islam. Unlike previous periods of Islamic reform and revival, these efforts to spread religious knowledge were conducted within the context of a new and growing hunger for knowledge of all kinds, not just religious knowledge. The advent of the printing press in Muslim countries led to the emergence of newspapers during the last quarter of the nineteenth century, and printed books began appearing on a variety of topics. For the first time, literate readers were frequently devouring material that informed them of political issues, popular science, health topics, and nonreligious history.

Both consciously and unconsciously, religious reformers were absorbing not only knowledge, but also new criteria for what constitutes "truth." Most reformers were no longer willing to accept the conclusions of generations of religious scholars, and insisted instead on returning to the original textual sources of the faith. The Qur'an and Hadith were no longer merely revered—they were studied and mined for clues to God's guidance for every issue that emerged in modern life. Fewer and fewer Sunnis expected the texts to have multiple or metaphorical meanings; the scriptures were inerrant and precise and were meant to be read literally. Readers assumed that the texts possessed objective and self-evident truth that the mind could apprehend directly. In a manner comparable to what was happening in the Christian fundamentalist movement that was emerging in the United States during this period, religion for many Muslims was becoming less a matter of the heart than a set of dogmas to be defended rationally against competing world views. Precisely because adherents assumed that the meaning of the scriptures was self-evident, they were less able than their predecessors to tolerate interpretations that differed from their own.

A major development of this period was the maturation of the South Asian and Southeast Asian Muslim communities as centers of independent thought and action. Both regions had already produced notable scholars, of course: Shah Wali Allah is indisputably one of the great figures in Islamic history, and other figures in both regions had been original thinkers. After the middle of the nineteenth century, however, a major shift in the center of gravity of the Muslim world took place. The variety of the movements of reform that emerged in India during the second half of the nineteenth century and the size and organizational features of the mass movements that arose in the Netherlands Indies on the eve of World War I are impressive achievements that dwarf developments in the rest of the Muslim world during that period. The distinct, independent, multicivilizational features of the Muslim world were becoming apparent. Moreover, British India was already home to the world's largest concentration of Muslims, and the Muslim population of the Netherlands Indies was rapidly expanding. These regions, which had once been on the periphery of the Dar al-Islam, had moved into the forefront of confronting the challenges of the modern world.

NOTES

1. Violent extremists of the past decade have adopted the term *salafi* for their own purposes, but their ideas and programs must not be confused with the movement that arose in the late nineteenth and early twentieth centuries.
2. For a representative sample of the conclusions of mainstream historians regarding this topic, see Erik J. Zürcher, *Turkey: A Modern History,* new ed. (London and New York: I. B. Taurus, 2004), 114–117; Ronald Grigor Suny, "Rethinking the Unthinkable: Toward an Understanding of the Armenian Genocide," from *Looking Toward Ararat: Armenia in Modern History* (Bloomington and Indianapolis: Indiana University Press, 1993), 94–115; Guenter Lewy, *The Armenian Massacres in Ottoman Turkey: A Disputed Genocide* (Salt Lake City: The University of Utah Press, 2005), and Taner Akçam, *A Shameful Act: The Armenian Genocide and the Question of Turkish Responsibility.* Translated by Paul Bessemer (New York: Metropolitan Books, 2006).

FURTHER READING

European Imperialism, 1875–1914 and Imperial Rule

Dupree, Louis. *Afghanistan.* Princeton, New Jersey: Princeton University Press, 1980.

Fieldhouse, D. K. *Economics and Empire 1830–1914.* Ithaca, New York: Cornell University Press, 1973.

Gowing, Peter Gordon. *Mandate in Moroland: The American Government of Muslim Filipinos, 1899–1920.* Quezon City, Philippines: New Day Publishers, 1983.

Hupchick, Dennis P. *The Balkans: From Constantinople to Communism.* New York: Palgrave, 2002.

Kanya-Forstner, A. S. *The French Conquest of the Western Sudan: A Study in French Military Imperialism.* London: Cambridge University Press, 1968.

Lovejoy, Paul E. *Transformations in Slavery: A History of Slavery in Africa,* 2d ed. Cambridge, U.K.: Cambridge University Press, 2000.

McCarthy, Justin. *The Ottoman Peoples and the End of Empire.* London: Arnold; New York: Oxford University Press, 2001.

McKenna, Thomas M. *Muslim Rulers and Rebels: Everyday Politics and Armed Separatism in the Southern Philippines.* Berkeley, Los Angeles, and London: University of California Press, 1998.

Saunders, Graham. *A History of Brunei.* Kuala Lumpur: Oxford University Press, 1994.

Webster, Anthony. *Gentlemen Capitalists: British Imperialism in South East Asia, 1770–1890.* London and New York: Tauris Academic Studies, 1998.

Encounters with Tradition

Abun-Nasr, Jamil N. *A History of the Maghrib in the Islamic Period,* 3d ed. Cambridge, U.K., and New York: Cambridge University Press, 1987.

Commins, David Dean. *Islamic Reform: Politics and Social Change in Late Ottoman Syria.* New York and Oxford, U.K.: Oxford University Press, 1990.

Daniel, Elton L. *The History of Iran.* Westport, Connecticut, and London: Greenwood Press, 2001.

Friedmann, Yohanon. *Prophecy Continuous: Aspects of Ahmadī Religious Thought and Its Medieval Background,* new ed. New Delhi and New York: Oxford University Press, 2003.

Gowing, Peter G. *Muslim Filipinos—Heritage and Horizon.* Quezon City, Philippines: New Day Publishers, 1979.

Hardy, Peter. *The Muslims of British India.* Cambridge, U.K.: Cambridge University Press, 1972.

Hupchick, Dennis P. *The Balkans: From Constantinople to Communism.* New York: Palgrave Macmillan, 2002.

Keddie, Nikki R. *An Islamic Response to Imperialism: Political and Religious Writings of Sayyid Jamāl ad-Dīn "al-Afghānī."* Berkeley and Los Angeles: University of California Press, 1983.

Kerr, Malcolm H.. *Islamic Reform: The Political and Legal Theories of Muhammad 'Abduh and Rashīd Ridā.* Berkeley: University of California Press, 1966.

Khalid, Adeeb. *The Politics of Muslim Cultural Reform: Jadidism in Central Asia.* Berkeley: University of California Press, 1998.

Landau, Jacob M. *The Politics of Pan-Islam: Ideology and Organization.* Oxford, U.K.: Clarendon Press; New York: Oxford University Press, 1990.

Lelyveld, David. *Aligarh's First Generation: Muslim Solidarity in British India,* 2d ed. Delhi and Oxford, U.K.: Oxford University Press, 1996.

Masselos, Jim. *Nationalism on the Indian Subcontinent: An Introductory History.* Melbourne: Thomas Nelson, 1972.

Melson, Robert. "A Theoretical Inquiry into the Armenian Massacres of 1894–1896." *Comparative Studies in Society and History,* 24 (July 1982): 481–509.

Metcalf, Barbara. *Islamic Revival in British India: Deoband, 1860–1900.* Princeton, New Jersey: Princeton University Press, 1982.

Ricklefs, M. C. *A History of Modern Indonesia Since C. 1200,* 3d ed. Stanford, California: Stanford University Press, 2001.

Sanyal, Usha. *Devotional Islam and Politics in British India: Ahmad Riza Khan Barelwi and His Movement, 1870–1920.* Delhi: Oxford University Press, 1996.

Troll, Christian W., ed. *Muslim Shrines in India: Their Character, History and Significance.* Delhi: Oxford University Press, 1989.

Troll, Christian W. *Sayyid Ahmad Khan: A Reinterpretation of Muslim Theology.* New Delhi: Vikas Publishing House, 1978.

The Impact of World War I

Adelson, Roger. *London and the Invention of the Middle East: Money, Power, and War, 1902–1922.* New Haven, Connecticut, and London: Yale University Press, 1995.

Brower, Daniel. *Turkestan and the Fate of the Russian Empire.* London and New York: RoutledgeCurzon, 2003.

Fromkin, David. *A Peace to End All Peace: The Fall of the Ottoman Empire and the Creation of the Modern Middle East,* 2d repr. ed. New York: Owl Books, 2001.

Macmillan, Margaret. *Paris 1919: Six Months That Changed the World.* New York: Random House, 2002.

Minault, Gail. *The Khilafat Movement: Religious Symbolism and Political Mobilization in India.* New York: Columbia University Press, 1982.

Ozcan, Azmi. *Pan-Islamism: Indian Muslims, the Ottomans and Britain (1877–1924).* Leiden, Netherlands, and New York: Brill Academic Publishers, 1997.

Yemelianova, Galina M. *Russian and Islam: A Historical Survey.* Houndmills, U.K., and New York: Palgrave Macmillan, 2002.

CHAPTER 10

The Interwar Years, 1920–1939

World War I is overshadowed in the modern consciousness by World War II, but the psychological and geopolitical impact of the former conflict was every bit as shattering as the latter. Terrible new weapons made their first appearance during this war, venerable empires collapsed, new countries were born, and ethnic conflicts broke out that have not been resolved to this day. World War I led to disillusionment among Europeans and Americans regarding assumptions of progress, rationality, and the supremacy of Western civilization, and it triggered an unprecedented wave of religious and political activism in the Muslim world.

During the period between the two world wars, Muslims found themselves in a variety of settings. Some formed the majority population in a handful of independent, Muslim-ruled states that had narrowly escaped imperialist domination. Others were part of Muslim minorities in large, independent states. The vast majority, as we have seen, were the subjects of imperial powers. Regardless of their political status, most Muslim societies underwent profound transformations. Each society had its own unique experience, but most shared in varying degrees the impact of the dissemination of modern technologies. Many people who had been accustomed to the rhythms of the agricultural cycle and immersed in the intimacies of village life began to punch a clock in factories and to subsist in the anonymity of urban apartment complexes. Radios and newspapers provided rapid distribution of news and propaganda alike. Rural-to-urban migration caused a major shift in political power away from rural elites and a corresponding shift toward individuals who understood the dynamics of mass politics. Larger numbers of students attended the secular schools that offered subjects like science and political thought, thereby becoming exposed to possibilities and explanations that had never been discussed in traditional religious schools. In most societies, mass organizations emerged whose goals might be independence, religious renewal, women's rights, or any of a number of other causes. The interwar period witnessed the rise of ideas and institutions that would provide the basis for important trends in the period of independence that followed World War II.

Independent Muslim States

On the eve of the war, most Muslims lived in regions that were controlled by non-Muslim governments, and almost all of the remaining Muslims were subjugated during or immediately after the war. A few countries managed to escape permanent occupation. Turkey was targeted for occupation but managed to secure its independence by war; great-power rivalry allowed Iran to end its occupation; and Afghanistan ceased recognizing Britain's claim to control its foreign affairs. Sectors of the Arabian Peninsula that held neither strategic significance nor any known natural resources managed to escape serious imperial interest until the 1930s, when imperial conquest had become unseemly.

The Republic of Turkey

The Treaty of Sèvres was never implemented. As early as spring 1919, many Ottomans were furious at the news that was filtering from the Paris Peace Conference regarding the delegates' plans for the empire. Several spontaneous resistance movements arose across Anatolia. Mustafa Kemal (1881–1938), a military officer who had won plaudits for his leadership during the war, became the most well-known dissident. The sultan, who was cooperating with the Allies, recalled Kemal to Istanbul in June 1919 in an attempt to calm the situation. Instead of obeying the orders, Kemal created an opposition government at the interior provincial capital of Ankara. From there, he conducted military operations designed to evict all foreign forces from what remained of the empire. He reclaimed the predominantly Kurdish areas, and he and the Soviet Union's leader, Lenin, agreed to divide Armenia between them. Italy and France signed agreements to evacuate Anatolia rather than fight Kemal's army.

The worst fighting took place between Kemal's forces and the army of Greece, which tried to expand the territory that it controlled in western Anatolia. The Greek army advanced almost all the way to Ankara before the Turkish nationalist army began pushing it back in 1922. By August 1922, the Turks surrounded Izmir, a predominantly Greek-speaking city, but one that was essential for the economy of Turkey. During the campaign, the two armies engaged in fierce fighting against each other and committed atrocities against the civilians of the region. Greek forces burned several Turkish towns and killed Turkish civilians indiscriminately. Kemal's soldiers, in turn, burned much of the Greek and Armenian quarters of Izmir to the ground, killed indiscriminately, and forced the evacuation of tens of thousands of people by ship.

Kemal then turned toward the straits, where Britain had primary responsibility for security. British political leaders were unable to obtain the support of their dominions (especially Canada, Australia, and South Africa) for a conflict with

Kemal for control of the waterway, and so they agreed to a new conference whose purpose was to review the Treaty of Sèvres. As the result of skillful negotiations on the part of the Turkish delegates, the Treaty of Lausanne (July 1923) recognized Turkish sovereignty over Anatolia and the region around Edirne in Europe, and it exempted Turkey from the hated Capitulations. Meanwhile, the government in Ankara abolished the sultanate in November 1922 and, in 1923, transferred the capital from Istanbul to Ankara, where the new Republic of Turkey was proclaimed. In March 1924, Kemal persuaded the assembly to abolish the caliphate. Henceforth, Turkey was a secular state.

The vicious fighting between Greeks and Turks during 1920–1922 convinced the leaders of both countries that the two peoples could not live together. Throughout the 1920s, Greece and Turkey engaged in a program of forcible population exchange. In conditions of great hardship, over one million Greek Orthodox Christians (many of whom spoke Turkish, not Greek) were deported from Turkey to Greece, and some 400,000 Muslims (most of whom spoke Greek, not Turkish) were deported from Greece to Turkey. As a result, Turkey became almost exclusively Muslim, in stark contrast to the multireligious nature of the Ottoman Empire at its height. The country was now largely Turkish, as well, but in the east it retained a large minority (perhaps twenty percent of the total population) of Kurds, whose dialects belong to a totally distinct linguistic family from that of the Turkish dialects (see Map 10.1).

Mustafa Kemal's exploits did not end with the creation of the republic. As president of the new country from its founding until 1938, he was the driving force behind the set of policies that was largely responsible for the ethos that has dominated Turkey to the present day. The title that his followers in the Assembly bestowed upon him in 1934—Ataturk, or "Father Turk"— was not inappropriate, for it is difficult to imagine another figure in modern times who left his imprint upon a country more decisively than Kemal did on Turkey. As a military officer, he had been embarrassed and humiliated by what he considered to be the backwardness of the Ottoman Empire despite decades of modernizing reforms. Like other secularists of the waning days of the Ottoman period, Kemal blamed Islam for his country's backwardness and regarded it as an obstacle to progress. Once he had swept aside the office of the caliphate, he began to implement a secular program for the country—known in Turkey as Kemalism—that was more radical than has ever been attempted in any other Muslim country. He succeeded in part because he was able to convert the high level of loyalty and admiration that he had won in nation-building into political acquiescence, and in part because he used brute force to coerce compliance.

Kemal accomplished most of his objectives during the first ten years of his rule. He abolished the Shari'a and replaced it with the Swiss civil code and the Italian penal code. He abolished madrasas and replaced them with state-run schools for preachers and a theological faculty at the University of Istanbul. He abolished all Sufi orders, triggering a revolt centered in the remote Kurdish regions; Kemal declared martial law and used the army to suppress the uprising. He outlawed the wearing of the fez and replaced it with the fedora-style, broad-brimmed hat. Turkish citizens had to learn to read and write the Ottoman Turkish language in the Latin alphabet instead of Arabic, and the language was purged of most of its Arabic and Persian loan words. The republic adopted the European clock and the Gregorian calendar; replaced Friday with Sunday as the official day of rest; and granted

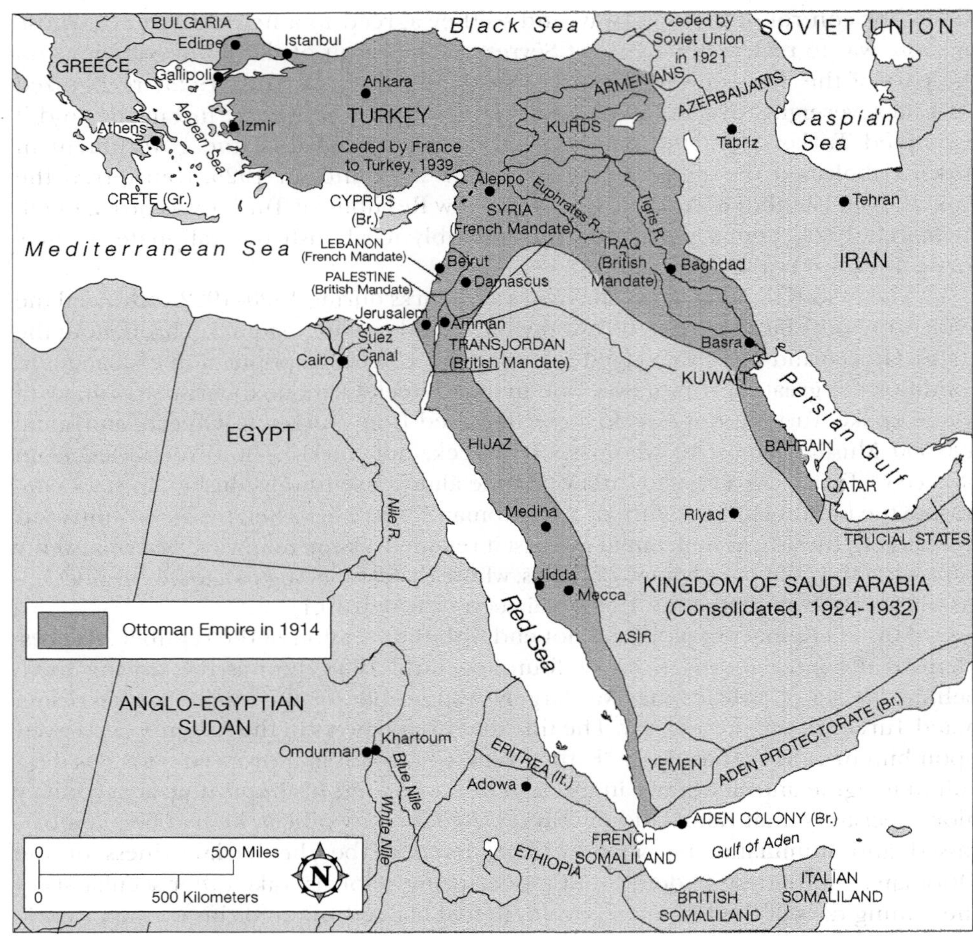

MAP 10.1 Dissolution of the Ottoman Empire.

women complete legal equality with men, including the right to vote and to be elected to political office.

In historical perspective, Kemal was completing the process of the secularization of the state, education, and law that Sultan Mahmut II (r. 1808–1839) had begun and that the Tanzimat had extended, but his more radical approach was the result of his renunciation of any ties with the Islamic past. He justified the claim of Turks to their country by declaring that all the ancient civilizations that had been based in Anatolia were Turkic, including the Hittite and Akkadian. In a challenge to his Egyptian contemporaries who were claiming that all civilizations derived from the Pharaonic civilization, Kemal claimed that all civilizations derived from the Turkish ones. Moreover, he declared that the Turkish language was the original language from which all others evolved. By using this interpretation, he assured Turks that they should not be reluctant to borrow technical terms from European languages—by doing so, they were merely reclaiming their own heritage.

In the aftermath of the horrifying circumstances of World War I and the struggle to free Turkey from foreign occupation, Kemal felt that he had to move quickly in order to create a society that would be strong enough to survive. His authoritarian methods were probably required for the purpose, because powerful social groups were opposed to radical change. Kemal's legacy contains many positive features, including a political system that has remained remarkably stable given the severity of the crises that it has weathered. It is the only example of a predominantly Muslim country that has functioned as a meaningful democracy for most of its history.

Kemal's legacy also contains two notably negative features. The draconian secularization of state and society, while welcomed by Westernized elites, had little impact on the thought or behavior of the large majority of the population, who lived in thousands of towns and villages where traditional customs persisted. The policy created a rift between the urban elites and the majority of the population that has lasted many decades. The other nagging problem that Kemal bequeathed to Turkey is the insistence on a Turkish identity for his people. By "Turks," Kemal meant the citizens of his republic rather than a particular ethnic group, because his purpose was to generate a dynamic, forward-looking nation that was united in its ambition to achieve parity with the leading nations in the world. His myth of Turkish homogeneity, however, ran headlong into the reality of the nation's large (twenty percent) Kurdish minority. Under the republic, Kurds have continued to exist on the margins of Turkish society. The government has never accepted the legitimacy of Kurdish identity, and until recently it even designated Kurds to be "Mountain Turks." It was illegal for spoken Kurdish to be used in courts or schools or for journals to be published in Kurdish. The result has been a profound feeling of alienation on the part of Kurds that has often taken the form of violence.

The Pahlavi Monarchy of Iran

In Iran, Reza Khan played a nation-building role almost as important as that of Kemal in Turkey. During the winter and spring of 1920–1921, tensions between Britain and the Soviet Union began to ease as the British made clear their plans to evacuate Iran. British officers in Tehran turned over their military duties to the Cossack Brigade after its Russian officers were removed. Meanwhile, Colonel Reza Khan of the Cossack Brigade marched a contingent of his troops into Tehran, declared martial law, and assumed the position of commander of the army. He allowed the government to appear to be functioning as usual, but he was the power who named and dismissed cabinet officials, reorganized the army, and arranged treaties.

In the fall of 1925, Reza Khan persuaded the Majlis to depose the young and incompetent Ahmad Shah, bringing the Qajar dynasty to a close. Reza Khan proposed abolishing the monarchy and creating a republic, but the ulama rejected that idea: They feared the implications of a republic for the Shari'a, whose influence in society was already in decline. In the following December, the constitution was amended to transfer the monarchy to Reza Khan. In April 1926, he crowned himself Reza Shah Pahlavi.

Reza Shah (1878–1941) was a commoner who joined the Cossack Brigade in the 1890s, when he was a teenager. As a member of the military unit, he learned firsthand how vulnerable the government was to tribal uprisings and provincial recalcitrance. When he became the ruler of the country, he was determined to build a powerful, modern state that exercised its authority over the entire nation. He conscripted a large, permanent standing army and equipped it with aircraft and motorized transport. He also built the Trans-Iranian Railroad and almost 16,000 miles of highways. Thus equipped, he moved to control the tribes by imprisoning or executing the leaders and forcibly settling their followers. By proving his indisputable mastery of the tribes, Reza Shah accomplished what neither the Mongols nor the Safavids had. The tribesmen's loss of freedom was traded for the security of the peasants and merchants and for the stability of the state.

Like Kemal, with whom he had good relations, Reza Shah wanted to create a strong national identity that trumped regional, ethnic, and religious identities. He insisted on using *Iran* as the name of the country instead of *Persia,* and he forced the Anglo–Persian Oil Company to change its name to Anglo–Iranian Oil Company. He also purged the Persian language of Arabic words. New government schools emphasized the pre-Islamic heritage of the country. Reza Shah also restructured the bureaucracy so that the central government's policies would be enforced at the provincial and local levels. In 1932, Reza Shah asserted Iran's new pride by canceling the concession for the Anglo–Iranian Oil Company when it became clear that the oil company was paying only one-fifth the amount that it should have. The World Court negotiated a settlement that renewed the concession on far better terms for Iran.

During the interwar period, the Iranian government was not as hostile to Islam as the new Turkish government was. Unlike Ataturk, Reza Shah did not blame Islam for Iran's backwardness, and he encouraged the enhancement of Qum's stature as a center of religious studies that rivaled Najaf and Karbala. Like Ataturk, however, Reza Shah had no intention of depending on the ulama for advice or expertise, and he developed a secular educational system that grew at the expense of the traditional religious schools. He also introduced judicial measures that encroached on the realm of the Shari'a courts. Reza Shah's modernization policies did not extend to the realm of the treasury, where he followed centuries-old policies of monarchs who regarded the national wealth to be indistinguishable from their personal wealth. By a variety of means—some quite brutal and dishonest—he acquired over 5000 square miles of personal property and deposited the equivalent of $150,000,000 in his own accounts in overseas banks.

States in the Arabian Peninsula

Two states in the Arabian Peninsula functioned independently after World War I. Yemen, which had expelled the Ottomans in the seventeenth century, faced them again soon after Britain occupied Aden in 1839. Istanbul was worried that British control of the strategic harbor at the entrance to the Red Sea would threaten Ottoman hegemony in southwestern Asia. The Ottomans occupied the Red Sea coast for two decades, and then tried to expand against the Zaydi Imam in 1872.

San'a was captured only after one Ottoman army was annihilated and a second one suffered serious losses. Even after the fall of San'a, the Imam's control of northern Yemen remained secure. After the Ottomans withdrew from the peninsula at the end of World War I, Imam Yahya (1904–1948) expanded his control to the Red Sea coast. He and Imam Ahmad (1948–1962) practiced a deliberate policy of keeping Yemen as isolated from the outside world as possible. When Ahmad died, army officers revolted against his son and declared a republic, inaugurating a bloody civil war that lasted until 1970.

Farther north, in the north-central section of the peninsula, the Sa'ud family was beginning to make a resurgence during the early years of the twentieth century. At that time, the second state (1843–1887) was but a nostalgic memory. The family had been forced to seek refuge in Kuwait in 1893 after being driven out of the Arabian interior by the Rashidi tribe. To all appearances, the family's prospects were grim, but great-power rivalry provided an opportunity for a revival. The Sa'ud family arrived in Kuwait as Great Britain was in the process of consolidating its position in the Gulf by means of treaties with regional rulers. Britain faced several challenges, however. The Ottoman sultan, Abdulhamit II, was concerned about Britain's growing strength in the region, and he was supported by Germany, which wanted to challenge Britain for global supremacy. The sultan granted Germany a concession to build railroads in his empire that would increase his control over his borderlands and simultaneously serve as a deterrent to any further expansion by the British. Russia, which was still competing with Britain in the Great Game, had plans to construct a railroad from the Caucasus to the Gulf.

The British realized that their position in the Gulf was being threatened, and they began looking for allies with whom to cooperate. The Ottomans did not wield direct control over central or eastern Arabia, but they did exercise indirect influence through a loyal and powerful tribal confederation led by the Rashidi tribe. It was in the British interest to weaken the Rashidis in order to reduce Ottoman influence in the region, and in 1902 they had their chance. In January of that year, twenty-two-year-old 'Abd al-'Aziz ibn Sa'ud and only forty followers made a daring raid on Riyad and captured it by stealth from the Rashidis. Over the next decade, with direct aid from Kuwait and indirect assistance from Britain, Ibn Sa'ud reestablished his family's power at Riyad.

During the period prior to World War I, Ibn Sa'ud slowly built up his power in the region. His purpose appeared to be nothing more than an effort to establish military and political power in the region; religion played little or no part in Ibn Sa'ud's campaigns. In 1913, however, Ibn Sa'ud began an alliance with a religious movement called the Ikhwan ("Brothers"). The precise origins of the group and their initial contacts with Ibn Sa'ud are obscure: Little is known for certain beyond their status—former bedouin who had been impelled by drought and economic necessity to settle into a life of agriculture—and their ideology—a set of teachings, behavior, and attitude that suggest a direct link to Wahhabism. They insisted on scrupulous performance of the Five Pillars of Islam, and they withdrew from regions in which they feared they might be spiritually polluted by contact with nominal Muslims or by Europeans. They created new settlements for their exclusive use. They called their settlements *hijras*, to convey the notion that they had performed a hijra from an ungodly society to a place where they could live an authentically Islamic life. Whereas bedouin had historically been notorious for their lack of religious zeal, these former bedouin considered themselves to be the only true Muslims. Everyone else—Muslims and non-Muslims alike—were "polytheists."

When World War I broke out, Britain offered to help arm Ibn Sa'ud against Arab tribes that were allied with the Ottomans. With material aid from the British and with the manpower reserves of the fierce Ikhwan, Ibn Sa'ud managed to prevent the Ottomans and their allies from making any gains in the central or eastern sectors of the Arabian Peninsula. In 1921, Ibn Sa'ud defeated the Rashidi tribe, gaining control of the central and northern sections of the Arabian Peninsula.

During the war, Britain also sent arms and technical assistance to the Sharif Husayn, who was the caretaker of the holy sites in Mecca and Medina. In 1916, he launched the Arab Revolt based on his understanding that Britain would recognize the independence of the Arab countries after the Ottomans had been defeated. The revolt, which was advised by T. E. Lawrence, was critical to British military success against the Ottomans, tying up 30,000 Ottoman troops between Yemen and Damascus. Despite this contribution and the written promises that the British had made to Husayn in the Husayn–McMahon Correspondence, the British and the French seized the region between Egypt and Iran at the conclusion of the war. Husayn was angered and disillusioned, but he gained a modicum of solace when the British named two of his sons as the nominal leaders of Transjordan and Iraq. In 1921, 'Abd Allah became the amir of Transjordan, and in 1922 Faysal became the king of Iraq.

Whereas Husayn took some satisfaction in these appointments, they provoked alarm in Riyad. Husayn's family, known as the Hashemites, now confronted Ibn Sa'ud on three of his frontiers. The showdown with Husayn, which would have been inevitable due to Ibn Sa'ud's desire to control Mecca and Medina, was now accelerated. Ibn Sa'ud captured Mecca in October 1924, and he took control of Medina and Jidda in December 1925.

After the fall of Jidda, the Ikhwan began criticizing Ibn Sa'ud for having signed treaties with the British that defined borders with Transjordan, Iraq, and Kuwait. The Ikhwan objected to making treaties with infidels and resented being denied the opportunity to raid areas that offered the prospect of plunder. Many of the Ikhwan were also disillusioned with Ibn Sa'ud when they learned that he was planning to use automobiles, airplanes, and radio, all of which they considered to be the work of the devil. From the end of 1925 to the end of 1929, Ibn Sa'ud had to fight a full-fledged civil war against the Ikhwan. After defeating them, he had to quell a challenge from Asir, which lies between the Hijaz and Yemen. He annexed Asir, and in 1932, he proclaimed the creation of the Kingdom of Saudi Arabia.

On the surface, the new kingdom appeared to be the fulfillment of the aspirations of many of the Muslim activists of the previous two centuries: a state committed to the defense, strengthening, and dissemination of a unified, normative Islam that was free of all local accretions. The kingdom was founded as a jihad state, and many of Ibn Sa'ud's subjects regarded him as a spiritual and political authority who was prepared at all times to lead his people, the "monotheists," into jihad against the "polytheists," namely, all other Muslims.

Ibn Sa'ud found that it was expedient to encourage his subjects to maintain this interpretation of himself, for it facilitated his efforts to create an independent, centralized state that ruled over the bulk of the peninsula. He accomplished a feat that eclipsed anything the region had witnessed since the time of the Prophet himself. In accordance with the Wahhabi–Ikhwan legacy, Ibn Sa'ud began to implement the Hanbali school of law as the standard framework for the kingdom. He had to overcome resistance on the part of the bedouin, who wished to retain their customary law, and on the part of urban dwellers, whom the Ottomans had allowed to use any of the four schools of the Shari'a.

Despite appearances, however, Ibn Sa'ud was not the single-minded religious warrior that many of his followers imagined. He was certainly not irreligious in the mold of Kemal, but he was pragmatic as well as devout. His defiance of the Ikhwan's criticism of his treaties with Britain revealed that feature of his personality. Moreover, although he consulted with the ulama and asked for their advice, on major issues of state—such as adopting modern technologies of radio, automobiles, and telegraph—he did not hesitate to act against their advice. He was adaptable, practical, and devoted to the preservation of his state.

Economically, the new kingdom appeared to have a precarious future. It possessed no known natural resources and played a negligible role in global commerce. Petroleum had been discovered in Iran in 1908 and in northern Iraq in 1927, but British geologists believed that the rock structures of the peninsula—which were quite different from those of the oil fields of Iraq and Iran—were unlikely to yield oil. American oil companies, by contrast, were eager to investigate the peninsula's potential for oil, because they had been excluded from exploring in the colonial possessions of Britain, France, and the Netherlands. Their interest in the country was reciprocated by Ibn Sa'ud, who needed revenue but distrusted the imperial record of the British. Standard Oil of California (later known as Chevron) signed an agreement with Ibn Sa'ud in 1933, and commercial quantities of petroleum were discovered five years later.

Geologists soon realized that the petroleum deposits in the country were among the richest in the world, and the oil fields became the focus of intense interest by both the Allied and Axis powers during World War II. During the war, the American government sold military equipment to Ibn Sa'ud on the Lend–Lease plan, and Franklin Roosevelt met with Ibn Sa'ud in the Suez Canal in February 1945 in order to cement the American–Saudi relationship. Production and distribution of oil continued to be an American monopoly under the Arabian–American Oil Company (Aramco), a corporation jointly operated by Chevron and three other American companies.

The revenue from royalties paid by Aramco enabled Ibn Sa'ud and his immediate successors to make important improvements to the kingdom's infrastructure, but dramatic changes did not show up prior to the mid-1970s. Until then, the rulers proceeded cautiously out of deference to the underlying hostility that conservatives expressed toward any kind of imported technology and concepts. It became increasingly difficult for the ruling family, many of whose members valued a Western education and enjoyed the amenities of secular life, to strike a balance between modernizing their country and retaining the allegiance of the sector of the population that remained xenophobic and religiously intolerant.

The Kingdom of Afghanistan

Afghanistan remained neutral during World War I, but the king had to resist enormous pressures to keep from entering the conflict. Widespread hostility persisted toward Britain and Russia due to the imposition of the Durand Line and the terms of the 1907 Russo–British agreement. When the Ottoman Empire entered the war, many Afghans expressed a desire to ally with it. The king, however, knew that any sign of sympathy with Germany would result in a partition of his country similar to that suffered by Iran. He was so cautious that he did not even take advantage of the war to renounce the terms of the 1879 treaty with Britain, according to which Afghanistan agreed not to conduct its own foreign relations without British consent. The king's inaction provoked a group to assasinate him. Immediately after the war, the new king unilaterally declared Afghanistan's unconditional independence from any outside constraints. This declaration led to an invasion by Britain in 1919 (the so-called Third Afghan War), but both countries were eager to end hostilities after a month of fighting. Reluctantly, Britain recognized Afghanistan's sovereignty in the Anglo–Afghan Treaty of 1921.

The fifteen years following World War I were characterized by political instability and chronic tribal conflict. Of the four kings who ruled from 1918 to 1933, one was deposed and exiled, and the other three were assassinated. In 1933, nineteen-year-old Zahir Shah inherited the throne and began the longest administration in modern Afghan history (1933–1973). Until 1953, his uncles served as regents. During those two decades, the country made modest, but meaningful, gains in the mileage of paved roads and the number of small industries. A guiding principle of the period was caution and discretion, for Afghan rulers faced daunting challenges as they tried to modernize their country. Although the level of opposition to innovation was not as high as in Saudi Arabia, government officials had to estimate the potential that any new measure would offend religious sensitivities, trigger tribal rivalries, or exacerbate tensions between the central government and the tribes.

Muslim Minorities in the USSR

Millions of Muslims lived in imperial Russia, which strongly supported the Orthodox Church. The communist revolution meant that Muslims would have to adapt to a government that was militantly atheistic. When the Bolsheviks seized power in late autumn of 1917, their true intentions for minorities were still largely unknown in non-communist circles. Prior to the revolution, Lenin had written extensively of the right of self-determination for nationalities. When the Bolsheviks were securely in power after the civil war of 1917–1921, however, one of their first priorities was to make sure that nationalities did not practice self-determination.

Although the vast majority of the Soviet Union's Muslims remained neutral during the civil war, the communist government faced fierce fighting in sections of the Caucasus, Azerbaijan, the Crimea, and Central Asia. Fearing the possibility of a general Islamic movement that would pose a threat to the officially atheistic state, the government set out to encourage Muslims to view themselves as members of nationalities rather than as Muslims. Between 1924 and 1936, the government created "soviet republics," "autonomous republics," and "autonomous regions" for numerous Muslim groups. It drew borders that had never existed before, gave new names to certain languages, and even fabricated national histories to justify the new administrative divisions.

The clearest illustration of the communists' methods and purposes was the disposition of the Uzbeks and Tajiks. The most urbanized of the khanates that imperial Russia conquered in the nineteenth century were Kokand and Bukhara, which were multiethnic societies ruled by Uzbek dynasties. The Uzbeks, a Mongol people who migrated from southern Siberia to the valley of the Syr Darya River in the early fifteenth century, adopted the local Chaghatay Turkish language as their everyday speech. Chaghatay Turkish was highly Persianized (sixty percent of its vocabulary was borrowed from Persian), and the Uzbeks retained literary Persian as the language of culture at the courts of Bukhara and Kokand. The descendants of the pre-Uzbek population spoke a dialect of Persian known as Tajik. Because the Uzbeks and Tajiks lived among each other and their languages shared such a large vocabulary, the vast majority of the population of Bukhara and Kokand were bilingual. Ethnic differences were recognized less by speech than by means of subsistence: The first language of most nomads and transhumants was Chaghatay, and the first language of most cultivators and urban merchants was Tajik.

It was not in the Soviet government's interest to foster the Persianized culture that the inhabitants of the region shared. The Tajiks were the wealthiest and best-educated segments of the population due to their dominance in the urban mercantile sector, and they were present in both of the former khanates. Working in conjunction with the Uzbeks, who had a legacy of wielding political power, they might constitute a formidable bloc of power. Soviet planners thus set out to create distinct Uzbek and Tajik nationalities.

One of the five Central Asian administrative districts that the Soviet government created was called Uzbekistan. Authorities designated its non-Russian population to be "Uzbeks," even though the new province contained the largely Tajik-speaking cities of Bukhara and Samarqand. The Soviet government also grafted to Uzbekistan an awkward eastern extension of the country that included most of the largely Tajik-speaking Fergana valley, including the city of Kokand. The inclusion of so many of the major cities of Central Asia made Uzbekistan the most populous of the new provinces. The Soviets soon moved its capital from Samarqand to Tashkent, in the eastern extremity of the country and away from the traditional centers of power.

Tajikistan was created to the east of Uzbekistan. It was allowed no major cities and had access to only one small strip of the Fergana valley. It was even separated from the eastern part of the valley by a strip of land that was given to Kyrgyzstan. The province contained ethnic groups other than Tajiks, but under the Soviet system, all the inhabitants were thenceforth identified as Tajiks.

After Stalin came to power in 1927, the Soviet Union's antireligion campaign shifted into high gear against Islam as well as Christianity. In 1929, the government replaced the Arabic alphabet—which was used for all the Turkic and Persian languages used by the country's Muslims—with the Latin alphabet; a decade later, it replaced the Latin alphabet with Cyrillic. As a result of the changes, Islamic religious scholars became cut off both from their own cultural heritage and from contact with Islamic scholarship in other Muslim lands.

The government closed madrasas and mosques alike. By the 1950s, of the hundreds of madrasas that had existed at the time of the communist revolution, only two—one in Bukhara and one in Tashkent—remained open, and of 26,000 mosques, only 400 were still functioning. Thousands of religious leaders were killed or fled to neighboring countries. Many Muslims continued to pray in secret, but the quality of religious leadership was low. Central Asia, which had once been a center of Islamic scholarship, was almost devoid of ulama.

Nationalist Movements

For most Muslim countries that were occupied by European powers, World War I intensified anti-imperialist sentiment and accelerated the process of developing organizations and ideologies that opposed foreign control. The outbreak of the four-year-long war in Europe had nothing to do with the direct interests of the imperial subjects, and yet it dislocated their economies and required the military services of more than one million of them. Throughout the British and French empires, a conviction arose that the sacrifices of the war demanded a quid pro quo in the form of independence or, at least, greater autonomy. When the imperial powers rejected any loosening of control, nationalist activity began in earnest.

North Africa

Large numbers of Europeans—primarily Spaniards, Frenchmen, Italians, and Maltese—settled in the most fertile regions of French-controlled North Africa. Algeria's European population (known as *pieds noirs*) was the largest and most politically active of the colonies in the region; its demographic weight peaked at fifteen percent of the population in the mid-1920s. Metropolitan areas such as Oran, Bone, and Algiers were thirty-five to fifty percent European. The *pieds noirs* wanted all the rights and privileges of citizens who lived in France, but they opposed the extension of those rights and privileges to Muslims. Moreover, as Europeans acquired more agricultural land in Algeria, economic pressure on Muslims increased. By the mid-1920s, 100,000 Algerian Muslims had migrated to France to look for employment. The irony of the exchange of populations was not lost on many Muslims.

The opposition by the *pieds noirs* to any governmental concessions to Muslim aspirations created a perpetual crisis atmosphere during the interwar period. Perhaps the most egregious instance occurred soon after World War I. More than 170,000 Algerian Muslims had served in the military during World War I, and 25,000 died. An attempt by the French government in 1919 to reward Muslims for their loyalty by granting them a limited degree of local political rights was sabotaged by the *pieds noirs*.

Throughout French North Africa, activist Muslims who sought relief for their community tended to consolidate into two major groups, one of which was secular and the other religious. The secularists were, in turn, divided into two further

Ataturk Mustafa dancing with his stepdaughter at her wedding, c. 1925. The clothing styles and mixed company contrasted sharply with wedding practices in the rest of the Muslim world.

groups. One advocated assimilation to French culture. This group was small—limited to those who had enjoyed the privilege of gaining a French education—but articulate and with many contacts among the French elite. Its members hoped that Muslims would be granted the full rights of French citizenship on the basis of their educational attainment and responsible actions. When the opportunity arose in 1936 for the government in Paris to do precisely that for Algerian Muslims, the *pieds noirs* once again scuttled the bill. The assimilationist model was thereafter largely discredited. The other secularist movement was much larger, for it recruited from among the working class. In many areas, it was imbued with Marxist ideas of class struggle, and it considered the French government to be as much of an enemy as the settlers were. It demanded independence, not French citizenship. During the period prior to 1945, its leaders were closely monitored and frequently jailed.

The politically active religious element of the Muslim population was the Salafiya movement, which was more visible in Morocco and Algeria than in Tunisia. The North African wing of the movement was faithful to Muhammad 'Abduh's argument that pristine Islam was a religion of progress that was compatible with the adoption of modern technology and organizational methods. The backwardness of Muslim countries, then, was the fault of irresponsible humans (especially

Sufis) and not anything inherent in original Islam. Leaders of the North African Salafiya worried that Francophone Muslims were in danger of losing their cultural identity, and they rejected the Marxist doctrine of class struggle. They resented the French occupation and settlement, but they were careful not to confront the French directly. They worked to create an alternative to French civilization by opening hundreds of schools to teach the Arabic language, Qur'an, and Hadith, as well as geography, mathematics, and, in some schools, science. Whenever possible, they cooperated with the secular Muslims, but such synergy happened much more regularly in Morocco than in Algeria.

Algerian nationalists were never able to cohere around a single charismatic personality or an ideology that synthesized variant world views. Moroccans, by contrast, did have a single figure around whom they could rally in opposition to the French. The French protectorate that was declared in 1912 preserved the head of the Alawite family in his position as the titular ruler of Morocco. He was a ruler only in name, for he had to defer to the French resident-general in all matters of substance. On the other hand, the sharifian status of the ruling family remained a powerful badge of legitimacy and of cultural authenticity if it were used skillfully. By the end of World War I, several decades had passed since a sultan had possessed the personal qualities that would reignite the charismatic potential of the sharifian lineage. That changed in 1927, when seventeen-year-old Muhammad V succeeded his father as sultan. The young ruler had to be cautious and circumspect in his dealings with the French, but he showed his sympathy for the nationalists and inspired loyalty by his integrity and courage. His accession to the throne inaugurated a long and ultimately fruitful relationship with the independence movement.

In Tunisia, as well, a major charismatic figure emerged during the interwar period, but he was unabashedly secular. The struggle for political rights began in 1920, when a new organization calling itself the Dustur (Constitution) Party demanded the establishment of a constitutional government in which Tunisians would share the same rights as Europeans. The French arrested the Dustur's leader, and the party never recovered its dynamism. In 1934, a young lawyer, Habib Bourguiba (1903–2000), split from the Dustur and created the Neo-Dustur Party. Bourguiba did not flinch from demanding total independence from France. Although he was a secularist, he was willing to use religious sentiment for political purposes: Even before breaking with the Dustur, he urged Tunisians to ignore French criticisms of traditional styles of clothing, including the veil. Appealing to Tunisian pride, he argued that the wearing of traditional forms of dress was an assertion of Tunisian identity against the French (although Bourguiba himself wore European-style suits). The Neo-Dustur became such a threat to the peace that officials arrested Bourguiba in 1938, and he served a total of nine years in jail.

Libya was the only North African country during the interwar period where the primary resistance to imperialism was led by an ostensibly religious organization. Whereas the French were able to co-opt Sufi orders in their protectorates, the Italian government faced a formidable opponent in the Sanusi Sufi order, based in Cyrenaica. It had sided with the Ottomans early in World War I and attacked both the Italians and the British. A new shaykh, Sayyid Muhammad Idris, negotiated peaceful arrangements with the Italians during the last stage of the war and in its aftermath, but the agreements left Sayyid Idris without the political power that Sanusi shaykhs had traditionally exercised. He left for Egypt in 1922, where he remained until 1947.

After Idris's departure, the Italians quickly took control of Tripolitania by exploiting tribal factionalism, but Cyrenaica became the setting for one of the most spectacular anticolonial struggles of the interwar period. Idris had delegated his authority in Cyrenaica to 'Umar al-Mukhtar, who subsequently led a fierce military resistance against the Italians that lasted until 1932. The war did not end until the Italians built long barbed-wire barriers, employed airplanes and armored vehicles, and herded 80,000 of the region's tribal population into crowded and unsanitary camps. Most of the lands of the Cyrenaican plateau were then opened to colonization by Italian immigrants. By 1939, Italians composed about one-tenth of the region's population.

For most of the colonial period, the inherent tensions in North Africa between Arabs (people who speak Arabic in the home) and Berbers (people who speak a dialect of Berber in the home) remained latent, because most of the indigenous people united against the European invaders. Arab–Berber issues were most salient in Morocco—where as many as forty percent of the population were Berber during the colonial period—and Algeria—where Berbers composed twenty percent of the population (Berbers constituted about one percent of Tunisia's population and about five percent of the population of Libya, where most were concentrated in Jabal Nafusa). French officials tried to implement different policies for the administration of the Berber populations in Morocco and Algeria in an effort to divide the nationalist movement, but the plans backfired, generating new enthusiasm for independence. The nationalist movements rallied around cultural themes that included the centrality of the Arabic language because of its status as the language of the Qur'an. Berber–Arab differences would have to wait until the period of independence to be faced squarely, often with tragic results.

The Eastern Arab World

Egypt was by far the most populous of the Arabic-speaking countries. It played an important role in Britain's economy by providing raw materials—especially cotton—and serving as a captive market for British manufactured goods. Its economic value was sufficient reason for Britain to want to possess it, but its strategic location was the motivation for Britain's conquest and continuing occupation. London was determined to control the Suez Canal and the Nile River because of their importance as transportation and communication routes linking the numerous components of the British Empire.

British officials' complacency regarding the security and permanence of their position in Egypt was shaken by a violent uprising in 1919 that caused a temporary loss of control over much of the country. London issued a Unilateral Declaration of Egyptian "independence" in 1922, but the imperial power continued to claim the sole right to provide for Egypt's defense, protect foreign interests and communities, oversee imperial communications (a term that included control of the Suez Canal), and administer Sudan. Britain retained and expanded its military base on the Suez Canal, and British troops continued to occupy barracks on the banks of the Nile in downtown Cairo. In the face of bitter Egyptian protests, Britain and other European nations also retained the Capitulations, which kept Egypt's economy and legal system in a straitjacket. Although Egyptians implemented a constitutional monarchy, the continuing British interference in Egyptian affairs distorted the country's political and economic life until the 1950s. Most of the energies that politically active Egyptians expended during those three decades were directed against the British presence rather than toward alleviating social problems.

The creation of the so-called mandates in the predominantly Arab regions of the former Ottoman Empire provoked a deep-seated sense of betrayal and anger among many of the inhabitants. Arabs who had been assured that their independence would be recognized if they organized an Arab Revolt against the Ottomans reacted with outrage when Britain and France carved up the lands of the Fertile Crescent.

An independent, Arab-ruled Syria was formed in Damascus when the forces of the Arab Revolt captured the city in October 1918. In March 1920, a Syrian congress selected Sharif Husayn's son Faysal, who had led the military forces of the Revolt, to be their king. When French soldiers marched in to claim Syria the following summer, they bombarded Damascus and occupied the country, forcing Faysal to flee. Syrian opposition to French control remained fierce, provoking colonial officials to inaugurate a policy of dividing the country administratively in an effort to weaken nationalist sentiment. They gave most of the Syrian coast to Lebanon, and they divided the remaining Syrian territory into provinces that were governed through totally separate administrations. In 1939, France ceded Alexandretta to Turkey. French officials also tried to limit Sunni Arab access to power by concentrating their recruiting efforts for security personnel among the Alawi population. The Alawis are regarded as heretical by most Sunnis because of their trinitarian conception of God (in which God manifests Himself as ʻAli, Muhammad, and Salman the Persian), a refusal to practice the Five Pillars, celebration of non-Islamic feast days, and other non-Sunni practices.

Under French control, Lebanon became a much more complex society than it had been prior to World War I. Historically, it had consisted only of the inland mountainous area that contained the bulk of the region's Christian Maronites (who have their own liturgy and clerical hierarchy but acknowledge the Pope as the head of the church) and Druze community (which broke away from Ismaʻili Islam early in the eleventh century). As a French mandate, Lebanon grew to include the cosmopolitan city of Beirut; the formerly Syrian coastal cities of Tyre, Sidon, and Tripoli; a largely Shiʻite territory that included the Baqaa' Valley and the hinterlands of Tyre and Sidon; and the largely Sunni hinterland of Tripoli. The Druze and Maronites were organized by clans that were led by feudal lords and were suspicious of anyone from outside the mountains. The inhabitants of the port cities were accustomed to a wide-ranging mercantile life and regarded the mountain people as bumpkins. The comfortable Sunnis of the north considered the poverty-stricken Shiʻites of the south and east of the country to be infidels. The French had created an ideally fragmented mosaic of peoples for their colonial purposes.

Britain's mandates included Palestine, Transjordan, and Iraq. Implementing the Balfour Declaration in Palestine proved to be considerably more difficult than issuing it. First came the task of determining where Palestine was, for it was not marked on any map. After drawing arbitrary borders in 1920, British officials separated the section east of the Jordan River (Transjordan) in 1921 and subsequently recognized Sharif Husayn's son 'Abdullah as its amir. Zionist settlement was excluded from it. Then, during the 1920s, Palestinian Arab opposition to the prospect that their ancestral home would become part of a Jewish state proved to be more vehement than Britain had anticipated, and Jewish immigration proved to be smaller than Zionist leaders had anticipated: Immigration during the 1920s averaged fewer than 10,000 annually, and there was actually a net loss of Jewish population in 1927. British commitment to Zionist aspirations became more ambivalent.

In 1933, Jewish immigration into Palestine surged, as German Jews flooded in after the accession to power of Adolf Hitler. Palestinian fears of being displaced by foreigners escalated, leading to the Great Revolt of 1936–1939, during which thousands of people lost their lives. In 1939, when war with Germany loomed, Britain issued a policy statement that decreed no more sales of Arab-owned land to Jews in most of the mandate, severe restrictions on Jewish immigration, and the goal of an independent, predominantly Arab, Palestine by 1949.

Britain also had unexpected difficulties in its mandate of Iraq. Iraq, like the other mandates of the post–World War I era, was a new state, not an Ottoman territorial entity under new management. The creation of Iraq was similar to the cobbling together of Lebanon: It was the forcing together of regions that had not been joined together in centuries. The overwhelming majority of people in the north were Kurds, who speak dialects that belong to the Persian language family. The vast majority of Kurds were Sunnis, but some were Twelver Shi'ite and others were Alawi. The central section of Iraq was dominated by Sunni Arabs. These were divided into nomadic groups, peasants working the irrigated river valleys, and urban dwellers, notably those of Baghdad. Baghdad also contained a large and wealthy Jewish population, the legacy of the Babylonian Captivity of the sixth century B.C.E. In the southern section of Iraq, most of the population were Shi'ite Arabs who lived in the marshes where the lower Tigris and Euphrates rivers meander. This population was the result of nineteenth-century migrations of nomadic Arab tribes into the region from the Arabian Peninsula. Originally lightly touched by Sunni Islam, they became acculturated to Shi'ite Islam radiating outward from Karbala and Najaf.

In 1920, a major revolt erupted among the tribes of the middle Euphrates, in modern Anbar province. More than 10,000 people were killed, including hundreds of British soldiers. In London, officials were becoming overwhelmed with crises in their far-flung empire, and they decided to cut their losses in Iraq. In 1921, they named Faysal, who had fled Syria a year earlier, king of Iraq. A series of treaties over the next decade granted Iraq increased autonomy over internal affairs, until formal independence was granted in 1932. Iraq then joined the League of Nations. British military forces remained in the country, however, on terms similar to those in Egypt.

Faysal was highly regarded by most Iraqis, and he ruled with skill. Unfortunately for Iraq, he died of heart problems in 1933, at the age of fifty. His playboy son, Ghazi, was uninterested in ruling and died in a sports car accident in 1939. His only heir was an infant son. Ghazi's weak leadership had already allowed a small group of Sunni Iraqi Arabs who had served under Faysal in the Arab Revolt to concentrate political and economic power in their hands. With the appointment of a regent for Ghazi's baby son, the process of concentration of power in Sunni hands accelerated, at the expense of the nation's Kurds and Arab Shi'ites. For the rest of the century, the history of Iraq was a violent and unstable one of Sunni Arabs quarreling over the politics of patronage and the distribution of the spoils.

South Asia

On the eve of World War I, the British administration in India was faced with opposition from both the Indian National Congress and the Muslim League. The latter had become incensed when, in 1911, the British succumbed to Hindu pressure and reversed the 1905 plan to partition Bengal. When the Ottoman Empire became an adversary of Britain in October 1914, the League had an additional reason to oppose the British. For the previous four decades, Muslims of India had followed the course of events in the Ottoman realm. As the only remaining independent Muslim state and the seat of a self-proclaimed caliphate, the Ottoman Empire became a beacon of hope and pride for Muslims who had lost their own independence. The Ottomans were also important in their role as keepers of the shrines in Mecca and Medina. During the Russo–Ottoman war of 1875–1877, Indian Muslims launched a fund-raising drive to aid their co-religionists. When the Ottomans became the wartime enemies of the Allies in 1914, British officials were in constant fear that their Indian Muslim subjects might rebel in the cause of loyalty to the caliph.

Indian Muslims did not rebel, but most of the politically conscious ones did become determined opponents of the British. A shared hostility toward the British allowed the League and the Congress to develop a working relationship. Muhammad Ali Jinnah, who was a member of both the League and Congress by the outbreak of the war, helped to negotiate an agreement between the two groups known as the Lucknow Pact of 1916. The League accepted Congress's demand for immediate self-government, and Congress accepted the principle of separate electorates for Muslims in the provincial assemblies.

Hindu–Muslim cooperation continued after the war when the organizers of the Khilafat Movement formed an alliance with Mohandas Gandhi as he began his first major noncooperation campaign. The Khilafat Movement was a response to the news that France and Britain had agreed to partition Ottoman territory. Muslim leaders from northern India began the Khilafat Movement in late 1919 as a means of preserving the integrity of the Ottoman Empire and the caliphate by applying diplomatic pressure on the Allies.

Gandhi, who had returned to India in 1915 after two decades in South Africa, saw in the Khilafat Movement an opportunity to advance the cause of Indian unity. He worked out an agreement with the Khilafat leaders according to which he would support their cause if they would support his noncooperation campaign of 1920. The conferences at San Remo and Sèvres of 1920 that authorized the mutilation of Ottoman territories so angered Indian Muslims that the deal was quickly made.

Unfortunately, fissures began to appear in the bonds of Muslim–Hindu harmony. Nationalist fervor had spiked in 1919 due to remarkably brutal British repression of nonviolent nationalist activity. Jinnah and other leaders, both Hindu and Muslim, wanted to employ legal and constitutional means for compelling

Britain to recognize India's independence. Gandhi, by contrast, was convinced that Indian nationalism had languished because it had never been a mass movement. His noncooperation campaign would employ the masses in a nonviolent campaign that would make British rule impossible. Jinnah feared that a mass movement would degenerate into chaos and widespread violence, making it impossible to effect a smooth transition to the anticipated independent government. At meetings, he was shouted down by Khilafatists and others, provoking him to resign from Congress in 1920.

The noncooperation campaign proceeded well for over a year, but several acts of violence committed by its participants began to make Gandhi uneasy. Increasingly concerned that his followers did not possess the self-discipline required, he abruptly called off the campaign in early 1922. The Khilafat Movement continued its agitation, but Turkey's abolition of the caliphate in early 1924 was an unexpected blow: It revealed that the Turks themselves were not as interested in a caliphate as some Indian Muslims were. To many Hindus, who never understood the rationale for the cause, the Khilafat Movement seemed to suggest that many Indian Muslims were more interested in an arcane issue half a world away than they were in the welfare of India.

It is hard to exaggerate the depth of the humiliation and despair that many Indian Muslims experienced due to the collapse of the noncooperation campaign and the Khilafat Movement. Both Muslims and Hindus were embarrassed at their failure to sustain a nonviolent campaign, and the Muslims felt that the Turks had made them look foolish on the caliphate issue. Moreover, Muslims had to concede the fact that the most severe of the episodes of violence during this period were initiated by members of the Muslim community. In 1921, Mappilas of Kerala had misinterpreted a speech given by a leader of the Khilafat Movement, inferring that the British had embarked upon a campaign to destroy Islam. Mappilas attacked British police and then began attacking Hindus. The British, who had developed a wariness of the Mappilas due to several revolts in Kerala during the nineteenth century, responded in a major reprisal, killing several thousand Mappilas before the violence was quelled in 1922.

The Mappila revolt of 1921–1922 was the last in the 400-year-long series of Mappila uprisings, but no one knew that at the time. Instead, Hindu and British commentators referred to this and other Muslim outbreaks of violence as part of the "jihad mentality" of Muslims, which cast doubt on their fitness to live in a modern state. Muslim resentment at these charges was aggravated by the emerging style of Gandhi's leadership of his mass movement. Although Gandhi wanted to lead an all-India campaign, he was most successful when he employed symbols and rhetoric that drew from Hindu sources. His idealization of primitive village life and agriculture made even the Hindu mercantile and industrial elites uneasy, but his rising influence caused many Muslims to fear that he was intending to create a Hindu-dominated India. Apart from a couple of short-lived joint Hindu–Muslim endeavors during the late 1920s and early 1930s, the brief period of Hindu–Muslim political cooperation was effectively over. Several outstanding leaders on both sides continued to labor for intercommunal cooperation—Abul Kalam Azad, the brilliant Muslim who was twice elected president of Congress, was just one of the most notable—but the trend was palpably in the direction of communalism. Jinnah became so disgusted with Gandhi's style of leadership and the ineffectiveness of the League that he moved to England in 1931.

Loyalty to the interests of one's own ethnic group rather than to those of society as a whole is not unusual, and its efflorescence in India at this time was a logical development. Hindu revivalist groups had arisen during the nineteenth century as British rule brought new opportunities for education, government employment, and education. Many Hindus wanted to assert their new-found power and skills. Muslims, by contrast, were on the defensive. The destruction of the Mughal dynasty in 1858 had been a powerful psychological shock to them, and over the next few years they discovered that, outside the Indo–Gangetic plain, their community lagged behind Hindus in educational achievement and commercial wealth. By the twentieth century, Hindus were making it clear that they wanted to have their fair share of whatever political influence could be wrung from the British, whereas Muslims—who composed a little more than one-quarter of the population—knew that their influence would be overwhelmed by the Hindu majority. Indians had no experience of democracy, either before the British period or under colonial rule. The transition to self-rule thus entailed as much anxiety as it did hope, because Indians could not know if it would mean more political freedom and economic opportunity than they had experienced under the British, or less.

Progress toward Indian independence proceeded in fits and starts throughout the 1920s and 1930s. Numerous organizations arose that worked toward a variety of goals with an equally diverse set of methods. Gandhi is the best-known leader of the period, but the only two civil disobedience campaigns that he led after 1922 were in 1930 and 1940. His potential for mobilizing millions of followers is what caused the British to be obsessed with him throughout this period. When British officials were not meeting with him, they often had him in jail. Recognizing that some concessions had to be made to Indian aspirations, London issued the Government of India Act in 1935. It provided for full responsible government at the provincial level and envisioned substantial Indian participation at the federal level for the future. Elections were scheduled for 1937.

Meanwhile, an idea began emerging that would have fateful consequences for Indian unity. It made its first appearance in the Muslim League presidential address given by Muhammad Iqbal in December 1930. Iqbal (1877–1938) had earned a degree in philosophy at Cambridge, qualified as a barrister at Lincoln's Inn in London, and received his doctorate in philosophy at the University of Munich. A gifted poet, he had been knighted in 1922 by King George V for his literary achievements and is widely considered to have been the greatest Urdu poet of the twentieth century. The themes of his poetry increasingly addressed the sense of crisis among Muslims that stemmed from their political weakness and the conviction that Islam was in need of reform.

In Iqbal's speech to the League, he proposed the "creation of a Muslim India within India." He also said that he foresaw the eventual creation of a self-governing Muslim state comprising Punjab, the North West Frontier Province, Sindh, and Baluchistan. During the winter of 1932–1933, four Muslims living in Cambridge called for the creation of an independent *Pakistan,* a name that was imaginatively derived from the provinces of *P*unjab, North-West Frontier Province ("*A*fghan Province"), *K*ashmir, *S*indh, and Baluchis*tan.* Whereas the derivation of the name had to be explained, its meaning was clear: In Urdu, it suggested "land of the pure."

From one point of view, the Pakistan idea was a natural outgrowth of the conviction of influential Muslims from at least the time of Sayyid Ahmad Khan that Muslims and Hindus constituted two separate nations. From another point of view, the idea was unnatural, for at least two reasons. One was that Hindus and Muslims who hoped to create a modern, multiethnic, liberal democracy were unable to understand why their two cultural communities could not coexist within the same country as long as legal safeguards were erected and enforced. The other reason that the Pakistan idea seemed unnatural to many Hindus and Muslims was the demographic problem involved. Muslims lived all over India, not just in the northwest—Bengal alone contained almost one-third of India's total Muslim population. Moreover, millions of Hindus lived in the regions targeted for the creation of the new country. The premise of the idea of Pakistan—that the Muslims of South Asia needed their own state—would require the uprooting of millions of people and a huge population transfer.

In 1934, Jinnah began to split his time between India and England and soon moved back permanently to India. He tried to organize support for the Muslim League's candidates for the 1937 elections, but the League garnered only four percent of all Muslim votes cast. Most Muslims voted for Congress candidates or for candidates from local parties. Congress won an overwhelming victory, but Congress politicians made the mistake of trying to discredit the League as being genuinely representative of India's Muslims. Jawaharlal Nehru, the leader of Congress, made derogatory comments about Jinnah and the League, and Congress accepted into the government only such Muslims as would join the Congress party itself. By 1939, Muslim–Hindu relations had never been so bad.

These actions of Congress confirmed for Jinnah and others that some Hindus were, in fact, determined to create a Hindu Raj to replace the British Raj. In 1940, the mounting tensions were the primary object of discussion at the Muslim League's meeting, held in Lahore. The conference issued the so-called Lahore Resolution, which, in a highly circuitous, deliberately obscure fashion, called for the creation of separate states in the Muslim-majority regions of India, but suggested that these "autonomous," "independent," and "sovereign" states would be under the constitution of independent India.

The Indian press immediately identified the resolution as the de facto adoption of the Pakistan idea by the League, although the text never mentions the concept. Jinnah himself soon began equating the object of the resolution with the Pakistan idea, and throughout the war, he engaged in a frenetic campaign to win support for Pakistan among India's Muslims. The ironies of the enterprise were remarkable: The aloof, private Jinnah had always distrusted the masses, and yet he spent the last years of his life trying—and largely succeeding—to win their support. Moreover, Jinnah, whom leading Hindus and Muslims had once considered the most likely to bring about a united India, became the single most important force that brought about partition.

Although Jinnah is often portrayed as having been dedicated to the creation of two separate states, one for Hindus and one for Muslims, his actual goal appears to have been more subtle—perhaps too subtle under the circumstances. If he had wanted an independent Muslim country, he would have discussed borders and ideology, but throughout the war, he consistently refused to discuss either topic. The prospect of drawing borders was patently absurd in light of the distribution of millions of Muslims throughout most of India. Ideologically, "a state for Muslims" was not necessarily an "Islamic state": Jinnah, who loved his Scotch whisky and ham sandwiches, clearly had a much different idea of what Pakistan would be like than those who looked forward to an Islamic state that would enforce the Shari'a.

When Jinnah's Pakistan campaign is considered in the context of themes that show up in the negotiating points that he used both during the 1920s and immediately after World War II, it appears that Jinnah was employing a tactic of demanding an independent state while expecting to be offered provincial autonomy within a federated India. Jinnah expected that Muslim-majority provinces would wield sufficient leverage in a future central government to be able to hold their own against Hindu-majority provinces. Jinnah's bluff might have worked under ordinary circumstances, but he was using it during a world war and as communal tensions were running high—communal tensions that he inadvertently helped to create.

During World War II, the British stifled the Congress's activities by jailing its leaders. The League, meanwhile, maintained a steady stream of warnings to the Muslim masses that "Islam" was in danger, without defining what "Islam" meant. Support for the League was strongest in the areas where Muslims were in a minority, and thus felt most vulnerable to the prospect of a multiethnic democracy. Many were convinced that, in a Hindu-dominated state, they would be forced to become vegetarian idolators.

Southeast Asia

In the Netherlands Indies, the so-called Ethical Policy, which had been implemented after the conclusion of the Aceh War in 1903, disintegrated in the interwar period. Dutch policies became more rigid and ruthless during the 1920s and 1930s, due to a combination of political challenges and the economic constraints of the Great Depression. A major factor in the hardening of imperial attitudes was the communist takeover of Sarekat Islam during the last years of World War I. The Bolshevik Revolution of November 1917 had inspired communists across the world with the hope of achieving a similar transformation of the political and social order. As radicals became more assertive in Sarekat Islam, many middle-class members stopped attending meetings. Emboldened by the decrease in opposition, the radicals escalated their demands and began attacking Dutch officials. In 1926–1927, communists in Sarekat Islam led the organization into an alliance with the Communist Party (founded in 1920) as the latter initiated violent rebellions against the government. In the bloody suppression that followed, Sarekat Islam was utterly discredited, and it practically disappeared.

In the aftermath of the failed revolt, other religious organizations avoided political themes. Thereafter, the nationalist movement was dominated by secular, Western-educated intellectuals who were inspired by liberal or socialist ideologies. As a result, many Muslims who were serious about their faith became politically marginalized during the interwar period, and the dynamic forces of the anti-imperialist struggle took on a decisively secular cast. To the nationalist leaders, Islam was not a viable basis for national unity. The development of a nationalist ideology was a difficult task in any protectorate, but nowhere was it more daunting than in the Netherlands Indies, with its thousands of islands and multiplicity of cultures. The large number of non-Muslims in the archipelago was not the only problem; the deep divisions within the Muslim community itself also seemed to preclude an agreement on a common ideology based on Islam.

After the collapse of Sarekat Islam, the major arena of political activism was that of so-called study clubs established by secondary and college students. In 1927, several study clubs cooperated to form the Indonesian National Association, which was dedicated to working toward independence. A prominent figure in this group was Sukarno (his only name), an engineering student from eastern Java. Sukarno (1901–1970) was a spell-binding orator and had a charismatic personality that thrust him into the center of attention. He was a major force in devising a set of principles for the new organization to agree on. These included renaming the Netherlands Indies to Indonesia and renaming Batavia to Jakarta, as well as adopting the Malay trade dialect as the national language of Indonesia.

By suggesting a dialect that was widely used in port cities, the nationalists avoided offending particular ethnic groups. The language project was highly successful. The dialect came to be known as *Bahasa Indonesia* ("The Language of Indonesia"), and today, of the roughly 240 million Indonesians, it is spoken by thirty million people as their first language and by 140 million more as a second language. The dramatic nature of the compromise on the language issue can be illustrated by noting that Javanese is the native language of seventy-five million people, more than twice as many as speak Indonesian as their first language.

Although the nationalists were able to develop powerful unifying symbols for Indonesians, the specific content of the nationalist ideology was vague and would not be formulated until the declaration of independence. The nationalist leaders were determined to avoid identifying their movement with Islam, class struggle, or a particular ethnic group, leaving them with few alternative themes that would inspire the mass support they needed. Sukarno himself had grown up imbibing the eclectic mixture of eastern Javanese animism, Buddhism, Islamic mysticism, and shadow plays based on Hindu epics. At school, he became enamored of Western ideas and values. He believed that all of these sources were valuable and that it did not matter which predominated in an individual's world view. What mattered was anti-imperialism.

Sukarno was influenced by the secular reforms that were taking place in contemporary Turkey and Iran. Like Kemal, he thought that the backwardness of the Muslim world was due to the influence of traditional religious leadership in the functions of the state. He was careful to say that he was not opposed to Islamic values, but he argued that the separation of religious institutions from the state machinery would make it possible for genuine Islamic values to flourish.

Sukarno and his fellow secular nationalists were concerned not only about the reaction of activist Muslims, but also of the Chinese community. Many Chinese feared Indonesian nationalism, for in many cases the nationalist sentiment was directed as much against themselves as the Dutch. The Chinese community in Batavia had suffered pogroms for two centuries. Many of the Malay Indonesians resented the powerful role that the Chinese played in the economy and the fact that few of the Chinese were Muslims. For many Indonesians (as well as Malayans and Filipinos), the Chinese played the role that Jews played in the minds of European anti-Semites: They were viewed as economic exploiters, and they were the religious Other.

The nationalist struggle was also complicated by a Dutch government that was unwilling to negotiate any issue. Unlike the British in India, the Dutch were not prepared to make concessions on autonomy, phased or otherwise. As a result, the nationalist movement was totally oppositional and lacked any element of compromise. The government often banished nationalist leaders without trial. Sukarno himself was in jail for most of the period between 1929 and the Japanese invasion of 1942.

By contrast with Java, the issues of religion and ethnicity were not major factors in the rice-based subsistence economies of the Malay Peninsula. In those areas, the population was overwhelmingly Malay and Muslim. In the regions where the tin and rubber industries developed, however, large numbers of Chinese and Indian workers poured in. By 1940, only half the population of the seven federated and unfederated states was Malay, whereas thirty-eight percent was Chinese and eleven percent was Indian. Religion and ethnicity became significant issues during the 1930s, when the global economic depression brought significant hardship to the region. Malays demanded that citizenship be reserved for them and denied to Chinese and Indians.

In the Philippines, euphoria greeted a 1934 bill from the American Congress implementing a ten-year "commonwealth" period that would serve as a transition toward independence for the Philippines. Filipinos were authorized to begin writing a constitution. This exhilarating news was soured for Moros when the constitutional convention refused to make special provisions for accommodating the Shari'a. Despite the fact that few Muslims were even familiar with the Shari'a, their self-appointed spokesmen hoped to see the day when their people adhered to it. An additional grievance arose in 1936, when the sultan of Sulu died. The nationalist government in Manila, led by commonwealth president Manuel Quezon, refused to recognize a successor to him. The sultanate was never revived, and the government in Manila never made serious efforts to integrate the Sulu archipelago into the nation's affairs.

The commonwealth period raised alarms among Moros for another policy that has had long-lasting consequences. As early as 1913, American officials had begun to create agricultural colonies on Mindanao for Christian Filipinos from the northern islands. The rationale was that, since the Moros had not been exposed to Spanish colonial administration or culture, they would become "civilized" faster if they had the benefit of living among people who had been exposed to Western culture. Under American auspices, only a few thousand Christians moved to predominantly Muslim territory, but during the commonwealth, tens of thousands of Christians resettled on Mindanao. The Quezon government gave them title to public lands and provided them with an array of government services to help them begin their new lives. Since the government declared all unregistered land on Mindanao to be public land, Muslims—the vast majority of whom had never had the occasion or necessity to register their land—were vulnerable to having their land seized and given to the settlers. Moreover, Muslims did not have access to the government services that were provided to the Christian settlers. Resentment, fear, and a sense of grievance began to fester, laying the foundation for an explosion of violence after independence was acquired.

Islamic Movements

Islamic religious leaders rarely played more than a supporting role in the major independence movements. Islamic organizations, however, were active and highly visible during the interwar period. They promoted education, health care, moral reform, and cultural pride. Whether they were actively involved in the nationalist movements or not, they were actively involved in debates on cultural identity.

The rise of the nationalist movements coincided with Kemal's abolition of the caliphate. The consequences of the conjunction of these two developments were enormous. Prior to World War I, the advocates of Pan-Islam had worked toward a global political union of Muslims as the means of defending religion and homeland. The destruction of the caliphate, which was unimportant in any tangible form outside Turkey, nevertheless entailed the loss of a symbol of global Sunni Islam in which many Muslims had invested their hopes and dreams. Simultaneously, because of the influence of contemporary nationalist movements, many Islamic organizations began to articulate their social and political identity in local terms. A major legacy of the nationalist period was a diminution of the concept of the global Umma, or Muslim community, and the substitution for it of national loyalties. The appeals for political Pan-Islam became harder to hear in an atmosphere of intense nationalist activity.

Tensions between Secular and Religious Muslims

The most influential nationalist movements in countries with Muslim majorities or large Muslim minorities had a secularist cast to them. They were led by intellectuals who were familiar with Western political thought and who communicated with the imperialist powers in the imperialists' own language. These activists objected to the fact of colonial rule, but they did not intend to eliminate the existing state machinery. They accepted models of the state from Europe—some preferred the liberal model, whereas others were socialists—and merely intended to transform the existing colonial state into one that reflected the voice of the ruled rather than the interests of the colonial master.

Religious Muslims were offended by the secularists' willingness—and even eagerness—to borrow from the West. They thought that secular nationalist values were an inadequate foundation on which to build a new political order. They were convinced that Islam, not secular liberalism or socialism, was the proper basis on which to build the nation. For them, secular nationalism evoked images of the tribal and ethnic loyalties that had divided the Arabs in pre-Islamic times and against which the Prophet had struggled. World War I only confirmed this impression, as the conflict appeared to be a vicious European civil war whose root cause was nothing more substantial than ethnic rivalries.

In order to combat the seductive modernity of the European models, the critics of secular nationalism began developing new theories regarding the nature of Islam. They argued that Islam both transcends ethnicity and provides a spiritual dimension that liberalism and socialism lack. Moreover, Islam is not merely a matter of individual piety and private belief, like post-Enlightenment Christianity. It is, rather, a complete and self-sufficient civilization that has no need to borrow from any other civilization. Because it is an integrated system, its components are mutually dependent and cannot be artificially separated from one another as Western liberalism's separation of religion and state require.

Throughout the interwar period, tension simmered between the religious activists and the secular Muslims who dominated the nationalist movements. Both groups wanted to be free of imperialist control, and in some cases secularists and religious activists formed tactical alliances in the cause of anti-imperialism. Despite the cooperation, a chasm separated their respective visions of the political futures of their countries.

Religious Activists: Reformers and Traditionalists

Religious activists in the twentieth century continued to be divided between reformers (sometimes called *modernists*) and traditionalists. The reformers continued the recent emphasis on returning directly to the Qur'an and Hadith rather than relying on the numerous commentaries on them that had accumulated through the centuries. They were confident that the meaning of the two sources was open to the honest seeker who read the texts for their literal meaning. The message of the text was plain and obvious to all and required no esoteric interpretation. In this sense, the reformers resembled Protestants of the sixteenth century and fundamentalist Christians of the late nineteenth and early twentieth centuries. The reformers, it should be stressed, did not ignore religious decisions made in previous centuries. The serious and well-educated ones reviewed the relevant decisions of past scholars before rendering a judgment on any subject. This process is the primary reason why the modern reformers remained well within the historic tradition despite their emphasis on original research.

A key element in the ferment of reformist ideas during this period was the spread of Salafi influence by means of Rashid Rida's journal, *al-Manar* ("The Lighthouse"). Rida (1865–1935) was a Syrian who emigrated to Cairo in order to study with Muhammad 'Abduh and became his biographer. He believed that he carried on 'Abduh's tradition, although by the end of his career his ideas sounded remarkably congruent with those of Wahhabism. The Salafiya movement influenced opinion from French North Africa to the Netherlands Indies. Its adherents continued the reformist effort to dissuade Muslims from engaging in tomb visits and saint worship and to emphasize the study of the Qur'an and Hadith for guidance in addressing contemporary issues.

Traditionalists, by contrast, were troubled by the enthusiasm of reformers for the widespread exercise of ijtihad. They suspected that reformers were too eager to claim the mantle of original interpretation. During the most formative period of the Shari'a, ijtihad had been the preserve of only the greatest of the ulama until its exercise was finally discouraged in most of the schools of law. When, in the early eighteenth century, Shah Wali Allah urged that ijtihad be practiced again, he made it clear that it was to be practiced only by highly qualified men. Traditionalists were confident that the accumulated consensus of the centuries was an approximation of the truth, much as Catholics respect the work of the Church Fathers. They argued that independent interpretation of the Qur'an and Hadith could be dangerous, leading to misinterpretation and error. It should be embarked upon only when the reasons are overwhelmingly compelling. The exercise of reason, these men thought, had become a modern fetish. They urged the reformers to recall that religious knowledge is a matter of faith and is not necessarily meant to be subject to the scrutiny of reason.

The Muslim Brothers

A major legacy of the Salafiya movement was the emergence of *al-Ikhwan al-Muslimin* ("the Muslim Brothers") in Egypt. It was founded in 1928 by twenty-two-year-old Hasan al-Banna (1906–1949), a school teacher. Banna was critical of corruption and mismanagement in the Egyptian government, and he condemned the growing influence of Western economic and cultural forces. He called for the implementation of "the Islamic order" (*al-nizam al-islami*). Unlike many other Egyptians of the 1920s, Banna was unconcerned about the issue of the caliphate. In fact, he never revealed an interest in discussing the structure of an ideal state, but he did insist that it must enforce and protect Islamic law.

The Muslim Brothers was an organization dedicated to moral reform, which its members viewed as more than merely a question of piety. Cultural, political, and economic issues were also involved. Members of the organization objected to what they considered to be the corrupting influence of features of Western culture that were flooding Egypt, particularly in the form of entertainment and styles of clothing. They bitterly criticized the dominant political influence that the British embassy continued to wield in Egyptian political life, but they reserved particular vitriol for the power that foreign economic interests—which they identified as Christian or Jewish—wielded in Egypt. Foreign control of the economy suggested Egyptian inferiority. For the Muslim Brothers, the economic issue was inseparable from cultural, religious, and personal humiliation, and was linked to a sense that Islam was in danger from hostile forces. The anger that derived from a sense of servility to a foreign and non-Muslim master has been a constant theme in the organization's doctrine throughout its history.

Banna's organization experienced steady but unspectacular growth during its first years, but it grew rapidly during the second half of the 1930s, as the Great Depression settled in. On the eve of World War II, its membership exceeded 100,000. As its presence became larger, several members of the group urged Banna to use forceful measures to take over the government in order to implement the Islamic order. When he refused, they left the organization in disgust and formed competing groups.

During World War II and its immediate aftermath, the Muslim Brothers became the largest, and possibly the most important, mass movement in Egyptian history. For many Egyptians, the combined effects of the war contributed to a sense that Egypt had lost its soul and was in need of reform: The British repeatedly humiliated the Egyptian government by selecting its ministers and dictating its policies; cultural conflicts were rife, as Egyptians came into personal contact with hundreds of thousands of Allied soldiers who passed through the country on the way to combat stations; and the postwar inflation and high unemployment rate were graphic indicators of a country out of control. Midway through the war, a group known as the "secret apparatus" was established within the Muslim Brothers. Scholars are still not certain whether it was initially established for purposes of self-defense or intimidation, or even whether the group was directed by Banna. It did carry out violent acts, including assassinations, and as a result, the government began to regard the Muslim Brothers as a whole as a threat.

Banna, meanwhile, was becoming famous for his outspoken criticism of the British occupation, and his organization began opening schools, small industries, scouting organizations, and social and medical services. The Muslim Brothers experienced explosive growth, and before the end of the decade it had 500,000 active members out of a total Egyptian population of twenty-one million. At least half a million more were enthusiastic supporters. The popularity of the Muslim Brothers stemmed from its fortuitous combination of anti-imperialist activity, demand for a society based on Islamic values, and provision of desperately needed social services that the state failed to provide. It stood in sharp contrast to both the corrupt, collaborating, and ineffective government and the majority of Sufi orders. Most of the Sufi orders had been slow to adapt their organization and message to the challenges of the industrial economy of large, modern cities. Once, they had served as the primary center for social and spiritual activities for most Muslims throughout the world, but modern society offered alternatives. Typically, they offered only a sense of escape from this world rather than a vision for changing it in order to comply with God's will. Organizations such as the Muslim Brothers offered ethical values, educational opportunities, a variety of wholesome social activities, and the goal of creating an independent Islamic state. They appealed to the new theme of individual responsibility and accountability. Banna himself had grown up as a Sufi, and he always spoke fondly of Sufism's deep spirituality. Like many other Islamic reformers of the modern era who also retained their nostalgia for the Sufi experiences of their youth, he felt compelled to become socially involved and politically active. Sufi movements that did not follow in that path declined in influence.

Abu'l A'la Mawdudi

While Banna's organization was emerging in Egypt, another highly influential reform program was underway in India that was the initiative of Abu'l A'la Mawdudi (1903–1979). Mawdudi lived an isolated life as a child and was home-schooled in traditional Islamic studies until the eighth grade. When he entered journalism as a young man after World War I, he began to study European social and political thought on his own. During the early 1920s, he was enthusiastic about both the Khilafat and Indian nationalist movements, and he wrote a glowing tribute to Gandhi. His views began to shift when the Khilafat Movement collapsed and Congress, under Gandhi's leadership, appeared increasingly to be a vehicle for Hindu aspirations. As Hindus and British officials denounced Islam as a religion of violence, and as Hindu revivalist organizations began their campaigns to convert lower-class Muslims to Hinduism, Mawdudi became defensive. His transformation into an apostle of communalism had begun.

Unlike Jinnah, Mawdudi did not regard the Muslim League to be an appropriate instrument for the achievement of Muslim aspirations. He despised most of the League's members for their Westernized habits, and he knew that most of them envisioned a future state that would be Western and secular. He, by contrast, sought to create a new identity for India's Muslims that would unite them in spite of their many cultural differences. It would be neither Western nor Indian, but authentically Islamic. He felt deeply the need to differentiate Muslims from Europeans and Hindus and to make it impossible for Muslim assimilation into either a Western culture or a Hindu-dominated, independent India. The only way to do that was to develop a Muslim identity rooted in the timeless features of Islam.

Mawdudi obtained a mouthpiece for his views in 1932 when he began a newspaper that he called *Tarjumanu'l-Qur'an* ("Translating the Qur'an"). Over the next nine years, he published a steady stream of articles and books that were so radical that they did not have an immediate impact; their influence would not become apparent until the last third of the century. One of the most novel ideas that Mawdudi introduced was that Islamic history has not been a history of Islam, but rather a history of *jahiliya. Jahiliya* is an Arabic word for "ignorance," and in the Qur'an it suggests "barbarism." In Islamic history, it is the designation for the condition of the world prior to the rise of Islam. Historically, the term has been heavily charged with negative meaning and has been contrasted with the period of truth, righteousness, and illumination that began with Muhammad's ministry. Mawdudi, however, used the term as a way of expressing his negative evaluation of the relevance of the traditional schools of Islamic law for his time. He claimed that, after the period of the first four caliphs (632–661), Muslims fell into a period of jahiliya of their own due to their borrowing of cultural elements from the Greeks, Iranians, Indians, and local pagan cults. Because Islamic jurisprudence had incorporated some of these features, it was fundamentally flawed and had no ultimate value. Only the Qur'an and Hadith can be regarded as valid sources for living the Islamic life.

Mawdudi also argued that Muslim political systems since the mid-seventh century were equally flawed and cannot serve as models for the twentieth century. The ideal society is one in which government and society reflect Islamic values, but Muslim history has been characterized by a de facto separation of religion and politics, a defining characteristic feature of jahiliya. That pattern must be reversed, for the practice of Islam is inseparable from an Islamic state. Mawdudi formulated an idea that has become a mantra within the groups that seek to create an Islamic state today: By creating a state based on God's law, man is freed from the servitude and exploitation that is entailed by being subject to laws made by men.

In Mawdudi's view, the revival of Islam cannot take place within existing political or cultural frameworks—there is no point in even trying to encourage people to follow God's will in an un-Islamic society. It is therefore incumbent upon Muslims to become politically active agents of God with the goal of creating an Islamic state. Only then can the history of Islam resume, after a 1300-year hiatus, and culminate in the creation of a genuinely Islamic society. Muslims should employ all modern means of political organization and technology. Mawdudi was an enthusiast for a value-free science and technology, and he eagerly sought to use them for the purpose of exerting Muslim power. He believed that traditional Islam had been a dead weight that had trapped Muslims in a state of backwardness and weakness; he understood his task to be that of providing a means of modernizing the Muslim world and changing the balance of power between the Muslim world and the West.

In his obsession with the modernization and empowerment of the Muslim world, Mawdudi echoed themes that had characterized the career of Jamal al-Din al-Afghani. Unlike Afghani, Mawdudi also provided his followers with detailed instructions on pious deportment. Much of the corpus of Mawdudi's writings is composed of detailed instructions regarding proper behavior, dress, and language, drawn from his reading of the Qur'an and Hadith. He required his followers to restate the *shahada,* or Islamic profession of faith, to signify that they had not been Muslims before coming under his guidance. Not to belong to his following was to commit apostasy.

Mawdudi was the first Islamic thinker in modern times to engage in a systematic exposition of the doctrine of jihad. The small booklet that he wrote on the subject in 1930 was a reaction to the chorus of accusations by Hindus and Christians that Islam was an intrinsically violent religion. The violent incidents following the collapse of the Khilafat Movement triggered the charges, and their advocates pointed out that history was replete with instances of jihad, from the original Arab conquests to the numerous jihads of the eighteenth and nineteenth centuries. Mawdudi was irritated by the caricatures of jihad as a militaristic operation that demanded a "convert or die" decision. In the style that became characteristic of his numerous writings over the next two decades, he redefined terms and used selective evidence to devise his own interpretation of jihad. He agreed that it is obligatory, but argued that it is entirely peaceful. Its purpose is to establish justice, and its means is preaching and teaching. A world characterized by jahiliya needs to be freed from the tyranny of men's laws and restored to the freedom that comes from obeying God's laws.

A major impulse for Mawdudi's desire to create an Islamic state was that he believed that the ethos of a society flowed from the elites to the masses. Thus, his project of jihad was geared to the education of Muslim elites, in order to persuade them not to be seduced by Congress's notions of democracy or the growing appeal of Western culture. He aspired to educate leading Muslims in the principles of Islam and to correct erroneous ways of thinking. He would do so through the organization of a disciplined group of Muslims who would not only preach and teach, but also be prepared to take over the leadership of the future independent state in order to build Muslim civilization. Once an Islamic state was established, it would be used as a base to transform the entire world.

The Muslim League's 1940 Lahore Resolution prompted Mawdudi to give institutional form to his plans, because he did not trust the League's Westernized elites to create a Pakistan that would be compatible with Islam. The following year, also in Lahore, he created the organization that he entrusted with the task of creating a state based on the Shari'a. It was called the Jama'at-i Islami (Islamic Party). Mawdudi attracted a group of highly dedicated followers, but his ideas also spawned bitter controversy. Leading members of the ulama from all the major traditions—Deobandi, Ahl-i Hadith, Barelwis, and others—criticized him for his emphasis on creating a political movement. They argued that he was defining Islam primarily as a political system, thereby distorting the very purpose of Islam, which they saw as engaging with the spiritual truths of the Qur'an. Where he saw Islam as political power, they saw Islam as faith in God's majesty and sovereignty, and as the cultivation of virtue in the believer. He believed that he was recovering true Islam, whereas they accused him of reducing Islam to a hollow shell of arid behavioral prescriptions.

Mawdudi became well known prior to the end of World War II, but his actual influence at that time was limited. Only a few hundred followers were able to meet his rigorous demands, and—with his elite audience in mind—he deliberately chose to write and give speeches in Urdu, which was spoken only in the region around Delhi. Throughout most of the war, Mawdudi rejected Jinnah's proposal for Pakistan, because he suspected that it would be secular. He advocated an idea that was even more difficult for most people to conceptualize, which was an Islamic state within India.

Unlike Banna, Mawdudi developed few ideas of social reform, and he reveals little understanding of the difficulties confronting the poor: His political views had little to do with day-to-day economic and political realities. Thus, his following came largely from the educated middle class, rather than from the masses. Nevertheless, his program ran parallel to that of other advocates for a separate Muslim political entity, whether geographic or institutional. The combination of Mawdudi's tenacity and the disciplined organization of the Jama'at-i Islami ensured that, when independence came, Mawdudi would be much more influential than the number of his followers would suggest.

Tablighi Jama'at

In 1927, as Mawdudi was beginning his transition away from Indian nationalism, a graduate of Deoband, Muhammad Ilyas (1885–1944), founded an organization called Tablighi Jama'at. *Tabligh* is a word of Arabic origin that connotes "propagation" or "conveyance" and is often used in the sense of *da'wa,* which suggests missionary activity. Ilyas was stimulated to act by the Hindu missionary groups of the postwar period that were working among nominal Muslims in the Mewat region west of Delhi. The self-identified Muslims of that area practiced birth, marriage, and burial ceremonies that were still heavily Hindu, and the Hindu missionaries were trying to pry them from their Islamic identity. Ilyas was convinced that their conversion to a Hindu identity would be apostasy, and thus could not be countenanced. Thus, Tablighi Jama'at did not originate as a proselytizing group, but as an organization for spiritual renewal among nominal Muslims.

Like Mawdudi, Ilyas was obsessed with the project of persuading fellow Muslims to live in accordance with the Shari'a. In sharp contrast to Mawdudi, however, Ilyas believed that religion could be dissociated from politics. His followers were strictly forbidden from discussing politics, and he had no interest in achieving political power. Ilyas represents a strand of Muslims who defy easy categorization or labeling. In some ways, he was a traditionalist, but he was also a dedicated reformer: He was a Sufi leader when he created Tablighi Jama'at, and he continued to use Sufi terms to make his teachings intelligible to the masses. Like Shah Wali Allah and many other reformers within Sufism, he tried to eliminate the more egregious abuses associated with the tradition.

The Tabligh movement is notable for several features that combine traditional Sufi values with radical social implications. Social egalitarianism is a major value: The society has no membership requirements, and all members wear the same simple garment. The central concept of the movement is that ordinary Muslims who are

Mawdudi on the Scope and Purpose of the Islamic State

Many Muslims in India would have been pleased with the formation of a government that was free of imperial control, protected its citizens from physical harm and discrimination, and provided the services that had become standard governmental functions in Europe, such as education, roads, and hospitals. Widespread support among Muslims for that political model exasperated Mawdudi, who had come to believe that the chief purpose of the state was to implement the will of God. The following selection provides a glimpse of how different Mawdudi's vision of the state was from the secular model. Notice how Mawdudi uses scattered passages from the Qur'an and the Hadith to weave a seamless argument.

What is the scope of activities of an Islamic state and the nature of limitations imposed thereon? . . . The answer is that as this state is a vicegerent of God and accepts His *de jure* sovereignty, the scope of its activities will naturally be restricted within the limits ordained by the Almighty Himself. This means that the state can act only within the framework of these limitations and is not empowered to infringe or overstep them. This is not only an inference deduced from the acceptance of God's sovereignty, but the Qur'an emphasizes it directly also and warns repeatedly in clear words: "These are the limits ordained by God; so do not transgress them. If any do transgress the limits ordained by God, such persons are the unjust." (2:229) According to the above injunction, obedience to the state is subject to the obedience to God and His Prophet and not independent of it; which clearly means that on insisting to violate the commands of God and the limitations prescribed by the Prophet (peace be on him), the state loses the right of claiming obedience from the people. . . .

What are the fundamental objects for which Islam advocates the establishment of an Islamic state? These objects, as defined and explained in the Qur'an and the Sunnah, are as follows:

The Qur'an says: "Certainly We sent our Messengers with clear proofs, and sent down with them the Book and the Balance, so that people may conduct themselves with equity." (57:25) At another place it has been said: "[Muslims are] those who, if We give them power in the land, establish the system of *salat* and *zakat* and enjoin virtue and forbid evil." (22:41). The Holy Prophet (peace be upon him) said: "Allah brings to an end through the state what He does not eradicate with the Qur'an" (quoted in the *Tafsir Ibn al-Kathir*).

In other words, the evils which are not eradicated through the preaching of the Qur'an need the coercive power of the state to eradicate them. This means that the main objects of an Islamic state are to enforce and implement with all the resources of its organized power that reformatory program which Islam has given for the betterment of mankind. Mere establishment of peace, mere protection of national frontiers, mere endeavor to raise the standard of living of the common man do not form its ultimate goal nor do they constitute the characteristics which distinguish the Islamic state from the non-Islamic states. Its distinction lies in the fact that it has to encourage and popularize those good practices which Islam desires humanity to adopt and to discourage, eradicate and crush with full force all those evils of which Islam aims to purge mankind.

SOURCE: Sayyid Abul A'lā Maudūdi, *First Principles of the Islamic State,* 6th ed. Translated and edited by Khurshid Ahmad (Lahore, Pakistan: Islamic Publications Limited, 1983), 27–28, 42–43.

dedicated to the cause of moral improvement can teach fellow Muslims the central Islamic principles and rituals. Despite the element of teaching, members of Tabligh place great emphasis on the recognition that they have much to learn, as well. The characteristic activity of the movement is the da'wa tour, which is organized on the basis of groups (*jama'at*) of about ten men. The tour can be as short as a day or as long as several months. Its purpose is twofold: It is designed to share knowledge of the acceptable practice of Islam with others, but by causing tour members to break with the routine of their daily life, the tour also forces them to depend upon each other and God. By washing their own clothes, cooking their own meals, and praying for the development of their character, the tour members cultivate the values of humility, gentleness, and self-criticism.

The projects of Ilyas and Mawdudi were quite different from each other. The Tabligh movement directed its efforts toward invigorating Islam at the individual level, whereas the Jama'at-i Islami was convinced that the revival of Islam required the acquisition of state power. Like Mawdudi, Ilyas encouraged scrupulous observance of universal Islamic norms, but he did not reject the legitimacy of the history of the faith. He accepted the notion of personal accountability to God, but in moral and religious, rather than political, terms.

Indonesian Religious Organizations

Indonesia is notable for three important religious organizations during the interwar period. A movement with striking similarities to the Muslim Brothers and the Jama'at-i Islami emerged in Bandung, in central Java, in 1923. Persatuan Islam ("Islamic Union") was aggressively reformist, and its members, called Persis, initiated vociferous debate with fellow reformist movements, secular nationalists, and traditional Muslims alike. Their program was similar to that of other modern reform movements of the period: It included a critique of traditionalist Islam and of secular nationalism, combined with an emphasis on the study of the Qur'an and Hadith. What distinguished the Persis in the Indies—but what they shared with the Muslim Brothers and Jama'at-i Islami—was their combative and uncompromising method of presenting their ideas. Thus, although their numbers have never been large, they played a large role in the colonial and early national periods as Indonesians were grappling with issues of identity.

Persis claimed to reject the authority of the Shafi'i school of Islamic law, which had predominated in Southeast Asia from the first appearance of Islam in the region. They insisted that the principles that they selected from the Qur'an and Hadith were the only valid Shari'a, and they insisted that society as a whole should adhere to them. In practice, like most reformers, they reviewed the corpus of fiqh literature—in this case, the legacy of the Shafi'i school—before issuing pronouncements on points of the Shari'a. Doing so allowed them to buttress their own ruling when their decisions agreed with tradition, and it gave them an opportunity to justify their rulings when they broke with tradition, by arguing the weaknesses of prior rulings.

Persis were prolific writers, and they published books and pamphlets in Bahasa Indonesia that provided behavioral instruction. They accused secular nationalism of being idolatrous for placing the nation higher than Islam, and they even accused fellow reformist Muslims—particularly those of Muhammadiya—of being unbelievers because their interpretation of the Qur'an and Hadith differed from that of Persatuan. They were particularly hostile toward the Ahmadiya, who entered Indonesia in 1925.

Nationalists and other reformist Muslims were forced to respond to the Persis' critiques, thus providing a rigorous exploration of possible political and social frameworks for an independent Indonesia. On the other hand, the Persis' fierce denunciations of traditionalist and nominal Islam created greater social cleavages within the Muslim community than before. The Persis developed a reputation for being intolerant and narrow-minded, and their legacy included the development of mistrustful factionalism in Indonesia as the colony approached independence.

The Muslim Brothers, Jama'at-i Islami, and Persatuan Islam are influential reformist or modernist Muslim organizations that developed reputations for being combative and intolerant of other viewpoints. Other important groups developed during this period that acquired quite different images. The Muhammadiya, which was organized in the Netherlands Indies simultaneously with Sarekat Islam in 1912, explicitly claimed to be part of the Salafi tradition, tracing its inspiration to Rashid Rida's *al-Manar.* The troubled history of Sarekat Islam convinced Muhammadiya's leaders to remain apolitical. The group has remained focused on educational and social services. It was active in promoting its reformist program, but it did so with less vitriol than Persatuan Islam.

Despite Muhammadiya's moderate tone, the profound differences that it had with traditionalist Islam inevitably led to bitter recriminations. Like Persatuan, it rejected strict adherence to the Shafi'i tradition, and its critique of traditional practices threatened mainstream ulama. Apart from the differences between Muhammadiya and traditionalist Muslims regarding acceptable rituals was Muhammadiya's repudiation of the pattern of charismatic leadership that was typical not only of mainstream Southeast Asian Islam, but of groups such as the Muslim Brothers and Jama'at-i Islam. It created organizations with rule-governed buraucracies and open elections. Muhammadiya provided education, social services, and religious guidance for anyone who chose to join. Its membership qualifications were not nearly as restrictive as those of Persatuan Islam, but the organization's goals were narrower. The organization grew rapidly, and today it has an estimated twenty-five million members.

The success of Muhammadiya and Persatuan Islam, both of which were reform groups, provoked the creation of an organization for Muslims who identified with traditional Southeast Asian Islam. Throughout the first quarter of the twentieth century, the leaders of Shafi'i Islam in the Netherlands Indies felt increasingly on the defensive. The Dutch kept them under surveillance as possible rebels, and members of the rapidly growing modernist movements attacked them as backward, ignorant, and responsible for the subjugation of Muslim society to imperialist powers. The mainstream ulama, of course, viewed the world through quite different lenses. They considered themselves to be the custodians of God's revelation, and they believed that their long years of rigorous study of the Shafi'i tradition qualified them to be the unchallenged religious leaders of their society. To have to bear the attacks of young reformers, only a handful of whom had any significant religious training at all, was too much to bear. A series of developments in the aftermath of

World War I persuaded many of the traditionalist leaders to band together before their influence was totally lost: Abroad, the caliphate had been abolished in Turkey; locally, communists were moving toward revolution, modernists were organizing, and the Ahmadiya were making numerous converts. In 1926, several prominent ulama from eastern Java created the Nahdatul Ulama ("Renaissance of the ulama"; often rendered *Nahdlatul Ulama*).

Membership in the Nahdatul Ulama (NU) was not limited to the ulama. The founders of the organization realized that they needed large numbers to counter the modernist movement. The organization's greatest support came from its heartland in eastern Java. For the remainder of the colonial period, the NU was more tolerant of nominal expressions of Javanese Islam than modernists were, and it refrained from involvement with western ideologies and from political action in general. Like the reformist organizations, it engaged in educational and welfare work, but it focused on helping peasants and the marginalized urban population. The NU, like Muhammadiya, became a mass organization, and in recent years it has become the largest in Indonesia, with an estimated thirty million members.

Women's Issues

During the first four decades of the twentieth century, furious debates raged over women's issues in the Muslim world. As we examine them, it is important not to lose sight of the global context: Debates over the roles and status of women were also raging among non-Muslims in the contemporary West. Women in the United States and

Abu'l 'Ala Mawdudi, the influential theoretician of the modern Islamic state.

Western Europe had been struggling since the mid-nineteenth century for legal equality with men regarding property rights, child custody, grounds for divorce, and even the right not to be subjected to genital mutilation without their consent.[1] Their demands were vehemently and sometimes violently resisted by men.

European and American women won several legal victories in the late nineteenth century, but American women obtained the vote on the same basis as men only in 1920, and British women gained it in 1928; French women first voted in 1945; and in one canton in Switzerland, women gained political rights equal to those of men only in 1990. During the 1920s, the issues of women's deportment and modesty became front-page news as young women flouted numerous social conventions by smoking and drinking in public, bobbing their hair, and wearing form-revealing dresses. Such behavior prompted outcries in the press and the pulpit, caused severe rifts within families, and even provoked some fathers and husbands to physical violence against their daughters and wives.

The advocacy of new patterns of gender roles provokes anxiety on a level matched by very few other social issues. The West has borne witness to that fact for more than a century and a half. The debate over gender roles within the Muslim world has been even more highly charged. There, it began within a colonial context and could never be fully extricated from suspicions that advocates for new roles for women were agents—consciously or unconsciously—of Western culture. For most Muslims, remaining faithful to Islamic norms was a major concern, and it was not always clear when "progress" in women's rights entailed cultural betrayal and religious apostasy. In some regions, deeply rooted concepts of family honor were also at stake in women's public behavior. Although these were pre-Islamic in origin and were characteristic of Christian Mediterranean societies as well as Islamic Arab and South Asian societies, many Muslims assumed they were Islamic values.

At the beginning of the twentieth century, Muslim women theoretically possessed certain advantages over their European and American counterparts. The Shari'a unequivocally declares their right to own and manage property, whereas Western women at the time were fighting bitterly for that right. The Shari'a also stipulates that women are to receive one-half of a brother's share of an estate as an inheritance, whereas Western women were dependent on their father's whim. The one-half share of the inheritance is an imperative that comes directly from the Qur'an, and the difference between a woman's share and that of her brother is usually explained on the basis of another provision of the Shari'a: the responsibility of the groom to bring to his bride a dower, which is hers to keep as her private property and to use as she pleases. It is also the husband's responsibility to provide his wife with food, clothing, and shelter, whatever her dower or other wealth may be.

The problem that Muslim women faced was that violations of the Shari'a's property provisions were not uncommon. In many places, customary law outweighed the Shari'a—in the Netherlands Indies, the property provisions of the Shari'a never took root, and they were rarely enforced in rural areas of any part of the Muslim world. In India, most Muslim communities set aside the groom's obligation to provide a dower and replaced it with the Hindu requirement that the bride's family pay a dowry. The dowry, rather than the dower, remains standard there to this day, despite women's protests.

At the beginning of the twentieth century, Muslim and Western women alike could be divorced by their husbands much more easily than they could divorce their husbands. Among Muslims, the four schools of Islamic law contained different provisions for women's divorce. The Maliki and Hanbali schools contained provisions favorable to women, but the Hanafi school—the dominant one in the Ottoman Empire and South Asia—provided virtually no grounds for a woman to extricate herself from an undesirable marriage unless (1) her husband was unable to consummate the marriage or (2) her husband was a missing person who was at least ninety years old.

A circumstance that Muslim women encountered but few of their Western counterparts did was polygyny. The practice of having multiple wives had always been restricted to the men who could afford to support more than one wife, but women were aware that the possibility existed for another wife (except in the few regions where the Hanbali law school allowed women to write a stipulation in the marriage contract that forbade her husband from taking another wife). In circumstances where being one of several wives made the workload easier or was a social marker of high status because of the wealth it reflected, some women did not mind the practice. On the other hand, court records, memoirs, and family histories reveal that most women feared the possibility of being one of several wives and resented the experience when it happened.

Modest dress was prescribed for respectable women in the West and the Muslim world alike. Most of us today gaze with fascination at photographs of European and American women taken during the decade prior to World War I. Whether at home, at the market, or at the beach, women were largely covered up. The distinguishing feature for Muslims was that wealthy families interpreted the rule to include a veil over the face, but peasants and the urban poor rarely wore a face veil—they would draw their head covering over their mouth when approaching a male in public. Muslim women and men were also forbidden to mix socially (the prohibition usually even applied to greeting acquaintances on the street), and many wealthy urban men kept their wives secluded in their homes. In a handful of extreme cases, husbands did not even allow their wives to attend their mother's funeral.

The "woman question" became increasingly salient in Western Europe after the 1790s, and a bit later in the United States. Public discussions of women's issues in the Muslim world began during the last third of the nineteenth century. In India, Egypt, and Anatolia, a handful of male novelists and educators voiced concern regarding the lack of educational opportunities (other than private tutors) for women, but even these influential men made no constructive efforts for girls outside the families of the governing elite.

During the 1890s, middle-class women in Egypt began to publish journals that addressed women's issues. Most of the earliest editors and writers were Syrian Christian women whose families had emigrated to Egypt in the 1860s and 1870s due to ethnic and religious conflicts in Lebanon. Syrian Christians had long had contacts with France, and it is not surprising that many of the articles in the new journals looked to certain features of European women's experience for guidance. These journals did not attract much notice, since they were read within circles of women whose families were already receptive to European influences.

The "woman question" rocked Egypt with an intellectual tsunami in 1899, when Qasim Amin, a lawyer, published *The Liberation of Women.* Amin was an admirer of Muhammad 'Abduh, and many of the ideas in the book reflect 'Abduh's own advocacy of public primary education for girls and the reform of laws on polygyny and divorce. Most of the book was unexceptional, but the book provoked outrage among many people because it criticized Egyptian women as ignorant and degraded, demanded that Egyptian women imitate European women's fashions and behavior uncritically, and asserted that the veil was an embarrassing symbol of Muslim inferiority that should be abandoned.

Amin had thrown down the gauntlet, and there was no shortage of respondents. His book provoked the publication of more than thirty others, most of which expressed outrage at his invidious comparisons of Egyptian Islamic culture with that of Europe. Amin's book gained wide distribution beyond Egypt, and the furor followed it everywhere it went. From that time on, women's issues—and in particular that of veiling—became enmeshed in the debate over the relative merits of local culture and Western culture, as well as a growing sense among many Muslims that Islam was under attack by sinister forces in the West.

Despite the uproar, there was no escaping the debate over the roles, rights, and status of women in the Muslim world. Muslim women quickly became the dominant voice in the discussions. Some, like the Egyptian Malak Hifni Nassef (1886–1918), revealed the complexity of issues such as veiling. Writing under the pseudonym Bahithat al-Badiya, Nassef asserted that whether a woman wears the veil or not should be her choice, and not the decision of Muslim males or of Europeans. Nassef preferred to wear it, and in a direct slap at Qasim Amin's derogatory descriptions of Egyptian women, she said that women needed the veil to protect them from the Egyptian male, who was the debased and debauched of the two sexes.

After the Young Turk revolution of 1908, many individuals among the social elites of the Ottoman Empire criticized the practices of veiling, seclusion, and polygyny. From that time on, upper-class women in the large cities of the empire and in Egypt began appearing without a veil, although they remained veiled in the towns. Some urban women began dressing in clothing that was clearly influenced by European styles. During World War I, the Ottoman government made the first changes in the laws of divorce by granting women the right to sue for divorce in cases of desertion or the existence of a husband's contagious disease. Thousands of Ottoman women worked in industries, just as their European and American counterparts did, leading to an increased level of public social contact between the sexes. It was still socially unacceptable for a woman to patronize a restaurant, even with her husband; swimming at the beach was not an option for her; and if she attended lectures, concerts, and plays, she did so at separate performances for female audiences.

After World War I, the most dramatic changes that affected Muslim women took place in the USSR, Turkey, and Iran, where autocratic leaders were able to overcome stiff opposition by force. Soviet leaders were convinced that all religions were doomed to fade into extinction when their function as the "opiate of the people" was no longer needed. In the meantime, it was helpful for the government to give religion a little shove toward its historical inevitability. While Soviet leaders destroyed churches and disrupted Orthodox Christian life, they launched an attack on Islam in 1927 and 1928. A major reason for communist officials to challenge traditional Islamic notions of women's roles was to create a home environment in which Soviet culture would have a better chance of taking root. In Soviet ideology, the equality of women played a prominent role, and that ideal stood in contrast to the domestic role for women that was standard among Muslims. Thus, the government closed Shari'a courts and prohibited child marriage and polygyny. Communist officials provided incentives for Muslim women to join the party and encouraged them to join the labor market. Other than among Tatar women, many of whom had already become Westernized before the Bolshevik Revolution, the Communist attempt to create a "Soviet woman" among Muslims failed. Few Muslim women joined the Party, and the vast majority continued to follow traditional marriage and family practices: In Central Asia, twenty percent still marry cousins or other close relatives, and most continue to wear traditional clothing.

In Turkey, the new legal code in 1926 abolished polygyny and provided equal access to divorce for men and women. The government also made efforts to promote new and different role models for women: professional women, pilots, opera singers, and beauty queens. Women gained the right to vote in 1930 and to stand for elections in 1934, but that achievement meant little at the time, due to the one-party political system. The new laws were enforced in cities, but life for women in rural areas continued unchanged for decades. In spite of legal changes, few women dared—or even knew—to assert their rights against their husbands, fathers, or brothers due to the powerful forces of tradition and kinship networks.

In Iran, Reza Shah was an advocate of equal rights for women and men within the limits of his autocratic system. He favored full educational access for women, and his wife and daughters appeared in public unveiled and in mixed company. His attempt to revise Iran's legal system was limited by the ulama's power to retain control over marriage, divorce, and child custody. He did manage to raise the minimum marriage age for females to fifteen and allowed women to include the right to divorce in their marriage contracts. Reza Shah pushed for the creation of a national education system to educate boys and girls equally, and he insisted that female as well as male students be admitted to the University of Tehran when it opened in 1936.

Whereas Ataturk had merely criticized the veil but failed to take action against the wearing of it, Reza Shah passed a law in 1934 that prohibited female students and teachers from wearing the chador in schools (the chador is a traditional, full-length body covering worn by women when they go out in public; it can be pulled over the face as a veil when in the presence of men). In 1936, the law was extended to apply to women in other public facilities, and Reza Shah initiated an occasionally brutal campaign to eradicate the wearing of the chador. Many traditional women were afraid to appear in public wearing the chador for fear of punishment, but were ashamed to appear in public without it. Some of these women, who had not been subject to seclusion before, now refused to go out in public at all, making it difficult for them to run their households.

A group of Egyptian women made news in 1919 by marching in support of Egyptian independence. They represented an influential, Westernized, upper middle class that had emerged in the larger towns and cities in the course of the previous century. During the interwar period, women from that stratum became active in creating institutions and organizing events to press for changes in laws affecting women and the family. One of the women nationalists, Huda Sha'rawi (1879–1947), founded the Egyptian Feminist Union in 1923. Her organization advocated women's suffrage, equal access to education, and reform of marriage laws.

Sha'rawi is also famous for her role in legitimizing the removal of the face veil in Egypt. Upon returning from an international women's meeting in 1923, she removed her veil when she disembarked from her train in downtown Cairo. This public act electrified the city, and Sha'rawi's social status and nationalist credentials made it socially acceptable for other urban women to discard their own veils. The topic was furiously debated by traditionalists, but it never became a legal issue. The veil practically disappeared in Egypt within a decade, evidence that it was not as important as the legal issues that concerned women.

Egypt's parliament was in a position to make substantive laws after the Unilateral Declaration of 1922. In 1923, it raised the minimum age of marriage for girls to sixteen; in 1925, primary education was made compulsory for girls as well as for boys; and a few years later women were admitted to the national university for the first time. On the other hand, efforts to modify divorce laws managed only to extend the grounds for divorce to failure of maintenance, desertion, communicable disease, and maltreatment. Obtaining a divorce was still much more difficult for a woman than for a man.

In the Netherlands Indies, women's issues also became a topic of intense public debate. In matriarchal Minangkabau, a newspaper for women opened as early as 1911, and on Java, Muhammadiya opened a women's section of the organization in 1917 called 'Aisyiya, after 'A'isha, the Prophet's youngest, most outspoken, and favorite wife. 'Aisyiya broadened the social roles of women by training female preachers, creating Muslim preschools, building the first prayer house for women, and establishing literacy courses for women. Subsequently, it built orphanages, birth clinics, programs for preventive health care, and a school for training nurses. The organization also called for restrictions on the practices of concubinage and temporary marriage.

Temporary marriage has historically been associated with Shi'ism. For centuries, Shi'ite ulama approved marriage contracts that specified a specific length of time—from a day to a few months—that the obligations of the marriages would be in force, usually for the convenience of merchants who traveled far from home. Sunnis often cited the practice when they discussed the inadequacies of Shi'ism. In Indonesia, however, some Sunnis practiced temporary marriage. The custom may have had its origins among the merchant class that came from the Gulf region. Whatever its origins, it became so entrenched that women's organizations continue to fight it in the twenty-first century.

In 1930, another organization, called Alert Women, began to demand equal rights for women and an end to polygyny. Alert Women represented the secular nationalist movement, and its demands provoked protests from those who were convinced that men and women inhabit separate spheres of responsibilities. 'Aisyiya, for example, defended polygyny, arguing that it had proven successful in preventing an increase in prostitution. The Dutch government made no legal changes in marriage or family law, for fear of provoking violence.

The issues of women's roles and rights were as controversial within Islamic reform groups as they were between religious and secular groups. Abu'l A'la Mawdudi and Hasan al-Banna, for example, both assumed that men and women inhabited "separate spheres" in society, but the way they interpreted that position differed dramatically. Mawdudi insisted on strict observance of purdah (except for his own wife, an independent-minded person who did not take orders from her husband). His visceral hatred for Western civilization made him hesitant to concede any changes in women's roles, polygyny, marriage law, or divorce law.

Banna argued that men and women should avoid social mixing when possible, and he advised women to use public transport only when necessary. On the other hand, he opposed seclusion. Women and men should both dress modestly, but he argued that the face veil is not authentically Islamic. He urged women to become educated so that they would be prepared to fulfill their primary function in life as wife and mother, but he grudgingly conceded that they are also allowed to specialize in such fields as chemistry, law, and engineering. He argued that the Qur'an's commandment to treat wives equally was in effect a prohibition on polygyny, since it would be impossible to be absolutely equitable to more than one. He also reminded his readers and listeners that the Hadith assert that divorce is the most hateful to God of all permitted acts. Whereas he did not advocate granting women equal rights to divorce, he urged men to seek mediation in the event of conflict with their wives.

Conclusion

For several decades prior to World War I, religious and political developments in the Muslim world had placed an increasing emphasis on individual initiative. Historically, the dominant tendency had been to defer to spiritual and political authorities, but most of the new religious organizations stressed the theme of personal accountability to God, and political activism reflected a growing sense of personal responsibility for replacing colonial administrations with self-government. The increasing sense of personal accountability had become palpable on the eve of the war; the events of the war served as the catalyst that precipitated the new attitude into organized, purposeful activity.

The leaders and the organizations of the interwar period exhibited several major differences from their prewar counterparts. Charismatic leadership continued to play an important role in many of the new activities, but charisma was no longer the monopoly of spiritual leaders. Several of the most inspiring leaders of the era were outspokenly secular. Another major difference in leadership in several countries was the active and public role that women took in effecting social change.

The period after the war was also notable for transformations in the nature of mass movements. Mass organizations had come into existence in the Muslim world prior to the war—the best-developed ones were in India and the Netherlands Indies—but during the interwar period they became much more sophisticated. Like trade union organizations, political parties, and social causes all over the world after World War I, Muslim religious and nationalist organizations took advantage of the radio, the telephone, the printing press, megaphones, microphones, newspapers, mass transportation, and theories of propaganda to build and mobilize their following. In a matter of only a few decades, the fragmented societies that the imperial armies had subjugated with little effort became so organized in their opposition that imperial governments would no longer be able to rule them.

NOTE

1. For a well-written summary of some of the challenges facing late-nineteenth-century women in Britain and the United States, see Susan Kingsley Kent, *Sex and Suffrage in Britain, 1860–1914* (Princeton, New Jersey: Princeton University Press, 1987).

FURTHER READING

Independent Muslim States

Atabaki, Touraj and Eric J. Zürcher, eds. *Men of Order: Authoritarian Modernization Under Atatürk and Reza Shah.* London and New York: I. B. Taurus, 2004.

Daniel, Elton L. *The History of Iran.* Westport, Connecticut, and London: Greenwood Press, 2001.

Ewans, Martin. *Afghanistan: A Short History of its People and Politics.* New York: HarperCollins Publishers, 2002.

Gowing, Peter G. *Muslim Filipinos: Heritage and Horizon.* Quezon City, Philippines: New Day Publishers, 1979.

Mango, Andrew. *Atatürk: The Biography of the Founder of Modern Turkey.* Woodstock, New York, and New York: The Overlook Press, 1999.

Vassiliev, Alexei. *The History of Saudi Arabia.* London: Saqi Books, 2000.

Zürcher, Eric J. *Turkey: A Modern History,* new ed. London and New York: I. B. Taurus, 2004.

Muslim Minorities in the USSR

Allworth, Edward. ed. *Central Asia: 120 Years of Russian Rule.* Durham, North Carolina, and London: Duke University Press, 1989.

Hunter, Shireen T. *Islam in Russia: The Politics of Identity and Security.* With Jeffrey L. Thomas and Alexander Melikishvili; foreword by James F. Collins. Armonk, New York, and London: M. E. Sharpe, 2004.

Roy, Olivier. *The New Central Asia: The Creation of Nations.* New York: New York University Press, 2000.

Yemelianova, Gina. *Russia and Islam: A Historical Survey.* Houndmills, U.K., and New York: Palgrave, 2002.

Nationalist Movements

Abun-Nasr, Jamil M. *A History of the Maghrib in the Islamic Period,* 3d ed. Cambridge, U.K., and New York: Cambridge University Press, 1987.

Benda, Harry J. *The Crescent and the Rising Sun: Indonesian Islam Under the Japanese Occupation, 1942–1945.* The Hague, Netherlands, and Bandung, Indonesia: W. Van Hoeve Ltd., 1958.

Cleveland, William L. *A History of the Modern Middle East,* 3d ed. Boulder, Colorado, and Oxford, U.K.: Westview Press, 2004.

Crowder, Michael. *West Africa Under Colonial Rule.* Evanston, Illinois: Northwestern University Press, 1968.

Harrison, Christopher. *France and Islam in West Africa, 1860–1960.* Cambridge, U.K.: Cambridge University Press, 2003.

Masselos, Jim. *Indian Nationalism: A History,* 5th rev. ed. Elgin, Illinois: New Dawn Press, 2005.

Roff, William R. *Origins of Malay Nationalism,* 2d ed. Kuala Lumpur, Malaysia, and Oxford, U.K.: Oxford University Press, 1994.

Islamic Movements

Ahmad, Mumtaz. "Islamic Fundamentalism in South Asia: The Jamaat-i-Islami and the Tablighi Jamaat of South Asia." In *Fundamentalisms Observed,* eds. Martin E. Marty and R. Scott Appleby, pp. 457–530. Chicago and London: University of Chicago Press, 1991.

Banna, Hasan. *Five Tracts of Hasan Al-Banna' (1906–1949): A Selection From the Majmu'at Rasa'il al-Imam al-Shahid Hasan al-Banna'.* Translated from the Arabic and annotated by Charles Wendell. Berkeley: University of California Press, 1978.

Federspiel, Howard. *Islam and Ideology in the Emerging Indonesian State: The Persatuan Islam (Persis), 1923 to 1957.* Leiden, Netherlands, and Boston: Brill, 2001.

Mitchell, Richard P. *The Society of the Muslim Brothers.* London: Oxford University Press, 1969.

Nash, Manning. "Islamic Resurgence in Malaysia and Indonesia." In *Fundamentalisms Observed,* eds. Martin E. Marty and R. Scott Appleby, pp. 691–739. Chicago and London: University of Chicago Press, 1991.

Nasr, Seyyed Vali Reza. *Mawdudi and the Making of Islamic Revivalism.* New York and Oxford, U.K.: Oxford University Press, 1996.

Noer, Deliar. *The Modernist Muslim Movement in Indonesia, 1900–1942.* Singapore and New York: Oxford University Press, 1973.

Sikand, Yoginder. *The Origins and Development of the Tablighi Jama'at (1920–2000): A Cross-Country Comparative Study.* Hyderabad, India: Orient Longman, 2002.

Smith, Wilfred Cantwell. *Modern Islām in India: A Social Analysis.* London: Victor Gollancz, Ltd., 1946.

Women's Issues

Ahmed, Leila. *Women and Gender in Islam. Historical Roots of a Modern Debate.* New Haven, Connecticut, and London: Yale University Press, 1992.

Baron, Baron. *Egypt as a Woman: Nationalism, Gender, and Politics.* Berkeley: University of California Press, 2005.

Berkes, Niyazi. *The Development of Secularism in Turkey.* New York: Routledge, 1998.

Meriwether, Margaret L., and Judith E. Tucker, eds. *A Social History of Women and Gender in the Modern Middle East.* Boulder, Colorado: Westview Press, 1999.

Shaarawi, Huda. *Harem Years: The Memoirs of an Egyptian Feminist.* Translated and introduced by Margot Badran. New York: Feminist Press at the City University of New York, 1986.

CHAPTER 11

Regaining Sovereignty, 1939–1970

The Great Depression of the 1930s still held the world in its grip when World War II erupted. The Depression had exposed the embarrassing reality that the imperial powers were unable to provide adequate sustenance for all of their citizens; the war soon revealed that some of them could not defend their citizens, either. Those revelations transformed the perceptions that the inhabitants of the far-flung imperial empires held of their ruling powers, resulting in a growing assertiveness on the part of nationalist leaders in their dealings with their administrations. In some protectorates—particularly those that had experienced considerable prewar nationalist organization or that came under enemy occupation during the war—nationalist leaders seized the advantage that wartime disruptions created and pushed for independence. Once the process of decolonization began, it proceeded much faster than had the race to create the empires in the first place: Whereas the period of the New Imperialism lasted a little more than four decades, the process of decolonization took less than half that time.

The advent of independence was greeted with euphoria in dozens of countries across the world. The imperial era, with its daily humiliations and manifold injustices, was over—ahead lay the future, full of glorious accomplishments, prosperity, and justice. Even seasoned and cynical political veterans shared in the excitement and joy of independence. But independence, as it turned out, was an anticlimactic experience. The meaning of the words *freedom* and *independence* had often been conflated during the nationalist period, but it soon became clear that a country could be independent while its citizens were not free. Moreover, in many countries, growing restrictions on political freedoms were accompanied by a fall in the standard of living. Few were nostalgic for the days of imperial rule—for the majority of people, the humiliation of being ruled by outsiders outweighed any benefits that imperialism might have conferred. On the other hand, the string of disappointments that characterized the period of independence left many people longing for an alternative to the dreary reality that had displaced their dreams.

World War Two

With signs of an impending war accumulating in the late 1930s, France and Britain once again expected to call on the vast resources of their imperial protectorates to aid them in what they expected would be a conflict fought primarily in Europe. World War II, however, proved to be quite different from its predecessor. Two differences are worth noting. First, whereas the western front in Europe was the defining feature of World War I for Britain and France, the second war had no western front between the fall of France in June 1940 and the Allied landing at Normandy in June 1944. Second, whereas most of the fighting in World War I took place in Europe and the Ottoman Empire, the action of the second war included the takeover of several major protectorates by enemies of, or collaborators with the enemies of, the imperial rulers. As a result, many of the protectorates were involved in the war firsthand rather than at the remove of hundreds, or even thousands, of miles. The nature of their wartime experience was decisive in shaping their individual paths to independence.

World War II began in Asia in the summer of 1937, when the Japanese invaded China. Two years later, in September 1939, it broke out in Europe when Germany and the Soviet Union divided Poland between themselves. Western Europe remained breathless for several months, wondering if the partition of Poland was, in fact, the last phase of German expansion that Hitler had engineered since 1936. In April 1940, the Führer put the debate to rest by attacking Scandinavia, and in May he attacked Belgium, the Netherlands, and France. By the end of June 1940, all of continental Western Europe was occupied by Germany, allied with it, or officially neutral. Only Britain remained defiant, surviving both the air war called the Battle of Britain (July 1940–October 1940) and the German saturation bombing of British urban areas called the Blitz (August 1940–May 1941). In France, Germany's army was concentrated on the coasts in order to repel a possible invasion, but French collaborators were allowed to operate a government at Vichy, a small town at the center of the country. Vichy loyalists were sent to the imperial possessions to replace officials whose allegiance lay with the noncollaborating, Free French faction under Charles De Gaulle, which was based in London.

The Middle East

The war's first serious impact in the Muslim world occurred in a region that was slowly coming to be known as the *Middle East.* The American naval historian Alfred Thayer Mahan coined the term in 1902. He had in mind a region centered on the Persian Gulf, for which the contemporary term *Near East* (with its connotations of the Holy Land) seemed inadequate, and which was certainly not the *Far East. Middle East* appeared again during World War I, when it was appropriated by the British army. The British deployed two armies against the Ottomans. One, based in Cairo, was called the Near East Forces (the one to which Lawrence of Arabia reported on his activities in the Arab Revolt), while the other, composed largely of Indian troops, fought in Iraq and was called the Middle East Forces.

In 1940, the British established a military headquarters in Cairo called General Headquarters–Middle East. The constant use of *Middle East* to describe the area controlled by this base of Allied operations made the term familiar to a large public in Britain, Australia, New Zealand, and the United States. Thereafter, it became a standard term for journalists, foreign service personnel, and scholars, despite the continuing lack of agreement regarding the exact territories included in the region. Most maps that purport to portray the Middle East include the region from Egypt to Iran, inclusive, and from Yemen to Turkey, inclusive. Some American journalists and government officials, however, use the term in a much more limited fashion to designate only the territory that once defined the mandate of Palestine (Israel, the West Bank, and Gaza).

As the Blitz was winding down in spring 1941, British officials became concerned about the security of their possessions in the Middle East. General Erwin Rommel had taken command of combined German and Italian forces in Libya, and during the spring and summer, he routed the British army from its newly-won position in Cyrenaica. He would have chased the British all the way to the Suez Canal if he had not outrun his supply lines. The military front remained stationary on the Libyan-Egyptian border for another year. Meanwhile, in Iraq, where the prime minister was blatantly pro-German, Iraqi army units began to skirmish with British-led Indian forces defending British military bases at Basra and Baghdad. Fighting broke out that lasted through April and May until the British secured control of the country and forced the prime minister to flee the country. An Iraqi puppet government ruled only in name for the rest of the war.

In Iran, Reza Shah had always been reluctant to cultivate relations with Britain and the Soviet Union because of his country's unpleasant history with the actors in the Great Game. Germany, which had its own rivalries with the British and the Soviets, was a great power that did not have obvious designs on Iranian sovereignty. Reza Shah encouraged a growing German presence in his country, both before and after Hitler's accession to power in January 1933. After Germany's invasion of the USSR in June 1941, Britain and the USSR overcame their mutual enmity and began to formulate a coordinated policy toward Iran. They agreed on the necessity of preventing Iran's oil fields from falling into German hands. When Reza Shah refused to submit to their joint ultimatum to expel German nationals, the two new allies invaded in August 1941 and once again divided the country into northern and southern zones of occupation. The following month, they forced Reza Shah to abdicate the throne. He went into exile in South Africa, where he died in 1944. His son, Muhammad Reza Pahlavi (1941–1979), replaced him under the cloud of having been installed by the two traditional enemies of Iran.

Meanwhile, the British were growing uneasy regarding developments in Syria and Lebanon, where Vichy officials were cooperating with German agents. In June 1941, British forces based in Palestine invaded two French mandates and removed their pro-German rulers. British officials continued to exert influence in the two mandates, much to the annoyance of the leaders of the Free French forces, who could not retake effective control due to lack of personnel.

Southeast Asia

In the Pacific, the attack on the American base at Pearl Harbor on December 7, 1941, was quickly followed by a Japanese attack on British and Dutch possessions in Southeast Asia. By February 15, 1942, Malaya and Singapore were overrun. Three weeks later, the Netherlands Indies government surrendered to Japanese forces, and the American military forces in the Philippines did so in May. The Japanese occupation of the Philippines and Malaya was brutal. Contemptuous treatment of Filipinos triggered a guerrilla war of resistance in which as many as one million Filipinos were killed, but which also tied down tens of thousands of Japanese soldiers. In Malaya, the Japanese promised to create a unified state composed of most of Malaya and Sumatra, which is also ethnically Malay. This plan won the Japanese considerable support among the Malay population during the early period of the occupation. As the war dragged on, however, the heavy-handed policies of the army alienated a large part of the population. Among the Chinese minority of Malaya and Singapore, the occupation was brutal from the beginning. The hatred and contempt that Japanese soldiers had demonstrated for the Chinese during the conquest of Shanghai and Nanking in 1937 was replicated in the peninsula. Throughout the war, the Chinese-dominated Malayan Communist Party allied with the British to fight the Japanese. The British provided supplies and arms, and the Party provided the fighters, who used bases in the rain forest to attack Japanese garrisons.

The Netherlands Indies was more decisively influenced by its experience of Japanese occupation than were the Philippines and Malaya. The Japanese occupation of the Philippines interrupted the transition toward independence that was almost completed. The occupation of Malaya substituted a brutal and exploitative Japanese administration for a British administration that both Malays and Chinese grudgingly admitted was benign. Moreover, the Malay and Chinese communities relied on the British to serve as arbiters between them. In the Netherlands Indies, by contrast, the Japanese replaced an increasingly harsh and repressive Dutch administration. The Japanese were occasionally harsh and brutal here, too, but they also released nationalist leaders from jail and gave them remarkable scope for activity. Some of the nationalist leaders refused to cooperate with the Japanese on the grounds that the occupiers were fascist, but Sukarno and other major figures argued that cooperation would be the best opportunity to secure independence.

The Japanese banned the use of the Dutch language, so that even the Dutch-educated Indonesians were forced to use Bahasa Indonesia or Japanese. Symbols of Dutch authority, such as statues and street names, were removed. Batavia was renamed Jakarta. The Japanese employed thousands of Indonesians in the bureaucracy and allowed them to create religious and even quasi-military organizations as long as they supported Japanese war aims. The Japanese were particularly impressed by Sukarno's popular appeal, and they carefully secured his cooperation. Relying upon his charisma and contacts, they used him to force several million Javanese manual laborers to work on economic and military projects. More than a quarter of a million of such workers were sent to the Outer Islands and Japanese-held territories, and fewer than one-fifth were ever seen again.

Africa

General Rommel's 1941 campaign to invade Egypt had stalled, but he launched another one a year later. During the first half of 1942, the Axis army appeared to be heading for success, but during the summer it was stopped at El Alamein, a little more than sixty miles west of Alexandria. That fall, the second battle of El Alamein resulted in the beginning of a retreat for Rommel. On November 9, 1942, the American army landed at Casablanca, Morocco, and at the Algerian cities of Oran and Algiers. This was the first step in the Allied military plan to squeeze the German and Italian armies between the American forces and the British army that was advancing westward from Egypt. After some awkward moments with the Vichy French forces—and even some fighting with them in Oran—the Allied advance to Tunisia was rapid. Tunisia was the battleground for fierce fighting between November 1942 and May 1943, when more than 250,000 Axis soldiers surrendered at Tunis.

During the course of the war in North Africa, the British army took over Cyrenaica and Tripolitania from the German and Italian armies between October 1942 and February 1943. Forces of the Free French then occupied Fezzan. In the Horn of Africa, Italy had avenged its late-nineteenth-century defeat by Ethiopia by conquering it in 1936, but a British army freed Ethiopia in 1941 and restored the emperor, Haile Selassie (ruled 1930–1974) to independent rule. British troops also chased Italian troops out of Italian Somaliland in 1941.

South Asia

In late 1939, Britain formally declared that India was a participant in the war, making its human and material resources accessible to the British war effort. The announcement provoked anger and dismay among Indians who remembered the unrequited sacrifices of World War I. Gandhi pointed out that India was being asked to support a war that was ostensibly fought for democratic freedom while being denied that freedom. In March 1942, after the Japanese conquest of Malaya and the Netherlands Indies, a British parliamentary delegation tried to mollify Indian opinion by offering internal autonomy after the war, with only control over foreign relations reserved to Britain.

The proposal was controversial in Britain and India alike. Prime Minister Churchill disowned the offer, declaring that he had no intention of presiding over the liquidation of the empire. The Indian National Congress rejected it as well, demanding full independence. During the summer, Congress launched the "Quit India" movement, which demanded immediate British evacuation of the country. Acts of civil disobedience as well as incidents of sabotage and violence stretched British security to its limits. The police made 100,000 arrests and killed hundreds more. Imperial anxiety was heightened by the knowledge that at least 40,000 Indian troops—most of whom were prisoners of war captured in Malaya and Singapore—joined the Indian National Army (INA), an auxiliary of the Japanese military that sought to capture India from the British. Millions of Indians were sympathetic to the cause of the INA. The authorities jailed the leaders of Congress for the rest of the war, and the INA failed in its attempt to capture Bengal. Nevertheless, the widespread disaffection of Indians demonstrated to subjects and rulers alike that the days of the British administration were numbered.

Not all Indians refused to cooperate with the British. In contrast to the INA were more than two million Indians who served in the Indian Army during the war. Tens of thousands of them served in North Africa against the Germans and Italians, in the Horn of Africa against the Italians, and in Burma against the Japanese. A counterpoint to Congress's refusal to participate in the government of a colony was the Muslim League's full cooperation with the authorities. The League, which had appeared to be politically dead after the 1937 elections, had recovered due to Jinnah's tireless campaigning and his unexcelled mastery of tactical maneuvers. He won British goodwill for his support of the empire's war effort, and he gradually won over Muslim support for his adoption of Sayyid Ahmad Khan's notion that Muslims and Hindus constitute two separate nations. The uncertainties and fears of the wartime experience helped Jinnah convince most Indian Muslims that, despite the linguistic, social, geographical, and religious differences that divided them, their status as Muslims was their most important identity marker. They became persuaded that the Muslim community in general, and Muslims as individuals, were at risk if Hindus were to gain a political majority after independence. Only a separate political structure, they believed, guaranteed Muslim welfare in South Asia.

Formal Independence

Among the war's numerous effects was a loosening of the grip that the imperial powers held on their protectorates, even in regions that were not occupied by enemy forces during the war. The disruption of communications between protectorates and their rulers, combined with the inevitable economic strains of the war effort, contributed to a growing dissatisfaction with the status of being ruled from afar. For varying periods of time, imperialists everywhere had been trying to rationalize the exploitation of their protectorates on the grounds that they were bringing good government, sound finances, and economic development to the subject populations. In most cases, however, the war exacerbated the hardship that a decade of economic depression had brought.

The most obvious impact of the war on the empires was the severing of the ties of communication and control that occurred in Southeast Asia when the Japanese occupied French, British, and Dutch possessions and in Africa and the Middle East when German-sponsored Vichy officials replaced noncollaborators. When, after several years, the Japanese and the collaborators with the Nazis were finally defeated, members of the old imperial regimes returned, expecting to resume operations as if nothing had happened. For many of the local inhabitants, however, the defeat of their rulers by the Germans and, especially, the Asian Japanese, had been a defining moment: They insisted on negotiating new terms for any future relationship.

The war and its aftermath had other consequences, as well. In several regions, the conflict provided a boost to the phenomenon of urbanization that had begun during the Great Depression. Peasants, caught between a double bind of falling prices for agricultural products and falling infant mortality rates that increased the size of their families, had begun migrating to the cities during the 1930s to search for employment. The conditions of war increased industrial employment—almost everywhere, local industries began manufacturing substitutes for goods that the imperial powers had provided before the disruptions of wartime conditions—but the number of applicants exceeded the available jobs. The displaced peasants sold matches and trinkets on sidewalks, lived off the generosity of their relatives, or turned to begging. After they filled up the older slums, they created shanty towns on the outskirts of the metropolis, perhaps next to the city dump. They were without running water, sewers, and electricity—they had lived without these conveniences in the village, but in the vast shanty towns they found it much more difficult to gain access to potable water and to dispose of waste than they had in the small rural village. Living near the modern city, with its neon signs and conveniences, the contrast between their own deprivation and the comforts enjoyed by the middle class became apparent to them for the first time. The vast population of the urban poor would thereafter be a potent source of support for political and religious leaders.

The war also accelerated the penetration of largely rural societies by modern technology. The war effort's need for efficient means of transportation and communication resulted in the construction of thousands of miles of new roads, telephone lines, and telegraph wires, as well as the introduction of radios into remote areas. Governments continued investing in these sectors of infrastructure after the war in an attempt to gain political legitimacy. These investments conferred benefits on the local populations, but they also had negative effects. The roads brought in automobiles and trucks, which damaged or obliterated freight and transport systems that had been based on the use of donkeys or camels. As the number of animals declined, the local population lost animal byproducts and opportunities for off-road mobility. When electronic technologies replaced word of mouth as the means of conveying information, people who lacked the disposable income to purchase telephones and radios were at a disadvantage compared to those who owned the devices.

The cumulative effects of World War II provided the shock to imperial systems that began the process of decolonization. The four-year German occupation of France and the Netherlands, and the Japanese conquest of most of Southeast Asia, transformed political reality and the terms of political discourse. New arrangements now seemed possible, and in some cases, the changes seemed realizable immediately: A handful of possessions declared their independence midway through the war. The war affected imperial territories in different ways, and the response of the colonized peoples varied from region to region, depending on local conditions. Once the process of decolonization began, however, the legitimacy of imperial rule became more difficult to defend everywhere, and the rationale for imperial "tutelage" sounded increasingly hollow. The most active period of decolonization lasted from 1943 to 1960.

The 1940s

Most of the violent and dramatic independence movements took place in the 1940s, when the process of the devolution of power was still a novelty. The French were the first to confront challenges to the reimposition of imperial control. After the British had evicted Vichy officials from Syria and Lebanon in July 1941, British and Free French representatives agreed on immediate and unconditional independence for the two mandates. When the Free French were reinstalled, however, they refused to countenance a withdrawal from the region. In 1943, elections in both mandates resulted in overwhelming victories for pro-independence forces. In Lebanon, Maronite Christians and Sunnis worked out a power-sharing agreement that came to be known as the National Pact. Among other provisions, the agreement included a power-sharing formula between Christians and Muslims that was based on the census of 1932. It stipulated that Christians and Muslims would share seats in the parliament on a ratio of six to five; the president would be Maronite; and the prime minister would be Sunni. Civil service positions and judicial appointments were also allocated on the basis of the ratio. This arrangement remained the basis for Lebanese confessional politics until a civil war began in 1975. It contained two fatal flaws that were ignored at the time: It made no provision for changes in the relative size of the religious communities, and it practically ignored the Shi'ite community of Lebanon. Maronites and Sunnis continued to be the power brokers in the country, although the Shi'ites, who constituted the poorest and most neglected religious community in the country, gradually became the single largest group.

During the remaining two years of the war, the Free French made repeated attempts to block the movement toward independence in Syria and Lebanon. To their anger and dismay, the United States and the Soviet Union recognized the independence of both countries in 1944. Refusing to accept defeat, French army units entered the country at the end of the war to try to reestablish French control, but they encountered stiff resistance. In a fit of spite, the French army bombarded Damascus, killing over four hundred civilians. The British intervened militarily at that point, forcing the French to begin withdrawing. They completed their pullout from both countries in 1946.

Meanwhile, the British were beginning to confront independence movements in India and Palestine that would prove to be political tsunamis. Two months after the war in Europe was over, the Labour Party won the British elections. In contrast to Churchill, the new prime minister, Clement Atlee, clearly understood that Britain would be unable to impose its rule on the "jewel in the crown" of the empire. In spring 1946, Atlee sent a commission to India to persuade Congress and the Muslim League to agree to a formula for independence. When Jinnah realized that the members of the commission were serious about granting independence, he agreed to the creation of a self-governing Pakistan within an Indian federal union. Negotiators for Congress, however, refused the plan, insisting on a unitary state. Recriminations began to fly again between Congress and the League, with each thinking the other was working with Britain to betray it. Operating within this bitter atmosphere, and knowing that time for defining a specific policy was short, Jinnah demanded a fully independent Pakistan. To force the hand of Congress, he called for "direct action" in Calcutta on August 16, 1946, and at least 4000 people were killed in rioting there. In retaliation, Hindus killed 7000 Muslims in Bihar.

In March 1947, the new Viceroy, Lord Louis Mountbatten, arrived in India and began accelerating the process for transferring power. He proceeded on the assumption that two separate political entities would be formed, one with a majority of Hindus and one with a majority of Muslims. He sent out surveyors to fix boundaries as quickly as possible in Bengal and the Punjab, where tens of millions of Hindus and Muslims lived next door to each other in mixed communities. The Punjab had the added complication of containing millions of Sikh inhabitants (see Map 11.1).

Despite all the complexities, fears, and uncertainties, the surveyors completed their work within a few months. At midnight on August 14–15, 1947, the British flag came down, and India and Pakistan were born. The new Muslim-majority state was composed of two regions, East and West Pakistan, that were separated by 1000 miles of Indian territory. All along the new borders, some fourteen million people fled their homes out of the fear that being the member of a minority ethnic group would be dangerous: Millions of frightened Hindus and Sikhs left Pakistan for India, and millions of Muslims left India for Pakistan. The fears and hatreds that had accumulated over the previous two decades now exploded, and crowds engaged in frenzied mass murder. An estimated one million refugees were butchered. Locomotives pulled into train stations with hundreds of dead passengers who had been killed en route. Gangs attacked buses, mutilating everyone on board. Individual families making their way along footpaths were hacked to death by total strangers.

By the terms of the independence agreement, the princely kingdoms that had not been under direct British rule were free to choose which country they wished to join. Most were surrounded by India, and the question was moot; British officials assumed that Kashmir would join Pakistan, because it had a large Muslim majority and it was adjacent to West Pakistan. Its ruler, however, was a Hindu, and he delayed making a decision, perhaps in hopes of retaining his independence. When Muslim tribesmen sought to depose him, he asked the Indian army to intervene. After India invaded from the south, Pakistan's army invaded from the north and west, initiating the first war between Pakistan and India. The war left the northern one-third of Kashmir, which is almost entirely Muslim, under Pakistan's control and the southern two-thirds, which has a sizeable Muslim majority and a large minority of Buddhists, under India's control. India promised to hold a plebiscite to determine the will of the people of the people under its control, but it has repeatedly found ways to avoid doing so.

The Indian problem alone would have been difficult for the British to manage, but during the same period they were also struggling with heightened tensions in Palestine. The Holocaust transformed the terms of the Zionist goal for Palestine from the desire for a Jewish homeland to the need for a Jewish haven from genocide. In order to force the British to grant a Jewish state, Jewish terrorists began to assassinate British officials and soldiers—the bombing of the King David Hotel in 1946, which killed almost one hundred people, was just one of many Jewish terrorist acts—and the international community placed heavy pressure on the British government to open the borders to unlimited Jewish immigration.

The British argued that removing the immigration restrictions would infringe on Arabs' rights, and Arabs argued that the problems generated by European anti-Semitism should be solved in Europe, not in Palestine. International opinion was

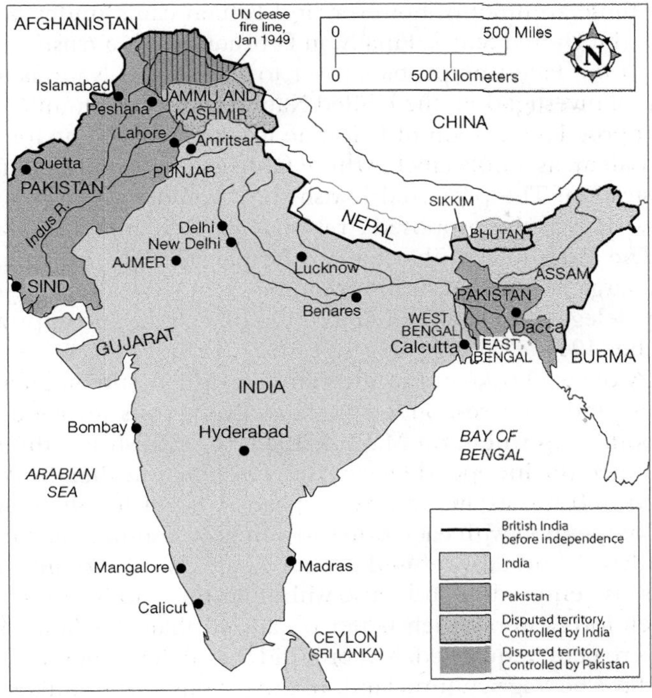

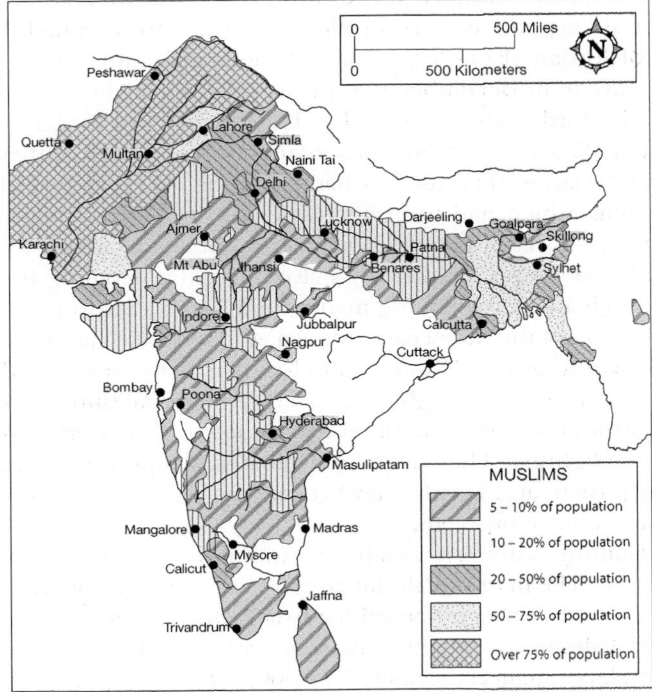

MAP 11.1 Partition of India.

not swayed by these arguments, however, and Britain came under heavy pressure, especially from the United States. Finally, in February 1947, a frustrated British government turned the Palestine problem over to the United Nations to solve. After several months of investigation, the United Nations Special Committee on Palestine (UNSCOP) proposed a partition of Palestine into two states, one for Jews and one for Arabs. Jerusalem, as a holy city for three faiths, would be placed under international administration. The proposed Jewish state would contain 500,000 Jews and 400,000 Arabs, whereas the proposed Arab state would contain 700,000 Arabs and 10,000 Jews. The Palestinians objected to the partition in principle and on the grounds that a large number of Arabs would be included within the Jewish state. A majority of the delegates in the UN ignored the objections and approved the partition in November 1947.

Sporadic violence broke out in the mandate, as Palestinian guerillas attacked Jewish positions and Jews responded in kind. Numerous atrocities had already occurred on both sides when, on May 14, 1948, the British left the mandate and Zionists proclaimed the independence of Israel. All-out war then broke out as army units from Egypt, Transjordan, and Syria invaded Israel for their own purposes. They were in competition with each other to annex Palestinian territory as much as they were with Israel, and they refused to coordinate efforts. Volunteers from other Arab countries also entered the fray, also with their own motivations.

The Israeli forces were much better organized than the Arab armies and, by late summer, were better equipped. Not only did they defend their own territory, but they also seized the best agricultural lands of the proposed Palestinian Arab state. By the end of the year, Israel controlled over three-fourths of what had been the Palestine Mandate; the Egyptian army controlled what came to be called the Gaza Strip; and the army of Jordan (King 'Abd Allah changed the name of his country from Transjordan to Jordan in December 1948) controlled what came to be known as the West Bank (of the Jordan River) (see Map 11.2). Israel and Jordan each occupied half of Jerusalem. The UN partition proposal had been modified beyond recognition: Israel was now larger than the UN had proposed, whereas the Palestinians had nothing. Jerusalem, which had been envisioned as an international city, was bifurcated into hostile enclaves, separated by a narrow but deadly no-man's land.

Many Arabs had expected an easy victory over the fledgling Jewish state. For Israel to win in such an overwhelming manner left the Arab world in a daze. Among Arabs, the conclusion of the war became known as the *nakba* ("catastrophe"), a humiliating event that continues to define the era for them. The Israelis had defeated the combined armies of its Arab neighbors. Some 750,000 Palestinians who had lived within the territories controlled by Israel had either fled or been driven from their homes during the fighting. They settled in wretched camps in Gaza, the West Bank, Lebanon, Syria, Jordan, and Egypt. They became the nucleus of what became known as the Palestinian refugee problem.

Israel had almost doubled its arable land with its conquests, and yet its Arab population plummeted. The mass of Palestinian refugees had fled from two distinct areas: the territory that the UN had proposed for Israel and the territory that the UN had intended to be a Palestinian state but that Israel conquered during the fighting. As a result, Israel's Arab population dropped from 400,000 in May 1948 to 160,000 in January 1949, even though the country had become significantly larger during that period.

Israel did not allow the refugees to return home. During the first few years of exile, the refugees expected the international community to force Israel to rescind its decision, but that never happened. As it became clear that the Palestinians were stateless, only Jordan made any meaningful provision for them to become citizens of their host countries. Most of the remainder—and their far more numerous descendants—persist in a condition of statelessness and abject poverty, vulnerable to the machinations of demagogues.

The Arabs who live within Israel itself have never qualified for equal treatment with their Jewish neighbors. The Israeli government expropriated forty percent of the land owned by the Arabs of Israel, and Israeli Arabs were subject to military, rather than civil, jurisdiction until 1966. Although Israeli Arabs were eventually granted citizenship, Israel's official status as a Jewish state has meant that, in practice, Arab villages still do not receive the same services that Jewish settlements do.

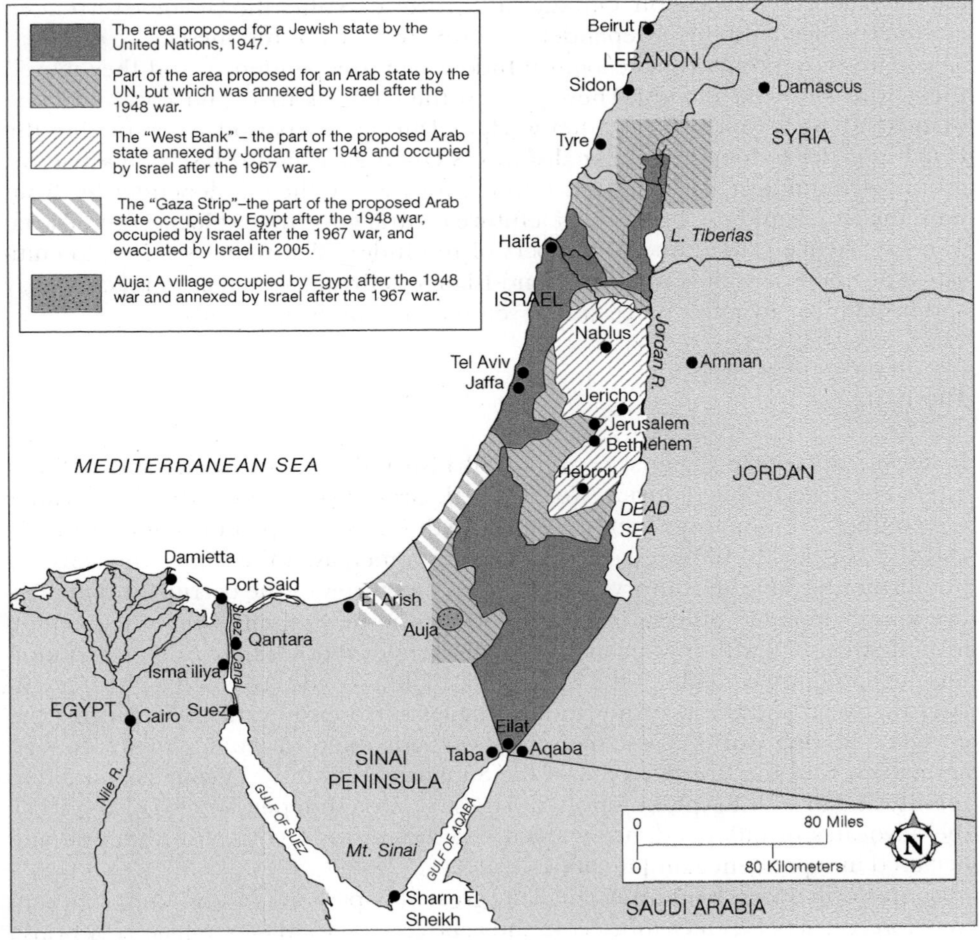

MAP 11.2 Partition of Palestine.

Thousands of miles from Palestine, in the South Pacific, most Filipinos welcomed the return of the Americans in 1945, both because the American occupation had been benign compared to that of the Japanese and because Filipinos knew that the Americans would not stay long due to the transition to independence that had already been set in motion in the mid-1930s. Formal independence was declared on July 4, 1946. The joy of independence was clouded by American insistence on ninety-nine-year leases on several military bases, free trade for American products for several years, and the granting to American citizens of equal rights with Filipinos in the exploitation of natural resources.

In the Netherlands Indies, the Japanese occupation became harsher toward the end of the war. The Japanese began requisitioning food supplies to such an extent that widespread famine occurred. On the other hand, in an effort to secure the continuing cooperation of nationalists, the occupiers allowed Sukarno and others to begin planning for independence. From March 1945 until the Japanese surrendered five months later, nationalists of a wide variety of ideologies met to hammer out the blueprint for a nation. On August 17, three days after the Japanese surrender, nationalists declared the independence of the Republic of Indonesia.

The Dutch refused to recognize Indonesian independence, and they moved their army into the islands. They gave up their efforts to regain control of the islands only after four years of bitter warfare. During that period, when neither the Dutch nor the Indonesian nationalist forces could exert control, several separatist groups—communist, Islamic, and ethnic—fought for their independence, from both the Dutch and the prospect of a future central government located at Jakarta. The experience caused many members of the Indonesian military forces to cultivate a deep mistrust of communism and Islamic activism, as well as to react quickly and brutally to any hint of secessionist sentiment in outlying islands.

The 1950s

In Egypt, resentment against continued British military, economic, and political interference accelerated during World War II. Growing discontent during and after the conflict led to massive membership growth for the Egyptian Communist Party and the Muslim Brothers alike. The 1948 *nakba* increased the anger and sense of humiliation within the country, provoking an overthrow of the corrupt and ineffective king by military officers in 1952. In 1954, the new regime began negotiating with the British to withdraw from the army base in downtown Cairo and to abandon the huge military base along the Suez Canal. The two sides reached an agreement later that year, and the British withdrew their last troops in June 1956. During the decade following World War II, nationalists in Sudan were also trying to work out an agreement with the British. A few of the Sudanese, and most Egyptians, wanted to reunite Sudan with Egypt, but most Sudanese wanted independence. During 1955, the advocates of independence worked out the terms for British withdrawal and declared independence on January 1, 1956.

In North Africa, World War II had the greatest impact on Libya, where the Italians were forced out between October 1942 and February 1943 and were replaced by British and French forces. After the war, Britain, France, and the United States supported

Italy's demand to reclaim Tripolitania after Italy renounced its claim to the other parts of Libya. Fear of returning to Italian control prompted Tripolitanian tribal leaders to work out agreements with their counterparts in other regions of the country to devise a federal state under a monarchy headed by Sayyid Idris, who had returned to Cyrenaica from Egypt in 1947. Libyans declared him to be king in December 1950, and the UN reluctantly recognized Libyan independence a year later. Of all the North African countries, Libya was the least developed in economic terms, and its predominantly nomadic society was characterized by tribal loyalties rather than national ones. The irony that it was the first country in the Maghrib to gain independence was not lost on the nationalists of the areas ruled by the French.

Restored to power in Morocco, Algeria, and Tunisia in 1943, the Free French authorities were dismissive of nationalist demands, even though most nationalists had remained loyal after the war broke out in hopes of being rewarded politically. The main nationalist grievance was that the French refused to grant citizenship to Muslims on the same basis as they did to Europeans. At the end of the war in 1945, brutal violence broke out in Algeria, with atrocities being committed on both sides. In 1948, several independence movements emerged that were dedicated to the use of violence. The most famous of the revolutionary movements, however, arose only in 1954: the Front de Libération Nationale (FLN). Its violent attacks were the most serious challenge that French political and military authorities in Africa had faced in the twentieth century.

The FLN's attacks coincided with the French humiliation in Indochina (Vietnam) at Dien Bien Phu, where Ho Chi Minh's irregulars defeated the French army, forcing the French evacuation of the protectorate. French dignity could not afford to suffer a similar humiliation in Algeria, which was regarded as an integral part of the nation itself, not a mere settler colony. Tens of thousands of French troops were sent to Algeria, where their indiscriminate violence against Muslims turned the attacks by a small, secret organization into a mass uprising. The conflict in Algeria evolved into the largest, most brutal war for independence of the entire global decolonization process. The ability of the French to concentrate on the uprising in Algeria was compromised by an upsurge of nationalist activity in postwar Morocco and Tunisia. French authorities quickly decided to cut their losses in those two colonies and focus on the struggle in Algeria.

By the time the Algerian and Indochinese problems coincided, the situation in Morocco was becoming tense. The sultan, Muhammad V, had become less cooperative with the French in the years since his coronation in 1927. After World War II, he became the focus of the nationalist impulse and a symbol of resistance to the French. The authorities became so irritated by the sultan's cautious but firm nationalism that they exiled him to Madagascar in 1954. Terrorist incidents that broke out in 1955 unnerved the authorities, however, and they began discussions for Moroccan independence. On March 2, 1956, Muhammad V became the King of Morocco.

Next door, in Spanish Morocco, the government came under intense pressure by January 1956. There, Moroccan activists demanded Spanish withdrawal and the union of their territory with the independent state that would soon be ruled by Muhammad V. In April, Spanish and Moroccan negotiators formally agreed upon independence, and Spanish territory—excluding the Spanish Sahara and the cities of Ceuta and Melilla—came under the control of Muhammad V. Over the next four years, Tangier made the transition from an international zone to a Moroccan city. Of the 500,000 European residents in the country (which had a total population of some 10,000,000), about 200,000 left the country over the next four years.

In Tunisia, the French negotiated with Tunisian nationalists between 1954 and 1956 over the issue of autonomy. Bourguiba returned from exile to become the directing hand in this process, which, in early 1956, abruptly turned into discussions regarding independence. On March 20, 1956, France recognized Tunisian independence, just two weeks after Morocco became independent. The following year, Bourguiba became both president and prime minister. Of the 250,000 European residents in the country (which had a total population of some 3,800,000), about 160,000 left the country over the next four years.

Meanwhile, in Algeria, the French built up their army to a force of over 400,000 troops (including 170,000 Muslims) in 1956. Terror was met with terror, and individual acts of violence were met with the destruction of entire villages. The brutality of the war caused many observers to think that the French army was willing to destroy Algeria in order to retain it. In 1958, the war had such a destabilizing effect that settlers and French military officers planned a coup d'état to overthrow the government in Paris, but they were placated when Charles de Gaulle came to power. Even he proved to be a disappointment to them, and the radicals made several attempts on his life. De Gaulle, realizing that the war was unwinnable in any meaningful way, recognized Algerian independence in March 1962. Estimates of the death toll in the eight-year-long war range from 250,000 to one million, and 800,000–900,000 of the one million European settlers who lived in Algeria (out of a total population of 10,900,000) had fled to France by the end of 1962.

As the Algerian conflict reached its climax, another long and bloody conflict in Malaya was in its last throes. It, however, was more complicated than simply a war for independence. It stemmed, rather, from linked issues of ethnicity and ideology. Two weeks after the Japanese surrender in August 1945, the British had returned to Malaya and found cheering crowds welcoming them back. Compared to the horrors of the Japanese occupation, the era of British rule seemed like "the good old days." Even though the reception was friendly, British officials were sufficiently aware of how different the postwar world was to announce a new policy that they thought was more enlightened than the old one. They planned to open citizenship to everyone, including the Chinese. The Chinese, who formed one-third of the population of Malaya, had not previously been allowed access to citizenship, under the fiction that they were merely descendants of immigrants who would undoubtedly "return home." The plan also entailed the creation of a new Malayan Union that would replace the six Federated States, the three Unfederated States, and the Straits Settlements. The plan aroused the ire of ethnic Malays who feared the political potential of the economically powerful Chinese, and the British had to drop the proposal.

In 1948, the Malayan Communist Party began a guerilla war against the British government, wealthy Chinese capitalists, and the traditional rule of Muslim sultans. The British and tens of thousands of noncommunist Malayans engaged in a ruthless, twelve-year war to extirpate the communists. New anti-insurgency techniques helped the process, but the most significant factor in the success of the campaign was a political one. The British unilaterally introduced self-government in phases in order to demonstrate to the Malayans that they had more to gain from supporting the British than by aiding the communists. In 1957, three years before the insurgency was finally suppressed, the British transferred sovereignty to the new Federation of Malaya.

The constitution of the new country was written with an eye toward the ethnic composition of the country. Written with the aid of British consultants, it was intended to protect the rights of non-Malays but also to secure a preeminent position for ethnic Malays and Islam. It states that Islam is the country's official religion, and it not only retains Shari'a courts, but requires that all Muslims use them for most aspects of family law and a few of criminal law. On the other hand, the constitution guarantees freedom of worship to members of all religions, and no mention is made of the Qur'an or Hadith as sources of national legislation. The document's most notable provision is Article 153, which recognizes the "special position" of ethnic Malays and states that it is the government's responsibility to ensure that they enjoy preferences in education and employment. An ethnic Malay is defined as a person who is a Muslim, speaks Malay, and adheres to Malay customs. Thus, to be considered a Malay, a person has to be a Muslim.

The new state was renamed Malaysia in 1963 when other British colonies in the region gained their independence and joined the federation: The addition of wealthy Singapore, with its overwhelmingly Chinese population, was balanced demographically by the addition of Sabah and Sarawak on northern Borneo, which were ethnically diverse. The Malay elites had gambled that they would be able to retain power even with the expansion of the federation, but they miscalculated. Animosity between Malays and Chinese in Singapore led to the outbreak of race riots in 1964, which caused ethnic tensions to rise throughout the region. Furthermore, Malay leaders in Kuala Lumpur belatedly realized that it was most unlikely that their city would ever eclipse Singapore as the dominant city of the peninsula. In 1965, the Malays ejected Singapore from the federation, and Singapore has been a sovereign state ever since.

The 1960s and 1970s

Nationalist activity in the French Sudan did not become a threat to French control until the end of World War II. Despite the much-publicized ideal of France's *mission civilisatrice,* only a tiny fraction of West Africans attended French schools other than in Senegal. In the rest of French West Africa, no town had more than 25,000 inhabitants, and French administrators found it easier and cheaper to maintain traditional arrangements by allying themselves with local chieftains. As a result, West Africa had few of the middle-class, Western-educated leaders who typically led the nationalist movements of the interwar period. The movement toward independence began during World War II, when the Vichy regime increased discontent among West African subjects by frequent demands for forced labor and the implementation of policies that were transparently racist. When the Free French took over from the collaborators of Vichy in late 1942 and early 1943, they repudiated the policies of the Vichy regime, but unrest against European rule had acquired its own dynamic. Recognizing the need to grant concessions to their imperial subjects,

French colonial officials began to offer new political and economic opportunities for colonial subjects, but they also made it clear that they would not countenance any moves toward independence such as were occurring in some of the British possessions. However, by granting the legal right to form political parties and trade unions, colonial officials inadvertently provided the institutions within which West Africans began to discuss new political arrangements.

During the decade following the war, West African elites were divided over tactics that should be used in negotiating with France. One group, led by Léopold Senghor of Senegal and Sékou Touré of Guinea, wanted to retain the overall unity of the federation that French colonial policy had created. Félix Houphouët-Boigny of the Ivory Coast, on the other hand, rejected the idea of a West African federation of independent states, because he feared that wealthier states such as his would subsidize their poverty-stricken inland neighbors. The conflicting visions came to the fore in 1958, when French president Charles de Gaulle took power in the political crisis generated by the war in Algeria. De Gaulle needed to concentrate his attention on the conflict in North Africa, and so he hoped to minimize the threat of violence in the protectorates of sub-Saharan Africa by offering them internal self-government within a French Community for which France would govern economic and foreign affairs. He arranged to hold a referendum on the issue, and he made it clear that any protectorate that voted for independence would be the target of French economic retribution.

All the protectorates except Guinea voted to accept de Gaulle's proposal. Sékou Touré persuaded his countrymen that the proposal would leave each protectorate vulnerable to French policies, and the proposal was overwhelmingly rejected there. Guinea gained its independence in October 1958. During the following year, the leaders of the other territories of West Africa were emboldened to demand independence; in 1960, France granted full independence to all of its West African territories. Some, such as Senegal and Ivory Coast, negotiated close economic relations. Others insisted on a full break.

Most British and Italian colonies in Africa with significant Muslim populations gained their independence during the same period. Nigeria—Africa's most populous nation by far—was more complex than most other colonies due to its size, its ethnic diversity, and its division into a predominantly Muslim north and a Christian and animistic south. It gained its independence in 1960. Sierra Leone, which the British had established in 1787 for freed slaves, gained its independence in a series of stages between 1951 and 1961. The Gambia became independent in 1965. Tanganyika gained its independence in 1961, and Zanzibar became independent in December 1963. Zanzibar's sultan was overthrown less than a month later, and in April 1964, Zanzibar and Tanganyika merged to form Tanzania. The UN placed Italian Somaliland under Italian administration as a UN Trust Territory from 1949 until 1960. In the latter year, both British Somaliland and Italian Somaliland gained their independence and merged, creating the Republic of Somalia.

In the Arabian Peninsula, the British had long maintained several spheres of influence that they valued for economic or strategic purposes. The two most valuable were Kuwait and Aden. Kuwait had been a British protectorate since the outbreak of World War I in 1914. Even though vast petroleum deposits were discovered there in 1938, Britain agreed to a negotiated independence in 1961. Aden, which had no natural resources but which had traditionally held great strategic importance for Britain, was a very different story.

After British India captured Aden in 1839, the port shared with Singapore the duty of giving London effective control of the Indian Ocean. In the late 1950s, Marxist and nationalist activism arose among the dock workers of Aden and spread to the young and educated tribesmen of the interior, who were discontented with the tribal chiefs with whom the British had signed treaties of protection. The rising tide of nationalist fervor became violent by the 1960s. To many observers outside Britain, it seemed that the decision to withdraw from Aden should be self-evident, particularly since the loss of India, the Suez military base, and Singapore had removed the rationale for retaining a military base in Aden. Leaders of the Conservative Party, however, realized that, by giving up Aden, Britain would be abandoning all pretense of being a great power. They were vehemently opposed to withdrawal, especially while under fire from nationalists.

The Labour Party, which won the 1964 elections, came into office with a tradition of criticizing imperialism, and it faced a gravely weak British economy. Withdrawal seemed to the party's leaders to be consistent with their traditional policy and a way to cut costs. The easy decision proved to be extremely hard to implement. The insurgents refused to negotiate a withdrawal, because they wanted to take credit for having expelled the imperial power. British troops had to pull out under fire in 1967. As the Conservatives had feared, the process appeared to be a humiliation for Britain. The withdrawing troops seemed to have been driven out, and the tribal chiefs of the interior, whom the Britain had promised to protect, had to flee if they wished to avoid being murdered.

In 1968, continuing economic challenges prompted the British government to announce that it was abdicating its role as protector of the Gulf. Bahrain, Qatar, and the seven members of the Trucial States (a seventh emirate joined the Trucial States in 1952) were concerned about their security without British support. The Trucial States felt vulnerable because Saudi Arabia had never agreed to define its border with them, and Iran coveted three small islands in the Strait of Hormuz that tribes of the Trucial States had used for several centuries. Iran also announced that it claimed Bahrain, making the shaykhdom fearful that it would soon be annexed. The Arab rulers held several meetings to discuss the feasibility of a union. In the end, Qatar and Bahrain chose to retain their individual identity, but the Trucial States agreed to remain confederated. In 1971, they formed the United Arab Emirates (UAE), even as Iran seized two of the disputed islands. The UAE's constitution accorded primacy to Abu Dhabi and Dubai due to their wealth (derived from the petroleum of the former and the commerce of the latter). This imbalance of power within the UAE was a potential tinderbox in the context of traditional tribal rivalries and jealousies, but observers have been impressed by how well the leaders of the two most powerful units have accommodated the needs and desires of the other five.

A handful of protectorates became independent in the 1970s. Increasingly violent protests in the Territory of the Afars and the Issas (originally known as French Somaliland) and pressure from the United Nations finally forced France to grant independence to the protectorate in 1977. Its new name was Djibouti. Portugal, too, was loath to relinquish control of colonies, laboring under the delusion that its overseas possessions regarded themselves as integral parts of the mother country. Its three major African colonies—Guinea–Bissau, Angola, and Mozambique—taught it a very hard lesson during the early 1970s, when they fought vicious guerilla wars against the mother country. Guinea–Bissau, an overwhelmingly Muslim territory, won its independence in 1974, and the other two became independent the following year.

Muslim Minorities in the USSR and China

The Muslim minorities of the Soviet Union and China lived in independent states, but they often felt as though they were under imperial masters. In the Soviet Union, the two regions where Muslims suffered the most were the Caucasus and the Crimea. During World War II, the Germans tried to foment anti-Soviet activity in the Caucasus. Some collaboration took place, and Stalin took advantage of it to expel Muslim populations that had long been viewed as unassimilable. The three target populations were the Chechens, Ingush, and Meskhetian Turks. As we saw in Chapter 8, the Chechens and Ingush live on the northern slopes of the Caucasus Mountains. Some 500,000–700,000 Chechens and Ingush were deported in 1943 to Siberia and Kazakhstan. Many—perhaps one-third—died or were massacred en route to their exile. In 1957, during Khrushchev's de-Stalinization program, the Chechen and Ingush exiles were informed that they were free to move wherever they wished. Many returned to their respective homelands, only to discover that Russian and other settlers had taken over their property. Conditions were very difficult for most of the returned exiles. Hostility simmered for years before erupting shortly after the collapse of the USSR in the early 1990s.

The Meskhetian Turks lived in Georgia. In 1944, they were deported to Central Asia. In 1958, they, too, were allowed to leave their exile, but their homeland remained beyond reach for most of them. Georgia allowed only those who claimed a Georgian (Christian) nationality to return. Tens of thousands settled along Azerbaijan's border with Georgia, and others have migrated all over the world.

Whereas the only German presence in the Caucasus during the war was that of *agents provocateurs*, the German regular army occupied the Crimea from the autumn of 1941 until the spring of 1944. In 1944, Stalin accused the entire Crimean Tatar population of having collaborated with the Nazis, and he ordered the expulsion of the total population of some 200,000 people. Half of them died en route to exile in Central Asia and Siberia. In 1989, under Gorbachev's liberalizing reforms, the Tatars were allowed to return to the Crimea. At least 150,000 have done so, but, like the Chechens and Ingush, they have experienced a bitter "homecoming." The Chechens and Ingush had been gone for little more than a decade when they returned; the vast majority of the Crimean Tatars who are still "returning" were born in exile. They demand the return of what they view as their rightful inheritance, but others have legal claim to the property that once belonged to the Tatars' parents or grandparents. The people who consider themselves robbed are viewed by others as unreasonable troublemakers.

The Muslims of China did not suffer the trauma of the Chechens, Ingush, Meskhetian Turks, or Crimean Tatars, but their experience under communism bore striking parallels with that of the Muslims of Soviet Central Asia. The fall of the corrupt and ineffective Ch'ing dynasty (1644–1911) early in the century caused euphoria among the urban, educated young people in China. Many were followers of Sun Yat-sen (1866–1925), who had led a long campaign for a democratic China free of the corrupt Ch'ing and exploiting foreigners alike. The high expectations were quickly dashed, however, as military generals and rural landlords quickly carved up the country into fiefdoms, and China entered a period of history known for its "warlordism." Sun Yat-sen's successor, Chiang Kai-shek, managed to unite the bulk of eastern China under his rule in 1926–1927, but central and western China, where most of the country's Muslims lived, remained beyond the reach of direct central control.

About half of China's twenty million Muslims live in Xinjiang, which contains both the Tarim Basin and Zungaria. The province was never fully incorporated under Ch'ing control, and it was lost to the central government during the interwar period. It was under the control of warlords during the 1920s and under Soviet influence during the 1930s. During World War II, Chiang Kai-shek was finally able to appoint a governor for the province, but Chiang and his followers were forced to flee to Taiwan in 1949 when Mao Zedong's communist movement took control of China.

The communist revolution in China brought significant changes to Islamic institutional life. The government eliminated the zakat, or alms tax, and placed imams on the state payroll. It also abolished Shari'a courts. The new government could not resist expropriating the wealth that was owned by tens of thousands of mosques, tomb complexes, and religious endowments. Since many of these were rural, officials rationalized the seizures as breaking the power of big landlords for the purpose of distributing the lands to the poor. The property seizures, however, were not merely a way to obtain more capital for the state to distribute among its citizens; primarily, they shattered the economic support system for institutional Islam, thus rendering Muslim religious authorities much weaker than before.

Mao continued the policy that Chiang had begun during World War II of settling Han Chinese in Xinjiang as a way of diluting the demographic weight of the Turkic Muslim population there. At the beginning of the war, Xinjiang's Muslims accounted for ninety-eight percent of the province's population; the Uighurs alone represented eighty percent of the total population. Unlike the country's Hui population, which was ethnically indistinguishable from non-Muslim Chinese and spoke the Chinese language, the Uighurs consciously retained their Turkic identity. According to the 1998 census, the settlement policy had reduced the Muslim component of Xinjiang's population to sixty percent of the total, and Uighurs accounted for forty-six percent. Uighurs numbered a little over eight million, more than one million were Kazakh, about three-quarters of a million were Hui, and several small ethnic groups comprised the remainder.

The Cultural Revolution of 1966–1976 was a time of great fear and suffering for much of China's population. Ostensibly a movement to identify "enemies of the revolution" within the country, it was actually Mao's effort to purge the Communist Party of critics who might be in a position to limit his power or even to replace him. He inspired his Red Guards—composed primarily of students in secondary schools and universities—to cast the net of suspicion as widely as possible in their search for elements of the population and culture that were incompatible with Mao's vision for the country. Accordingly, the Red Guards destroyed Buddhist temples and Christian churches, paintings, books, and antiques of all kinds. All mosques were closed and some were destroyed; many Qur'ans were destroyed; and many imams were publicly ridiculed and even killed. The worst period was 1966–1969, but the witch hunt persisted until Mao's death in 1976. Two years later, the new Chinese leadership affirmed a policy of religious toleration, and religious communities began the slow process of recovery.

Disillusionment with Secular Nationalism

Few of the leaders of new countries began as radicals in religion or politics. The vast majority were secular modernists who objected to colonial rule, but who intended to take over the existing colonial state and turn it to new purposes rather than eliminate it. They paved roads, launched programs of mass education, and revised imperial tariff regulations. Many of them redistributed land from a handful of magnates to at least part of the peasant population.

All of the leaders knew that their task was formidable, but they could not know just how difficult it would prove to be. They came to power during the Cold War, which meant that they were forced to consider what the American or Soviet reaction would be to any foreign policy decision. Economically, the treaties of independence typically granted the former imperial power privileges that allowed it to continue to exercise a degree of control over the local economy. Most of the former colonies had few natural resources on which to base a thriving economy; in some cases, they had only a single cash crop or mineral to export, a condition that made their markets vulnerable to price fluctuations. In domestic politics, the various ethnic groups that the colonial borders had thrust together had to find ways to share power and not feel threatened by the others. Unfortunately, the parliamentary system that departing Europeans recommended as a remedy was not designed to accommodate the dynamics of tribal-based societies or the politics of religious communalism. Moreover, the experience of imperialism had convinced some elements of the population that communism or the creation of an Islamic state was the simple solution to all problems; these advocates had no patience for leaders who did not immediately implement the reforms that they demanded.

Pakistan

Pakistan confronted some of the most daunting problems of any new country. It was divided into two wings that were separated by 1000 miles of hostile Indian territory. West Pakistan's major ethnic groups—the Pashtuns, Punjabis, Sindhis, and Baluchis—had long been involved in rivalries with each other. The lines of demarcation among these groups were obscured when millions of Muslim refugees from India arrived, lacking homes and livelihood. About ninety-seven percent of West Pakistan's inhabitants were Muslim, but the Shi'ites (about one-fifth of the population) and the Sunnis typically regarded each other as infidels.

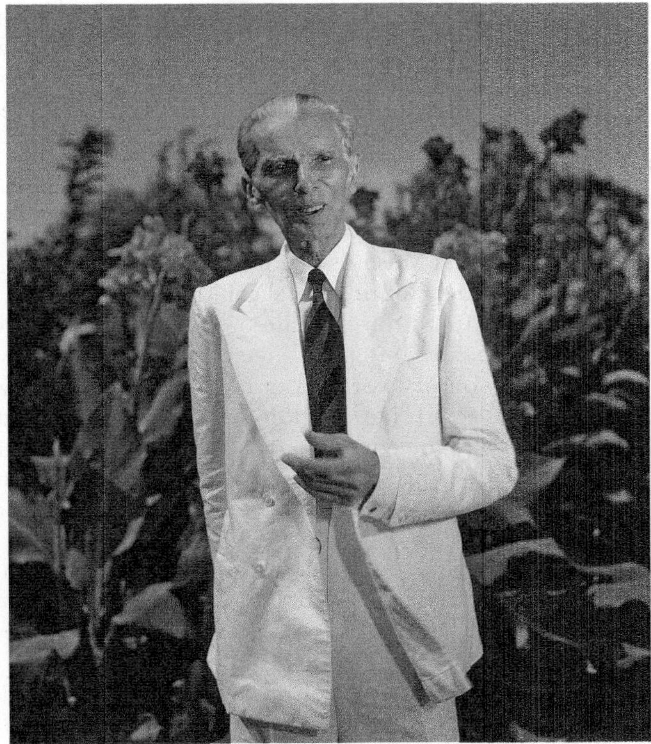

Jinnah

Despite their differences, all of these West Pakistani groups had more in common with each other than any of them had in common with the inhabitants of East Pakistan. The latter spoke Bengali (Bangla), which was largely unintelligible to the western groups; they ate rice and fish instead of wheat and red meat; and they lived in a wet, subtropical ecosystem rather than in a semiarid, continental climate. Moreover, many Punjabi and Pushtuns considered Bengalis to be an "effeminate" population that required the protection of the "martial" ethnic groups of West Pakistan.

The scale of the problem of agreeing upon the new country's identity is revealed in the determination of the country's official language. The people of East Pakistan (eighty-three percent of whom were Muslim) accounted for fifty-two percent of the country's total population. Their language of Bengali is written in a script closely related to the Devanagari script used in Hindi and Sanskrit. In West Pakistan, Punjabis were the largest ethnic group, with about forty-eight percent of the population there (or about twenty-three percent of the country's total population), and Sindhis were the second-largest group, representing twelve percent of the population in the west. The government declared Urdu to be the official state language. This solution had the virtue of not favoring any particular ethnic group, but its profound disadvantage was the fact that Urdu was spoken by only a handful of people. Although it had become the primary language of written communication among the north Indian Muslim elite, it was spoken at home by only one or two percent of the population even in West Pakistan and by no one in East Pakistan. Urdu shared the Arabic alphabet with the other West Pakistani languages, so it would be easy for West Pakistanis to learn, but in Bengal, only the religious elite were familiar with Arabic notation.

The multitude of cleavages within Pakistani society meant that its leaders would have to devise a state thoughtfully and with great sensitivity in order to create one that would allow the various constituencies to feel represented. The rationale for the creation of Pakistan was that Muslims needed a state of their own, but opinions differed regarding what the shape of that state would be. Throughout his campaign for a Pakistan, Jinnah had refused to speculate on the future framework of its government. Finally, four days before independence was achieved, he gave a speech in which he declared that the country would offer equal rights to all citizens, irrespective of creed or ethnicity. He said that religion would have nothing to do with the state and would be relegated to the conscience of individuals. His several references to England during the speech expressed his assumption—shared by many others of the Westernized elite—that European democracies would be the model for the new country.

The writing of a constitution for Pakistan proceeded slowly. The first year of independence was consumed with the settlement of refugees, the war with India over Kashmir, and the myriad details that had to be addressed in the creation of a new country. Jinnah died at the end of the year, allowing advocates of an Islamic state to express their views more assertively. These advocates included Mawdudi, who ordered his followers not to take an oath of allegiance to the state until it became Islamic. Due to such pressure, in March 1949 the Constituent Assembly passed the Objectives Resolution in an attempt to reassure advocates of an Islamic state that the constitution would be acceptable to them. Its language, skillfully crafted by secular elites, allowed both secularists and the advocates of an Islamic state to find their goals affirmed. The resolution stated that the Islamic meanings of democracy, freedom, equality, tolerance, and social justice would be fully implemented in the new state, and that Muslims would "be enabled to order their lives in the individual and collective spheres in accordance with the teachings of Islam as set out in the Holy Quran and Sunnah." Despite the Islamic nature of the state and society, the resolution continued, minority groups would be able to practice their religious faiths freely.

Meanwhile, several hard-line Sunni groups became enraged that members of the Ahmadiya had become high-ranking members of the Pakistan government. Beginning with a vicious anti-Ahmadiya propaganda campaign in 1949, these activists began conducting pogroms against Ahmadis in 1953, killing hundreds of them. A government commission investigated the disturbances. The report of the commission was issued in 1954 as the *Report of the Court of Inquiry Constituted under Punjab Act II of 1954 to Enquire into the Punjab Disturbances of 1953*, but is popularly known as the Munir Report, after the chair of the commission. It is a remarkable document, and perhaps one of the most important documents in modern Muslim history.

The commission conducted interviews with numerous members of the ulama. One of the questions asked was to define the irreducible minimum requirement for someone to be considered a Muslim. None of the ulama could agree upon the definition. The range of opinion extended from the assertion that uttering the *shahada* ("There is no god but God, and Muhammad is his messenger") was sufficient, to the insistence that there were too many requirements to be able to list them all. A second question asked how an Islamic state should be structured, and none agreed on that issue either. The ulama were also asked if apostasy should be punished by death, and they unanimously agreed that it should. The authors of the Munir Report were aware that Sunnis and Shi'ites regarded each other as apostates, and that Deobandis, Ahl-e Hadith, Barelwis, Ahmadis, and others had all declared each other apostates at one time or another. They concluded that, given the irreconcilable views among religious leaders regarding the structure of an Islamic state and even what it means to be a Muslim, it would be a mistake for religion and the state to mix. If they were to do so, one sect or the other would gain control of the state and use it as an instrument of persecution against all the others.

A constitution was finally approved for Pakistan in 1956, but regional and sectarian violence became so serious that military officers abrogated the constitution in 1958 and placed the country under martial law. It remained under martial law until 1962, when the army placed it under emergency rule (with civil liberties suspended) from 1965 to 1968. Meanwhile, throughout the 1950s and 1960s, the resentment of Bengalis was building up toward West Pakistan. East Pakistan produced seventy percent of the country's exports, and yet the West Pakistan–dominated central government allocated it only a third of the proceeds from economic growth. It received less than its share of foreign aid and of development projects, as well. The Awami League, under the leadership of Mujib al-Rahman (sometimes transliterated as Mujibur Rahman), began to advocate economic autonomy for East Pakistan.

In November 1970, just a month before the country's first national election was scheduled, a cyclone (hurricane) struck East Pakistan. It generated a tidal wave thirty feet high that killed between 300,000 and one million people. The slowness and inefficiency of the government's emergency relief efforts angered the large majority of the population of East Pakistan, which gave the Awami League 160 of the national assembly's 313 seats. The Awami League's achievement dwarfed that of the second-largest party: Zulfikar Ali Bhutto's socialist Pakistan People's Party, based in West Pakistan, won only eighty-one seats. The election results should have automatically placed Mujib al-Rahman in the position of prime minister, but Bhutto and other West Pakistan politicians blocked him from taking over the reins of power.

In March 1971, East Pakistani frustration over the blocked election results boiled over into riots. In retaliation, the army—overwhelmingly composed of West Pakistanis—began the indiscriminate murder of Bengalis. Mujib al-Rahman was arrested and jailed in West Pakistan, but Major Zia al-Rahman (sometimes transliterated as Ziaur Rahman; he was unrelated to Mujib), proclaimed the independence of the eastern province. Soon, the new country was named Bangladesh ("Country of Bengal"). A Bangladeshi government in exile was formed across the border in Calcutta. The West Pakistan army conducted a brutal, scorched-earth policy that some have characterized as genocide. As many as one million Bangladeshis were killed; eight million fled to India; and twenty million were displaced from their homes. Bangladesh appealed to India for help, and the Indian army required only the first two weeks of December 1971 to crush the army of West Pakistan, which soon became known simply as Pakistan. The humiliation by the Indian army added to Pakistan's list of grievances against its neighbor—many Pakistanis even believed that the whole affair was an Indian plot from the beginning—but Bangladesh concluded a twenty-five-year treaty of friendship and a trade agreement with India.

Indonesia

The idea of Indonesia, like that of Pakistan, was a leap of faith. The 17,000 islands of the Netherlands Indies had never functioned as a unified state, and their rulers maintained a variety of arrangements with the Dutch. A myriad of languages, religions, customs, and traditional rivalries yielded profound diversity. Only the historical accident of Dutch rule united the islands; had that not occurred, it is unlikely that Indonesia would exist today.

The struggle to create Indonesia was exhausting. Between March and August 1945, with Japanese approval, leaders from throughout the archipelago engaged in intense discussions regarding the nature of the independent nation that they planned to create once the war was over. Representatives of the major Islamic groups insisted on a statement of Islamic identity for the country, but Sukarno and others argued that such a provision would be fatal to national unity, given the large number of Christians, Hindus, and nominal Muslims in the country. Sukarno wanted to find a set of principles with which the wide variety of peoples and cultures throughout the archipelago could identify. He proposed the *Pancasila,* or Five Principles: monotheism, nationalism, humanitarianism, social justice, and democracy. These became the ideological foundation for the new country.

The new country had a difficult birth. The Japanese had shattered its economy in an effort to supply its army; the Dutch fought for four years (1945–1949) to regain control of its colony; and isolated groups of Muslims and communists rebelled in vicious separatist wars. The first elections were held in 1955. These were the focus of considerable excitement, because their purpose was to determine the members of a constituent assembly that would write a permanent constitution to resolve the question of whether Indonesia's government would be secular or Islamic. The results of the vote were inconclusive, for twenty-eight parties split the seats in the assembly. The secular Nationalist Party won 22.3 percent, two Islamic parties split 40 percent of the vote almost evenly, and the Indonesian Communist Party (PKI) won 16.4 percent. The inability of any coalition of parties to form a government led to a stalemate. Sukarno took advantage of the political paralysis to consolidate power into his own hands.

Sukarno used the euphemism "Guided Democracy" to describe the period of martial law that he oversaw from 1957 to 1963. He was determined to maintain a secular government, and so he excluded members of Muslim political parties from positions of power. He also wanted to distance himself from the powerful influence that the military had built up over the first decade of the nation's history. One element of his policy was to cultivate close ties with members of the PKI, and he brought several of them into the government. The policy was fraught with peril, because the leading army officers loathed communism. Since Sukarno depended on the military to preserve martial law, he was forced to give its leadership major concessions. It soon became difficult to tell where the lines of authority lay between the civilian and military leadership.

Sukarno himself was not a communist, but his experience under Dutch imperialism made him suspicious of the exploitative aspects of capitalism. His ideology employed the rhetoric of revolution, and he embarked upon a series of socialist reforms, including the nationalization of Dutch- and British-owned property. In the international arena, he became famous as one of the leaders of the nonaligned movement that protested the bipolar geopolitical framework of the Cold War. In practical terms, however, he had much warmer relations with the Soviet Union and China than with the United States.

In 1965, Sukarno lost his high-stakes gamble that he could balance the growing communist presence in his government with the continued support of the army. In September 1965, the murder by communists of the most influential anticommunist army officers provoked a backlash against the PKI that resulted in blood-letting on a scale that defies comprehension. An army general, Suharto (his only name), called upon the people to destroy communism. The mounting tensions and uncertainties of the previous few years burst open in a murderous frenzy that lasted several weeks. Many people—Hindus, Chinese, Christians, and nominal Muslims—were killed who had no connection with communism at all, but were targeted by neighbors who wanted to settle scores, seize their property, or kill someone—anyone—before they were killed themselves. Some 500,000 people were murdered, and many hundreds of thousands were imprisoned.

Suharto allowed Sukarno to remain the titular ruler for two more years before placing him under house arrest and taking his place. His so-called New Order turned Indonesia into a bastion of anticommunism and moved the country into the American orbit. His three decades in power included some positive features: He presided over an era of impressive economic growth, launched educational programs that raised literacy rates from forty percent to ninety percent, and implemented a successful, noncoercive family planning program. His rule also had some significant negative features. He ruled as a dictator and ruthlessly crushed dissent. He and his family practiced corruption on a colossal scale: By 1990, they were estimated to have deposited thirty billion dollars of bribes and kickbacks in foreign banks.

Muslim politicians who had been frustrated by Sukarno's ban on Muslim political parties hoped that Suharto would remove the restrictions. They were bitterly disappointed, because although Suharto's New Order had abandoned Sukarno's flirtation with communism, it continued the tradition of militantly secular rule that Sukarno had practiced. Traditional Muslims were alarmed when Suharto moved to restrict polygyny, gave women greater rights in divorce proceedings, and removed most authority for marriage and divorce from Islamic courts to civil courts. Although these measures were similar to ones long advocated by Muhammadiya, their implementation by a secular military regime provoked fears of government control of Islam. In 1973, Suharto forced the existing four Muslim political parties to combine into one, and he forbade the new organization to use Islamic symbols or even to call itself an Islamic party. The new organization had to use the Pancasila as its platform, with its vague reference to monotheism. The mid-1970s were years of pessimism and despair for many Muslims who had hoped to reshape society along Islamic lines.

Iran

World War II served as a time warp for Iranians who were old enough to recall their experience in World War I. Their country was divided into zones of influence by their huge neighbor to the north and by the British; the shah could not make any important policy decisions without the approval of the ambassadors representing those two countries; and, in the hinterlands, movements for tribal and regional autonomy erased the work of years of careful centralization of government power. The British evacuated their troops at the end of the war, but Iran had to appeal to the United Nations to secure the withdrawal of Soviet troops a year later. Continuing Soviet interference in Iran's northern provinces was one of the factors that led to the declaration of the Truman Doctrine, which stated American determination to help countries resist Soviet expansionism. Iran's long border with the USSR became an increasingly important issue in American foreign policy.

In the immediate postwar period, the major political topic in the country was the long-simmering issue of the petroleum concession held by the Anglo–Iranian Oil Company (AIOC). Iranians' bitter experience with foreign occupation during the war had heightened their sensitivity to any perception of being exploited by foreigners, and it had become clear that AIOC's contract with Iran provided less control and smaller royalties to the host country than those that Arab countries had with American oil companies. Demands arose for the government to nationalize the company. When the contract came up for renewal in 1949, AIOC proposed more favorable terms, but it was too late to turn the tide of public sentiment. By the summer of 1951, the new prime minister, Muhammad Mosaddeq, had secured a bill of nationalization in the Majlis over the objections of Muhammad Reza Shah. At the time, Mosaddeq enjoyed the enthusiastic support of an unlikely coalition of communists, religious leaders, and traditional merchants.

The nationalization measure made provisions for compensation to the owners of AIOC, but the timing was unfortunate. Although the British government had been nationalizing its own large industrial enterprises in the years since World War II, the Iranian action was an intolerable reminder of Britain's rapid slide from superpower status to secondary status in the world. London reacted as if Iran had declared war. It quickly organized a boycott and blockade of Iran's oil exports. The United States joined the boycott after the British convinced the government that communists were responsible for the nationalization.

By the summer of 1953, the boycott had successfully reduced the Iranian economy to shambles. Mosaddeq lost the support of the military and, more critically, the ulama and their large following. In August, the American Central Intelligence Agency (CIA) advised the shah to leave Tehran temporarily, and then it provided support for a coup that removed Mosaddeq from power. When the shah returned to the capital, the Americans helped to negotiate a new arrangement for Iran's oil. Iran would subsequently own the petroleum, but the refining and production were allocated to the AIOC (forty percent), American companies (forty percent), and European companies (twenty percent). The new arrangement for Iran's oil reflected the fact that the United States had become the major foreign power in Iran, replacing the British and Russians. In 1955, the United States persuaded Iran to join the Central Treaty Organization (CENTO; also known as the Baghdad Pact), which linked Turkey, Iraq, Iran, and Pakistan in a belt of anticommunist states along the USSR's frontier.

As Muhammad Reza Shah became aware of the important role that Iran had come to play in American Cold War strategy, he began to take advantage of it for his own purposes. Like his father, he wanted to modernize Iran quickly, and he needed to be able to quash any dissent that might arise. In 1957, he created the internal security agency known as SAVAK (an acronym for Organization for Intelligence and National Security). Trained by the CIA and Israel's Mossad, SAVAK became notorious the world over for its techniques of torture and murder of those bold or careless enough to voice criticism of the shah. In the 1960s, the shah embarked upon a program of reforms called the White Revolution ("white" suggested that it was not a "red," or communist, revolution) that included the creation of a literacy corps, land reform, and women's suffrage.

To many Americans, the shah's reforms were the work of an enlightened ruler trying to drag his country into the twentieth century. The shah's subjects saw another side to him, and some of his policies made them uneasy or even angry. He rammed a bill through the rubber-stamp Majlis that granted Americans exemption from Iranian laws, he became openly contemptuous of the ulama and tried to destroy their economic base through the land reform program, and he deposited a large portion of Iran's oil revenue in his own bank accounts. By the mid-1960s, many thoughtful Iranians—even secular ones—were also becoming concerned that the rapid Westernization of Iran's culture was causing Iranians to lose their Iranian and Islamic identity.

The Arab World

In most of the Arabic-speaking countries, the period from independence to the 1970s was one of great instability. The countries that were in the greatest turmoil were Jordan, Egypt, Syria, and Iraq. Their governments suffered challenges to their legitimacy due to the shock of the Israeli military victory over the combined Arab forces in 1948. King 'Abd Allah of Jordan (ruled 1921–1951) was criticized for his habit of conferring with Israeli leaders, and in 1951, he was assassinated by a Palestinian who suspected that he was about to sign a separate treaty with Israel (no Arab government signed a treaty with Israel until 1979). In 1962, his grandson, King Husayn (Hussein; ruled 1952–1999), conveyed the security-conscious nature of his reign by titling his autobiography (written when he was only twenty-seven years old) *Uneasy Lies the Head.*

In Egypt, the military officers who seized power in July 1952 had originally intended only to exile the despised king. They did not exile his infant son, who remained the heir to the monarchy. The officers initially planned to return the government to civilian leaders. They soon realized, however, that the civilian leaders were the same corrupt politicians who had been so ineffective for the previous three decades. They began reconsidering their earlier plans, and by the end of its first year, the officers' Revolutionary Command Council (RCC) abolished all political parties and the monarchy.

Some leading members of the Muslim Brothers thought that the time had arrived for their organization to begin shaping national policy, and they demanded positions in the government. Although some members of the RCC were sympathetic to the Muslim Brothers, the dominant figure within the RCC by 1954 was Jamal 'Abd al-Nasir (Gamal Abdel Nasser), a confirmed secularist. 'Abd al-Nasir harbored a deep mistrust of the Muslim Brothers that was only reinforced when members of the group began making threats to seize power. Following an apparent attempt to assassinate 'Abd al-Nasir in October 1954, the government outlawed the Muslim Brothers, and anyone found to be supporting the movement was sent to prison, where torture was routine and murder was not uncommon.

The new Egyptian government began on good terms with the United States, and with American advice it passed a land reform law that broke the power of the small landed elite that had dominated Egyptian life for centuries. Relations with the United States deteriorated quickly, however, when Egypt insisted on maintaining a neutral stance in the Cold War. Egypt's refusal to join CENTO, within the context of other "nonaligned" foreign policy decisions, provoked the United States and Britain to withdraw a commitment to provide financial support for a projected Aswan High Dam, which was the centerpiece of Egypt's plan for economic modernization. In retaliation, 'Abd al-Nasir nationalized the Suez Canal in July 1956 and gave the contract for the dam to the USSR.

The majority of shareholders in the company that owned the Suez Canal were British and French citizens. Britain and France, reduced to bit players in the Cold War and forced to withdraw from imperial possessions all over the world, chose to fight on this issue. Comparing 'Abd al-Nasir to Hitler, they recruited Israel into an alliance that invaded Egypt in late October 1956. The American president, Eisenhower, who had not been informed in advance of the attack, was outraged. He had been trying to focus world attention on the Soviet Union's brutal suppression of Hungarian resistance to the Soviet occupation, but the attack on Egypt by leading members of the "Free World" negated his efforts. Eisenhower threatened economic retaliation against all three invading countries if they did not withdraw. The USSR, glad to have the world's attention distracted from Budapest, threatened to use military force against Britain and France. The invasion was interrupted, and the invading forces had to withdraw.

The Suez crisis radicalized the political climate of the Arab world. Britain and France, the former imperial powers in the region, were totally discredited, and Israel, the local upstart, was forced to back down. The United States, which was most instrumental in stopping the invasion of Egypt, did not receive credit for it in the Arab world: Its threat to undercut the financial solvency of Britain and France was not nearly as dramatic as the Kremlin's blustering threat to rain missiles on London. But nothing the United States did at that point was likely to win over Arab opinion due to resentment toward three years of heavy-handed American pressure to influence the foreign policies of Arab governments. The Soviet Union was lauded as the champion of anticolonialism and justice, and diplomatic opportunities in the area were suddenly opened to it.

'Abd al-Nasir used the Suez crisis as a pretext to nationalize other foreign-owned property in Egypt, beginning a policy that led to the creation of a huge public sector. During the early 1960s, he nationalized large Egyptian-owned firms, as well. He called the new system Arab Socialism, although it was not based on the Soviet model. Despite his increasing military ties with the USSR, he was wary of that country and did not allow it to exercise influence over his policies. Egyptian Marxists frequently found themselves languishing alongside Muslim Brothers in Egypt's notorious prisons. 'Abd al-Nasir resisted becoming an extension of either Soviet or American interests, and he tried to play the two superpowers against each other to his advantage.

The Suez episode lasted from July to November 1956, and it turned the relatively unknown 'Abd al-Nasir into a hero among most Arabs. Many invested profound hopes in his ability to restore pride and power to the Arab world. Only a year after the termination of hostilities along the Suez Canal, a delegation of Syrian politicians visited him, begging him to allow their country to unite with Egypt. Syria had become politically unstable, and these individuals were afraid that communists would seize power there.

'Abd al-Nasir was quite aware that Egypt and Syria had been linked together in political unions for much of history ever since Pharaonic times, but Palestine had always been a key element in those unions, forming the land bridge between them. Now, with a hostile Israel between Syria and Egypt, 'Abd al-Nasir was skeptical of the viability of the proposed union, but his ego could not resist the prospect of moving forward with the project. He agreed to the merger, and Syria and Egypt became yoked together in an unstable partnership that was called the United Arab Republic (UAR). Egyptians insisted on dominating the civilian and military positions of power, even those in Syria, provoking Syria to break away from the union in 1961.

The Syrian–Egyptian union was ill fated, but it was symptomatic of the emergence of a powerful collective consciousness known as Arab nationalism, or Pan-Arabism, during the 1950s and 1960s. Many Arabs were convinced that their lack of wealth and standing in the world was due, first, to their dominance by the Ottomans, and then to their subjection to the imperialist powers. They developed the notion that the great cultural achievements of Islamic civilization during the first six centuries of Islamic history had taken place during a period of Arab political unity and that, if the Arabs overcame the artificial divisions imposed on them by outsiders, their "Arab nation" would once again become great.

After the Suez crisis, when 'Abd al-Nasir became a charismatic figure, a pan-Arab movement arose called Nasirism, which espoused Arab unity, modernization, and anti-imperialism. Nasirism attracted followers in several Arab countries, although it stressed the centrality of 'Abd al-Nasir himself as the figure under whose leadership the Arabs would be united. Arab nationalism was particularly strong in Syria and Iraq. Nasirism played a significant role there, but several other pan-Arab groups were even more popular. The one with the greatest staying power was devised by two Syrians during the 1940s. Michel Aflaq, a Greek Orthodox Christian, and Salah al-Din al-Bitar, a Sunni Muslim, collaborated on devising a movement that they called the *Ba'th* ("Renaissance"). Its ideals and goals were vague and romantic notions about Arab unity, freedom, modernization, anti-imperialism, and opposition to large land holdings, but they appealed to young men in Syria and Iraq who were frustrated by a growing sense of Arab powerlessness. By the late 1940s, the Ba'th party had developed a slogan of "unity, freedom, and socialism," although it was anticommunist. The movement was outlawed in Iraq in 1949 due to its criticism of landowners and the British.

Ba'thist regimes came to power in both Syria and Iraq during the 1960s, a tumultuous decade in those countries. The civilian government that had been formed in Syria after the 1961 secession from the UAR proved to be too conservative for young military officers who were watching developments in the world at large. In February 1963, Ba'thist military officers seized power and declared martial law. Land reforms that the Egyptians had begun were continued, and all major industrial and commercial firms were nationalized over the next decade.

The Ba'thist officers originally represented Syria's Sunni, Alawi, and Druze communities. During the first three years of the military regime, they engaged in fierce and bloody clashes over ideology and strategy. Although the disagreements were over political and economic issues rather than religious ones, sectarian affinities tended to drive the alignment of factions. By 1966, Alawis dominated the government, and few individuals from the other groups were represented at the higher levels of civilian or military offices. Ironically, a movement advocating the supranational union of all Arabs led to the domination of Syria by a subnational, clannish group that had historically been confined to the coast. It represented only ten percent of the population and was considered heretical by the majority of the country.

In Iraq, Ghazi's son Faysal II was just coming of age in 1958 when he was killed in a bloody military coup led by General 'Abd al-Karim Qasim. Qasim was neither a Ba'thist nor a communist, but he shared in the widespread revulsion directed toward the 2800 landlords who owned half the agricultural land in the country. One of his several social reforms was the seizure of their large estates. In 1959, Qasim withdrew from CENTO and turned to the Soviet Union for the bulk of Iraq's military supplies.

The first five years of the new Iraqi republic were filled with violence. Communists, Ba'thists, and Nasirists battled each other in the streets, and long-simmering Kurdish grievances exploded into a full-scale revolt. In 1963, a military coup overthrew Qasim, and two Nasirist brothers ruled in succession until 1968. During that time, the Nasirists were hopeful that 'Abd al-Nasir would annex Iraq, but the Egyptian leader was still reeling from the humiliation of Syria's secession from the UAR in 1961. The Nasirists nationalized the country's large industrial and commercial enterprises in emulation of 'Abd al-Nasir's policies in Egypt.

In 1968, two more military coups took place in Iraq. The second one, led by Ahmad Hasan al-Bakr, brought Ba'thist officers to power. The new government was beset by enemies: Communists and conservatives wanted them overthrown, and the Kurdish revolt continued to flare. The Syrian Ba'thists who were in power from 1966 to 1970 had adopted the ideology of Leninism and were pressuring al-Bakr to adopt it as well. He refused, which led to a permanently hostile relationship between the Syrian and Iraqi Ba'thist groups, even after Syria abandoned Leninism in 1970. The development of the rift between the two Ba'thist organizations fatally compromised their effectiveness outside those two countries: If the two major branches of a Pan-Arab movement could not maintain a civil relationship with each other, how could they lead the movement for Arab unity?

The new Iraqi government enacted draconian security measures to protect its power, turning Iraq into a police state. Al-Bakr's young cousin, Saddam Husayn (Hussein), quickly rose to the second position of power in the country and was largely responsible for personnel decisions. He was most comfortable appointing relatives and people he knew from Tikrit, a town north of Baghdad that was the home of both al-Bakr and Saddam. Soon, Tikritis held the most important posts in the government. Few Shi'ites were to be found in the upper ranks, although the reason was not sectarian—the Tikriti Sunnis were not known for their piety—but rather geographical: Although Shi'ites formed a slight majority of the country's population, almost all lived in the southern half of the country. Thus, as in Syria, the Ba'thists of Iraq came to prominence espousing a supranationalist ideology but became entrenched as the monopoly of power of a subnational group. Saddam Husayn's thirst for power eventually led him to overthrow al-Bakr in 1979, and he became the absolute ruler of Iraq.

The countries of North Africa followed distinct paths of political development. Libya was a poor country that sought international aid. One way it collected rent was by leasing military bases to Britain and the United States. The country's poverty came to an end in 1959, when large quantities of oil and natural gas were discovered. The new wealth contributed to a growing sense of dissatisfaction among some of the population regarding the government's close ties with the West. Nasirism was popular among the urban youth because of its anti-imperialism. Demonstrations by young people in 1964 forced the government to request Britain and the United States to remove their troops from the country and to begin evacuating the military bases. In September 1969, a Nasirist army captain, Mu'ammar al-Qadhdhafi, led an overthrow of the government and exiled King Idris to Egypt. Qadhdhafi was a staunch advocate of Arab unity. His hero, 'Abd al-Nasir, died a year after his coup, and Qadhdhafi made it his mission to fulfill the dream of Nasirism. He suggested several unity plans to the leaders of Tunisia, Sudan, Egypt, and Syria, but managed only a short-lived arrangement with Syria in 1980. Today, he is better known for his long-time support of violent political movements from Ireland's Irish Republican Army to left-wing organizations in Japan.

Next door, in Tunisia, Habib Bourguiba was skeptical of visions of Arab unity. Although he had fought the French for Tunisian independence, he admired French culture. Forthright in his secularist values, he aspired to achieve high levels of education and health for his country. Within a few months after Tunisia won its independence, Bourguiba's government seized religious endowments and absorbed the Shari'a courts into the state judicial system. It also passed a Personal Status Code that gave women new rights of divorce and child custody, outlawed polygyny, and set a minimum age for marriage. Major efforts were made to raise the rates of women's literacy and to make family planning services available to women. These policies had supporters as well as opponents, but Bourgiba persuaded only a handful when he urged Tunisians to abandon the practice of fasting during Ramadan, on the grounds that fasting lowered worker productivity. He justified his antifasting initiative as an example of the analogical reasoning that was characteristic of traditional Islamic jurisprudence: Tunisians were engaged in a "jihad" in the cause of economic development, and so they were entitled to exemption from fasting just as warriors in defense of Islam were exempt. This rationalization only convinced the ulama and other committed Muslims that a Bourgiba-dominated government was the enemy of Islam.

In Algeria, the leaders of the epic struggle against French domination were not able to savor their triumph. Almost immediately, factions arose among the participants. Some of the tensions were due to ideological commitments, others were the result of ethnic or other cultural factors, and still others were the outgrowth of the fact that the leaders of the revolt had undergone different experiences, depending on whether they had been prisoners in France, exiles in Egypt, or leaders of independent combat groups in the war itself. Bitter fighting among the victors left 15,000 dead during the first summer until order was restored and Ahmad Ben Bella, the most famous of the revolutionaries, secured his power. His rule lasted only three years (1962–1965) until he was overthrown by Houari Boumedienne (1965–1978).

The new rulers declared Algeria to be a one-party, socialist state, and by 1971, the major sectors of the economy were nationalized. Changes in women's status were minimal compared to developments in Tunisia and Morocco: Because the French had tried to "liberate" Muslim women, the issue of women's rights absorbed the taint of imperialist values. As a result, the independence movement incorporated elements of Islamic and traditional patriarchal values. The only significant reform of women's status during the first two decades of independence was raising the age of marriage for girls to sixteen, which was accomplished in 1963.

Other problematic issues arose regarding the nature of Algerian identity. Many of the educated elite were more comfortable using the French language than Arabic, but nationalists and traditionalists—including Boumedienne—insisted on the need to

The longest and most destructive of the wars for independence after World War II was fought in Algeria. Here, French soldiers, coping with urban guerilla warfare, round up a group of Muslim men for questioning.

Arabize Algerian culture. Arabization proceeded fitfully due to a lack of qualified teachers for the schools and to resistance by the country's large Berber minority. Berbers, who represented about twenty percent of the nation's population, felt as marginalized by the dominant culture as Kurds did in Turkey and Iraq. Berbers had borne the brunt of the fighting during the revolution, but Arabs from the leadership-in-exile took over the reins of power at independence. When the government implemented the Arabization program, it simultaneously suppressed Berber studies at the University of Algiers. Berbers also noticed that economic development programs focused on urban industries, while agriculture—the pursuit of most Berbers—was relatively neglected.

In Morocco, King Muhammad V continued to be popular until his unexpected death in 1961 following minor surgery. He was succeeded by his son Hasan (Hassan) II (ruled 1961–1999), who gained a reputation as a ruthless suppressor of dissent. When he did allow parliamentary elections, he rigged them in favor of parties that were allied with his interests. Opposition to the king spread to the military; in 1971, army cadets made an attempt on his life, and a year later, air force pilots tried to shoot down the royal airliner as the king was returning from a visit to France. In 1975, the king won widespread popularity among the masses—but condemnation around the world—when he claimed the Western Sahara for Morocco after Spain evacuated it.

Turkey

Turkey's leaders wished to remain neutral during World War II but were afraid of offending either side. As a result, they signed both a mutual assistance pact with the Allies and a nonaggression pact with Germany. In February 1945, just three months before the end of the war in Europe, Turkey declared war on Germany. After the war, the Soviet Union's continued occupation of Eastern Europe and its support of communists within Turkey drew the country into the orbit of the United States. It joined the North Atlantic Treaty Organization (NATO) in 1952, the same year that its bitter enemy Greece joined the organization.

One of Turkey's problems during the postwar decades was that it had to shelter several waves of refugees, just as the Ottoman Empire had had to do during the 1860s and 1870s. Modern Bulgaria, which was part of the Soviet-dominated Warsaw Pact, had never assimilated its Muslim population. When Turkey sent troops to help South Korea resist North Korea's attack in 1950, Bulgaria's communist government expelled 250,000 of its Muslim citizens to Turkey. It expelled another 50,000 during the following eighteen years. The Bulgarian government began another series of anti-Muslim measures in 1985 that culminated in the expulsion of 360,000 Muslims in 1989, just before national elections swept the communists from power.

Turkey's political life was utterly transformed after World War II. During the war, Kemal's Republican People's Party (RPP) had yielded to domestic and foreign pressure to end its one-party rule. The first multiparty elections were held in 1946, allowing the new Democratic Party (DP) to win seats in the legislature. The DP administered an overwhelming defeat to the RPP in 1950, marking the first time that the RPP was not in power since its formation in 1923. The transition to multiparty politics in 1946 provided an opportunity to modify the state's implementation of Kemalism. The radical secularism of the RPP's version of Kemalism reflected the world view of only a small percentage of the country's population, largely confined to the ranks of civil servants, teachers and professors, and military officers. Members of these groups had been taught to fear the influence of religion in political life, and they owed their positions to their advocacy of the principles of secularism and Western values. Any modification of the practice of radical secularism not only would challenge their basic assumptions about the respective roles of government and religion, but would potentially challenge their careers. For the vast majority of Turks, however, religious values provided the basic framework of their world view. Turkish Muslims adhered to a wide spectrum of theological beliefs and ritual practices, and their notions of what role Islam should play in public life differed just as greatly, but they were all convinced that religious values and practice should not be treated as enemies of the state and society.

Turkish social life did not feature the presence of mass-membership, voluntary organizations such as Muhammadiya, the Muslim Brothers, or Jama'at-i Islami. As a result, the impulse for revising the interpretation of the principle of secularism took place within political parties. The first, tentative steps were taken while the RPP still held the reins of power, during the 1946–1950 period. Once the DP won power in 1950, however, it immediately began making significant breaches in the wall that had excluded Islam from public life. It passed bills that allowed the call to prayer to be given once again in Arabic, allowed religious radio programming, and introduced religious lessons into the schools. Opponents of Kemalism throughout the country saw the opportunity to overturn secularization entirely: Vandals damaged statues of Ataturk, and some members of the DP demanded the restoration of the fez for men and the veil for women, as well as the replacement of the Latin script by the Arabic. The DP leaders, however, were as committed to the principle of a secular government as those of the RPP, and fought against radical attempts to Islamize the country. The DP was more willing than the RPP to recognize a legitimate place for religion in public life, but only as long as it did not infringe on the basic course set by Kemal. Throughout the 1950s, both parties shamelessly exploited religious sentiments during election campaigns while remaining committed to slightly different interpretations of Kemalism.

The transition to multiparty politics in 1946 was peaceful, but it took a while before politicians learned how to rule without trying to crush their opponents. During the period that the DP held power (1950–1960), the RPP became increasingly antagonistic, rejecting and criticizing almost everything the government proposed. In response, the DP became increasingly heavy-handed and repressive in its treatment of the expression of political dissidence. Hostility between the two major parties reached a breaking point in 1960, prompting the army to intervene in May of that year. Military officers directed the government for more than a year and supervised a trial of major DP political figures, executing three of them, including the former prime minister. Civilians regained control of the government in late 1961, but political tensions did not abate. Leftist groups became active among the working class and peasants, and groups advocating right-wing social and economic agendas allied with religious activists. Both challenged the Kemalist center. Widespread and intense violence provoked the military to intervene again in 1971 and 1980 to remove politicians and restart the process.

Throughout the period, major issues included economic justice, political rights, Turkey's relationship with Europe on the one hand and the rest of the Muslim world on the other, and the legal status of Turkey's Kurdish population. The Kurdish issue became prominent in 1974, when activists formed the Kurdish Workers' Party. In 1984, it began a violent campaign for separatism, claiming as a goal the creation of a Kurdistan that would contain the Kurds of Turkey, Iran, Iraq, and Syria. Both the Kurdish Workers' Party and the army engaged in massacres of civilians who did not make clear their loyalty to the appropriate side in the conflict. The war subsided only in 1999, when the leader, Abd Allah Ojalan, was captured. By then, over 30,000 people had been killed. The violence of this internal war, coupled with the human rights abuses of the early 1980s, cast a cloud over Turkey's reputation that the country is only now dispelling.

Voices of Urgency

Consumerism and secularism struck quickly in large parts of the Muslim world compared to their subtle emergence in the West. As early as the 1920s, European styles of dress for both men and women became popular among the middle class. Billboards offered products that promised beauty, status, and cures for every ill. Clothing, household utensils, and devices of every kind could be imported from abroad, often more cheaply than buying them from local craftsmen. Listening to the radio and phonograph increasingly took the place of listening to folk songs and folk tales; as fewer individuals learned the traditional songs and stories, fewer people knew them well enough to pass them on to the next generation. Entire sections of the economy and culture were being obliterated by modernization.

Major institutions became secularized. The imperialist legacy and policies of Muslim rulers themselves had progressively narrowed the scope allowed to the Shari'a to the point that, in most countries, it covered only family and inheritance issues. In China and the Soviet Union it had no authority at all. Moreover, the Qur'an schools, where most Muslims gained their knowledge of the Qur'an—and, in non-Arab countries, of the Arabic language—were replaced by government schools that offered a modern curriculum. The schools offered very little that dealt specifically with Islam or Islamic culture, and in non-Arab countries, they offered Western languages rather than Arabic. Students who were enrolled in programs in engineering, the natural sciences, the social sciences, or law were particularly vulnerable to the conclusion that the world that they were being prepared to enter was the product of the foreigners whom their fathers had fought against and whom their political leaders criticized in speeches.

The growth of consumerism and secularization, and the concomitant disappearance of traditional cultural markers, stimulated a rethinking of cultural identity. A growing number of writers raised questions that struck a chord in millions of people: What does it mean to be a Muslim in the modern world when so much that is quintessentially Islamic seems to be disappearing? What will be the fate of local culture, given the fact that many of the most desirable aspects of consumer culture are imported from abroad and reflect Western culture? Does an examination of the Islamic legacy offer meaningful alternatives to the policies of the ruling elites that are betraying the hopes and dreams that had been invested in them?

In Iran, the shah's rush to Westernize the country spawned a wide range of reactions that eventually proved to be the foundations for a revolution. One Iranian cultural critic was Jalal Al-i Ahmad (1923–1969), who came from a family with a reputation for producing ulama. As a youth, he attended both a madrasa and a government secondary school. When he adopted a secular world view rather than a religious one, his father disowned him. After earning a graduate degree in Persian literature, he became a teacher and one of the most famous writers of Persian short stories. For several years, he was a member of socialist parties, but he eventually became disenchanted with the subservience of Iranian socialists toward Moscow. He embarked upon an intensive study of Iranian peasants—which included extended periods of living in villages with them—in order to write stories about them.

By the early 1960s, Al-i Ahmad's immersion in peasant values and rhythms of life had made him outspokenly critical of what he considered to be the crass materialism and superficiality of the increasingly Westernized culture of the large cities. He contrasted the simplicity and purity of peasant values and social behavior with those of the uncritical imitators of the West, who he thought had lost their souls. In describing the urban middle- and upper-class Iranians who were mindlessly striving to be modern, he used the concept *gharbzadegi*, which has been variously translated as "Westoxication," "Occidentosis," and "Euromania." The term suggests a frantic, uncritical adoption of Western technologies, styles of dress, and manners that left many middle- and upper-class Iranians neither European nor Iranian.

Al-i Ahmad offered no practical suggestions for Iranians to follow in constructing an alternative to the existing situation. He had become an incorrigible romantic, and his sympathy for the peasants had become warped into an idealization of their rustic way of life, which was devoid of electricity, plumbing, literacy, and rudimentary medical care. Moreover, Al-i Ahmad was ambivalent regarding Islam: He suggested that Islam was the only element that could elicit a total commitment from most Iranians, and yet he could never recapture his own childhood commitment to it. He opposed the White Revolution, but not just for its aggrandizement of monarchical power: He feared that the land reform and literacy programs would spread the contagion of gharbzadegi to the villages. On the other hand, his widely read critique of Iranian culture caused many Iranians to reflect upon issues of cultural authenticity.

One appreciative reader of Al-i Ahmad was Ruhallah Khomeini (Ruh Allah Musavi Khumayni; 1902–1989), a mujtahid who taught in Qum. Khomeini, who was unusual among mujtahids for his deep interest in the 'irfan tradition of Mulla Sadra, personally thanked Al-i Ahmad for his cultural critique. Khomeini became famous during 1963–1964 for his plain-spoken criticism of the shah. For a year and a half, he blasted the shah's arbitrary and brutal rule, economic and legal concessions to the United States, and dismissal of the Majlis. Khomeini was arrested three times, and would have been executed the third time were it not for several ayatollahs who certified that he had risen to ayatollah status himself: The execution of an ayatollah would have risked provoking a major uprising. Khomeini was sent into exile, instead. He made his way to Najaf, where he taught for over a decade.

Khomeini continued his opposition to the shah from Iraq. In 1970, he pronounced the Iranian government to be anti-Islamic after it abandoned the use of the Islamic calendar. The following year, he published his most famous book, *Islamic Government.* It is composed of transcripts of a series of lectures that he had delivered early in 1970 in Najaf. The thesis of the book is that, in the absence of the Hidden Imam, his right to rule devolved upon mujtahids in their role of providing *velayat-i faqih* ("guardianship of the jurist").

Velayat-i faqih was a traditional term for the responsibility of the Shi'ite mujtahid to provide religious guidance and ensure social welfare (as distinct from the responsibility of the ruler to provide security). Khomeini, though, was not merely suggesting how mujtahids could do a better job in their role as spiritual resources: He was challenging the political authority of the shah, and his argument was a major innovation in the history of Shi'ite political thought. Throughout the centuries, Shi'ite veneration for the religious and political authority of the Imam had profound consequences. The Friday noon prayer never took on the preeminence among Shi'ites the way it did among Sunnis, because only the Imam had the right to preside over it. Because only the Imam has the right to rule, Shi'ites argued that all governments established in his absence are illegitimate. This tenet is the basis for their rejection of all the caliphs except 'Ali.

During the late Safavid period, some mujtahids became so critical of the shahs that they insisted on acting as their advisors, but no consensus on this issue was possible. The lack of an agreement on the role of the mujtahid was vividly apparent in the fierce and bloody battles between the Akhbaris and Usulis regarding even their religious authority. The Usulis won that battle, at least for the interim. Khomeini's contribution to the historic debate was to expand the Usuli position to argue that, in the absence of the Imam, mujtahids are the supreme authorities in both religious and political affairs.

Khomeini's argument in *Islamic Government* was not the result of an evolving theme in his sermons and corpus of writings, but rather a sharp reversal in his lifelong assumptions. Previously, he had spoken admiringly of the framers of the 1906 Iranian Constitution, and his criticisms of the monarchy had been directed against abuses of power, not the legitimacy of the institution itself. In *Islamic Government,* however, Khomeini condemns the constitution and the monarchy alike as plots by enemies of Islam.

Khomeini begins his exposition by deflecting attention away from the innovative element of his own position. He argues that it is self-evident from reading the Qur'an and Hadith that the Prophet and the Imams intended for mujtahids to establish a government, and that it is only because of the machinations of Jews and imperialists that Muslims do not understand that point today. The Prophet, Imam 'Ali, and Imam Husayn were political activists as well as spiritual leaders. Their struggles against oppression and injustice occurred simultaneously with their provision of religious guidance. Pointing to them as exemplars of the authentic Islamic life, Khomeini can assert that Islam is the religion of militants who seek truth and justice, freedom and independence. It is not possible to live in accordance with Islam while suffering oppression from an un-Islamic regime. Thus, the traditional pattern of behavior by Shi'ites to acquiesce to an unjust regime is un-Islamic behavior. God expects his people to fight against secular regimes and to establish a government directed by mujtahids.

Khomeini does not discuss the structure of his proposed government by mujtahids. He is careful to assert that the purpose of the government is not to legislate, because the Shari'a provides all necessary legislation, which comes from God. The primary purpose of government is to implement the Shari'a; beyond that function, he envisions only a number of planning agencies headed by mujtahids who consult with technicians and specialists before making appropriate decisions regarding policy.

A third Iranian during this period inspired numerous followers with quite a different message. 'Ali Shari'ati (1933–1977) had a modern education in Iran and then earned his Ph.D. at the Sorbonne, in Paris. Handsome, articulate, and charming, he returned to Iran in 1965. In Tehran, he attracted large audiences of young people to his scheduled lectures that centered on the theme of "return to self." Like Al-i Ahmad, he sought to articulate what it meant to be authentically Iranian and Islamic in the modern age.

Shari'ati criticized the shah's despotic regime, secular intellectuals, and obscurantist ulama alike for being equally irrelevant to Iran's needs. He was a first-rate, Western-educated intellectual himself, heavily influenced by French and German philosophy, but he was most intrigued by the critiques of colonialism and racism by such writers as Franz Fanon and Jean-Paul Sartre. He stressed the need for Iranians to overcome their traditional political quietism and to cultivate a sense of responsibility for creating and maintaining a just society. Shari'ati's ability to explicate the Islamic theme of social justice within the framework of radical social theory convinced many discontented young Iranians that they could struggle to build a better society under the flag of Islam rather than as a member of Tudeh, Iran's perennially popular communist party.

Shari'ati's ridicule of the ulama as obscurantist, incompetent, and hypocritical unleashed a barrage of criticism from them, and his unflinching critique of the shah led to his being arrested and tortured several times. He was finally expelled from Iran in 1977. He flew to London, where he died three weeks later. Many Iranians assumed that this was another case of SAVAK's having murdered a critic of the shah.

Al-i Ahmad, Khomeini, and Shari'ati wrote within the context of Iranian Shi'ism. Despite their shared background, they differed greatly from each other in their basic assumptions and their prescriptions for the future. Al-i Ahmad could not shake his secular assumptions sufficiently to "go home again" to the religious beliefs of his childhood. Having rejected both socialism and capitalism as well as Islam, he took refuge in a romantic vision of peasant life as an alternative to the coarsening of Iranian culture. His personal odyssey echoed those of Tolstoy and Turgenev, who wrote wistfully of peasant life during the period of the rapid industrialization of Russia, when their country seemed to be losing its own soul. Khomeini was a mujtahid who reached the limit of his patience with the Pahlavi regime. A basic tenet of Shi'ism is that the only legitimate government is one led by the Twelfth Imam. In his absence, the Imam provides guidance through intermediaries: the spiritually and intellectually elite class of mujtahids. When Khomeini realized that Muhammad Reza Shah was not merely negligent in his religious duties but actually an enemy of Islam, he felt compelled to challenge the legitimacy of his entire system of government. Khomeini's advocacy of velayat-i faqih was novel, but within the context of the two-hundred-year history of the rise in status of mujtahids and the loss of spiritual qualities on the part of the office of the shah, it was a logical development. Shari'ati combined a highly developed religious sensitivity with a loathing of dogma, and a brilliant mind with an uncommon ability to communicate to non-specialists. By making enemies of both the shah and the religious hierarchy, however, he was left with no institutional base for his ideas, and the influence of his ideas died with him.

Whereas Shi'ites place a premium on the guidance of the Twelfth Imam, Sunnis have traditionally been less concerned about the unique status of their ruler or their religious leadership than in whether people have the opportunity to follow the teachings and example of the Prophet. Religious scholars attempted to codify these teachings and behaviors in the Shari'a. In the eighteenth century, the Sunni reform movement that insisted on the primacy of the Qur'an and Hadith, and that claimed the right to exercise ijtihad, was a major break with tradition. Since the reformers insisted that the authentic Shari'a is to be found in the Qur'an and Hadith, and not necessarily in the accumulated works of mujtahids over the centuries, it was not clear what the specific content of the Shari'a was for them. The issue of the Shari'a became even more complicated when the modernizing Muslim governments and the imperial regimes implemented secular laws that restricted the scope of the Shari'a courts. During the era of imperialism, whatever concerns Muslims might have had about the weakened influence of the Shari'a, they could assure themselves that, with independence, the Shari'a would be restored to its rightful role in society. That, of course, did not happen. The contrast between the ideal Muslim state and the sordid reality of the new independent states was painfully obvious to all who thought in those terms. In the morass of corruption and crass materialism, it seemed to some activists that it had become impossible to follow the Shari'a. The compelling necessity was to replace the hypocrites who claimed to be Muslim and to establish a regime staffed by true Muslims. This was the conviction of the most influential theorist within Sunni Islam in the post–World War II era, Sayyid Qutb.

Qutb (1906–1966) was a teacher of Western literature in the Egyptian government schools before he became an inspector of schools for the Ministry of Education. In his spare time, he published literary criticism and wrote a novel. Like many of his fellow countrymen, Qutb was radicalized by his experience during World War II. The monarchy and the Wafd Party were made subservient to the demands of the hated British; hundreds of thousands of Allied soldiers who passed through Egypt in transit to their assignments were often rowdy and contemptuous of Egyptians; and the wartime and postwar dislocations of the economy created enormous hardships for much of the population. After the war, he wrote *Social Justice in Islam,* which contained a critique of Egypt's social elites and an argument that the concept of social justice was the single most important theme in Islam.

In 1948, the Ministry of Education sent Qutb on a study mission to the United States, where he earned a master's degree in 1951. His experience in America only confirmed his disillusionment with the West. He complained that his dark skin color made him the victim of racism, he was stunned to discover that churches sponsored dances in their own buildings, and he was outraged by widespread support for Zionism in the United States. He returned to Egypt, convinced that Muslims must choose Islam as an alternative to both capitalism and communism.

The next four years of Qutb's life were a period of frenetic activity. Shortly after his return home, he joined the Muslim Brothers and became the editor of the group's newspaper. Soon, too, the writings of Mawdudi appeared in Egypt in Arabic translation. Qutb discovered a kindred spirit in the Pakistani activist, and he devoured all of Mawdudi's books that he could get his hands on. Then, in July 1952, the monarch was overthrown. The RCC included a number of officers who were sympathizers of the Muslim Brothers and who genuinely sought their guidance in the creation of a new government. The secular members of the RCC hoped to exploit the organization's mass membership and organizational structure. For several months, Sayyid Qutb served as a cultural advisor to the RCC.

By 1954, however, the Muslim Brothers became disillusioned with the RCC for not prohibiting the sale of alcohol and for making concessions to the British in the 1954 treaty that began the withdrawal of British troops from Egypt. Its criticism of the government became so strident that the government banned it. Then, in October, the government accused one of its members of shooting at 'Abd al-Nasir when he was giving a speech. Many members of the organization were arrested, several were executed, and Qutb was sentenced to a prison term of fifteen years. He was repeatedly tortured, and his health was broken. He was released in December 1964, but he was rearrested in August 1965 and hanged the following summer.

While he was in prison, Qutb wrote letters and began a monumental commentary on the Qur'an, *In the Shade of the Qur'an.* In 1964, before his release from prison, his followers published a small book, *Milestones,* that contained several of his letters from prison as well as selections from his commentary. *Milestones* proved to be exceedingly popular and was translated into several languages. Many analysts believe that its popularity sealed Qutb's fate.

The central idea in Qutb's thought was that Islam is a comprehensive guide to living in accordance with God's will and that it cannot function if it does not emanate from the state itself. He was convinced that the West and Westernized elites in the Muslim world were determined to confine Islam to the private sphere and bar it from exercising dominion over the full range of human activity. The state must not be secular, because then it would be dominated by ruthless men who impose their will on others, and society would be corrupted by self-interest and hedonism. That state of affairs is the plight of the present world, and Qutb acknowledged his debt to Mawdudi in appropriating the concept of jahiliya to describe the situation. Again echoing Mawdudi, Qutb argued that it is the God-ordained duty of true Muslims to devote their lives to the cause of creating a genuinely Islamic state, and that doing so is to engage in jihad. Unlike Mawdudi, who insisted that jihad was nonviolent, Qutb made it clear that the jihad to create an Islamic state would entail force.

Qutb vehemently denied that jihad is merely defensive, as some Muslim apologists and Western scholars asserted. Its primary purpose, he argued, is to make it possible for people to follow Islam. It may take several forms. It may, indeed, be defensive in the sense of fighting against invaders. But jihad may also take the form of conquering non-Muslim societies to provide people of other religions the opportunity of becoming Muslims: Polytheists would have to convert, but Jews and Christians could continue to adhere to their religions by paying the traditional tax that Muslim rulers typically levied on their non-Muslim subjects throughout history. Qutb devoted most of his discussion of jihad, however, to a third purpose of jihad: removing from power "those who have usurped God's authority." He had in mind the Muslim rulers who do not implement the Shari'a.

Qutb's Two-Pronged Approach to Political Change

From 1954 to 1964, Sayyid Qutb was a political prisoner in the most notorious of Egypt's jails, where torture and degradation were part of his daily routine. He was released in 1964, only to be rearrested in 1965 and summarily executed. Despite the brutal prison conditions, Qutb managed to write a commentary on part of the Qur'an as well as a collection of essays that became his most famous book: Ma'alim fi al-Tariq, *which has been variously translated as* Milestones *or* Signposts Along the Road. *Throughout the book, Qutb stresses the obligations on the believer to be actively engaged in God's work. As reflected in the selections reproduced here, he taught that the first priority was preaching and persuasion, but that an organized movement would be required to remove oppressors by force.*

To establish God's rule means that His laws be enforced and that the final decision in all affairs be according to these laws. The establishing of the dominion of God on earth, the abolishing of the dominion of man, the taking away of sovereignty from the usurper to revert it to God, and the bringing about of the enforcement of the Divine Law (Shari'a) and the abolition of man-made laws cannot be achieved only through preaching. Those who have usurped the authority of God and are oppressing God's creatures are not going to give up their power merely through preaching; if it had been so, the task of establishing God's religion in the world would have been very easy for the Prophets of God! This is contrary to the evidence from the history of the Prophets and the story of the struggle of the true religion, spread over generations.

This universal declaration of the freedom of man on the earth from every authority except that of God, and the declaration that sovereignty is God's alone and that He is the Lord of the universe, is not merely a theoretical, philosophical, and passive proclamation. It is a positive, practical, and dynamic message with a view to bringing about the implementation of the Shari'a of God and actually freeing people from their servitude to other men to bring them into the service of God, the One without associates. This cannot be attained unless both "preaching" and "the movement" are used. This is so because appropriate means are needed to meet any and every practical situation.

Because this religion proclaims the freedom of man on the earth from all authority except that of God, it is confronted in every period of human history—yesterday, today, or tomorrow—with obstacles of belief and concepts, physical power, and the obstacles of political, social, economic, racial, and class structures. In addition, corrupted beliefs and superstitions become mixed with this religion, working side by side with it and taking root in peoples' hearts.

If through "preaching" beliefs and ideas are confronted, through "the movement" material obstacles are tackled. Foremost among these is that political power which rests on a complex yet interrelated ideological, racial, class, social, and economic support. Thus these two—preaching and the movement—united, confront "the human situation" with all the necessary methods. For the achievement of the freedom of man on earth—of all mankind throughout the earth—it is necessary that these two methods should work side by side. This is a very important point and cannot be overemphasized.

Source: Sayyid Qutb, *Milestones*. Cedar Rapids, Iowa: The Mother Mosque Foundation, n.d., 58–59.

Qutb organizes his discussion of jihad around his central assumption, which he repeats numerous times in his exposition: Islam's purpose is to free humans from servitude to others so that they can recognize God's authority as Lord of the universe. Islam is the perfect freedom to serve God. It is the duty of Muslims, therefore, to be engaged in a long regimen of spiritual discipline, educating others, and recruiting kindred spirits into the movement. Eventually they will be ready to eliminate the obstacles that prevent God's purposes from being implemented. The chief obstacles to the unfettered expression of Islam are those who usurp God's authority in their role as secular rulers.

Qutb's ideas are the logical extension of Mawdudi's ideology. Mawdudi broke with Islamic tradition by equating Islam with state-building and the designation of Muslim societies as being in a condition of jahiliya; Qutb used those concepts to build a case for advocating the violent overthrow of Muslim-led governments. Throughout history, the overwhelming majority of Sunni political theorists had consistently urged Muslims not to take criticism of an unjust ruler to the point of risking the outbreak of large-scale violence. Three massive civil wars during the first century of Islamic history were so destructive and traumatic that subsequent generations were cautioned to bear the exactions of oppressive rule rather than risk a conflagration. They assumed that God is in control of history and that His purposes are often inscrutable. The bias against changing rulers by force meant that ulama usually joined revolts against rulers only when the rebellions were led by self-proclaimed Mahdis, when participants believed that mundane history was drawing to a close. The passivity and fatalism that the traditional attitude reflected was slowly undermined by the cumulative effects of eighteenth- and nineteenth-century demands for the practice of ijtihad, the charismatic influence of Jamal al-Din al-Afghani, the growing consciousness of personal responsibility and accountability that the reform movements cultivated, and the work of twentieth-century activists, especially Hasan al-Banna and Mawdudi.

Qutb legitimized rebellion by recasting it as jihad. His claim that the concept of jihad could embrace a rebellion against one's own Muslim-dominated government was a step of breath-taking audacity. First, Qutb was not a member of the ulama, and he had no formal education in the religious sciences. His challenge to the provisions of Islamic jurisprudence regarding the conduct of jihad was a clear example of his contempt for the labor of centuries of Muslim scholars. Qutb's radicalism extended to a skepticism of the authenticity of many of the Hadith—he urged his readers to consult only the Qur'an.

Second, Qutb was undoubtedly aware that many individuals who were familiar with Islamic history would associate him with Kharijism for the same reason that Ibn 'Abd al-Wahhab was accused of being a Kharijite. Qutb asserted that secular rulers usurp the authority of God—the greatest sin possible—and that people who follow the man-made laws of such rulers are equally guilty of being outside God's religion. Both ruler and ruled are infidels, even if they claim to profess Islam. Qutb did not live long enough to work out the details of how to determine who is a Muslim and who is not, but the events of the next few years inspired a critical mass of Sunni Muslims to adopt his writings as their primary guide to the meaning of Islam.

It is easy to see why Qutb had a powerful influence on many people. At a time when many principled people were in despair over the condition of Egypt's government and spiritual welfare, Qutb issued a clarion call for resolute action. His own courageous martyrdom demonstrated that he was no parlor warrior, calling on others to risk punishment while he was preoccupied with more important pursuits. As a professional writer and literary critic, Qutb's books were expressed in elegant prose and reveal a spiritual sensitivity that can inspire a receptive reader. What Qutb did not do, as none of the Sunni reformers had done to that point, was to clarify his vision for the Islamic state that he wished to create after removing the secular rulers. Since he rejected any authority except the Qur'an, there was no description of a twentieth-century Islamic state. He seems to have assumed that true Muslims would find their course of action self-evident, and would work in harmony as they established its structure.

Conclusion

World War II provided the seismic shocks that caused load-bearing walls of a great imperial structure to buckle and fold. When one end of the complex collapsed, it dragged down the rest of the edifice. Even though the empires of several nations were involved, their fates were interlinked because of the fact that the entire imperial project was, at its base, an elaborate con game. Once the victims of the con game realized what was happening, the game was over. As the historians of empire put it in more elegant terms, none of the protectorates could have existed without indigenous collaboration. There simply was not enough imperial manpower to control a protectorate; the system required economic and political cooperation on the part of a critical mass of the population. By World War II, the purported economic benefits of the imperial project had not materialized, and large numbers of people in the protectorates had begun to reassess the bargain that they had made. When the defeats that France and Britain suffered in the war provided some of the protectorates the opportunity to sever imperial ties, many others in distant imperial possessions demanded the same option. The imperial powers found fewer and fewer subjects who were willing to provide the necessary collaboration, and the empires collapsed.

The new leaders were men who spoke the language of the former imperial masters, and they often admired much about imperial culture. Typically, they were people who could not feel entirely at home in their fathers' culture, and yet they had not been fully accepted within European social circles. They aspired to create independent states that retained vestiges of local traditions, but that also offered the best of European thought and technology. They faced daunting economic and political problems that were largely the legacy of the imperial legacy. The Europeans had shaped the local economies to service their own interests, and they had carefully and systematically ensured that no indigenous organization would challenge their political power. As a result, the economies of the new states typically made little progress, and many of the new political systems were characterized by nepotism and violent struggles for power.

In Muslim countries, the squalid features of the new regimes were particularly disappointing. At the heart of the Islamic vision is the conviction that social justice and harmony are the natural consequences of the implementation of the will of God. In the era of independence after World War II, Muslims began to realize that an Islamic government did not spontaneously arise with the departure of the imperialists. Self-identified Muslims who held the reins of state power had no interest in establishing an Islamic state. During the 1960s, a handful of talented Iranian and Arab writers pilloried the political and cultural life of their countries. By combining trenchant criticism of the present with a yearning for the ideal society, their critiques resonated with large audiences. For all their differences in assumptions and proposals, they stimulated a widespread movement of change that challenged the very foundations of their governments. It remained to be seen whether critics of the status quo could agree on a framework for the ideal state for Muslims.

FURTHER READING

World War II

Benda, Harry J. *The Crescent and the Rising Sun: Indonesian Islam Under the Japanese Occupation, 1942–1945.* The Hague, Netherlands, and Bandung, Indonesia: W. Van Hoeve Ltd., 1958.

Crowder, Michael. *West Africa under Colonial Rule.* London: Hutchinson, 1968.

Hutchins, Francis G. *India's Revolution: Gandhi and the Quit India Movement.* Cambridge, Massachusetts: Harvard University Press, 1973.

Kirk, George. *The Middle East in the War.* Oxford, U.K., and New York: Oxford University Press, 1952.

Kratoska, Paul H. *The Japanese Occupation of Malaya: A Social and Economic History.* Honolulu: University of Hawai'i Press, 1997.

Moorehead, Alan. *Desert War: The North African Campaign, 1940–1943.* New York: Penguin Books, 2001.

Tarling, Nicholas. *A Sudden Rampage: The Japanese Occupation of Southeast Asia, 1941–1945.* Honolulu: University of Hawai'i Press, 2001.

Formal Independence

Abun-Nasr, Jamil M. *A History of the Maghrib in the Islamic Period,* 3d ed. Cambridge, U.K., and New York: Cambridge University Press, 1987.

Chafer, Tony. *The End of Empire in French West Africa: France's Successful Decolonization?* Oxford, U.K., and New York: Berg, 2002.

Cleveland, William L. *A History of the Modern Middle East,* 3d ed. Boulder, Colorado, and Oxford, U.K.: Westview Press, 2004.

Gifford, Prosser, and Wm. Roger Louis. *Decolonization and African Independence: The Transfers of Power, 1960–1980.* New Haven, Connecticut, and London: Yale University Press, 1988.

Holland, R. F. *European Decolonization 1918–1981: An Introductory Survey.* New York: St. Martin's Press, 1985.

Jalal, Ayesha. *The Sole Spokesman: Jinnah, the Muslim League and the Demand for Pakistan.* Cambridge, U.K.: Cambridge University Press, 1985.

Lapping, Brian. *End of Empire.* New York: St. Martin's Press, 1985.

Lumby, E. W. R. *The Transfer of Power in India, 1945–7.* New York: Praeger, 1954.

Reid, Anthony. *The Indonesian National Revolution.* Hawthorn, Victoria, Australia: Longman, 1974.

Muslim Minorities in the USSR and China

Gladney, Dru. *Muslim Chinese: Ethnic Nationalism in the People's Republic.* Cambridge, Massachusetts: Council on East Asian Studies, Harvard University: Distributed by Harvard University Press, 1996.

Hunter, Shireen T. *Islam in Russia: The Politics of Identity and Security.* With Jeffrey L. Thomas and Alexander Melikishvili; foreword by James F. Collins. Armonk, New York, and London: M. E. Sharpe, 2004.

Ro'i, Yaacov. *Islam in the Soviet Union: From the Second World War to Gorbachev.* New York: Columbia University Press, 2000.

Rossabi, Morris, ed. *Governing China's Multiethnic Frontiers.* Seattle and London: University of Washington Press, 2004.

Roy, Olivier. *The New Central Asia: The Creation of Nations.* New York: New York University Press, 2000.

Yemelianova, Gina. *Russia and Islam: A Historical Survey.* Houndmills, U.K., and New York: Palgrave, 2002.

Starr, S. Frederick, ed. *Xinjiang: China's Muslim Borderland.* Armonk, New York, and London: M. E. Sharpe, 2004.

Disillusionment with Secular Nationalism

Ahmad, Feroz. *The Turkish Experiment in Democracy, 1950–1975.* Boulder, Colorado: Westview Press, for the Royal Institute of International Affairs, London, 1977.

Cleveland, William L. *A History of the Modern Middle East,* 3d ed. Boulder, Colorado, and Oxford, U.K.: Westview Press, 2004.

Keddie, Nikki.*Modern Iran: Roots and Results of Revolution,* updated ed. New Haven, Connecticut, and London: Yale University Press, 2006.

Report of the Court of Inquiry Constituted under Punjab Act II of 1954 to Enquire into the Punjab Disturbances of 1953. Lahore, Pakistan: Superintendent, Government Printing, Punjab, 1954.

Ricklefs, M. C. *A History of Modern Indonesia since c. 1200,* 3d ed. Stanford, California: Stanford University Press, 2001.

Ziring, Lawrence. *Pakistan in the Twentieth Century: A Political History.* Karachi, Pakistan, and New York: Oxford University Press, 1997.

Voices of Urgency

Ahmad, Jalal Al-e. *Occidentosis: A Plague from the West.* Translated by R. Campbell. Annotations and introduction by Hamid Algar. Berkeley, California: Mizan Press, 1984.

Boroujerdi, Mehrzad. *Iranian Intellectuals and the West: The Tormented Triumph of Nativism.* Syracuse, New York: Syracuse University Press, 1996.

Khumayni, Ruh Allah. *Islam and Revolution: Writings and Declarations of Imam Khomeini.* Translated and annotated by Hamid Algar. Berkeley, California: Mizan Press, 1981.

Qutb, Sayyid. *Social Justice in Islam.* Translated from the Arabic by John B. Hardie. Translation revised and introduction by Hamid Algar. Oneonta, New York: Islamic Publications International, 2000.

Qutb, Sayyid. *Milestones.* Cedar Rapids, Iowa: The Mother Mosque Foundation, n.d.

Shari'ati, Ali. *On the Sociology of Islam.* Translated from the Persian by Hamid Algar. Berkeley, California: Mizan Press, 1979.

Chapter 12

New Directions, 1970s–Present

Disillusionment with the results of independence coincided with a larger, global phenomenon that surprised political elites and political analysts alike in the last third of the twentieth century. Contrary to the assumptions of most politicians and the theories of social scientists, distinctly religious themes began to color political discourse in many societies. The growing influence of religion in politics occurred in several regions of the world, whether they were predominantly Christian, Jewish, Islamic, or Hindu, and whether they were "developed" or "undeveloped." One of the most intriguing elements shared by all of the religious movements responsible for this phenomenon was that, although they claimed to be promoting the authentic, original form of their religions, their doctrines and practices were distinctly new, original, and imbued with modern assumptions.

A corollary of the rise of religiously inspired political movements has been the emergence of a strand of religious violence. The rise of religious violence is a global phenomenon, afflicting all the major religions. Only a few activists within any of the religions engage in violence, but their horrific acts express general anxieties that affect a much larger number of people.[1] Within Islam, activists who were influenced by the innovations of Mawdudi and Qutb continued to expand on those scholars' reinterpretations of the doctrine of jihad, providing opportunities for a diverse set of militants to incite followers into highly destructive and even suicidal missions by using appeals to religious duty and religious reward. The terrorists who acted in the name of Islam were relatively small in number, but their spectacularly destructive acts created a linkage between Islam and violence in the minds of most people in the non-Muslim world. Millions of Muslims who had made their homes in Europe and North America during the last third of the twentieth century suddenly found themselves members of a suspect population. A new urgency fueled the efforts already underway to articulate expressions of Islam that were demonstrably compatible with democratic political values.

The Watershed Years

Between 1967 and 1979, large numbers of Muslims across the world became convinced that their societies were spiritually bankrupt. At the beginning of this period, the arguments by Islamic activists were widely disseminated, but they had not yet made an impression beyond small groups of enthusiasts. The growing estrangement of many citizens from their postcolonial regimes, however, began to have an effect on perceptions. Dashed expectations, economic hardship, and political repression led to disillusionment with secular ideologies of both the left and the right. Anger, suffering, and a sense of humiliation were widespread in many countries during the 1960s. The fact that acceptance of the prevailing order lasted as long as it did was due in large part to the high value that most of these societies have traditionally placed on the virtues of patience and fortitude when confronted by hardship.

Then, during little more than a decade, a series of major disturbances swept the Muslim world that seemed to demonstrate that Muslim societies were on the verge of collapse or that Islam itself was under attack; other events provided reassurance that God would ensure triumph for those who struggled against internal and external enemies. Some Muslims became convinced that further patience might actually be an offense against God. They realized that the events of this period might well have cosmic significance, for the fourteenth century on the Islamic calendar was due to end in November 1979 on the Gregorian calendar.

The Arab World

In 1967, a thunderbolt struck the Arab world. Tensions had been growing between Syria and Israel, as both nations encroached upon parcels of land whose ownership had been left unresolved after the 1948 war. Syria persuaded ʻAbd al-Nasir of Egypt to promise military aid in the event of a conflict, and King Husayn of Jordan was pressured into joining the new alliance. The Arab states' propaganda machinery began threatening Israel with annihilation during the spring of the year. When the Arab governments mobilized their troops, Israel responded with a preemptive attack that destroyed their air forces. The June War, or Six-Day War, was over before many people could adjust to the fact that the region was embroiled in conflict. Israel seized Golan from Syria, the West Bank and East Jerusalem from Jordan, and the Gaza Strip and the Sinai Peninsula from Egypt.

The overwhelming victory was a heady experience for the Israelis. Before the end of June, Israel annexed East Jerusalem, raising the question of the fate of the other occupied regions. Some of Israel's senior statesmen advised the government to withdraw unilaterally from the captured land to show that Israel was not an expansionist country, but sentiment to retain control of the territories ran high. In August, the Arab leaders declared a policy of "no peace, no recognition, and no negotiation" with Israel. Their intransigence played into the hands of Israeli expansionists, and the territories remained under Israel's control.

The war had major repercussions. Israel's capture of East Jerusalem and the West Bank—the sites of Judaism's holiest shrines—fired the religious imagination of Jews around the world. Since the beginning of the twentieth century, the driving force behind Zionism and the creation of Israel had been secular socialism, but the war created a loud and vociferous religious nationalist group whose influence was out of all proportion to its numbers. In October 1967, one prominent rabbi declared that religious law denied the government the right to yield a single inch of the West Bank, and settlements soon began to sprout in parts of the occupied territories.

Only a few Israeli Jews faced up to the demographic implications of the occupation, and their voices were not heard by their fellow citizens. The Jewish population of Israel was 2.4 million, and its Arab population was 400,000. Adding the one million Palestinians of the West Bank and Gaza created an Arab minority of almost thirty-seven percent within the boundaries of the old mandate of Palestine, and the rate of population growth was higher among Arabs than among Jews. If those trends continued, Israel would eventually have to confront the reality that it could remain a Jewish state only if it withdrew from the territories or engaged in mass expulsions of Palestinians from the West Bank and Gaza.

The June War turned the Arab–Israeli conflict into a major theater of the Cold War. When the Soviets began rearming Syria and Egypt after their devastating defeat, the United States ended its policy of an arms embargo to the Middle East and became the primary supplier of military supplies to Israel. From that time on, the United States identified its interests in the region with those of Israel, thereby sharing with Israel the hostility of the Palestinians Arabs who felt the brunt of Israeli occupation.

The 1967 war was an impressive display of Israeli military superiority over its combined enemies. Whereas the 1948 Arab "catastrophe" had dragged out over several months, the June War was over for practical purposes in three days—it lasted six days only because Israel made a belated decision to capture Golan. The June War ended the "honeymoon" period for the modernizing regimes of the Arab world. Arab public opinion had been willing to overlook the economic and political shortcomings of the first several years of independence, realizing that the international and domestic challenges facing the new leaders were enormous. The ineptitude of the Arab effort in the war was so shocking, however, that a feeling of revulsion toward the regimes swept the region. ‘Abd al-Nasir was forced to make political concessions in Egypt, the Nasirist regime in Iraq was overthrown in 1968, and the Leninist oligarchy that dominated the Syrian Ba‘th regime was overthrown by a more pragmatic—but no less authoritarian—Ba‘thist faction in 1970. Many Arabs who lived under the defeated secular regimes interpreted the results of the war as a judgment by God for having failed to live according to the clear instructions of the Qur'an.

The defeat sent a different message to most Palestinians. For two decades, they had looked to Arab governments to reclaim for them the land that they lost in 1948, but they now came to the conclusion that their fate lay in their own hands. What is striking is how few of them saw a religious meaning in the defeat of the Arab governments. A few months after the June War, Yasir ‘Arafat took control of the Palestine Liberation Organization (PLO), which had been a tool of the Egyptian government up to that point. After 1968, the PLO became an umbrella organization for a number of rival guerrilla groups. Several of the Palestinian resistance militias were led by men whose backgrounds were Muslim, and two of the most influential groups had Christian leaders (George Habash and Nayef Hawatma), but all of them were explicitly secular in values and goals.

Members of the guerilla factions had given up on their expectation that the world community would take steps to bring about justice for the Palestinians in their conflict with Israel. Hence, they embarked upon a series of terrorist attacks on civilian targets in order to draw attention to their plight. In Europe and the United States, such acts squandered much of the sympathy that the Palestinians had earned as refugees. In much of the Muslim world, by contrast, the Palestinian violence echoed as cries of despair with which a large proportion of the population could identify. As far away as India and Indonesia, the Palestinian cause came to be viewed as a classic struggle against imperialism. Even more significant as an indicator of the changing mood of the period was that, in the larger Muslim world outside Palestine itself, the Palestinian cause—despite its secular character—became interpreted as a defense of Islam against non-Muslims.

In 1973, the Arab–Israeli conflict erupted again when Egypt and Syria attempted to recover lands that they had lost to Israel in 1967. The Israelis were caught unprepared, and they had to struggle before repulsing the attacks. The war had important local and global consequences. It achieved Egyptian President Anwar Sadat's purpose of forcing the Americans to intervene in the stalemate between Egypt and Israel over the territorial issue. With their help, he managed to recover the Sinai Peninsula in stages during the remainder of the decade. In Israel, the revelation of the country's vulnerabilities convinced Jewish religious nationalists that the war was a punishment from God for not having appropriated the "promised land" of the West Bank and Gaza. The subsequent colonization of those two areas by hundreds of thousands of Jews provoked growing resistance from the Palestinians.

On the global scale, the war transformed the petroleum industry. Prior to 1973, prices had been set by negotiations between oil company executives and the rulers of oil-producing countries. Company executives had held the trump card of excess capacity in the world: The United States, in particular, could pump additional oil if the ruler was reluctant to accept the company's price. By 1973, conditions had changed. The world was operating at full capacity, and the reserves of the United States were no longer sufficient to make up for any shortfall.

The 1973 war prompted Arab members of the Organization of Petroleum Exporting Countries (OPEC) to use their petroleum as a weapon against the countries—particularly the United States—that had aided Israel during the conflict. As they cut production by five percent per month, the price of petroleum on the world market skyrocketed. Panic ensued in the industrialized countries. The shah of Iran, who had no stake in the Arab–Israeli conflict, saw the crisis as an opportunity to gain the revenues that he needed to finance his grand ambitions. At the OPEC meeting of December 1973, he persuaded the Arab members of OPEC to set the group's price at $11.65 per barrel, which doubled the price for the second time in two months. High demand had raised the price of petroleum to $2.90 in mid-1973 from its 1970 price of $1.80; the 1973 OPEC decisions raised it to $5.12 in October and $11.65 in December.

The flood of oil revenue into the coffers of the OPEC members, combined with the turmoil that the shortages caused in Europe and the United States, gave a big boost to the confidence and self-esteem of Arabs who had considered themselves to be mere pawns in the Cold War. Even Arabs from countries that were not major oil producers felt a share in the sense of triumph. Some interpreted the wars of 1967 and 1973 and the new oil wealth as a series of events that God was using to call Muslims to reverse their abandonment of Islam and to begin actively propagating the true faith.

In Saudi Arabia, the ruling family believed that its petroleum-derived wealth had allowed it to buy its subjects' loyalty. In 1979, oil revenues were more than thirty times as great as they had been in 1970. During that decade, mud-brick villages were transformed into gleaming, skyscraper-studded metropolises. The world's greatest architects were commissioned to design universities, airports, and palaces, ordinary citizens were guaranteed jobs, free education, and free lifetime health care. Then, on 20 November 1979, the last day of the fourteenth Islamic century, the Saudi monarchy faced the most serious crisis in half a century when a group of several hundred armed men seized the Grand Mosque in Mecca. They denounced the moral laxity of the royal family and demanded the expulsion of the foreign military and civilian specialists whom the government had hired to operate its sophisticated infrastructure. Members of the group expected that God was about to reveal that one of their two leaders, Muhammad ibn 'Abd Allah al-Qahtani, was the Mahdi, who would bring history to a close.

The Saudi political authorities obtained a fatwa from the ulama that allowed them to storm the mosque and kill or capture the rebels. The royal family, stung by charges of moral laxity, quickly issued several new regulations designed to purify the kingdom. To accomplish that goal, the government prohibited television and radio stations from playing music, banned women from appearing on television, and ordered all retail establishments to close during the five daily prayers. It gave Wahhabi ulama greater latitude to control educational materials and to harass non-Wahhabi Islamic groups.

Iran

In Iran, Muhammad Reza Shah's success in consolidating his power during the two decades after 1953 transformed a shy and insecure young man into a middle-aged autocrat. He began systematic efforts to push Islam to the margins of society. In addition to accelerating his attacks on the Shi'ite ulama, he appropriated symbols of the Achaemenid dynasty that ruled Iran 2500 years earlier to endow his reign with pre-Islamic grandeur. He claimed that he was not just the political leader of Iran, but also the country's teacher and spiritual leader. At designated times, the national broadcasting service filled television screens with a photograph of the shah's face; rays of light radiated outward from behind his head, suggesting supernatural qualities.

The shah's accomplishment of doubling the price of oil in December 1973 yielded undreamed-of wealth. Iran's annual income from oil sales rose from $1 billion in 1970 to $20 billion in 1975. After 1973, the mushrooming of national revenue made possible enormous investments in the economic infrastructure of Iran, but Iranians also experienced rapid inflation and heard rumors that the shah's family was appropriating vast sums of the nation's oil revenues. In 1975, the shah decided to rein in his subjects' growing criticism. He abolished the existing political parties and required all Iranians of voting age to join the new Rastakhiz ("Resurgence") Party. Those who failed to join were branded as traitors and terrorized. The Rastakhiz was intended to be a means of monitoring and controlling the behavior of each of the shah's subjects. Its leaders blamed the rising inflation on merchants in the traditional bazaars and organized gangs of ruffians to wage a violent campaign against them.

With no recourse to secular political mechanisms of opposition, the Iranian people took their political activity to other institutions. The merchants of the bazaar and the craftsmen sought aid and consolation at the mosques, where the ulama maintained their traditional status as independent spiritual authorities and guardians of national honor and values. Students at the modern universities visited cultural centers, ostensibly to hear poetry readings or musical performances but actually for the purpose of venting their opposition to the shah. In early 1977, growing international criticism of the government's repression prompted the shah to relax some of his repressive policies. For the rest of the year, a rising tide of criticism emanated from students and from the professional and traditional classes.

In January 1978, the government's retaliation for the criticism came in the form of a crude attack on what it called "reactionary" clerics. A government newspaper singled out Khomeini for special vilification, accusing him of being a foreigner who, in his youth, had led a licentious life and served as a British spy. The article outraged the students and faculty members of the seminaries in Qum, who poured into the streets in angry demonstrations. Police and soldiers fired on the demonstrators, killing several. Traditionally, a ceremony of mourning the dead is practiced in private, forty days after the funeral. This time, however, the mourning took the very public form of further demonstrations against the government, during which the police and soldiers created more martyrs. The cycle repeated itself every forty days throughout 1978.

During this period of street demonstrations, Ayatollah Khomeini increasingly became the symbolic expression of opposition to the shah. His courage and integrity inspired the entire spectrum of the political opposition. 'Ali Shari'ati had died under mysterious circumstances in London the previous year, and many of his followers joined merchants from the bazaars, workers, and seminary students in mass rallies in support of the return of the elderly scholar and the abdication of the shah. Young, secular women even donned the chador—a black, body-length robe that drapes over the head and is held together in front by the hands—as a statement of their appreciation for Khomeini's symbolic representation of Iran's cultural roots. By December, as many as two million people were attending rallies.

The secular liberals and communists who participated in the rallies fully expected to ease Khomeini aside into a comfortable retirement once the shah was removed, but they realized the tremendous political benefit that came from having the vast majority of the country united in a single movement. Muhammad Reza Shah became so concerned with Khomeini's popularity that, in September 1978, he requested that the Iraqi government expel him. Iraqi Vice President Saddam Husayn, who despised and feared religious activists himself, was only too glad to do so.

Khomeini moved to France, but he remained in constant touch with his young followers by means of audio tapes and printed sermons.

By December 1978, general strikes had paralyzed Iran, and the shah left Iran in January 1979. The following month, Ayatollah Khomeini returned in triumph to the country amid a tumultuous celebration. Some of his followers even called him "Imam," revealing their desperate hope that he was the Hidden Imam who had returned after more than a millennium in order to bring history to a close and inaugurate an age of justice and righteousness. The ayatollah's followers proved to be better organized, more unified, and more ruthless than their secular competition, and they jailed or killed those who resisted the implementation of the Islamic Republic of Iran.

It is hard to overstate the impact of the overthrow of the shah's regime and its replacement by a government that aspired to implement God's will. In the West, government and academic specialists were in the thrall of social science theories that assumed the irrelevance of religion in public affairs. The revolution, in the eyes of many, was a fluke that could not be taken seriously. Despite the remarkably innovative features of Khomeini's plan for governance and his obvious appreciation of modern technology, the most common evaluation of him was that he was a medieval atavism who wanted to "return Iran to the seventh century." Few believed that ulama would be in important positions for very long.

In the Muslim world, the event had an even greater impact. Secular Muslims in the Middle East were aghast that a cleric had seized the reins of power in an oil-rich nation, and some Arab Sunnis were so hostile to Shi'ites or wary of Iranian power that they were hostile to the revolution. Among many pious Sunnis and Shi'ites, on the other hand, the revolution was an eye-popping revelation of God's power. Many Sunnis openly admired it and were profoundly inspired by it. Among the Shi'ites of Iran and Lebanon, a major shift occurred in political assumptions: The passive wait for the Hidden Imam to return was replaced by a new militancy. Many Shi'ites concluded that the reason that the Imams had never become the political leaders of the Muslim world was the timidity of their followers. The success of the Iranian revolution inspired them to believe that revolutionary involvement was the answer for the troubles of the Muslim world.

South Asia

In Pakistan, the secession of Bangladesh and the crushing military defeat at the hands of India left much of the country gripped by emotions of anger, betrayal, and humiliation. Ali Bhutto led the government during the difficult time from December 1971 until July 1977. He was a member of the country's social elite: The scion of one of Sindh's wealthiest landowning families, he held academic degrees from the University of California–Berkeley and Oxford University. Despite his own social background, Bhutto appealed to the masses on a socialist platform that had resonated with a large segment of the population prior to the civil war. After 1971, however, the issues of national identity and purpose eclipsed those of justice and economic well-being.

The secession of Bangladesh brought into sharp focus a fact that most Pakistanis had tried to avoid addressing: The assertion of a shared Muslim identity had not been sufficient to close the deep social and cultural cleavages among Pakistanis. The Bengalis were not the only ethnic group that held grievances. In the new, smaller Pakistan, rumblings of discontent were also being heard: Separatist movements arose in Baluchistan, where the creation of Pakistan had never been popular; no one had any illusions regarding the loyalty of the tribal population in the North West Frontier Province; and in Sindh, the Muhajir community was becoming increasingly vocal about its grievances.

Muhajir is the term given to migrants to Pakistan from the territory that was destined to become independent India. As a whole, the Muhajirs were more educated than most of the indigenous Pakistanis, and they were more involved in the Muslim League's efforts to create the new country. Thus, they dominated the government until the 1960s, when local resentment led to the imposition of discriminatory policies against them. Limits were placed on their admission to universities and to government positions despite their higher qualifications. In addition, because the Muhajirs were the most successful of Pakistan's merchant and industrial class, their enterprises were disproportionately affected by Bhutto's nationalization policies. Many began to wonder how their condition could have been worse if they had stayed in Hindu-majority India.

The turmoil and insecurities of the period led to a desperate search both for a purpose that would unite the country and for scapegoats upon whom the country could vent its anger against India and Bangladesh. The unifying purpose would be Islam: Mawdudi's Jama'at-i Islami and other organizations attributed both the secession and the military defeat to the failure to establish Pakistan as an Islamic state. The scapegoat would be individuals and groups that could be portrayed as un-Islamic. The focal point of the efforts of the first two years following the civil war was the writing of a new constitution that would reflect the new geographical reality of Pakistan. Despite the efforts of the religious parties, the 1973 constitution did not establish Islam as the basis for the state, but the document did declare that Ahmadis were not Muslims for the purposes of the constitution or the law. In 1975, Ahmadis were purged from the army and civilian government, and they were even barred from performing the hajj.

Bhutto's plans to implement a socialist system were stymied both by the turmoil of the period and by his own failures. He ran the government and his party as personal fiefdoms. He antagonized provincial governments by refusing to accept requests for greater autonomy, and he alienated the leading military officers by creating a private, independent army that enforced his decrees against dissenters. Moreover, the evidence supports the charges against him that, when the prospects for his party looked bleak in the 1977 elections, he rigged the results. At that point, officers in the military staged a coup and arrested him. Two years later, Bhutto was executed.

The new leader of Pakistan was Zia ul-Haq, whom Bhutto had appointed as his chief of staff because of Zia's reputation for piety, a trait that Bhutto had hoped would appease the growing number of proponents of an Islamic state. Upon becoming the leader of the government, Zia banned all political parties and began Islamizing the country. He declared that all laws passed by legislative bodies had to conform to

Islamic law of the Hanafi school, and any that were already in force would be nullified if they were determined to be contrary to Islamic law. Zia also announced his intention to bring the country's financial institutions into conformity with Islamic law, including the Shari'a's prohibition on interest. He built new madrasas, and he declared madrasa certificates to be equivalent to university degrees. The system of government schools with modern curricula, on the other hand, was chronically underfunded.

At first, Zia's Islamization program was greeted with mixed reviews, because many Pakistanis suspected that, despite Zia's undoubted piety, the proposals were the result of equal parts of piety and of the cynical use of religion to enhance his own power. During 1979, however, Zia's program began to win widespread support due to the convergence of international and domestic events. First, previously noncommittal Sunnis were gradually won over as the Iranian revolution resulted in the overthrow of the shah in January 1979: The emergence of an explicitly Shi'ite state on the western border of Pakistan unsettled many members of Pakistan's large Sunni majority, who subsequently felt the need for explicit assertions of their own Sunni identity. Second, Zia's program was endorsed by Mawdudi, just before the latter's death later that year. And third, the Soviet Union invaded Afghanistan in December, triggering a sense that the world of Islam was under attack.

Afghanistan

The Soviet invasion of Afghanistan capped a year of electrifying events in the Muslim world. The return of Khomeini to Iran in February, the signing of the Camp David Accords in March (discussed later in this chapter), and the invasion of Afghanistan each qualified to be the event of the decade; in combination, they transformed the consciousness of millions of Muslims. The Soviets assumed that the invasion of Afghanistan would prove to be a low-cost military and political venture. Not only would the ill-equipped Afghans be rapidly subdued by modern military technology, but Afghanistan's remote location meant that the foray would not threaten American interests sufficiently to provoke a major crisis. The Soviets' risk analysis proved to be as faulty as Gavrilo Princip's assumption that, in shooting Archduke Franz Ferdinand in Sarajevo that June morning in 1914, he was just killing an Austrian prince.

Six years before the invasion, Afghanistan's monarchy had come to an end when Muhammad Da'ud Khan deposed his cousin, King Zahir Shah (r. 1933–1973), and declared a republic. Da'ud Khan had served as Zahir Shah's prime minister from 1953 to 1963 and had devised a foreign policy that was as authentically "nonaligned" as that of any other country during the Cold War. During that period, he purchased military equipment from the Soviet Union, a policy that he resumed after his 1973 coup. Despite his friendly relations with Moscow, he ran afoul of Marxists in his own army. In 1978, communist officers massacred Da'ud and his entire family and installed a new president. Factions among the communists who took over the government then fought each other for precedence while revolts against the central government erupted in the countryside. The rebellion of a warlord in Herat in March 1979 provoked a bombing raid from the government that killed an estimated 20,000 civilians.

As the communist regime became increasingly unstable, Soviet intelligence agents thought that they detected an American plot to recruit the new Afghan president to the American sphere of interest. Soviet prestige was at stake, and Moscow was determined not to lose its leverage in Afghanistan the way the United States had lost its leverage in Iran earlier in the year, when Khomeini replaced Muhammad Reza Shah. When, in November 1979, the United States became fixated on the safety of sixty American citizens who had been taken hostage at the American embassy in Tehran, the Soviets saw their opportunity to act. In December, their tanks began to rumble across their border with Afghanistan. KGB agents killed the ineffectual communist leaders and installed a president of their choice.

When Afghanistan's rough-hewn tribesmen put up stiff resistance to the invaders, they became folk heroes around the world. In the United States, they were frequently called "freedom fighters" because their resistance was placed within the context of the Cold War. In the Muslim world, they were known as *mujahidun* ("those who engage in jihad") because they were defending a Muslim country against the invading army of a non-Muslim government. Their active engagement in fighting the infidel, only a few months after the unexpected overthrow of the shah by religious activists, inspired Muslims throughout the world, a topic to which we will return.

Southeast Asia

Malaysia's expulsion of Singapore in 1965 was an attempt by Malay elites to ensure the continuation of their own political dominance over the economically powerful Chinese, but it soon became clear that the ethnic issue had not been resolved. During the first few years of independence, many young Malays left their farming villages and migrated to the cities in search of education or economic opportunity. There they discovered that Chinese dominated the economy and that the English language was the lingua franca of the business world. The Malays, most of whose backgrounds were in agriculture and fishing, could not compete. In 1969, major riots broke out in Kuala Lumpur against the Chinese population after a Chinese political party won an election. For two months, the Chinese population suffered arson, rape, and murder; estimates of the dead range from 178 to over 1000.

The 1969 riots loom large in Malaysia's history. Today, they are referred to as "the May 13 incident," and they mark two major changes in the country. The first was the implementation of government policies to protect a particular ethnic group—the Malay majority, not the Chinese minority that had been victimized by the riots. The government implemented the so-called New Economic Policy, the goal of which was to enlarge the share of the national wealth held by Malays. According to international estimates, Malays owned a mere 1.5 to 2.5 percent of the national wealth, Chinese held almost a quarter of it, and foreigners controlled almost all of the rest. In order to redistribute the wealth, ethnic Malays were to receive at least thirty percent of the shares of publicly held companies, most government offices and government contracts, quotas for university admissions, and discounts on housing and automobiles. By 1990, the policy had raised the Malay share of Malaysian firms to almost twenty percent.

The other major effect of May 13 was the emergence of a yearning within many young Malays to ground their identity in something more substantial than ethnicity alone. The 1957 constitution had equated status as a Malay with Muslim identity, and yet the Islamic features of Malay society were superficial and perfunctory. At the national level, the state was openly secular. In the nine federated and unfederated states, the sultans retained the authority that British imperial rule had granted them for all matters pertaining to Islam, including the issuing of fatwas and the banning of unacceptable forms of Islamic practice. The sultans, who were hereditary rulers, often made decisions that were transparently self-serving, provoking widespread cynicism regarding their integrity.

Just as the May 13 incident stimulated an awareness of Muslim identity in Malaysia, it was ethnic violence that provoked an awakening of Muslim consciousness in the Philippines. The government policy of settling Christians on Mindanao, and of providing land and services to them alone, had transformed the Muslims of the island into an impoverished minority in their homeland by the 1960s. In 1968, the growing disaffection of many Filipino Muslims climaxed with the news that Christian army officers had shot and killed as many as two dozen Muslim army recruits without investigation or trial. Demonstrations erupted at schools, and a political separatist movement emerged that was led by Muslim university graduates.

The leader of the separatist movement, Nur Misuari, confronted the problem that the Muslims of the Philippines were members of several cultural groups that spoke mutually unintelligible languages and were divided by deep traditional rivalries. Thus, he needed to find a unifying concept for the movement. He found it in the term *Moro,* which Christians had long used as a derisive slang word. For separatists, it established a proud identification with the independent Muslim sultanates that had resisted Spanish subjugation for three centuries. The goal of the new movement was the creation of an independent nation of Bangsamoro ("Moro Nation"). Bangsamoro's secular architects, like those of Pakistan, envisioned a country for Muslims, not an Islamic state.

Increasing tension in Mindanao sparked an outbreak of communal violence in 1970. Repeated attacks by Christians on Muslims, and by Muslims on Christians, killed hundreds over the next two years. In 1971, growing involvement of government security personnel with Christian attacks prompted the creation of the Moro National Liberation Front (MNLF), an armed separatist movement. Its founders invited Misuari to become its chairman. Then, in 1972, after a six-month lull in the violence, the government of President Ferdinand Marcos declared martial law, targeting the Muslim community for repressive measures. In response, the MNLF launched a revolt. Between 10,000 and 30,000 insurgents fought the Philippine army to a stalemate in a war that killed tens of thousands of civilians. In 1976, both sides were eager to begin talks, which were held in Tripoli, Libya. The negotiations resulted in an agreement signed by the government to create a Muslim Autonomous Region. When the government made it clear that it was not serious about implementing the agreement, the insurgency broke out again within a year. This time, however, the Moro leadership splintered into factions that mirrored the ethnic and geographical differences of the Muslim population of Sulu and Mindanao.

Women marching for Khomeini

Responding to the Divine Imperative: Political Islamism

The cumulative effect of the explosive developments of the period 1967–1979 was to sensitize Muslims all over the world to issues of identity, power, and piety. The events generated intense discussions about their meaning and significance. Books, magazines, newspapers, pamphlets, sermons, and radio and television broadcasts analyzed them endlessly. Almost no one was left untouched by them, and some were provoked to action. One of the major consequences of this dramatic era was that the legacies of Mawdudi and Qutb became shared by a critical mass of disciples.

A discussion of the political and militant activism that was spawned during the 1970s has to be prefaced by a reminder that the number of people who have become activists is a tiny percentage of the total Muslim population. Small cults are able to keep the majority of their members involved in specified programs, but the adherents of the great world religions are not easily mobilized for sustained action. Muslims are no exception. Whereas the events of the period 1967–1979 affected the consciousness of everyone in the Muslim world, the responses of self-identified Muslims varied widely. Many gained a new perspective on world events but did not change their behavior in noticeable ways. They are nominal Muslims who attend mosques only occasionally or not at all. They think that an occasional beer is no great sin. They keep movie theaters, nightclubs, coffee houses, and soccer stadiums as full as ever, and they find televisions and video games to be more interesting than prayer vigils. In spite of the urging of Islamic activists who demand allegiance to their particular groups and political goals, most Muslims prefer to live their private lives. They would be satisfied with a secular government that provided basic services, treated its citizens with justice, and was not riddled with corruption.

Another large sector of the Muslim population is observant but not activist. Many Muslims responded to the crises of the period by wanting to demonstrate their commitment to Islam in a deeper fashion, but they did not join activist movements because they were too involved with their families or their jobs, or they felt inadequate to participate meaningfully. They were, however, able to make symbolic gestures, even if it was only to place a copy of the Qur'an in a velvet-lined box located on the dashboard of their car—a gesture not unlike the posting of a copy of the Ten Commandments in American culture.

Observant Muslims also engaged in nonpolitical action that was substantial rather than symbolic, and that changed the tone of society. Regular travelers to Muslim-majority countries detected palpable, visible changes from the early 1970s to the early 1980s. Radio and television stations included more religious content in their programming. Mosque attendance rose, and in many cases, worshipers had to place their mats on sidewalks outside the mosque due to overcrowding. On the campuses of universities, students appropriated rooms for performing the salat, and female students began wearing head coverings. Some young women even covered their faces, prompting their mothers and grandmothers to marvel that the young women were dressing more modestly than they themselves had when they were that age.

In Saudi Arabia, certain individuals were inspired to give away large sums of money in a program that appeared apolitical but that would have a powerful political impact in other countries. Several pious millionaires realized that their new oil wealth provided them the means to disseminate Wahhabi teachings to other parts of the world. They began building mosques and schools in numerous countries and sent Wahhabi-trained imams to lead the new institutions. They were particularly effective in Indonesia, East Africa, and Pakistan.

The reaction of most people in the Muslim world to the upheavals of the period 1967–1979 was unremarkable. They either went on with their lives as they had before or merely engaged in more pious behavior. What made the events so significant was the reaction to them by a relatively small but intensely focused sector of the population. These were the people who subsequently have been called *Islamists* due to their commitment to Islamism. *Islamism* is a term coined to express the ideological use of Islam to create an Islamic state. It should be clear by now that Islamists regard Islamism to be the authentic and original Islam that became corrupted, whereas other Muslims consider Islamism to be a novel adaptation of the Islamic legacy to specific social circumstances; some ulama even consider it to be a heresy. At the heart of Islamism is the conviction that a commitment to God requires active and unceasing efforts to create an Islamic state, but Islamists do not agree on what form the state should take. In fact, what some analysts consider to be the most remarkable feature of Islamism is that the vast majority of the thinking, writing, discussion, and energy invested in it has focused on the tactics for achieving an Islamic state rather than on the mechanisms of the future state itself.

It is important to distinguish between two distinct types of Islamists. *Political Islamists* chose nonviolent methods to accomplish their goals, whereas *jihadi Islamists* rejected the political system and insisted that a violent jihad is the only religiously responsible way of achieving an Islamic state. Political Islamists chose to work within the existing system in order to educate their fellow citizens regarding the need for a reformed society and an Islamic state. They wanted to create political parties to contest local and national elections in order to be able to implement a Shari'a-based state as an expression of the will of the majority. Only rarely, however, did secular states allow Islamic parties to form, and so these Islamists became active in indirect ways that would influence the values and attitudes of a growing number of people. They established publishing houses, medical centers, schools and after-school programs, day-care centers, job-training centers, tutoring programs, Islamic banks, and boys' and girls' organizations. In some countries, they assumed the leadership of the national medical and legal professional associations, and, when possible, their members contested for seats in the parliament in the name of a secular party.

Egypt and Jordan

During the 1970s, many political Islamist groups emerged all over the Muslim world, but the two best-known had been founded decades earlier: the Muslim Brothers and Pakistan's Jama'at-i Islami. The Muslim Brothers' largest branch, in Egypt, was notable precisely because its leaders responded to the brutal repression at the hands of the government of 'Abd al-Nasir by nonviolent and constructive measures. After President Sadat allowed the group to reorganize after the 1973 war with Israel, it created numerous medical, social, and educational programs, and it gained international attention in 1992 when it responded much more effectively than the government did to the needs of the people of Cairo in the aftermath of an earthquake. In 2005, its candidates won twenty percent of the seats in the national legislature as independent candidates. The Jordanian branch of the Muslim Brothers is the only one that is allowed to operate as a political party. In 2003 it won a quarter of the seats in the House of Representatives.

Pakistan

Zia ul-Haq of Pakistan should be viewed as a political Islamist: He was clearly an Islamist, but there is no evidence that his military coup was undertaken for the purpose of creating an Islamic state. He had long been an admirer of Mawdudi—who advocated a nonviolent approach to creating an Islamic state—and received the latter's imprimatur in 1979. Once he was in power, he easily rationalized his Islamization policies as the natural extension of the increasing prominence of Islamic symbols and policies that had already been taking place under Bhutto.

Zia's Islamization program, which began in mid-1977, was accelerated by the Soviet invasion of Afghanistan in December 1979. Regardless of the invasion's rationale in Moscow, within the Muslim world the war was widely perceived as an attack on Islam. More than three million Afghan refugees sought refuge in Pakistan, the vast majority of whom settled in camps in North West Frontier Province. The crisis placed an overwhelming burden on Pakistan's resources, but it also provided Zia with a rallying cry for Pakistani unity. By linking the humanitarian effort with a call for protecting and enhancing the country's Islamic heritage, he managed to gain a wide and deep current of support.

Zia's program of increasing the number of madrasas in Pakistan was also affected by the refugee crisis. Saudi private and government aid was already pouring into the country to help the refugees, but when Zia asked for additional support to provide religious education for them, the quantity of aid from those sources mushroomed. The introduction of madrasas into the refugee camps resulted in a phenomenal expansion of these institutions: Between 1971 and 1988, the total number of madrasas in Pakistan expanded from 900 to 33,000. Although the schools were nominally affiliated with the Deoband system, the sheer quantity of schools made it impossible to maintain any meaningful oversight of them. As a result, most offered rudimentary education at best, and some became little more than indoctrination centers for a variety of marginal groups. They made a mockery of Zia's announcement that they would offer an education equivalent to that of a university.

Under Zia's leadership, Pakistan achieved an explicitly Islamic identity for the first time. Due to the country's strategic position as a conduit for American and Saudi aid to Afghan resistance fighters, Pakistan also gained wealth and unprecedented standing among other Muslim countries. Although most of the country's social elites were secular, a growing percentage of army officers and members of the intelligence services were cultivating an Islamic set of values and commitments.

The transition to an Islamic state did not unify the country as Zia had hoped. The identification of the Shari'a with the Hanafi school of Islamic law entailed the imposition of a Sunni system on the twenty percent of the population that was Shi'ite. When Sh'ites protested, they were accused of constituting a fifth column for the Iranian regime and were persecuted. Sunni groups demonstrated in the streets to demand the restoration of party politics and were met with rifle fire. Muhajirs created vigilante groups to protect their interests, particularly in the city of Karachi. Karachi, which contained significant concentrations of Shi'ites and Muhajirs alike, experienced repeated waves of violence and developed a reputation during the 1980s as the most dangerous city in the world. The country's violence culminated in 1988, when an explosive device detonated aboard an airplane carrying Zia, the American ambassador, and Pakistan's leading military officers. Everyone on the airplane was killed.

Southeast Asia

In Malaysia, a number of Islamic groups emerged in the aftermath of the May 13 riots, ranging from pietistic study groups and social welfare movements to armed rebel organizations. The most numerous and influential were for the purpose of *dakwa* (the Malay variant of *da'wa,* the Arabic word suggesting missionary work and a call to commitment). By the end of the 1970s, the new dakwa groups were exerting considerable pressure on the government for Islamization measures. The Islamic Party of Malaysia (PAS), which since its founding in 1951 had exerted its influence primarily for implementing Malay ethnic preferences, became the most vociferous and antagonistic advocate for the creation of an Islamic state. In response, the ruling National Front—composed of the three major secular parties that represented the interests of Malays, Chinese, and Indians—decided to take the initiative away from the Islamic groups and PAS by instituting its own Islamic reforms. During the two decades of leadership by Prime Minister Mahathir Mohamad (1981–2003), the self-described secular government implemented policies that were attempts to placate the new demands. Notable examples of new initiatives were the creation of an Islamic university and an Islamic bank.

In Indonesia, the world's largest Muslim nation, Suharto's New Order ended in chaos in 1998. It was the victim of Suharto's increasingly corrupt governing style and a 1997 financial collapse that affected several East Asian economies. The economic crisis hurt Indonesia worse than any of the other countries: The Indonesian currency, the rupiah, lost seven-eighths of its value in nine months, and millions of Indonesians were plunged into poverty. Massive riots forced Suharto to resign in May 1998. With the removal of Suharto's heavy hand, Indonesians wanted to express themselves politically. Numerous groups arose to try to influence the direction of the country. Secular and Islamist groups alike formed parties, forty-eight of which contested the elections of June 1998. Some Muslims, influenced by international jihadi networks, ignored the political process and created armed groups instead.

Over the next eight years, four different people served as Indonesia's president. The challenges were enormous: Government ministers could not agree on a coherent program to rejuvenate the economy; a separatist movement in Aceh that had broken out in 1989 became more violent in 1998; Islamic extremist groups carried out bloody attacks on crowded restaurants; a tsunami killed 150,000 people in Aceh in December 2004; and other natural disasters continued to wreak havoc in the country.

In the first decade of the twenty-first century, Indonesia became a major arena for Islamism of both the nonviolent and violent forms. It surprised no one to see it manifested in Aceh and western Java, which have long histories of Islamic activism, but Islamists are now prominent in the political debates in other regions, as well. The political frustrations that built up during the four decades of the Sukarno and Suharto regimes, combined with the economic collapse at the end of the twentieth century, seem to have convinced many Indonesians that there are no viable secular alternatives to an Islamic state. As in other regions of the world, Islamists are not the majority of Muslims, but their salience within the educated classes of Indonesia has been a surprise for a people who are accustomed to a mystical approach to Islam.

North Africa

Algeria and Tunisia provide illustrations of political Islamist organizations that spawned violent movements when repressive governments appeared to be thwarting what the Islamists considered to be the popular will. The ruling clique of the FLN, which had dominated Algeria's government since independence in 1962, finally removed restrictions on Islamic parties in 1988. In response, Islamists formed the Islamic Salvation Front (FIS, from the French *Front Islamique du Salut*).

Public disgust with the FLN led to a spectacular rise in the popularity of FIS. In 1991, its success in preliminary elections made it clear that it was on its way to winning a majority of seats in parliament.

In January 1992, just before the last stage of the Algerian election process, the military canceled the elections in order to thwart an FIS victory. The army then jailed the leaders of the party and banned the party itself. Radical groups from within the FIS coalition, some of which were already grumbling that democracy was un-Islamic, broke away from the main body of members and declared a jihad against the government. Sometimes the various groups fought the army; sometimes they fought each other; and sometimes they killed Algerian and European civilians. The most notorious was the Armed Islamic Group (GIA), which was responsible for numerous massacres. In some cases, the massacre of entire villages was due to the murderers' decision that the villagers were not Muslim since they did not share all of the GIA's beliefs, and sometimes the cause seems to have been ethnic hostilities between Berbers and Arabs. The scale of the violence was immense—human rights groups estimate that 150,000 people died during the decade—but what outsiders found even more inexplicable than the sheer number of deaths was the apparent practice of mass murder. By 1997, members of the urban middle class, which had supported FIS during the election campaign, had become so repelled by the murders that they began supporting the military government against the rebels, and the level of violence dropped precipitously.

In Tunisia, Habib Bourguiba dominated politics from the achievement of independence in 1956 until 1987. Under his secular and authoritarian leadership, the standard of living of most Tunisians actually declined. In 1981, several religious groups formed the Islamic Tendency Movement (MTI). MTI had a comprehensive platform. It called for greater adherence to Islamic values in individual lives and for access to the political system. It also recommended specific changes in economic policies. In particular, it proposed greater self-reliance in agriculture and industrial production.

Bourguiba had a deep-seated antipathy toward religious groups. He not only refused to allow MTI to organize as a political party, but he also jailed its leaders in retaliation for any demonstrations or riots in Tunisia, even when there was no connection between the organization and the events. In 1987, as his rule became more brutal and his decision making more capricious, Bourguiba's prime minister, Zine al-'Abidine ben 'Ali, removed the eighty-four-year-old leader and assumed the presidency. At first, Ben 'Ali seemed to have achieved a working relationship with MTI, but he refused to recognize it as a political party when it recast itself as Hizb al-Nahda ("Renaissance Party"). Militants within the party began attacking the government, leading Ben 'Ali to begin a brutal crackdown on the organization.

The simultaneous rise of FIS in neighboring Algeria, followed by ghastly violence there, left many Tunisians ambivalent about their own government's repressive measures against Hizb al-Nahda. They had hoped that a new era of political freedom was dawning, but Westernized Tunisians, like their Algerian counterparts, were already made uneasy by aspects of the Islamist program. At least some prominent spokesmen within both Hizb al-Nahda and FIS called for restrictions on women's employment, the enforced wearing of a head covering for women, segregation of the sexes at all levels of education, and revisions to modern divorce laws. Some leading ulama suggested that their party would outlaw all other political parties when it got the chance. Thus, many middle-class Algerians and Tunisians were genuinely torn between their advocacy of political freedom, on the one hand, and their fear of Islamist totalitarianism, on the other.

Turkey

In Turkey, three small parties merged in 1970 to form the National Salvation Party. At the center of its platform was the demand for the restoration of Islamic law and practice in the country, whose rulers had zealously maintained a secular state since 1923. The division of the vote among multiple parties allowed the National Salvation Party to be involved in several coalition governments during the decade. Its threat to Kemalism, however, meant that it was a target of secularists, including the leadership of the military. It was outlawed soon after the 1980 military coup.

In spite of the hostility of Kemalist military officers toward religious parties, they thought that religion could serve the instrumental function of inoculating the country's young people against leftist ideas and corrupt values. As a result, during their period in power, 1980–1982, they implemented a policy of requiring religious instruction at every level of precollegiate schooling. Turkey's young people began acquiring a much deeper knowledge of Islam than most of their elders possessed, and many of them asked questions about the relationship of religion to society that Kemalism had never bothered to answer. Some turned to the Welfare Party, founded in 1983 by members of the outlawed National Salvation Party. It became the nation's largest party by 1995, and its leader formed a coalition that allowed him to become prime minister in early 1996. The party had campaigned on Islamist rhetoric and hostility to the previous government's attempts to join the European Union, but the cabinet proceeded carefully once in power, in an attempt not to provoke the Kemalist army. Local party leaders failed to exercise such discretion, and some of their actions led the army to force the Welfare Party from power in 1997. Military leaders arranged to have the party banned in January 1998.

In 2001, Recep Tayyip Erdoğan led a moderate faction of the Welfare Party to create the Justice and Development Party. Erdoğan, who had won widespread admiration among Islamists and secularists alike for his performance as mayor of Istanbul, led his party to victory in the 2002 election. The pattern of the election results showed that the Justice and Development Party won because of the voters' hopes that it could fight poverty and corruption more than for its Islamist identity. Erdoğan was careful not to lose that trust during his first few years as prime minister. He confounded the expectations of skeptics by working conscientiously to respect the secular, democratic framework of Turkish society. He sought to deepen an appreciation for Islamic values while working energetically toward qualifying Turkey for membership in the European Union, cultivating close ties with the United States, strengthening the economy, and eliminating abuses of human rights. He developed warm relations with Greece and developed a higher image for Turkey among Europeans than his secular predecessors had.

Responding to the Divine Imperative: Jihadi Islamism

In Algeria and Tunisia, movements founded by political Islamists tragically collapsed and became violent when they were thwarted in their political aspirations. Other Islamists chose the path of violence from the beginning. Why certain individuals chose one path or the other is hard to determine. Social scientists have discovered that the leading members of political Islamist groups typically came from small towns, were the first in their families to finish college, and earned degrees in the sciences, medicine, engineering, or law. Sharing an identical educational and social background with the political Islamists were other Islamists, who, by contrast, contemptuously rejected the method of working through the existing political system and argued that change could come about only through jihad. They first gained notoriety in Egypt in the mid-1970s and included members of the Muslim Brothers who responded to state repression in a diametrically different manner from that of the leaders of the group. Initially, an Islamist who engaged in jihad as the method of establishing an Islamic state was referred to by the traditional Arabic term of *mujahid,* but by the 1990s even the participants themselves often called such a person a *jihadi,* which is not a word that an Arab would have recognized half a century ago.

The concepts of *jihad* and *jihadi* are difficult for many non-Muslims to grasp because they are elements of a particular religious world view. The task of understanding them is made even more difficult by the fact that different types of activists use the terms for their own purposes. Jihadi Islamism takes three major forms. In its most easily identifiable form, it is the use of violence in an attempt to overthrow one's own secular state and replace it with an Islamic state. A second type of jihadi Islamism is the attempt to remove by force a foreign military occupation of one's homeland. Rather than using mere patriotism as the rallying cry of liberation, the fighters in this effort employ the concept of defensive jihad to characterize their struggle. Their implicit or explicit goal after evicting the occupying forces is the creation of an Islamic state. The third form of jihadi Islamism is called global jihad. Unlike the first two types, which have local goals, global jihad involves striking at perceived enemies far from the homeland. It is a response to the failure of jihadi Islamism to overthrow secular states, and its practitioners try to appropriate the aura of national liberation of the second type of jihadi Islamism. By claiming to strike at a global conspiracy that seeks to destroy Islam, global jihadis attempt to mobilize Muslims into a worldwide liberation movement that will result in a global Islamic state.

Jihad as the Means to Implement an Islamic State

Jihadis lionized Sayyid Qutb for his analysis and personal sacrifice, but they elevated a secondary theme of his—jihad—to primacy of place. Qutb's first objective in writing was to explicate the meaning of the Qur'an and its impact on the believer's daily life. His conviction that an Islamic state was required in order to live an authentic Islamic life led him logically to address the subject of jihad, because he saw that the ruthless military regimes of the era would not give up their power willingly. Jihadis, by contrast, give primacy of place to jihad rather than to cultivation of the spiritual life or the organization of social services.

An important theoretician for the jihadi perspective was an Egyptian, Muhammad 'Abd al-Salam Faraj. Faraj, an electrician at Cairo University, wrote a manual on jihad entitled *The Neglected Duty*, which reveals the direction that Qutb's ideas had taken by the late 1970s. For Faraj, jihad is more than a means to an end, and even more than a mere duty; it is, rather, the defining characteristic of Islam. The Muslim world's abandonment of jihad is the primary reason for the weak position of Islam in the world today, and the resumption of jihad will restore the glory of Islam. The highest priority for Muslims is to remove the apostates who rule their countries and to create an Islamic state. Nothing else—social reforms, economic reforms, the struggle against Zionism, or even the cultivation of a deeper spiritual life—can take precedence over armed action.

Faraj argued that true Muslims had an obligation to fight any self-identified Muslim who did not scrupulously adhere to the obligations of Islam. The obligation was the same whether the target was a farmer who failed to observe the Ramadan fast or a ruler who failed to enforce the whole of the Shari'a. Like the early nineteenth-century Wahhabis who needed to find a justification to declare a jihad against the Ottomans in order to capture Mecca and Medina, Faraj turned to the writings of the thirteenth-century scholar Ibn Taymiya. Ibn Taymiya had declared the Il-khanid regime to be the target of an obligatory jihad due to its practice of allowing parts of the Mongol traditional law to be observed alongside the Shari'a. Faraj claimed that opposition to secular Muslim regimes was analogous to the Mamlukes' war against the Il-khanids, because self-proclaimed Muslims who failed to implement the Shari'a, and the Shari'a alone, were apostates. He considered the overthrow of apostate Muslim regimes to be merely the first step in a global conquest in the name of Islam, with the eventual goal of creating a worldwide caliphate. He was insistent, however, that the war against the "near enemy"—the secular Muslim regimes—must take precedence over attacks on the "far enemy"—Israel or the superpowers that supported the Muslim regimes. Faraj considered jihad to be the defining element of Islam. Mawdudi and Qutb, in their respective ways, had interpreted jihad to be a means of releasing humanity from its bondage to the tyranny of man-made laws into the freedom to serve God; Faraj saw jihad as an Islamic permanent revolution that would take the Muslim world from a state of degradation and humiliation to that of world dominance.

By the late 1970s, Faraj and other jihadis were convinced that conditions in Egypt had become even more hostile to Islam than they had been in the 1950s and 1960s. In the aftermath of the 1973 war with Israel, President Sadat began a program of economic liberalization of Egypt's stagnant economy. In contrast to 'Abd al-Nasir's policies of import substitution, Sadat removed many import restrictions, allowing luxury goods and cheap manufactured goods alike to flood into the country, and he began privatizing businesses in Egypt's large public sector.

The policies benefitted many in the middle and upper classes: Capitalist ventures opened opportunities to become wealthy, and Western consumer goods were finally available to those who could afford them. Expensive German automobiles began sharing Cairo's streets with the ubiquitous donkey carts. The poor, on the other

The Neglected Duty

The following extracts are from The Neglected Duty, by 'Abd al-Salam Faraj. Throughout his manual, Faraj cites the Qur'an extensively, but in the section on fighting apostates he relies more heavily on Ibn Taymiya, the thirteenth-century scholar who vehemently denied that the Il-khans of Iran could be true Muslims on the grounds that they had not abandoned every feature of Mongol customary law. Here, Faraj quotes extensively from Ibn Taymiya because of the myriad of opportunities that his diatribe against the Mongols provided for finding fault with a self-identified Muslim. It is interesting to compare the passages that he took from Ibn Taymiya with the manifesto of jihad by Uthman dan Fodio that is reproduced in Chapter 8.

The Rulers of this age are in apostasy from Islam. They were raised at the tables of imperialism, be it Crusaderism, or Communism, or Zionism. They carry nothing from Islam but their names, even though they pray and fast and claim (*idda'a*) to be Muslim.

Ibn Taymīyah says on p. 293: "It is a well-established rule of Islamic Law that the punishment of an apostate will be heavier than the punishment of someone who is by origin an infidel, and this in many respects. For instance, an apostate has to be killed in all circumstances, he does not have the right to profess his new religion against the payment of the head tax, and there can be no Covenant of Protection unlike the case with someone who has always been an infidel. For instance, an apostate has to be killed even if he is unable to go to war. Someone, however, who is by origin an infidel and who is unable to go to war should be not killed, according to leading Muslim scholars like Abu Hanifah and Malik and Ahmad ibn Hanbal"

What then, is the position of the Muslims in relation to these people?

Ibn Taymīyah also says, in the same chapter on p. 281: "Any group of people that rebels against any single prescript of the clear and reliably transmitted prescripts of Islam has to be fought, according to the leading scholars of Islam, even if the members of this group pronounce the Islamic Confession of Faith. If such people make a public formal confession of their faith but, at the same time, refuse to carry out the five daily prayer ceremonies, then it is obligatory to fight them. If they refuse to pay *zakāt*, it is obligatory to fight them until they pay the *zakāt*. Similarly, if they refuse to keep the Fast of the Month of Ramadan or to perform the Pilgrimage to the Ancient House (the Ka'bah), and similarly if they refuse to forbid abominations or adultery or gambling or wine or anything else that is forbidden by the laws of Islam. Similarly, if they refuse to apply on matters of life and property, or merchandise and commodities of any kind the Judgment of the Book and the Example (of the Prophet). Similarly, if they refuse to compel what is good and to prohibit what is bad and refuse to fight the infidels (*jihād al-kuffār*) until they surrender and humbly pay the head tax. Similarly, if they introduce innovations that are contrary to the Book and the Example and that are not consistent with the example of the Pious Forefathers, like introducing deviating opinions concerning the Names of God, or His Signs, or disbelieving in the Signs of God and His Properties, or disbelieving His Omnipotence, or disbelieving anything on which the community of Muslims agreed in the period of the rightly guided Caliphs."

SOURCE: Johannes J. G. Jansen, *The Neglected Duty: The Creed of Sadat's Assassins and Islamic Resurgence in the Middle East* (New York: Macmillan Publishing Company; London: Collier Macmillan Publishers, 1986), 169–171.

hand, were ambivalent. While the new measures allowed the importation of some goods that were cheaper than those available locally, the relaxed tariffs stimulated inflation, and the sale of publicly owned businesses resulted in layoffs of employees. Sadat also yielded to pressure from the World Bank to remove subsidies on basic foodstuffs. A sudden, thirty-one-percent spike in the cost of the necessities of life caused the simmering tensions to boil over, and massive riots broke out in the large cities during January 1977.

In 1978, Sadat met with American President Jimmy Carter and Israeli Prime Minister Menachem Begin at Camp David. The Camp David Accords that were signed in March 1979 had two elements: the first peace treaty between an Arab state and Israel, and a five-year plan for granting "autonomy" to Palestinians under Israeli control rather than recognizing their independence. The two documents caused an uproar throughout the Arab world, where Sadat was accused of betraying the Arab cause. Most Arab countries withdrew their ambassadors from Cairo in protest, and members of the Arab League voted to evict Egypt.

The first jihad groups to gain publicity in Egypt were composed of impulsive and reclusive amateurs, far removed from the ideal of patient professionals that Qutb had envisioned. They were convinced that a dramatic action would trigger a mass uprising that would lead to the fulfillment of their goals. In 1974, a group of jihadis attacked and killed cadets at an Egyptian military academy, and in the summer of 1977, another group kidnapped and murdered a member of the Egyptian cabinet. In October 1981, a group of jihadis assassinated Sadat as he watched a military parade celebrating the 1973 war. The group that killed him included 'Abd al-Salam Faraj, who was arrested and executed in 1982.

Among those arrested during the investigation of Sadat's murder were Ayman al-Zawahiri and 'Umar 'Abd al-Rahman. 'Abd al-Rahman was released, and al-Zawahiri served only three years, although he underwent torture. Little noticed at the time, the two men eventually gained worldwide notice as leaders of jihad groups. Al-Zawahiri was a physician who went to Pakistan in 1986, where he worked in a hospital on the Afghan border. He viewed the war in Afghanistan as an opportunity to build a jihad organization called Egyptian Islamic Jihad. His primary purpose for remaining in Afghanistan was to gain combat experience in preparation for toppling the Egyptian regime. After the Soviets withdrew from Afghanistan, he found a home in Sudan, where he directed attacks against Egyptian government officials and institutions, including Egyptian embassies.

'Umar 'Abd al-Rahman was a revered religious scholar within al-Jama'at al-Islamiya ("The Islamic Group"), which was by far the largest jihad group in Egypt, with thousands of members. 'Abd al-Rahman won the gratitude of the CIA for recruiting heavily for volunteers to go to Afghanistan during the Soviet occupation. The Egyptian government, by contrast, viewed him as a security threat, and arrested him several times during the 1980s. Finally, on the eve of yet another arrest, he moved to Sudan and applied for a visa to the United States. He obtained it in 1989 as a reward for his recruiting efforts in Afghanistan. He settled in Jersey City, where he continued to communicate with his organization from a distance and fulminated against corruption in American society. In 1992, his mosque in Jersey City became the center of a plot to bomb the World Trade Center and other sites in New York City. The only site that suffered damage and casualties was the World

Trade Center, which was bombed in February 1993. The explosion was the idea of Ramzi Yusuf, a Baluchi who grew up in Kuwait. Yusuf also planned to blow up several American airliners over the Pacific, but was arrested before he could carry out the project. Both ʻAbd al-Rahman and Yusuf were sentenced to life in prison.

Between 1992 and 1997, the Egyptian government found itself in a desperate struggle with jihadis, especially from al-Jamaʻat al-Islamiya. Cabinet officials, police officers, tourists, and innocent bystanders were killed by jihadis' bombs and shootings. In response, the government engaged in a massive effort to crush the movement. Tens of thousands of Islamists—including political Islamists—and unlucky people who happened to have Islamist brochures in their possession were arrested and tortured. Relatives of jihadis were harassed. Over one thousand people were killed. The government's efforts slowly but surely wore the jihadis down, and by mid-decade, the organizations were facing shortages of personnel and funding. In 1997, al-Jamaʻat al-Islamiya launched a spectacular attack at the world-famous tourist spot of Luxor, in southern Egypt. Fifty-eight tourists and four Egyptians—three police officers and a tour guide—were killed by the murderers. The result was the opposite of what the perpetrators had envisioned: The Egyptian public condemned the attack, leading al-Jamaʻat al-Islamiya to announce a cease-fire and renounce the killing of tourists or other foreigners. In a striking coincidence, the bloody period of jihadi violence in Algeria and Egypt began and waned in the same year.

Jihad as National Liberation

The canonical texts of Islamic jurisprudence do not address the concept of jihad against a repressive Muslim government, but they do stress the duty of jihad against an infidel power that attempts to dominate Muslim territory. Such defensive action is the "individual duty" of jihad that is incumbent on every Muslim. During the last quarter of the twentieth century, resistance movements claimed the mantle of individual jihad in numerous regions across the world.

The Philippines

In the Philippines, the long-simmering struggle for Moro autonomy led to the formation of armed groups that claimed to be pursuing jihad. When Nur Misuari accused the government of failing to implement the autonomy agreement signed at Tripoli, he ordered the MNLF to resume fighting in 1977. His decision was challenged by Hashim Salamat, his vice-chairman, who had been involved in Islamic reform movements for over a decade. Salamat began a struggle for the leadership of the MNLF and even negotiated on his own with the government. By 1984, realizing that he could not wrest control of the MNLF from Misuari, Salamat announced the creation of the Moro Islamic Liberation Front (MILF).

Salamat was one of several hundred Philippine Muslims who received scholarships from the Egyptian government during the period from the mid-1950s to the mid-1970s to study at the venerable al-Azhar in Cairo. After eight years of study, he returned home in 1967, committed to Islamic reform. He joined the MNLF in the early 1970s, but the period of peace negotiations enabled him to seize the opportunity to abandon the secular MNLF and lead a movement focused on Islamic reform. He was supported by hundreds of ulama who, like him, had been educated abroad and represented the first meaningful wave of Islamic reform in the region. They were dedicated to the task of bringing Philippine Islam into accord with the practices that they had been taught in the Middle East.

The MILF was an armed movement that competed for influence with the MNLF (and other Moro groups that arose after 1977), and it self-consciously proclaimed itself to be engaged in a jihad. In spite of its jihadi identity and its formal demands for independence, the MILF, like the MNLF, was willing to negotiate with the government for autonomy rather than independence. Neither the MILF nor the MNLF was satisfied with the plan implemented by the government of Corazon Aquino that created the Autonomous Region in Muslim Mindanao in 1990, although several regional provinces voted to accept it. The MILF and MNLF demanded that it be expanded to three times its size.

By the 1990s, the government in Manila discovered that it had no serious problems with the major armed Moro groups as long as the national military maintained a low profile and the legislature did not implement policies that could be interpreted as favoring Christians. The Moro groups were divided along ethnic, as well as religious, lines—the MNLF was based in Sulu, where Misuari was born, and the MILF was based on Mindanao, the homeland of Salamat—and they fought each other more than they fought the government.

The most notorious Moro organization to arise was the Abu Sayyaf Group, which had its origins among the cohort of several hundred Moros who fought in Afghanistan. Usama bin Laden provided financial backing for it and sent Ramzi Yusuf to the Philippines to train members in bomb-making. The group's first bombing took place in 1991. Since then, it has become infamous for random murders and kidnaping for ransom. It has attracted only a few hundred members, many of whom were common criminals, but it provides a base for extremists from all over the world.

Lebanon

In Lebanon, the emergence of Hizb Allah ("The Party of God," also spelled *Hizbullah* and *Hezbollah*) was a response to the occupation of the southern sector of the country by the Israeli Defense Forces. Israel invaded the region in June 1982 in order to rid Lebanon of the PLO and install a friendly government over Lebanon. After fleeing to southern Lebanon from Jordan in 1970, the PLO had created a state-within-a-state in which the authority of the government in Beirut carried little weight. The PLO was highly unpopular among the Shi'ites of southern Lebanon due to its heavy-handed tactics at checkpoints, its extortion of money from local residents, and its provocation of Israel, which resulted in devastating artillery barrages from across the Israeli border. Thus, when Israeli soldiers invaded in 1982, many Shi'ites responded with joy and gratitude for the expulsion of the PLO. When it became clear that Israel intended to install Maronites over them and to prolong the military occupation of the south, resistance broke out. Hizb Allah was established by Shi'ite ulama at the suggestion of Ayatollah Khomeini, who promised Iranian financial and technical assistance.

Hizb Allah declared a jihad whose original purpose was to drive the Israeli army out of Lebanon. It became notorious for its use of suicidal attacks (or, as it preferred to call them, "martyrdom operations") and seizure of hostages. The first suicidal attack was in November 1982, against the Israeli military headquarters in Tyre. When the American and French military established a presence in the Beirut area, they were perceived as props for the Maronite president, and thus became targets. Subsequent attacks in 1983 on the American embassy and on American and French military barracks bore the hallmarks of Hizb Allah, but the organization has denied responsibility. Hizb Allah also captured foreign hostages and hijacked airplanes throughout the decade; the goal was usually the release of prisoners. Hizb Allah's relentless attacks on the Israelis and their proxy militia, known as the South Lebanon Army, finally forced all traces of the Israeli military to evacuate southern Lebanon in 2000. The group's leaders justified their possession of a vast and sophisticated arsenal after the Israeli withdrawal by claiming that Israel remained in occupation of a small slice of Lebanese territory, although the UN and Syria agreed that the territory in question had belonged to Syria before Israel occupied it in 1967.

Hizb Allah's leaders were ulama, in accord with the Shi'ite tradition that mujtahids have access to spiritual insights not available to others. The ulama, in turn, acknowledged spiritual dependency upon Iran's spiritual guide as well as financial dependency upon its treasury: They recognized the spiritual supremacy of Khomeini and then of his successor, Ayatollah 'Ali al-Khamene'i. Like the Iranians, they rejected the political quietism and withdrawal that characterized Shi'ism for most of the past millennium. Although martyrdom continued to permeate their interpretation of the past, they no longer expected to be passive martyrs. They believed that God favors strength and boldness, and they were eager to confront enemies.

Like Iranian Shi'ites, Hizb Allah also rejected the notion that the state is illegitimate in the absence of the Hidden Imam. In fact, the absence of the Imam accentuates the need to create a state that guarantees a just social order. Accordingly, Hizb Allah used its armed might to defeat rival militias in the Shi'ite-majority regions of Lebanon (the southern and eastern regions) and became the de facto government there. It operated schools, courts, hospitals, and utilities independently of the Lebanese government. In 2005, it participated in Lebanese national elections, winning over ten percent of the seats in the Lebanese parliament.

Palestinian Territories

In Gaza, a spin-off from the local branch of the Muslim Brothers became a rival of the PLO for leadership of the Palestinian national movement. Gaza covers an area about twice the size of Washington, D.C., but it contains almost three times the population of the American capital. Its inhabitants are overwhelmingly the descendants of Palestinian refugees from the 1948 and 1967 wars, in contrast to the Palestinian inhabitants of the West Bank, most of whom have indigenous roots. Under Israeli occupation from 1967 to 2005, Gazans were not citizens of any country, and they could not leave the confines of Gaza unless they had a permit to work in Israel, in which case they had to return to Gaza by nightfall. They did not qualify for passports, and so they could not travel to foreign countries except by special dispensation from the Israeli government. Gaza did not have the rich links with Jewish history that the West Bank did, and so it attracted far fewer Jewish settlers and improvements to the infrastructure than did the West Bank. Gaza, which had been a fertile citrus-growing area during the Mandate, became one of the three or four most squalid places on earth under Egyptian (1948–1967) and Israeli (1967–2005) occupation.

The Muslim Brothers provided religious and charitable services in Gaza for decades. Then, in December 1987, the Palestinian uprising known as the Intifada broke out in Gaza and the West Bank. Members of the Muslim Brothers established a military arm of the organization known as Hamas. *Hamas* is a word that serves a dual role: It means "zeal" in Arabic and is also an acronym for an Arabic phrase that means "Islamic Resistance Movement." Hamas was founded just as the PLO began to edge toward a public recognition of the right of Israel to exist and to advocate the creation of a secular Palestinian state in Gaza and the West Bank. Hamas, by contrast, stated as its objective the creation of an Islamic state in all of the former Mandate of Palestine, a goal that would require the elimination of the Israeli government.

During the Intifada of 1987–1993, Hamas gained a reputation for violent attacks against Israeli civilian targets at a time when the PLO was exiled in Tunis. When the PLO negotiated the Oslo Accords with Israel in 1993, Hamas rejected the agreement because it entailed the recognition of Israel. In late winter 1994, Hamas began using suicidal attacks to inflict terror on Israel after an Israeli settler killed twenty-nine Palestinians at prayer in a mosque. Over the next decade, hundreds of bombers and Israelis died. Clashes also occurred between Hamas and the PLO following the latter's return to the West Bank and Gaza from exile in Tunis in July 1994.

The PLO's political achievement of having negotiated the Oslo Accords gained it a huge advantage in Palestinian popularity, but by 2000, the gap between it and Hamas closed. The PLO lost support when it turned out to be infested with corruption and incompetence, and its achievement of the Oslo Accords was diminished when the policies of a series of Israeli prime ministers either deliberately (Benjamin Netanyahu and Ariel Sharon) or inadvertently (Ehud Barak) had the effect of wrecking the agreement. When Intifada II broke out in September 2000, Prime Minister Sharon blamed the PLO and began systematically to destroy the political and security infrastructure that it had set up. The PLO's inability to defend itself allowed Hamas to fill the void, and it won the Palestinian elections of 2006. Its unexpected victory placed it in a quandary. Having always played a role of opposition—both to the secularism of the PLO and the existence of Israel—it was not clear how a jihadi organization would operate a government that would have to accommodate a large, secular Palestinian middle class and find a modus vivendi with Israel.

Afghanistan

World opinion was divided on the legitimacy of the use of violence by Muslim groups in the Philippines and the Middle East. In Afghanistan, the issue seemed more clear-cut: An outside power had invaded the country, and the indigenous population was defending itself. The "jihad" by Afghans won widespread support across the world, but the battleground there became the incubator for a new strand of militancy that appropriated the label of jihad for a totally new form of violence.

The mujahidun who responded to the Soviet invasion of Afghanistan were a diverse assortment of individuals. Among their ranks were members of Sufi orders, militant Islamic groups, and local tribes, all of whom fought for their own reasons. Some of the members of Islamic organizations had adopted the ideas of Mawdudi and Qutb. The works of both men had been translated into Dari and Pashtu by the early 1970s and became popular among university students.

The war was devastating for Afghanistan, which was one of the poorest countries in the world even before the invasion. In addition to the three million refugees who poured into Pakistan, another two million crossed the border into Iran, complicating that country's efforts to consolidate its recent revolution. Millions of land mines that were laid by both sides maimed and killed children almost every day. The destruction of the central government allowed tribal warlords to reemerge as regional powers.

The conflict attracted the interest of foreign countries. Some officials in the United States relished the opportunity for the Soviets to experience their own "Vietnam." In cooperation with Saudi Arabia and Pakistan, the United States began aiding Afghan resistance groups. Members of Saudi Arabia's ruling family and wealthy individuals outside the government saw the war as an opportunity to strike against Soviet influence and to expand Wahhabi influence into South Asia. During the early 1980s, the United States provided an average of $600 million of aid per year, and the Arab Gulf states—primarily Saudi Arabia—matched that amount.

For Pakistan's Zia ul-Haq, the timing of the Soviet invasion was fortuitous. His execution of former president Bhutto in March 1979 had made him a pariah in Europe and the United States, but within a year he had become the indispensable channel for most of the aid that flowed into Afghanistan. The United States was forced to work closely with him, and a sizable percentage of the aid remained in Pakistan by virtue of creative bookkeeping techniques.

Pakistan was also fixated upon the conflict due to the huge numbers of Pashtun refugees from Afghanistan who poured across the border into Pakistan. This was not only a major strain on Pakistan's humanitarian aid resources; it also threatened to metastasize the cancer called the Durand Line. In Chapter 9, we saw that the British unilaterally fixed this line in 1893 to mark the boundary between Afghanistan and India. It divided the huge Pashtun population, leaving millions of Pashtuns on both sides of the border. Over the decades, occasional demands were made to unite the Pashtun population into a "Pashtunistan." Between 1953 and 1963, Muhammad Da'ud Khan had made the creation of Pashtunistan a major focus of his foreign policy when he served as Afghanistan's prime minister. Like other Afghans, he intended for it to become a province of Afghanistan. Pakistan, of course, rejected the notion of yielding a large chunk of its territory to its neighbor. A high level of tension led to outbreaks of violence and the closing of the border between the two countries for years at a time.

With millions of Afghan Pashtuns settling in refugee camps in the Pashtun-majority region of Pakistan after 1979, Zia had to become involved in the conflict in order to retain control over his own territory. Pakistani activity took two major forms: aid to jihad groups and policies directed toward the refugee camps. Aid to jihad groups was facilitated by channels that already existed. During the 1970s, during Da'ud's presidency, Pakistan had funneled aid to Islamist groups in order to distract Da'ud from his continuing interest in the Pashtunistan project. Under the new circumstances of Soviet occupation, Pakistan's increasingly Islamized intelligence services funneled the majority of American and Saudi military aid—which was intended for resistance fighters in general—to Islamist groups rather than to secular warlords.

Within the Pakistan refugee camps, the scope of the humanitarian crisis was mind-boggling. Food, shelter, clothing, and sanitation services had to be provided on a daily basis for millions of people. As we have seen, Zia and wealthy families from Saudi Arabia also realized the opportunity to provide madrasa educations to a new audience. The rapid expansion of the madrasa system in Pakistan had fateful consequences. Refugee families gratefully accepted the opportunity to send their sons off to boarding schools where they could obtain a religious education. Once at school, the Pashtun boys mixed with many other ethnic groups and had little contact with their families. The school became their "family," and they absorbed its values and norms rather than those of their blood relatives. Living in the disembodied world of the madrasa, the *taliban* ("students") knew almost nothing of how governments worked or of the dynamics of tribal loyalties. They were easily persuaded by their poorly educated instructors that the doctrines and fatwas that they heard in school could—and should—be implemented within society at large. The Deobandis had not been associated with violence before, but the graduates of the Deoband-affiliated schools in Pakistan during this period became increasingly militant. In addition to crossing the border to fight the Soviets, they formed the core of the militants who slipped into Kashmir to fight the Indian administration there.

By 1985, the conflict in Afghanistan had become a cause célèbre for Muslims across the world. Many sent aid as a humanitarian issue for fellow Muslims, but increasing numbers of volunteers came to fight. At least 8000—and perhaps as many as 25,000—such volunteers entered the country. Most of them saw the conflict in terms of the duty of jihad. Fighters came from many countries, but volunteers from the Arab countries formed the single biggest ethnic group.

In 1987, the Soviet government began trying to find a way to withdraw its army from Afghanistan. It began negotiations with the Americans and Pakistanis, and it built up the army of the communist-led government in Kabul in order to equip it for the post-Soviet period. By the end of 1989, Soviet troops had left the country, and the seven major groups of resistance fighters began trying to overthrow the communist government. The Kabul government survived much longer than observers had predicted, and it was not overthrown until 1992. When it fell, many people assumed that Afghanistan's agonies were over, and that the time for rebuilding was at hand. More than one million of the country's citizens had been killed, five million were refugees in surrounding countries, the cities lay in ruins, and the farms and grazing lands were littered with explosives.

Rather than bringing an end to more than a decade of suffering, however, the capture of Kabul merely began yet another chapter of a vicious war. Once the capital had been taken, the various groups of armed Afghan units turned on each other in order to assert their dominance. Previously, the enemy had been communists, the majority of whom wore Soviet uniforms. Now it was fellow Muslims. Security totally collapsed. The United States government, faced with a myriad of issues in the post–Cold War world, withdrew its diplomatic and intelligence personnel from the country and abandoned it to its fate. Most foreign Muslim fighters also left Afghanistan to carry the jihad against the corrupt and repressive regimes of their own countries.

As Afghanistan collapsed into a maelstrom of warfare, banditry, extortion, and rape, a group of Pashtuns in south-central Afghanistan began to punish some of the worst gangs in the area around Qandahar. As their reputation as a constructive force grew in late 1994, people in surrounding areas called upon them for protection against lawless forces. Soon hundreds—and then thousands—of *taliban* from the madrasas in the Pakistani refugee camps enlisted in their militia. They proudly adopted the name Taliban for their movement, and they became a beacon of hope for the end to the conflict in the country. In September 1995, the Taliban captured Herat, and in September 1996, after a long and bloody siege, they captured Kabul. Soon they controlled all of Afghanistan except for small sectors in the north-central and northeastern parts of the country.

Many of the Afghans who had welcomed the Taliban's victories with relief and gratitude were soon to be bitterly disappointed. The Taliban were pious, but they were remarkably ignorant, bigoted, and cruel. They were unlike any of the other Islamist groups, whose members were typically educated. The Taliban's madrasa "education" proved to be a mockery, for their members knew little about the Qur'an or the history of Islamic thought, and they confused the Shari'a with Pashtun tribal code. The overwhelming majority of the Taliban came from rural, poverty-stricken backgrounds or from the all-male boarding schools of the refugee camps, and their attitudes toward Shi'ites, women, modern technology, and entertainment were shaped by that reality. They closed all girls' schools, discouraged women from appearing in public (even when wearing the *burqa,* or face veil), and prohibited Afghans from watching television, listening to radio, playing music or chess, flying kites, and playing soccer. Their hatred of Shi'ism provoked them to massacre thousands of Shi'ites of the Hazara ethnic group in central Afghanistan.

The Balkans

Beginning in 1992, some of the jihadis who had gone to Afghanistan to defend Muslims against the Soviet invasion traveled to the Balkan Peninsula to defend Muslims from Serbs. This was the region that the Ottomans had called Rumelia, and it was the heart of the Ottoman Empire for several centuries. Despite the anti-Ottoman nationalist movements and secessions that occurred prior to World War I, several million Muslims still lived in the Balkans. The heaviest concentrations today are in Albania (2.5 million Muslims, seventy percent of the country's population), Bosnia–Herzegovina (1.8 million, forty percent of the population), Serbia (1.5 million, sixteen percent of the population), Bulgaria (0.9 million, twelve percent of the population), and Macedonia (0.5 million, twenty-five percent of the population). Ethnic tensions in the area are occasionally the result of simple bigotry—the expulsion of 600,000 Bulgarian Muslims by their communist government during the four decades following World War II is an example—but usually they are the result of complex and deep-seated factors that are not always obvious even to the participants, much less to outsiders. The horrors that were committed during the collapse of Yugoslavia fall into the latter category.

The creation of Yugoslavia after World War I was the result of a relentless campaign on the part of Slavic nationalists, particularly in Serbia, for a South Slav nation–state. The new country proved to be an unstable union. As we saw in Chapter 3, the Slovenes, Croats, Serbs, and Bosniaks were all South Slavs who migrated into the region over one thousand years ago, but they developed cultural differences thereafter: The Slovenes and Croats, like their Austrian overlords, adhered to the Catholic faith and used the Latin alphabet; the Serbs were proudly Orthodox and used the Cyrillic alphabet; and most of the Bosniaks, who were caught between these two rival cultural zones, adopted Islam after the Ottoman conquest. During World War II, the cultural antagonisms spilled over during the Axis occupation. Nationalist and cultural rivalries resulted in the deaths of hundreds of thousands of people.

Under the communist rule of Josip Tito (1945–1980), Yugoslavs were forced to forgo their ethnic identities in favor of an official "proletarian" one. When Tito died in 1980, however, no one leader could command the respect that he had. With economic conditions deteriorating in the late 1980s, nationalist aspirations once again filled the air. In 1991, Slovenia and Croatia seceded from Yugoslavia, provoking a war with the latter, but their success was ensured when the European Community intervened in December 1991. When that happened, Bosnia–Herzegovina and Macedonia announced their independence, as well. About forty percent of Bosnia–Herzegovina's population was Serb, and the province was adjacent to the Serb heartland centered around Belgrade. The Yugoslav president, Slobodan Miloševic, a Serbian nationalist, was determined not to allow the province to secede. He engineered a major military expedition to retain it, and, according to the charges that were later filed against him at a United Nations war crimes tribunal, he approved numerous massacres of Bosnian Muslims at the hands of paramilitary squads. During the war, which lasted from 1992 until 1995, an estimated 100,000 civilians were murdered—the vast majority of whom were Muslims—and 1.8 million people—of all ethnic groups—lost their homes.

The numerous massacres and mass rapes that occurred in Bosnia–Herzegovina provoked horror all over the world, but their effect was most pronounced in the Muslim world. The perpetrators of the killings and rapes of Muslims were Christians; the results of the atrocities were televised globally; and yet the historically Christian nations of Europe and the United States did not intervene until the United States sent troops in late summer 1995. To many Muslims, the conflict appeared to be a clear-cut case of a religious war whose goal was to destroy the Muslim community in the region. As early as the summer of 1992, the Bosnian conflict had become a major issue among Muslim university students throughout the world, and several hundred Muslim volunteers from various countries slipped into the country to fight as jihadis. Analysts of the conflict agree that their impact was minimal, in part because their radicalism and aggressiveness alienated many of the very people whom they had come to help. Their military contribution was not as important as their symbolic presence was to Muslims observing the conflict from afar.

The Caucasus

During the second half of the Bosnian conflict, yet another vicious war began that Muslims interpreted as a Christian attack on Islam. Beginning in 1994, Chechnya experienced the horrors of a war that evoked accounts of the scorched-earth policy of the Russian conquest of the region in the mid-nineteenth century. Its roots lay in an attempted coup against Soviet premier Mikhail Gorbachev in late August 1991. The coup was suppressed in three days, but the event provided Boris Yeltsin, the president of the Russian Republic, the opportunity to press for the dissolution of the Soviet Union and the independence of its constituent republics. Over the next few months, the leaders of the fifteen Soviet republics engaged in tumultuous debate regarding the proposal. Finally, the advocates of dissolution won, and on December 25 of that year, Gorbachev's resignation officially terminated the Union of Soviet Socialist Republics.

Meanwhile, in Chechnya, which was an Autonomous Republic and therefore officially subject to the Russian Republic, a powerful separatist movement was growing. Its leaders declared independence six weeks before the dissolution of the Soviet Union. Russia did not accept the action, but Chechnya proceeded as though it were an independent state. In 1994, Yeltsin sent troops into Chechnya to reassert Russian authority. A brutal war broke out that destroyed most of Grozny, the Chechnyan capital, a city of 400,000 people. The Russians were unable to suppress the nationalists, and they withdrew in humiliation in 1996.

The departure of the Russian army did not bring peace to Chechnya. Various indigenous factions fought each other for dominance, causing anarchic conditions. In addition, jihadis from several countries had poured in during the Russian occupation and established bases in the mountains. Although they brought welcome military manpower and financial aid, they were also critical of local Islamic practice. Violent altercations broke out between them and local Sufi groups. Then, in 1999, Russia invaded again, determined to complete the task that it had begun in 1994. As brutal as the first war had been, the so-called Second Chechnyan War was even more pitiless. Grozny was utterly destroyed, and each side inflicted massacres on the other. Because Chechnya was dangerous for news teams to enter, few outside Chechnya could see the atrocities that the Russians inflicted—even the scale of the destruction in Grozny was not widely reported in the news media of the West. When Chechen fighters, on the other hand, committed atrocities—most notably a hostage-taking attempt in a Moscow auditorium and the murder of 331 people at a school in Beslan, North Ossetia—they were publicized around the globe. The large Russian army managed to establish bases around the country, but resistance continued, and jihadi versions of Islam thrived on the festering conflict.

Global Jihad

Because of the spectacular jihadi attacks that began in the 1990s against Western targets, it is now common among non-Muslims everywhere to associate the term *Islamist* or *Islamic fundamentalist* with someone who wishes to harm non-Muslims. As we have seen, however, political Islamists have sought to change their society by peaceful and legal means, and jihadis—whether Islamists or members of national liberation movements—rarely went outside their own societies in search of targets. The phenomenon of global jihad that has spawned attacks in the United States and Western Europe is a byproduct of the war in Afghanistan and the failure of jihadi Islamists.

The war in Afghanistan produced yet another theoretician of jihad, 'Abd Allah 'Azzam (1941–1989), a Palestinian. Between 1959 and 1966, 'Azzam studied the religious sciences in Damascus, where he joined the Muslim Brothers. After the June War of 1967, he joined the PLO and fought in several skirmishes, but he became disillusioned with the secular nationalism of the PLO and dreamed of helping to establish a Pan-Islamic nation. He studied at al-Azhar and then taught at various Islamic institutions in Jordan and Saudi Arabia. When the Soviet Union invaded Afghanistan in 1979, he moved to Pakistan. He soon settled in Peshawar, on the Pakistan–Afghanistan border, where he established the Service Bureau, a center for training and supplying jihadis. He also engaged in recruiting missions throughout the Muslim world and wrote tracts on the necessity of jihad.

'Azzam's contribution to the jihad movement was an elaboration of the thesis of 'Abd al-Salam Faraj. 'Azzam argued that participation in the Afghan jihad was an individual duty for Muslims everywhere. He argued that, once Afghanistan was freed, the obligation to participate in jihad continued until all lands that were once under Muslim rule had been reconquered. These included not only Palestine and Central Asia, but also Andalus and the Philippines. Like Faraj, he insisted that participation in jihad is the decisive factor for determining whether a person is a genuine Muslim or an infidel. 'Azzam's most distinctive contribution to the theory of jihad was his glorification of martyrdom. He argued that the ink of scholars and the blood of martyrs were the twin factors that would inspire Muslims to engage in God's work. The Arabs in Afghanistan who were inspired by him became noted for their habit of weeping after a comrade had been killed in battle—not because of the loss of their friend, but because they, themselves, had not experienced the "joy" of martyrdom, as well. The Afghans, who were fighting for their freedom, considered such behavior bizarre.

An admirer of 'Azzam was Usama bin Laden. Bin Laden's Yemeni father had emigrated to Saudi Arabia and subsequently became a multimillionaire by virtue of his construction company, which won many of the contracts of the Saudi royal family. The son went to college, but dropped out and worked for his father. Not long thereafter, in 1980, Bin Laden joined the Afghan resistance against the Soviet Union. He had already met 'Azzam at King 'Abd al-'Aziz University in Saudi Arabia, when he was a student and 'Azzam was a professor. In Peshawar, Bin Laden helped 'Azzam build his Service Bureau, and the two men worked together on numerous projects. Bin Laden also met Zayman al-Zawahiri in Peshawar in 1986, and they remained in communication with each other thereafter. Bin Laden had some combat experience in Afghanistan, but his most important roles were training and disciplining impulsive young jihadis, supplying large sums of money to the jihad, and exploiting his own extensive contacts in Saudi Arabia to facilitate further aid.

After the Soviets withdrew from Afghanistan, some of the foreign volunteers remained to fight against the communist-led government in Kabul, but as the Afghans became more factionalized during the conflict, most of the foreigners slowly drifted away. Many sought venues for jihad in other countries. They had various motives for doing so: Some agreed with 'Azzam regarding the obligation of a continuous jihad; others could not go home due to their prior reputation as security threats; still others found the life of the jihadi to be a glorious adventure. Whatever their motivation, many veterans of the Afghan conflict wound up in conflicts as far-flung as Bosnia, Chechnya, and Kashmir.

Participation in the multinational force of Muslims in Afghanistan had been an inspirational and transforming experience for most of the fighters, but nobody was more affected than Bin Laden. His combination of wealth and international contacts led him to act upon the notion of Faraj and 'Azzam of conducting a global jihad. Just as those two men's ideas were vague and utopian, Bin Laden began with the simple notion that he could provide both financial support and military training camps for Muslims anywhere in the world to conduct jihad against corrupt governments. His inchoate ideas began to take more concrete form in late summer of 1990, when Saddam Husayn invaded and annexed Kuwait.

Saddam Husayn was a hated and despised figure among Islamists due to his reputation as an utterly irreligious figure who flaunted his secularism and his contempt for religion. In the wake of the invasion, Bin Laden quickly offered a formal proposal to Saudi Arabia's King Fahd to organize 12,000 of the jihadis who had fought in Afghanistan to protect the kingdom from any possible threat from Iraq's forces in Kuwait. Bin Laden expected the offer to be accepted; when the Saudi rulers rebuffed him in favor of the American-led coalition, he was humiliated as well as indignant. His jihadi force had been refused in favor of infidels, whose armies would defile the land containing the holy cities of Mecca and Medina.

The American presence in Saudi Arabia caused a permanent rift between Bin Laden and the Saudi government, but more important, it led Bin Laden to narrow the focus of his hostility on the United States. After spending the period 1992–1996 in Sudan, he returned to Afghanistan, which by 1996 was coming under the control of the Taliban. The Taliban, who were focused on establishing an Islamic state in Afghanistan and were uninterested in the outside world, nevertheless admired Bin Laden for having sacrificed his comfortable and carefree life to participate in the jihad against the Soviets. They agreed to allow him to continue to operate training camps. Soon after his arrival, he issued a public declaration of jihad on the United States, calling upon all Muslims to join him in driving the Americans out of the Gulf region.

In public statements that he began issuing in the mid-1990s, Bin Laden made clear his belief that the continuing American military presence in the Gulf was the prelude to an attempt by a Jewish cabal to exploit the oil wealth of the region. He believed that Jews dominated the American government, and he envisioned that this group, in coordination with Israel, was determined to impoverish the Muslim world and to destroy Islam. He became impatient with jihadi Islamists who were trying to overthrow their governments, and he argued that they should realize that their efforts to that point had been fruitless as well as excessively costly in terms of human lives and financial resources. The priority should be to attack the United States in the region. Such an approach required far fewer assets and would cause the removal of American support for corrupt regimes, making it easier to overthrow them later. By 1998, Bin Laden had convinced Ayman al-Zawahiri of the Egyptian Islamic Jihad to abandon his efforts to overthrow the Egyptian government and join his group, al-Qa'ida ("the base"), in the war against the United States.

Al-Zawahiri's decision triggered an impassioned debate among jihadi Islamists. Many of them were vehemently opposed to the notion of attacking American targets, either in the Muslim countries or anywhere else in the world, on two grounds. First, they argued that the Qur'an specifies attacks on the "near" enemy before attacks on the "far" enemy. Second, and no doubt more important for many of the jihadis, was the concern that American security and intelligence forces would start pursuing them. At the time, many jihadis were able to gain asylum in several European countries, and they did not want to lose that privilege due to American pressure. Many members of Egyptian Islamic Jihad refused to recognize the actions of al-Zawahiri, and members of other jihadi Islamist organizations also condemned the action. Later in 1998, the fears of the jihadi Islamists were confirmed when al-Qa'ida attacked American embassies in Tanzania and Kenya. European countries began deporting or arresting jihadis of various types. The attacks by al-Qa'ida continued, although many Americans and Europeans did not realize what a serious threat the organization posed until the attacks on New York and Washington on September 11, 2001.

Al-Qa'ida's increasing provocation of the United States sharpened the debate among Islamists regarding the wisdom of the policy. Increasingly on the defensive, al-Zawahiri wrote a book to explain his position. It was found in manuscript form in a cave in Afghanistan after the American defeat of the Taliban in November 2001. In *Knights Under the Prophet's Banner,* al-Zawahiri insists that the secular regimes of the Muslim world were still his primary targets, but he admits that Egyptian Islamic Jihad and al-Jama'at al-Islamiya did not win the support of a sufficiently large mass of the Muslim public to allow them to succeed. Muslim public opinion was ambivalent about attacking the "near enemy" in the form of Muslim regimes, but it had frequently rallied against external enemies such as imperialism and Zionism. Thus, al-Qa'ida's tactic was to create an "external enemy" against which the Muslim public would mobilize. By provoking the United States to attack Muslim targets in retaliation for bombings of American facilities, the Muslim public would see that fellow Muslims were under attack by the United States and that jihadis were in the vanguard of defending them against the infidels. Public opinion would rally around the call to jihad against the United States and its ally Israel. With the jihadi mind-set established, leaders could then redirect it against the infidel regimes of the Muslim world. Thus, al-Zawahiri explains that the attacks on the United States were primarily attempts to provoke American military assaults on Muslim territory in the expectation that such warfare would create mass support for jihadi rebellions against Muslim governments.

At the beginning of the twenty-first century, a small but efficient movement had emerged within Islam that was an outgrowth of Mawdudi's politicization of Islam and Qutb's insistence that infidel governments would have to be removed by force. In spite of its intellectual debt to these two men, it developed original doctrines of jihad and martyrdom in order to accomplish its purposes. By making the United States and its allies its primary targets, it capitalized on the feelings of anger, humiliation, and failure that were widespread throughout the Muslim world. After the collapse of the Soviet Union, the United States enjoyed not having to share the status of superpower with another country; the disadvantage was that it could no longer compare itself favorably with its "evil twin." Free-floating resentment fastened on to it, and conspiracy theorists found it to be the natural actor in all calamities. Its inability to distinguish between support for the existence of Israel, on the one hand, and support for Israeli territorial expansion at the expense of Palestinians, on the other; its heavy-handed advocacy of free-trade policies during the 1990s; and its flawed policies toward Iraq after 1991 were easily exploited by clever jihadi leaders.

Twenty-First-Century Challenges and Opportunities

During the opening years of the twenty-first century, Muslims across the world felt that they were in the grip of a crisis that struck at the very heart of their identity. In some cases, their physical survival itself was at stake; in most cases, the problem was how to determine an appropriately Islamic response to a myriad of formidable economic, political, and ethical problems. How these issues were resolved would determine not only the physical welfare and political rights of the people living in particular societies, but also the future content of Islam itself.

A Siege Mentality

One of the most problematic features of the global concern over religious violence is a stark difference in the perspectives of Muslims and non-Muslims regarding the cause of much of the violence. Many Muslims have the vague, but deep-seated, conviction that Islam is under assault by powerful forces. They are convinced that their secular Muslim rulers and Western business interests alike consider Islam to be the major obstacle in the way of their attempts to dominate political and economic affairs in Muslim-majority countries. They believe that a "war against Islam" explains much of the violence in the world over the past few years: the interminable Palestine conflict, the Soviet invasion of Afghanistan, the utter destruction of much of Chechnya by Russian forces, the genocide in Bosnia, attacks on mosques by Hindu extremists in India, Chinese attempts to de-Islamize Xinjiang, two recent American wars against Iraq, and the Christian settlement of Moro lands in Mindanao.

This interpretation of recent world events is incomprehensible to many non-Muslims in the West. In the world view of the latter, an expansionist, violence-prone "Islam" is the aggressor in each of the conflicts, and Muslims have no one to blame but themselves for the casualties. It is difficult for most non-Muslims in highly developed countries to realize why a sense of humiliation, helplessness, and frustration pervades much of the Muslim world. In order to understand the Muslim sense of siege, it is useful to remind ourselves that a small but vocal sector of the American evangelical Christian population also proclaims its conviction that its religion is under assault by hostile forces. The sense that Christian values were under siege was a major stimulus for the emergence of the American Christian fundamentalist movement during the half-century from 1870 to 1920. It was also a component of the rise of the so-called Christian Right in the 1970s, when supporters were mobilized by warning cries that Christianity was under attack. By the first decade of the twenty-first century, there was even a heated debate regarding whether major corporations and media outlets had begun to wage a "war on Christmas."

American Christians use the terms *attack* and *war* in a metaphorical sense—they do not think that they are in danger of being shot for their religion—but they are not speaking hyperbolically. They interpret the secularization of society as a conscious plot by vague but real enemies ("Hollywood," "liberals," etc.) to undermine religious values. Historical development, in their view, is the result of a cosmic contest between good and evil, not a natural process. Thus, as an example, "taking God out of the public schools" expresses the conviction that the imposition of restrictions on sectarian religious practice in public schools is the result of a deliberate policy to destroy religion. It is a victory by the forces of darkness, rather than a logical development within a nonsectarian constitutional system when a formerly homogeneous society becomes increasingly pluralistic.

The sense that one's religious heritage is under siege has been a common theme of the global religious revival that began in the 1970s. It is prominent in Jewish and Hindu revival movements as well as among fundamentalist Christians. Pious individuals in the predominantly Muslim world feel the impact of secularization even more than the members of most other religious communities do, as a result of their conviction that God provided the Shari'a to offer guidance in every facet of individual and social life. The striking difference between the siege mentality of Muslims and that of American evangelicals is the context of their respective struggles to reverse the process of the desacralization of society. American evangelicals act with the tacit knowledge that they live in the most powerful nation on earth, and they assume that they can transform their society by employing an electoral process to vote into office like-minded believers. Muslims, by contrast, are acutely aware of the deaths of hundreds of thousands of fellow believers by non-Muslims. The economies of Muslim-majority countries are mere tributaries of more powerful ones, and the popular cultures of their societies absorb Western influences that are offensive to religious sensitivities. When citizens of Muslim-majority countries attempt to reform their own societies, they often encounter a closed political process, and those who are courageous enough to try to breach the barriers can be jailed or even killed.

The accumulation of defeats has led to a widespread sense of humiliation in the Muslim community. The themes of individual and collective humiliation appear repeatedly in the literature of the jihadi movements. Engaging in jihad is a way to overcome individual humiliation and regain dignity, for it aligns the fighter on the side of God in the war against the enemies of Islam. Islamists of all stripes expect the creation of an Islamic state to overcome collective humiliation, for it will bring God's blessing upon the country as a whole, enabling it to exert power and influence in the world at large.

Many jihadis aspire to create a global caliphate, transcending the nation-state. This, too, is a reflection of a desire to overcome weakness: When Muslim states were among the most powerful on earth—the era of the Ottoman, Mughal, and Safavid empires—individuals did not theorize about jihad, nor did they dream of a worldwide caliphate. The theme of a caliphate was resurrected after centuries of disuse only in the late nineteenth century, when countries were falling into the clutches of imperialists and desperate Muslims placed their hope in the power of the Ottoman Empire. After a period of dormancy that lasted several decades, it reemerged again in response to the ineffectiveness of Muslim states in global affairs.

A Crisis of Authority

A perceived state of siege is normally addressed by rallying around a leader whose role is to organize resistance to the threat to the community. Much of the turmoil within the Muslim world in the twenty-first century derives from a crisis of authority that afflicts both the political and religious spheres. The crisis of political authority is one that we have been tracing since the decolonization process. The crisis of religious authority is an outgrowth of developments that have occurred since the eighteenth century. Because that theme was extended over several chapters, it is useful to review it.

Throughout the bulk of Sunni Islamic history, Muslims were confident that they had access to religious truth by virtue of chains of transmission that linked them with the Prophet. Sufi shaykhs believed that they could trace their spiritual lineage through a line of teachers who had faithfully passed down the Prophet's teachings on spiritual exercises. Scholars who sought to provide guidelines for behavior assumed that pious men and women in each generation had passed on to the next generation the knowledge of doctrines, rituals, and deportment as the Prophet taught and modeled them. Apart from the Qur'an itself, the Hadith were the first link in this chain. Their authenticity was considered to be validated by the chain of names of pious men and women who were said to have transmitted the accounts through the years. Scholars analyzed these documents and wrote commentaries on them, using rational methods that had been approved by a consensus of the scholars. Later generations of scholars studied the commentaries and added their own perspectives. After the twelfth century, the study of these scholarly works, sometimes highly philosophical in nature, typically took place in a madrasa.

By the seventeenth century, Sufis still maintained a sharp consciousness of their links with the Prophet, but the emerging cluster of religious reformers found it increasingly difficult to see how the work of scholars reflected concerns of the generation of the Prophet. The *ijaza,* or document by which an established scholar certified that a student had mastered specific texts, was the instrument devised to provide the desired chain of transmission. Reformers, however, realized that the texts that students mastered were several layers of analysis removed from the Qur'an and Hadith themselves: Some of them were commentaries on commentaries.

What had happened was the natural development of an evolving educational system. A student who aspired to become a member of the ulama spent many years at a madrasa. During the most advanced stages of study, the student spent most of his time mastering the commentaries on the Qur'an and Hadith rather than studying the primary sources themselves. Virtuosity of reasoning and argumentation were more highly prized than spiritual sensitivity or profundity of interpretation of the scriptures. The ulama were not always spiritual men, but they had quick, supple minds that qualified them for positions of great responsibility in government, where they could quickly master the technical details of office. The system had parallels with that of higher education in contemporary Western Europe, which produced men like Richelieu, Mazarin, and Wolsey. All were cardinals in the Church, but no one doubted their ability or qualifications to wield enormous temporal power.

By the eighteenth century, a handful of Sunni ulama were criticizing the pedagogical techniques of the madrasa. They argued for the need to place primacy on the study of the Qur'an and Hadith, and they insisted on the right to exercise ijtihad rather than to practice taqlid. They also encouraged all literate believers, not just scholars, to join them in this new venture. The reformers' encouragement of literate Muslims to study the Qur'an and Hadith for themselves was part of the same impulse that inspired their Shi'ite contemporaries, the Akhbaris. The Akhbaris and the Sunni advocates of ijtihad shared many impulses, and they both worked furiously in the eighteenth century to accomplish their goal. Whereas the former lost to their rivals, the Usulis, the cause of the Sunni reformers made incremental gains against determined conservative opposition for more than a century and a half.

The pioneers of the Sunni "back to the sources" movement, notably India's Shah Wali Allah, were men who had undergone years of rigorous training in grammar, logic, jurisprudence, and the critical reading of conflicting arguments. They were sensitized to detect nuances, inconsistencies, and implications. They assumed that their new approach, although open to all, would be overseen by men who shared their educational background, ensuring that the interpretation of the Qur'an and Hadith would be grounded in sober scholarship and an awareness of the pitfalls of the unlimited use of the imagination. The question of who had the authority to determine what would be a valid interpretation of the Qur'an and Hadith did not arise with them. Sunni Islam has never had a central religious authority that can be compared to a rabbinical council, a presbytery, or the papacy. The ulama, operating on the basis of the consensus of their peers, developed the Shari'a and the institutions for the reproduction of knowledge, including the madrasa. The eighteenth-century reformers were themselves members of the ulama who reacted against a system that had grown formulaic and largely irrelevant to the needs of daily life.

The outcome of the struggle between the two Sunni camps took place much later than that of the Shi'ites, and it was decisively influenced by outside forces. The first generation of Sunni reformers fully expected that the ulama would guide the practice of ijtihad, but they could not have anticipated that the influence of the ulama would rapidly decline. The introduction of secular schools in the nineteenth century had a devastating impact on the class of religious scholars, because the graduates of the new schools were favored in the competition for employment in government and business. As the scope of the Shari'a was circumscribed by modernizing governments and imperial regimes, even opportunities to serve as qadis were reduced. The rigorous course of study in madrasas, which could last for two decades, became less attractive to all but those individuals who were committed to a life within a specifically religious institution.

By the dawn of the twentieth century, reformers such as Muhammad 'Abduh were proposing curricular changes in the great madrasas such as al-Azhar in Cairo, but the schools' leaders refused to make more than token changes. As a result, their students were not exposed to the subjects taught in the private and public modern schools. The narrowly trained ulama increasingly lost touch with the world view and spiritual needs of members of the modern middle class, who were products of the modern schools.

Bereft of meaningful religious guidance, members of the new middle class began to study the Qur'an and Hadith on their own. With no formal training in principles of exegesis, they interpreted the Qur'an and Hadith within the framework of their own education and social setting. Some were successful in devising interpretations of Islam that provided structure and meaning to the lives of people for whom the events of the twentieth century had brought confusion and anxiety. By the middle decade of the twentieth century, figures such as Mawdudi (a journalist) and Qutb (a writer) were preparing their own commentaries on the Qur'an. During the last quarter of the century, Faraj (an electrician) was writing a manual on jihad; al-Zawahiri (a physician) was assuring his followers that they had a God-given obligation to overthrow their government; and Bin Laden, who studied business administration before dropping out of college and returning to his father's construction company, was issuing fatwas, a function that was traditionally the prerogative of the most accomplished religious scholar in society.

The democratization of ijtihad was a development that Shah Wali Allah and the other pioneer advocates of ijtihad could never have imagined and would never have sanctioned. It has had several important consequences, two of which are worth stressing. The first is that charismatic leaders who do not have a grounding in systematic principles of scriptural interpretation are free to manipulate scripture in any way that they choose. The capricious use of scripture has ominous implications today because of the fact that many of the new movements within the global religious revival—whether Islamic, Christian, Jewish, or Hindu—consider themselves to be at war with the forces of darkness on behalf of God. Their adherents choose to emphasize scriptures that glorify war and apocalyptic imagery. David Koresh's Branch Davidian group was a notorious Christian example. The new interpretations of jihad that sanction mass murder of bystanders in the cause of toppling unrighteous governments have a remarkable parallel in the Christian Identity movement, with which both Timothy McVeigh and Eric Rudolph were associated. The jihadi movements are as different from the Islam of Muhammd 'Abduh as the Christian Identity movement is from the Christianity of Billy Graham.

Another consequence of the unrestricted practice of ijtihad is the advent of an era that will match any in Islamic history for its fateful consequences. Islam is being reconstituted as profoundly as Western Christianity was during the Protestant Reformation. Pundits who assert that the solution for the turmoil in the Muslim world today would be an Islamic Reformation are missing the point: The turmoil is a *result* of an Islamic Reformation that has already begun. The assertion of the right to interpret the Qur'an and Hadith is accompanied by a demotion of Islamic tradition to a secondary source of religious authority. The parallels with the movement that Luther initiated are remarkably close. Both Reformations began in the context of profound anxiety caused by social, political, and economic uncertainties. Luther insisted on the uniqueness of the Bible's authority and a demotion of Christian tradition to a secondary status as a source of religious authority.

Like Luther, the advocates of ijtihad have never faced up to the consequences of encouraging ordinary believers to engage in scriptural interpretation. Luther assumed that all critics of the Catholic Church would join his movement. He accused Protestants who disagreed with him of doing so because of bad faith rather than because of genuine disagreements over the meaning of biblical passages. Also worth noting is the fact that the Protestant Reformation triggered a period of religious violence among Christians that lasted for two centuries until the secular forces of the Enlightenment ushered in the age of religious toleration that the West takes for granted today. As we observe the turmoil within Islam today, we should keep in mind the fact that, although both Protestants and Catholics seized upon certain scriptural passages to justify acts of violence during the Protestant Reformation, historians do not conclude that Christianity is essentially a violent religion. In Islam, the wide range of interpretation of the scripture enables progressive reformers and jihadis alike to find support for their movements in the Qur'an, just as Anabaptists and Anglicans used a wide range of biblical passages to justify their actions and doctrines centuries ago.

Baitul Futuh Mosque

Economic and Social Issues

Political and religious crises in the Muslim world are compounded by economic ones. Only seven Muslim countries have a higher gross national income (GNI) per capita than the world average: the six Gulf countries of Bahrain, Kuwait, Oman, Qatar, Saudi Arabia, and the United Arab Emirates—all of which depend heavily on revenue from petroleum—and Malaysia, whose economy is largely in the hands of non-Muslim Chinese. The majority of Muslims live in grinding poverty. One way of comprehending the meaning of that bald fact is to compare the GNI per capita of four countries that contain almost half of the world's Muslims with the GNI per capita of Mexico ($10,000), which is roughly the world average. Mexico's GNI per capita is three times that of either India or Indonesia, four times that of Pakistan, and five times that of Bangladesh.[2]

The Gulf states have been fortunate to possess petroleum deposits, but economists who specialize in economic development argue that the countries without petroleum reserves cannot avoid responsibility for their backwardness. Economic growth depends on a country's policies, not its natural resources. Countries such as the Netherlands, Israel, Singapore, Hong Kong, Taiwan, Japan, and South Korea have developed their human resources to such a degree that their lack of natural resources is not a handicap. Although some Muslim countries have made impressive gains in developing their human resources, none are close to matching the East Asian countries. As a result, they have little to export. A 1995 study by the World Bank made the point with stunning clarity with regard to the Muslim countries that stretch from Morocco to Iran, inclusive. The non-oil exports of that entire region of 260 million people were less than Finland's, with five million people.[3]

In most Muslim countries, economic development faces numerous obstacles. State-protected monopolies are widespread, and since they distribute much of their profit to government officials, the officials have no incentive to break them up. Corruption is rife due to low salaries for bureaucrats; the court system is rarely independent of the executive; and the process of obtaining permits and licenses requires weeks or months. Training in science and mathematics is at a low level, and in the countries where the new type of madrasa has become entrenched, a large sector of the population will remain entirely bereft of the knowledge and skills necessary for improving the standard of living in their countries.

When members of any society sense that they are competing for scarce resources with others, latent social tensions among ethnic groups are exacerbated. In many parts of the Muslim world, a decline in the standard of living has, indeed, been accompanied by a rise in social conflict. An example occurred in Indonesia during the worst period of the 1997–1998 financial collapse in East Asia. Prior to the crisis, the Chinese of Indonesia accounted for only three percent of the population, but they exerted much more influence on the economy than their numbers would suggest. Most were small shopkeepers, but a few were wealthy cronies of Suharto who had benefitted from his corrupt financial dealings. Resentment toward the men involved in corruption became directed toward the Chinese community in general during the 1990s. In early 1998, as the financial crisis was in its most severe phase, mobs of Indonesian Muslims began roaming the streets, looking for villains to punish. They burned shops belonging to Chinese, raped and killed individual Chinese, and destroyed over 400 Chinese Christian churches. Over 2000 people were killed, and many of the wealthiest Chinese fled the country, taking some $40–100 billion in capital with them.

Perhaps the most-studied instance of ethnic group relations within the Muslim world is that of Hindu–Muslim interaction, because some Muslims' fears of being submerged in an independent, Hindu-majority India were the catalyst for creating Pakistan. As many observers during the 1940s predicted would happen, almost a third of British India's Muslims remained in the Republic of India after partition. The percentage of Muslims in India dropped from approximately thirty percent during the British period to about eleven percent after partition. Despite Indian Muslims' status as a small minority (they are now thirteen percent of the population), they are the third largest concentration of Muslims in the world due to India's huge overall population.

Even though the percentage of Muslims in India dropped by two-thirds at independence, the nightmarish visions of what life would be like for them once the British left did not materialize. Most continued to live in villages and small towns with non-Muslims, remained neighbors with them, and spoke the same languages. Ordinary Hindus and Muslims typically interacted with each other properly even when they did not have warm relations with each other. Children from the two communities played together and developed life-long friendships, even if their parents were not interested in meeting each other. Occasional, small-scale communal violence did take place, as it had in the past, but these incidents were usually the result of a deliberate provocation by individuals on one side or the other, not the result of a constant state of vigilance and fear.

It would be a distortion to describe the conditions of life for Indian Muslims during the first three decades of independence as halcyon, but it is also hard to sustain an argument that Indian Muslims were worse off than those in East and West Pakistan. Indian Muslims voted equally with Hindus in democratic elections from the beginning, whereas Pakistan's first election was the one in 1970 that triggered the secession of Bangladesh. Two Muslims have served as India's president, whose role is largely ceremonial, as it is in most parliamentary republics. The first woman to serve on the Indian supreme court was a Muslim, and Muslim women have served as governors of several Indian states; Muslims are among the most popular movie stars and singers of the country; and a Muslim was the architect of India's missile program.

In a well-meaning attempt to correct long-standing injustices suffered by the lower castes and to make ethnic minorities feel welcome, India's leaders implemented a program of affirmative action that guaranteed quotas for the lower castes and the untouchables in education and government employment. The program also allowed Christians and Muslims to follow their own codes of family law. By the 1970s, members of the higher castes were expressing their anger that they were being denied admission to schools and opportunities for employment despite being more highly qualified than the lower castes. They also questioned why Christians and Muslims were being given special religious concessions when India was theoretically a secular state.

The growing resentment led to the creation of a Hindu nationalist organization, the Bharatiya Janata Party (BJP). The BJP struck a chord among many Hindus by arguing that the attempts by the government to be secular had led to a diminution of the country's Hindu identity and special privileges for non-Hindus. The generalized resentment and anger latched on to a concrete, if obscure, symbol in the small town of Ayodhya. The BJP claimed—without adducing historical evidence—that the Mughal ruler Babur had destroyed a temple in Ayodhya that had been built to mark the birthplace of the god Ram. The Mughal ruler allegedly then built the Babri Mosque on the ruins of the destroyed temple. In December 1992, tens of thousands of Hindu nationalists broke through police barriers and destroyed the mosque. A wave of communal violence swept parts of India, and thousands of people were killed. The large majority of the victims were Muslims. Since that time, communal tensions have remained high, particularly in the state of Gujarat, where several lethal riots have occurred and where Muslims continue to be the majority of the victims.

Analysts of Indian society hoped that the concentration of attacks on Muslims in only a few regions was a sign that specific social circumstances were playing the leading role in the violence. The surprising loss experienced by the BJP in the 2004 national elections was another encouraging sign that the majority of Hindus were more interested in developing their country as a secular democratic state than in asserting a particular identity. Unfortunately, a new development occurred simultaneously with the defeat of the BJP that had the potential of exacerbating communal tensions: Non-Indian Muslim extremists began bombing trains and other crowded venues, hoping to incite Hindus to attack Muslim neighborhoods. Using the same methods that al-Qa'ida had pioneered, these terrorists hoped to provoke Hindu massacres of Muslims that would in turn generate a jihadi mentality among Indian Muslims, who had not thought in those terms up to that time.

Although some features of communal relations in India took a turn for the worse in the 1980s, others have continued to exhibit encouraging signs. The Khoja and Bohra Isma'ilis, who were forced to live reclusive lives for centuries due to persecution, participate openly and fully in modern society. The Khojas are the largest component of the worldwide community of Nizari Isma'ilis, who are led by Aga Khan IV (b. 1936). The Nizaris have gained a reputation as an educated, wealthy, and cosmopolitan group of people who contribute enormous sums to economic development, health programs, and cultural projects around the world. Like the Khojas, the Da'udi (Dawoodi) Bohras boast rates of literacy that are unsurpassed in India, and the curricula of their educational institutions prepare students for admission to leading American and European universities. Like the Khojas, the community has managed to find a way to celebrate tradition while adapting to a rapidly changing world.

Another positive development in the Indian Muslim community is the reintegration of the Mappila Muslims of Kerala into their society. The Mappilas had lived harmoniously and prosperously with their Hindu neighbors until the advent of the Portuguese in the early sixteenth century. In response to the ruthless treatment of the Mappilas by the Portuguese and their Dutch successors, the Mappila community developed a reputation for being violent xenophobes. The turmoil of the period of the European trade monopolies also disrupted traditional economic and social relations between Mappilas and Hindus, and the Muslims began to view the Hindus, too, with suspicion and hostility.

After the British conquered Kerala in the late eighteenth century, they had to quell several Mappila revolts. The largest outbreak of violence was the rebellion of 1921, discussed in Chapter 10. That orgy of violence was so destructive that the community itself was shocked, and it withdrew into a shell. By the 1960s, however, the Muslims of Kerala had begun to participate in Indian political life and were sending their children to secular schools. They had fewer communal problems with their Hindu and Christian neighbors than Muslims in other regions of India did. They actively explored how to combine the experience of being a religious minority with an authentically Islamic practice.

In Africa, several social conflicts pose difficult problems. The attempts by the Sudanese government since 1989 to impose the Shari'a on the non-Muslim southern half of the country continues to fuel a secessionist movement in the south. In Nigeria, the predominantly Muslim northern half of the country—the region of the former Sokoto Caliphate—expresses its sense of alienation from political domination by the predominantly non-Muslim southern half by insisting on the application of the Shari'a, even on non-Muslims. In Algeria, Berbers compare themselves to the Kurds of Turkey: They have resisted the Arabization program of the government that at one time limited the broadcasts of the one Berber-language radio station to four hours a day, prohibited giving children Berber names, and banned explicitly Berber festivals and musical groups. Many Berbers believe that the massacres of Berber villagers during the civil war of the 1990s were acts of rage by Arab jihadis directed against rural Berbers' non-Arab identity and their lack of scrupulous religiosity.

The Prospects for Islamism and Sufism

The rise of Islamism is the latest in a series of challenges to the practice of Sufism that began in the eighteenth century. Sufism has a long history, and so it is has much "baggage" that its critics can attack. Islamism, by contrast, is not only a recent development, but it has accomplished very little by which it can be judged. It still remains largely an aspiration. The two movements actively compete with each other for followers, and the future of Islam will be determined by which trend dominates.

It is common to meet Muslims who joined Islamist movements after becoming disillusioned with secular ideologies. For others, Islamism's appeal is its logical analysis of Muslim history: Muslim society achieved greatness when it followed God's laws; it declined when its governments became secular; and God will reward it when it restores an Islamic state. The many currents of Islamism share little in the way of political thought beyond the conviction that Islam orders all of life and the determination to create a state that enforces the tenets of Islam. An obstacle to harmony among Islamists is the issue of the institutional structure of a future Islamic state. The Qur'an and Hadith provide no guidance on this issue, with the result that some Islamists anticipate a strong executive, whereas others want strong parliamentary and judicial branches to balance the power of the executive. If by "Islam" the Islamists referred to a fixed tradition that has been passed down through the centuries, they would at least agree on the rituals and the civil and criminal statutes that the Islamic state would enforce. Because of widespread agreement among Islamists that the exercise of ijtihad is obligatory, however, modern Islamists interpret the Qur'an and Hadith in radically different ways and come to the radically different conclusions that one would expect. Vehement disagreements arise among Islamists over such questions as whether the Qur'an prohibits paying any interest on loans or only exorbitant interest; gender issues, such as polygyny, the use of the veil, the social mixing of men and women, and equal rights before the law; and the limits of religious toleration and civic equality of non-Muslims.

Islamists have rarely been allowed to implement their vision. Secular Muslims and Western states have united in opposing them out of a fear that they would create a system that would harass or persecute nonconformists. Two of the most egregious examples are the military coup that took place in Algeria in early 1992 on the eve of a certain Islamist electoral victory and the outlawing of Islamic parties in Egypt when it became clear that the Muslim Brothers might win open and fair elections. Critics of these actions have argued that, as long as Islamists are banned from taking power, the Islamist vision remains a powerful ideal that raises unrealistic expectations of a utopian future and nurses a deep sense of injustice and oppression as a result of the hostility of the secular state. According to this argument, only by allowing the Islamist ideal to engage with the grimy reality of day-to-day administration can Muslims begin to see what is feasible in an Islamic state and what is not. It is instructive in this regard to see how successful some of the self-identified Islamic states have been. We will briefly examine three of them: Saudi Arabia, Pakistan, and Iran.

The oldest of the Islamic states is that of the Saudi monarchy, established in the 1930s. Because it was created in a tribal society, its institutional structure is primitive. It has no parliament or independent judiciary, and it has functioned on the basis of negotiations among the king, tribal leaders, and Wahhabi ulama. During the oil boom of the 1970s, the country rapidly urbanized, modernized, and became wealthy. Intense strains came to bear on the system, and these were magnified by the controversial occupation of the country by the American military in 1990 after Iraq's annexation of Kuwait. Members of the country's growing middle class have become increasingly dissatisfied with the economic and political privileges of the ruling family and with features of the country's educational system, legal procedures, and regulations governing women. From the other end of the spectrum, Islamists also criticize the organization of the kingdom, but they do so largely on the basis that it is a monarchy, which is not a Qur'anic concept. Jihadi Islamists consider the members of the dynasty to be hypocrites and apostates, and therefore illegitimate rulers. They have carried out several terrorist attacks against the government in an attempt to destabilize the country in preparation for a violent takeover. Analysts are unanimous in agreeing that the state has to engage in a dramatic reorganization in order to survive.

In Pakistan, the Islamization policies of Zia al-Haqq helped him to consolidate power, but his authoritarian methods provoked a pro-democracy backlash. In 1988, three months after his assassination, Benazir Bhutto gained revenge for the 1977 deposition and execution of her father when her party gained the largest bloc of votes. She became prime minister in a coalition government. Bhutto, however, was dogged by accusations of corruption during her two administrations (1988–1990, 1993–1996). Her chief rival, Nawaz Sharif, a wealthy landowner, also disillusioned many of his followers by using political office for personal gain during his tenure as prime minister (1990–1993, 1997–1999). In 1999, General Pervez Musharraf overthrew Sharif in yet another of Pakistan's series of military coups.

Pakistan entered the twenty-first century with the world's second largest Muslim population and sixth largest total population. Its poverty, continuing divisions regarding its national identity, and ethnic and social diversity prevented Pakistan from wielding the influence that the size of its population might suggest. Vast swaths of Baluchistan and the Pashtun tribal regions along the Afghan frontier were still not under the direct control of the government and demonstrated no loyalty to the nation of Pakistan. Mutually hostile groups of Islamists aspired to seize control of the government and convert it to an Islamic state of their own design. The country's secular military leaders faced daunting obstacles as they tried to forge national unity and provide opportunities for a majority of the citizens to live comfortably in the global economy.

In 1979, many Shi'ites had reason to hope that the creation of the Islamic Republic of Iran was a harbinger of the imminent return of the Hidden Imam. Even among secular Iranians, only hard-core supporters of the shah could resist harboring hopes that the new republic would cultivate the theme of social justice for which Shi'ism has historically yearned. Most were to be disappointed. The government immediately became embroiled in a clash with leftists, and it engaged in a ruthless campaign to exterminate all opponents. In September 1980, Iraq's Saddam Husayn attacked, thinking that he would be able to take advantage of the turmoil in the country and the collapse of the shah's military machine. He miscalculated: The war continued until 1988, causing hundreds of billions of dollars of damage and one million casualties. Meanwhile, the price of petroleum fell precipitously in the mid-1980s, causing a severe economic crisis. Then, in 1989, Khomeini died, removing the charismatic and unifying figure who had made the revolution possible.

The Iranian government had been able to mobilize support during the war with Iraq by calling on the faithful to defend God's holy project. Once the war was over and Khomeini had died, the regime drifted. Competing interest groups thwarted the implementation of each other's programs. The government enacted few economic or social reforms, and the ulama who dominated it gained a reputation for wanting to control the levers of power, not for improving the lives of the country's citizens. In 1997 and 2001, the platform of presidential candidate Muhammad Khatami included a slate of proposals that would have reversed many of the policies of the regime. He drew seventy percent of the votes in both elections, but conservative resistance blocked the implementation of his proposed reforms during both of his terms in office. In 2005, economic distress brought to power a populist candidate, Mahmud Ahmadinejad. Once again, the results of the elections disappointed the voters, because the government's revenues from the sale of petroleum were not nearly sufficient for Ahmadinejad to meet the pressing economic needs of his people. Moreover, when demonstrations occurred or criticism of the new government appeared in newspapers, the government harshly suppressed the dissenters. More than a quarter of a century after the implementation of *velayat-i faqih,* most Iranians were deeply dissatisfied with their government.

Whereas Islamists are floundering in their efforts to create Islamic states that are not deeply compromised by human foibles, Sufism exhibits signs of revival after many observers had written its obituary. For more than two centuries, Islamic reformers dismissed Sufism as a bundle of superstitions and a departure from the teachings of the Qur'an and Hadith; recent reformers accused it of being a means for unscrupulous men to exploit the uneducated and desperate masses and criticized it for neglecting the duty of building a Shari'a-enforcing state. Simultaneously, agrarian reforms undermined the economic foundations of Sufi orders, the secularization of education challenged central elements of Sufism's world view, and the social service agencies of modern governments encroached on a traditional function of the orders. The rapid pace and new rhythms of industrialized urban life presented formidable obstacles to the practice of spending sustained periods of quiet time in meditation. In the post–World War II era, religious reformers and secular political leaders alike assumed that Sufism was moribund.

Despite these ominous developments, Sufism shared in the global religious revival of the last quarter of the twentieth century. Some of the features of its growing salience may have been superficial: It is hard to know if spiritual insight or the quest to be chic is the motive for the recent popularity in Europe and North America of Sufi poetry by such luminaries as the thirteenth-century Jalal al-Din al-Rumi and the music of the Pakistani Chishti singer Nusrat Fateh Ali Khan (d. 1997), whose work appeared in Hollywood soundtracks as well as on more than fifty compact disks. In the predominantly Muslim world, the motives are more clear. Sufis share with Islamists the desire to reform a corrupt and materialistic society. Whereas Islamists intend to effect reform by enforcing certain behaviors by the power of the state, however, Sufis seek a transformation of the soul. In many cases, the rigidity and sterility of much of the Islamist project has prompted Muslims to seek a religious life that cultivates the inner life. This phenomenon is more than merely interesting: The quest for a deep spiritual life that transcended ritual duties was the stimulus for the emergence of Sufism in the first place, at the dawn of Islamic history. The violence of the jihadis in the 1990s, and al-Qa'ida's attacks on the United States and Europe in the early years of this century, only accentuated this trend. When it became clear that fifteen of the nineteen attackers involved in the attacks on New York and Washington were Saudi citizens, the Saudi government began reassessing some of its religious policies. In 2003, the government reversed the long-standing Wahhabi ban on participation in Sufi festivals, citing the need for greater recognition and acceptance of different religious practices.

Sufis have begun an active preaching and publication campaign to refute criticisms made by Islamists and to try to win new members into their organizations. Like the Islamists, they attract people from all social ranks and professions, but whereas the Islamists' weak spot in recruitment is their focus on correct behavior at the expense of the life of the spirit, Sufis' vulnerability is the traditional framework for conceptualizing the ascent of the soul to God, which is based on an earth-centered cosmology and a series of "heavens" through which the soul ascends to its goal. Sufis with modern world views are working to bring the cosmology and overall values of their tradition into harmony with the spiritual and intellectual tastes of modern men and women.

New Frontiers

A major development in Muslim history and the history of Islam itself was the late-twentieth-century growth of Muslim communities in Western Europe and North America. Tiny communities of Muslims had lived in both regions from the late nineteenth century on, but their presence was little noticed until after 1960, when millions of people from predominantly Muslim countries began migrating to both continents. The Muslim population then became a critical mass in a non-Muslim society, and a new experiment began.

The significance of what has happened can be appreciated only if we recall that, throughout history, Muslims assumed that they should not, and could not, live in non-Muslim countries. The ulama explicitly taught that no Muslim should voluntarily move to an area not ruled by Muslims. The ulama also taught that when Muslim territory was conquered by non-Muslims—as in the case of the Reconquista—Muslims should "perform hijra" (i.e., move away from a situation not conducive to living the Islamic life to a place where it was possible). Performing hijra was not always feasible because of economic or other reasons, but the doctrine caused many people to experience anxiety for continuing to remain under the rule of non-Muslims.

The experience of imperialism desensitized many Muslims to non-Muslim rule: Although the importance of the Shari'a courts continued to shrink during the imperial period, freedom of worship was not restricted by government officials. After the period of decolonization, political refugees and people in search of greater economic opportunity emigrated from their homelands to the countries that had been their former imperial masters. Countries like Norway and Sweden, which had not been active imperialists, also attracted migrants. A shortage of labor in Germany led to agreements with several Muslim countries to recruit workers, most of whom came from Turkey.

The emergence of sizable Muslim communities in Western countries is generating new expressions of Islam. At this point, unfortunately, it is too early to be able to make many generalizations about the Muslim experience in North America and Europe. Because the communities are so new, much about their religious and social experience is rapidly changing, and the diversity of the ethnic groups involved is as almost as great as that which exists in the world as a whole. Another problem that limits our knowledge is that no one knows exactly how many Muslims there are in North America and Western Europe. Religious affiliation is not a component of many national censuses; mosques typically do not keep membership rolls; and many people identify culturally as Muslims without being active religiously. Estimates of the number of Muslims in the United States, for example, range from a little over one million to over seven million. With these caveats in mind, it can be stated that most scholars studying Muslims in the West find the following population estimates reasonable for the first decade of the twenty-first century: three to five million in the United States; half a million in Canada; and twelve to fifteen million in Western Europe.

Between one-fourth and one-third of the Muslims in the United States are converts, and most of the converts are African American. From the 1950s to the late 1970s, many Americans in the larger cities associated Islam with the Nation of Islam, a black nationalist movement that appropriated several features of Islam into its own, distinctive ideology. Most Sunni and Shi'ite ulama, however, did not recognize the Nation of Islam as an Islamic group due to its identification of God with Wali Fard Muhammad, the attribution of prophethood to Elijah Muhammad, the movement's racist creation myth, and ritual features such as the substitution of December for Ramadan as the month of fasting. In 1976, Elijah Muhammad's son and successor, Warith Deen Muhammad, led his followers into Sunni Islam, while Louis Farrakhan led a splinter group that remained largely faithful to the tradition of Elijah Muhammad.

The turmoil within the Nation of Islam took place during the decade that witnessed an acceleration of the rate of immigration of Muslims into the United States. Most of the immigrants were well educated, and many took employment as professionals. The average income of immigrant Muslims is substantially higher than the national average. The new residents represent the Sunni, Twelver Shi'ite, Isma'ili, and Ahmadi traditions, and they come from dozens of countries.

Because Warith Deen Muhammad's attempts to bring his movement into the mainstream of Sunni practice required the efforts of a decade, most immigrant Muslims were initially wary of existing mosques in the United States, suspicious that they were tainted by Elijah Muhammad's doctrines. As a result, little interaction has developed between African American congregations and the new mosques that immigrants established. Even within the mosques of the immigrants, considerable debate takes place regarding ritual and doctrine, as one would expect when the representatives of traditions as radically different as those of Wahhabism and Indonesian *kejawen* pray together. In an effort to overcome such differences, American Muslims have created several organizations to facilitate communication with each other and to provide services for individuals and congregations. The largest of these organizations is the Islamic Society of North America (ISNA).

ISNA also has many Canadian members. Most Canadian Muslims are immigrants and, at least until the late 1990s, were predominantly from the professional classes. Most live in Ontario, and the majority of those live in the Toronto metropolitan area. Beginning in the 1990s, Canada began accepting a growing number of Muslim political refugees, an issue that became politically sensitive in the aftermath of al-Qa'ida's attacks on New York and Washington, D.C. in 2001.

In Europe, the largest populations of Muslims are in France, Germany, and the United Kingdom. Over half of France's estimated four to five million Muslims have roots in the country's former North African protectorates; two-thirds of Germany's estimated three million trace their family histories to Turkey; and the single largest group of the U.K.'s estimated one and one-half million Muslims is composed of Pakistanis (one-third of the total). The immigrant Muslim population in each European country is every bit as diverse as that of North America. The multiplicity of nationalities is not the only problem that complicates Muslim unity among immigrants. Social class differences are hard to overcome, as are the barriers among the various religious factions: The Britons of Pakistani background are proud of their shared roots, but their religious identity may be Barelvi, Ahl-i Hadith, Deobandi, Tablighi, Shi'ite, or Ahmadi, to name only a few of the possibilities for conflict.

Europe boasts many examples of individual success stories among its Muslims, but most immigrants who came for improved economic opportunities were unprepared to cope with cultural differences and insufficiently educated to compete in a modern economy. In contrast to the immigrant Muslims of North America, most European Muslims were manual laborers when they arrived, and they now suffer from high rates of unemployment. Many live in depressing urban housing projects, and when they interact with the majority society, they often encounter prejudice based on race, religion, or social class distinctions.

A shared sense of estrangement and alienation has led some immigrants to choose to cluster in neighborhoods composed of their ethnic and religious group. Although this action removes much of the stress of interacting with an unfamiliar culture, it also makes it difficult, if not impossible, to assimilate into the larger society. Under any circumstances, the creation of ghettos is an indicator of a malfunction in society, but given the known susceptibility to radical Islamist groups on the part of young men who feel alienated from their environment, these insulated neighborhoods also pose a potential threat to national security.

The permanent settlement of millions of Muslims in Europe has surprised native Europeans and the immigrants alike. The first wave of immigrants, in the 1960s and 1970s, expected to be temporary workers. Due to extended labor shortages and relaxed immigration policies, families soon followed the primary wage earner to Europe. As economies cooled and unemployment rates rose, some non-Muslims began to resent the new settlers. The rise of the European Union, with its search for a European identity that could be shared by all member states, also opened the question of how Muslims fit into the Western, Christian legacy, even though relatively few Europeans are practicing Christians today.

The Muslim presence in the West will continue to grow. This will occur most dramatically in Europe, where overall fertility rates are so low that immigration has to be encouraged or octogenarians will outnumber children by midcentury. The Muslim communities of Europe and North America are developing forms of Islam that have never been seen before. Individuals and groups are exploring how to live an authentically Islamic life within a culture that, on the one hand, did not have centuries of exposure to Islam, but, on the other hand, offers the advantage of being legally bound to a statement of universal human rights and the rule of law. Tariq Ramadan of Switzerland and Khaled Abou El Fadl of the United States are just two of the many thinkers who are attracting attention to their work in this field. The nature of the synthesis between new forms of Islam and Western culture will be determined by how Muslims and non-Muslims choose to relate to each other.

Conclusion

By the early twenty-first century, the determined efforts of a small group of Muslim militants had caused the word *Muslim* to become linked with violence in the minds of non-Muslims around the world. Today it is hard to comprehend that, prior to the last quarter of the twentieth century, people in Europe and North America who played word association games commonly identified *Muslim* with flying carpets, Aladdin's lamp, and a popular television show called *I Dream of Jeannie,* and almost never with violence. The terrorists who frightened Europeans and Americans during the 1970s were not Muslims, but rather secular, leftist, European and American young people who belonged to organizations like the Baader–Meinhof Group, the Symbionese Liberation Army, and Weatherman.

The ideology of global jihad is a new phenomenon in history, and it is the result of a particular historical trajectory. It is a potentially lethal threat to the world's population for which security measures must be devised, but it is a transitory phenomenon that will pass as the circumstances that created it change. Meanwhile, other developments within the Muslim community are taking shape that offer the prospect of a modern and egalitarian version of the ways that Muslims and members of other religious communities interacted harmoniously in the past. In an era characterized by the widespread practice of ijtihad, the future trajectory of change in Islamic thought depends in large part on whether Muslims feel secure and confident in the future, on the one hand, or fear that their religion and culture are threatened by sinister forces, on the other.

NOTES

1. See the excellent analysis by Mark Juergensmeyer, *Terror in the Mind of God: The Global Rise of Religious Violence.* 3d ed. Berkeley: University of California Press, 2003.
2. Data from the World Development Indicators Database of the World Bank, 1 July 2006. Comparisons are made using the PPP method. http://siteresources.worldbank.org/DATASTATISTICS/Resources/GNIPC.pdf
3. *Claiming the Future: Choosing Prosperity in the Middle East and North Africa.* Washington, D.C.: The World Bank, 1995, 4.

FURTHER READING

The Watershed Years

Cleveland, William L. *A History of the Modern Middle East,* 3d ed. Boulder, Colorado, and Oxford, U.K.: Westview Press, 2004.

Isaacson, Jason F., and Colin Rubenstein, eds. *Islam in Asia: Changing Political Realities.* New Brunswick, New Jersey, and London: Transaction Publishers, 2002.

Keddie, Nikki. *Modern Iran: Roots and Results of Revolution,* updated ed. New Haven, Connecticut, and London: Yale University Press, 2006.

Smith, Charles D. *Palestine and the Arab-Israeli Conflict,* 5th ed. New York: Bedford/St. Martin's, 2004.

Ziring, Lawrence. *Pakistan in the Twentieth Century: A Political History.* Karachi, Pakistan, and New York: Oxford University Press, 1997.

Responding to the Divine Imperative

Burg, Steven L., and Paul S. Shoup. *The War in Bosnia–Herzegovina: Ethnic Conflict and International Intervention.* Armonk, New York: M. E. Sharpe, 2000.

Coll, Steve. *Ghost Wars: The Secret History of the CIA, Afghanistan, and bin Laden, from the Soviet Invasion to September 10, 2001.* New York: Penguin Books, 2004.

Cook, David. *Understanding Jihad.* Berkeley and Los Angeles: University of California Press, 2005.

Gerges, Fawaz. *The Far Enemy: Why Jihad Went Global.* New York: Cambridge University Press, 2005.

Gilsenan, Michael. *Recognizing Islam: Religion and Society in the Modern Arab World.* New York: Pantheon Books, 1982.

Glenny, Misha. *The Balkans: Nationalism, War and the Great Powers, 1804–1999.* London: Viking, 2000.

Hefner, Robert W. *Civil Islam: Muslims and Democratization in Indonesia.* Princeton, New Jersey, and Oxford, U.K.: Princeton University Press, 2000.

Isaacson, Jason F., and Colin Rubenstein, eds. *Islam in Asia: Changing Political Realities.* New Brunswick, New Jersey, and London: Transaction Publishers, 2002.

Jansen, Johannes J. G. *The Neglected Duty: The Creed of Sadat's Assassins and Islamic Resurgence in the Middle East.* New York: Macmillan Publishing Company; London: Collier Macmillan Publishers, 1985.

Kepel, Gilles. *Jihad: The Trail of Political Islam.* Translated by Anthony F. Roberts. Cambridge, Massachusetts: Harvard University Press, 2002.

McKenna, Thomas M. *Muslim Rulers and Rebels: Everyday Politics and Armed Separatism in the Southern Philippines.* Berkeley: University of California Press, 1998.

Mansfield, Laura. *His Own Words: Translation and Analysis of the Writings of Dr. Ayman al-Zawahiri.* n.p.: TLG Publications, 2006.

Militant Ideology Atlas. William McCants, editor and project director; Jarrett Brachman, project coordinator. West Point, New York: Combating Terrorism Center, U.S. Military Academy, 2006.

Mishal, Shaul, and Avraham Sela. *The Palestinian Hamas: Vision, Violence, and Coexistence,* new ed. New York: Columbia University Press, 2006.

Norton, Augustus Richard. *Hezbollah: A Short History.* Princeton, New Jersey, and Oxford, U.K.: Princeton University Press, 2007.

Scheuer, Michael. *Through Our Enemies' Eyes: Osama bin Laden, Radical Islam, and the Future of America.* Washington, D.C.: Brassey's, 2002.

Roy, Olivier. *The Failure of Political Islam.* Translated by Carol Volk. Cambridge, Massachusetts: Harvard University Press, 1994.

Roy, Olivier. *Globalized Islam: The Search for a New Ummah.* New York: Columbia University Press; Paris: In association with the Centre d'Études et de Récherches Internationales, 2004.

Sageman, Marc. *Understanding Terror Networks.* Philadelphia: University of Pennsylvania Press, 2004.

Tishkov, Valery. *Chechnya: Life in a War-Torn Society.* Berkeley: University of California Press, 2004.

al-Zayyat, Montasser. *The Road to al-Qaeda: The Story of Bin Laden's Right-Hand Man.* Translated by Ahmed Fekry. Edited by Sara Nimis. London and Sterling, Virginia: Pluto Press, 2004.

Twenty-First-Century Challenges and Opportunities

Abou El Fadl, Khaled. *The Great Theft: Wrestling Islam from the Extremists.* New York: HarperSanFrancisco, 2005.

Browers, Michaelle, and Charles Kurzman, eds. *An Islamic Reformation?* Lanham, Maryland: Lexington Books, 2004.

Commins, David. *The Wahhabi Mission and Saudi Arabia.* London and New York: I. B. Taurus, 2006.

Ernst, Carl W., and Bruce B. Lawrence. *Sufi Martyrs of Love: The Chishti Order in South Asia and Beyond.* New York: Palgrave Macmillan, 2002.

Haddad, Yvonne. *Muslims in the West: from Sojourners to Citizens.* New York and Oxford, U.K.: Oxford University Press, 2002.

Hasan, Mushirul. *Legacy of a Divided Nation: India's Muslims Since Independence.* Boulder, Colorado: Westview Perss, 1997.

Hoffman, Valerie J. *Sufism, Mystics, and Saints in Modern Egypt.* Columbia, South Carolina: University of South Carolina Press, 1995.

Hunter, Shireen T. *Islam, Europe's Second Religion: The New Social, Cultural, and Political Landscape.* Foreword by Charles Buchanan. Westport, Connecticut: Praeger, 2002.

Jackson, Sherman A. *Islam and the Blackamerican: Looking Toward the Third Resurrection.* Oxford, U.K., and New York: Oxford University Press, 2005.

Liebeskind, Claudia. *Piety on its Knees: Three Sufi Traditions in South Asia in Modern Times.* Delhi and New York: Oxford University Press, 1998.

Miller, Roland E. *Mappila Muslims of Kerala: A Study in Islamic Trends.* New Delhi: Orient Longman, 1976.

Nielsen, Jorgen. *Towards a European Islam.* New York: St. Martin's 1999.

Nasr, Seyyed Vali Reza. *Islamic Leviathan: Islam and the Making of State Power.* Oxford, U.K., and New York: Oxford University Press, 2001.

Rabasa, Angel M. et al. *The Muslim World after 9/11.* Santa Monica, California: The RAND Corporation, 2004.

Ramadan, Tariq. *Western Muslims and the Future of Islam.* New York and Oxford, U.K.: Oxford University Press, 2004.

Roberson, B. A., ed. *Shaping the Current Islamic Reformation.* London and Portland, Oregon: Frank Cass, 2003.

Trofimov, Yaroslav. *Faith at War: A Journey on the Frontlines of Islam, from Baghdad to Timbuktu.* New York: Henry Holt, 2005.

Vassiliev, Alexei. *The History of Saudi Arabia.* London: Saqi Books, 2000.

Wiktorowicz, Quintan. *Radical Islam Rising: Muslim Extremism in the West.* Lanham, Maryland: Rowman & Littlefield Publishers, Inc., 2005.

Glossary

(See the guide to pronunciation in the front matter of the book.)

'abd: Arabic term meaning "slave" or "servant." In conjunction with the name of God or one of his attributes, the word is a component of many Muslim names: 'Abd Allah (or 'Abdullah) 'Abd al-Rahman, 'Abd al-Karim, etc. (It is worth noting that "Abdul" ["'Abd al-"] is not a name, despite popular representations of it in English; it must be followed by the name of God or one of his attributes.)

abu: Arabic term meaning "father." Many Arab men often consider it a point of pride to be called the father of their first-born son. Hence, Abu Hasan is a nickname for someone who was born with a name such as Mahmud until his son Hasan was born, at which time he became known as Abu Hasan.

A.H. Abbreviation of the Latin phrase *anno hejirae,* referring to the dating system based on the Islamic calendar. Muslims decided to use the year of the Hijra (622 C.E.) to begin their calendar and to use a lunar, rather than a solar, calculation, resulting in a calendar of 354 days rather than 365/366 days. As a result, it gains a year on the Gregorian calendar approximately every thirty-three years. Thus, the year A.H. 100 did not begin, as one might think, in 722 C.E., but rather extended from August 718 through July 719.

Alid: a lineal descendant of 'Ali.

Anatolia: Asia Minor, or the section of western Asia that juts westward between the Black Sea and the Mediterranean Sea. Anatolia comprises the bulk of modern Turkey.

Ashura: Islamic holy day observed on the tenth day of Muharram, the first month of the Islamic calendar. The Prophet Muhammad had designated Ashura to be a day of voluntary fasting, but it became most celebrated when Husayn, the elder son of 'Ali by Fatima, was killed at Karbala. Because of this tragedy, Ashura became the major religious day of the year among Shi'ites. Many of them dedicate the first ten days of the month to fasting, reading from the Qur'an, prayers, and reenactments of the martyrdom. Many Sunnis also observe Ashura, but on a more subdued note, and normally only on the tenth day.

caliph (KAY-lif)**:** An English derivation of the Arabic word *khalifa,* which can mean either "deputy" or "successor." Leading members of the Prophet's companions chose the first few caliphs, who possessed moral, political, and military authority, but not prophetic authority. The caliphate rapidly became dynastic, causing the office to lose much of its legitimacy in the eyes of many, and then a multiplicity of simultaneous caliphates arose, further diluting its authority. Moreover, Shi'ites have recognized only the fourth caliph, 'Ali, as legitimate, claiming that 'Ali and his descendants, called Imams, are the only legitimate spiritual and political rulers.

dar: Arabic term meaning "abode" or "dwelling." Often used metaphorically, as in *Dar al-Islam,* the term used for the lands under Muslim rule, and *Dar al-Kufr* ("Abode of Unbelief") and *Dar al-Harb* ("Abode of War"), terms used for the lands not yet under Muslim rule.

dargah: The word used in South Asia to denote the shrine of a holy man.

dervish: Turkish variant of Persian *darvish,* literally meaning "poor" (*faqir* in Arabic). Sometimes it is used as a synonym for *Sufi,* and sometimes it is used to designate a wandering, mendicant spiritualist.

devshirme (DEV-shir-muh): Turkish term for the levy of young Christian boys that was begun in the late fourteenth century to staff the infantry and higher civil administration in the Ottoman realm.

dhimmi (THIM-mee; ZIM-mee): A free non-Muslim subject living in a Muslim country who, in return for paying a head tax, was granted protection and safety.

dhikr (thikr; zikr): Arabic term for "recollection" or "memory." The term is used for Sufi devotional practices intended to accentuate the awareness of the presence of God. In later Sufi history the various *tariqa*s were differentiated in part by their distinctive *dhikr*s.

faqir (fà QEER): An Arabic term that literally means "poor man." Because poverty was held as an ideal by most Sufis, the term came to denote a dervish.

fatwa: Arabic term for a ruling made by a very high government-appointed authority on the Shari'a (*mufti*) on a point of Islamic law; became important in the Muslim empires that emerged in the fifteenth and sixteenth centuries.

fiqh: Arabic term for Islamic jurisprudence, the method of determining the Shari'a. The jurist who follows the method is called a *faqih* (fă-QEEH).

gazi: A Turkish derivative of an Arabic term for "raider." After the frontiers between the Dar al-Islam and Byzantine territory became relatively stabilized, Turks who migrated into Anatolia after the eleventh century found Byzantine settlements attractive targets to plunder. The plunderers became known as gazis. As Muslims attacking Christian targets, they acquired the status of *mujahid*s, even though their goals and tactics did not resemble the classic definition of jihad.

ghulam (ghoo-LÄM): Literally, "boy" or "servant," but in the Safavid Empire, the term was applied to the slave soldiers from Georgia, Armenia, and Circassia that became the standing army for 'Abbas I and subsequent shahs.

ghulat (ghoo-LÄT): Literally, "exaggerators," or "those who go beyond the proper bounds." This is a term usually applied to certain Shi'ites who claimed a divine status for 'Ali, believed in metempsychosis, and engaged in rituals which seemed to other Muslims to violate Islamic norms.

Hadith (ha-DEETH): A "report" of something that takes place. In religious usage, it means reports (sometimes called "traditions") of what the Prophet said or did.

These accounts were passed down through the generations, documented by chains of transmissions in the form, "So-and-So told So-and-So that the Prophet said such-and-such." The Hadith were compiled into collections and became a source of religious authority second only to the Qur'an itself.

hijra: The noun form of the Arabic verb meaning to "emigrate," "abandon," or "renounce." The most famous hijra was Muhammad's trek from Mecca to Medina in 622 after it became clear that Meccans were not going to accept his message. Throughout history, Muslims have spoken of "performing hijra" in emulation of the Prophet when circumstances make it impossible to live an authentically Islamic life. It entails leaving one's home and moving to a land where the Shari'a is enforced.

Hui (whey): The Muslims of central and eastern China who speak Chinese as their native language and do not identify with a non-Sinitic ethnic group.

Ibadi (i-BĂ-dee): A sect of Islam that has its origins in the schismatic Kharijite group of the seventh century. Whereas the Kharijites were notorious for their tendency to kill Muslims who did not agree with them, the Ibadis abandoned that tactic in favor of withdrawing from sinful society. Their major settlements were in the deserts of North Africa and in Oman.

ibn: The Arabic word for "son." Just as Arab men often are known to their friends as the "Father of So-and-So," their sons are often known as the "Son of So-and-So" rather than by their personal name: Ibn Sina, Ibn Khaldun, Ibn Battuta, etc. It is often abbreviated, as in Ahmad b. Hanbal, and is sometimes rendered "Bin," as in Usama bin Laden. It is a convention to capitalize *ibn* and *bin* only when the person's given name is not used: Usama bin Laden, but Bin Laden

ijaza (i-JAA-za): An Arabic term indicating an authorization or license to teach a certain book on the grounds that the recipient of the *ijaza* has shown that he or she fully understands it. The *ijaza* that a student receives is one in a long chain of such licenses that extends from teacher to teacher, all the way back to the original author of the text, guaranteeing that the chain of authorities who have taught the material have conveyed the intent of the author.

ijtihad (ij-ti-HAD): An Arabic term denoting the independent judgment that is exercised when ruling upon a given point in the field of Islamic jurisprudence. One who exercises *ijtihad* is a *mujtahid.* Contrasts with *taqlid.*

imam (i-MÄM): An Arabic word that literally means "before" or "in front of." The term came to be applied to the prayer leader at a mosque within the Sunni tradition of Islam

Imam (i-MÄM): The recognized leader of Shi'ite Islam. Shi'ite sects have defined the characteristics of their Imams in different ways over the centuries, but generally the Imam is understood not to have prophetic status. He does, however, provide religious guidance that is indispensable, and he is the rightful head of the entire Muslim community. Some Shi'ite groups consider their Imam to be in seclusion, awaiting the time to return to lead the world; others have a "visible" Imam who lives among them.

'irfan (ir-FAN): A Persian borrowing of an Arabic word suggesting gnosis, a type of knowledge accessible only to spiritual adepts. Thus, it is the type of mystical knowledge that Sufis and other mystics can acquire only through rigorous training and special techniques, and is comparable to the concept of "enlightenment" that is found in many mystical traditions.

jahiliya (ja-hi-LEE-ya): An Arabic word whose root means "ignorance" or "barbarism." Traditionally in Islamic history, it is a term that designates the condition of humanity prior to the advent of Islam.

jihad (ji-HAD): An Arabic word connoting "struggle" or "exertion." The schools of Islamic law drew up detailed regulations concerning the execution of jihad. Jihad could be aggressive, for the expansion of the Dar al-Islam, or defensive, for the protection of the Dar al-Islam.

khanaqa: The term for a Sufi lodge, or *zawiya,* in Persian-language areas.

Kharijite (KHA-ri-jite): A name given to seventh-century Muslims with a perfectionist ethic who did not tolerate leaders who engaged in acts that they considered unworthy. The first Kharijites killed the caliph ʻAli when he agreed to negotiate with a rival: ʻAli preferred to negotiate rather than shed the blood of fellow Muslims, but the Kharijites said that his willingness to negotiate proved that he was not God's chosen leader after all, but an impostor. Some Kharijites advocated the position that any Muslim who sinned should be killed, but most preferred to "perform hijra" and leave the corrupting influences of society.

Khorasan (kho-ra-SAN): A region in northeastern Iran whose area has been defined differently over the centuries, but prior to the demarcation of modern national boundaries it approximated the area bounded on the west by the Dasht-e Kavir desert of Iran, on the south by the Dasht-e Lut desert of Iran, and on the north by the Amu Darya River, and it comprised the western quarter of modern Afghanistan.

madhhab (math-hab; maz-hab): An Arabic term indicating a formalized system or method of determining *fiqh.* It is often translated as "school of (Islamic) law." Hundreds of such schools arose during the early history of Islam, but four dominated by the thirteenth century: the Hanifi, Maliki, Hanbali, and Shafiʻi schools.

madrasa (ma-DRA-sa): A cognate of the Arabic word to "study," it denotes a school for the study of Islamic jurisprudence, Qur'an interpretation, Hadith, biographies of great Muslims, and dialectic.

Maghrib (MA-ghrib): Literally, "West." Throughout most of Muslim history, it denoted North Africa west of Tripoli, Libya, but some commentators use it to denote all of North Africa west of Egypt, and still others use it to identify the area comprising Tunisia, Algeria, and Morocco.

mahdi (MAHH-dee): An Arabic term meaning "the guided one," an eschatological figure who first emerged in the writings of the first century of Islam. He is usually considered to be a Muslim leader who will be sent by God at the end of history to bring an end to the corruption and injustice of a wicked world and to implement God's will. Within Shiʻism the use of the term is usually understood to mean the Imam.

majlis: An Arabic term meaning "council" or "meeting," it has been adopted to denote "parliament."

mamluk (mam-LUKE): An Arabic term meaning "owned," it usually connotes a slave soldier, most often of Turkish origin.

Moghulistan: A region that approximates modern Xinjiang (i.e., the Tarim Basin and Zungaria, separated by the Tien Shan).

Monophysitism: A Christian doctrine adopted by the Coptic Church of Egypt and the Armenian Church, among others. Whereas the Orthodox Church adopted the doctrine that Christ had two separate human and divine natures united in one "person" (or being), Monophysites denied that the two natures were separate. In practice, they normally stated that Christ had a single, divine nature. The differences between the two doctrines led to schisms, riots, and executions by rival groups.

muhajir (moo-HA-jir)**:** One who performs a *hijra,* whether for the purpose of separating oneself from a non-Islamic area or of fleeing danger, as happened during the partition of India in 1947.

mujahid (moo-JA-hid)**:** One who engages in jihad. Plural: mujahidun (moo-ja-hi-doon) and mujahidin (moo-ja-hi-deen).

mujtahid (muj-TA-hid)**:** One who engages in *ijtihad.*

murid (moo-REED)**:** A Sufi *shaykh* or *pir.*

murshid (MOOR-shid)**:** A Sufi student or disciple, the follower of a *murid/ shaykh/ pir.*

Pancasila (pan-cha-SEE-la)**:** The five principles that Sukarno identified as the ideological basis of independent Indonesia: belief in the one and only God; the subsuming of ethnic identities into an Indonesian nationalism; humanitarianism, in the sense of treating all human beings with dignity; representative democracy; and social justice.

pir (peer)**:** Persian term for a Sufi master who leads disciples on the mystical way. It is used in South Asia as well as in Iran.

pirzada (peer-ZA-da)**:** The administrator of a *dargah.*

Punjab: Also "Panjab." A geographical region deriving its name from the words *punj* meaning "five," and *aab* meaning "waters,"referring to five rivers that are tributaries of the Indus River: the Sutlej, Beas, Ravi, Chenab, and Jhelum rivers. Today the Punjab is divided between Pakistan and India.

qadi (qaw-dee)**:** A member of the ulama who sits in a Shari'a court and rules on cases, using as his reference the body of jurisprudence (*fiqh*) developed by scholars over the centuries.

Qipchaqs: A group of Turks who dominated the so-called Qipchaq steppe north of the Black Sea. They were the primary source for the ruling elite of the Mamluke Empire from 1260 to 1382 and were the core population group of the Golden Horde.

Reconquista (ray-con-kees-tah)**:** Spanish term literally meaning "reconquest" that was applied to the process by which the Christian kingdoms of the northern Iberian Peninsula conquered Muslim-ruled regions in the southern part of the peninsula over a period of four centuries.

ribat (ri-BÄT)**:** Originally, a fort that guarded frontier areas in North Africa and al-Andalus. It served as a garrison for what was often a volunteer force serving at least in part out of religious commitment, and thus became associated with religious devotionals as well as with the idea of a garrison. When conditions changed, and a ribat was no longer need for defensive purposes, it might become a Sufi lodge. In North Africa, Sufi lodges, whether they had originally been used as forts or built new for specifically devotional purposes, were typically called ribats.

Rum (room)**:** The name given by Arabs to the Byzantine Empire, which viewed itself as the successor to Rome. Since Anatolia was the part of the empire that most Muslims encountered, it was known as Rum for several centuries even after the Byantines lost it at the Battle of Manzikert (1071). The Saljuq Turks even established the Sultanate of Rum in western Anatolia.

Rumelia: The Balkan region of the Ottoman Empire.

Shari'a (sha-REE-'a): Arabic word originally connoting "the approach to a watering hole" in the desert; later identified with Islamic law, derived from the Qur'an, Hadith, analogy, and consensus.

sharif (sha-REEF): An Arabic word literally meaning "illustrious" or "distinguished." It is used to denote descendants of the Prophet, who continue to maintain a high social status.

shaykh: Arabic term connoting "elderly man" or "venerable gentleman." It is also used to denote a chieftain or a Sufi leader.

sipahi (si-pä-hee): An Ottoman cavalryman.

South Asia: The term usually applied to those countries south of the Hindu Kush and Himalayan mountain ranges.

sunna: "Customary practice." In religious usage, it came to mean the ritual and ethical practice of (1) the Companions of the Prophet or (2) the Prophet himself. The ideal religious life is to emulate the Sunna of the Prophet, which can be found in the Hadith.

taqiya (tä-QEE-yah): A doctrine within the Shi'ite community that allows a believer who is being persecuted to dissimulate: to deny his or her beliefs.

taqlid (täq-LEED): An Arabic word that has the connotation of "uncritical, unquestioning acceptance" of an earlier decision in Islamic jurisprudence. Used as a contrast to *ijtihad* in the debate over how much latitude a Muslim jurist had to exercise his own judgment.

Tarim (tä-REEM): A basin in the western extremity of Xinjiang province of China, bounded on the north by the Tien Shan mountain range, on the south by the Kunlun Shan range, and on the west by the Pamir Mountains. Historically, it was a major gateway through the mountains for armies and merchants and was of great importance for the Silk Roads.

tariqa (taw-REE-qa): A Sufi order. Literally meaning "path" or "route," the term technically applies to the method of spiritual growth that the eponymous founder of the order reputedly taught and which distinguishes it from other orders.

timar (ti-MAR): The grant of land given to an Ottoman sipahi for his sustenance.

Transoxiana (also rendered "Transoxania"): The area known by the Arabs as *ma wara an-nahr,* or "that which lies beyond the (Amu Darya) river." Usually the term refers to the area between the Oxus (Amu Darya) and Jaxartes (Syr Darya) rivers, but sometimes connotes areas beyond the Syr Darya, as well.

tuğra (too-ra): The calligraphic signature or "logo" of an Ottoman sultan.

'ulama' (oo-lah-MAA): An Arabic word literally meaning "scholars," it usually denotes the specialists in Qur'an, Hadith, and religious law. Rendered "ulama" in this book for simplicity.

umma: An Arabic word meaning "nation," "people," or "generation," it normally denotes the entire community of Muslims.

Uighur (wee-ghurr): A Turkic Muslim people of Central Asia. Often rendered "Uyghur."

vizier (vi-ZEER): The English transliteration of the Turkish word for *wazir.*

wazir (wah-ZEER): An Arabic word denoting the chief administrative officer to the head of state (caliph or sultan) in a premodern Muslim state. In the modern era, the term usually denotes the head of a ministry or department within the national government.

Xinjiang (shin-zhang): The westernmost province of China. It comprises the historic regions of the Tarim Basin and Zungaria. Sometimes transliterated *Sinkiang,* particularly on older maps.

zawiya (ZAA-wee-ya): Arabic term for a lodge that Sufis visit or live in, in order to pursue the mystical way.

Zionism: A Jewish nationalist movement whose goal was the creation of a state for Jews in Palestine. Although it was in one sense a continuation of an ancient religious longing for Palestine, its leaders were explicitly secular and westernized.

Zungaria: The triangular basin to the north of the Tien Shan range, defined by the Altay Mountains on the east and the Yili River valley and Lake Balkash to the west. Also transliterated in several other ways; in European publications, it is usually rendered *Dzungharia.*

Credits

Chapter 1

Page 10: The Pierpont Morgan Library/Art Resource, NY.
Page 21: Courtesy of Historic Photogrphs, Fine Arts Library, Harvard College Library.

Chapter 2

Page 40: Bodleian Library, University of Oxford.
Page 55: Vernon O. Egger.

Chapter 3

Page 86: Ughra of Sultan Sulaiman the Magnificent, Ottoman Period (c.1280-1924). Ink, colors, and gold on paper. Height: 20 1/2 in. (52.1 cm); Width: 25 3/8 in. (64.5 cm). Rogers Fund, 1938 © The Metropolitan Museum of Art/Art Resource, NY.
Page 99: Vernon O. Egger.

Chapter 4

Page 127: © Corbis. All Rights Reserved.
Page 139: Saudi Aramco World/PADIA/Stephanie Hollyman.

Chapter 5

Page 167: Alamy Images/imagebroker.
Page 175: Alamy Images/Bernard O'Kane.

Chapter 6

Page 192: © Christophe Boisvieux/Corbis. All Rights Reserved.
Page 210: Alamy Images/Tibor Bognar.

Chapter 7

Page 243: Alamy Images/World Religious Photo Library.
Page 250: Courtesy of the Library of Congress.

Chapter 8

Page 267: © Ali Jasim/Corbis. All Rights Reserved.
Page 307: Hulton Archive/Getty Images.

Chapter 9

Page 348: Wikipedia, The Free Encyclopedia.
Page 357: The Granger Collection.

Chapter 10

Page 381: Hulton Archive/Getty Images.
Page 403: Wikipedia, The Free Encyclopedia.

Chapter 11

Page 433: © Bettmann/Corbis. All Rights Reserved.
Page 444: Getty Images Inc. - Hulton Archive Photos.

Chapter 12

Page 469: © Bettmann/Corbis. All Rights Reserved.
Page 497: Corbis/Reuters America LLC/David Bebber.

Index

2 020000 048572